msdn training

D1457974

2310B: Developing
Microsoft® ASP.NET Web
Applications Using
Visual Studio® .NET

Microsoft®

Course Number: 2310
Part Number: X09-90419
Released: 07/2002

END-USER LICENSE AGREEMENT FOR MICROSOFT OFFICIAL CURRICULUM COURSEWARE –STUDENT EDITION

PLEASE READ THIS END-USER LICENSE AGREEMENT ("EULA") CAREFULLY. BY USING THE MATERIALS AND/OR USING OR INSTALLING THE SOFTWARE THAT ACCOMPANIES THIS EULA (COLLECTIVELY, THE "LICENSED CONTENT"), YOU AGREE TO THE TERMS OF THIS EULA. IF YOU DO NOT AGREE, DO NOT USE THE LICENSED CONTENT.

1.   **GENERAL.** This EULA is a legal agreement between you (either an individual or a single entity) and Microsoft Corporation ("Microsoft"). This EULA governs the Licensed Content, which includes computer software (including online and electronic documentation), training materials, and any other associated media and printed materials. This EULA applies to updates, supplements, add-on components, and Internet-based services components of the Licensed Content that Microsoft may provide or make available to you unless Microsoft provides other terms with the update, supplement, add-on component, or Internet-based services component. Microsoft reserves the right to discontinue any Internet-based services provided to you or made available to you through the use of the Licensed Content. This EULA also governs any product support services relating to the Licensed Content except as may be included in another agreement between you and Microsoft. An amendment or addendum to this EULA may accompany the Licensed Content.

2.   **GENERAL GRANT OF LICENSE.** Microsoft grants you the following rights, conditioned on your compliance with all the terms and conditions of this EULA. Microsoft grants you a limited, non-exclusive, royalty-free license to install and use the Licensed Content solely in conjunction with your participation as a student in an Authorized Training Session (as defined below). You may install and use one copy of the software on a single computer, device, workstation, terminal, or other digital electronic or analog device ("Device"). You may make a second copy of the software and install it on a portable Device for the exclusive use of the person who is the primary user of the first copy of the software. A license for the software may not be shared for use by multiple end users. An "Authorized Training Session" means a training session conducted at a Microsoft Certified Technical Education Center, an IT Academy, via a Microsoft Certified Partner, or such other entity as Microsoft may designate from time to time in writing, by a Microsoft Certified Trainer (for more information on these entities, please visit www.microsoft.com). WITHOUT LIMITING THE FOREGOING, COPYING OR REPRODUCTION OF THE LICENSED CONTENT TO ANY SERVER OR LOCATION FOR FURTHER REPRODUCTION OR REDISTRIBUTION IS EXPRESSLY PROHIBITED.

3.   **DESCRIPTION OF OTHER RIGHTS AND LICENSE LIMITATIONS**

   3.1   *Use of Documentation and Printed Training Materials.*

          3.1.1   The documents and related graphics included in the Licensed Content may include technical inaccuracies or typographical errors. Changes are periodically made to the content. Microsoft may make improvements and/or changes in any of the components of the Licensed Content at any time without notice. The names of companies, products, people, characters and/or data mentioned in the Licensed Content may be fictitious and are in no way intended to represent any real individual, company, product or event, unless otherwise noted.

          3.1.2   Microsoft grants you the right to reproduce portions of documents (such as student workbooks, white papers, press releases, datasheets and FAQs) (the "Documents") provided with the Licensed Content. You may not print any book (either electronic or print version) in its entirety. If you choose to reproduce Documents, you agree that: (a) use of such printed Documents will be solely in conjunction with your personal training use; (b) the Documents will not republished or posted on any network computer or broadcast in any media; (c) any reproduction will include either the Document's original copyright notice or a copyright notice to Microsoft's benefit substantially in the format provided below; and (d) to comply with all terms and conditions of this EULA. In addition, no modifications may made to any Document.

          Form of Notice:

          © 2002. Reprinted with permission by Microsoft Corporation. All rights reserved.

          Microsoft and Windows are either registered trademarks or trademarks of Microsoft Corporation in the US and/or other countries. Other product and company names mentioned herein may be the trademarks of their respective owners.

   3.2   *Use of Media Elements.* The Licensed Content may include certain photographs, clip art, animations, sounds, music, and video clips (together "Media Elements"). You may not modify these Media Elements.

   3.3   *Use of Sample Code.* In the event that the Licensed Content includes sample code in source or object format ("Sample Code"), Microsoft grants you a limited, non-exclusive, royalty-free license to use, copy and modify the Sample Code; if you elect to exercise the foregoing rights, you agree to comply with all other terms and conditions of this EULA, including without limitation Sections 3.4, 3.5, and 6.

   3.4   *Permitted Modifications.* In the event that you exercise any rights provided under this EULA to create modifications of the Licensed Content, you agree that any such modifications: (a) will not be used for providing training where a fee is charged in public or private classes; (b) indemnify, hold harmless, and defend Microsoft from and against any claims or lawsuits, including attorneys' fees, which arise from or result from your use of any modified version of the Licensed Content; and (c) not to transfer or assign any rights to any modified version of the Licensed Content to any third party without the express written permission of Microsoft.

3.5 *Reproduction/Redistribution Licensed Content.* Except as expressly provided in this EULA, you may not reproduce or distribute the Licensed Content or any portion thereof (including any permitted modifications) to any third parties without the express written permission of Microsoft.

4. **RESERVATION OF RIGHTS AND OWNERSHIP.** Microsoft reserves all rights not expressly granted to you in this EULA. The Licensed Content is protected by copyright and other intellectual property laws and treaties. Microsoft or its suppliers own the title, copyright, and other intellectual property rights in the Licensed Content. You may not remove or obscure any copyright, trademark or patent notices that appear on the Licensed Content, or any components thereof, as delivered to you. **The Licensed Content is licensed, not sold.**

5. **LIMITATIONS ON REVERSE ENGINEERING, DECOMPILATION, AND DISASSEMBLY.** You may not reverse engineer, decompile, or disassemble the Software or Media Elements, except and only to the extent that such activity is expressly permitted by applicable law notwithstanding this limitation.

6. **LIMITATIONS ON SALE, RENTAL, ETC. AND CERTAIN ASSIGNMENTS.** You may not provide commercial hosting services with, sell, rent, lease, lend, sublicense, or assign copies of the Licensed Content, or any portion thereof (including any permitted modifications thereof) on a stand-alone basis or as part of any collection, product or service.

7. **CONSENT TO USE OF DATA.** You agree that Microsoft and its affiliates may collect and use technical information gathered as part of the product support services provided to you, if any, related to the Licensed Content. Microsoft may use this information solely to improve our products or to provide customized services or technologies to you and will not disclose this information in a form that personally identifies you.

8. **LINKS TO THIRD PARTY SITES.** You may link to third party sites through the use of the Licensed Content. The third party sites are not under the control of Microsoft, and Microsoft is not responsible for the contents of any third party sites, any links contained in third party sites, or any changes or updates to third party sites. Microsoft is not responsible for webcasting or any other form of transmission received from any third party sites. Microsoft is providing these links to third party sites to you only as a convenience, and the inclusion of any link does not imply an endorsement by Microsoft of the third party site.

9. **ADDITIONAL LICENSED CONTENT/SERVICES.** This EULA applies to updates, supplements, add-on components, or Internet-based services components, of the Licensed Content that Microsoft may provide to you or make available to you after the date you obtain your initial copy of the Licensed Content, unless we provide other terms along with the update, supplement, add-on component, or Internet-based services component. Microsoft reserves the right to discontinue any Internet-based services provided to you or made available to you through the use of the Licensed Content.

10. **U.S. GOVERNMENT LICENSE RIGHTS**. All software provided to the U.S. Government pursuant to solicitations issued on or after December 1, 1995 is provided with the commercial license rights and restrictions described elsewhere herein. All software provided to the U.S. Government pursuant to solicitations issued prior to December 1, 1995 is provided with "Restricted Rights" as provided for in FAR, 48 CFR 52.227-14 (JUNE 1987) or DFAR, 48 CFR 252.227-7013 (OCT 1988), as applicable.

11. **EXPORT RESTRICTIONS**. You acknowledge that the Licensed Content is subject to U.S. export jurisdiction. You agree to comply with all applicable international and national laws that apply to the Licensed Content, including the U.S. Export Administration Regulations, as well as end-user, end-use, and destination restrictions issued by U.S. and other governments. For additional information see <http://www.microsoft.com/exporting/>.

12. **TRANSFER.** The initial user of the Licensed Content may make a one-time permanent transfer of this EULA and Licensed Content to another end user, provided the initial user retains no copies of the Licensed Content. The transfer may not be an indirect transfer, such as a consignment. Prior to the transfer, the end user receiving the Licensed Content must agree to all the EULA terms.

13. **"NOT FOR RESALE" LICENSED CONTENT.** Licensed Content identified as "Not For Resale" or "NFR," may not be sold or otherwise transferred for value, or used for any purpose other than demonstration, test or evaluation.

14. **TERMINATION.** Without prejudice to any other rights, Microsoft may terminate this EULA if you fail to comply with the terms and conditions of this EULA. In such event, you must destroy all copies of the Licensed Content and all of its component parts.

15. **DISCLAIMER OF WARRANTIES.** **TO THE MAXIMUM EXTENT PERMITTED BY APPLICABLE LAW, MICROSOFT AND ITS SUPPLIERS PROVIDE THE LICENSED CONTENT AND SUPPORT SERVICES (IF ANY)** *AS IS AND WITH ALL FAULTS,* **AND MICROSOFT AND ITS SUPPLIERS HEREBY DISCLAIM ALL OTHER WARRANTIES AND CONDITIONS, WHETHER EXPRESS, IMPLIED OR STATUTORY, INCLUDING, BUT NOT LIMITED TO, ANY (IF ANY) IMPLIED WARRANTIES, DUTIES OR CONDITIONS OF MERCHANTABILITY, OF FITNESS FOR A PARTICULAR PURPOSE, OF RELIABILITY OR AVAILABILITY, OF ACCURACY OR COMPLETENESS OF RESPONSES, OF RESULTS, OF WORKMANLIKE EFFORT, OF LACK OF VIRUSES, AND OF LACK OF NEGLIGENCE, ALL WITH REGARD TO THE LICENSED CONTENT, AND THE PROVISION OF OR FAILURE TO PROVIDE SUPPORT OR OTHER SERVICES, INFORMATION, SOFTWARE, AND RELATED CONTENT THROUGH THE LICENSED CONTENT, OR OTHERWISE ARISING OUT OF THE USE OF THE LICENSED CONTENT. ALSO, THERE IS NO WARRANTY OR CONDITION OF TITLE, QUIET ENJOYMENT, QUIET POSSESSION, CORRESPONDENCE TO DESCRIPTION OR NON-INFRINGEMENT WITH REGARD TO THE LICENSED CONTENT. THE ENTIRE RISK AS TO THE QUALITY, OR ARISING OUT OF THE USE OR PERFORMANCE OF THE LICENSED CONTENT, AND ANY SUPPORT SERVICES, REMAINS WITH YOU.**

16. **EXCLUSION OF INCIDENTAL, CONSEQUENTIAL AND CERTAIN OTHER DAMAGES.** **TO THE MAXIMUM EXTENT PERMITTED BY APPLICABLE LAW, IN NO EVENT SHALL MICROSOFT OR ITS SUPPLIERS BE LIABLE FOR ANY SPECIAL, INCIDENTAL, PUNITIVE, INDIRECT, OR CONSEQUENTIAL DAMAGES WHATSOEVER (INCLUDING, BUT NOT**

LIMITED TO, DAMAGES FOR LOSS OF PROFITS OR CONFIDENTIAL OR OTHER INFORMATION, FOR BUSINESS INTERRUPTION, FOR PERSONAL INJURY, FOR LOSS OF PRIVACY, FOR FAILURE TO MEET ANY DUTY INCLUDING OF GOOD FAITH OR OF REASONABLE CARE, FOR NEGLIGENCE, AND FOR ANY OTHER PECUNIARY OR OTHER LOSS WHATSOEVER) ARISING OUT OF OR IN ANY WAY RELATED TO THE USE OF OR INABILITY TO USE THE LICENSED CONTENT, THE PROVISION OF OR FAILURE TO PROVIDE SUPPORT OR OTHER SERVICES, INFORMATION, SOFTWARE, AND RELATED CONTENT THROUGH THE LICENSED CONTENT, OR OTHERWISE ARISING OUT OF THE USE OF THE LICENSED CONTENT, OR OTHERWISE UNDER OR IN CONNECTION WITH ANY PROVISION OF THIS EULA, EVEN IN THE EVENT OF THE FAULT, TORT (INCLUDING NEGLIGENCE), MISREPRESENTATION, STRICT LIABILITY, BREACH OF CONTRACT OR BREACH OF WARRANTY OF MICROSOFT OR ANY SUPPLIER, AND EVEN IF MICROSOFT OR ANY SUPPLIER HAS BEEN ADVISED OF THE POSSIBILITY OF SUCH DAMAGES. BECAUSE SOME STATES/JURISDICTIONS DO NOT ALLOW THE EXCLUSION OR LIMITATION OF LIABILITY FOR CONSEQUENTIAL OR INCIDENTAL DAMAGES, THE ABOVE LIMITATION MAY NOT APPLY TO YOU.

17. <u>LIMITATION OF LIABILITY AND REMEDIES.</u> NOTWITHSTANDING ANY DAMAGES THAT YOU MIGHT INCUR FOR ANY REASON WHATSOEVER (INCLUDING, WITHOUT LIMITATION, ALL DAMAGES REFERENCED HEREIN AND ALL DIRECT OR GENERAL DAMAGES IN CONTRACT OR ANYTHING ELSE), THE ENTIRE LIABILITY OF MICROSOFT AND ANY OF ITS SUPPLIERS UNDER ANY PROVISION OF THIS EULA AND YOUR EXCLUSIVE REMEDY HEREUNDER SHALL BE LIMITED TO THE GREATER OF THE ACTUAL DAMAGES YOU INCUR IN REASONABLE RELIANCE ON THE LICENSED CONTENT UP TO THE AMOUNT ACTUALLY PAID BY YOU FOR THE LICENSED CONTENT OR US$5.00. THE FOREGOING LIMITATIONS, EXCLUSIONS AND DISCLAIMERS SHALL APPLY TO THE MAXIMUM EXTENT PERMITTED BY APPLICABLE LAW, EVEN IF ANY REMEDY FAILS ITS ESSENTIAL PURPOSE.

18. **APPLICABLE LAW.** If you acquired this Licensed Content in the United States, this EULA is governed by the laws of the State of Washington. If you acquired this Licensed Content in Canada, unless expressly prohibited by local law, this EULA is governed by the laws in force in the Province of Ontario, Canada; and, in respect of any dispute which may arise hereunder, you consent to the jurisdiction of the federal and provincial courts sitting in Toronto, Ontario. If you acquired this Licensed Content in the European Union, Iceland, Norway, or Switzerland, then local law applies. If you acquired this Licensed Content in any other country, then local law may apply.

19. **ENTIRE AGREEMENT; SEVERABILITY.** This EULA (including any addendum or amendment to this EULA which is included with the Licensed Content) are the entire agreement between you and Microsoft relating to the Licensed Content and the support services (if any) and they supersede all prior or contemporaneous oral or written communications, proposals and representations with respect to the Licensed Content or any other subject matter covered by this EULA. To the extent the terms of any Microsoft policies or programs for support services conflict with the terms of this EULA, the terms of this EULA shall control. If any provision of this EULA is held to be void, invalid, unenforceable or illegal, the other provisions shall continue in full force and effect.

Should you have any questions concerning this EULA, or if you desire to contact Microsoft for any reason, please use the address information enclosed in this Licensed Content to contact the Microsoft subsidiary serving your country or visit Microsoft on the World Wide Web at http://www.microsoft.com.

Si vous avez acquis votre Contenu Sous Licence Microsoft au CANADA :

DÉNI DE GARANTIES. Dans la mesure maximale permise par les lois applicables, le Contenu Sous Licence et les services de soutien technique (le cas échéant) sont fournis *TELS QUELS ET AVEC TOUS LES DÉFAUTS* par Microsoft et ses fournisseurs, lesquels par les présentes dénient toutes autres garanties et conditions expresses, implicites ou en vertu de la loi, notamment, mais sans limitation, (le cas échéant) les garanties, devoirs ou conditions implicites de qualité marchande, d'adaptation à une fin usage particulière, de fiabilité ou de disponibilité, d'exactitude ou d'exhaustivité des réponses, des résultats, des efforts déployés selon les règles de l'art, d'absence de virus et d'absence de négligence, le tout à l'égard du Contenu Sous Licence et de la prestation des services de soutien technique ou de l'omission de la 'une telle prestation des services de soutien technique ou à l'égard de la fourniture ou de l'omission de la fourniture de tous autres services, renseignements, Contenus Sous Licence, et contenu qui s'y rapporte grâce au Contenu Sous Licence ou provenant autrement de l'utilisation du Contenu Sous Licence. PAR AILLEURS, IL N'Y A AUCUNE GARANTIE OU CONDITION QUANT AU TITRE DE PROPRIÉTÉ, À LA JOUISSANCE OU LA POSSESSION PAISIBLE, À LA CONCORDANCE À UNE DESCRIPTION NI QUANT À UNE ABSENCE DE CONTREFAÇON CONCERNANT LE CONTENU SOUS LICENCE.

<u>**EXCLUSION DES DOMMAGES ACCESSOIRES, INDIRECTS ET DE CERTAINS AUTRES DOMMAGES.**</u> **DANS LA MESURE MAXIMALE PERMISE PAR LES LOIS APPLICABLES, EN AUCUN CAS MICROSOFT OU SES FOURNISSEURS NE SERONT RESPONSABLES DES DOMMAGES SPÉCIAUX, CONSÉCUTIFS, ACCESSOIRES OU INDIRECTS DE QUELQUE NATURE QUE CE SOIT (NOTAMMENT, LES DOMMAGES À L'ÉGARD DU MANQUE À GAGNER OU DE LA DIVULGATION DE RENSEIGNEMENTS CONFIDENTIELS OU AUTRES, DE LA PERTE D'EXPLOITATION, DE BLESSURES CORPORELLES, DE LA VIOLATION DE LA VIE PRIVÉE, DE L'OMISSION DE REMPLIR TOUT DEVOIR, Y COMPRIS D'AGIR DE BONNE FOI OU D'EXERCER UN SOIN RAISONNABLE, DE LA NÉGLIGENCE ET DE TOUTE AUTRE PERTE PÉCUNIAIRE OU AUTRE PERTE**

DE QUELQUE NATURE QUE CE SOIT) SE RAPPORTE DE QUELQUE MANIÈRE QUE CE SOIT À L'UTILISATION DU CONTENU SOUS LICENCE OU À L'INCAPACITÉ DE S'EN SERVIR, À LA PRESTATION OU À L'OMISSION DE LA 'UNE TELLE PRESTATION DE SERVICES DE SOUTIEN TECHNIQUE OU À LA FOURNITURE OU À L'OMISSION DE LA FOURNITURE DE TOUS AUTRES SERVICES, RENSEIGNEMENTS, CONTENUS SOUS LICENCE, ET CONTENU QUI S'Y RAPPORTE GRÂCE AU CONTENU SOUS LICENCE OU PROVENANT AUTREMENT DE L'UTILISATION DU CONTENU SOUS LICENCE OU AUTREMENT AUX TERMES DE TOUTE DISPOSITION DE LA U PRÉSENTE CONVENTION EULA OU RELATIVEMENT À UNE TELLE DISPOSITION, MÊME EN CAS DE FAUTE, DE DÉLIT CIVIL (Y COMPRIS LA NÉGLIGENCE), DE RESPONSABILITÉ STRICTE, DE VIOLATION DE CONTRAT OU DE VIOLATION DE GARANTIE DE MICROSOFT OU DE TOUT FOURNISSEUR ET MÊME SI MICROSOFT OU TOUT FOURNISSEUR A ÉTÉ AVISÉ DE LA POSSIBILITÉ DE TELS DOMMAGES.

LIMITATION DE RESPONSABILITÉ ET RECOURS. MALGRÉ LES DOMMAGES QUE VOUS PUISSIEZ SUBIR POUR QUELQUE MOTIF QUE CE SOIT (NOTAMMENT, MAIS SANS LIMITATION, TOUS LES DOMMAGES SUSMENTIONNÉS ET TOUS LES DOMMAGES DIRECTS OU GÉNÉRAUX OU AUTRES), LA SEULE RESPONSABILITÉ 'OBLIGATION INTÉGRALE DE MICROSOFT ET DE L'UN OU L'AUTRE DE SES FOURNISSEURS AUX TERMES DE TOUTE DISPOSITION DEU LA PRÉSENTE CONVENTION EULA ET VOTRE RECOURS EXCLUSIF À L'ÉGARD DE TOUT CE QUI PRÉCÈDE SE LIMITE AU PLUS ÉLEVÉ ENTRE LES MONTANTS SUIVANTS : LE MONTANT QUE VOUS AVEZ RÉELLEMENT PAYÉ POUR LE CONTENU SOUS LICENCE OU 5,00 $US. LES LIMITES, EXCLUSIONS ET DÉNIS QUI PRÉCÈDENT (Y COMPRIS LES CLAUSES CI-DESSUS), S'APPLIQUENT DANS LA MESURE MAXIMALE PERMISE PAR LES LOIS APPLICABLES, MÊME SI TOUT RECOURS N'ATTEINT PAS SON BUT ESSENTIEL.

À moins que cela ne soit prohibé par le droit local applicable, la présente Convention est régie par les lois de la province d'Ontario, Canada. Vous consentez Chacune des parties à la présente reconnaît irrévocablement à la compétence des tribunaux fédéraux et provinciaux siégeant à Toronto, dans de la province d'Ontario et consent à instituer tout litige qui pourrait découler de la présente auprès des tribunaux situés dans le district judiciaire de York, province d'Ontario.

Au cas où vous auriez des questions concernant cette licence ou que vous désiriez vous mettre en rapport avec Microsoft pour quelque raison que ce soit, veuillez utiliser l'information contenue dans le Contenu Sous Licence pour contacter la filiale de succursale Microsoft desservant votre pays, dont l'adresse est fournie dans ce produit, ou visitez écrivez à : Microsoft sur le World Wide Web à http://www.microsoft.com

Contents

Module 17: Review

Appendix A: Lab Recovery

Appendix B: Debugging with Microsoft Visual Studio .NET

Appendix C: Using Templates with List-Bound Controls

Appendix D: XML Web Service Responses

Course 2310: Index

About This Course

This section provides you with a brief description of the course, audience, suggested prerequisites, and course objectives.

Description

This course provides students with the knowledge and skills that are needed to develop Web applications by using Microsoft® Visual Studio® .NET and Microsoft ASP.NET.

Audience

This course is designed for two types of students: beginner Web developers and Microsoft Visual Basic® or C# developers who want to learn Visual Studio .NET and ASP.NET:

- *Beginner Web developer.* These developers have minimal experience with programming. However, they should know the basic constructs of programming, such as loops and conditional statements. Beginning Web developers need to have experience with Hypertext Markup Language (HTML) and some scripting language, such as Visual Basic Scripting Edition or Microsoft JScript®.

  This audience includes both HTML developers and dynamic HTML (DHTML) developers.

- *Visual Basic developer.* These developers have experience developing Microsoft Windows® applications by using Visual Basic 6.

Student prerequisites

This course requires that students meet the following prerequisites:

- Knowledge of HTML or DHTML, including:
  - Tables
  - Images
  - Forms
- Programming experience using Visual Basic .NET, including:
  - Declaring variables
  - Using loops
  - Using conditional statements

The completion of either Course 2559, *Introduction to Visual Basic .NET Programming with Microsoft .NET*, or Course 2373, *Programming with Microsoft Visual Basic .NET*, satisfies the preceding prerequisite skills requirements.

Course objectives

After completing this course, the student will be able to:

- Describe the Microsoft .NET Framework and ASP.NET.
- Create an ASP.NET Web application project by using Visual Studio.NET.
- Create a component in Visual Basic .NET or C#.
- Add server controls to an ASP.NET page.
- Add functionality to server controls that are located on an ASP.NET page.
- Use the tracing features of Visual Studio .NET.
- Use validation controls to validate user input.

- Create a user control.

- Access data by using the built-in data access tools that are in Visual Studio .NET.

- Use Microsoft ADO.NET to access data in an ASP.NET Web application.

- Call a stored procedure from an ASP.NET Web application.

- Access Extensible Markup Language (XML) data and read it into a **DataSet** object.

- Consume and create an XML Web service from an ASP.NET Web application.

- Store ASP.NET Web application and session data by using a variety of methods.

- Configure and deploy an ASP.NET Web application.

- Secure an ASP.NET Web application by using a variety of technologies.

Appendices

There are four appendices included with Course 2310B, *Developing Microsoft ASP.NET Web Applications Using Visual Studio .NET*:

- Appendix A, "Lab Recovery"

  This appendix provides the steps that are required to recover from an incomplete or broken lab solution.

- Appendix B, "Debugging with Microsoft Visual Studio .NET"

  This appendix is an optional lesson for Module 6, "Tracing in Microsoft ASP.NET Web Applications." This Appendix is a lesson that includes three topic slides and one demonstration; it should take 30 minutes to deliver this appendix.

- Appendix C, "Using Templates with List-Bound Controls"

  This appendix is an optional lesson for Module 9, "Accessing Relational Data Using Microsoft Visual Studio .NET." This appendix lesson includes two topic slides and one demonstration; it should take 15 minutes to deliver this appendix.

- Appendix D, "XML Web Service Responses"

  This appendix is an optional lesson for Module 13, "Consuming and Creating XML Web Services." This lesson includes three topic slides and one demonstration; it should take 20 minutes to deliver this appendix.

Student Materials Compact Disc Contents

The Student Materials compact disc contains the following files and folders:

- *Autorun.exe.* When the compact disc is inserted into the CD-ROM drive, or when you double-click the **Autorun.exe** file, this file opens the compact disc and allows you to browse the Student Materials compact disc.

- *Autorun.inf.* When the compact disc is inserted into the compact disc drive, this file opens Autorun.exe.

- *Default.htm.* This file opens the Student Materials Web page. It provides students with resources pertaining to this course, including additional reading, review and lab answers, lab files, multimedia presentations, and course-related Web sites.

- *Readme.txt.* This file explains how to install the software for viewing the Student Materials compact disc and its contents and how to open the Student Materials Web page.

- *2310B_ms.doc.* This file is the Manual Classroom Setup Guide. It contains a description of classroom requirements, classroom setup instructions, and the classroom configuration.

- *Democode.* This folder contains demonstration code.

- *Flash.* This folder contains the installer for the Macromedia Flash 5 browser plug-in.

- *Fonts.* This folder contains the fonts that are required to view the PowerPoint presentation and Web-based materials.

- *Labfiles.* This folder contains files that are used in the hands-on labs. These files may be used to prepare the student computers for the hands-on labs.

- *Media.* This folder contains files that are used in multimedia presentations for this course.

- *Mplayer.* This folder contains the setup file to install Microsoft Windows Media™ Player.

- *Practices.* This folder contains files that are used in the hands-on practices.

- *Webfiles.* This folder contains the files that are required to view the course Web page. To open the Web page, open Windows Explorer, and in the root directory of the compact disc, double-click **Default.htm** or **Autorun.exe**.

- *Wordview.* This folder contains the Word Viewer that is used to view any Word document (.doc) files that are included on the compact disc.

Document Conventions

The following conventions are used in course materials to distinguish elements of the text.

Convention	Use
bold	Represents commands, command options, and syntax that must be typed exactly as shown. It also indicates commands on menus and buttons, dialog box titles and options, and icon and menu names.
italic	In syntax statements or descriptive text, indicates argument names or placeholders for variable information. Italic is also used for introducing new terms, for book titles, and for emphasis in the text.
Title Capitals	Indicate domain names, user names, computer names, directory names, and folder and file names, except when specifically referring to case-sensitive names. Unless otherwise indicated, you can use lowercase letters when you type a directory name or file name in a dialog box or at a command prompt.
ALL CAPITALS	Indicate the names of keys, key sequences, and key combinations—for example, ALT+SPACEBAR.
`monospace`	Represents code samples or examples of screen text.
|	In syntax statements, separates an either/or choice.
▶	Indicates a procedure with sequential steps.
...	Represents an omitted portion of a code sample.

msdn® training

Introduction

Contents

Microsoft®

Introduction

- Name
- Company affiliation
- Title/function
- Job responsibility
- Programming, networking, and database experience
- ASP.NET and Visual Studio .NET experience
- Expectations for the course

Course Materials

- **Name card**
- **Student workbook**
- **Student Materials compact disc**
- **Course evaluation**

The following materials are included with your kit:

- *Name card.* Write your name on both sides of the name card.

- *Student workbook.* The student workbook contains the material that is covered in class, in addition to the hands-on lab exercises.

- *Student Materials compact disc.* The Student Materials compact disc contains the Web page that provides you with links to resources pertaining to this course, including additional readings, review and lab answers, lab files, multimedia presentations, and course-related Web sites.

> **Note** To open the Web page, insert the Student Materials compact disc into the CD-ROM drive, and then in the root directory of the compact disc, double-click **Autorun.exe** or **Default.htm**.

- *Course evaluation.* To provide feedback on the course, training facility, and instructor, you will have the opportunity to complete an online evaluation near the end of the course.

To provide additional comments or inquire about the Microsoft Certified Professional program, send an e-mail message to mcphelp@microsoft.com.

Prerequisites

> - **Knowledge of HTML or DHTML, including:**
>   - Using tables
>   - Displaying images
>   - Using forms
> - **Programming experience using Visual Basic .NET or C#, including:**
>   - Declaring variables
>   - Using loops
>   - Using conditional statements

This course requires that you meet the following prerequisites:

- Knowledge of Hypertext Markup Language (HTML) or dynamic HTML (DHTML), including:

  - Tables

  - Images

  - Forms

- Programming experience using Microsoft Visual Basic® .NET, including:

  - Declaring variables

  - Using loops

  - Using conditional statements

The completion of either Course 2559, *Introduction to Visual Basic .NET Programming with Microsoft .NET*, or Course 2373, *Programming with Microsoft Visual Basic .NET*, satisfies the preceding prerequisite skills.

- Programming experience using Microsoft Visual C#™ .NET, including:

  - Declaring variables

  - Using loops

  - Using conditional statements

The completion of either Course 2609, *Introduction to C# Programming with Microsoft .NET*, or Course 2124, *Programming with C#*, satisfies the preceding prerequisite skills.

Course Outline

- ■ **Module 1: Overview of the Microsoft .NET Framework**
- ■ **Module 2: Using Microsoft Visual Studio .NET**
- ■ **Module 3: Using Microsoft .NET–Based Languages**
- ■ **Module 4: Creating a Microsoft ASP.NET Web Form**
- ■ **Module 5: Adding Code to a Microsoft ASP.NET Web Form**
- ■ **Module 6: Tracing in Microsoft ASP.NET Web Applications**

Module 1, "Overview of the Microsoft .NET Framework," discusses how the .NET Framework represents a major change in the way that Web applications are built and run. After completing this module, you will have a greater understanding of the .NET Framework in general and Microsoft ASP.NET specifically. At the end of this module, you will have the opportunity to examine the complete ASP.NET Web application that you will build in the labs throughout this course.

Module 2, "Using Microsoft Visual Studio .NET," describes how to use the primary features of Microsoft Visual Studio® .NET to create ASP.NET Web applications. After completing this module, you will be able to navigate the Visual Studio .NET integrated development environment (IDE), and be able to create, build, and view an ASP.NET Web application project.

Module 3, "Using Microsoft .NET–Based Languages," introduces the different languages that are available for use when developing .NET-based Web applications. After completing this module, you will be able to identify the languages that support the .NET Framework, and be able to choose an appropriate development language for your needs.

Module 4, "Creating a Microsoft ASP.NET Web Form," describes how to create and populate Web Forms. Web Forms are programmable Web pages that serve as the user interface (UI) for an ASP.NET Web application project. After completing this module, you will be able to add a Web Form to an ASP.NET Web application project and use the Visual Studio .NET toolbox to add server controls to a Web Form.

Module 5, "Adding Code to a Microsoft ASP.NET Web Form," describes the various methods that can be used to add code to your ASP.NET Web application. After completing this module, you will be able to create event procedures for server controls, use code-behind pages in a Web application, and use **Page** events in a Web application.

Module 6, "Tracing in Microsoft ASP.NET Web Applications," describes how to catch runtime errors by using the **Trace** object. After completing this module, you will be able to use the **Trace** object to view runtime information about a Web application.

Course Outline *(continued)*

- Module 7: Validating User Input

- Module 8: Creating User Controls

- Module 9: Accessing Relational Data Using Microsoft Visual Studio .NET

- Module 10: Accessing Data with Microsoft ADO.NET

- Module 11: Calling Stored Procedures with Microsoft ADO.NET

- Module 12: Reading and Writing XML Data

Module 7, "Validating User Input," describes the input validation controls that are available in ASP.NET, and describes how to add these controls to an ASP.NET Web Form by using Visual Studio .NET. After completing this module, you will be able to identify when input validation is appropriate, use input validation controls to verify user input, and verify that all of the validation controls on a page are valid.

Module 8, "Creating User Controls," describes how user controls provide an easy way to reuse common UI components and code throughout an ASP.NET Web application. After completing this module, you will be able to create a user control, and then add that user control to an ASP.NET Web Form.

Module 9, "Accessing Relational Data Using Microsoft Visual Studio .NET," describes what Microsoft ADO.NET is, and describes how you can incorporate ADO.NET into an ASP.NET Web application by using the data tools that are built into Visual Studio .NET. After completing this module, you will be able to create a connection to a database by using ADO.NET, and then display data in a Web Form.

Module 10, "Accessing Data with Microsoft ADO.NET," describes how to manually add data access to your Web application. After completing this module, you will be able to programmatically connect to a Microsoft SQL Server™ database by using **SqlConnection** and **SqlDataAdapter** objects, store multiple tables of data in a **DataSet** object, and then display that data in **DataGrid** controls. Finally, you will be able to manually read data from a SQL Server database by using a **SqlDataReader** object, and bind a list-bound server control to a **DataSet**, or to a **DataReader** control.

Module 11, "Calling Stored Procedures with Microsoft ADO.NET," describes how to accomplish data access tasks from your Web application by using stored procedures. After completing this module, you will be able to explain the reasons for using stored procedures with a database and be able to call stored procedures.

Module 12, "Reading and Writing XML Data," describes how to read, write, and display Extensible Markup Language (XML) data. After completing this module, you will be able to read and write XML data into a **DataSet** object. You will also be able to store, retrieve, and transform XML data by using **XmlDataDocument** and **XslTransform** objects, and be able to use the XML Web server control to load and save XML data.

Course Outline *(continued)*

- **Module 13: Consuming and Creating XML Web Services**
- **Module 14: Managing State**
- **Module 15: Configuring, Optimizing, and Deploying a Microsoft ASP.NET Web Application**
- **Module 16: Securing a Microsoft ASP.NET Web Application**
- **Module 17: Review**

Module 13, "Consuming and Creating XML Web Services," describes how to call an XML Web service directly with a browser, and programmatically call an XML Web service from a Web Form. Also covered in this module is the creation and publishing of XML Web services by using Visual Studio .NET. After completing this module, you will be able to call an XML Web service directly from a browser, and be able to create a Web reference to programmatically call an XML Web service from a Web Form. You will also be able to build and publish an XML Web service.

Module 14, "Managing State," describes how to maintain state in an ASP.NET Web application. State is the ability to retain user information in a Web application. After completing this module, you will be able to manage state in an ASP.NET Web application by using application and session variables. You will also be able to use cookies and cookieless sessions to manage state.

Module 15, "Configuring, Optimizing, and Deploying a Microsoft ASP.NET Web Application," describes how to set up and deploy your ASP.NET Web application. After completing this module, you will be able to use the **Cache** object and page output caching, and be able to configure a Web application by using the Machine.config and Web.config files. You will also be able to deploy an ASP.NET Web application.

Module 16, "Securing a Microsoft ASP.NET Web Application," describes how to use Microsoft Windows®-based and Forms-based authentication. A discussion of Microsoft Passport authentication is also included. After completing this module, you will be able to secure ASP.NET Web applications by using Windows-based or Forms-based authentication.

Module 17, "Review," consists of a review of the main concepts that you have learned throughout this course. In this module, you will have an opportunity to apply your new knowledge in Lab 17, which is an interactive review game.

Setup

> ■ **Windows XP Professional Edition**
>
>   • Internet Information Services
>
>   • Internet Explorer 6
>
> ■ **SQL Server 2000 Developer Edition**
>
>   • SQL Server 2000 Service Pack 2
>
> ■ **Visual Studio .NET Enterprise Developer Edition**
>
>   • Microsoft .NET Framework Service Pack 1
>
> ■ **Macromedia Flash Player 5**

Software

The following software will be used in the classroom:

- Windows XP Professional Edition
  - Internet Information Services (IIS)
  - Microsoft Internet Explorer 6
- SQL Server 2000 Developer Edition
  - SQL Server 2000 Developer Service Pack 2
- Visual Studio .NET Enterprise Developer Edition
  - Microsoft .NET Framework Service Pack 1
- Macromedia Flash Player 5

Course files

There are files that are associated with the labs in this course. The lab files are located in the *install folder*\Labfiles\Lab*XXLL* folder on the student computers where *XX* is the Module number and *LL* is the language used, either VB for Visual Basic .NET or CS for C#.

Classroom setup

The classroom is configured in the workgroup model. Each student computer in the classroom has Windows XP Professional installed as a member of that workgroup.

Microsoft Official Curriculum

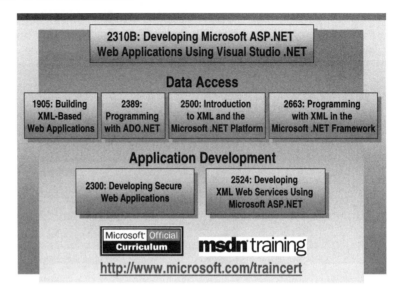

Introduction

Microsoft Training and Certification develops Microsoft Official Curriculum (MOC), including MSDN® Training, for computer professionals who design, develop, support, implement, or manage solutions by using Microsoft products and technologies. These courses provide comprehensive skills-based training in instructor-led and online formats.

Additional recommended courses

After you complete this course, there are several follow-up courses that are available that will allow you to focus in greater depth on subjects that are covered in this course.

For more information about the curriculum paths, see the Microsoft Official Curriculum Web page at http://www.microsoft.com/traincert/training/moc.

Data access

The following table lists courses would be an appropriate continuation of the data access sections of this course.

Course	Title and description
1905	*Building XML-Based Web Applications,* is a five-day course that covers how to structure and validate data in a document by using document type definitions (DTDs). Students also learn how to get data from a database by using XML, and how to present that data by using the Extensible Stylesheet Language (XSL).
2389	*Programming with ADO.NET,* is a five-day course that covers accessing data sources from Windows-based applications, Web applications, and Web services by using ADO.NET.

(continued)

Course	Title and description
2500	*Introduction to XML and the Microsoft .NET Platform*, is a two-day course that provides a technological overview of the structure and programming techniques of XML. This course shows where XML figures into the Microsoft .NET vision and into the larger world of distributed standards-based computing.
2663	*Programming with XML in the Microsoft .NET Framework*, is a three-day course for programmers who have some experience with XML. This course covers programming that uses XML in the .NET Framework.

Application development

The following table lists courses would be an appropriate continuation of the Web application development sections of this course.

Course	Title and description
2300	*Developing Secure Web Applications*, is a three-day course that teaches Web developers the knowledge and skills that are required to build Web applications by using secure coding techniques. This course also covers the security features that are available in Windows XP, IIS, ASP.NET, and ADO.NET. Students learn how to identify Web site security vulnerabilities and understand the trade-offs between functionality and speed when choosing the appropriate security mechanisms. Students will also learn how to use the security features that are available in Windows 2000, SQL Server, ASP.NET, and ADO.NET.
2524	*Developing XML Web Services Using Microsoft ASP.NET*, is a three-day course that covers how to build and deploy Web services by using Visual Studio .NET.

Microsoft Training and Certification information

Other related courses may become available in the future, so for up-to-date information about recommended courses, visit the Training and Certification Web site at http://www.microsoft.com/traincert.

Microsoft Certified Professional Program

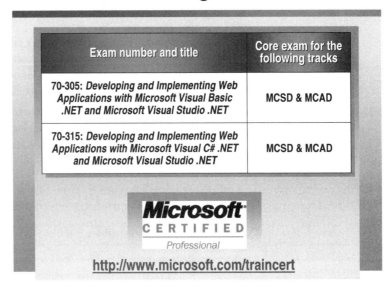

Exam number and title	Core exam for the following tracks
70-305: *Developing and Implementing Web Applications with Microsoft Visual Basic .NET and Microsoft Visual Studio .NET*	MCSD & MCAD
70-315: *Developing and Implementing Web Applications with Microsoft Visual C# .NET and Microsoft Visual Studio .NET*	MCSD & MCAD

Microsoft
C E R T I F I E D
Professional
http://www.microsoft.com/traincert

Introduction

Microsoft Training and Certification offers a variety of certification credentials for developers and IT professionals. The Microsoft Certified Professional program is the leading certification program for validating your experience and skills, keeping you competitive in today's changing business environment.

Related certification exams

The following exams relate to ASP.NET Web Application design:

- Exam 70-305: *Developing and Implementing Web Applications with Microsoft Visual Basic .NET and Microsoft Visual Studio .NET*, measures your ability to develop and implement Web applications with Web Forms, ASP.NET, and the .NET Framework.

  When you pass the *Developing and Implementing Web Applications with Microsoft Visual Basic .NET and Microsoft Visual Studio .NET* exam, you achieve Microsoft Certified Professional status. You also earn credit toward the following certifications:

  - Core credit toward Microsoft Certified Solution Developer for Microsoft .NET certification.

  - Core or elective credit toward Microsoft Certified Application Developer for Microsoft .NET certification.

- Exam 70-315: *Developing and Implementing Web Applications with Microsoft Visual C# .NET and Microsoft Visual Studio .NET*, measures your ability to develop and implement Web applications with Web Forms, ASP.NET, and the .NET Framework.

  When you pass the *Developing and Implementing Web Applications with Microsoft Visual C# .NET and Microsoft Visual Studio .NET* exam, you achieve Microsoft Certified Professional status. You also earn credit toward the following certifications:

  - Core credit toward Microsoft Certified Solution Developer for Microsoft .NET certification.

  - Core or elective credit toward Microsoft Certified Application Developer (MCAD) for Microsoft .NET certification.

MCP certifications

The Microsoft Certified Professional program includes the following certifications.

- MCAD

  The Microsoft Certified Application Developer (MCAD) for Microsoft .NET credential is appropriate for professionals who use Microsoft technologies to develop and maintain department-level applications, components, Web or desktop clients, or back-end data services, or who work in teams developing enterprise applications. The scope of responsibility of MCADs is a subset of MCSDs.

- MCSD

  The Microsoft Certified Solution Developer (MCSD) credential is the premier certification for professionals who design and develop leading-edge business solutions with Microsoft development tools, technologies, platforms, and the Microsoft Windows DNA architecture. The types of applications MCSDs can develop include desktop applications and multi-user, Web-based, N-tier, and transaction-based applications. The credential covers job tasks ranging from analyzing business requirements to maintaining solutions.

- MCSA on Microsoft Windows 2000

  The Microsoft Certified Systems Administrator (MCSA) certification is designed for professionals who implement, manage, and troubleshoot existing network and system environments based on Microsoft Windows 2000 platforms, including the Windows .NET Server family. Implementation responsibilities include installing and configuring parts of the systems. Management responsibilities include administering and supporting the systems.

- MCSE on Microsoft Windows 2000

  The Microsoft Certified Systems Engineer (MCSE) credential is the premier certification for professionals who analyze the business requirements and design and implement the infrastructure for business solutions based on the Microsoft Windows 2000 platform and Microsoft server software, including the Windows .NET Server family. Implementation responsibilities include installing, configuring, and troubleshooting network systems.

- MCDBA on Microsoft SQL Server 2000

  The Microsoft Certified Database Administrator (MCDBA) credential is the premier certification for professionals who implement and administer Microsoft SQL Server databases. The certification is appropriate for individuals who derive physical database designs, develop logical data models, create physical databases, create data services by using Transact-SQL, manage and maintain databases, configure and manage security, monitor and optimize databases, and install and configure SQL Server.

- MCP

  The Microsoft Certified Professional (MCP) credential is for individuals who have the skills to successfully implement a Microsoft product or technology as part of a business solution in an organization. Hands-on experience with the product is necessary to successfully achieve certification.

- MCT

  Microsoft Certified Trainers (MCTs) demonstrate the instructional and technical skills that qualify them to deliver Microsoft Official Curriculum through Microsoft Certified Technical Education Centers (Microsoft CTECs).

Certification requirements

The certification requirements differ for each certification category and are specific to the products and job functions addressed by the certification. To become a Microsoft Certified Professional, you must pass rigorous certification exams that provide a valid and reliable measure of technical proficiency and expertise.

For More Information   See the Microsoft Training and Certification Web site at http://www.microsoft.com/traincert.

You can also send an e-mail to mcphelp@microsoft.com if you have specific certification questions.

Acquiring the skills tested by an MCP exam

MOC and MSDN Training Curriculum can help you develop the skills that you need to do your job. They also complement the experience that you gain while working with Microsoft products and technologies. However, no one-to-one correlation exists between MOC and MSDN Training courses and MCP exams. Microsoft does not expect or intend for the courses to be the sole preparation method for passing MCP exams. Practical product knowledge and experience is also necessary to pass the MCP exams.

To help prepare for the MCP exams, use the preparation guides that are available for each exam. Each Exam Preparation Guide contains exam-specific information, such as a list of the topics on which you will be tested. These guides are available on the Microsoft Training and Certification Web site at http://www.microsoft.com/traincert.

Facilities

Facilities

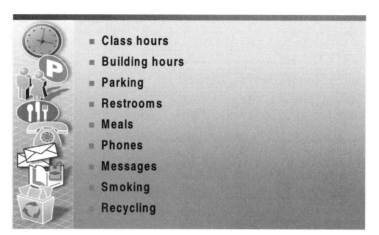

msdn training

Module 1: Overview of the Microsoft .NET Framework

Contents

Overview

- ■ **Introduction to the .NET Framework**
- ■ **Overview of ASP.NET**
- ■ **Overview of the Lab Application**
- ■ **Resources**

Introduction

The Microsoft® .NET Framework represents a major change in the way that Web applications are built and run. Microsoft ASP.NET is one of numerous technologies that are part of the .NET Framework. In this module, you will learn about the .NET Framework and ASP.NET. You will then have an opportunity to examine the complete Web application that you will build in the labs throughout Course 2310B, *Developing Microsoft ASP.NET Web Applications Using Visual Studio .NET*.

Objectives

After completing this module, you will be able to:

- ■ Explain the advantages of using the .NET Framework.

- ■ Understand the key functionality and purpose of ASP.NET in developing Web applications.

- ■ Understand the basic functionality of the Web site that you will build in the labs in Course 2310B.

Lesson: Introduction to the .NET Framework

- **What is the .NET Framework?**

- **What Problems Does .NET Solve?**

- **The .NET Framework Components**

- **Benefits of Using the .NET Framework**

- **Visual Studio .NET: The Tool for .NET Development**

Introduction

In this lesson, you will learn about the .NET Framework. You will learn about some of the problems that developers confront while developing Web applications and understand how the .NET Framework solves these problems. You will also be introduced to Microsoft Visual Studio® .NET, which is the development tool that you will use to develop Web applications with the .NET Framework.

Lesson objectives

After completing this lesson, you will be able to:

- Differentiate between Microsoft .NET and the .NET Framework.

- List the benefits of using .NET, based on the perspective of the problems that .NET solves.

- Identify the features of Visual Studio .NET.

What is the .NET Framework?

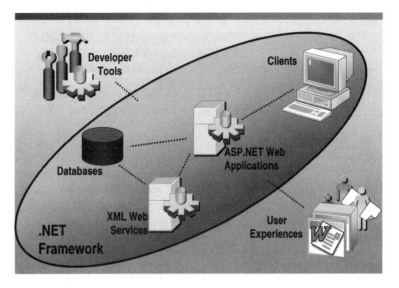

Introduction

.NET is Microsoft's development model in which software becomes platform- and device-independent, and data becomes available over the Internet. The .NET Framework is the infrastructure of .NET.

What is the .NET platform?

.NET is built from the ground up on open architecture. .NET is a platform that can be used for building and running the next generation of Microsoft Windows® and Web applications. The goal of the Microsoft .NET platform is to simplify Web development. The.NET platform consists of the following core technologies:

- The .NET Framework
- The .NET Enterprise Servers
- Building block services
- Visual Studio .NET

The .NET platform spans clients, servers, and services, and it consists of:

- A programming model that enables developers to build Extensible Markup Language (XML) Web services and applications.
- A set of building block services that are a user-centric set of XML Web services that move control of user data from applications to users. For example, Microsoft Passport is a core component of the.NET initiative that makes it easier to integrate various applications.

- A set of .NET Enterprise Servers, including Windows 2000, Microsoft SQL Server™, and Microsoft BizTalk® Server, that integrate, run, operate, and manage XML Web services and applications.

- Client software, such as Windows XP and Windows CE, which helps developers deliver a comprehensive user experience across a family of devices.

- Tools, such as Visual Studio .NET, which can be used to develop XML Web services and Windows and Web applications for an enriched user experience.

What is the .NET Framework?

The .NET Framework provides the foundation upon which applications and XML Web services are built and executed. The unified nature of the .NET Framework means that all applications, whether they are Windows applications, Web applications, or XML Web services, are developed by using a common set of tools and code, and are easily integrated with one another.

The .NET Framework consists of:

- *The common language runtime* (known hereafter as runtime). The runtime handles runtime services, including language integration, security, and memory management. During development, the runtime provides features that are needed to simplify development.

- *Class libraries*. Class libraries provide reusable code for most common tasks, including data access, XML Web service development, and Web and Windows Forms.

What Problems Does .NET Solve?

- **Even with the Internet, most applications and devices have trouble communicating with each other**

- **Programmers end up writing infrastructure instead of applications**

- **Programmers have had to limit their scope or continually learn new languages**

Introduction

The .NET Framework was developed to overcome several limitations that developers have had to deal with when developing Web applications, and it makes strong use of the Internet as a means for solving these limitations.

Pre-.NET issues

Even with the advent of a global, easily accessible network for sharing information (the Internet), few applications work on more than one type of client or have the ability to seamlessly interact with other applications. This limitation leads to two major problems that developers must confront:

- Developers typically have to limit their scope.

- Developers spend the majority of their time rewriting applications to work on each type of platform and client, rather than spending their time designing new applications.

The .NET Framework solves the preceding two problems by providing the runtime, which is language-independent and platform-independent, and by making use of the industry-standard XML. Language independence in .NET allows developers to build an application in any .NET-based language and know that the Web application will work on any client that supports .NET.

The runtime also controls much of the application infrastructure so that developers can concentrate on the application-specific logic.

XML Web services use XML to send data, thereby ensuring that any XML-capable client can receive that data. Since XML is an open standard, most modern clients, such as computer operating systems, cellular telephones, personal digital assistants (PDAs), and game consoles, can accept XML data.

The .NET Framework Components

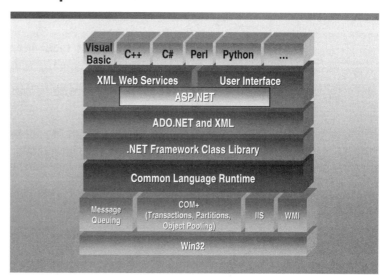

Introduction

The .NET Framework provides the necessary compile-time and run-time foundation to build and run .NET-based applications.

The .NET Framework

The .NET Framework consists of different components that help to build and run .NET-based applications:

- Platform Substrate

    The .NET Framework must run on an operating system. Currently, the .NET Framework is built to run on the Microsoft Win32® operating systems, such as Windows 2000, Windows XP, and Windows 98. In the future, the .NET Framework will be extended to run on other platforms, such as Windows CE.

- Application Services

    When running on Windows 2000, application services, such as Component Services, Message Queuing, Internet Information Services (IIS), and Windows Management Instrumentation (WMI), are available to the developer. The .NET Framework exposes application services through classes in the .NET Framework class library.

- .NET Framework Class Library

    The .NET Framework class library exposes features of the runtime and simplifies the development of .NET-based applications. In addition, developers can extend classes by creating their own libraries of classes.

    The .NET Framework class library implements the .NET Framework. All applications (Web, Windows, and XML Web services) access the same .NET Framework class libraries, which are held in namespaces. All .NET-based languages also access the same libraries.

■ Common Language Runtime

The common language runtime simplifies application development, provides a robust and secure execution environment, supports multiple languages, and simplifies application deployment and management.

The common language runtime environment is also referred to as a managed environment, in which common services, such as garbage collection and security, are automatically provided.

■ Microsoft ADO.NET

ADO.NET is the next generation of Microsoft ActiveX® Data Objects (ADO) technology. ADO.NET provides improved support for the disconnected programming model. ADO.NET also provides extensive XML support.

Note To learn more about ADO.NET, see Modules 9, 10, and 11 in Course 2310B, *Developing Microsoft ASP.NET Web Applications Using Visual Studio .NET.*

■ ASP.NET

ASP.NET is a programming framework that is built on the common language runtime. ASP.NET can be used on a server to build powerful Web applications. ASP.NET Web Forms provide an easy and powerful way to build dynamic Web user interfaces (UIs).

■ XML Web Services

XML Web services are programmable Web components that can be shared among applications on the Internet or the intranet. The .NET Framework provides tools and classes for building, testing, and distributing XML Web services.

Note To learn more about XML Web services, see Module 13 in Course 2310B, *Developing Microsoft ASP.NET Web Applications Using Visual Studio .NET.*

■ User Interfaces

The .NET Framework supports three types of UIs:

● Web Forms, which work through ASP.NET and the Hypertext Transfer Protocol (HTTP)

● Windows Forms, which run on Win32 client computers

● The Command Console

■ Languages

Any language that conforms to the Common Language Specification (CLS) can run with the common language runtime. In the .NET Framework, Microsoft provides support for Microsoft Visual Basic® .NET, Microsoft Visual C++® .NET, C#, and Microsoft JScript® .NET. Third parties can provide additional languages.

Note For more information on the .NET-based languages, see Module 3, "Using Microsoft .NET-Based Languages," in Course 2310B, *Developing Microsoft ASP.NET Web Applications Using Visual Studio .NET.*

Benefits of Using the .NET Framework

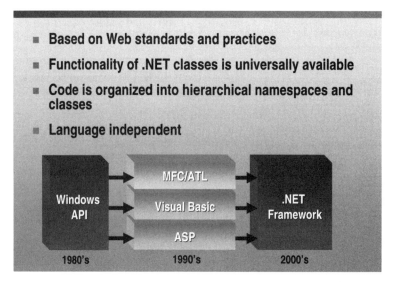

- Based on Web standards and practices
- Functionality of .NET classes is universally available
- Code is organized into hierarchical namespaces and classes
- Language independent

Windows API	MFC/ATL	.NET Framework
Visual Basic	
ASP	
1980's	1990's	2000's

Introduction

During the early years of Windows application development, all applications were written to the Windows application programming interface (API) in C or C++.

With the advent of Visual Basic, and then the Internet, developers had to specialize in developing C and C++ (MFC/ATL) applications, Visual Basic applications, or Active Server Pages (ASP) applications. With the .NET Framework, you can use your skills to develop any type of application.

Benefits

The benefits of using the .NET Framework for developing applications include:

- Based on Web standards and practices

  The .NET Framework fully supports existing Internet technologies, including Hypertext Markup Language (HTML), HTTP, XML, Simple Object Access Protocol (SOAP), Extensible Stylesheet Language Transformation (XSLT), XML Path Language (XPath), and other Web standards.

- Designed using unified application models

  The functionality of a .NET class is available from any .NET-compatible language or programming model. Therefore, the same piece of code can be used by Windows applications, Web applications, and XML Web services.

- Easy for developers to use

  In the .NET Framework, code is organized into hierarchical namespaces and classes. The .NET Framework provides a common type system, referred to as the unified type system, which can be used by any .NET-compatible language. In the unified type system, all language elements are objects. These objects can be used by any .NET application written in any .NET-based language.

- Extensible classes

  The hierarchy of the .NET Framework is not hidden from the developer. You can access and extend .NET classes (unless they are protected) through inheritance. You can also implement cross-language inheritance.

Visual Studio .NET: The Tool for .NET Development

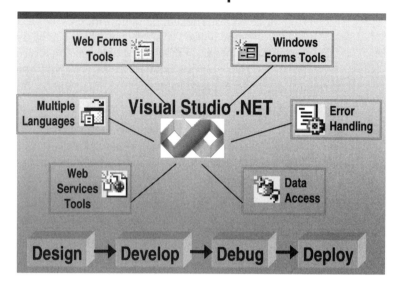

Introduction

Visual Studio .NET constitutes the core of .NET development.
Visual Studio .NET is a complete development environment in which you can design, develop, debug, and deploy your .NET applications and XML Web services.

Features of Visual Studio .NET

Visual Studio .NET, as a development tool, provides the following:

- Support for various development languages.

> **Note** For more information on the available .NET-based languages, see Module 3, "Using Microsoft .NET-Based Languages," in Course 2310B, *Developing Microsoft ASP.NET Web Applications Using Visual Studio .NET.*

- Tools for building Web applications, Windows applications, and XML Web services.
- Data access tools.
- Complete error handing, including local debugging, remote debugging, and tracing.

Optional practice

You will be using Visual Studio .NET throughout this course. In this practice, you will pin Visual Studio .NET to your **Start** menu, making it easily available, and then open Visual Studio .NET.

▶ **Pin a program to the Start menu**

- On the **Start** menu, click **All Programs**, point to **Microsoft Visual Studio .NET**, right-click **Microsoft Visual Studio .NET**, and then click **Pin to Start menu**.

  The Visual Studio .NET icon and name appear near the top left side of the **Start** menu.

▶ **Start and then close Visual Studio .NET**

1. Click **Start**, and then on the list on the upper left side of the **Start** menu, click **Microsoft Visual Studio .NET**.

   Visual Studio .NET opens and displays the start page.

   Note You will learn more about the Visual Studio .NET IDE in Module 2, "Using Microsoft Visual Studio .NET," in Course 2310B, *Developing Microsoft ASP.NET Web Applications Using Visual Studio .NET*.
   ---

2. On the **File** menu, click **Exit** to close Visual Studio .NET.

Lesson: Overview of ASP.NET

- **What is ASP.NET?**
- **ASP.NET Web Application**
- **Multimedia: ASP.NET Execution Model**

Introduction

ASP.NET is a programming framework built on the .NET Framework that is used to build Web applications. ASP.NET Web Forms, which are part of an ASP.NET Web application, provide an easy way to build dynamic Web sites. ASP.NET also includes the needed technology to build XML Web services, which provide the building blocks for constructing distributed Web-based applications.

Lesson objectives

After completing this lesson, you will be able to:

- Explain the difference between ASP.NET Web Forms and Web applications.
- Describe the parts of an ASP.NET Web application.

What is ASP.NET?

- **Evolutionary, more flexible successor to Active Server Pages**
- **Dynamic Web pages that can access server resources**
- **Server-side processing of Web Forms**
- **XML Web services let you create distributed Web applications**
- **Browser-independent**
- **Language-independent**

Introduction

For many years, developers have been using ASP technology to build dynamic Web pages. Similar to ASP, ASP.NET runs on the Web server and provides a way for you to develop content-rich, dynamic, personalized Web sites. In addition, ASP.NET offers many improvements over ASP.

What is ASP.NET?

Developing ASP.NET Web applications in the .NET Framework is similar to developing Windows applications. The fundamental component of ASP.NET is the Web Form. A Web Form is the Web page that users view in a browser. An ASP.NET Web application comprises one or more Web Forms. A Web Form is a dynamic page that can access server resources.

For example, a traditional Web page can run script on the client to perform basic tasks. An ASP.NET Web Form, conversely, can also run server-side code to access a database, to generate additional Web Forms, or to take advantage of built-in security on the server.

In addition, because an ASP.NET Web Form does not rely on client-side scripting, it is not dependent on the client's browser type or operating system. This independence allows you to develop a single Web Form that can be viewed on practically any device that has Internet access and a Web browser.

Because ASP.NET is part of the .NET Framework, you can develop ASP.NET Web applications in any .NET-based language.

XML Web services

The ASP.NET technology also supports XML Web services. XML Web services are distributed applications that use XML for transferring information between clients, applications, and other XML Web services.

Note You will learn how to consume and create XML Web services in Module 13, "Consuming and Creating XML Web Services," in Course 2310B, *Developing Microsoft ASP.NET Web Applications Using Visual Studio .NET*.

ASP.NET Web Application

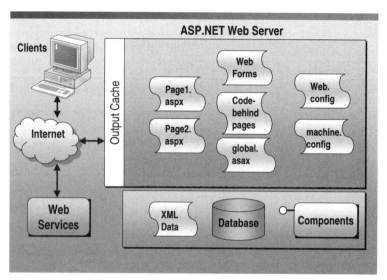

Introduction

An ASP.NET Web application contains different parts and components. Creating ASP.NET Web applications involves using and working with all of its parts and components.

In this topic, you will learn what constitutes an ASP.NET application.

Part of an ASP.NET Web application

The parts of an ASP.NET Web application include:

- *Web Forms, or .aspx pages*

  Web Forms and .aspx pages provide the UI for the Web application.

- *Code-behind pages*

  Code-behind pages are associated with Web Forms and contain the server-side code for the Web Form.

- *Configuration files*

  Configuration files are XML files that define the default settings for the Web application and the Web server. Every Web application has one Web.config configuration file. In addition, each Web server has one machine.config file.

- *Global.asax file*

  Global.asax files contain the needed code for responding to application-level events that are raised by ASP.NET.

- *XML Web service links*

  XML Web service links allow the Web application to send and receive data from an XML Web service.

- *Database connectivity*

  Database connectivity allows the Web application to transfer data to and from database sources.

- *Caching*

  Caching allows the Web application to return Web Forms and data more quickly after the first request.

Multimedia: ASP.NET Execution Model

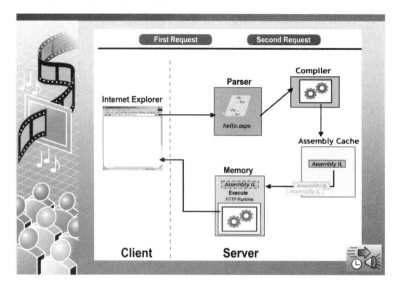

Introduction

In this animation, you will see how ASP.NET works to send information to a requesting client.

First request

When the client requests a Web page for the first time, the following set of events take place:

1. The client browser issues a GET HTTP request to the server.

2. The ASP.NET parser interprets the source code.

3. If the code was not already compiled into a dynamic-link library (DLL), ASP.NET invokes the compiler.

4. Runtime loads and executes the Microsoft intermediate language (MSIL) code.

Second request

When the user requests the same Web page for the second time, the following set of events take place:

1. The client browser issues a GET HTTP request to the server.

2. Runtime loads and immediately executes the MSIL code that was already compiled during the user's first access attempt.

Lesson: Overview of the Lab Application

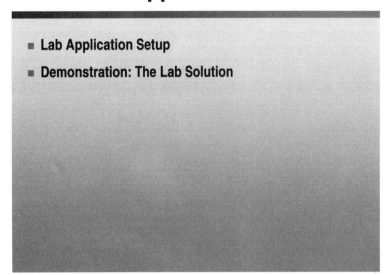

Introduction

In this lesson, you will be introduced to the lab application that you will build throughout the remainder of Course 2310B, in Labs 2 through 17. You will also have the opportunity to explore a complete version of the lab application and understand some of its functionality.

Lesson objective

After completing this lesson, you will be able to:

- Understand the basic functionality and features of the Lab application that you will build in the remaining labs in this course.

- List the software that is required to run the labs in this course.

Lab Application Setup

- **3 Projects**
  - Web Application
  - Class Library
  - XML Web Service
- **12 Web Forms**
- **3 Databases**
  - Doctors
  - Dentists
  - Coho

Introduction

In the labs in this course, you will build a complete ASP.NET Web application that simulates an internal Web site for the fictitious company, Coho Winery. This fictitious Web site, which you will build on your computer, provides information to employees about their benefit options.

Details

The Benefits Web application that you will develop includes the following:

- Three projects, including a Web application, a class library, and an XML Web service.
- 12 Web Forms that are used for displaying the employee benefits information.
- Three SQL Server databases.

Note Throughout this course, you will be given the choice between developing lab solutions by using either Visual Basic .NET or C#.

The Visual Basic .NET and C# components of the Benefits Web application are listed in the following table.

Visual Basic .NET Page	C# Page	Description	Labs
default.aspx default.aspx.vb	default.aspx default.aspx.cs	The home page. Calls the BenefitsList component and lists the benefits options in a **CheckBoxList** control.	4, 5, 14
dental.aspx dental.aspx.vb	dental.aspx dental.aspx.cs	Calls the XML Web service to get a listing of dentists.	13
doctors.aspx doctors.aspx.vb	doctors.aspx doctors.aspx.cs	Lists the primary care physicians from the doctors SQL Server database.	9, 10, 11, 15
dsDoctors.vb dsDoctors.xsd	dsDoctors.cs dsDoctors.xsd	Contains the schema of the **DataSet** that is used in the doctors.aspx Web form.	9
growth.xml lgcap.xml midcap.xml smcap.xml	growth.xml lgcap.xml midcap.xml smcap.xml	XML files with the prospectus information.	12
header.ascx	header.ascx	User control that is the header of each page.	4, 5, 15
life.aspx life.aspx.vb	life.aspx life.aspx.cs	Input form for life insurance data. Uses validation controls.	4, 7, 14
login.aspx login.aspx.vb	login.aspx login.aspx.cs	Logon page for the Web site.	17
medical.aspx medical.aspx.vb	medical.aspx medical.aspx.cs	Input form for medical data. The page used for selecting primary care physician from the doctors.aspx page.	8, 15
mutual_funds.xml	mutual_funds.xml	XML file containing the list of mutual funds.	12
namedate.ascx namedate.ascx.vb	namedate.ascx namedate.ascx.cs	User control that is used to gather name and birth date information. Used on the medical.aspx page.	8, 14
nestedData.aspx nestedData.aspx.vb	nestedData.aspx nestedData.aspx.cs	Allows you to create a nested XML file from the several tables that comprise the Doctor database.	12
prospectus.aspx prospectus.aspx.vb	prospectus.apsx prospectus.aspx.cs	Displays a retirement fund prospectus from a given XML file by using a style sheet file.	12
prospectus_style.xsl	prospectus_style.xsl	Style sheet file for displaying the prospectus.	12
register.aspx register.aspx.vb	register.aspx register.aspx.cs	Adds new users to the Coho Winery database.	16
retirement.aspx retirement.aspx.vb	retirement.aspx retirement.aspx.cs	Displays XML data from the mutual_funds.xml file in an HTML format.	12, 14
securitytest.aspx securitytest.aspx.vb	securitytest.aspx securitytest.aspx.cs	Displays the identity and the authentication method that is used to authenticate the current user, to test the security system.	16

(continued)

Visual Basic .NET Page	C# Page	Description	Labs
signout.aspx	signout.aspx	Allows the user to sign out of the system.	16
signout.aspx.vb	signout.aspx.cs		
Web.config	Web.config	This is a configuration file.	14, 15, 16
BenefitsListVB component project	BenefitsListCS component project	This project contains a Visual Basic .NET or C# component named Class1.vb or Class1.cs that returns a list of benefit options.	3
DentalService Web service project	DentalService Web service project	This project contains an XML Web service named DentalService.asmx (DentalService.asmx.vb and DentalService.asmx.cs). This XML Web service reads information from the dentists SQL Server database and returns the information as a **DataSet**.	13

Demonstration: The Lab Solution

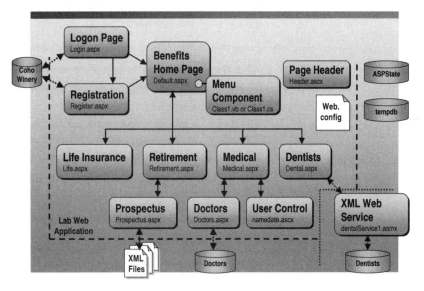

Introduction

In this demonstration, the instructor will show you the features and functionality of the Benefits Web application.

The default.aspx Web Form is the home page for the Benefits Web application. From this page, users can browse to other Web Forms, including to pages to enter information about specific benefits, such as Life Insurance, Retirement, Medical, and Dental coverage.

▶ **Run the application**

1. On the **Start** menu, click **Visual Studio .NET**.

2. Open **2310LabApplication**.

   Point out the three projects by using Solution Explorer. Each project is provided in Visual Basic .NET and C# versions.

   Point out the databases by using Server Explorer.

3. Build **2310LabApplication**.

4. Open Microsoft Internet Explorer and navigate to http://localhost/BenefitsVB/default.aspx to demonstrate the Visual Basic .NET solution and navigate to http://localhost/BenefitsCS/default.aspx to demonstrate the C# solution.

   The Web application is secured, so you are redirected to the login.aspx page to log in. This is set up in the Web.config file. The login.aspx page compares user data to the user names and passwords that are stored in the Coho SQL Server database.

Note If you receive a SQL permission error when trying to browse the Benefits Web site, open Windows Explorer, browse to C:\Program Files\MSDNTrain\2310\LabFiles\Lab16VB\Starter and then double-click **Lab16.bat**. Close Windows Explorer, and then refresh Microsoft Internet Explorer.

---

5. Click **Click here!**

   Because you are a new user, the register.aspx page is used to add yourself to the list of registered users for the Benefits Web application.

6. Enter user information and then click **Save**.

   After the register.aspx page adds you to the database and logs you on, the default.aspx page is displayed because that is the page you originally requested.

   The default.aspx page has a user control which is a page banner with links across the top. This user control reads from the same component as the list of check boxes on the page.

7. Select some check boxes and click **Submit**.

   When **Submit** is clicked, the page reads which check boxes are selected and displays an output list.

8. Click **Life Insurance**.

   The Life Insurance page uses server controls, validation controls, and a summary validation control. A calendar control displays todays date.

9. Enter incorrect information and click **Save**.

   The Error messages are displayed in a Validation Summary control.

10. Enter correct information and click **Save**.

11. Click **Medical**.

   This page uses a user control and session variables to display the same name and birth date as you entered on the Life Insurance page.

12. Click **Select a doctor**.

   This link redirects you to the doctors.aspx page. The doctors.aspx page uses a database connection and **DataGrid** control. The doctors.aspx page calls stored procedures and performs sorting and paging of the data.

13. Click **Select** to select a doctor, and then click **Submit**.

   The selected doctor information is passed back to the medical.aspx page in the Uniform Resource Locator (URL).

14. Click **Retirement Account**.

   This page obtains its information from various XML data documents.

   A page counter displays the number of visits that have been made to the page.

15. Click **Dental**.

   The dental.aspx page connects to the DentalService XML Web service, which reads a list of dentists from the **dentists** SQL Server database.

Lesson: Resources

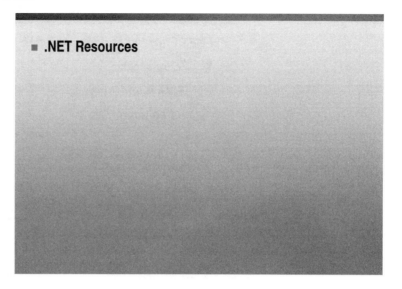

■ .NET Resources

Introduction

In this lesson, you will learn about some of the resources that are available to you as you develop Web applications in Visual Studio .NET.

Lesson objective

After completing this lesson, you will be able to find the information that you need for developing ASP.NET Web applications.

.NET Resources

> ■ **.NET Framework documentation**
>   ● Code samples
>   ● Quick Start tutorials
> ■ **Online communities**
> ■ **Web sites**
>   ● www.gotdotnet.com
>   ● www.ibuyspy.com
>   ● www.asp.net
>   ● msdn.microsoft.com
>   ● www.google.com

Resources

While learning to develop in .NET, you may need to research solutions to problems. The following list of resources is intended to give you a starting point for finding more information about .NET, along with answers to specific questions:

■ *The .NET Framework documentation.* The .NET Framework documentation is found in two places.

  ● On a computer with Visual Studio .NET installed, you can access the documentation from within Visual Studio .NET (on the **Help** menu, or by pressing **F1**).

  ● Another way to view the documentation is on the **Start** menu, point to **All Programs**, point to **Microsoft .NET Framework SDK**, and then click **Documentation**.

The .NET Framework documentation contains code samples in many languages, in addition to Quick Start tutorials.

■ *Online communities.* Online communities are .NET-specific newsgroups.

■ *External Web sites.* There are a few external Web sites that provide in-depth knowledge about .NET development:

  ● The first site, http://www.gotdotnet.com, provides detailed developer information, code samples, links to.NET communities, and more.

  ● The second site, http://www.ibuyspy.com, is a fictitious company store that shows how ASP.NET development can be used for e-commerce. The http://www.ibuyspy.com Web site is part of the more general http://www.asp.net site, which is an entire Web site that is dedicated to ASP.NET developers.

  ● You can also access the resources that are available at http://www.msdn.microsoft.com.

  ● The Web site http://www.google.com is another good source to search for information on .NET development.

Review

- **Introduction to the .NET Framework**
- **Overview of ASP.NET**
- **Overview of Lab Application**
- **Resources**

1. What is the Microsoft .NET Framework?

2. What are the core technologies in the .NET platform?

3. List the components that comprise the .NET Framework.

4. What is the purpose of the common language runtime?

5. What is the purpose of Common Language Specification?

6. What is an XML Web service?

7. What is a managed environment?

msdn® training

Module 2: Using Microsoft Visual Studio .NET

Contents

Overview

■ Overview of Visual Studio .NET

■ Creating an ASP.NET Web Application Project

Introduction

In this module, you will learn how to use the primary features of Microsoft® Visual Studio® .NET to create Microsoft ASP.NET Web applications.

Visual Studio .NET is the comprehensive development environment that can be used to create powerful, reliable, enterprise Web solutions. By offering end-to-end Web development capabilities and scalable, reusable server-side components, Visual Studio .NET will increase your productivity and help you to more effectively create applications and ASP.NET Web sites.

Objectives

After completing this module, you will be able to:

■ Navigate the Visual Studio .NET integrated development environment (IDE).

■ Create, build, and view an ASP.NET Web application project.

Lesson: Overview of Visual Studio .NET

- Why Visual Studio .NET?
- Start Page
- Available Project Templates
- Practice: Select the Project Template
- Integrated Development Environment (IDE)
- Demonstration: Using the Visual Studio .NET IDE
- Practice: Using the Visual Studio .NET IDE

Introduction

This lesson introduces the Visual Studio .NET IDE. The IDE is the common user interface (UI) and set of tools that are used for all of the different project types and programming languages that are supported by Visual Studio .NET.

Lesson objectives

After completing this lesson, you will be able to:

- Explain the purpose of Visual Studio .NET.
- Explain the IDE opening screen links.
- Identify the available project types and templates.
- Identify the available windows in the IDE.

Why Visual Studio .NET?

- **One IDE for multiple languages and multiple project types**
- **Multiple languages within a project**
- **Multiple project types within a solution**
- **Integrated browser**
- **Debugging support**
- **Customizable interface**

Introduction

Visual Studio .NET simplifies the development of powerful, reliable enterprise Web solutions and increases developer efficiency by providing a familiar, shared development environment. Pre-built components, programming wizards, and the ability to reuse components that are written in any language can reduce development time significantly. Microsoft IntelliSense®-based code completion enables you to produce accurate code more quickly. Powerful, end-to-end, cross-language debugging support, together with cross-language debugging, helps you make your applications operational.

One IDE

Visual Studio .NET has a single IDE that provides a consistent look and feel, regardless of the programming language being used or the application type being developed. Features that were available for only one language are now available to all languages.

Multiple languages

Visual Studio .NET supports development in a number of the Microsoft .NET-based languages. This support of various and diverse languages allows developers to work in their own preferred language, because they no longer need to learn a new language for each new project.

The languages that are included with Visual Studio .NET are:

- Microsoft Visual Basic® .NET
- C#
- Microsoft Visual C++®

Note For more information on the available .NET-based languages, see Module 3, "Using Microsoft .NET-Based Languages," in Course 2310B, *Developing Microsoft ASP.NET Web Applications Using Visual Studio .NET.*

Multiple project types

Visual Studio .NET supports the development of multiple project types, ranging from Microsoft Windows®-based applications, to ASP.NET Web applications, to XML Web services.

This support for multiple project types allows you to simultaneously work on several projects without having to change development environments and learn new tool interfaces or languages.

Integrated browser

Visual Studio .NET contains a built-in browser that is based on Microsoft Internet Explorer. The browser is integrated into the IDE and can be accessed from multiple windows and menus.

This browser accessibility allows you to view your Web site during the development cycle without having to transfer to another program and retype Uniform Resource Locator (URL) strings.

Debugging support

Visual Studio .NET is designed to support debugging from your initial code through to the application release. Debugging support includes breakpoints, break expressions, watch expressions, and the ability to step through code one statement or one procedure at a time.

Note For more information on debugging, see Module 6, "Tracing in Microsoft ASP.NET Web Applications," in Course 2310B, *Developing Microsoft ASP.NET Web Applications Using Visual Studio .NET*.

Customizable interface

Because the Visual Studio .NET IDE can be customized at the window and tool level, you can show only those tools or windows that you are using at any given time and hide the remainder.

Start Page

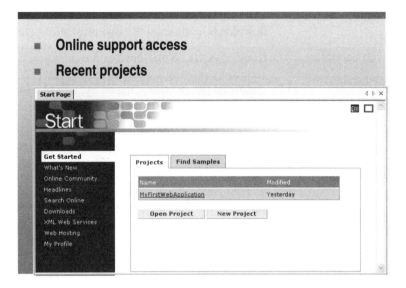

Introduction

Each time you start Visual Studio .NET, the Start page is displayed. This page provides an essential location for setting preferred options, reading product news, accessing discussions with fellow developers, and obtaining other information that can be used to get started within the Visual Studio .NET environment.

You can view the Start page at any time when you are working in the development environment.

To view the Start Page

- On the **Help** menu, click **Show Start Page**.

Get Started

Clicking **Get Started** sets Dynamic Help to display topics about starting new projects, and displays the following two folders:

- **Projects**

  The Projects folder displays links to the latest projects that you have been working on. This folder allows you to quickly open Visual Studio .NET and load all of the files that are related to your current projects.

- **Find Samples**

  The Find Samples folder displays a search engine that finds code samples by language and keyword online from ms-help://MS.VSCC.

What's New

Clicking **What's New** provides you with access to updates on Visual Studio Resources, Partner Resources, and Product Information.

Online Community

Clicking **Online Community** provides you with access to the Microsoft Visual Studio .NET Web sites and related newsgroups.

Headlines

Clicking **Headlines** provides you with access to Visual Studio .NET features, technical articles, and the Microsoft Visual Studio .NET Knowledge Base.

Search Online

Clicking **Search Online** provides you with a search engine that accesses the Microsoft MSDN® Online Library.

Downloads

Clicking **Downloads** provides you with access to Visual Studio .NET-related downloads, code samples, and reference materials.

XML Web Services

Clicking **XML Web Services** provides you with tools to find an XML Web service by running a query in a directory of XML Web services called Universal Description, Discovery, and Integration (UDDI) Service. In addition, you can use the **XML Web Services** selection to register an XML Web service in the UDDI directory.

Web Hosting

Clicking **Web Hosting** provides you with a list of links to hosting providers.

My Profile

Clicking **My Profile** allows you to set a user profile that adjusts the Toolbox, Default New Project, and Dynamic Help to match your programming preferences. You can change your profile at any time to modify these custom settings.

You have the option of choosing a pre-existing profile, such as Visual Basic Developer, or modifying each profile item manually.

Available Project Templates

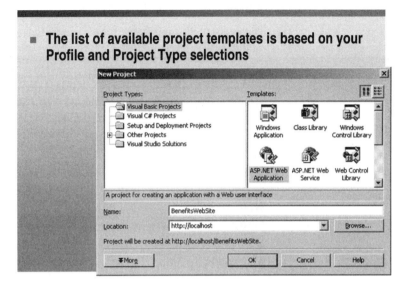

Introduction

Visual Studio .NET provides templates that support the creation of a number of common project types. These templates contain all of the required files and work with your profile to adjust the IDE into the correct configuration for the selected project.

These templates allow you to make use of your time by focusing on adding functions to the project and avoiding having to set up the infrastructure every time you change project types.

Solutions and projects

When you create a project in Visual Studio .NET, you also create a larger container called a Solution. This Solution can contain multiple projects in the same way that a project container can contain multiple pages.

Solutions allow you to concentrate on the project or set of projects that are required to develop and deploy your application, instead of having to focus on the details of managing the objects and files that define them. In using the concept of a *Solution* as a container, a solution allows you to:

- Work on multiple projects within the same instance of the IDE.

- Work on items, settings, and options that apply to a group of projects.

- Manage miscellaneous files that are opened outside the context of a Solution or a Project.

- Use Solution Explorer, which is a graphical view of your solution, to organize and manage all of the projects and files that are needed to design, develop, and deploy an application.

Project templates

Visual Studio .NET includes multiple project templates that are sorted by language and type. To select the correct template, you first need to specify the language in which you will be working.

The available Visual Basic project and Microsoft Visual C#™ project templates include:

Project templates	Description
Windows Application	The **Windows Application** project template is used to create standard Windows applications. This template automatically adds the essential project references and files that are needed as a starting point for your application.
Class Library	The **Class Library** template is used to create reusable classes and components that can be shared with other projects.
Windows Control Library	The **Windows Control Library** template is used to create custom controls that are to be used on Windows Forms.
ASP.NET Web Application	The **ASP.NET Web Application** project template is used to create an ASP.NET Web application on a computer that has Internet Information Services (IIS) version 5.0 or later installed. This template creates the basic files that are needed on the server to help you start designing your application.
ASP.NET Web Service	The **ASP.NET Web Service** project template is used to write an XML Web service that can be consumed by other Web services or applications on a network.
	XML Web services are components that are available over the Internet and are designed to only interact with other Web applications.
Web Control Library	The **Web Control Library** template is used to create custom Web server controls. This template adds the necessary project items that are needed to start creating a control that can then be added to any Web project.
Console Application	The **Console Application** project template is used to create console applications. Console applications are typically designed without a graphical UI and are compiled into a stand-alone executable file. A console application is run from the command line with input and output information being exchanged between the command prompt and the running application.
Windows Service	The **Windows Service** template is used to create Windows Service applications, which are long-running executable applications that run in their own Windows session.
Empty Project	The **Empty Project** template is used to create your own project type. The template creates the necessary file structure that is needed to store application information. Any references, files, or components must be manually added to the template.

(continued)

Project templates	Description
Empty Web Project	The **Empty Web Project** template is for advanced users who want to start with an empty project. This template creates the necessary file structure for a server-based project on an IIS server. References and components (such as Web Forms pages) must be added manually.
New Project in Existing Folder	The **New Project in Existing Folder** project template is used to create a blank project within an existing application directory. You can then choose to add the files from the preexisting application directory into this new project by right-clicking each of these items in Solution Explorer and selecting **Include in Project** on the shortcut menu.

The following table lists the additional project templates that are available in Visual Studio .NET.

Template Group	Description
Visual C++ Projects	Templates include: ■ Active Template Library (ATL) projects ■ Managed Applications ■ Managed Class Library ■ Managed Web Services
Setup and Deployment Projects	The **Setup and Deployment Projects** template allows you to create installers to distribute an application. The resulting Windows Installer (.msi) file contains the application, any dependent files, information about the application, such as registry entries, and instructions for installation.
Other Projects	Templates include: ■ Database projects ■ Enterprise projects ■ Extensibility projects ■ Application center test projects

Note The Class Library, Empty project, New Project in Existing Folder, Web Control Library, Windows Service, Windows Control Library, and Empty Web Project templates are not available in the Standard Edition of Visual Studio .NET.

Practice: Select the Project Template

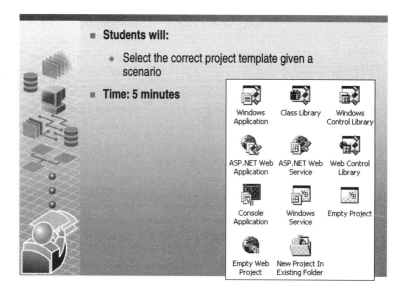

Choose the appropriate project template for each of the following scenarios

You want to create a control with a UI that you can reuse in any Windows application.

_____

_____

You want to build an application that will run on a single computer running Windows.

_____

_____

You want to create a dynamic Web application that includes Web pages and may use XML Web services.

_____

_____

You want to create a reusable component that is accessible to several Windows or Web applications.

_____

_____

You want to create a user-defined Web control that can be used in several Web pages.

_____

_____

You want to create an application that will run from a command line.

_____

_____

You want to create a class in which the methods are accessible through the Internet by any Web application.

_____

_____

You want to create a Windows service that will run continuously, regardless of whether a user is logged on or not.

_____

_____

Integrated Development Environment (IDE)

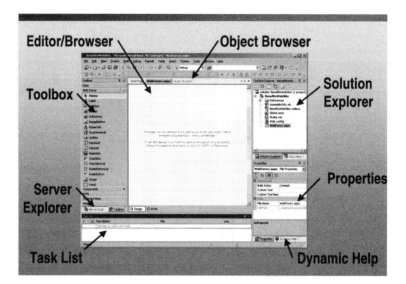

Introduction

The Visual Studio .NET IDE contains multiple windows that provide a variety of tools and services. Many of the features of Visual Studio .NET are available from several of the IDE windows, menus, and toolbars.

You can move or hide IDE windows depending on your personal preference. Use the **View** menu to select which windows to display. Click the thumbtack **Auto Hide** button to turn static windows into pull-out windows.

Editor/browser

The editor/browser is the primary interface window in Visual Studio .NET. In editor mode, the editor/browser displays code for editing and provides a What You See Is What You Get (WYSIWYG) graphical interface for control placement. You can use drag-and-drop editing to create the visual design of your application. You can then manage the logical design of your application by modifying the default Web control code.

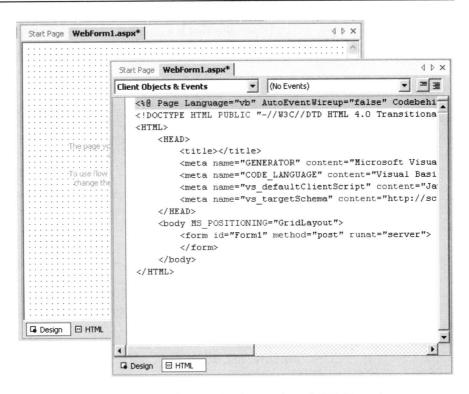

The screen options for the editor are Design mode and HTML mode:

- Design mode

  In Design mode, the editor allows you to move controls and graphic elements around the window by a simple drag-and-drop operation. Visual Studio .NET provides two control positioning schemes for designing Web pages: **FlowLayout** and **GridLayout**. In **FlowLayout**, controls follow each other across the page, while **GridLayout** allows you to exactly position each control by automatically adding dynamic Hypertext Markup Language (DHTML) tags to the controls.

  When you add a control to a Web page in **Design** mode, Visual Studio .NET adds the supporting code and default properties to the Web Form. You can then switch to **HTML** mode to bring up that code for you to edit.

- HTML mode

  In HTML mode, Visual Studio .NET highlights your code so that the different elements, such as variable names and key words, are instantly identifiable. The IntelliSense feature provides you with auto completion suggestions and allows you to build functions by simply selecting from lists of available syntax.

  When you use the editor window in HTML mode, two drop-down lists appear at the top of the window: the **Class Name** list, which is on the left, and the **Method Name** list, which is on the right. The **Class Name** list shows all of the controls on the associated form. If you click a control name in the list, the **Method Name** list then shows all of the events for that control. Events are actions that the control can perform and that can be interpreted by your application. By using the **Class Name** and **Method Name** lists together, you can quickly locate and edit the code in your application.

Object Browser

The Object Browser is a tool that provides information about objects and their methods, properties, events, and constants.

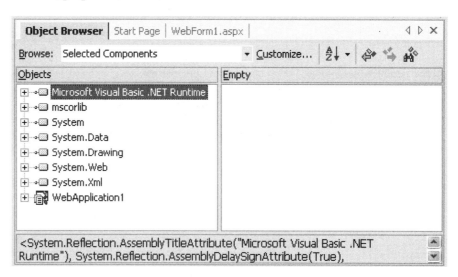

Solution Explorer

Solution Explorer displays the hierarchy of project files. From this window, you can move and modify files, including:

- Use a drag-and-drop operation to rearrange items.

- Select an item in Solution Explorer and the Properties window will show that item's properties. This allows you to change properties at the project or page level.

- Right-click the file, project, or solution to see the available options, including adding, building, and editing pages.

The file types shown in Solution Explorer include:

- Project References that list the classes that are used by the page and Web controls.

- All of the Web Forms in the project.

- All of the code-behind pages that contain the logic that supports the Web Forms.

- Project-related folders and sub-items.

Dynamic Help

Dynamic help provides access to local and online help topics, based on the settings in **My Profile**, the **Project Type**, and the present location of the cursor. As you move around the IDE or edit code, the available options in dynamic help adjust to match your activity.

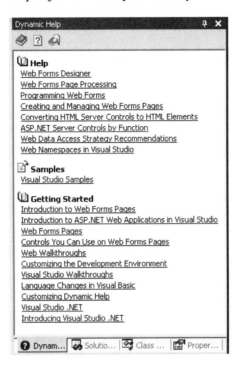

Properties

Visual Studio .NET lets you adjust the properties of documents, classes, and controls by using a common Properties window. When you create or select an item, the Properties window automatically displays the related properties. As shown on the following illustration, the available properties are listed in the left column, while the settings are listed on the right.

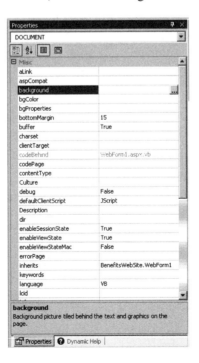

Task List

The Task List allows you to track the status of tasks as you develop applications. Visual Studio .NET also uses the Task List to flag errors when you build your application.

There are a number of ways to add a task to the Task List, including:

- Adding tasks manually by clicking the Task List and entering items.

  The top task in the following Task List screen shot is a manually added task.

- Visual Studio .NET automatically adds a task for tokens, such as the 'TODO comment in the code.

  The second task in the following screen shot was automatically added by Visual Studio .NET because of a 'TODO comment in the code. To access this section of code, click the item in the Task List and Visual Studio .NET will open the preferred page at that comment line.

  There are a number of preset tokens that you can use in your code and they will automatically add a task to the Task List.

  ▶ **To view and add to the list of tokens**

  a. On the **Tools** menu, click **Options**.

  b. In the **Options** dialog box, on the **Environment** folder, click **Task List**.

- Visual Studio .NET automatically adds build errors to the Task List.

  The bottom task in the following screen shot was added automatically when the page was built. To access this section of code, click the item in the task list and Visual Studio .NET will then open the preferred page at the line containing the error.

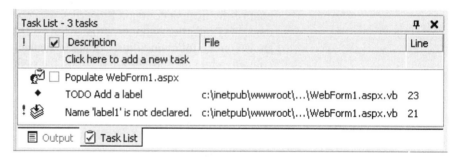

Server Explorer

Server Explorer allows you to view local data connections, servers, and windows services. Server Explorer supports the integration of external services into your Web site.

Toolbox

The Toolbox allows you to use a drag-and-drop operation on the controls in your application.

The available tools are grouped by category, in the following menus:

■ **Data**

This category contains objects that allow your application to connect and access the data in a Microsoft SQL Server™ and other databases.

■ **Web Forms**

This category contains a set of server controls that you can add to Web pages.

■ **Components**

This category contains components that support the infrastructure of your application.

■ **HTML**

This category contains a set of HTML controls that you can add to your Web page. Theses controls can run on either the server side or the client side.

Demonstration: Using the Visual Studio .NET IDE

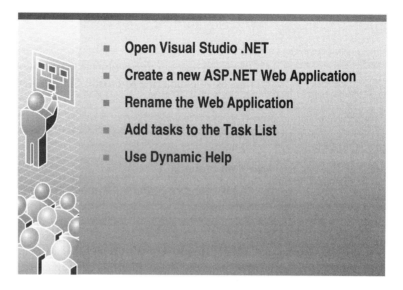

- Open Visual Studio .NET
- Create a new ASP.NET Web Application
- Rename the Web Application
- Add tasks to the Task List
- Use Dynamic Help

In this demonstration, you will learn how to use the Visual Studio .NET IDE to create an ASP.NET Web application project, add tasks to the Task List, use Dynamic Help, and use Server Explorer.

▶ **To run this demonstration**

Create a Visual Studio .NET solution

1. Open Visual Studio .NET.

2. Show the features of the Start Page, such as **What's New**, **Search Online**, and **My Profile**.

3. Using Visual Studio .NET, create a new blank solution named **MyFirstSolution**:

   a. On the **File** menu, point to **New**, and then click **Blank Solution**.

   b. In the **New Project** dialog box, type **MyFirstSolution** in the **Name** text box, and then click **OK**.

   The **MyFirstSolution** solution will contain several projects. The solution serves as a container to group these related projects.

Create an ASP.NET Web Application project within the solution

4. Create a new ASP.NET Web Application project named **MyFirstWebApplication** in the **MyFirstSolution** solution:

   a. On the **File** menu, point to **New**, and then click **Project**.

   b. In the **New Project** dialog box:

Visual Basic .NET

   In the **Project Types list**, click **Visual Basic Projects**. In the **Templates list**, click **ASP.NET Web Application**, set the **Location** to **http://localhost/MyFirstWebApplicationVB**, click **Add to Solution**, and then click **OK**.

C#

   In the **Project Types list**, click **Visual C# Projects**. In the **Templates list**, click **ASP.NET Web Application**, set the **Location** to **http://localhost/MyFirstWebApplicationCS**, click **Add to Solution**, and then click **OK**.

View where the new files are located

5. Using Solution Explorer, show the files that were created when the Web application was created.

6. Using Windows Explorer, show where the files were created in the file system.

   The solution files are located in the **\My Documents\Visual Studio Projects\MyFirstSolution** folder.

   The Visual Basic .NET project files are located in the **\Inetpub\wwwroot\MyFirstWebApplicationVB** folder and the C# project files are located in the **\Inetpub\wwwroot\MyFirstWebApplicationCS** folder.

View the properties of the Web Form

7. In Visual Studio .NET Solution Explorer, select **WebForm1.aspx** and show the properties that are listed in the Properties window.

8. Using the Toolbox, add a **Label** control and a **Button** control to the Web Form.

   Notice that the Properties window now shows properties for the **Button** control.

Dynamic Help

9. On the **Help** menu, click **Dynamic Help**.

   The Dynamic Help window opens with topics about the **Button** control.

10. Click the **Label** control.

    The Dynamic Help window displays topics about the **Label** control.

11. Click the Label **Members (System.Web.UI.WebControls)** topic.

    The topic is displayed in the main Visual Studio .NET window.

    Show the **Text** and the **Visible** properties.

Server Explorer

12. In Server Explorer, expand **Servers**, expand *machinename*, expand **SQL Servers**, and then expand *machinename*.

    The list of databases installed on the local computer running SQL Server is displayed.

13. For instance, open the **dentists** table of the **dentists** database.

Task List

14. If the Task List is not visible, on the **View** menu, click **Show Tasks**, and then click **All** to display the Task List window.

15. Insert the following tasks:

    - Add a new ASP.NET Web Form

    - Add a new project to the solution

16. On the **File** menu, click **Save All**.

Practice: Using the Visual Studio .NET IDE

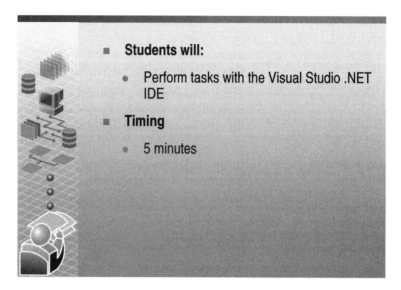

Complete the following tasks and list which window(s) you used

Create a new Web application project.

_____

_____

Add a **Button** control to the default Web Form.

_____

_____

Add a task to the project.

_____

_____

View the properties of the Web application project.

_____

_____

Determine what SQL Server databases are installed on your computer.

_____

_____

Lesson: Creating an ASP.NET Web Application Project

- **The Development Process**
- **Web Application Files**
- **Web Application File Structure**
- **Demonstration: Creating a Web Application Project**

Introduction

In this lesson, you will learn how to create, build, and view an ASP.NET Web application.

Lesson objectives

After completing this lesson, you will be able to:

- Explain how ASP.NET Web application pages are developed.
- Identify the function of the files that are used by Visual Studio .NET solutions.
- Explain the build process for ASP.NET Web application.
- Create, build, and view an ASP.NET Web application.

The Development Process

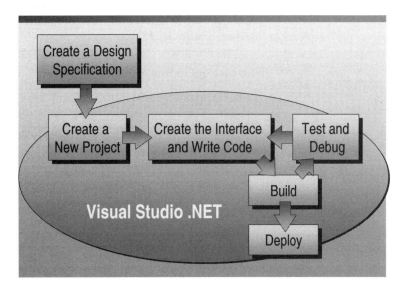

Introduction

Visual Studio .NET contains everything you need to build your own ASP.NET Web application from start to finish.

Creating an ASP.NET Web application with Visual Studio .NET involves the following basic steps:

1. Create a design specification

    The design specification is the blueprint that you will use when you create a Web application. Take time before writing any code to design the application that you will be creating. Although Visual Studio .NET provides tools to help you quickly develop a solution, having a clear understanding of the user needs and initial feature set will help you to be more efficient in your development efforts. By first coming up with a design specification, it will also help you save time by minimizing the potential for rewriting code because of a poor or nonexistent design specification.

2. Create a new project

    When you select a new project template, Visual Studio .NET automatically creates the files and the default code that are needed to support the project.

    As part of this initial project creation, you should transfer the main coding tasks from your design specification into the Visual Studio .NET Task List. This transfer allows you to track your development against the specification.

3. Create the interface

    To create the interface for your Web application, you will first need to place controls and objects on the Web pages by using the Editor/Browser window in Design mode.

    As you add objects to a form, you can set their properties from the table in the Properties window or as code in the Editor window.

> **Note** For more information on adding controls to an ASP.NET Web Form, see Module 4, "Creating a Microsoft ASP.NET Web Form," in Course 2310B, *Developing Microsoft ASP.NET Web Applications Using Visual Studio .NET.*

4. Write code

   After you have set the initial properties for the ASP.NET Web Form and its objects, you can write the event procedures that will run when different actions are performed on a control or object.

   You may also need to write code to add business logic and to access data.

   > **Note** For more information on writing code in ASP.NET Web Forms, see Module 5, "Adding Code to a Microsoft ASP.NET Web Form," in Course 2310B, *Developing Microsoft ASP.NET Web Applications Using Visual Studio .NET.*

5. Build

   When building a project, you compile all of the code in the Web pages and other class files into a dynamic-link library (DLL) called an *assembly*.

   Visual Studio .NET has two build options: debug and release. When you are first developing a project, you will build debug versions. When you are ready to release the project, you will create a release build of the project.

6. Test and debug

   Testing and debugging is not a one-time step, but rather something that you do iteratively throughout the development process. Each time you make a major change, you will need to run a debug build of the application to ensure that it is working as expected.

   Visual Studio .NET offers numerous debugging tools that you can use to find and fix errors in your application.

   > **Note** For more information on debugging, see Module 6, "Tracing in Microsoft ASP.NET Web Applications," in Course 2310B, *Developing Microsoft ASP.NET Web Applications Using Visual Studio .NET.*

7. Deploy

   When a project is fully debugged and a release build has been built, you can deploy the necessary files to a production Web server.

   > **Note** For more information on deploying an ASP.NET Web application, see Module 15, "Configuring, Optimizing, and Deploying a Microsoft ASP.NET Web Application," in Course 2310B, *Developing Microsoft ASP.NET Web Applications Using Visual Studio .NET.*

Web Application Files

- **Solution files (.sln, .suo)**
- **Project files (.vbproj, .csproj)**
- **Web application files**
  - ASP.NET Web Forms (.aspx)
  - ASP.NET Web services (.asmx)
  - Classes, code-behind pages (.vb or .cs)
  - Global application classes (.asax)
  - Web.config file
  - **Project assembly (.dll)**

Introduction

When you create a new project or work with existing projects, Visual Studio .NET creates a number of files that support your development.

Solution files

When you create a new project, a solution is also created, even if you only have one project in the solution. A folder is created for each solution in the **\My Documents\Visual Studio Projects** folder that contains the .sln and .suo files.

- Solution files (.sln)

  The *SolutionName*.sln file extension is used for solution files that link one or more projects together, and it stores certain global information. .sln files are similar to Visual Basic group (.vbg) files, which appear in previous versions of Visual Basic.

- Solution User Options (.suo)

  The *SolutionName*.suo file extension is used for Solution User Options files that accompany any solution records and customizations that you add to your solution. This file saves your settings, such as breakpoints and task items, so that they are retrieved each time you open the solution.

Project files

Each project is a single Web application stored in its own folder. Inside the project folder are the project configuration file and the actual files that make up the project. The Project Configuration file is an Extensible Markup Language (XML) document that contains references to all of the project items, such as forms and classes, in addition to project references and compilation options.

Visual Basic .NET project files use a .vbproj extension, while C# uses .csproj. These extensions enable you to differentiate between files that are written in other .NET-compatible languages and make it easy to include multiple projects that are based on different languages within the same solution.

Web application projects are created in a new folder in the **\Inetpub\wwwroot** folder. In addition, a virtual directory that points to the project folder is created in IIS.

Web application files
Visual Studio .NET supports a number of application file types and extensions:

- ASP.NET Web Forms (.aspx)

  ASP.NET Web Forms are used when you need to build dynamic Web sites that will be accessed directly by users.

  ASP.NET Web Forms may be supported by a code-behind page that is designated by the extension *WebForm*.aspx.vb or *WebForm*.aspx.cs.

- ASP.NET Web services (.asmx)

  Web services are used when you want to create dynamic Web sites that will only be accessed by other programs.

  ASP.NET Web services may be supported by a code-behind page that is designated by the extension *WebService*.asmx.vb or *WebService*.asmx.vb.

- Classes and code-behind pages (.vb or .cs)

  Previous versions of Visual Basic used different file extensions to distinguish between classes (.cls), forms (.frm), modules (.bas), and user controls (.ctl). Visual Basic .NET allows you to mix multiple types within a single **.vb** file.

  Code-behind pages carry two extensions, the page type (.aspx or .asmx) and the Visual Basic extension (.vb) or the C# extension (.cs). For example, the full file name for the code-behind page for a default ASP.NET Web Form is WebForm1.aspx.vb for a Visual Basic .NET project, and for a C# project it is WebForm1.aspx.cs.

  Note You will learn more about code-behind pages in Module 5, "Adding Code to a Microsoft ASP.NET Form," in Course 2310B, *Developing Microsoft ASP.NET Web Applications Using Visual Studio .NET*.

- Discovery files (.disco and .vsdisco)

  Discovery files are XML-based files that contain links (URLs) to resources that provide discovery information for an XML Web service. These files enable programmatic discovery of XML Web services.

- Global application classes (global.asax)

  The Global.asax file, also known as the ASP.NET application file, is an optional file that contains code for responding to application-level events that are raised by ASP.NET or raised by HttpModules. At runtime, Global.asax is parsed and compiled into a dynamically generated .NET Framework class that is derived from the **HttpApplication** base class.

- Resource files (.resx)

    A resource is any non-executable data that is logically deployed with an application. A resource might be displayed in an application as error messages or as part of the UI. Resources can contain data in a number of forms, including strings, images, and persisted objects. Storing your data in a resource file allows you to change the data without recompiling your entire application.

- Styles.css

    Styles.css is the default stylesheet file for the Web application.

- Web.config file

    This Web.config file contains configuration settings that the common language runtime reads, such as assembly binding policy, remoting objects, and so on, and settings that the application can read. Web.config files also contain the global application classes that support a project.

Other files

Any files that are not based on a programming language will have their own extensions. For example, a Crystal Report file uses the .rpt extension, and a text files uses .txt.

Project assembly

When a Web project is compiled, two additional types of files are created:

- Project Assembly files (.dll)

    All of the code-behind pages (.aspx.vb and .aspx.cs) in a project are compiled into a single assembly file that is stored as *ProjectName*.dll. This project assembly file is placed in the /bin directory of the Web site.

- AssemblyInfo.vb or AssemblyInfo.cs

    The AssemblyInfo file is used to write the general information, specifically assembly version and assembly attributes, about the assembly.

Note For more information on files that support ASP.NET Web applications, see the Visual Studio .NET documentation.

Web Application File Structure

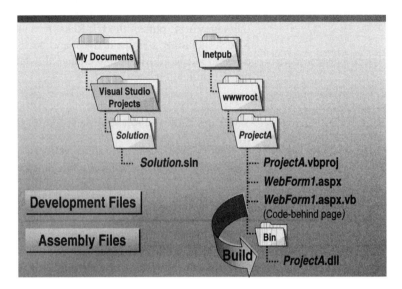

Introduction	When you create an ASP.NET Web application, Visual Studio .NET creates two folders to store the files that support that application. When you compile a project, a third folder is created to store the resulting .dll file.
My Documents	Visual Studio .NET creates a folder for the solution, *ProjectA,* containing the file *ProjectA*.sln. This file is a map of all of the various files that support the project.
	You can also create a blank solution and then add projects to it. By creating a blank solution, you will have a solution that has a different name than the project.
Inetpub	Visual Studio .NET also creates a folder named *ProjectA*, in the Inetpub\wwwroot folder, that contains the files that are required by the Web application. These files include:

- The project file, *ProjectA*.vbproj or *ProjectA*.csproj, which is an XML document that contains references to all project items, such as forms and classes, in addition to project references and compilation options.

- ASP.NET Web Forms, *WebForm1*.aspx, or XML Web services, *WebService*.asmx.

- Code-behind pages, *WebForm1*.aspx.vb, *WebService1*.asmx.vb, *WebForm1*.aspx.cs or *WebService1*.asmx.cs.

- A Web.config file, which contains the configuration setting for the Web application.

- A Global.asax file that handles events that are fired while the Web application is running.

The Assembly	When you build a Web application project, Visual Studio .NET creates an assembly in the Inetpub\wwwroot*ProjectA*\bin folder. An assembly is one .dll file that is created from all of the code-behind pages that make up a Web application.

Demonstration: Creating a Web Application Project

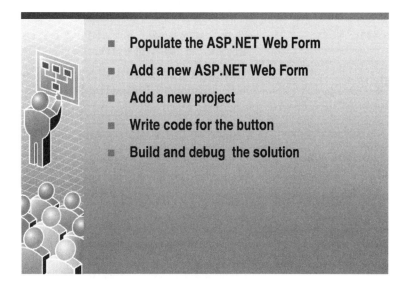

- Populate the ASP.NET Web Form
- Add a new ASP.NET Web Form
- Add a new project
- Write code for the button
- Build and debug the solution

In this demonstration, you will learn how to add Web Forms to a Web Application project, add a new project to a solution, and build and run a Web Application project.

▶ **To run this demonstration**

1. Open the MyFirstSolution solution file.

Populate an ASP.NET Web Form

2. Open the WebForm1.aspx file in Design view.

3. There are already two controls, a **Button** control and a **Label** control, that you placed in the previous demonstration.

4. Select the label and change the **ID** property to **lblMessage** in the Properties window.

5. Double-click the **Button** control to open the code-behind page for the Web Form, and add the following comment to the event procedure:

Visual Basic .NET

```
'TODO: Write Hello World
```

C#

```
//TODO: Write Hello World
```

A new task is automatically added to the Task List because of the TODO token.

Add a new ASP.NET Web Form

6. On the **Project** menu, click **Add Web Form**.

7. In the **Add New Item** dialog box, change the default name to login.aspx, and click **Open**.

Note You can also add an ASP.NET Web Form to a project by right-clicking the project in Solution Explorer, clicking **Add**, and then clicking **Add Web Form**.

---

8. In the Task List, select the **Add a new ASP.NET Web Form** task check.

Add a new project	9. In Solution Explorer, right-click the solution, click **Add**, and then click **New Project**.
	10. In the **Add New Project** dialog box:
Visual Basic .NET	Click **Visual Basic**, click **ASP.NET Web Service**, set the location to **http://localhost/MyFirstWebServiceVB**, and then click **OK**.
C#	Click **Visual C#**, click **ASP.NET Web Service**, set the location to **http://localhost/MyFirstWebServiceCS**, and then click **OK**.
	The new project also contains a XML Web service.
	11. In the Task List, check the **Add a new project to the solution** task.
Write code for a button control	12. In the Task List, double-click the **TODO: Write Hello World** task.
	The correct file is opened and the cursor is placed at the correct spot in the code.
	13. Write the following code:
Visual Basic .NET	`lblMessage.Txt = "Hello World!"`
C#	`lblMessage.Txt = "Hello World!";`

> **Note**   This is a syntax error because the code sets the **Txt** property instead of the **Text** property. This error is there to show you what happens when the build fails.

14. Remove the **TODO** from the **TODO: Write Hello World** comment.

    The TODO task disappears automatically from the Task List.

Build and run the solution

15. Verify that MyFirstWebApplicationVB or MyFirstWebApplicationCS is the startup project. In Solution Explorer, MyFirstWebApplicationVB or MyFirstWebApplicationCS should appear in bold text.

> **Note**   To set **MyFirstWebApplicationVB or MyFirstWebApplicationCS** as the startup project, right-click the **MyFirstWebApplicationVB** or **MyFirstWebApplicationCS** project in Solution Explorer and click **Set as StartUp Project**.

16. On the **Build** menu, click **Build Solution** to build the solution.

    Both **MyFirstWebApplicationVB** or **MyFirstWebApplicationCS** and **MyFirstWebServiceVB** or **MyFirstWebServiceCS** are built, but the Output window displays the following error condition:

    `Build: 1 succeeded, 1 failed, 0 skipped`

    And an error message is added to the Task List because Txt is not a member of System.Web.UI.WebControls.Label.

17. To view all of the tasks from both projects, on the **View** menu, click **Show Tasks**, and then click **All**.

18. Double-click the error message in the Task List. The cursor jumps to the correct spot in the code.

19. Correct the syntax error.

   The correct code should look like the following:

Visual Basic .NET

```
lblMessage.Text = "Hello World!"
```

C#

```
lblMessage.Text = "Hello World!";
```

   For Visual Basic .NET, when you move the cursor off of the corrected line of code, the error is removed from the Task List.

20. On the **Build** menu, click **Rebuild Solution** to rebuild the solution.

   Verify that you have the following message in the Output window:

```
Rebuild All: 2 succeeded, 0 failed, 0 skipped
```

View the result

21. To view the Web page in a browser, right-click **WebForm1.aspx** in the **MyFirstWebApplicationVB** or **MyFirstWebApplicationCS** project in Solution Explorer, and then click **View in Browser**.

Note You can build and browse a Web Form in one step by right-clicking the page in Solution Explorer and then clicking **Build and Browse**.

---

22. In the browser, click the button on the Web Form, and make sure that you see the message **Hello World**.

Review

- Overview of Visual Studio .NET
- Creating an ASP.NET Web Application Project

1. What is the difference between a Visual Studio .NET solution and a
    Visual Studio .NET project?

2. What is the difference between Server Explorer and Solution Explorer in
    Visual Studio .NET?

3. How do you add a new Web Form to a project?

4. When you create a Web application project, where are the project files
    stored?

5. When you build a project, what file(s) is created?

6. How do you view a Web Form in the Visual Studio .NET browser?

Lab 2: Using Microsoft Visual Studio .NET

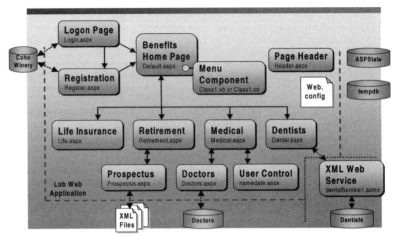

Lab 2: Using Microsoft Visual Studio .NET

Objectives

After completing this lab, you will be able to:

- Create a Microsoft® Visual Studio® .NET solution.
- Create a Web Application project.
- Add files to a Web Application project.

Note   This lab focuses on the concepts in this module and as a result may not comply with Microsoft security recommendations.

Prerequisites

There are no prerequisites for this lab.

Scenario

Coho Winery offers several benefits to its employees. In the labs for Course 2310B, *Developing Microsoft ASP.NET Web Applications Using Visual Studio .NET*, you will create a Web site that enables employees to select and set up their chosen benefits.

In this lab, you will create a Microsoft ASP.NET Web Application project for the Web site. You can work through the labs by using either C# or Microsoft Visual Basic® .NET.

Estimated time to complete this lab: 15 minutes

Exercise 1
Creating an ASP.NET Web Application Project

In this exercise, you will create the ASP.NET Web Application project that will be used for the Benefits Web site that is built throughout the labs that comprise Course 2310B, *Developing Microsoft ASP.NET Web Applications Using Visual Studio .NET.*

▶ **Create the ASP.NET Web application and add the starter files**

1. Using Visual Studio .NET, create a new blank solution named **2310LabApplication**:

    a. On the **File** menu, Point to **New**, and then click **Blank Solution**.

    b. In the **New Project** dialog box, type **2310LabApplication** in the **Name** text box, and then click **OK**.

    The 2310LabApplication solution contains several projects. Each project represents a different application or component. The solution serves as a container to group these related projects.

2. Create a new ASP.NET Web Application project named **BenefitsVB** or **BenefitsCS** in the 2310LabApplication solution:

    a. On the **File** menu, Point to **New**, and then click **Project**.

    b. In the **New Project** dialog box, in the **Project Types** list, click **Visual Basic Projects** or **Visual C# Projects**.

    c. In the **Templates** list, click **ASP.NET Web Application**.

    d. Set the **Location** to **http://localhost/BenefitsVB** for a **Visual Basic .NET** project, or to **http://localhost/BenefitsCS** for a C# project.

    e. Click **Add to Solution** and then click **OK**.

Caution   When adding projects to the solution, the capitalization of the project name is important. Because you may be using some prebuilt Web Forms in this and other labs in Course 2310B, *Developing Microsoft ASP.NET Web Applications Using Visual Studio .NET*, you must verify that you have capitalized the Benefits project as shown.

Visual Studio .NET creates a virtual root named **BenefitsVB** or **BenefitsCS**. List the 6 files for a Visual Basic project or 5 files for a C# project that appear in Solution Explorer.

_____

_____

The Benefits project will be the main Web application that you will build throughout the labs in Course 2310B, *Developing Microsoft ASP.NET Web Applications Using Visual Studio .NET*. Two versions of the project can be created: **BenefitsVB** is a **Visual Basic .NET** solution and **BenefitsCS** is a C# solution.

3. Add the starter lab files to the Benefits project:

   a. In Solution Explorer, right-click **BenefitsVB** or **BenefitsCS**, point to **Add**, and then click **Add Existing Item.**

   b. For the Visual Basic .NET Project, browse to the *install folder*\Labfiles\ Lab02\VB\Starter\BenefitsVB folder for the Visual Basic .NET files.

      For the Visual C# project, browse to the *install folder*\Labfiles\Lab02\CS\Starter\BenefitsCS folder for the C# files.

   Note   The default installation folder for this class is C:\Program Files\Msdntrain\2310.

   ---

   c. In the **Files of type** box of the **Add Existing Item – Benefits** dialog box, select **All Files (*.*)**.

   d. Select all of the files in this folder, and then click **Open**.

   e. Click **Yes** if asked if you want to create a new class file for the medical.aspx Web Form.

   When you add files to the Benefits project, they become part of the Benefits Web application. The files that you copied in the preceding step provide a foundation upon which you will build your Web application.

4. Right-click the **WebForm1.aspx** page in Solution Explorer and then click **Build and Browse**.

   When you build and browse a project, the code files are compiled and the default Web Form is displayed in the built-in browser in Visual Studio .NET.

   At this stage, WebForm1.aspx is blank. The browser displays a blank Web page.

5. Each project in Visual Studio .NET has its own virtual directory in Internet Information Services (IIS). Using Windows Explorer, find where the files were created for the Benefits project. Fill in your answer below.

   _____

   _____

Exercise 2
Using Visual Studio .NET

In this exercise, you will set up a profile, configure the Benefits project, and then add tasks to the Task List.

▶ **Set attributes for a profile**

1. Click the **Start Page** tab to view the Start page of Visual Studio .NET.

   If the **Start Page** tab is not available, on the **Help** menu, click **Show Start Page**.

2. Click **My Profile** to open the profile attribute section.

3. In the **Help Filter** drop-down list, click **.NET Framework SDK**.

   Setting a profile allows Visual Studio .NET to customize the interface for the type of development you are doing.

▶ **Set properties for the Visual Basic .NET project**

1. In Solution Explorer, right-click the **BenefitsVB** project, and then click **Properties**.

2. In the **BenefitsVB Property Pages** dialog box, in the Common Properties folder, click **Build**.

3. In the **Option Strict** drop-down list, click **On**, and then click **OK** to apply the changes.

   Enabling Option Strict causes Visual Basic .NET to enforce stronger data type conversion rules, and helps to ensure a well-running Web application.

▶ **Set properties for the Visual C# project**

- Option Strict does not need to be set for a Microsoft Visual C# project because C# enforces stronger type conversion rules by definition.

▶ **Add tasks to the Task List**

1. On the **View** menu, point to **Show Tasks**, and then click **All** to display the Task List.

2. On the Task List, click the area labeled **Click here to add a new task**. In the **Description** field, type **Build the BenefitsList component** and then press ENTER.

3. Create a second task named **Build the Benefits Web application** and then press ENTER.

   The Task List is a convenient place to list the tasks that you have yet to accomplish.

4. On the **File** menu, click **Exit**.

5. Click **Yes** to save changes.

msdn training

Module 3:
Using Microsoft .NET-
Based Languages

Contents

Microsoft

Overview

- ■ **Overview of the .NET-Based Languages**
- ■ **Comparison of the .NET-Based Languages**
- ■ **Creating a Component Using Visual Studio .NET**

Introduction

In this module, you will gain an understanding of the Microsoft® .NET development languages. You will be introduced to the different languages that are available for use when developing .NET applications and learn how the Microsoft .NET Framework uses different languages. You will also learn some of the fundamental aspects of writing code and creating components by using two of the .NET-based languages, Microsoft Visual Basic® .NET and C#.

Objectives

After completing this module, you will be able to:

- ■ Identify the languages that support the .NET Framework.
- ■ Choose an appropriate development language for your needs.
- ■ Create a component by using Visual Basic .NET or Microsoft Visual C#™.

Lesson: Overview of the .NET-Based Languages

- ■ **Multiple Language Support**
- ■ **The Common Language Runtime**
- ■ **The Common Language Runtime Components**
- ■ **Runtime Compilation and Execution**
- ■ **What are Namespaces?**
- ■ **Using Namespaces**

Introduction

In this lesson, you will learn about the programming languages that are supported by the .NET Framework. You will see how the .NET Framework is designed to support an unlimited number of development languages, assuming those languages conform to .NET requirements.

You will also learn about namespaces, which are a fundamental feature of the .NET Framework and the .NET-based languages.

Lesson objectives

After completing this lesson, you will be able to:

- ■ Name several of the .NET development languages.
- ■ Explain how the .NET Framework supports multiple development languages.
- ■ Explain the functionality of the common language runtime.
- ■ Illustrate the process that a Web application goes through when it is compiled and executed by the common language runtime.
- ■ Add a namespace to a page.

Multiple Language Support

- **The .NET Framework is designed to support many languages**
  - More than 20 languages currently supported
  - Microsoft provides Visual Basic .NET, C#, Visual J# .NET, and JScript .NET
- **Benefits of multiple-language support**
  - Code modules are reusable
  - API access is the same for all languages
  - The right language is used for the right task
  - Performance is roughly equal between all languages

Introduction

The .NET Framework was developed so that it could support a theoretically infinite number of development languages. Currently, more than 20 development languages work with the .NET Framework.

Multiple language support

The design of the .NET Framework allows developers to use their preferred language when developing .NET applications. Currently, the .NET Framework supports more than 20 languages, including those shown in the following table.

.NET Languages

Visual Basic .NET	C#	Microsoft Visual J#™ .NET
Microsoft JScript® .NET	Oberon	Scheme
Perl	Python	COBOL
Haskell	Pascal	ML
Mercury	Eiffel	ADA
SmallTalk	CAML	Microsoft Visual C++®
APL	C	n/a

Benefits of multiple language support

Because the .NET Framework supports multiple development languages, you gain the following benefits over single-language frameworks:

- Code modules are reusable. A code module written in one language can be used by an application written in a different language.

- The object library is the same for all languages. All languages use the same object model, which is supplied by the .NET Framework class library.

- Language flexibility allows you to choose the right language for the task. For example, Perl is a better choice for regular expressions, whereas COBOL was the preferred language for business applications for many years. Language flexibility not only lets you choose the right language for new projects, but it also allows you to upgrade existing applications with new technologies, without rewriting the entire application in a new language.

- All languages that are supported by the .NET Framework offer essentially equal performance. Every .NET-based language compiles to the Microsoft intermediate language (MSIL), and all MSIL is then compiled to native code, at run-time, by the same compiler.

The Common Language Runtime

- **One runtime for all . NET-Based Languages**
- **Manages threads and memory**
  - Garbage collection
- **Enforces code security**
- **Eliminates DLL versioning problems**
  - Multiple versions of a DLL can run simultaneously
  - Applications can specify a version of a DLL to use

Introduction	The common language runtime (hereafter referred to as "runtime") is the runtime engine of the .NET Framework. The runtime also provides several other services, including code security and solving dynamic-link library (DLL) versioning problems.
Manages threads and memory	The runtime manages application threading, providing application memory isolation. When objects are no longer used by a .NET application, the runtime performs *garbage collection*, which frees up the memory that was used by those objects.
Code security	The runtime ensures that a .NET application is secure and will run properly. The runtime provides type safety, and also ensures that there are:

- No unsafe casts.
- No uninitialized variables.
- No out-of-bounds array indexing.

The runtime also performs exception handling for applications.

DLL versioning

Prior to the .NET Framework, applications shared DLL files. If one application needed a newer version of the DLL, it would update the DLL during application installation. As a result of this update, other programs using the DLL may no longer function properly. These DLL versioning issues are commonly referred to as "DLL Hell."

With the runtime, versioning is part of a DLL's identity, not something the developer has to set. If an application requires a particular version of a DLL, you can specify that version in the application. The runtime ensures that the correct version of the DLL is available for the application. Thus, the runtime allows multiple versions of a DLL to exist and run at the same time.

Note You specify a DLL version for an application in Extensible Markup Language (XML)-based configuration files. Applications can be configured to always use a specific version, or to always use the latest version of a DLL.

The Common Language Runtime Components

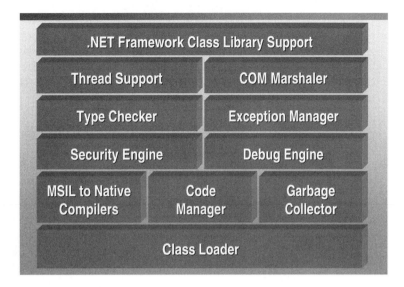

Introduction

Because the common language runtime is an integral part of developing applications with Microsoft Visual Studio® .NET, it is important to be familiar with the internal components of the runtime.

Components of the runtime

The runtime is referred to as a *managed* environment, one in which common services, such as garbage collection and security, are automatically provided. The following table describes the features of the common language runtime.

Component	Description
Class loader	Manages metadata, in addition to the loading and layout of classes.
MSIL to native compiler	Converts MSIL to native code (just-in-time [JIT] compilation).
Code manager	Manages code execution.
Garbage collector	Provides automatic lifetime management of all of your objects. This is a multiprocessor, scalable garbage collector.
Security engine	Provides evidence-based security that is based on the origin of the code and the user.
Debug engine	Allows you to debug your application and trace the execution of code.
Type checker	Will not allow unsafe casts or uninitialized variables. MSIL can be verified to guarantee type safety.
Exception manager	Provides structured exception handling, which is integrated with Microsoft Windows® structured exception handling (SEH).
Thread support	Provides classes and interfaces that enable multithreaded programming.
COM marshaler	Provides marshaling to and from COM.
.NET Framework Class Library support	Integrates code with the runtime that supports the .NET Framework Class Library.

Runtime Compilation and Execution

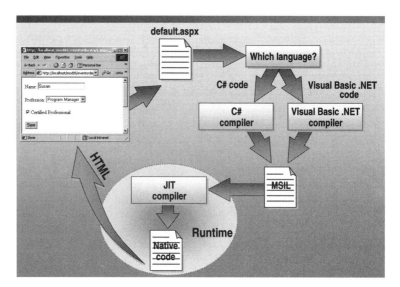

Introduction

Each .NET-compatible language provides its own compiler to compile code to MSIL. After the code is compiled in MSIL, the runtime compiles the MSIL to native code and then runs the application.

Language compilation

As shown in the preceding illustration, a Web browser requests a Web page from a Web server that is running Internet Information Services (IIS). The requested Web page, default.aspx, is compiled with the appropriate language compiler, depending on the language that is used to write the page. Regardless of the compiler and language used, the application is compiled to MSIL.

JIT compilation

The MSIL is handled by the runtime. The runtime uses a JIT compiler to compile the MSIL to native code. After the application is JIT-compiled, it is cached so that it does not need to be recompiled for each request.

Application execution

After the application is compiled, the runtime executes the application on the Web server and then generates the Hypertext Markup Language (HTML) and script that is returned to the client.

Note In the example provided on the preceding slide, the application being compiled is a Web application that was requested by a Web browser. The process of compilation and execution is the same for Microsoft Windows® applications. After the application is JIT-compiled, it is executed.

What are Namespaces?

> - **Group related classes**
>   - Logical, not physical, grouping
>   - Namespaces are hierarchical
> - **Decrease naming conflicts**
> - **Imports keyword in Visual Basic .NET code**
>
>   ```
>   Imports System.Data.SqlClient
>   ```
>
> - **Using keyword in C# code**
>
>   ```
>   using System.Data.SqlClient;
>   ```

Introduction

The .NET Framework class library, an object-oriented library, is composed of namespaces. The library is a collection of reusable types (classes, structures, enumerations, delegates, and interfaces) that reduces development time and increases cross-language support.

Note Do not confuse the .NET Framework namespaces with XML namespaces. Although they share the same name, the two concepts are entirely different.

Definition

Namespaces provide a logical grouping of classes that can be used by all .NET-compatible development languages. Each namespace contains types that you can use in your application. The namespaces are arranged hierarchically, which helps reduce naming conflicts and increases the reusability of code.

Importing namespaces

To use classes within a namespace, you can fully qualify each type with the full namespace hierarchy, or you can provide a declarative statement at the beginning of the application. To issue a declarative statement, you use the **Imports** statement in Visual Basic .NET or the **using** keyword in C#.

Example of importing namespaces

The following code shows you how to import a namespace in Visual Basic .NET:

```
Imports System.Data.SqlClient
```

The following code shows the same declaration in Visual C#:

```
using System.Data.SqlClient;
```

Note All namespaces provided by Microsoft begin with either Microsoft or System.

Using Namespaces

- **Implicit object declaration**

```
Imports System.Web.UI.WebControls
...
Dim listBox1 As New ListBox()
listBox1.Items.Add("First Item")
```

```
using System.Web.UI.WebControls;
...
ListBox listBox1 = new ListBox();
listBox1.Items.Add("First Item");
```

- **Explicit object declaration**

```
Dim listBox1 As New System.Web.UI.WebControls.ListBox()
listBox1.Items.Add("First Item")
```

```
System.Web.UI.WebControls.ListBox listBox1 =
        new System.Web.UI.WebControls.ListBox();
listBox1.Items.Add("First Item");
```

Introduction

When using namespaces, you can import the namespace by using a declarative statement at the beginning of the application, or you can explicitly use the namespace within your code.

Implicit object declaration

When you use the **Imports** statement (or, in Visual C#, the **using** keyword), you can then reference a method within the namespace by using only the method name. The following code demonstrates using the **listBox** class of the **System.Web.UI.WebControls** namespace:

Visual Basic .NET

```
Imports System.Web.UI.WebControls
...
Dim listBox1 As New ListBox()
listBox1.Items.Add("First Item")
```

C#

```
using System.Web.UI.WebControls;
...
ListBox listBox1 = new ListBox();
listBox1.Items.Add("First Item");
```

Explicit object declaration

If you do not use the **Imports** statement or **using** keyword, you must specify the entire namespace name with the method, as shown in the following code:

Visual Basic .NET

```
Dim listBox1 As New System.Web.UI.WebControls.ListBox()
listBox1.Items.Add("First Item")
```

C#

```
System.Web.UI.WebControls.ListBox listBox1 = new
        System.Web.UI.WebControls.ListBox();
listBox1.Items.Add("First Item");
```

Advantages and disadvantages

Although both methods of using namespaces are valid, there are distinct advantages to both. Implicit namespace use almost always reduces the amount of code. If you use a type from a namespace more than once in an application, you save time by declaring the namespace. Explicit use may make your code more readable and understandable to someone else, because every type you use is shown with its namespace.

Lesson: Comparison of the .NET-Based Languages

- **Visual Basic .NET**
- **C#**
- **Choosing a Language**
- **Practice: Language Translation**

Introduction

Visual Studio .NET is shipped with two .NET-based languages: C# and Visual Basic .NET, which are the two most popular .NET-based languages.

In this lesson, you will be introduced to Visual C# and Visual Basic .NET. Some of the advantages and disadvantages of these two languages will be explained, and you will be provided with guidance in choosing a development language to meet your needs.

Lesson objectives

After completing this lesson, you will be able to:

- List the common features of C#.
- List the common features of Visual Basic .NET.
- Pick the appropriate .NET development language for your needs.

Visual Basic .NET

- ■ **Visual Basic .NET is the latest version of Visual Basic**
- ■ **True object-oriented language**

```
Private Sub Button1_Click(ByVal sender As System.Object, _
    ByVal e As System.EventArgs) Handles Button1.Click
        Dim i As Integer = 0
        Dim x As Double = TextBox1.Text
        For i = 0 To 4
            x *= 2
            Label1.Text = Label1.Text & x & ","
        Next
End Sub
```

- **Visual Basic Scripting Edition (and JScript) are still used for client-side script**

Introduction

Visual Basic .NET is the latest version of Microsoft Visual Basic, but it should not be viewed as simply the next version after Visual Basic 6.0. The language has been rewritten for the .NET Framework, and it is now a true object-oriented language.

Features of Visual Basic .NET

Visual Basic .NET, like its predecessor Visual Basic 6.0, is a good language to use for rapid application development. However, Visual Basic .NET has many enhancements over Visual Basic 6.0:

- ■ Inheritance
- ■ Overloading
- ■ Parameterized constructors
- ■ Free threading
- ■ Structured exception handling
- ■ Strict type checking
- ■ Shared members
- ■ Initializers

Tip Unlike C#, Visual Basic .NET is not case-sensitive.

The following code example shows an event procedure written in Visual Basic .NET:

```
Private Sub Button1_Click(ByVal sender As System.Object, _
    ByVal e As System.EventArgs) Handles Button1.Click
  Dim i As Integer = 0
  Dim x As Double = TextBox1.Text
  For i = 0 To 4
    x *= 2
    Label1.Text = Label1.Text & x & ","
  Next
End Sub
```

Note Although Visual Basic .NET replaces Visual Basic 6.0 as a development language for .NET applications, Visual Basic Scripting Edition is still used for client-side scripting in Web pages. JScript also remains a suitable choice for client-side script.

C#

- **C# is a new language**

- **Similar to Java, Visual C++, and Pascal**

```
private void Button1_Click(object sender,
        System.EventArgs e)
{
   int i = 0;
   double x = Convert.ToDouble(TextBox1.Text);
   for (i=0; i<=4; i++)
   {
       x *= 2;
       Label1.Text = Label1.Text + x + ",";
   }
}
```

Introduction

C# is a new language, introduced with the .NET Framework. It has its origin in C and Visual C++, but it is an entirely new language that takes full advantage of the object-oriented nature of .NET development.

Features of Visual C#

C# is very closely related to Visual C++, Pascal, and Java. C# is a true object-oriented language. Features of Visual C# include:

- It is an object oriented programming (OOP) language

- Type safety

- Automatic garbage collection

- It is case-sensitive

- All class and pointer attributes are accessed by a dot (.)

- Everything is treated as an object (class, structure, array, etc.)

The following code example shows an event procedure written in C#:

```
private void Button1_Click(object sender, System.EventArgs e)
{
  int i = 0;
  double x = Convert.ToDouble(TextBox1.Text);
  for (i=0; i<=4; i++)
  {
      x *= 2;
      Label1.Text = Label1.Text + x + ",";
  }
}
```

Choosing a Language

- **.NET Framework class library is the same regardless of language**
- **Performance**
  - All languages are compiled to MSIL
  - Only performance difference is how each language compiler compiles to MSIL
  - The runtime compiles all MSIL the same, regardless of its origin
- **Development experience**
  - C# is similar to Java, C, Visual C++, and Pascal
  - Visual Basic .NET is similar to Visual Basic
- **Browser compatibility**
  - ASP.NET code is server-side code, so browser compatibility is not an issue

Introduction

Because the .NET Framework uses a runtime, and because all .NET-based languages compile to MSIL, there is little difference between the two languages. Choosing which language to use when developing your Web application mainly depends on your previous development experience.

Performance

Because all of the .NET-based languages are compiled to MSIL and the JIT compiler treats all MSIL the same, there is no noticeable performance difference amongst the different languages. The only difference is how each language-specific compiler writes the MSIL. In general, these differences are small and have an insignificant effect on performance.

Development experience

Because performance is not a factor in choosing the .NET-based language with which you will develop your application, you should consider your existing language experience and background. If you are familiar with Java, C# is an appropriate choice. If your background is in C and Visual C++ development, C# is a clear choice for .NET applications. If you are a Visual Basic 6.0 developer, you should choose Visual Basic .NET.

Browser compatibility

Because ASP.NET code runs only on the server, browser compatibility is not a consideration when choosing a .NET-based development language. The ASP.NET code runs on the server, and the server then returns the appropriate HTML and client-side script to the client's browser.

Practice: Language Translation

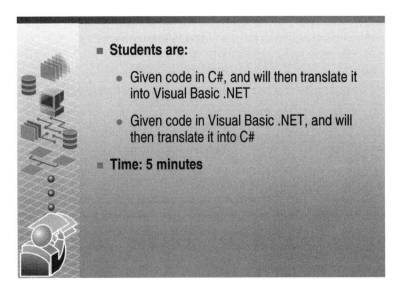

In this practice, you will translate Visual Basic .NET code into C#. You will then translate C# code into Visual Basic .NET.

▶ **Perform the following translations**

Visual Basic .NET code to translate:

```
Function getPi() As Double
    Dim pi As Double
    pi = 4 * System.Math.Atan(1)
    return pi
End Function
```

C# code to translate:

```
string Test()
{
    string sReturn = "";
    int j = 1;
    while (j < 10)
    {
        sReturn += j;
        j += 2;
    }
    return sReturn;
}
```

_____

_____

Lesson: Creating a Component Using Visual Studio .NET

- **What are Classes and Components?**
- **Creating a Class**
- **Using Components in an ASP.NET Web Form**
- **Demonstration: Creating a Class in Visual Studio .NET**

Introduction

In this lesson, you will be introduced to classes and components. You will then create a component by using Visual Studio .NET and learn how to use that component in other applications.

Lesson objectives

After completing this lesson, you will be able to:

- Distinguish between a class and a component.
- Create a class.
- Use a component from another application.
- Build a component in Visual Basic .NET or C#.

What are Classes and Components?

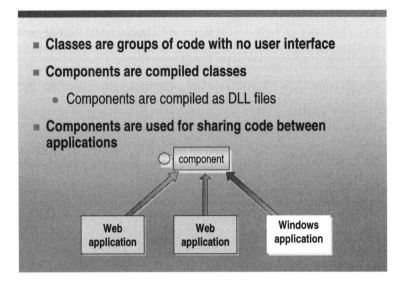

- Classes are groups of code with no user interface
- Components are compiled classes
  - Components are compiled as DLL files
- Components are used for sharing code between applications

component

Web application   Web application   Windows application

Introduction	When developing in an object-oriented language (such as Visual Basic .NET or C#), you can make of use existing classes and components. For example, the .NET Framework class library is comprised of many classes.
Class definition	Classes are groups of code statements that have no user interface (UI). Classes provide functionality within an application and can be shared amongst different parts of an application. Classes are used to organize functions and give them a single name by which they are referenced. Classes also have properties and methods. Whereas properties are the way you set the characteristics of a class, methods are the way that you invoke the actions of a class. When you want to use a class and its methods, you actually use an object of that class. An object is an instantiation of the class.
Component definition	Components are classes that are compiled into a DLL file. Because the component is its own file, the functionality of a component can be shared among different applications. You reference a component from an application by using the component's namespaces and class names.

Example of component sharing

For example, suppose you build a component that calculates the salary increase that an employee receives. This calculation is based on numerous formulas that are specific to your organization, including current base salary, performance rating, and tenure at the company. The calculations are very complex and time-consuming to develop. In addition, the company frequently changes the formula by which raises are calculated.

After the component is created and compiled as a DLL file, other applications can use it. For example, you might have a Windows application that the Human Resources department uses to determine an employees new salary for their next paycheck. You might also build a Web application that employees can use to determine what their new salary will be. You may also have an additional Web application, available only to managers, that also uses the component.

By using a component to handle the calculations, you only need to create the complicated algorithm once—after that, all applications can use it. Furthermore, when changes occur, you can update the component without needing to update the applications that use the component.

Creating a Class

■ **Create a Class Library project in Visual Studio .NET**

  ● Visual Studio .NET creates a default namespace

■ **Create methods of the class**

```
Public Class Shipping
  Function ShippingCost _
    (ByVal sngPrice As Single) As Single
    '…
    Return (sngShipping)
  End Function
End Class
```

```
public class Shipping
{
  public Single ShippingCost (Single sngPrice)
  {
    //…
    return sngShipping;
  }
}
```

Introduction

In object-oriented languages, the concept of abstraction is important. Abstraction is a form of organization in which methods, data, and functions that serve a common purpose are grouped together. A fundamental component of abstraction is the creation and use of classes.

Definition

A class is a template for an object. This template defines attributes for storing data and defines operations for manipulating that data. A class also defines a set of restrictions that can be used to allow or deny access to its attributes and operations.

Creating a new class

You can create a class in any Visual Studio .NET project. You can also create a new class library, which contains only the class and its methods, but no UI (windows or forms). If you create a class within an existing project, the class exists within the project namespace. If you create a new class library, Visual Studio .NET creates a default namespace and places that new class within that namespace.

When you create a class within a project, the class file is compiled into the application DLL and cannot be reused by other applications. If you create a class library, you are creating a component that can be reused.

▶ **To create a new class**

1. Open a solution in Visual Studio .NET.

2. On the **File** menu, point to **New**, and then click **Project**.

3. In the **Project Types** dialog box, select the language that you want to use. In the **Templates** pane, select **Class Library**. Click **Add to solution** to add the new project to the current solution.

4. In the **Name** box, type the name of your new class library, and then click **OK**.

Visual Studio .NET creates a new class file with a template for the class, as shown in the following code:

Visual Basic .NET

```
Public Class Class1

End Class
```

C#

```
using System;
namespace ClassLibrary1
{
    public class Class1
    {
        public class1()
        {
        }
    }
}
```

Visual Basic .NET

Visual Basic .NET creates a default namespace for the class that has the same name as the project. To change the namespace name, follow these steps:

a. Right-click the project in the Solution Explorer, and then click **Properties**.

b. In the **Property Pages** dialog box, on the **General Properties** tab, set the **Root namespace** to the new name for your component.

C#

If you are using C#, the namespace is contained in the class file and can be changed by editing the file, as shown in the following code:

```
namespace ClassLibrary1
{
    public class Class1
    {

    }
}
```

5. Build the project to create the component for your new class.

Creating the methods for a class

After the class is created, you add the methods (functions and sub procedures) that are contained within the class. The following code example shows the new class, **Shipping**. The class contains a single function, named **ShippingCost**:

Visual Basic .NET

```
Public Class Shipping
    Function ShippingCost(ByVal sngPrice As Single) _
      As Single
      ' . . .
      Return sngShipping
    End Function
End Class
```

C#

```
public class Shipping
{
    public Single ShippingCost (Single sngPrice)
    {
        //...
        return sngShipping;
    }
}
```

Using Components in an ASP.NET Web Form

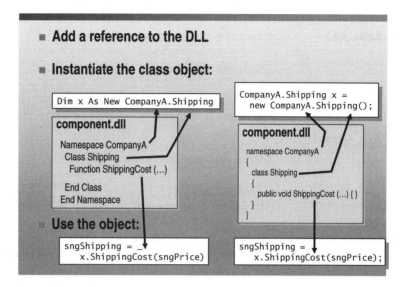

- Add a reference to the DLL

- Instantiate the class object:

```
Dim x As New CompanyA.Shipping
```

component.dll

```
Namespace CompanyA
  Class Shipping
    Function ShippingCost (...)

  End Class
End Namespace
```

```
CompanyA.Shipping x =
   new CompanyA.Shipping();
```

component.dll

```
namespace CompanyA
{
  class Shipping
  {
    public void ShippingCost (...) { }
  }
}
```

Use the object:

```
sngShipping = _
    x.ShippingCost(sngPrice)
```

```
sngShipping =
    x.ShippingCost(sngPrice);
```

Introduction

Classes created within a component are available to other programs. First, you must reference the component (DLL). Then, to access the methods within the class, you instantiate the class object by referencing its namespace and class name.

Referencing the DLL

Before using the classes in a component, you must first add a reference to the component within your project.

▶ **To add a reference to the DLL**

1. Open a Web application project in Visual Studio .NET.

2. Right-click the project in the Solution Explorer and then click **Add Reference**.

3. In the **Add Reference** dialog box, on the **Projects** tab, double-click the class library project, and then click **OK**.

   The component is added to the **References** folder in Solution Explorer.

   The reference makes the namespace of the component accessible to the application.

Tip If you keep the Web application project and the class library project in the same solution, any changes you make to the component are automatically reflected by the reference.

Instantiating the object   After you add a reference to the component, you instantiate the class object. The following line of code declares a new variable named *x* of the class **Shipping**, within the **Company** namespace:

Visual Basic .NET

```
Dim x As New CompanyA.Shipping
```

C#

```
CompanyA.Shipping x = new CompanyA.Shipping();
```

You can also use the **Imports** or **using** statement to import the namespace, and then instantiate the class directly, as shown in the following code:

Visual Basic .NET

```
Imports CompanyA
Dim x As New Shipping
```

C#

```
using CompanyA;
Shipping x = new Shipping();
```

Using the object   After it is instantiated, the object is used like any other object in your project. All of the public methods within the class are available for use. For example, the following line of code passes one parameter to the **ShippingCost** function of the **Shipping** class and assigns the returned value to the **sngShipping** variable:

Visual Basic .NET

```
sngShipping = x.ShippingCost(sngPrice)
```

C#

```
sngShipping = x.ShippingCost(sngPrice);
```

Demonstration: Creating a Class in Visual Studio .NET

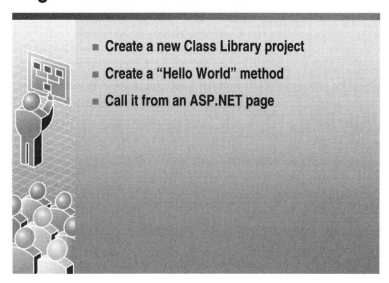

- Create a new Class Library project
- Create a "Hello World" method
- Call it from an ASP.NET page

▶ **To run the demonstration**

1. In Visual Studio .NET, create a new Class Library project in Visual Basic .NET or C# named **HelloWorld**.

   You can use the solution that you created in Module 2 to run this demonstration, or you can create a new solution.

2. Show the Class1.vb or Class1.cs file. A default class, Class1, is created.

3. Create a **Hello** method:

Visual Basic .NET

```
Function Hello() As String
    Return "Hi from Visual Basic .NET component."
End Function
```

C#

```
public string Hello()
{
    return "Hi from C# component.";
}
```

4. Build the project.

5. Create a new Web application project and add it to your current solution.

6. In the Web application, add a reference to the **HelloWorld** component.

7. Expand the bin folder in the Web application project and show that the HelloWorld.dll file has been copied there. Ensure that **Show All Files** is selected in Solution Explorer.

8. Open the default WebForm1.aspx page in the Web application project.

9. Place a **Button** control on the page and create a **Click** event procedure for it.

Note You will learn more about event procedures in Module 5, "Adding Code to a Microsoft ASP.NET Web Form," in Course 2310B: *Developing Microsoft ASP.NET Web Applications Using Visual Studio .NET.*

Add the following code to the **Click** event procedure, showing the Microsoft IntelliSense® for the HelloWorld component and the *x* variable.

Visual Basic .NET
```
Dim x As New HelloWorld.Class1()
Button1.Text = x.Hello()
```

C#
```
HelloWorld.Class1 x = new HelloWorld.Class1();
Button1.Text = x.Hello();
```

10. Build and browse the WebForm1.aspx page and click the button.

Review

- Overview of the .NET-Based Languages
- Comparison of the .NET-Based Languages
- Creating a Component Using Visual Studio .NET

1. How would you select a .NET-based language to create a new Web application project?

2. What role does the common language runtime play in running an ASP.NET page?

3. What is the role of the just-in-time (JIT) compilation?

4. List four languages that are currently supported by .NET.

5. What is garbage collection and why is it so useful in the .NET Framework?

6. Why would you create a component for a Web application?

Lab 3: Building a Microsoft Visual Studio .NET Component

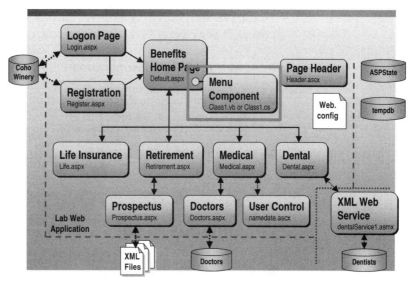

Objectives

After completing this lab, you will be able to:

- Create a component in Microsoft® Visual Studio® .NET.
- Add a reference to a component in Visual Studio .NET.

Note This lab focuses on the concepts in this module and as a result may not comply with Microsoft security recommendations.

Prerequisites

Before working on this lab, you must have:

- Knowledge of how to write a Microsoft Visual Basic® or C# function.
- Knowledge of how to create a Visual Basic structure or C# structure.

Scenario

Coho Winery offers several benefits to its employees. In the labs for Course 2310B, *Developing Microsoft ASP.NET Web Applications Using Visual Studio .NET*, you will create a Web site that enables employees to select and set up their chosen benefits.

The list of benefits that are offered by Coho Winery is displayed on a number of pages in the Web site. Rather than code the list on every Web page that displays the offered benefits, you have been asked to develop a component that returns the benefit names.

In this lab, you will create a component. The component you create will contain an array that holds the benefit name and the name of the Web page that implements that benefit.

Estimated time to complete this lab: 30 minutes

Exercise 0
Lab Setup

To complete this lab, you must have created a Benefits Web Application project. If you have not created this project, complete the following steps:

▶ **Create the 2310LabApplication solution**

Important Only perform this procedure if you have not created a 2310LabApplication solution file.

---

1. Using Visual Studio .NET, create a new blank solution named 2310LabApplication:

   a. On the **File** menu, point to **New**, and then click **Blank Solution**.

   b. In the **New Project** dialog box, in the **Name** text box, type **2310LabApplication**, and then click **OK**.

▶ **Create the Benefits solution**

Important Only perform this procedure if you have not previously created a Benefits project, or if you have removed the Benefits project according to the steps in Appendix A, "Lab Recovery," in Course 2310B, *Developing Microsoft ASP.NET Web Applications Using Visual Studio .NET*.

---

1. Create a new Microsoft ASP.NET Web Application project, named BenefitsVB or BenefitsCS, in the 2310LabApplication solution:

   a. On the **File** menu, point to **New**, and then click **Project**.

   b. In the **New Project** dialog box, in the **Project Types** list, click **Visual Basic Projects** or **Visual C# Projects**.

   c. In the **Templates** list, click **ASP.NET Web Application**.

   d. Set the **Location** to **http://localhost/BenefitsVB** for a Visual Basic .NET project or to **http://localhost/BenefitsCS** for a Visual C# project.

   e. Click **Add to Solution**, and then click **OK**.

Caution When adding projects to the solution, the capitalization of the project name is important. Because you may be using some pre-built Web Forms in this and other labs in Course 2310B, *Developing Microsoft ASP.NET Web Applications Using Visual Studio .NET*, you must verify that you have capitalized the Benefits project as shown. Two versions of the project can be created; **BenefitsVB** would be a **Visual Basic .NET** solution and **BenefitsCS** would be a **Visual C#** solution.

Exercise 1
Creating a Class

In this exercise, you will first create a Visual Basic .NET or Visual C# Class Library project and then create a class that returns a string of names.

▶ **Update the Benefits project**

1. In Visual Studio .NET, open the 2310LabApplication solution file.

2. In Solution Explorer, right-click **BenefitsVB** or **BenefitsCS**, point to **Add**, and then click **Add Existing Item**.

For the Visual Basic .NET project

   a. Browse to the *install folder*\Labfiles\Lab03\VB\Starter\BenefitsVB folder for the Visual Basic .NET files.

   b. In the **Files of type** box of the **Add Existing Item – BenefitsVB** dialog box, click **All Files**.

For the C# project

   a. Browse to the *install folder*\Labfiles\Lab03\CS\Starter\BenefitsCS folder for the Visual C# files.

   b. In the **Files of type** box of the **Add Existing Item – BenefitsCS** dialog box, click **All Files**.

3. Select all of the files in this folder, and then click **Open**.

4. Click **Yes** if prompted to overwrite or reload files.

▶ **Create a Class Library project**

1. In Visual Studio .NET, open the 2310LabApplication solution:

   a. On the **File** menu, click **Open Solution**.

   b. In the My Documents\Visual Studio Projects\2310LabApplication folder, select **2310LabApplication.sln**, and then click **Open**.

Tip If 2310LabApplication is listed in the list of projects on the Start Page, you can click the **2310LabApplication** link in the list to open the solution.

---

2. Create a new Visual Basic or Visual C# Class Library project:

   a. On the **File** menu, point to **New**, and then click **Project**.

   b. In the **New Project** dialog box, in the **Project Types** list, click **Visual Basic Projects** or **Visual C# Projects**.

   c. In the **Templates** list, click **Class Library**, set the **Name** to **BenefitsListVB or BenefitsListCS**, click **Add to Solution**, and then click **OK**.

Caution When adding projects to the solution, the capitalization of the project name is important. Because you may be using some pre-built Web Forms in this and other labs in Course 2310B, *Developing Microsoft ASP.NET Web Applications Using Visual Studio .NET*, you must verify that you have capitalized the BenefitsListVB or BenefitsListCS project as shown.

Visual Studio .NET creates a new class library named BenefitsListVB or BenefitsListCS and adds this project to the 2310LabApplication solution. List the two new files that appear in Solution Explorer, under the BenefitsListVB or BenefitsListCS project:

_____

_____

3. In Windows Explorer, find where the files were created. Fill in your answer below.

_____

_____

4. In Solution Explorer, double-click the **Class1.vb** file or the **Class1.cs** file to open it.

5. What is the name of the class that is created by default?

_____

_____

6. In Solution Explorer, right-click the **BenefitsListVB** or **BenefitsListCS** project, and then click **Properties**.

7. What is the name of the namespace that is created by default?

_____

_____

▶ **Create the component methods**

1. In the **Class1.vb** or **Class1.cs** file, change the name of the class to **Benefits**. In the **Class1.cs** file change the name of the constructor to **Benefits**.

Note   When using C#, the class constructor must have the same name as the class.

---

2. In the Benefits class in the Class1.vb or Class1.cs file, create a custom structure to hold the name of the benefit and the name of the Web page that implements it, as shown in the following code:

In the Visual Basic .NET class

```
Structure BenefitInfo
    Dim strName As String
    Dim strPage As String
End Structure
```

In the C# class

```
public struct BenefitInfo
{
    public string strName;
    public string strPage;
}
```

3. In the **Benefits** class, create a method named **GetBenefitsList** that creates an array of **BenefitInfo** structures, fills in the structures with the information that is shown in the following table, and then returns the array to the calling component.

strName	strPage
Dental	dental.aspx
Medical	medical.aspx
Life Insurance	life.aspx

In the Visual Basic .NET class

Your code should look like the following:

```
Public Function GetBenefitsList() As BenefitInfo()
    Dim arBenefits(2) As BenefitInfo
    arBenefits(0).strName = "Dental"
    arBenefits(0).strPage = "dental.aspx"
    arBenefits(1).strName = "Medical"
    arBenefits(1).strPage = "medical.aspx"
    arBenefits(2).strName = "Life Insurance"
    arBenefits(2).strPage = "life.aspx"
    Return arBenefits
End Function
```

In the C# class

Your code should look like the following:

```
public BenefitInfo[] GetBenefitsList()
{
BenefitInfo[] arBenefits = new BenefitInfo[3];
    arBenefits[0].strName = "Dental";
    arBenefits[0].strPage = "dental.aspx";
    arBenefits[1].strName = "Medical";
    arBenefits[1].strPage = "medical.aspx";
    arBenefits[2].strName = "Life Insurance";
    arBenefits[2].strPage = "life.aspx";
    return arBenefits;
}
```

4. Save your changes.

5. Right-click **BenefitsListVB** or **BenefitsListCS** in Solution Explorer and then click **Build** to build the BenefitsList project.

Exercise 2
Calling the Component

In this exercise, you will call the component that you created in the preceding exercise, Exercise 1, from an ASP.NET page.

▶ **Add a reference to the Benefits project**

1. In the Benefits project in the 2310LabApplication solution, complete the following steps to add a reference to the **BenefitsList** component that you just created.

   a. Right-click the **BenefitsVB** or **BenefitsCS** project in Solution Explorer and then click **Add Reference**.

   b. In the **Add Reference** dialog box, on the **Projects** tab, double-click the **BenefitsListVB** or **BenefitsListCS** project, and then click **OK**.

   The component is added to the References folder in Solution Explorer.

2. Open the test.aspx.vb or test.aspx.cs code-behind page and look at the code that is already there.

   Which line(s) of code instantiate the component?

   _____

   _____

3. Right-click the **test.aspx** page in Solution Explorer and then click **Build and Browse**.

   A browser window opens in Visual Studio .NET that displays the test.aspx page. test.aspx displays all of the benefits options from the component.

▶ **Make a change in the component**

1. Edit the Class1.vb or Class1.cs file in the BenefitsList project.

2. Increase the size of the array by one, as shown in the following code:

Visual Basic .NET

```
Dim arBenefits(3) as BenefitInfo
```

C#

```
BenefitInfo[] arBenefits = new BenefitInfo[4];
```

3. Add another benefit to the array, as shown in the following code:

Visual Basic .NET

```
arBenefits(3).strName = "Retirement Account"
arBenefits(3).strPage = "retirement.aspx"
```

C#

```
arBenefits[3].strName = "Retirement Account";
arBenefits[3].strPage = "retirement.aspx";
```

4. Build the component.

5. Refresh the browser that is displaying the test.aspx page.

You should see the new benefit option. Notice that you did not have to rebuild the Web application, because it automatically uses the new dynamic-link library (DLL).

▶ **Test a C# component**

For the Visual Basic .NET project

1. Remove the BenefitsListVB reference from the BenefitsVB project:

   a. In Solution Explorer, expand **References**.

   b. Right-click **BenefitsListVB** and then choose **Remove**.

2. Add a reference to the C# BenefitsList component, BenefitsListCS.dll, which is in the *install folder*\Labfiles\Lab03\VB\Starter\bin folder:

   a. Right-click the **BenefitsVB** project in Solution Explorer and then click **Add Reference**.

   b. In the **Add Reference** dialog box, click **Browse**.

   c. In the **Select Component** dialog box, navigate to the *install folder*\ Labfiles\Lab03\VB\Starter\bin folder, select the **BenefitsListCS.dll** file, and then click **Open**, and then click **OK**.

   The component is added to the References folder of the Benefits project, in Solution Explorer.

3. Modify the code to use the new component.

   a. In the **test.aspx** page, modify the code to match the new component, as shown in the following code:

   ```
   Dim clBenefits As New BenefitsListCS.Benefits()
   Dim bi As BenefitsListCS.Benefits.BenefitInfo
   ```

4. Right-click the test.aspx page in Solution Explorer and then click **Build and Browse**.

   You should see new benefits options from the C# component.

▶ **Test a Visual Basic .NET component**

For the Visual C# project

1. Remove the BenefitsListCS reference from the BenefitsCS project:

   a. In Solution Explorer, expand **References**.

   b. Right-click **BenefitsListCS** and then choose **Remove**.

2. Add a reference to the Visual Basic BenefitsList component, BenefitsListVB.dll, which is in the *install folder*\Labfiles\ Lab03\CS\Starter\bin folder:

   a. Right-click the **BenefitsCS** project in Solution Explorer and then click **Add Reference**.

   b. In the **Add Reference** dialog box, click **Browse**.

   c. In the **Select Component** dialog box, navigate to the *install folder*\ Labfiles\Lab03\CS\Starter\bin folder, select the **BenefitsListVB.dll** file, and then click **Open**, and then click **OK**.

   The component is added to the **References** folder of the Benefits project, in Solution Explorer.

3. Modify the code to use the new component:

   a. In the **test.aspx**, modify the code to match the new component, as shown in the following code:

```
BenefitsListVB.Benefits clBenefits = new
   BenefitsListVB.Benefits();
foreach(BenefitsListVB.Benefits.BenefitInfo bi in
   clBenefits.GetBenefitsList())
```

4. Right-click the **test.aspx** page in Solution Explorer and then click **Build and Browse**.

   You should see new benefits options from the Visual Basic .NET component.

Note Code changes to the test.aspx page are only required because of the different naming system that is used for BenefitsListCS and BenefitsListVB. When interchanging equivalent Visual Basic .NET and C# components with the same names, no further code modification is required.

▶ **Reset to the original component**

1. Remove the BenefitsList reference in the Benefits project.

2. Add a reference to the Visual Basic .NET or Visual C# BenefitsList component that you created previously in this lab.

3. Remove the code modification in test.aspx.

4. Right-click the **test.aspx** page in Solution Explorer and then click **Build and Browse**.

   You should see your original list of benefits options.

msdn training

Module 4: Creating a Microsoft ASP.NET Web Form

Contents

Overview

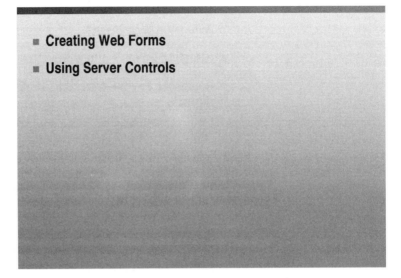

- Creating Web Forms
- Using Server Controls

Introduction

In this module, you will learn how to create and populate Web Forms. Web Forms are programmable Web pages that serve as the user interface (UI) for a Microsoft® ASP.NET Web Application project. A Web Form presents information to the user in any type of browser, and it implements application logic by using server-side code.

Objectives

After completing this module, you will be able to:

- Add a Web Form to an ASP.NET Web Application project.

- Use the Microsoft Visual Studio® .NET toolbox to add server controls to a Web Form.

Lesson: Creating Web Forms

- What is a Web Form?

- Creating a Web Form with Visual Studio .NET

- Demonstration: Converting an HTML Page to a Web Form

Introduction

In this lesson, you will learn how to create a Web Form. You will also learn how to identify the key characteristics of Web Forms.

Lesson objectives

After completing this lesson, you will be able to:

- Identify and explain the Hypertext Markup Language (HTML) code that comprises a Web Form.

- Create a Web Form by using Visual Studio .NET.

What Is a Web Form?

- **.aspx extension**
- **Page attributes**
  - **@ Page** directive
- **Body attributes**
- **Form attributes**

```
<%@ Page Language="vb" Codebehind="WebForm1.aspx.vb"
  SmartNavigation="true"%>
<html>
  <body ms_positioning="GridLayout">
    <form id="Form1" method="post" runat="server">
    </form>
  </body>
</html>
```

Introduction

Web Forms consist of a combination of HTML, code, and controls that execute on a Web server that is running Microsoft Internet Information Services (IIS). Web Forms display a UI by generating HTML that is sent to the browser, while the supporting code and controls that run the UI stay on the Web server. This split between client-side interface and server-side code is a crucial difference between Web Forms and traditional Web pages. While a traditional Web page requires all of the code to be sent to and be processed at the Browser, Web Forms need to send only the interface controls to the browser, and the page processing is kept on the server. This UI/code split increases the range of supported browsers while increasing the security and functionality of the Web page.

.aspx extension

Web Forms are commonly referred to as ASP.NET pages or ASPX pages. Web Forms have an .aspx extension and work as the containers for the text and controls that you want to display on the browser.

ASP.NET (.aspx) pages and Active Server Pages (ASP) (.asp) can coexist on the same server. The file extension determines whether ASP or ASP.NET processes it.

Web Forms are often comprised of two separate files: the .aspx file contains the UI for the Web Form, while the .aspx.vb or .aspx.cs file, which is called a *code-behind page,* contains the supporting code.

Page attributes

The functions of a Web Form are defined by three levels of attributes. Page attributes define global functions, body attributes define how a page will be displayed, and form attributes define how groups of controls will be processed.

The **<@Page>** tag defines page-specific attributes that are used by the ASP.NET page parser and compiler. You can include only one <@ **Page**>tag per .aspx file. The following examples are typical <@ **Page**>tags for Microsoft Visual Basic® .NET and for Microsoft Visual C#™ .NET:

Visual Basic .NET

```
<%@ Page Language="vb" Codebehind="WebForm1.aspx.vb"
SmartNavigation="true" %>
```

C#

```
<%@ Page Language="c#" Codebehind="WebForm1.aspx.cs"
SmartNavigation="true" %>
```

The attributes of an <@ **Page**>tag include:

- **Language**

  The **Language** attribute defines the language in which the script on the Web page is written. Some of the values for this attribute are: **vb**, **c#**, and **JScript**.

- **Codebehind** page

  The **Codebehind** page attribute identifies the code-behind page that carries the logic that supports the Web Form. When Visual Studio .NET creates a Web Form, such as *WebForm1*.aspx, it also creates a code-behind page, *WebForm1*.aspx.vb or *WebForm1*.aspx.cs.

  Note For more information about code-behind pages, see Module 5, "Adding Code to a Microsoft ASP.NET Web Form," in Course 2310B, *Developing Microsoft ASP.NET Web Applications Using Visual Studio .NET*.

- **SmartNavigation**

  The **SmartNavigation** attribute in ASP.NET allows the browser to refresh only the sections of the form that have changed. The advantages of Smart Navigation are that the screen does not flash as it updates; instead, the scroll position is maintained and the "last page" in history is maintained. Smart navigation is only available to users with Microsoft Internet Explorer 5 or later.

Body attributes

The **<Body>** tag attributes define the appearance of objects that are displayed on the client's browser. The following is a typical **<Body>**tag:

```
<body ms_positioning="GridLayout">
```

The attributes of a **<Body>**tag include:

■ **PageLayout**

The **pageLayout** attribute (tagged as **ms_positioning**) determines how controls and text are positioned on the page. There are two options for **pageLayout**:

• **FlowLayout**

In **FlowLayout,** the text, images, and controls wrap across the screen, depending on the width of the browser window.

• **GridLayout**

In **GridLayout**, the text fields, images, and controls on a page are fixed by absolute coordinates. **GridLayout** is the default **pageLayout** for Visual Studio .NET.

The following code example shows how to implement **GridLayout** and locate a text box:

```
<body ms_positioning="GridLayout">
    <form id="Form1" method="post" runat="server">
        <asp:textbox id="txtField1" style="Z-INDEX: 101;
        LEFT: 65px; POSITION: absolute; TOP: 98px"
    runat="server" Height="26px" Width="194px">
    </asp:textbox>
    </form>
</body>
```

Form attributes

The **<Form>** tag defines how groups of controls will be processed. The **<Form>** tag is different from the Web Form term that is used to define the entire Web page. **<Form>** tag attributes define how controls will be processed. Although you can have many HTML forms on a page, you can only have one server-side form on an .aspx page.

The following is a typical **<Form>**tag:

```
<form id="Form1" method="post" runat="server">
  ...
</form>
```

Attributes of a **<Form>** tag include:

- **Method**

  The **Method** attribute identifies the method of sending control values back to the server. The options for this attribute are:

  - **Post**

    Data is passed in name/value pairs within the body the Hypertext Transfer Protocol (HTTP) request.

  - **Get**

    Data is passed in a query string.

- **Runat**

  A key feature of a Web Form is that the controls run on the server. The **runat="server"** attribute causes the form to post control information back to the ASP.NET page on the server where the supporting code runs. If the **runat** attribute is not set to **"server"**, the form works as a regular HTML form.

Visual Basic .NET example

The following code is from the default Web Form that Visual Studio .NET creates when you create a new ASP.NET Web Application project using Visual Basic .NET:

```
<%@Page Language="vb" AutoEventWireup="false"
Codebehind="WebForm1.aspx.vb"
Inherits="WebApplication1.WebForm1"%>
<!DOCTYPE HTML PUBLIC "-//W3C//DTD HTML 4.0 Transitional//EN">
<html>
  <head>
    <title>WebForm1</title>
    <meta name="GENERATOR" content="Microsoft Visual
    Studio.NET 7.0">
    <meta name="CODE_LANGUAGE" content="Visual Basic 7.0">
    <meta name="vs_defaultClientScript"
    content="JavaScript">
    <meta name="vs_targetSchema"
    content="http://schemas.microsoft.com/intellisense/ie5">
  </head>
  <body MS_POSITIONING="GridLayout">
    <form id="Form1" method="post" runat="server">
        'HTML and controls go here
    </form>
  </body>
</html>
```

C# example

The following code is from the default Web Form that Visual Studio .NET creates when you create a new Visual C# ASP.NET Web Application project:

```
<%@ Page language="c#" Codebehind="WebForm1.aspx.cs"
AutoEventWireup="false" Inherits="WebApplication1.WebForm1" %>
<!DOCTYPE HTML PUBLIC "-//W3C//DTD HTML 4.0 Transitional//EN">
<html>
  <head>
    <title>WebForm1</title>
      <meta name="GENERATOR" Content="Microsoft Visual
      Studio 7.0">
      <meta name="CODE_LANGUAGE" Content="C#">
      <meta name="vs_defaultClientScript"
      content="JavaScript">
      <meta name="vs_targetSchema"
      content="http://schemas.microsoft.com/intellisense/ie5">
  </head>
  <body MS_POSITIONING="GridLayout">
    <form id="Form1" method="post" runat="server">
        'HTML and controls go here
    </form>
  </body>
</html>
```

Creating a Web Form with Visual Studio .NET

- **New ASP.NET Web Applications create a default Web Form: WebForm1.aspx**

- **Create additional Web Forms from the Solution Explorer**

- **Upgrade existing HTML pages into Web Forms**

Introduction

Depending on where you are in your development cycle, there are several ways that you can create a Web Form.

New Web applications

When you create a new project in Visual Studio .NET, a default Web Form named WebForm1.aspx is automatically included in the project.

▶ **To create a new ASP.NET Web Application project and a default Web Form**

1. In Visual Studio .NET, on the Start Page, click **New Project**.

2. In the **New Project** dialog box, click **ASP.NET Web Application**, type the project name in the **Location** field, and then click **OK**.

   Visual Studio .NET creates a new Web application and a default Web Form that is named WebForm1.aspx.

Creating additional Web Forms

If you are expanding an existing project, you can use Solution Explorer to quickly add additional Web Forms.

▶ **To add additional Web Forms to a Web Application project**

1. In the Solution Explorer window, right-click the project name, point to **Add**, and then click **Add Web Form**. The **Add New Item -** *ProjectName* dialog box opens.

2. In the **Add New Item -** *ProjectName* dialog box, change the name of the Web Form, and then click **Open**.

   A new Web Form will be created and added to the project.

Upgrading HTML pages

If you are revising an existing Web site, you can import HTML pages into Visual Studio .NET and then upgrade those pages to Web Forms.

▶ **To upgrade existing HTML pages**

1. In Solution Explorer, right-click the project name, point to **Add**, and then click **Add Existing Item**.

2. In the **Add Existing Item** dialog box, navigate to the location of the HTML file, click the file name, and then click **Open**.

3. Rename the file from *fileName*.htm to *fileName*.aspx, and then click **Yes** when asked if you are sure that you want to change the file extension.

4. When prompted whether to create a new class file now, click **Yes**.

Demonstration: Converting an HTML Page to a Web Form

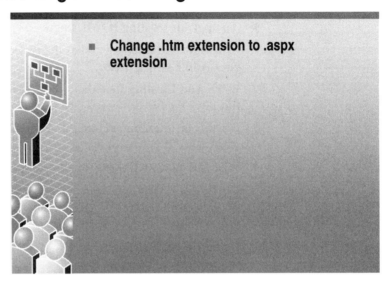

One quick way to create ASP.NET Web pages is to convert existing HTML pages.

▶ **To run this demonstration**

1. Start Visual Studio .NET.

2. Create a new **ASP.NET Web Application** project and set the location to **http://localhost/Mod04**.

3. Click **Add Existing Item** on the **File** menu.

4. In the **Files of type** box of the **Add Existing Item** dialog box, click **All Files (*.*)**.

5. Select the **HTMLPage.htm** page in the *install folder*\DemoCode\Mod04 folder, and then click **Open**.

6. Open the HTMLPage.htm page and switch to HTML view.

7. Add a fourth option to the list box containing **Lead Program Manager** to show that the contextual Microsoft IntelliSense® is working in the HTML file.

   Your code should look like the following:

   ```
   <option>Lead Program Manager</option>
   ```

8. Save your changes to the page.

9. In Solution Explorer, right-click **HTMLPage.htm** and then click **Rename**. Change the .htm extension of the page to .aspx, click **Yes** when asked if you are sure, and then click **Yes** again when you are asked to create a new class file.

10. In the HTMLPage.aspx page, point out that an @**Page** directive was added to the page.

11. Click **Show All Files** in Solution Explorer to show the code-behind page that was created.

12. Click **Save All** to save the project.

13. Right-click **HTMLPage.aspx** in Solution Explorer, then click **Build and Browse** to build the project and view the page in the Visual Studio .NET browser.

    You must build the project because Visual Studio .NET needs to compile the new code-behind page.

14. Type a name in the **Name** text box, click a profession in the **Profession** list, and then click **Save**.

    When the page is displayed again, the information in the controls is lost. This is the default behavior of HTML forms.

15. Right-click the page and then click **View Source** to show the source HTML on the client.

    The HTML delivered to the client is the same as the HTML created on the server.

16. Close the view of the HTML source code in the browser.

Lesson: Using Server Controls

- What is a Server Control?

- Types of Server Controls

- Saving View State

- Demonstration: Converting HTML Controls to Server Controls

- HTML Server Controls

- Web Server Controls

- Practice: Identifying the HTML Generated by Web Server Controls

- Selecting the Appropriate Control

- Demonstration: Adding Server Controls to a Web Form

Introduction

In this lesson, you will learn how to use ASP.NET server controls, such as buttons, text boxes, and drop-down lists. These server controls are different from HTML controls in that the supporting logic is run on the server and not on the user's browser.

Lesson objectives

After completing this lesson, you will be able to:

- Describe the features of server controls.

- Describe the available server control types.

- Explain how Web Forms save Web server control ViewState.

- Add HTML server controls to Web Forms.

- Add Web server controls to Web Forms.

- Select the appropriate control for a situation.

What is a Server Control?

```
<asp:Button id="Button1" runat="server"
Text="Submit"/>
```

- **Runat="server"**
  - Events happen on the server
  - View state saved
- **Have built-in functionality**
- **Common object model**
  - All have **Id** and **Text** attributes
- **Create browser-specific HTML**

Introduction

ASP.NET server controls are components that run on the server and encapsulate UI and other related functionality. Server controls are used in ASP.NET pages and in ASP.NET code-behind classes. Server controls include buttons, text boxes, and drop-down lists.

The following is an example of a **Button** server control:

```
<asp:Button id="Button1" runat="server" Text="Submit" />
```

Runat="server"

Server controls have a **runat="server"** attribute, the same attribute as Web Forms. This means that the logic in the control runs on the server and not on the user's browser. Server controls are different from HTML controls in that they run only on the client's browser and have no action on the server.

Another feature of server controls is that the view state, the settings, and the user input of the control are automatically saved when the page is sent back and forth between the client and the server. Traditional HTML controls are stateless and revert to their default setting when the page is returned from the server to the client.

Built-in functionality

The functionality of a control is what happens when the user clicks a button or a list box. These processes are called event procedures. As the Web Form programmer, you determine the event procedures that are associated with each server control.

Note For more information about server control functionality, see Module 5, "Adding Code to a Microsoft ASP.NET Web Form," in Course 2310B, *Developing Microsoft ASP.NET Web Applications Using Visual Studio .NET.*

Common object model

In ASP.NET, server controls are based on a common object model, and as a result, they share a number of attributes with each other.

For example, when you want to set the background color for a control, you always use the same **BackColor** attribute, irrespective of the control. The following HTML for a Web server control button shows some of the typical attributes of a server control:

```
<asp:Button id="Button1" runat="server" BackColor="red"
Width="238px" Height="25px" Text="Web control"></asp:Button>
```

Create browser-specific HTML

When a page is rendered for a browser, the Web server controls determine which browser is requesting the page and then delivers the appropriate HTML.

For example, if the requesting browser supports client-side scripting, such as Internet Explorer version 4.0 or later, the controls create client-side script to implement their functionality. But, if the requesting browser does not support client-side script, the controls create server-side code and require more round trips to the server to obtain the same functionality.

The following is the ASP.NET HTML from a Web Form that you would write to create a text box with the default text: "Enter your Username"

```
<asp:TextBox id="TextBox1" runat="server" Width="238px"
Height="25px">Enter your Username</asp:TextBox>
```

When this page is accessed by a user with Internet Explorer 6, the common language runtime creates the following HTML customized for Internet Explorer 6:

```
<input name="TextBox1" type="text" value="Enter your Username"
id="TextBox1" style="height:25px;width:238px" />
```

Because the server control creates customized HTML for the features that are available in the client's browser, you can write for the latest browsers without worrying about browser errors blocking your less up-to-date users.

Types of Server Controls

- ■ **HTML server controls**

- ■ **Web server controls**

  - ● Intrinsic controls

  - ● Validation controls

  - ● Rich controls

  - ● List-bound controls

  - ● Internet Explorer Web controls

Introduction

There are many types of sever controls that are available in ASP.NET. Some server controls closely resemble traditional HTML controls, while others are new in ASP.NET. This wide range of controls enables you to customize your Web Form to match the application that you are creating.

HTML server controls

By default, HTML elements on a Web Forms page are not available to the server; HTML elements are treated as opaque text that is passed through to the browser. However, adding the **runat="server"** attribute converts HTML elements to HTML server controls, thereby exposing them as elements that you can program with server-side code.

Web server controls

Web server controls include not only form-type controls, such as buttons and text boxes, but also special-purpose controls, such as a calendar. Web server controls are more abstract than HTML server controls in that their object model does not necessarily reflect HTML syntax.

Web server controls are categorized as follows:

- ■ Intrinsic controls

  Intrinsic controls match the simple HTML elements, such as buttons and listBoxes. You use these controls in the same way that you use HTML server controls.

- ■ Validation controls

  Validation controls incorporate logic that allows you to test a user's input. To test a user's input, you attach a validation control to the input control and specify the conditions of correct user input.

Note For more information about validation controls, see Module 7, "Validating User Input," in Course 2310B, *Developing Microsoft ASP.NET Web Applications Using Visual Studio .NET.*

■ Rich controls

Rich controls are complex controls that include multiple functions. Examples of rich controls include the **AdRotator** control, which is used to display a sequence of advertisements or the **Calendar** control, which provides an appointment calendar.

■ List-bound controls

List-bound controls can display lists of data on an ASP.NET Web page. These controls enable you to display, reformat, sort, and edit data.

Note For more information about list-bound controls and data access, see Module 9, "Accessing Relational Data Using Microsoft Visual Studio .NET," and Module 10, "Accessing Data with Microsoft ADO.NET," in Course 2310B, *Developing Microsoft ASP.NET Web Applications Using Visual Studio .NET.*

■ Internet Explorer Web controls

Internet Explorer Web controls are a set of complex controls, such as the **MultiPage**, **TabStrip**, **Toolbar**, and **TreeView** controls, which can be downloaded from the Internet and integrated into the Visual Studio .NET environment for reuse in any ASP.NET Web application. These controls can render in all commonly used browsers, while also taking advantage of powerful features that are supported by Internet Explorer 5.5 or later versions. You can download these controls from: http://msdn.microsoft.com/library/default.asp?url=/workshop/webcontrols/overview/overview.asp.

Example of equivalent controls

This example shows the HTML for three button controls: an **HTML button**, an **HTML server control button**, and a **Web server control button**. All button controls appear identical on the user's browser. The **HTML button** can only raise client-side events, while the **HTML server control button** and the Web server control button raise server-side events.

■ The following is an **HTML button** control:

```
<INPUT type="button" value="HTML Button">
```

■ Adding the attribute **runat="server"** converts the preceding **HTML button** control to an HTML server control that will run on the server. Note that in addition to the **runat="server"** attribute, you also need to add an **id** attribute for the control to function as a server control.

The **HTML server control button** is shown in the following example:

```
<INPUT type="button" value="HTML Server Control"
id="button1" runat="server">
```

■ The Web server control button uses ASP.NET HTML:

```
<asp:Button id="Button1" runat="server" Text="Web
control"/>
```

Saving View State

- **Hidden ViewState control of name-value pairs stored in the Web Form**

```
<input type="hidden" name="__VIEWSTATE"
  value="dDwtMTA4MzEOMjEwNTs7Pg==" />
```

- **On by default, adjustable at Web Form and control level**

```
<%@ Page EnableViewState="False" %>

<asp:ListBox id="ListName"
  EnableViewState="true" runat="server">

</asp:ListBox>
```

Introduction

One of the problems for Web sites is how to save the state of controls (settings and user input) on a Web page as the HTML travels back and forth between the client and the server. As is true for any HTTP-based technology, Web Forms are stateless, which means that the server does not retain any information on prior client requests.

ASP.NET Web Forms handle this problem of storing Web server control state by adding a hidden control named **_VIEWSTATE** that records the state of the controls on the Web Form. Specifically, **_VIEWSTATE** is added to the server-side form denoted by the tag **<Form ... runat**="server">, and only records the state of controls in this section. As the page travels back and forth from the client to the server, Web server control state is kept with the page and can be updated at either end of the transaction (at the client or the server).

Because the state of the Web page is kept inside the server form, the Web page can be randomly routed in a Web server farm and does not need to keep returning to the same server. The advantage of the **_VIEWSTATE** process is that the programmer can focus on the page design and does not need to build the infrastructure to keep track of the page state.

Hidden control

The _**VIEWSTATE** control is a hidden control containing a string value of name-value pairs that lists the name of each control and the last value of that control.

With each request, the _**VIEWSTATE** control is updated and sent to the server. The server response may in turn update the _**VIEWSTATE** control, which is then returned with the response. The result is that the settings in the page remain consistent from one request to the next.

The following is the HTML that is generated by a Web Form and sent to the client:

```
<form name="Form1" method="post" action="WebForm1.aspx"
  id="Form1">
    <input type="hidden" name="__VIEWSTATE"
    value="dDw3NzE0MTExODQ7Oz4=" />
  'HTML here
</form>
```

Disabling and enabling ViewState

By default, a Web Form saves the view state of the controls on the Web Form. But for Web Forms with multiple controls, the size of the _**VIEWSTATE** properties value field can slow performance. To maximize page performance, you may want to disable the **ViewState** attribute at the page level and enable **ViewState** for selected controls only.

To disable saving view state at the Web page level, set the **EnableViewState** attribute of the @**Page** directive, as shown in the following code:

```
<%@ Page EnableViewState="False" %>
```

To enable saving view state for a specific control, set the **EnableViewState** attribute of the control as shown in the following code:

```
<asp:ListBox id="ListName" EnableViewState="true"
runat="server"></asp:ListBox>
```

Note For more information about saving state, see Module 14, "Managing State," in Course 2310B, *Developing Microsoft ASP.NET Web Applications Using Visual Studio .NET.*

Demonstration: Converting HTML Controls to Server Controls

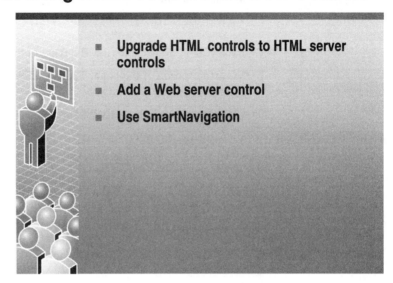

- Upgrade HTML controls to HTML server controls
- Add a Web server control
- Use SmartNavigation

Visual Studio .NET makes it easy to convert HTML controls into server controls.

▶ **To run this demonstration**

1. View the HTMLPage.aspx page that you converted from an HTML page in the previous demonstration, in HTML view, and then add a **runat="server"** attribute to the text box, select, and submit controls.

2. Click **Save All** to save the project.

3. View the HTMLPage.aspx page in the browser by right-clicking the page in Solution Explorer and then clicking **View in Browser**. You do not have to rebuild the project because you did not change any code.

4. View the source of the page to show the changes that were made. Notice that a **name** attribute was added to each server control.

5. Close the view of the HTML source code in the browser.

6. In the browser, enter information in the controls, and then click **Save**. The controls still lose their values.

7. Edit the page and add a **runat="server"** attribute to the form.

8. Save your changes and view the page in the browser again. You do not have to rebuild the project because you did not add any code.

9. View the source of the page to show the changes that were made. Among other changes made, **action** and **method** attributes were added to the form tag and a hidden control named **__VIEWSTATE** was created.

10. Close the view of the HTML source code in the browser.

11. Enter information in the controls and click **Save**. The controls now save their values.

Add a label to the Web Form

12. Edit the page and add a **Label** Web server control to the Web Form, below the **Save** button:

```
<asp:label id="lblMessage" runat="server">Label</asp:label>
```

13. Save your changes and view the page in the browser.

14. View the source of the page. The **Label** Web server control generates a <span> element.

15. Close the view of the HTML source code in the browser.

Using SmartNavigation

16. View the page http://localhost/Mod04/HTMLPage.aspx in Internet Explorer and resize the browser to vertically show less than the whole page. The vertical scroll bar should be visible.

17. Scroll down, and click **Save**. You are redirected to the top of the page because of the postback.

18. Close the browser.

19. Edit the page in HTML view and add **SmartNavigation= "true"** to the @ **Page** directive.

    Your HTML should look like the following:

Visual Basic .NET

```
<%@ Page SmartNavigation="true" Language="vb"
CodeBehind="HTMLPage.aspx.vb" AutoEventWireup="false"
Inherits="Mod04.HTMLPage" %>
```

C#

```
<%@ Page SmartNavigation="true" Language="c#"
CodeBehind="HTMLPage.aspx.cs" AutoEventWireup="false"
Inherits="Mod04.HTMLPage" %>
```

20. Save your changes and view the page in another resized browser.

21. Scroll down and click **Save**. This time you are not redirected to the top of the page during the postback, as the page maintains its current position.

22. View the source of the page in the browser. In Internet Explorer 4.0 and later, the **SmartNavigation** attribute creates IFrames to refresh only the changed portion of the page.

23. Close the view of the HTML source code in the browser.

HTML Server Controls

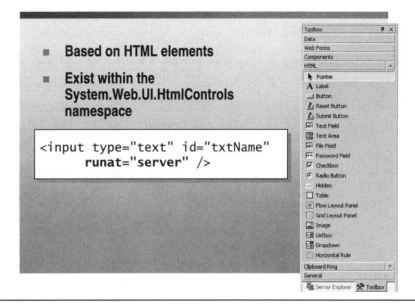

Introduction

HTML controls on a Web Form are not available to the server. By converting HTML controls to HTML server controls, you can expose them as elements to your server-side code. This conversion enables you to use the controls to trigger events that are handled on the server.

HTML server controls include the **runat="server"** attribute, and must reside within a containing <form ...runat="server">...</form> tag.

The advantage of HTML server controls is that they enable you to quickly update existing pages to Web Forms. In addition, you can optimize the performance of a page by adjusting which controls work locally on the browser and which controls are processed on the server.

Example

The following code example shows a simple HTML text box control that is processed on the client side by the browser:

```
<input type="text" id="txtName" >
```

Adding the **runat="server"** attribute converts the control to an HTML server control that is processed on the server side by ASP.NET:

```
<input type="text" id="txtName" runat="server" />
```

Web Server Controls

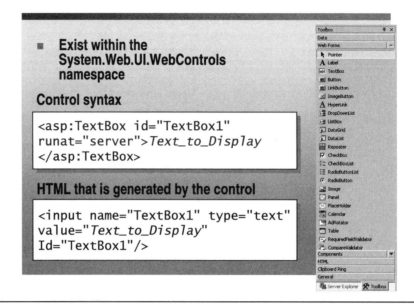

Introduction

Web server controls are server controls that are created specifically for ASP.NET. Unlike HTML server controls, Web server controls will not function if the **runat="server" attribute** is missing.

As Web server controls are based on a common object model, all controls share several attributes, including the tag **<asp:*ControlType* ...>**, and an **id** attribute. Web server controls exist within the **System.Web.UI.WebControls** namespace and may be used on any Web Form.

Intrinsic Web server controls

Intrinsic Web server controls correspond to simple HTML elements. Some of the commonly used intrinsic Web server controls are shown in the following table.

Web server control	HTML control equivalent	Web server control function
<asp:button>	**<input type=submit>**	Creates a button that sends a request to the server.
<asp:checkbox>	**<input type=checkbox>**	Creates a check box that can be selected by clicking.
<asp:hyperlink>	**<a href="..."> </a>**	Creates a hyperlink to an HTML anchor tag.
<asp:image>	**<img src="...">**	Creates an area that is used to display an image.
<asp:imagebutton>	**<input type=image>**	Creates a button that incorporates the display of an image instead of text.
<asp linkButton>	None	Creates a button that has the appearance of a hyperlink.
<asp:label>	**<span> </span>**	Creates text that users cannot edit.
<asp:listbox>	**<select size="5"> </select>**	Creates a list of choices. Allows multiple selections.

(continued)

Web server control	HTML control equivalent	Web server control function
<asp:panel>	<div> </div>	Creates a borderless division on the form that serves as a container for other controls.
<asp:radiobutton>	<input type=radiobutton>	Creates a single radio button control.
<asp:table>	<table> </table>	Creates a table.
<asp:textbox>	<input type=text>	Creates a text box control.

Validation controls

Validation controls are hidden controls that validate the user's input against predetermined patterns. Some of the commonly used validation controls are shown in the following table.

Control	Function
CompareValidator	Requires that the input match a second input or existing field.
CustomValidator	Requires that the input match a condition such as prime or odd numbers.
RangeValidator	Requires that the input match a specified range.
RegularExpressionValidator	Requires that the input match a specified format such as a U.S. telephone number or a strong password with numbers and letters.
RequiredFieldValidator	Requires that the user enter some value before the control is processed.
ValidationSummary	Collects all of the validation control error messages for centralized display.

Note For more information about validation controls, see Module 7, "Validating User Input," in Course 2310B, *Developing Microsoft ASP.NET Web Applications Using Visual Studio .NET.*

Rich controls

Rich controls provide a rich functionality to your Web Form by inserting complex functions into your Web Form. The presently available rich controls are shown in the following table.

Control	Function
AdRotator	Displays a sequence (pre-defined or random) of images.
Calendar	Displays a graphic calendar on which users can select dates.

List-bound controls

List-bound controls can display data from a data source. Some of the commonly used list-bound controls are shown on the following table.

Control	Function
CheckBoxList	Displays data as a column of check boxes.
Repeater	Displays information from a data set by using a set of HTML elements and controls that you specify. The **Repeater** control repeats the element once for each record in the **DataSet**.
DataList	Similar to the **Repeater** Control, but with more formatting and layout options, including the ability to display information in a table. The **DataList** control also allows you to specify editing behavior.
DataGrid	Displays information, usually data-bound in tabular form, with columns. Also provides mechanisms to allow editing and sorting.
DropDownList	Displays data as a drop-down menu.
Listbox	Displays data in a window.
RadioButtonList	Displays data as a column of option buttons.

Note For more information about list-bound controls and data access, see Module 10, "Accessing Data with Microsoft ADO.NET," in Course 2310B, *Developing Microsoft ASP.NET Web Applications Using Visual Studio .NET.*

Practice: Identifying the HTML Generated by Web Server Controls

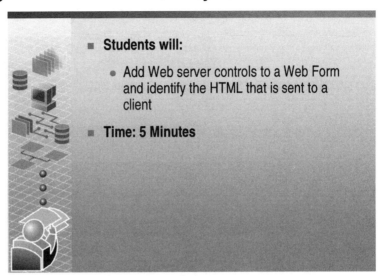

In this practice, you will add Web server controls to a Web Form and then view the source in a browser to see what HTML was sent to the client.

▶ **Fill out the table below by following the steps**

1. Start Visual Studio .NET.

2. Create a Web Application project and set the location to **http://localhost/Mod04Practice**.

3. Open the WebForm1.aspx page.

4. Add **TextBox**, **Button**, **Label**, **ListBox**, **Image**, **Hyperlink**, and **Calendar** controls to the Web Form.

5. Right-click **WebForm1.aspx** in Solution Explorer and click **Build and Browse**.

6. Right-click in the browser and click **View Source** to view the HTML that was sent to the client.

7. Fill out the following table with the HTML tags for the control.

Web server control	HTML Sent to the Client
asp:textbox	
asp:button	
asp:label	
asp:listbox	
asp:image	
asp:hyperlink	
asp:calendar	

Selecting the Appropriate Control

Use HTML Server Controls if:	Use Web Server Controls if:
You prefer an HTML-like object model	You prefer a Visual Basic-like programming model
You are working with existing HTML pages and want to quickly add ASP.NET Web page functionality	You are writing a page that might be used by a variety of browsers
The control will interact with client and server script	You need specific functionality such as a calendar or ad rotator
Bandwidth is limited	Bandwidth is not a problem

Introduction

When you create ASP.NET pages, you have the option of using HTML server controls or Web server controls. You can mix these control types on the same page as a means of quickly updating an HTML page.

As an example of mixing control types, your ASP.NET page might include an HTML span element that lists the local time, an HTML server control button converted from an HTML element, and a Web server control text box that accesses data from the server.

The best practice is to avoid HTML server controls. Web server controls are more capable and have a richer object model than HTML server controls.

HTML server controls

HTML server controls are modified HTML elements that run on the server instead of on the client browser.

Use HTML server controls if:

- You prefer an HTML-like object model. HTML server controls have almost the same HTML as the basic HTML controls. HTML server controls also have server-side functionality just like Web server controls.

- You are working with existing HTML pages and you want to quickly add Web Form functionality. Because HTML server controls map exactly to HTML elements, you do not need to replace controls and risk substitution errors or page formatting problems.

- The control needs to run both client-side and server-side script. You can write a client-side script and target a regular HTML control because the controls are visible in the client. At the same time, you can have server-side code because it is also a sever control.

- Bandwidth is limited and you need to do a large amount of client side processing to reduce bandwidth usage.

Web server controls

ASP.NET Web server controls not only approximate HTML controls, but they also include a number of new controls that do not exist in HTML.

Use Web server controls if:

- You prefer a Visual Basic-like programming model. You will be able to use object-oriented programming, identify controls by their **ID** attribute, and easily separate the page logic from the UI. With Web server controls, you can also create applications with nested controls and catch events at the container level.

- You are creating a Web page that might be viewed by a variety of browsers. Because the logic inside the Web server controls is able to create HTML that is tailored to the features that are available in the client's browser, you can write for the latest browsers without worrying about browser errors keeping your less up-to-date users from accessing all of the Web page functions.

- You need specific functionality, such as a calendar or advertisement, or ad rotator, that is available only as a Web server control.

- Your bandwidth is not limited and the request-response cycles of Web server controls will not cause bandwidth problems.

Demonstration: Adding Server Controls to a Web Form

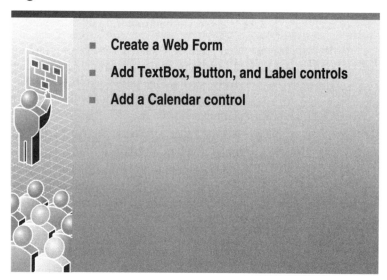

- Create a Web Form
- Add TextBox, Button, and Label controls
- Add a Calendar control

In this demonstration, you will see how to add Web server controls to a Web Form.

▶ **To run this demonstration**

Adding simple Web server controls

1. Open the WebForm1.aspx page in the Mod04 Web Application project.

2. Add a **TextBox**, a **Button**, and a **Label** Web server control to the WebForm1.aspx page.

3. Using the Properties window, set the **ID** and **Text** properties of the controls to the values in the following table.

Control	ID	Text
TextBox	txtName	Name
Button	cmdSubmit	Submit
Label	lblMessage	Message

4. View the page in HTML view.

    Notice that the Web Form was created with the **runat="server"** attribute, and that **style** attributes were added to the controls to place them on the Web Form in **GridLayout** mode.

    Point out how the **ID** and **Text** properties were implemented in HTML for the different controls.

5. Build and browse WebForm1.aspx.

6. Enter some text in the text box and then click **Submit** to show that the value is preserved.

7. View the source of the page. Notice that the positioning of the controls is done by using DHTML.

8. Close the source view of the page.

Change the target browser

9. Right-click the form in Design view and then click **Properties**.

10. Change the **Target Schema** to **Internet Explorer 3.02 / Navigator 3.0**, and then click **OK**.

11. Save your changes and view the page in the browser again.

12. View the source of the page.

    Notice that now the positioning of the controls is done by using HTML tables.

13. Close the source view of the page.

14. Right-click the form in Design view and then click **Properties**.

15. In the **Property Pages** dialog box, return the **Target Schema** to **Internet Explorer 5.0**.

Change the page layout

16. In the **Property Pages** dialog box, select **FlowLayout** (instead of **GridLayout**) in the **Page Layout** field, and then click **OK**.

    The grid disappears.

17. Add a **Button** control to the Web form, and view the page in HTML view.

    The new button does not have a **style** attribute.

Add a Calendar control

18. In Design view, add a **Calendar** Web server control onto the Web Form, and then view the page in HTML view.

    Locate the HTML for the **Calendar** control:

    ```
    <asp:Calendar id="Calendar1" runat="server"></asp:calendar>
    ```

19. Save your changes and view the page in the browser, and then view the source of the page.

    Notice all of the HTML that is generated by the **Calendar** control.

20. Close the source view of the page.

21. Edit the WebForm1page and point out the properties of the **Calendar** control in the Properties window.

22. Right click the **Calendar** control on the Web Form in Design view and select **Auto Format** to show the different styles in the **Calendar Auto Format** dialog box. Click **Colorful 1**, and then click **OK**.

23. Save your changes and view the page in browser again to see the new appearance of the **Calendar** control.

Review

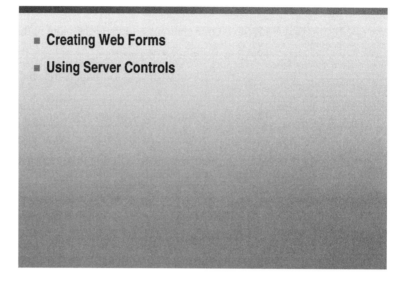

■ Creating Web Forms

■ Using Server Controls

1. If you were given a Web page with an .aspx extension, what would you look for to verify that it is a Web Form?

2. If you were given a Web page with an .aspx extension, what would you look for to see if there are Web server controls?

3. What type of code or script does a Web server control generate on the client?

4. What is the difference between **FlowLayout** and **GridLayout**?

5. How does ASP.NET save the state of Web server control during the client-server roundtrip?

Lab 4: Creating a Microsoft ASP.NET Web Form

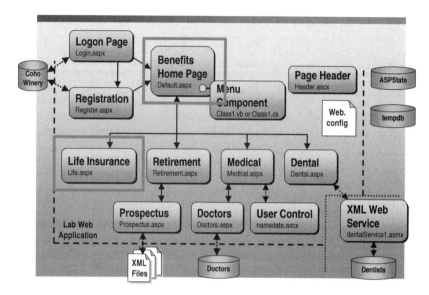

Objectives

After completing this lab, you will be able to:

- Create a Microsoft® ASP.NET Web Form and populate it with Web controls.
- Set properties of Web controls on an ASP.NET Web Form.

Note This lab focuses on the concepts in this module and as a result may not comply with Microsoft security recommendations.

PrerequisitesBefore working on this lab, you must have knowledge of the Microsoft Visual Studio® .NET integrated development environment (IDE).

ScenarioCoho Winery offers several benefits to its employees. In the labs for Course 2310B, *Developing Microsoft ASP.NET Web Applications Using Visual Studio .NET*, you will create a Web site that enables employees to select and set up their chosen benefits.

In Lab 2, "Using Microsoft Visual Studio .NET," in Course 2310B, *Developing Microsoft ASP.NET Web Applications Using Visual Studio .NET*, you created a Visual Studio .NET solution and a Web Application project for the Benefits Web Application.

In this lab, you will create the user interface (UI) of the default.aspx and life.aspx Web Form pages in the Benefits Web Application. The default.aspx Web Form is the home page for the Benefits Web site. The default.aspx Web Form displays the list of benefits that are offered by your company. The life.aspx Web Form allows a user to enter life insurance information, such as their name, birth date, and coverage amount.

Estimated time to complete this lab: 30 minutes

Exercise 0
Lab Setup

To complete this lab, you must have created a Benefits Web Application project and a BenefitsList Class Library project. These projects can be created by using Visual Basic .NET or Visual C# .NET.

If you have not created these projects, complete the following steps:

▶ **Create the 2310LabApplication solution**

Important   Perform this procedure only if you have not created a 2310LabApplication solution file.

1. Using Visual Studio .NET, create a new blank solution named **2310LabApplication**:
   a. On the **File** menu, point to **New**, and then click **Blank Solution**.
   b. In the **New Project** dialog box, type **2310LabApplication** in the **Name** text box, and then click **OK**.

▶ **Create the Benefits solution**

Important   Only perform this procedure if you have not previously created a Benefits project, or if you have removed the Benefits project according to the steps in Appendix A, "Lab Recovery," in Course 2310B, *Developing Microsoft ASP.NET Web Applications Using Visual Studio .NET.*

1. Create a new ASP.NET Web Application project, named **BenefitsVB** or **BenefitsCS**, in the 2310LabApplication solution:
   a. On the **File** menu, point to **New**, and then click **Project**.
   b. In the **New Project** dialog box, on the **Project Types** list, click **Visual Basic Projects** or **Visual C# Projects**.
   c. In the **Templates** list, click **ASP.NET Web Application**.
   d. Set the **Location** to **http://localhost/BenefitsVB** for a Visual Basic .NET project or to **http://localhost/BenefitsCS** for a Visual C# project, click **Add to Solution**, and then click **OK**.

Caution   When adding projects to the solution, the capitalization of the project name is important. Because you may be using some pre-built Web Forms in this and other labs in Course 2310B, *Developing Microsoft ASP.NET Web Applications Using Visual Studio .NET*, you must verify that you have capitalized the Benefits project as shown.

▶ **Update the Benefits project**

1. In Visual Studio .NET, open the 2310LabApplication solution file.

2. In Solution Explorer, right-click **BenefitsVB** or **BenefitsCS**, point to **Add**, and then click **Add Existing Item**.

3. Browse for project files

For the Visual Basic .NET project

Browse to the *install folder*\Labfiles\Lab04\VB\Starter\BenefitsVB folder.

For the Visual C# project

Browse to the *install folder*\Labfiles\Lab04\CS\Starter\BenefitsCS folder.

4. In the **Files of type** box of the **Add Existing Item – Benefits** dialog box, click **All Files (*.*)**.

5. Select all of the files in this folder, and then click **Open**.

6. Click **Yes** if prompted to overwrite or reload files.

▶ **Create the BenefitsList class library**

Important   Perform these steps only if you have not previously created a BenefitsList project, or if you have removed the BenefitsList project according to the steps in Appendix A, "Lab Recovery," in Course 2310B, *Developing Microsoft ASP.NET Web Applications Using Visual Studio .NET*.

1. Create a Class Library Project

For a Visual Basic .NET Project

Create a new Microsoft Visual Basic® .NET Class Library project, name it **BenefitsListVB**, and then add it to the 2310LabApplication solution:

a. On the **File** menu, point to **New**, and then click **Project**.

b. In the **New Project** dialog box, in the **Project Types list**, click **Visual Basic Projects**. On the **Templates** list, click Class **Library**, set the **Name** to **BenefitsListVB**, click **Add to Solution**, and then click **OK**.

For a Visual C# Project

Create a new Microsoft Visual C#™ .NET Class Library project, name it **BenefitsListCS**, and then add it to the 2310LabApplication solution:

a. On the **File** menu, click **New**, and then click **Project**.

b. In the **New Project** dialog box, in the **Project Types** list, click **Visual C# Projects**. On the **Templates** list, click **Class Library**, set the **Name** to **BenefitsListCS**, click **Add to Solution**, and then click **OK**.

Caution   Verify that you have capitalized the BenefitsList project as shown.

▶ **Update the BenefitsList project**

1. In Visual Studio .NET, open the 2310LabApplication solution file.

2. In Solution Explorer, right-click **BenefitsListVB** or **BenefitsListCS**, point to **Add**, and then click **Add Existing Item**.

3. Browse for project files:

For the Visual Basic .NET project

Browse to the *install folder*\Labfiles\Lab04\VB\Starter\BenefitsListVB folder.

For the Visual C# project

Browse to the *install folder*\Labfiles\Lab04\CS\Starter\BenefitsListCS folder.

4. In the **Files of type** box of the **Add Existing Item – BenefitsList** dialog box, click **All Files (*.*)**.

5. Select all of the files in this folder, and then click **Open**.

6. Click **Yes** if prompted to overwrite or reload files.

▶ **Create a reference to the BenefitsList component in the Benefits project**

1. In the **Benefits** project in the 2310LabApplication solution, complete the following steps to add a reference to the **BenefitsList** component that you just created:

   a. Right-click the **BenefitsVB** or **BenefitsCS** project in Solution Explorer and then click **Add Reference**.

   b. In the **Add Reference** dialog box, on the **Projects** tab, double-click the **BenefitsListVB** or **BenefitsListCS** project.

   c. In the **Selected Components** list, select the **BenefitsListVB** or **BenefitsListCS** component, and then click **OK**.

   The component is added to the References folder in Solution Explorer.

Exercise 1
Creating the Default.aspx Web Form

In this exercise, you will create a new Web Form named default.aspx. You will then add a user control, a list-bound control, a **Button** control, and a **Label** control to the default.aspx page. Finally, you will set attributes of the list-bound control to display a static list of information.

▶ **Place controls on a Web Form**

1. Create a new Web Form named default.aspx. This Web Form will serve as the main entry page for your Web application. To create the Web Form:

   a. Right-click the **BenefitsVB** or **BenefitsCS** project, point to **Add**, and then click **Add Web Form**.

   b. In the **Add New Item** dialog box, type **default.aspx** in the **Name** field and then click **Open**.

2. From Solution Explorer, use a drag-and-drop operation to place the file header.ascx from Solution Explorer to the top of the Web Form.

   Note You will learn more about user controls in Module 8, "Creating User Controls," in this Course 2310B, *Developing Microsoft ASP.NET Web Applications Using Visual Studio .NET*.

   ---

3. From the Toolbox, drag a **CheckBoxList** control, a **Button** control, and a **Label** control onto the Web Form. Your Web Form should look like the following illustration.

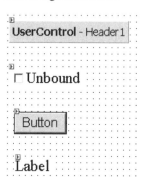

4. Set the **ID** and **Text** properties for the **CheckBoxList**, **Button**, and **Label** controls as shown in the following table.

Control	ID	Text
CheckBoxList	chkListBenefits	*None*
Button	cmdSubmit	Submit
Label	lblSelections	Selected items:

5. View the page in Hypertext Markup Language (HTML) view by clicking the **HTML** tab located at the bottom left of the editor window.

   Notice the dynamic HTML (DHTML) that was added by Visual Studio .NET to the **CheckBoxList**, **Button**, and **Label** controls. The **style** attribute containing **Z-INDEX**, **LEFT**, **POSITION**, and **TOP** parameters positions the controls on the page.

6. Right-click the **default.aspx** page in Solution Explorer and then click **Build and Browse**.

Note You have to build the project even though you have not written any code. This is because when you add UI components to the page Visual Studio .NET generates code to support those UI elements.

The page should look like the following illustration, with nothing in the **CheckBoxList** control.

Home Dental Medical Retirement Account Life Insurance

Benefits Selection Site

Submit

Selected items:

▶ **Add items to the CheckBoxList control**

1. View the default.aspx page in Design view.

2. Click the **chkListBenefits CheckBoxList** control on the **default.aspx Web Form**.

3. In the Properties window, click the **Items** property and then click the **...** button to open the **ListItem Collection Editor** dialog box.

4. In the **ListItem Collection Editor** dialog box, add the items that are shown in the following table (with the property **Selected** set to **False**).

Text	Value
First Item	First Item
Second Item	Second Item
Third Item	Third Item

5. Click **OK** to close the **ListItem Collection Editor** dialog box.

6. Save your changes to default.aspx and view the page in the browser.

   Now that you have added items to the **CheckBoxList** control, the list of items overwrites the **Submit** button.

7. View the default.aspx page in Design view again.

8. Click the background of the default.aspx page, and in the Properties window, set the **pageLayout** property to **FlowLayout** (instead of **GridLayout**).

   While **FlowLayout** makes page design slightly more difficult, it allows the UI elements to move automatically when other items on the page change size. For example, when the **chkListBenefits** control had more items added to the list, it wrote over the **Submit** button. By using **FlowLayout**, the button will move automatically to make room for a longer list.

9. Move the controls on the page, by using carriage returns, to make your page look like the following illustration.

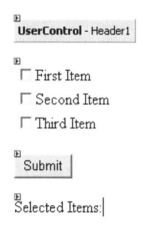

10. View the page in the browser again.

    Now the list of check boxes does not overwrite the **Submit** button.

11. Close the browser window.

Exercise 2
Creating the Life.aspx Web Form

In this exercise, you will create the UI for the life.aspx page. This page implements the life insurance benefit for your company.

▶ **Add controls to the life.aspx page**

1. Create a new Web Form named life.aspx. To create the Web Form:

    a. Right-click the **BenefitsVB** or **BenefitsCS** project, point to **Add**, and then click **Add Web Form**.

    b. In the **Add New Item** dialog box, type **life.aspx** in the **Name** field and then click **Open**.

2. Put a Calendar control on the Web Form.

3. Right click the **Calendar** control in **Design** view and then select **Auto Format** to open the **Calendar Auto Format** dialog box.

4. Click **Colorful 1** in the **Select a scheme** list, and then click **OK**.

5. Put the header.ascx user control, three **TextBox** controls, two **CheckBox** controls, one **Button**, and five **Label** controls on the page.

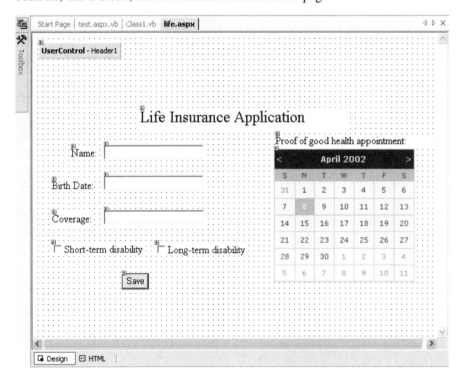

6. Set the **ID** and **Text** properties of each control as shown in the following table.

Control	ID	Text
Name text box	txtName	*none*
Birth date text box	txtBirth	*none*
Coverage text box	txtCoverage	*none*
Short-term disability check box	chkShortTerm	Short-term disability
Long-term disability check box	chkLongTerm	Long-term disability
Save button	cmdSave	Save
Label1	*default*	Life Insurance Application
Label2	*default*	Proof of good health appointment
Label3	*default*	Name:
Label4	*default*	Birth Date:
Label5	*default*	Coverage:

Note   To change the font size for Label1, in the Properties window for the label, expand **Font**, select **Size**, and then choose **Large**.

7. Right-click the life.aspx page in Solution Explorer and then click **Build and Browse**.

8. Type your name and birth date in the fields and then click **Save**. The values that you entered should remain on the page.

msdn training

Module 5: Adding Code to a Microsoft ASP.NET Web Form

Contents

Overview

- **Using Code-Behind Pages**
- **Adding Event Procedures to Web Server Controls**
- **Using Page Events**

Introduction

In this module, you will learn about the various methods that can be used for adding code to your Microsoft® ASP.NET Web application. You will also learn about event procedures for Web server controls, how to use them, and the order in which they work. You will then learn how to use code-behind pages, which are the Microsoft Visual Studio® .NET preferred method for adding code to Web pages. Finally, you will learn how page events, especially the **Page_Load** event, are used.

Objectives

After completing this module, you will be able to:

- Use code-behind pages in a Web application.
- Create event procedures for Web server controls.
- Use Page events in a Web application.

Lesson: Using Code-Behind Pages

- How to Implement Code
- Writing Inline Code
- What are Code-Behind Pages?
- Understanding How Code-Behind Pages Work

Introduction

In this lesson, you will learn how to implement code with Visual Studio .NET. You will also learn how code-behind pages are used and how they are different from inline code.

Lesson objectives

After completing this lesson, you will be able to:

- Identify the three ways to implement code in an ASP.NET Web Form.
- Use code-behind pages.

How to Implement Code

- **Three methods for adding code:**
  - Put code in the same file as content (mixed)
  - Put code in a separate section of the content file (inline code)
  - Put code in a separate file (code-behind pages)
- **Code-behind pages are the Visual Studio .NET default**

Implementing code

You can add code to your Web Form in the following three ways:

- **Mixed code**. The code is in the same file as the Web content, intermingled with the Hypertext Markup Language (HTML). This method is the least preferred, as it is difficult to read and work with such a file. However, this is the method that is often used in Active Server Pages (ASP).

- **Inline code**. The code is in a separate **SCRIPT** section of the same file as the HTML content.

- **Code-behind**. The code is in a separate file from the HTML content. The code file is called a code-behind page. When using Visual Studio .NET, the default method is to place all of the code in a code-behind page.

Writing Inline Code

- **Code and content in the same file**
- **Different sections in the file for code and HTML**

```
<HTML>
<asp:Button id="btn" runat="server"/>
</HTML>
<SCRIPT Language="vb" runat="server">
    Sub btn_Click(s As Object, e As EventArgs) Handles btn.Click
    ...
    End Sub
</SCRIPT>
```

```
<HTML>
<asp:Button id="btn" runat="server"/>
</HTML>
<SCRIPT Language="c#" runat="server">
  private void btn_Click(object sender, System.EventArgs e)
  {
    . . .
  }
</SCRIPT>
```

Introduction

Although the default method for implementing server-side code in Visual Studio .NET is to use a code-behind page, you might encounter pages that use inline code, especially pages that were developed for ASP.

Inline code

When inline code is used on a Web page, the HTML and code are in separate sections of a single .aspx file. This separation is for clarity when reading the page; functionally, the code and HTML can exist anywhere on the page.

The following is an example of inline code:

Visual Basic .NET

```
<HTML>
<asp:Button id="btn" runat="server"/>
...
</HTML>

<SCRIPT Language="vb" runat="server">
   Sub btn_Click(s As Object, e As EventArgs) _
     Handles btn.Click
   ...
   End Sub
</SCRIPT>
```

C#

```
<HTML>
<asp:Button id="btn" runat="server" />
...
</HTML>

<SCRIPT Language="c#" runat="server">
  private void btn_Click(object sender, System.EventArgs e)
    {
       . . .
    }
</SCRIPT>
```

What are Code-Behind Pages?

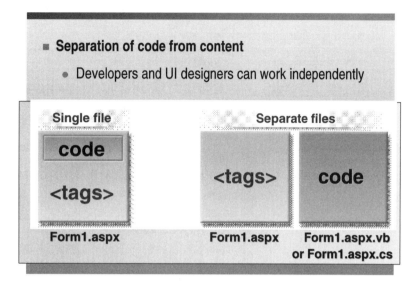

- ■ **Separation of code from content**
  - ● Developers and UI designers can work independently

Single file	Separate files	
code		
<tags>	<tags>	code
Form1.aspx	Form1.aspx	Form1.aspx.vb or Form1.aspx.cs

Introduction

The default method for implementing server-side code in Visual Studio .NET is to use code-behind pages. When you use code-behind pages, the programming logic is in a separate file than the visual elements of the page. Separating the logic from the design allows developers to work on the code-behind page while user interface (UI) designers work on the ASP.NET page.

Naming code-behind pages

Code-behind pages contain all of the programming logic for a single Web page. Each Web page in a Web application has its own code-behind page. By default, a code-behind page has the same name as the Web page with which it is associated; however, the code-behind page also has an .aspx.vb or .aspx.cs extension, depending on the language that is used in the code-behind page. For example, the Web page Form1.aspx will have a Microsoft Visual Basic® .NET code-behind page named Form1.aspx.vb or a C# code-behind page named Form1.aspx.cs.

Note A code-behind page can only contain code in a single language. You cannot mix Visual Basic .NET and C# in the same code-behind page.

Understanding How Code-Behind Pages Work

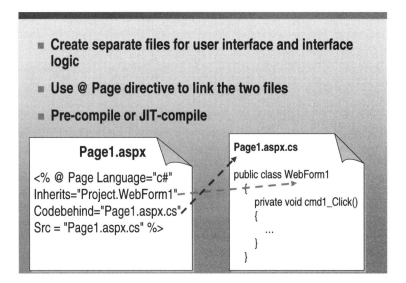

| Introduction | For code-behind pages to work, each .aspx page must be associated with a code-behind page, and that code-behind page must be compiled before information is returned to a requesting client browser.

Although each Web Form page consists of two separate files (the .aspx page and the code-behind page), the two files form a single unit when the Web application is run. The code-behind page can either be precompiled by Visual Studio .NET when you build the Web application project, or can be just-in-time (JIT) compiled the first time that a user accesses the page. |
|---|---|
| Linking the two files | The .aspx page must be associated with the code-behind page. Visual Studio .NET adds the following three attributes to the @ **Page** directive of the .aspx page to accomplish this association:

■ **Codebehind**. This is the attribute that Visual Studio .NET uses internally to associate the files.

■ **Src**. This attribute is the name of the code-behind page, and it is used if the Web application is not precompiled.

■ **Inherits**. This attribute allows the .aspx page to inherit classes and objects from the code-behind page. |

Note   The **Inherits** attribute is case-sensitive.

An example @ **Page** directive for a file named Page1.aspx is shown in the following code:

Visual Basic .NET

```
<%@ Page Language="vb" Inherits="Project.WebForm1"
  Codebehind="Page1.aspx.vb" Src="Page1.aspx.vb" %>
```

C#

```
<%@ Page Language="c#" Inherits="Project.WebForm1"
  Codebehind="Page1.aspx.cs" Src="Page1.aspx.cs" %>
```

JIT compile

When a page is JIT compiled, the code-behind pages are compiled the first time that a client requests the .aspx page. After the first request, all subsequent requests use the existing compiled file. Therefore, the first request of a page is longer, but subsequent requests are faster.

If you want to use JIT compiling for a page, you would use the **Src** attribute of the @ **Page** directive.

Note JIT compiling will keep the size of the project small and allow for code updates without recompiling the entire site.

Execution

When a user requests the .aspx page, the dynamic-link library (DLL) file processes the incoming request and responds by creating the appropriate HTML and script and returning them to the requesting browser.

Precompilation

If you omit the **Src** attribute from the @ **Page** directive in an .aspx file, the page is precompiled when you build the application in Visual Studio .NET. By default, Visual Studio .NET does not add the **Src** attribute, so all of the code-behind pages for Web Forms in a project are compiled when the project is built. This process saves considerable processing time on the Web server.

Precompiling code-behind pages also simplifies the deployment of the Web site because you do not have to deploy the code-behind pages along with the .aspx pages.

Note For more information about Web site deployment, see Module 15, "Configuring, Optimizing and Deploying a Microsoft ASP.NET Web Application," in Course 2310B, *Developing Microsoft ASP.NET Web Applications Using Visual Studio .NET.*

Lesson: Adding Event Procedures to Web Server Controls

- **What are Event Procedures?**
- **Demonstration: Using Events**
- **Client-Side Event Procedures**
- **Server-Side Event Procedures**
- **Multimedia: Client-Side and Server-Side Events**
- **Creating Event Procedures**
- **Instructor-Led Practice: Creating an Event Procedure**
- **Interacting with Controls in Event Procedures**

Introduction

In this lesson, you will learn about event procedures and how to add them to Web server controls. You will learn to distinguish between the two types of events (server-side and client-side) and understand when it is appropriate to use each kind.

Lesson objectives

After completing this lesson, you will be able to:

- Identify event procedures.
- Distinguish between server-side and client-side events.
- Create a server-side event procedure.
- Interact with controls in event procedures.

What are Event Procedures?

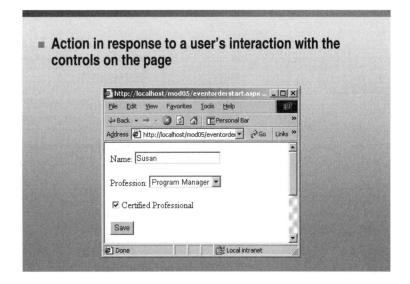

Introduction	Dynamic, interactive Web Forms typically react to user input. Event procedures are used to handle user interactions on a Web Form.
Definition	When a user interacts with a Web Form, an event is generated. You design your Web application to perform an appropriate task when the event is generated. An event procedure is the action that occurs in response to the generated event.
Example of an event procedure	Many Web Forms allow the user to enter information and then click a **Submit** button. An event is generated when the user clicks the **Submit** button. For example, an event procedure for an event might be to send the user information to a Microsoft SQL Server™ database.

Demonstration: Using Events

- Open an ASP.NET page with controls and client-side and server-side event procedures

- Click on the controls to view client-side and server-side events running

- In the browser, view the source of the page

- In the editor, view the event procedure code

Introduction

This demonstration can be performed using either the Visual Basic .NET or the Microsoft Visual C#™ project. In this demonstration, you will see how client-side and server-side event procedures run in a Web site.

▶ **To run the demonstration**

1. In Visual Studio .NET, open the eventorderstart.aspx page in the Mod05VB or Mod05CS project in the 2310Demos solution.

2. View the page in the browser. It is not necessary to build the project first.

3. Click the controls in the page. Each control has a client-side event procedure that outputs a string when it runs.

4. Click **Save**. This submits the form and causes all of the server-side event procedures to run.

5. In the browser, view the source of the page. Only the code for the client-side event procedures is visible.

6. Close the source view of the page.

7. In Visual Studio .NET, open the page in HTML view. There is code for both client-side and server-side event procedures.

Client-Side Event Procedures

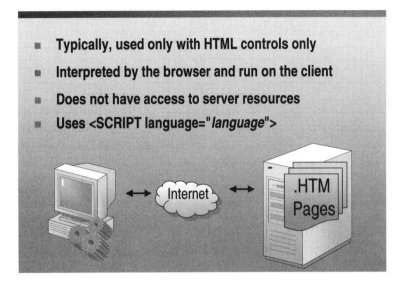

- Typically, used only with HTML controls only
- Interpreted by the browser and run on the client
- Does not have access to server resources
- Uses <SCRIPT language="*language*">

Introduction

There are two types of event procedures: client-side and server-side. There are advantages and disadvantages to both client-side and server-side event procedures.

Client-side event procedures

Client-side event procedures are events that are handled on the computer that requests the Web Form (the client). When an event is generated, no information is sent to the server. Instead, the client browser interprets the code and also performs the action.

Client-side event procedures can only be used with HTML controls. In addition, client-side event procedures never have access to server resources. For example, you cannot use client-side script to access a SQL Server database.

Uses for client-side event procedures

Client-side event procedures are useful for events that you want to happen immediately because they do not require a round trip to the Web server (sending information to the Web server and waiting for a response). For example, you may want to validate information in a text box before it is submitted to the server. You can use client-side script to validate the information quickly and effectively before sending the user information to the Web server for further processing.

Specifying client-side event procedures

You specify a client-side event procedure by creating a <SCRIPT> block in the Web page, as shown in the following code:

```
<SCRIPT language="javascript">
```

Server-Side Event Procedures

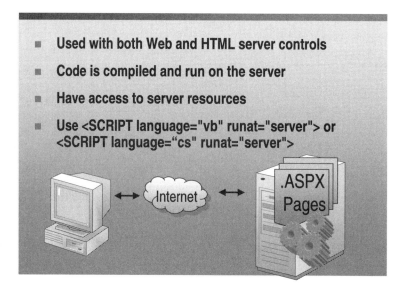

- **Used with both Web and HTML server controls**

- **Code is compiled and run on the server**

- **Have access to server resources**

- **Use <SCRIPT language="vb" runat="server"> or <SCRIPT language="cs" runat="server">**

Introduction

Unlike client-side event procedures, server-side event procedures require information to be sent to the Web server for processing. Although there is a time cost to using server-side event procedures, they are much more powerful than client-side event procedures.

Server-side event procedures

Server-side event procedures consist of compiled code that resides on the Web server. Server-side event procedures can be used to handle events that are generated from both Web and HTML server controls. Server-side event procedures have access to server resources that are normally unavailable to client-side event procedures.

You specify a server-side event procedure by using the **runat="server"** attribute in the **script** tag, as shown in the following code:

Visual Basic .NET

```
<SCRIPT language="vb" runat="server">
```

C#

```
<SCRIPT language="c#" runat="server">
```

Event Support

Because server-side event procedures require a round trip to the Web server, there are a limited number of types of control events that are supported. With client-side event procedures, you can include code to process mouse key events and **onChange** events. While server-side event procedures support click events and a special version of the **onChange** event, they cannot support events that occur frequently, like mouse key events.

Multimedia: Client-Side and Server-Side Events

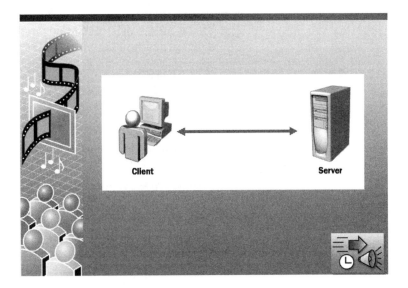

Introduction

In this animation, you will see how client-side and server-side event procedures are processed on the client and on the server.

1. The client requests an ASP.NET page from the Web server.

2. The server returns a page containing HTML and script to the client. The page includes a text box control and a **Submit** button. The page also contains client-side script that validates the contents of the text box.

3. The user enters invalid information into the text box, and the client-side script generates a message box.

4. Because no information has been sent to the server, client-side processing reduces network traffic and response times.

5. The user corrects the information in the text box, and then clicks the **Submit** button.

6. The information is validated on the client side, and then sent to the server, where server-side processing can take place.

7. The server repeats the validation and stores the information from the text box in a database.

8. Because the client-side script cannot access server resources, server-side processing offers a greater range of flexibility in data processing.

Creating Event Procedures

- **Visual Studio .NET declares variables and creates an event procedure template**

```
Protected WithEvents cmd1 As System.Web.UI.WebControls.Button
Private Sub cmd1_Click(ByVal s As System.Object, _
        ByVal e As System.EventArgs) Handles cmd1.Click
```

```
protected System.Web.UI.WebControls.Button cmd1;
private void InitializeComponent()
{
  this.cmd1.Click += new System.EventHandler(this.cmd1_Click);
  this.Load += new System.EventHandler(this.Page_Load);
}
private void cmd1_Click(object s, System.EventArgs e)
```

- **Using the Handles keyword adds many event procedures to one event**

Introduction

Creating a server-side event procedure in Visual Studio .NET involves two steps. In the first step, you create the control that generates the event on the Web Form. Secondly, you provide the code on the code-behind page that is needed to handle the event.

Creating a server-side event procedure

When you double-click a control in Visual Studio .NET, Visual Studio .NET declares a variable (with the same name as the **id** attribute of the control) and creates an event procedure template. When you use Visual Basic .NET, Visual Studio .NET also adds the **Handles** keyword, which attaches the event procedure to the control. The **Handles** keyword allows you to create multiple event procedures for a single event.

Note By default, Visual Studio .NET uses the **Handles** keyword because the **AutoEventWireup** attribute of the @ **Page** directive is set to **false**. If this attribute is set to **true**, controls are bound to event procedures through specific names, which is how event procedures are handled in Visual Basic 6.0.

The following HTML code shows a Web Form that has a single button with an **id** attribute of cmd1; the click event for the button will be handled on the server:

```
<form id="form1" method="post" runat="server">
  <asp:Button id="cmd1" runat="server"/>
</form>
```

The following Visual Basic .NET code shows the variable declaration that is needed in the code-behind page.

```
Protected WithEvents cmd1 As _
  System.Web.UI.WebControls.Button
```

In the preceding code, the name of the variable must match the **id** of the Web control, and you must use the **WithEvents** keyword to indicate that this control causes event procedures to run.

In the following Visual Basic .NET code, which shows the event procedure for the **Click** event, the **Handles** keyword indicates that the event procedure runs in response to the **Click** event of the cmd1 control:

```
Private Sub cmd1_Click(ByVal s As System.Object, _
  ByVal e As System.EventArgs) _
  Handles cmd1.Click
...
End Sub
```

Event arguments

All events pass two arguments to the event procedure: the sender of the event, and an instance of the class that holds data for the event. The latter is usually of the type **EventArgs**, and it often does not contain any additional information; however, for some controls, it is of a type that is specific to that control.

For example, for an **ImageButton** Web control, the second argument is of the type **ImageClickEventArgs**, which includes information about the coordinates where the user clicked. The following event procedure outputs the coordinates of the location where a click occurs within a **Label** control:

```
Sub img_OnClick(ByVal s As System.Object, _
  ByVal e As System.Web.UI.ImageClickEventArgs) _
  Handles ImageButton1.Click
  Label1.Text = e.X & ", " & e.Y
End Sub
```

Creating a server-side event procedure in C#

In C#, the way that you create an ASP.NET event procedure is slightly different than how you would create it in Visual Basic .NET. C# does not support the **Handles** keyword. Instead, in C#, you add the event procedure to the event property of the control.

For example, the following is the same HTML form as shown in the preceding code:

```
<FORM ID="Form1" runat="server">
  <asp:Button id="cmd1" runat="server" />
</FORM>
```

In the code-behind page, a variable is created with the same name as the control. In the **InitializeComponent** method, you add the event procedure to the event property of the control. The **Click** property of the cmd1 variable is handled as follows:

```
public class WebForm1 : System.Web.UI.Page
{
  protected System.Web.UI.WebControls.Button cmd1;

  private void InitializeComponent()
  {
     this.cmd1.Click += new
        System.EventHandler(this.cmd1_Click);
     this.Load += new System.EventHandler(this.Page_Load);
  }

  private void cmd1_Click(object sender, System.EventArgs e)
  {
  ...
  }
}
```

Instructor-Led Practice: Creating an Event Procedure

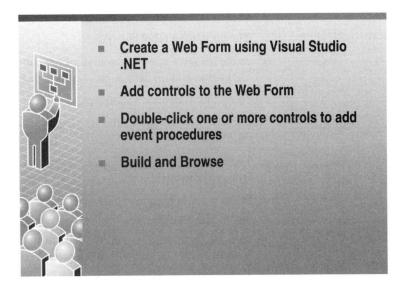

Introduction

This instructor-led practice can be performed by using either the Visual Basic .NET files or the Visual C# files.

In this practice, you will see how to add an event procedure to a Web control by using Visual Studio .NET.

▶ **To run the practice**

1. In Visual Studio .NET, add a new Web Form named events.aspx to the Mod05VB or Mod05CS project, in the 2310Demos solution.

2. Open the events.aspx page.

3. Put a **Button** and a **Label** Web Form control on the form.

   The controls are assigned a default ID that you can view and change in the Properties window.

4. In Design view, double-click the **Button** control to open the code-behind page and create a **Click** event procedure.

   In the code-behind page, notice the variable that is declared and the event procedure template that is created by Visual Studio .NET.

5. Enter the following code in the **Click** event procedure:

Visual Basic .NET

```
Label1.Text = "You clicked the button"
```

C#

```
Label1.Text = "You clicked the button";
```

Visual Basic .NET

6. Notice the **Handles** keyword on the **Button1_Click** event procedure.

C#

C# does not support the Handles keyword, instead C# binds a procedure to an event in the **InitializeComponent** procedure. To see the binding for Button1_Click, expand the **Web Form Designer generated code** section in the code window. Find the **InitializeComponent** procedure and notice the event handler binding.

7. In Solution Explorer, right-click the **events.aspx** page and then click **Build and Browse**.

8. In the browser, click the button on the form.

   The text of the label changes.

9. In the browser, view the source of the page to show that there is no client-side code. There is just server-side code.

10. Close the source view of the page.

11. In Design view, change the ID property of the **Button** control to **cmdSubmit**.

Visual Basic .NET

12. In the code-behind page, notice that the **Handles** keyword was removed from the **Button1_Click** event procedure.

C#

In the code-behind page, notice that the event binding in the **InitializeComponent** has changed to the new button name.

Visual Basic .NET

13. Add the **Handles** keyword to the **Button1_Click** event procedure to run the procedure for the **cmdSubmit.Button** event, as shown in the following code:

```
Private Sub Button1_Click(ByVal sender As System.Object,
    ByVal e As System.EventArgs) Handles cmdSubmit.Click
```

C#

The **Handles** keyword is not supported in C#. Instead the procedure is bound to the event in the **InitializeComponent** procedure. Visual Studio adds the correct binding, as shown in step 12.

14. Build and Browse the page.

   The **Click** event procedure still fires with the new name of the control.

Interacting with Controls in Event Procedures

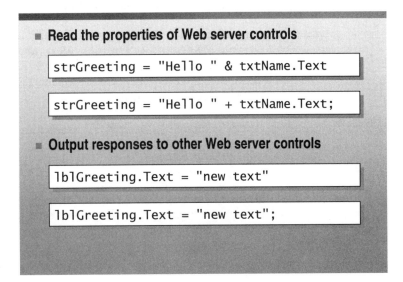

- Read the properties of Web server controls

```
strGreeting = "Hello " & txtName.Text
```

```
strGreeting = "Hello " + txtName.Text;
```

- Output responses to other Web server controls

```
lblGreeting.Text = "new text"
```

```
lblGreeting.Text = "new text";
```

Introduction

In many Web applications, you need to read from and write to controls on a form. You can do this within server-side event procedures.

Reading properties from a server control

Within a server-side event procedure, you can read information from a server control. For example, if you have the following form with a **Textbox** and a **Button** control:

```
<FORM id="Form1" runat="server">
    <asp:TextBox id="txtName" runat="server" />
    <asp:Button id="cmd1" runat="server" />
</FORM>
```

When the user clicks the button, you can read the text that the user typed into the text box. The following code assigns the string variable **strGreeting** to a concatenation of the text "Hello" and the text in the **txtName** text box:

Visual Basic .NET

```
Dim strGreeting As String = "Hello " & txtName.Text
```

C#

```
string strGreeting = "Hello " + txtName.Text;
```

For example, if a user typed "Shannon" in the **txtName** text box, the **strGreeting** variable would contain the text string "Hello Shannon".

Outputting to a Web server control

You can output information directly to a Web server control by using the control's properties. For example, suppose you have a **Label** Web server control on the ASP.NET page, as follows:

```
<asp:Label id="lblGreeting"
    runat="server">Greeting</asp:Label>
```

The following server-side code assigns the **Text** property of **lblGreeting** Web server control to a text string:

Visual Basic .NET

```
lblGreeting.Text = "new text"
```

C#

```
lblGreeting.Text = "new text";
```

Tip In ASP, you use the **Request.Forms** collection to read the properties of controls on a form, and use **Response.Write** to output text. Although these methods still work with ASP.NET, they are not the preferred methods. Instead, you will want to use server control labels and spans.

Lesson: Using Page Events

- **Understanding the Page Event Life Cycle**
- **Multimedia: The PostBack Process**
- **Demonstration: Handling Events**
- **Practice: Placing Events in Order**
- **Handling Page.IsPostback Events**
- **Linking Two Controls Together**
- **Demonstration: Linking Controls Together**

Introduction

In this lesson, you will learn how to use page events. You will first learn about the page event life cycle. You will then see how the postback process works, and then learn about event order. You will also see how to work with the **Page_Load** event. The lesson ends with linking controls together.

Lesson objectives

After completing this lesson, you will be able to:

- Describe the page event life cycle.
- Use postback forms.
- Link one control to another control.

Understanding the Page Event Life Cycle

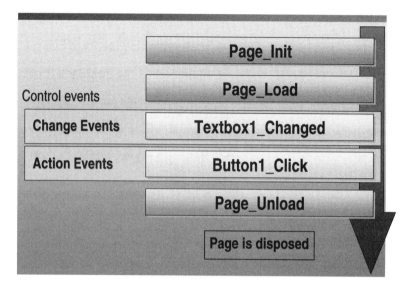

Introduction

When an ASP.NET page is requested, there are a series of page events that occur. These events always occur in the same order, which is referred to as the page event life cycle.

The page event life cycle

The page event life cycle consists of the following page events, which occur in the following order:

1. **Page_Init**. This page event initializes the page by creating and initializing the Web server controls on the page.

2. **Page_Load**. This page event runs every time the page is requested.

3. **Control** events. This page event includes change events (for example, **Textbox1_Changed**) and action events (for example, **Button1_Click**).

4. **Page_Unload**. This page event occurs when the page is closed or when the control is passed to another page.

The end of the page event life cycle includes the disposal of the page from memory.

Most control events do not occur until the Web Form is posted back to the server. For example, **Change** events are handled in a random order on the server after the form is posted. Conversely, **Click** events can cause the form to be sent to the server immediately.

If, for example, a user enters text into a number of controls on a form and then clicks a **Submit** button, the **Change** events for the text controls will not be processed until the form is sent to the server by the **Click** event.

Note For more information on page events, see "Page Members" and "Control Execution Lifecycle" in the Visual Studio .NET online documentation.

Postbacks

In ASP.NET, forms are designed to post information back to the sending ASP.NET page for processing. This process is called postback. Postbacks may occur with certain user actions. By default, only **Button** click events cause the form to be posted back to the server. However, if you set the **AutoPostBack** property of a control to **true**, a postback is forced for events of that control.

For example, the following HTML code is an example of using **AutoPostBack** on a list box. Every time the user changes the value of the list box, the **SelectedIndexChanged** event will be raised on the server and it will update the text box:

```
<asp:DropDownList id="ListBox1" runat="server"
        AutoPostBack="True">
  <asp:ListItem>First Choice</asp:ListItem>
  <asp:ListItem>Second Choice</asp:ListItem>
</asp:DropDownList>
```

The code in the code-behind page is as follows:

Visual Basic .NET

```
Private Sub ListBox1_SelectedIndexChanged _
  (ByVal s As System.Object, ByVal e As System.EventArgs) _
  Handles ListBox1.SelectedIndexChanged
      TextBox1.Text=ListBox1.SelectedItem.Value
End Sub
```

C#

```
private void ListBox1_SelectedIndexChanged
  (object sender, System.EventArgs e)
{
      TextBox1.Text = ListBox1.SelectedItem.Value;
}
```

Multimedia: The Postback Process

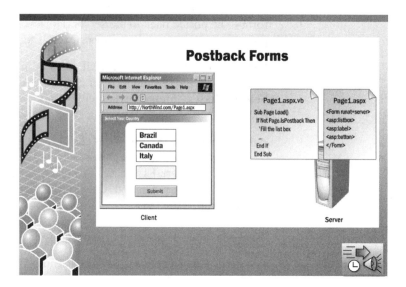

Introduction

In this animation, you will see how forms work in ASP.NET and how the **Page_Load** event can be coded to only run the first time a page is displayed, and how controls can be made to post immediately to the server.

- The first time that a user requests a page from the server, the test for **Page.IsPostBack** in the **Page_Load** event succeeds and the code in the block runs. In this example, the code fills in a list box.

- The server then returns the page to the user. In this example, the page has a **ListBox**, a blank **Label**, and a **Submit** button on it.

- When the user changes the selection in the list box, and then clicks the **Submit** button, the information is sent back to the server.

- The server can determine that this is a page that is being posted back to itself, and so the test for **Page.IsPostBack** in the **Page_Load** event fails and the code in the block does not run.

- Instead, the event procedures for the controls on the form (the list box and the button) run and in this scenario, the list box event procedure changes the label to reflect the new list box selection.

- Then, the server returns the updated information to the client. The user sees the same page, but the label has now changed to reflect the list box selection.

- If you want the new value of the list box to be sent to the server immediately, and not wait for the user to click the **Submit** button, you can set the list box control's **AutoPostBack** property to **True**.

- With the **AutoPostBack** property set to **True**, as soon as the user changes the selection in the list box, the information is sent to the server.

- The server updates the label to reflect the change, and then sends the updated information back to the client.

Demonstration: Handling Events

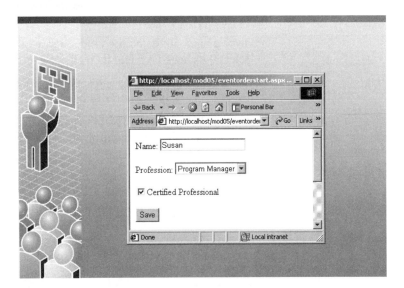

Introduction	This demonstration can be performed by using the Visual Basic .NET project or the Visual C# project.
	In this demonstration, you will see how HTML and Web server controls can support both client-side and server-side events.
	The completed code for this demonstration is in the:
Visual Basic .NET	*install folder*\DemoCode\Mod05VB\eventorderFinal.aspx page.
C#	*install folder*\DemoCode\Mod05CS\eventorderFinal.aspx page.
	The eventorderFinal.aspx page is also in the Mod05VB and Mod05CS projects in the 2310Demos solution.

▶ **To run the demonstration**

1. In Visual Studio .NET, view the page eventorderstart.aspx in the Mod05VB or Mod05CS project in the browser.

   Type a name in the **Name** field, click a value in the **Profession** list box, select the check box, and then click **Save**.

   The page has client-side and server-side event procedures for the text box, list box, check box, button, and the page.

2. In Visual Studio .NET, edit the page in HTML view and change the check box into a Web server control, adding a **Text** attribute, as shown in the following code:

```
<asp:checkbox onclick="checkClick()"
   onserverclick="checkServerClick"
   onserverchange="checkServerChange"
   runat="server"
   id="Checkbox1"
   Text="Certified Professional"/>
```

Note Although the **onclick**, **onserverclick**, and **onserverchange** attributes are not recognized by the syntax checker, you can leave them in the code.

---

3. View the page in the browser again.

   Type a name in the **Name** field, click a value in the **Profession** list box, select the check box, and then click **Save**.

   The check box only fires client-side events now.

   While the client event still runs because <asp:checkbox> generates <input type=checkbox>, the server event does not run because the name of the server event is **oncheckedchange**, not **onserverchange**.

4. Edit the page in HTML view and change the name of the server-side event procedure attribute from **onserverchange** to o**ncheckedchange**, as shown in the following code:

```
<asp:checkbox onclick="checkClick()"
   onserverclick="checkServerClick"
   oncheckedchanged="checkServerChange"
   runat="server"
   id="Checkbox1"
   Text="Certified Professional"/>
```

5. View the page in the browser again.

   Enter a name in the **Name** field, click a value in the **Profession** list box, select the check box, and then click **Save**.

   Both client and server event procedures run again.

6. Edit the page and set the **AutoPostBack** attribute to **true** for the check box.

7. View the page in the browser again.

   When you select the check box, you get the client-side event and then the server-side event.

8. In the browser, view the source of the page to see how **AutoPostBack** is implemented.

9. Close the source view page.

10. Edit the page and add a **Page.IsPostBack** test to the **Page_Load** event procedure, as shown in the following code:

Visual Basic .NET

```
Sub Page_Load(s As Object, e As EventArgs)
    If Not Page.IsPostback Then
        Label1.Text &= "<P>Page_Load first time, "
    Else
        Label1.Text &= "<P>Page_Load postback, "
    End If
End Sub
```

C#

```
void Page_Load(object s, System.EventArgs e)
{
    if (!Page.IsPostBack)
    {
        Label1.Text += "<P>Page_Load first time, ";
    }
    else
    {
        Label1.Text += "<P>Page_Load postback, ";
    }
}
```

11. View the page in the browser again.

While the form is loaded the first time, and then posted back, you can see the different messages displayed.

Practice: Placing Events in Order

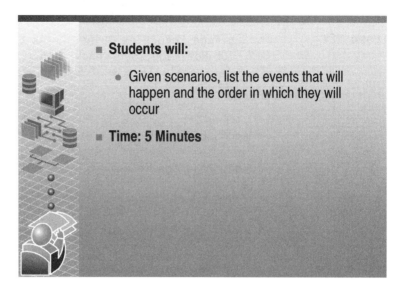

Introduction

In this practice, you will predict what events will happen for given scenarios. The events to include are: page load, *control* change, and *control* click.

▶ **List the order of events for the following scenarios**

Enter Name, enter age, click **Female**, and click **Submit**.

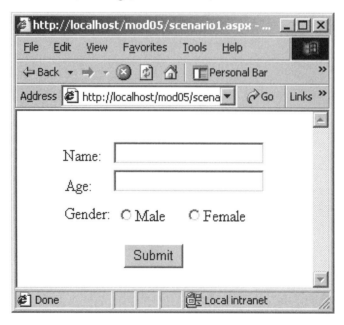

Select state, and click **Submit**.

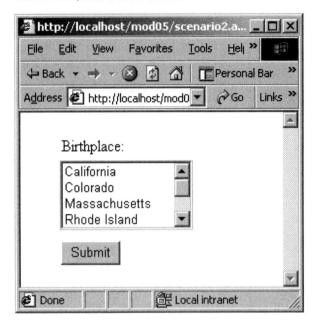

Select start date, select end date, and click **Submit**.

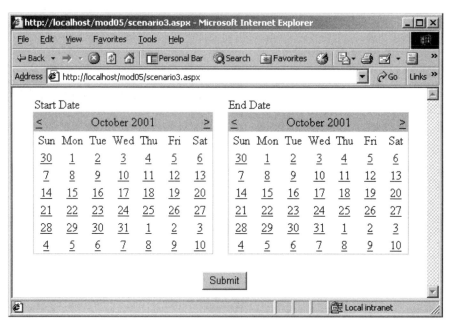

Handling Page.IsPostback Events

■ **Page_Load fires on every request**

  ● Use **Page.IsPostBack** to execute conditional logic

```
private void Page_Load(object sender, System.EventArgs e)
{    if (!Page.IsPostBack)
        {
            // executes only on initial page load
        }
    //this code executes on every request
}
```

```
Private Sub Page_Load(ByVal s As System.Object, _
    ByVal e As System.EventArgs) Handles MyBase.Load
    If Not Page.IsPostBack Then
       'executes only on initial page load
    End If
    'this code executes on every request
End Sub
```

● **Page.IsPostBack** prevents reloading for each postback

Introduction

The **Page_Load** event runs on every request for a page, whether it is the first request of the page or a postback.

Using Page.IsPostBack

Because the **Page_Load** event runs with every request for a page, all of the code within the **Page_Load** event will execute each time the page is requested. However, when you are using postback events, you may not want all of the code to execute again. If this is the case, you can use the **Page.IsPostBack** property to control which code executes only when the page is initially requested, as shown in the following code:

Visual Basic .NET

```
Private Sub Page_Load(ByVal s As System.Object, _
    ByVal e As System.EventArgs) _
    Handles MyBase.Load
    If Not Page.IsPostBack Then
       'executes only on initial page load
    End If
    'this code executes on every request
End Sub
```

C#

```
private void Page_Load(object sender,
    System.EventArgs e)
{
    if (!Page.IsPostBack)
    {
        // executes only on initial page load
    }
    //this code executes on every request
}
```

Linking Two Controls Together

- **Linking one control to another is useful for taking values from list boxes or drop-down lists**

```
<asp:DropDownList id="lstOccupation"
    autoPostBack="True" runat="server" >
You selected: <asp:Label id="lblSelectedValue"
    Text="<%# lstOccupation.SelectedItem.Text %>"
    runat="server" />
```

- **Data binding**

```
private void Page_Load(object sender, System.EventArgs e)
{
    lblSelectedValue.DataBind();
}
```

```
Sub Page_Load(s As Object, e As EventArgs) Handles MyBase.Load
    lblSelectedValue.DataBind()
End Sub
```

Introduction

You can link one control to the contents of another. Linking is particularly useful for displaying values from list boxes or drop-down lists.

The following code example demonstrates how to link a **Label** control to the contents of a drop-down list. Using the linking tags **<%#** and **%>,** you set the **Text** attribute of the **Label** control to the **SelectedItem** of the list box:

```
<asp:Label id="lblSelectedValue" runat="server"
  Text="<%# lstOccupation.SelectedItem.Text %>" />
```

The following example shows the code in a Web Form that is used to link the **Label** control to the list box:

```
<form runat="server">
  <asp:DropDownList id="lstOccupation"
      autoPostBack="true" runat="server" >
      <asp:ListItem>Program Manager</asp:ListItem>
      <asp:ListItem>Tester</asp:ListItem>
      <asp:ListItem>User Assistance</asp:ListItem>
  </asp:DropDownList>
  <p>You selected: <asp:Label id="lblSelectedValue"
      Text="<%# lstOccupation.SelectedItem.Text %>"
      runat="server" />
  </p>
</form>
```

In the preceding code, notice that the **AutoPostBack** property of the drop-down list is set to **True**, which causes automatic postback whenever the value of the list box changes.

In the **Page_Load** event procedure, you call the **DataBind** method of either the entire page or just the **Label** control, as shown in the following code:

Visual Basic .NET

```
Sub Page_Load (s As Object, e As EventArgs) _
  Handles MyBase.Load
  lblSelectedValue.DataBind()
End Sub
```

C#

```
private void Page_Load(object sender, System.EventArgs e)
{
  lblSelectedValue.DataBind();
}
```

You can use **Page.DataBind()** if you want the page to data bind all of the elements on the page. The preceding code example binds only the **Label** control to data, thereby using the *control*.DataBind() syntax, where *control* is the **id** attribute of the **Label** control.

Demonstration: Linking Controls Together

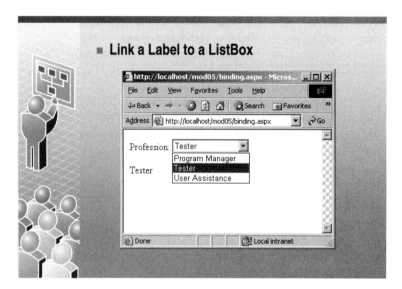

Introduction

This demonstration can be performed by using either the Visual Basic .NET or Visual C# project files.

In this demonstration, you will see how to link controls together.

The completed code for this demonstration is in the:

Visual Basic .NET

install folder\DemoCode\Mod05VB\binding.aspx page.

C#

install folder\DemoCode\Mod05CS\binding.aspx page.

The eventorderFinal.aspx page is also in the Mod05VB and Mod05CS projects in the 2310Demos solution.

▶ **To run the demonstration**

1. In Visual Studio .NET, edit the page beforebinding.aspx in the Mod05 project. There is a **DropDownList** and a **Label** control on this page. View the HTML for the page. Note the **AutoPostBack** attribute for the **DropDownList**.

2. Link the **Label** control to the **DropDownList** control by setting its **Text** attribute, as shown in the following code example:

```
<asp:label id="lblListValue"
Text="<%# lstTitle.SelectedItem.Text %>" runat="server"/>
```

3. Create a **Page_Load** event procedure and call lblListValue.DataBind(), as shown in the following code example:

Visual Basic .NET

```
Private Sub Page_Load(ByVal sender As System.Object, _
    ByVal e As System.EventArgs) Handles MyBase.Load
    lblListValue.DataBind()
End Sub
```

C#

```
private void Page_Load(object sender, System.EventArgs e)
{
    lblListValue.DataBind();
}
```

4. Build and browse to view the page in Microsoft Internet Explorer.

When you select an item in the **DropDownList,** the value is reflected in the **Label** control.

Review

- **Using Code-Behind Pages**
- **Adding Event Procedures to Web Server Controls**
- **Using Page Events**

1. What is the advantage of using code-behind pages when adding functionality to a Web Form?

2. How is an event procedure associated with an event of a server control?

3. What are the two arguments to an event procedure?

4. How is a code-behind page associated with an .aspx page?

5. List the three ways you can add code to an ASP.NET page.

6. Why would you want to set up your code-behind pages to be precompiled instead of "just-in-time"?

7. When does a form post back to itself?

8. How can you determine through code if the **Page_Load** event is being run as a result of a postback?

Lab 5: Adding Functionality to a Web Application

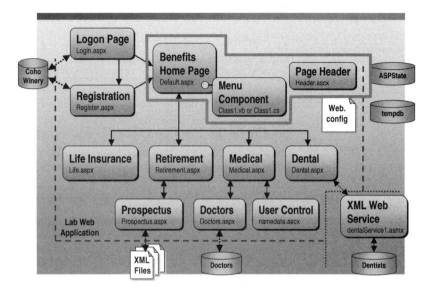

Objectives

After completing this lab, you will be able to:

- Create a **Page_Load** event procedure for a Microsoft® ASP.NET Web page.
- Create **Click** event procedures for Web controls on an ASP.NET Web page.

Note This lab focuses on the concepts in this module and as a result may not comply with Microsoft security recommendations.

Prerequisites

Before working on this lab, you must have:

- Knowledge of how to call a Microsoft Visual Basic® .NET function.
- Knowledge of how to use Web controls on a Web Form.

Scenario

Coho Winery offers several benefits to its employees. In the labs for Course 2310B, *Developing Microsoft ASP.NET Web Applications Using Visual Studio .NET*, you will create a Web site that enables employees to select and set up their chosen benefits.

In Lab 3, "Building a Microsoft Visual Studio .NET Component," in Course 2310B, *Developing Microsoft ASP.NET Web Applications Using Visual Studio .NET*, you created a component that returned a list of all the benefits that are offered by your company. In this lab, you will call that component from the default.aspx page of your company's Web site, display the information in a **CheckBoxList** control, and then implement the **Submit** button on the form to display which benefits are selected.

Estimated time to complete this lab: 45 minutes

Exercise 0
Lab Setup

To complete this lab, you must have created a Benefits Web Application project and a BenefitsList Class Library project. These projects may be created by using Visual Basic .NET or Microsoft Visual C#™ .NET.

If you have not created these projects, complete the following steps:

▶ **Create the 2310LabApplication solution**

Important   Only perform this procedure if you have not created a 2310LabApplication solution file.

---

1. Using Microsoft Visual Studio® .NET, create a new blank solution named **2310LabApplication**:

    a. On the **File** menu, point to **New**, and then click **Blank Solution**.

    b. In the **New Project** dialog box, type **2310LabApplication** in the **Name** text box, and then click **OK**.

▶ **Create the Benefits project**

Important   Only perform this procedure if you have not previously created a Benefits project, or if you have removed the Benefits project according to the steps in Appendix A, "Lab Recovery," in Course 2310B, *Developing Microsoft ASP.NET Web Applications Using Visual Studio .NET*.

---

1. Create a new ASP.NET Web Application project, named **BenefitsVB** or **BenefitsCS**, in the 2310LabApplication solution:

    a. On the **File** menu, point to **New**, and then click **Project**.

    b. In the **New Project** dialog box, in the **Project Types** list, click **Visual Basic Projects** or **Visual C# Projects**.

    c. In the **Templates** list, click **ASP.NET Web Application**, set the **Location** to **http://localhost/BenefitsVB** for the Visual Basic .NET project or to **http://localhost/BenefitsCS** for the Visual C# project.

    d. Click **Add to Solution**, and then click **OK**.

Caution   When adding projects to the solution, the capitalization of the project name is important. Because you may be using some pre-built Web Forms in this and other labs in Course 2310B, *Developing Microsoft ASP.NET Web Applications Using Visual Studio .NET*, you must verify that you have capitalized the Benefits project as shown.

▶ **Update the Benefits project**

1. In Visual Studio .NET, open the 2310LabApplication solution file.

2. In Solution Explorer, right-click **BenefitsVB** or **BenefitsCS**, point to **Add**, and then click **Add Existing Item**.

3. Browse the Benefits project.

For the Visual Basic .NET Project

Browse to the *install folder*\Labfiles\Lab05\VB\Starter\BenefitsVB folder for the Visual Basic .NET files.

For the Visual C# Project

Browse to the *install folder*\Labfiles\Lab05\CS\Starter\BenefitsCS folder for the Visual C# files.

4. In the **Files of type** box of the **Add Existing Item – Benefits dialog box**, choose **All Files (*.*)**.

5. Select all of the files in this folder, and then click **Open**.

6. Click **Yes** if prompted to overwrite or reload files.

▶ **Create the BenefitsList class library**

Important   Only perform these steps if you have not previously created a BenefitsList project, or if you have removed the BenefitsList project according to the steps in Appendix A, "Lab Recovery," in Course 2310B, *Developing Microsoft ASP.NET Web Applications Using Visual Studio .NET.*

1. Create a Class Library project.

For the Visual Basic .NET Project

Create a new Visual Basic .NET Class Library project, name it **BenefitsListVB**, and then add it to the 2310LabApplication solution:

a. On the **File** menu, point to **New**, and then click **Project**.

b. In the **New Project** dialog box, in the **Project Types** list, click **Visual Basic Projects**.

c. In the **Templates** list, click **Class Library**, and then set the **Name** to **BenefitsListVB**.

d. Click **Add to Solution**, and then click **OK**.

For the Visual C# Project

Create a new Visual C# .NET Class Library project, name it **BenefitsListCS**, and then add it to the 2310LabApplication solution:

a. On the **File** menu, point to **New**, and then click **Project**.

b. In the **New Project** dialog box, in the **Project Types** list, click **Visual C# Projects**.

c. In the **Templates** list, click **Class Library**, and then set the **Name** to **BenefitsListCS**.

d. Click **Add to Solution**, and then click **OK**.

Caution   Verify that you have capitalized the BenefitsList project as shown.

▶ **Update the BenefitsList project**

1. In Visual Studio .NET, open the 2310LabApplication solution file.

2. In Solution Explorer, right-click **BenefitsListVB** or **BenefitsListCS**, point to **Add**, and then click **Add Existing Item**.

3. Browse the BenefitsList project.

For the Visual Basic .NET Project

Browse to the *install folder*\Labfiles\Lab05\VB\Starter\BenefitsListVB folder.

For the Visual C# Project

Browse to the *install folder*\Labfiles\Lab05\CS\Starter\BenefitsListCS folder.

4. In the **Files of type** box of the **Add Existing Item – BenefitsList** dialog box, click **All Files (*.*)**.

5. Select all of the files in this folder, and then click **Open**.

6. Click **Yes** if prompted to overwrite or reload files.

▶ **Create a reference to the BenefitsList component in the Benefits project**

1. In the Benefits project in the 2310LabApplication solution, complete the following steps to add a reference to the **BenefitsList** component that you just created:

   a. Right-click the **BenefitsVB** or **BenefitsCS** project in Solution Explorer and then click **Add Reference**.

   b. In the **Add Reference** dialog box, on the **Projects** tab, double-click the **BenefitsListVB** or **BenefitsListCS** project.

   c. In the **Selected Components** list, select the **BenefitsListVB** or **BenefitsListCS** component, and then click **OK**.

   The component is added to the References folder in Solution Explorer.

Exercise 1
Creating a Page_Load Event Procedure

In this exercise, you will create the **Page_Load** event procedure for the default.aspx page. In the **Page_Load** event procedure, you will add code to read the list of benefits from the BenefitsListVB or BenefitsListCS component that you created in Lab 3, "Building a Microsoft Visual Studio .NET Component," in Course 2310B, *Developing Microsoft ASP.NET Web Applications Using Visual Studio .NET*. You will then display the benefits in a **CheckBoxList** control.

▶ **Call the BenefitsListVB or BenefitsListCS component**

1. Using Visual Studio .NET, open the 2310LabApplication solution.

2. Open the default.aspx page in the BenefitsVB or BenefitsCS project.

3. Double-click the background of the default.aspx page in Design view to create a **Page_Load** event procedure.

   The code-behind page opens and a template is added for the **Page_Load** event procedure, which contains the following code:

Visual Basic .NET
```
Private Sub Page_Load(ByVal sender As System.Object, _
    ByVal e As System.EventArgs) Handles MyBase.Load
    'Put user code to initialize the page here
End Sub
```

C#
```
private void Page_Load(object sender, System.EventArgs e)
{
    // Put user code to initialize the page here
}
```

4. Create a new instance of the BenefitsList.Benefits class and save it in a variable named **clBenefits**.

   Your code should look like the following:

Visual Basic .NET
```
Dim clBenefits As New _
    BenefitsListVB.Benefits()
```

C#
```
BenefitsListCS.Benefits clBenefits = new
    BenefitsListCS.Benefits();
```

5. If you are completing this lab in Visual Basic .NET, declare a variable of type BenefitsListVB.Benefits.BenefitInfo and name it **bi**.

   Your code should look like the following:

Visual Basic .NET
```
Dim bi As BenefitsListVB.Benefits.BenefitInfo
```

C#
If you are completing this lab in Visual C#, the variable **bi** is declared in the **foreach** loop later in this lab.

6. Call the **GetBenefitsList** method of the class, which returns an array of BenefitsListVB.Benefits.BenefitInfo or BenefitsListCS.Benefits.BenefitInfo variables.

7. Iterate through the returned array with a For Each loop.

8. For each item in the array, generate a string of the following format:

```
<a href=item.strPage> item.strName </a>
```

Add the string to the **Items** collection of the **chkListBenefits** CheckBoxList control by using the **chkListBenefits.Items.Add** method.

Your code should look like the following:

Visual Basic .NET

```
For Each bi In clBenefits.GetBenefitsList()
    chkListBenefits.Items.Add("<a href=" & bi.strPage & _
        ">" &  bi.strName & "</a>")
Next
```

C#

```
foreach (BenefitsListCS.Benefits.BenefitInfo bi
    in clBenefits.GetBenefitsList())
{
    chkListBenefits.Items.Add("<a href=" + bi.strPage +
        ">" + bi.strName + "</a>");
}
```

9. Right-click the **default.aspx** page in Solution Explorer and then click **Build and Browse**.

The **chkListBenefits** list now contains hyperlinks to other pages, in addition to the initial collection of values, as shown in the following illustration.

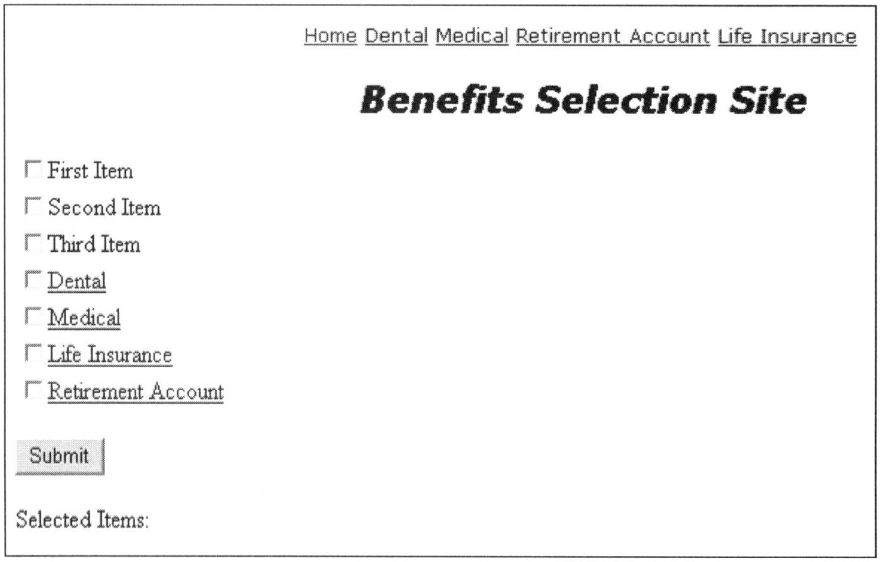

10. Click the **Life Insurance** hyperlink.

The life.aspx page is displayed.

11. Click the **Home** hyperlink to return to the default.aspx page.

12. Click **Submit** twice. What happens? Why?

_____

_____

The **chkBenefitsList** list box display should only display the benefits list that was provided by the BenefitsList component, not the first three temporary items. Furthermore, the list of benefits should not be added to the list box with every refresh of the page. To fix these issues, perform the following procedures.

▶ **Remove temporary list items**

1. Open the default.aspx page.

2. Select the **chkListBenefits** list box control.

3. In the Properties window, click **Items**, and then click the **...** next to **(Collection)**.

4. In the **ListItem Collection Editor**, select an item in the **Members** list and then click **Remove**. Repeat this step until all three members have been removed from the collection, and then click **OK**.

▶ **Add a Page.IsPostBack test**

1. In the default.aspx page, add a **Page.IsPostBack** test to the **Page_Load** event procedure.

Only add items from the component to the **CheckBoxList** control if the page is being displayed for the first time.

When complete, the entire **Page_Load** event procedure should look like the following (the new code is in bold font):

Visual Basic .NET

```
Private Sub Page_Load(ByVal sender As System.Object, _
    ByVal e As System.EventArgs) Handles MyBase.Load
    If Not Page.IsPostBack Then
        Dim clBenefits As New BenefitsListVB.Benefits()
        Dim bi As BenefitsListVB.Benefits.BenefitInfo

        For Each bi In clBenefits.GetBenefitsList()
            chkListBenefits.Items.Add("<a href=" & _
                bi.strPage & ">" & bi.strName & "</a>")
        Next
    End If
End Sub
```

C#

```
private void Page_Load(object sender, System.EventArgs e)
{
    if (!Page.IsPostBack)
    {
        BenefitsListCS.Benefits clBenefits = new
            BenefitsListCS.Benefits();

        foreach (BenefitsListCS.Benefits.BenefitInfo bi
            in clBenefits.GetBenefitsList())
        {
            chkListBenefits.Items.Add("<a href=" +
                bi.strPage + ">" + bi.strName + "</a>");
        }
    }
}
```

2. Build and browse the default.aspx page.

   The list now only displays the items from the BenefitsList component.

3. Click **Submit** two or more times. What happens? Why?

   _____

   _____

Exercise 2
Creating Click Event Procedure

In this exercise, you will create a **Click** event procedure for the **Submit** button on the default.aspx page. When the user clicks **Submit**, the event procedure will read the list of benefits and output the benefits in the list that are selected to a label on the default.aspx page.

▶ **Read benefits checked**

1. Open the default.aspx page.

2. Double-click the **Submit** button in Design view to create a **Click** event procedure for the **Submit** button.

   The default.aspx.vb or default.aspx.cs page opens with the new **cmdSubmit_Click** event procedure already created.

3. In the **Click** event procedure, iterate through the list of items in the **CheckBoxList** control. For each item, if the **Selected** property is **True**, then add a string to the **Text** property of the **lblSelections Label** control.

   Your code should look like the following:

Visual Basic .NET

```
Dim li As ListItem
For Each li In chkListBenefits.Items
    If li.Selected Then
        lblSelections.Text &= ", " & li.Value
    End If
Next
```

C#

```
foreach (ListItem li in chkListBenefits.Items)
{
    if (li.Selected)
    {
        lblSelections.Text += ", " + li.Value;
    }
}
```

4. Build and browse the default.aspx page.

5. Select a few benefits from the list, and then click **Submit**.

   The label displays a list of the selected items as hyperlinks.

Exercise 3 (If Time Permits)
Using a Component in a User Control

Each page of the Benefits Web site displays some of the same information. This information is stored in a user control that is named header.ascx. This header control does not read its list of benefits from the BenefitsList component. Rather, the list of benefits is hard-coded in the page.

In this exercise, you will redesign the header.ascx page to read the list of benefits from the BenefitsList component and then display them in hyperlink controls.

Note You will learn more about user controls in Module 8, "Creating User Controls," in Course 2310B, *Developing Microsoft ASP.NET Web Applications Using Visual Studio .NET.*

▶ **Call the BenefitsList component**

1. Open the header.ascx page.

2. Complete the following steps to change each of the four benefit hyperlinks that are across the top of the page, excluding the **Home** hyperlink, to Web server controls:

   Note Do not perform the following steps for the **Home** hyperlink. That hyperlink will remain hard-coded in this lab.

   ---

   a. In Design view, right-click each hyperlink and then click **Run as Server Control**.

   b. Click the **HTML** button to View the Hypertext Markup Language (HTML) for the page.

   List the **id** of each of the four hyperlink controls that are used for the benefits:

   _____

   _____

3. Create a **Page_Load** event procedure for the header.ascx page.

4. Create a new instance of the BenefitsList.Benefits class and save it in a variable that is named **clBenefits**.

5. Declare an array of BenefitsList.Benefits.BenefitInfo variables that is named **arBenefits**.

6. Call the **GetBenefitsList** method of the class, which returns an array of BenefitsList.Benefits.BenefitInfo variables.

7. Set the **HRef** and **InnerText** properties of each hyperlink to the **strPage** and **strName** properties of an item in the returned array.

   Your code should look like the following:

Visual Basic .NET

```
Dim clBenefits As New BenefitsListVB.Benefits()
Dim arBenefits As BenefitsListVB.Benefits.BenefitInfo()

arBenefits = clBenefits.GetBenefitsList()
A1.HRef = arBenefits(0).strPage
A1.InnerText = arBenefits(0).strName
A2.HRef = arBenefits(1).strPage
A2.InnerText = arBenefits(1).strName
A3.HRef = arBenefits(2).strPage
A3.InnerText = arBenefits(2).strName
A4.HRef = arBenefits(3).strPage
A4.InnerText = arBenefits(3).strName
```

> **Tip** You can copy-and-paste the preceding code from the file *install folder*\Labfiles\Lab05\VB\Solution\header.aspx.vb.

C#

```
BenefitsListCS.Benefits clBenefits = new
    BenefitsListCS.Benefits();
BenefitsListCS.Benefits.BenefitInfo[] arBenefits;

arBenefits = clBenefits.GetBenefitsList();
A1.HRef = arBenefits[0].strPage;
A1.InnerText = arBenefits[0].strName;
A2.HRef = arBenefits[1].strPage;
A2.InnerText = arBenefits[1].strName;
A3.HRef = arBenefits[2].strPage;
A3.InnerText = arBenefits[2].strName;
A4.HRef = arBenefits[3].strPage;
A4.InnerText = arBenefits[3].strName;
```

> **Tip** You can copy-and-paste the preceding code from the file *install folder*\Labfiles\Lab05\CS\Solution\header.aspx.cs.

8. Build the Benefits project.

   Because header.ascx is a user control, you cannot view it directly in a browser.

9. View the default.aspx page in a browser.

   The page looks the same, but if you change the items that were returned by the BenefitslistVB or BenefitsCS component, both the **chkListBenefits** control on the default.aspx Web Form and the set of hyperlinks on the header.ascx user control will reflect the change.

msdn®training

Module 6: Tracing in Microsoft ASP.NET Web Applications

Contents

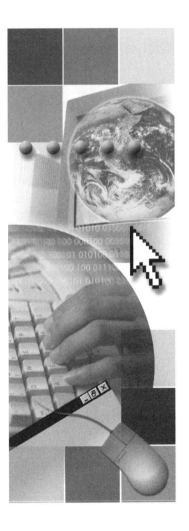

Overview

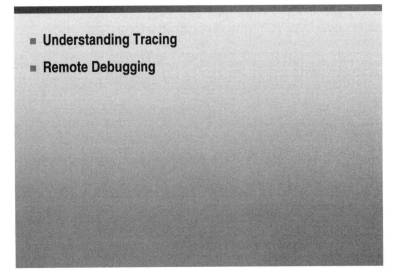

■ **Understanding Tracing**

■ **Remote Debugging**

Introduction

It is difficult, if not impossible, to catch every possible error in code when you first develop the Web application. Errors can either be compile-time errors or run-time errors. Compile-time errors are found by the Microsoft® Visual Studio® .NET compiler. To find runtime errors, you can use the Visual Studio .NET debugger, the **Trace** object, or the **Debug** object.

Objectives

After completing this module, you will be able to:

■ Use the **Trace** object to view runtime information about a Web application.

■ Use the **Debug** object to view runtime information about a Web application.

■ Debug applications remotely.

Lesson: Understanding Tracing

- ■ **Runtime Information**
- ■ **Enabling Tracing**
- ■ **Using the Trace Object**
- ■ **Viewing Trace Results**
- ■ **Using Application-Level Trace**
- ■ **Demonstration: Tracing Through a Web Application**
- ■ **Tracing into a Component**

Introduction

Tracing means receiving informative messages about the execution of a Web application at runtime. These informative messages from the running Web application can help diagnose problems or analyze performance.
Visual Studio .NET offers two objects that can be used for gathering such information during runtime: the **Debug** object and the **Trace** object.

Lesson objectives

After completing this lesson, you will be able to:

- ■ Identify the types of information that can be collected during runtime.
- ■ Use the **Debug** object to display runtime information in the Visual Studio .NET debugger.
- ■ Enable tracing on a Web Form.
- ■ Use the **Trace.Write** and **Trace.Warn** methods.
- ■ Use application-level tracing.
- ■ Interpret trace results.
- ■ Trace into a component.

Runtime Information

- **During runtime, you can:**
  - Output values of variables
  - Assert whether a condition is met
  - Trace through the execution path of the application
- **You can collect runtime information using:**
  - The **Trace** object
  - The **Debug** object

Introduction

You can collect information while your Web application is running by using the **Debug** and **Trace** objects.

Note If you want to refresh your debugging knowledge, see Appendix B, "Debugging with Microsoft Visual Studio .NET" at the end of the workbook.

Types of information

You can perform the following steps during runtime:

- Output values of variables.

- Determine whether certain conditions have been met. For example, there is a **Trace.WriteIf** method that only outputs a message if the condition is met.

- Follow the execution path of the application. You can follow the programming logic of a Web Form while it is executing to ensure that processing is occurring properly.

Runtime objects

There are two objects that you use for displaying debugging information during runtime. Those objects are:

- The **Trace** object. The **Trace** object in Microsoft ASP.NET enables you to display information on a Web page or save it in memory.

  In traditional ASP pages, you use **Response.Write** statements to track a Web application's progress. The advantage of using the **Trace** object over using **Response.Write** statements, or outputting debug information to labels on a Web Form, is that all of the tracing can be enabled or disabled by changing a single setting in the Web.config file. Therefore, you do not have to revise all of your code; you just remove the trace statements on a production server.

- The **Debug** object. You can also use the **Debug** object to output debugging information. Statements that use the **Debug** object will only run when they are compiled in debug mode and when the Web application is run in the debugger. If you create a release build, the statements will not run.

  With the **Debug** object, messages are displayed in the Output window of the debugger.

  When you use the **Debug** object to print debugging information and check your logic, you can make your code more stable without impacting the final product's performance or code size.

Note To use the **Debug** object, you need to import the **System.Diagnostics** namespace.

Enabling Tracing

- Page-level tracing displays trace statements only on the configured page
- Enabling page-level tracing

```
<%@ Page Language="vb" Trace="true" %>
```

```
<%@ Page Language="c#" Trace="true" %>
```

- Application-level tracing displays trace information for all pages in a Web application
- Enabling application-level tracing in the Web.config file

```
<trace enabled="true" pageOutput="true"
localOnly="true"/>
```

- Practice: Check default settings

Introduction

When you use tracing, you can write trace statements directly to the page or to a storage object.

Page-level tracing

When you use page-level tracing, all trace messages are appended to the end of the Web page, which allows you to quickly view trace messages at the same time that you are viewing the Web page.

To enable page-level tracing for a page, you set the **Trace** attribute of the @ **Page** directive to **true**, as shown in the following code:

```
<%@ Page Language="vb" Trace="true" %>
-or-
<%@ Page Language="c#" Trace="true" %>
```

After tracing is enabled, all **Trace.Write** statements in your code will appear on the page. When you are finished using trace, you can disable trace rather than removing all **Trace.Write** statements from your code.

Application-level tracing

When you enable application-level tracing, you enable tracing for all of the pages in the Web application. Application-level tracing also allows you more flexibility in writing trace statements. For example, with page-level tracing, all trace messages are appended to their page, whereas with application-level tracing, you can write trace messages to the page or to memory. Trace statements that are saved to memory are accessible by the application-level trace viewer, trace.axd.

To enable application-level tracing, you need to configure the Web.config file for the Web application, as shown in the following code:

```
<configuration>
  <system.web>
      <trace enabled="true"/>
  </system.web>
</configuration>
```

To configure trace messages to be written to the page, you use the **pageOutput** attribute of the **trace** element. A setting of **true** writes trace statements to each page. A setting of **false** writes trace statements to memory, where they are then accessible by the application-level trace viewer, trace.axd, as shown in the following code:

```
<trace enabled="true" pageOutput="true|false"/>
```

You can also set the **localOnly** attribute of the **trace** element to ensure that trace messages are only visible on the local computer, as shown in the following code:

```
<trace enabled="true" pageOutput="true" localOnly="true"/>
```

Practice (optional)

In Visual Studio .NET, open the benefits project. From Solution Explorer, double-click the **Web.config** file. What are the default settings for application-level tracing?

_____

_____

Using the Trace Object

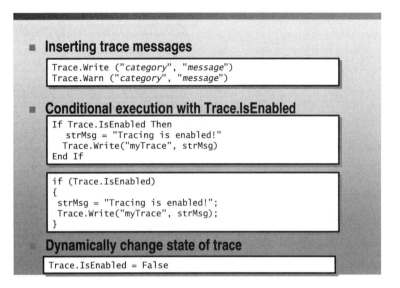

Inserting trace messages

```
Trace.Write ("category", "message")
Trace.Warn ("category", "message")
```

Conditional execution with Trace.IsEnabled

```
If Trace.IsEnabled Then
   strMsg = "Tracing is enabled!"
  Trace.Write("myTrace", strMsg)
End If
```

```
if (Trace.IsEnabled)
{
  strMsg = "Tracing is enabled!";
  Trace.Write("myTrace", strMsg);
}
```

Dynamically change state of trace

```
Trace.IsEnabled = False
```

Introduction

To write trace messages on a page (or in memory), you use the **Trace.Write** and **Trace.Warn** methods. You can use the **IsEnabled** property of the **Trace** object to dynamically change the state of tracing in a page.

Trace.Write and Trace.Warn

You use the **Write** and **Warn** methods of the **Trace** object to output trace messages. **Trace.Write** and **Trace.Warn** work exactly the same way, except that **Warn** writes trace messages in the color red.

When using the **Write** and **Warn** methods, you provide a message to be written, along with a corresponding category for the message, as shown in the following code:

Visual Basic .NET

```
Trace.Write ("category", "message")
Trace.Warn ("category", "message")
```

C#

```
Trace.Write ("category", "message");
Trace.Warn ("category", "message");
```

Note The category parameter is used to classify and group trace messages. For example, you can set the sort order of trace messages to display messages of the same category together.

Example using Write and Warn

The following code writes two trace messages to a page, with the second trace message appearing in red, because it is using the **Warn** method:

Visual Basic .NET

```
Trace.Write("Custom Trace", "Beginning User Code...")
Trace.Warn("Custom Trace", "Array count is null!")
```

C#

```
Trace.Write("Custom Trace", "Beginning User Code...");
Trace.Warn("Custom Trace", "Array count is null!");
```

The resulting trace messages appear as shown in the following illustration.

Trace.IsEnabled

There are situations when you may want to generate trace messages only when tracing is enabled for Web page or Web application. For these situations, the **Trace** object has a Boolean property named **IsEnabled** that allows you to call the **Write** and **Warn** methods only when tracing is enabled, as shown in the following code:

Visual Basic .NET

```
If Trace.IsEnabled Then
  strMsg = "Tracing is enabled!"
  Trace.Write("myTrace", strMsg)
End If
```

C#

```
if (Trace.IsEnabled)
{
   strMsg = "Tracing is enabled!";
   Trace.Write("myTrace", strMsg);
}
```

You can also use the **IsEnabled** property to dynamically change the state of tracing for a page, as show in the following code:

Visual Basic .NET

```
Trace.IsEnabled = False
```

C#

```
Trace.IsEnabled = false;
```

Viewing Trace Results

Introduction

Page-level trace results are appended to the bottom of the .aspx page for which they are enabled. An abundant amount of information is displayed in the trace results, along with the custom messages that you created with the **Trace.Write** and **Trace.Warn** statements.

Trace categories

There are several categories of information that are displayed in the trace results. The following table lists each category and the description of the type of information it contains.

Category	Description
Request Details	Information about the request: session identification (ID), time of request, type of request, and request status.
Trace Information	Output from standard and custom trace statements. The "From First(s)" column contains the total time since execution until the trace is executed, and the "From Last(s)" column displays the increment duration.
Control Tree	List of all of the items that are on the page, along with the size of each item.
Cookies Collection	List of cookies that are being used.
Headers Collection	List of items in the Hypertext Transfer Protocol (HTTP) header.
Form Collection	List of the controls, and their values, on the form that is being posted.
Server Variables	List of all the server variables and their values.

Using Application-Level Trace

Page	Application	Result
Trace=True	Trace=True or Trace=False	▪ Trace results are displayed on page
Trace=False	Trace=True or Trace=False	▪ Trace results are not displayed
Trace not set	Trace=True	▪ Trace results are displayed on page

▪ **Application-level trace statements are displayed on individual pages**

▪ **Set pageOutput=false in the Web.config file and trace results are viewable by trace viewer**

```
http://server/project/trace.axd
```

Introduction

For a Web application, you enable application-level tracing in the Web.config file. After application-level tracing is enabled, you can view trace statements on individual pages or in the trace viewer.

Trace settings

When you enable application-level tracing, the page-level trace settings remain in effect. For example, if you disable page-level tracing for a page, and that page is part of a Web application in which application-level tracing is enabled, tracing is disabled for that specific page. The following table shows possible combinations of enabling and disabling tracing and the corresponding result for that page.

Page setting	Application setting	Result for page
Trace=True	Trace=True or Trace=False	Trace results are displayed on the page.
Trace=False	Trace=True or Trace=False	Trace results are not displayed on the page.
Trace not set	Trace=True	Trace results are displayed on the page.

Displaying trace messages

You can display application-level trace messages in two places: on the page itself, or in the trace viewer. To determine how trace results are displayed, you set the **pageOutput** attribute of the **trace** element in the Web.config file. While a setting of **true** displays the results on the page, a setting of **false** keeps the trace messages in memory. The following code shows an example of disabling output to the page:

```
<configuration>
  <system.web>
      <trace enabled="true" pageOutput="false"/>
  </system.web>
</configuration>
```

If page output is disabled for application-level tracing, the trace messages are stored in memory. The trace messages can then be viewed by using the trace viewer, which is a Web page that is included with each Web application. You use the trace viewer by viewing the trace.axd page in a browser:

```
http://servername/projectname/trace.axd
```

For security reasons, you may want to disable the trace viewer. You can disable the trace viewer for a Web server by editing the machine.config file. The machine.config file is found in the following directory:

```
system folder\Microsoft.NET\Framework\version number\Config\
```

Within the machine.config file, the reference to trace.axd (the trace viewer) is in the httpHandlers section:

```
<httpHandlers>
  <add verb="*" path="trace.axd"
      type="System.Web.Handlers.TraceHandler"/>
</httpHandlers>
```

To disable the trace viewer, set the path attribute to an empty string (path="").

Tip   The **localOnly** attribute that is used for tracing in ASP.NET pages also applies to the trace.axd page. If **localOnly** is set to **true**, the trace.axd page can only be viewed from the local computer.

Demonstration: Tracing Through a Web Application

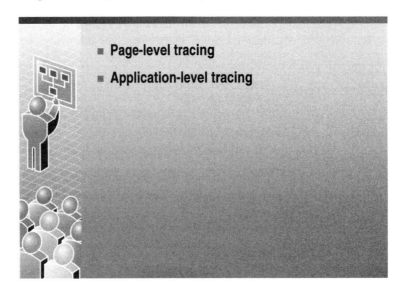

In this demonstration, you will see how to enable page-level and application-level tracing and to add trace statements to a Web Form.

To run the demonstration using Microsoft Visual Basic® .NET

1. In Visual Studio .NET, open the CallClassVB project in the 2310Demos solution.

2. In the CallClassVB project, turn tracing on in the CallClassLibraries.aspx page, by including the **Trace** attribute in the @ **Page** directive, as shown in the following code:

```
<%@ Page Language="vb" Trace="true"
  Codebehind="CallClassLibraries.aspx.vb"
  AutoEventWireup="false"
  Inherits="CallClassVB.CallClassLibraries" %>
```

Note Trace information shows up best on pages that are built with **flowLayout**. If a page is built with **gridLayout**, the trace messages show up behind the page content.

---

3. Add two custom trace messages to end of the **cmdUseVb_Click** event procedure in the CallClassLibraries.aspx.vb code behind page, as shown in the following code:

```
Trace.Write("UseVB", "price = " & CStr(TextBox1.Text))
Trace.Warn("UseVB", "shipping cost = " & CStr(sngShipping))
```

4. Build and browse the CallClassLibraries.aspx page.

    Trace information is shown on the page.

5. Enter a price, and then click **VB .NET Shipping Cost**.

    Point out the custom trace messages.

6. Disable tracing for the page, and then view the page again.

Note You do not have to rebuild the project because you did not change any code.

No trace messages are shown on the page.

7. Turn tracing on at the application level by editing the trace tag in the Web.config file. Set the **pageOutput** attribute to **true**, as shown in the following code:

```
<trace enabled="true" requestLimit="10" pageOutput="true"
    traceMode="SortByTime" localOnly="true" />
```

Notice that the **localOnly** attribute is set to **true**. This allows only local browsers to see trace information.

8. Refresh the view of the CallClassLibraries.aspx page and note that trace messages are not displayed because trace is explicitly turned off for this page.

9. Build and browse the VBForm.aspx page. These pages do not have tracing turned on, but the trace results show anyway because application-level tracing is turned on.

10. Have a student browse to the VBForm.aspx page on the instructor computer. They should not see the trace output because the **localOnly** attribute is set to **true**.

11. Add the following trace statement to the CSharpForm.aspx page in the **button1_onclick** event procedure:

```
Trace.Warn ("C#", "Value to double " + Textbox1.Text)
```

12. Build and browse the CSharpForm.aspx page. This page also does not have tracing turned on, but the trace results, including the custom message you just added, are shown anyway.

13. Change the trace tag in the Web.config to turn off **pageOutput**:

```
<trace enabled="true" pageOutput="false"/>
```

14. View the VBForm.aspx page in the browser. The trace output is not displayed on the page; instead, it is written to memory.

15. View the http://localhost/CallClassVB/trace.axd page to see the trace statements that were saved to memory.

To run the demonstration using C#

1. In Visual Studio .NET, open the CallClassCS project in the 2310Demos solution.

2. In the CallClassCS project, turn tracing on in the CallClassLibraries.aspx page, by including the **Trace** attribute in the @ **Page** directive, as shown in the following code:

```
<%@ Page Language="c#" Trace="true"
  Codebehind="CallClassLibraries.aspx.cs"
  AutoEventWireup="false"
  Inherits="CallClassCS.CallClassLibraries" %>
```

Note Trace information shows up best on pages that are built with **flowLayout**. If a page is built with **gridLayout**, the trace messages show up behind the page content.

---

3. Add two custom trace messages to end of the **cmdUseCSharp_Click** event procedure in the CallClassLibraries.aspx page, as shown in the following code:

```
Trace.Write("UseC#", "price = " +
  Convert.ToString(TextBox1.Text));
Trace.Warn("UseC#", "shipping cost = " +
  Convert.ToString(sngShipping));
```

4. Build and browse the CallClassLibraries.aspx page.

    Trace information is shown on the page.

5. Enter a price, and then click **C# Shipping Cost**.

    Point out the custom trace messages.

6. Disable tracing for the page, and then view the page again.

Note You do not have to rebuild the project because you did not change any code.

No trace messages are shown on the page.

7. Turn tracing on at the application level by editing the trace tag in the Web.config file. Set the **pageOutput** attribute to **true**, as shown in the following code:

```
<trace enabled="true" requestLimit="10" pageOutput="true"
  traceMode="SortByTime" localOnly="true" />
```

Notice that the **localOnly** attribute is set to true. This allows only local browsers to see trace information.

8. Refresh the view of the CallClassLibraries.aspx page and note that trace messages is not displayed because trace is explicitly turned off for this page.

9. Build and browse the VBForm.aspx page. These pages do not have tracing turned on, but the trace results are shown because application-level tracing is turned on.

10. Have a student browse to the VBForm.aspx page on the instructor computer. They should not see the trace output because the **localOnly** attribute is set to **true**.

11. Add the following trace statement to the VBForm.aspx page in the **button1_onclick** event procedure:

```
Trace.Warn ("VB", "Value to double " + Textbox1.Text);
```

12. Build and browse the VBForm.aspx page. This page also does not have tracing turned on, but the trace results, including the custom message you just added, show anyway.

13. Change the trace tag in the Web.config to turn off **pageOutput**:

```
<trace enabled="true" pageOutput="false"/>
```

14. View the VBForm.aspx page in the browser. The trace output is not displayed on the page; instead, it is written to memory.

15. View the http://localhost/CallClassCS/trace.axd page to see the trace statements that were saved to memory.

Tracing into a Component

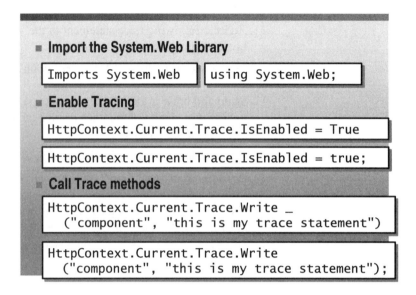

Introduction	If you have a component that is called from a Web Form, you can add trace statements to that component, which then allows you to generate trace messages for both the Web Form and the component.
Tracing in a component	To use trace in a component, you must import the **System.Web** namespace, enable tracing in the component, and then add the trace messages by using the **Write** and **Warn** methods.

To add trace to a component

1. At the top of the component, import the **System.Web** namespace:

Visual Basic .NET

```
Imports System.Web
```

C#

```
using System.Web;
```

2. In the constructor of the class to which you want to add trace statements, enable tracing with the following statement:

Visual Basic .NET

```
HttpContext.Current.Trace.IsEnabled = True
```

C#

```
HttpContext.Current.Trace.IsEnabled = true;
```

Because trace is attached to a page, you need to determine which page is running the component. In the preceding code, this is accomplished by using **HttpContext.Current**, which gets the **Context** object for the current request.

3. In the method in which you want to generate trace messages, use **Trace.Write** or **Trace.Warn**:

Visual Basic .NET

```
HttpContext.Current.Trace.Write _
    ("component", "this is my trace statement")
```

C#

```
HttpContext.Current.Trace.Write
    ("component", "this is my trace statement");
```

When trace is enabled in a component, trace results are written to any page that accesses the component, even if trace is disabled for that page.

The following table lists results of enabling or disabling trace on a page or in a component.

Component setting	Page setting	Result
Trace is enabled in the constructor	Trace disabled	Trace is enabled when calling all of the component methods.
Trace is enabled in a method	Trace disabled	Trace is enabled when calling only that one method.
Trace is disabled in the constructor	Trace enabled	Trace is disabled when calling the component methods.
Trace is not set in the component	Trace enabled	Trace is enabled when calling the component methods.

Important Trace messages in a component will appear in any trace-enabled page that calls the component if trace is not intentionally disabled in the component.

Lesson: Remote Debugging

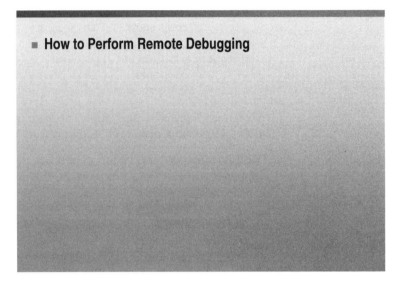

How to Perform Remote Debugging

Introduction

Debugging is generally used to catch errors during the creation of a Web application. Most debugging occurs locally; that is, you run the Visual Studio .NET debugger on the computer that hosts the Web application. Remote debugging enables you to debug a Web application running at a remote location. In this lesson, you will learn how to perform remote debugging.

Lesson objectives

After completing this lesson, you will be able to debug applications remotely.

How to Perform Remote Debugging

- **Remote debugging:**
  - Debug Web applications remotely
  - Simplifies team development
  - Simplifies Web site management
- **Requirements for remote debugging:**
  - Requires Visual Studio .NET or remote components on the server
  - Visual Studio .NET must be installed on the client
  - Requires administrative access to the server
  - Requires access for the user who is performing debugging

Introduction

Remote debugging is the process of debugging Web applications that are running on a separate server. Remote debugging enables you to debug Web applications on numerous disparate servers from a single workstation.

Requirements for remote debugging

For remote debugging to work, the following conditions must be met:

- Either Visual Studio .NET or the remote components of Visual Studio .NET must be installed on the server that hosts the Web application you want to debug.

- Visual Studio .NET must be installed on the client computer, which is the workstation from which debugging will occur.

- You must have administrative access to the server that hosts the Web application.

- The remote server must grant access to the user performing the debugging. To grant access to a user, you add the user to the **Debugger Users** group on the server. This permission is required even if the user is an administrator on the remote server.

Remote debugging procedure

▶ **To debug remotely**

1. On the client computer, start Visual Studio .NET.

2. On the **File** menu, click **Open**, and then click **Project From Web**.

3. In the **Open Project From Web** dialog box, type the Uniform Resource Locator (URL) of the server from which you want to open the project, and then click **OK**.

4. In the **Open Project** dialog box, navigate to the project on the remote server and click **Open**.

5. After you open the project, you can set breakpoints and run the Web application in debug mode, exactly as you would run a local application.

Note For more information about remote debugging, see "Debugging Web Applications on a Remote Server" and "Setting Up Remote Debugging" in the Microsoft .NET Framework software development kit (SDK).

Review

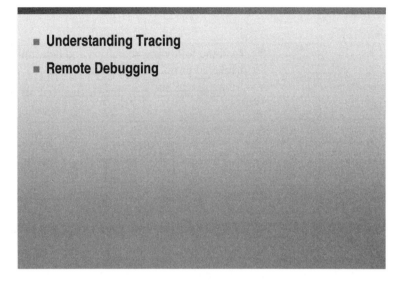

- Understanding Tracing
- Remote Debugging

1. What is the difference between using the **Trace** object and using the **Debug** object?

2. What is the difference between page-level tracing and application-level tracing?

3. How do you enable application-level tracing?

4. How do you configure trace so that trace information is visible only to local users of your Web site?

5. Read the following scenarios and determine whether trace messages will be displayed or not.

   a. Trace turned on in page1.aspx, but off in Web.config. View page1.aspx.

   b. Trace turned off in page1.aspx, but on in Web.config. View page1.aspx.

   c. Trace turned on in page1.aspx, but off in Web.config. View page2.aspx.

   d. Trace turned on in page1.aspx, and on in Web.config. View page2.aspx.

   e. Trace turned off in page1.aspx, but on in component A. View page1.aspx and click a button that calls component A.

   f. Trace turned on in page1.aspx, but off in component A. View page1.aspx and click a button that calls component A.

   g. Trace turned on in page1.aspx, and not explicitly set in component A. View page1.aspx and click a button that calls component A.

Lab 6: Tracing in Microsoft ASP.NET Web Applications

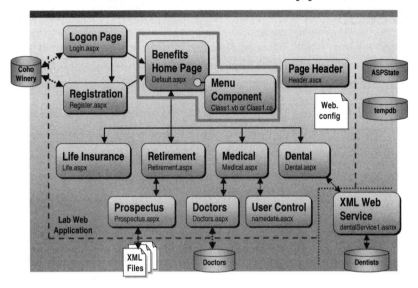

Objectives

After completing this lab, you will be able to:

- Add trace statements to a Microsoft® ASP.NET Web Form.
- Turn **Trace** on and off at the page and application level.
- Trace into a component.

Note This lab focuses on the concepts in this module and as a result may not comply with Microsoft security recommendations.

Prerequisites

Before working on this lab, you must have:

- Knowledge of how to build a class library.
- Knowledge of how to add a reference to a project.

ScenarioCoho Winery offers several benefits to its employees. In the labs for Course 2310B, *Developing Microsoft ASP.NET Web Applications Using Visual Studio .NET*, you will create a Web site that enables employees to select and set up their chosen benefits.

In this lab, you will trace through the execution of the Benefits Web application.

Estimated time to complete this lab: 30 minutes

Exercise 0
Lab Setup

To complete this lab, you must have created a Benefits Web Application project and a BenefitsList Class Library project. If you have not created these projects, complete the following steps:

▶ **Create the 2310LabApplication solution**

Important   Only perform this procedure if you have not created a 2310LabApplication solution file.

---

1. Using Microsoft Visual Studio® .NET, create a new blank solution named **2310LabApplication**:

   a. On the **File** menu, point to **New**, and then click **Blank Solution**.

   b. In the **New Project** dialog box, type **2310LabApplication** in the **Name** text box, and then click **OK**.

▶ **Create the Benefits project**

Important   Only perform this procedure if you have not previously created a Benefits project, or if you have removed the Benefits project according to the steps in Appendix A, "Lab Recovery," in Course 2310B, *Developing Microsoft ASP.NET Web Applications Using Visual Studio .NET*.

---

1. Create a new ASP.NET Web Application project, named **BenefitsVB** or **BenefitsCS**, in the 2310LabApplication solution:

   a. On the **File** menu, point to **New**, and then click **Project**.

   b. In the **New Project** dialog box, in the **Project Types** list, click **Visual Basic Projects** or **Visual C# Projects**.

   c. In the **Templates** list, click **ASP.NET Web Application**, and then set the **Location** to http://localhost/BenefitsVB for the **Visual Basic .NET** project or to http://localhost/BenefitsCS for the **Visual C#** project.

   d. Click **Add to Solution**, and then click **OK**.

Caution   When adding projects to the solution, the capitalization of the project name is important. Because you may be using some pre-built Web Forms in this and other labs in Course 2310B, *Developing Microsoft ASP.NET Web Applications Using Visual Studio .NET*, you must verify that you have capitalized the Benefits project as shown. Two versions of the project can be created; **BenefitsVB** would be a **Visual Basic .NET** solution and **BenefitsCS** would be a **Visual C#** solution.

▶ **Update the Benefits project**

1. In Visual Studio .NET, open the 2310LabApplication solution file.

2. In Solution Explorer, right-click **BenefitsVB** or **BenefitsCS**, point to **Add**, and then click **Add Existing Item**.

In the Microsoft Visual Basic .NET project

    a. Browse to the *install folder*\Labfiles\Lab06\VB\Starter\BenefitsVB folder for the Visual Basic .NET files.

    b. In the **Files of type** box in the **Add Existing Item – BenefitsVB** dialog box, click **All Files**.

In the Visual C# project

    a. Browse to the *install folder*\Labfiles\Lab06\CS\Starter\BenefitsCS folder for the Visual C# files.

    b. In the **Files of type** box in the **Add Existing Item – BenefitsCS** dialog box, click **All Files**.

3. Select all of the files in this folder, and then click **Open**.

4. Click **Yes** if prompted to overwrite or reload files.

▶ **Create the BenefitsList class library**

Important   Only perform these steps if you have not previously created a BenefitsList project, or if you have removed the BenefitsList project according to the steps in Appendix A, "Lab Recovery," in Course 2310B, *Developing Microsoft ASP.NET Web Applications Using Visual Studio .NET*.

---

1. Create a new Visual Basic .NET Class Library project, name it **BenefitsListVB** or **BenefitsListCS**, and then add it to the 2310LabApplication solution.

    a. On the **File** menu, point to **New**, and then click **Project**:

In the Visual Basic .NET project

      i. In the **New Project** dialog box, in the **Project Types** list, click **Visual Basic Projects**.

      ii. In the **Templates** list, click **Class Library**, and then set the **Name** to **BenefitsListVB**.

      iii. Click **Add to Solution**, and then click **OK**.

In the Visual C# project

      i. In the **New Project** dialog box, in the **Project Types** list, click **Visual C# Projects**.

      ii. In the **Templates** list, click **Class Library**, and then set the **Name** to **BenefitsListCS**.

      iii. Click **Add to Solution**, and then click **OK**.

Caution   Verify that you have capitalized the BenefitsListVB or BenefitsListCS project as shown.

▶ **Update the BenefitsList project**

1. In Visual Studio .NET, open the 2310LabApplication solution file.

2. In Solution Explorer, right-click **BenefitsListVB** or **BenefitsListCS**, point to **Add**, and then click **Add Existing Item**.

3. Copy the files from Labfiles folder:

In the Visual Basic .NET project

  a. Browse to the *install folder*\Labfiles\Lab06\VB\Starter\BenefitsListVB folder.

  b. In the **Files of type** box of the **Add Existing Item – BenefitsListVB** dialog box, click **All Files (*.*)**.

In the Visual C# project

  a. Browse to the *install folder*\Labfiles\Lab06\CS\Starter\BenefitsListCS folder.

  b. In the Files of type box of the Add Existing Item – BenefitsListCS dialog box, click All Files (*.*).

4. Select all of the files in this folder, and then click **Open**.

5. Click **Yes** if prompted to overwrite or reload files.

▶ **Create a reference to the BenefitsList component in the Benefits project**

1. In the Benefits project in the 2310LabApplication solution, complete the following steps to add a reference to the BenefitsList component that you just created:

  a. Right-click the **Benefits** project in Solution Explorer and then click **Add Reference**.

  b. In the **Add Reference** dialog box, on the **Projects** tab, double-click the **BenefitsListVB** or the **BenefitsListCS** project.

  c. In the **Selected Components** list, select the **BenefitsListVB** or the **BenefitsListCS** component, and then click **OK**.

  The component is added to the References folder in Solution Explorer.

Exercise 1
Using Trace Statements

In this exercise, you will enable and disable tracing and add custom messages to the trace output.

▶ **Enable tracing on a page**

1. In Visual Studio .NET, open the 2310LabApplication solution.

2. In the BenefitsVB or the BenefitsCS project, open the default.aspx file.

3. In the default.aspx page, switch to Hypertext Markup Language (HTML) view.

4. Modify the existing @ **Page** directive by adding a **Trace** attribute and setting its value to **true**.

   The @ **Page** directive should look like the following code, with the addition in bold font:

Visual Basic .NET
```
<%@ Page Language="vb" AutoEventWireup="false"
    Codebehind="default.aspx.vb"
    Inherits="BenefitsVB._default" Trace="true" %>
```

C#
```
<%@ Page Language="c#" AutoEventWireup="false"
    Codebehind="default.aspx.cs"
    Inherits="BenefitsCS._default" Trace="true" %>
```

5. Save default.aspx.

   You do not need to build the page because you did not change any of the code. Changes to the HTML only require you to save the page.

6. View the default.aspx page in the browser.

   The trace information appears at the bottom of the page.

▶ **Add custom trace messages**

1. Go to the beginning of the **Page_Load** event procedure for the default.aspx page, which is located in the default.aspx.vb or default.aspx.cs code-behind page. Add a trace message that displays the message **Beginning of Page_Load** in a category that is named **2310**.

   Your code should look like the following:

Visual Basic .NET
```
Trace.Warn("2310", "Beginning of Page_Load")
```

C#
```
Trace.Warn("2310", "Beginning of Page_Load");
```

2. In the **Page_Load** event procedure, immediately below the first trace message, add another trace message that displays the value of the **Page.IsPostBack** property.

   Your code should look like the following:

Visual Basic .NET
```
Trace.Warn("2310", "IsPostBack=" & Page.IsPostBack)
```

C#
```
Trace.Warn("2310", "IsPostBack=" + Page.IsPostBack);
```

3. Build and browse the default.aspx page.

    You should see your custom messages in the **Trace Information** section, as shown in the following illustration.

▶ **Use application-level tracing**

1. Open the life.aspx.vb or life.aspx.cs file in the BenefitsVB or the BenefitsCS project.

2. In the **Page_Load** event procedure, add a trace statement that you will easily recognize in the trace output. Using **2310** for the category will help you to find the trace statement.

3. Build and browse the life.aspx page.

    Is trace information displayed on the page? Why or why not.

    _____

    _____

4. Open the Web.config file for the Benefits project and locate the **trace** element.

5. List and define below the attributes that are set for the **trace** element. Use the Visual Studio .NET documentation to discover what the attributes are for.

   _____

   _____

6. In the Web.config file, enable application-level tracing by setting the **enabled** attribute of the **trace** element to **true**.

7. View the life.aspx page in the browser again.

   Is trace information displayed on the page? Why or why not.

   _____

   _____

8. In the Web.config file, set the **pageOutput** attribute of the **trace** element to **true**.

9. View the life.aspx page in the browser again.

   Is trace information displayed on the page? Why or why not.

   _____

   _____

   Why is the information displayed as it is?

   _____

   _____

Exercise 2
Tracing into a Component

In this exercise, you will add **Trace** statements to the BenefitsList component that is called from the default.aspx page.

▶ **Enable tracing in the BenefitsList component**

1. In the BenefitsList project, add a reference to the System.Web.dll by completing the following steps:

   a. In the BenefitsListVB or the BenefitsListCS project, right-click the References folder and then click **Add Reference**.

   b. In the **Add Reference** dialog box, on the **.NET** tab, in the list of components, double-click **System.Web.dll**, and then click **OK**.

2. Open Class1 file:

In the Visual Basic .NET project

In the BenefitsListVB project, open the Class1.vb file.

In the Visual C# project

In the BenefitsListCS project, open the Class1.cs file.

3. In the **GetBenefitsList** method, enable tracing by setting the **HttpContext.Current.Trace.IsEnabled** property to **True**.

   Your code should look like the following:

Visual Basic .NET

```
System.Web.HttpContext.Current.Trace.IsEnabled = True
```

C#

```
System.Web.HttpContext.Current.Trace.IsEnabled = true;
```

Note   You can also put the Trace.IsEnabled command in the constructor of the class if you need to use tracing in the whole component.

▶ **Add custom trace messages**

1. Add a custom trace message to the **GetBenefitsList** method that displays the message "Beginning of GetBenefitsList" in the category named **BenefitsList component**.

   Your code should look like the following:

Visual Basic .NET

```
System.Web.HttpContext.Current.Trace.Warn _
    ("BenefitsList component", _
    "Beginning of GetBenefitsList")
```

C#

```
System.Web.HttpContext.Current.Trace.Warn
    ("BenefitsList component",
    "Beginning of GetBenefitsList");
```

2. Add another trace message at the end of the procedure (but before the **Return** command) that displays the message "End of GetBenefitsList".

Your code should look like the following:

Visual Basic .NET

```
System.Web.HttpContext.Current.Trace.Warn _
    ("BenefitsList component", _
    "End of GetBenefitsList")
```

C#

```
System.Web.HttpContext.Current.Trace.Warn
    ("BenefitsList component",
    "End of GetBenefitsList");
```

▶ **Save and test**

1. Save your changes to the Class1 file, and the build the project.

2. View the default.aspx page in Microsoft Internet Explorer.

   You should see your custom messages from the page and from the component in the **Trace Information** section, as shown in the following illustration.

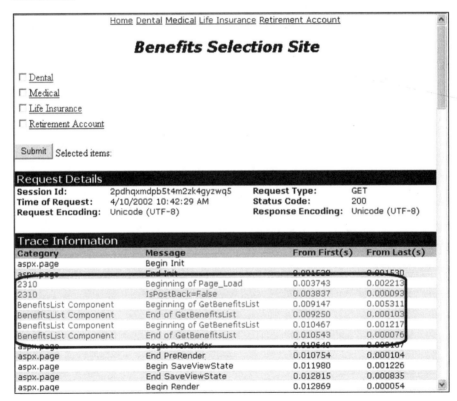

Why is the **GetBenefitsList** method called twice?

_____

_____

3. Open the header.ascx.vb or header.ascx.cs page.

4. In the **Page_Load** event procedure, add two **Trace.Warn** messages, both
   with a **Category** parameter of **Header**:

   a. Place one message at the beginning of the event procedure, and set its
      message text to **Start Header**.

   b. Place the second message at the end of the **Page_Load** event procedure,
      and set its message text to **End Header**.

   Your code should look like the following:

Visual Basic .NET
```
System.Web.HttpContext.Current.Trace.Warn _
   ("Header", "Start Header")
System.Web.HttpContext.Current.Trace.Warn _
   ("Header", "End Header")
```

C#
```
System.Web.HttpContext.Current.Trace.Warn
   ("Header", "Start Header");
System.Web.HttpContext.Current.Trace.Warn
   ("Header", "End Header");
```

5. Build and browse default.aspx.

   The trace information now includes two **Header** trace messages, one before
   and one after the second set of **BenefitsList Component** trace messages.

▶ **Disable tracing**

1. Disable application-level tracing in Web.config.

2. Disable page-level tracing in the default.aspx page.

3. Disable **Trace.Warn** messages in the header.aspx **Page_Load** event.

4. View the default.aspx page in the browser again.

   Is trace information displayed on the page? Why or why not?

   _____

   _____

   If trace information is displayed on the page, which custom trace messages
   are displayed? Why?

   _____

   _____

5. Remove or comment out the trace messages that you added in this lab, according to the following table.

Page	Code to remove
default.aspx.vb or default.aspx.cs	Two lines in the **Page_Load** event procedure.
life.aspx.vb or life.aspx.cs	One line in the **Page_Load** event procedure.
header.ascx.vb or header.ascx.cs	One line at the start of the **Page_load** event procedure, and one line at the end.
Class1.vb or Class1.cs	Three lines in the **GetBenefitsList** method.

You are removing these lines of code so that the pages do not look cluttered in future labs.

6. Rebuild both the Benefits (BenefitsVB or BenefitsCS) project and the BenefitsList (BenefitsListVB or BenefitsListCS) project.

7. Browse default.aspx to verify that trace messages are no longer displayed on the page.

msdn training

Module 7: Validating User Input

Contents

Overview

- ■ **Overview of User Input Validation**
- ■ **Using Validation Controls**
- ■ **Page Validation**

Introduction

When you create an input control, such as a **TextBox** control, you have expectations for the type of input that the user will enter into that control. Incorrect input will, at a minimum, delay the user, and may even break your Web application. To verify that the input meets your expectations, you must check the input against the value, range, or format that you expect to receive from the user. To create this check, you link at least one input validation control to the input control and then test the users input against your expectations.

In this module, you will learn about the input validation controls that are available in Microsoft® ASP.NET. You will also learn how to effectively apply these controls to an ASP.NET Web Form by using Microsoft Visual Studio® .NET.

Objectives

After completing this module, you will be able to:

- ■ Identify when input validation is appropriate in Web Forms.
- ■ Use input validation controls to verify user input on a Web Form.
- ■ Verify that all validation controls on a page are valid.

Lesson: Overview of User Input Validation

- What Is Input Validation?
- Client-Side and Server-Side Validation
- ASP.NET Validation Controls

Introduction

In this lesson, you will learn how input validation verifies that the user has correctly filled in input controls on a Web Form, before a request is processed on the server. You will also learn about the types of input validation controls that are available in ASP.NET.

Lesson objectives

After completing this lesson, you will be able to:

- Explain the concept of validation.
- Explain the difference between client-side and server-side validation.
- Match the appropriate types of ASP.NET validation controls for given input requirements.

What Is Input Validation?

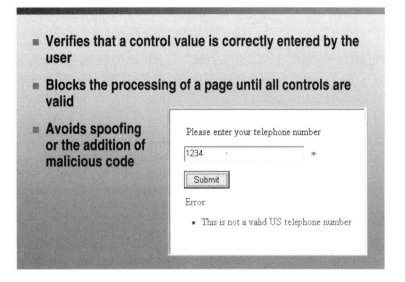

Introduction

Input validation is the process of verifying that a user's input on a Web Form matches the expected data value, range, or format. Input validation improves a user's experience with the Web site by reducing the wait time for error messages and the likelihood of incorrect returns or Web site crashes due to problems with the user's input. When combined with understandable and useful error messages, input validation controls can greatly improve the usability of a Web application, thereby improving the customer's perception of the Web site's overall quality.

Input validation controls act to verify that the user has correctly filled in an input control, such as a **TextBox** control, before the request is processed on the server. The input validation controls on a Web Form act as data filters before the page or server logic is processed.

In ASP.NET, input validation always runs on the server side, and can run on the client side, if the client browser supports validation. If the browser supports client-side validation, the input validation controls do error checking on the client before posting the data to the server. The user receives immediate feedback on whether the data that he or she entered is valid or not. For security reasons, any input validation that is run on the client side is then repeated on the server side.

Verify control values

Input validation works by comparing user input against a predetermined input format. These predetermined input formats may include the number of characters, the use of digits and/or letters, the value range, a specific character string, or a mathematical formula.

For example, a user input control that requests the user to enter his or her telephone number could have an attached input validation control that verifies that the user has only entered numbers in a telephone number format. Entering letters or too few numbers would trigger the input validation control to validate the input.

Errors block processing   User input that matches the predetermined format is processed by the Web Form. User input that does not match the predetermined format triggers an error message and stops the Web Form from processing. Further processing of the page is blocked until the user input is corrected to meet the expected format and the page has been resubmitted for processing.

Spoofing and malicious code   Validation controls protect Web Forms against two main dangers: spoofing and malicious code. By running all validation controls on the server side, regardless of client-side validation, ASP.NET protects against these threats:

- Spoofing

  Spoofing is when a user modifies the Hypertext Markup Language (HTML) page that is sent to him or her, and then returns values that make it appear that he or she has entered valid data or passed an authorization check. Validation is only susceptible to spoofing on the client side, because the user can turn off client-side script by changing browser options and not run the client-side validation code, which creates a false level of authorization.

  With ASP.NET, client-side input validation is always repeated on the server side, where users cannot modify or disable the validation control.

- Malicious code

  When a user can add unlimited text to a Web page through user input controls that do not have input validation, they may enter malicious code. When the user sends the next request to the server, this added code could be very disruptive to the Web server and any connected applications.

  For example, if you decided not to validate a **UserName** field because you have international customers and could not think of a universal name format to validate against, a malicious user could exploit this lack of validation to cause a number of problems, including:

  - Creating a buffer overrun and crashing the server by entering a name with several thousand characters.

  - Creating and authenticating a new user account.

  - Adding privileges to their own account, and removing privileges from other accounts.

  - Sending an SQL Query to your customer database and downloading all of the data that is present, including user names, addresses, passwords, and credit card numbers.

Client-Side and Server-Side Validation

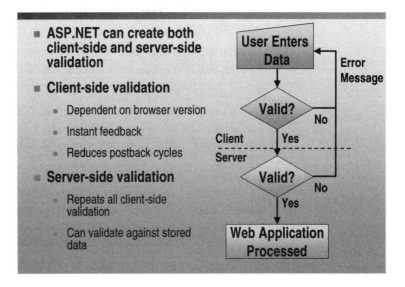

Introduction	Input validation can take place on both the server and the client. Although server-side validation is always required by ASP.NET, client-side validation is an option with some browsers.

Input validation can take place on both the server and the client. Although server-side validation is always required by ASP.NET, client-side validation is an option with some browsers.

The validation controls in ASP.NET have both client-side and server-side support. Client-side validation uses JavaScript and dynamic HTML (DHTML) scripts. Server-side validation can be written in any Microsoft .NET-based language, and it is compiled into Microsoft intermediate language (MSIL). Both client-side and server-side validation use the same programming model, although variations between languages may create minor differences in the validation functions.

Client-side validation

Client-side validation enhances the usability of the Web Form by checking user input as the user enters data. By checking for errors when data is being entered, client-side validation allows errors to be detected on the client before the Web Form is submitted, thereby preventing the round trip that is necessary for server-side validation.

Writing multiple versions of validation code to support both the server and several different browsers can be extremely time-consuming for developers. ASP.NET validation controls eliminate this problem because the validation logic is encapsulated within the controls. The controls create browser-specific code so that users with client-side script support will have client side input validation. Browsers that do not support scripts will not receive client-side validation scripts.

In browser versions that support input validation, such as Microsoft Internet Explorer 4 or later, client-side validation occurs when the user clicks the **Submit** button. The page will not be posted back to the server until all client-side validation is true. In Internet Explorer 5 or later, using the TAB key to move from one input control to the next runs the client-side validation for the completed input control. This validation by using the TAB feature gives the user immediate feedback on their input.

Server-side validation   All input validation controls run on the server side. Client-side validations are repeated on the server side when the page is posted back to the server. This repetition avoids spoofing by users who bypass the client-side script and try to use invalid input.

Server-side validation controls can be written in any .NET-based language, and are compiled into MSIL before being run on the server.

In addition to validating input format, server-side validation controls can be used to compare user input with stored data. This ability to compare user input with stored data allows validation against a variety of items, such as stored passwords and geographic restrictions, including local laws and taxes.

ASP.NET Validation Controls

ASP.NET provides validation controls to:

- Compare values
- Compare to a custom formula
- Compare to a range
- Compare to a regular expression pattern
- Require user input
- Summarize the validation controls on a page

Validation controls

The ASP.NET page framework includes the validation controls that are shown in the following table.

Validation control	Function
CompareValidator	Compares an input control to another input control, a fixed value, a data type, or a file. For example, this control can be used for password verification fields.
CustomValidator	Allows you to write your own code to create the validation expression. For example, this control can be used to verify that the input value is a prime number.
RangeValidator	Similar to the **CompareValidator** control, but this control can verify that the user input is between two values or the values of other input controls. For example, this control can be used to verify that the user matches the expected age range.
RegularExpression Validator	Verifies that the entry matches a pattern that has been defined by a regular expression. This validation control allows you to check for predictable sequences of characters, such as those in social security numbers, e-mail addresses, telephone numbers, and postal codes. Visual Studio .NET provides pre-defined patterns for common expression such as telephone numbers.
RequiredFieldValidator	Checks whether a value has been entered into a control. This is the only validation control that requires a value. All of the other input validation controls will accept an empty control as a valid response.
ValidationSummary	Displays a summary of all of the validation errors for all of the validation controls on the page. This control is typically placed near the **Submit** button to provide immediate feedback on the page input status.

Lesson: Using Validation Controls

- Adding Validation Controls to a Web Form
- Positioning Validation Controls on a Web Form
- Combining Validation Controls
- Input Validation Controls
- Using the RegularExpressionValidator Control
- Demonstration: Using Validation Controls
- Using the CustomValidator Control
- Demonstration: Using the CustomValidator Control

Introduction

In this lesson, you will learn how to apply input validation controls to user input controls on an ASP.NET Web Form.

Validating user input used to be difficult process. For each input control, you first had to write validation code for the server in one language. Then, if you were going to do client-side validation, you had to write the equivalent client-side validation for each expected browser in a different script. ASP.NET and Visual Studio .NET have made validating user input easier by providing input validation controls that provide server-side and client-side code when you add them to your Web Form.

Lesson objectives

After completing this lesson, you will be able to:

- Add a validation control to a Web Form and associate that validation control with an input control.
- Position validation controls on a Web page to support the correct use of the associated input control.
- Use the **RequiredInputValidator**, **CompareValidator**, and **RangeValidator** validation controls to validate user input.
- Use the **RegularExpressionValidator** control to validate user input.
- Use the **CustomValidator** control to validate user input.
- Associate multiple input validation controls to a single input control.

Adding Validation Controls to a Web Form

1. **Add a validation control**
2. **Select the input control to validate**
3. **Set validation properties**

```
<asp:TextBox id="txtName" runat="server" />
```

```
<asp:Type_of_Validator
   id="Validator_id"
   runat="server"
   ControlToValidate="txtName"
   ErrorMessage="Message_for_error_summary"
   Display="static/dynamic/none"
   Text="Text_to_display_by_input_control">
</asp:Type_of_Validator>
```

Introduction

Because all of the input validation controls share a common object model, the process of adding validation controls to a page is the same for all of the controls. In Visual Studio .NET, you simply drag the input validator control onto the page, select the input control to validate, and then set the properties.

Add a validation control

To add a validation control, open the **Web Forms** toolbox, select one of the available validation controls, and then drag the validation control next to the input control that you want to validate.

Select the input control to validate

You select the input control to validate by opening the Properties window and selecting the appropriate input control ID from the drop-down list that is next to the **ControlToValidate** property. You can attach multiple validation controls to a single input control. All of the attached validation controls must evaluate as **True** before that input control is accepted and the ASP.NET Web Form can be processed.

Set validation properties

After the input validation control is placed on the page, use the Properties window to enter the control-specific properties, such as the validation expression, error message, and text message.

The shared syntax for input validation controls is as follows:

```
<asp:type_of_validator id="validator_id" runat="server"
   ControlToValidate="control_id"
   ErrorMessage="error_message_for_error_summary"
   Display="static/dynamic/none"
   Text="Text_to_display_by_input_control">
</asp:type_of_validator>
```

Each validation control has additional unique properties that define how the control will perform. Two of the properties that are shared with all validation controls, with the exception of the **ValidationSummary** control, are **Type** and **EnableClientScript**:

- **Type**

  The **Type** property is the data type that will be validated.
  Visual Studio .NET will automatically adjust the data type to match the attached input control when you select the **ControlToValidate**.

  Available data types include String, Integer, Double, Date, and Currency.

- **EnableClientScript**

  The **EnableClientScript** property indicates whether to perform client-side validation. This property is set to true by default.

  ASP.NET creates client-side validation procedures in Microsoft JScript® .NET, and creates server-side validation procedures in C# and Microsoft Visual Basic® .NET. This language difference can lead to minor differences between the client-side and server-side validation control implementations.

Positioning Validation Controls on a Web Form

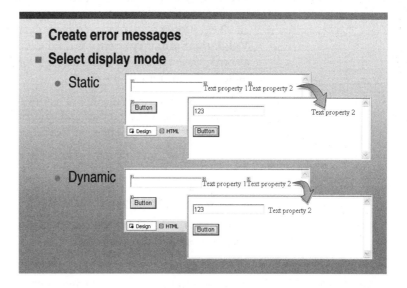

Introduction

Input validation controls can display an error message when an input violation has occurred. It is important to position input validation controls so that it is clear to the user which control has the incorrect input. In Visual Studio .NET, you must position the validation control on the page where the error message text should appear.

The standard HTML for an input validation control is as follows:

```
<asp:type_of_validator id="validator_id" runat="server"
  ControlToValidate="control_id"
  ErrorMessage="error_message_for_error_summary"
  Display="static|dynamic|none"
  Text="Text_to_display_by_input_control">
</asp:type_of_validator>
```

Error messages

ASP.NET input validation controls contain two error message properties, an **ErrorMessage** property and a **Text** property, both of which can be displayed at the location of the input validation control. The distinction between these two error message properties is:

■ **ErrorMessage** property

The **ErrorMessage** property is the error message that is displayed at the location of a validation control when the validation control is triggered, if the **Text** property is not set. This message will also be included in a **ValidationSummary** control if one is used on the Web Form.

■ **Text** property

The **Text** property is the alternative text that will be displayed at the location of the validation control when both the **ErrorMessage** property and **Text** property are used, and the validation control is triggered. If a **ValidationSummary** control is used to collect error messages, a red asterisk (*) is typically used to the right of the invalid input control to indicate the location of the error.

In Visual Studio .NET, the default script for the **Text** property is to print the **Text** content between the start and stop tags of the validation control, as shown in the following code:

```
<asp:type_of_validator...>Text</asp:type_of_validator>
```

Throughout this module, you will see the Text property explicitly declared, as shown in the following code:

```
<asp:type_of_validator...Text="Text">
</asp:type_of_validator>
```

Setting the Display property

The **Display** property sets the spacing of error messages from multiple validation controls when the Web Form is displayed in **FlowLayout**. The **Display** property only affects error messages at the validation control location. Messages that are displayed in the **ValidationSummary** are not affected by the **Display** property.

The following table describes the **Display** property options.

Options	Description
Static	Defines a fixed layout for the error message, causing each validation control to occupy space, even when no error message text is visible. This option allows you to define a fixed layout for the page as shown on the preceding illustration.
	Visual Studio .NET, by default, uses **Display="static"** to position the error message text.
Dynamic	Enables validation controls to render in the page as part of the text flow. Using this option prevents blank spaces from being displayed on the page when input validation controls are not triggered, as shown in the preceding illustration. This option sometimes causes controls to move on the Web Form when error messages are displayed.
None	Blocks the display of the error message at the location of the validation control.

Combining Validation Controls

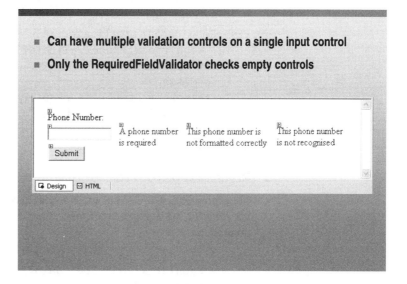

Introduction	Sometimes a single validation function or control is not sufficient to verify that the user has correctly entered data into an input control.

For example, a telephone number **TextBox** control may require an input, must conform to one of several telephone number patterns, and must be checked against a stored telephone number database. In this scenario, the **TextBox** would need to be linked to a **RequiredFieldValidator** control, a **RegularExpressionValidator** control with several patterns, and a **CustomValidator** control with access to a database.

Multiple validation controls on a single input control

You can associate multiple validation controls to a single input control. This many-to-one association of validation controls allows you to check the user's input for more than one validation requirement.

Example

The following code example shows a single input control for a telephone number. The input control is checked for content by using a **RequiredFieldValidator** control, and checked for correct format by using a **RegularExpressionValidator** control:

- Input control

  The following code defines the **TextBox** control that is being validated:

```
<asp:TextBox id="txtPhone1" runat="server" >
</asp:TextBox>
```

- **RequiredFieldValidator** control

   The following code defines the **RequiredFieldValidator** control that verifies that there is an input in **txtPhone1**:

```
<asp:RequiredFieldValidator
   id="RequiredtxtPhone1Validator1"
   runat="server"
   ErrorMessage=
   "A telephone number is required"
   ControlToValidate="txtPhone1"
   Text="*">
</asp:RequiredFieldValidator>
```

- **RegularExpressionValidator** control

   The following code defines the **RegularExpressionValidator** control that verifies that the input in **txtPhone1** matches the United States telephone number pattern:

```
<asp:RegularExpressionValidator
   id="RegulartxtPhone1Validator1"
   runat="server"
   ErrorMessage=_
   "This telephone number is not formatted correctly"
   ControlToValidate="txtPhone1"
   ValidationExpression=
   "((\(\d{3}\) ?)|(\d{3}-))?\d{3}-\d{4}"
   Text="*">
</asp:RegularExpressionValidator>
```

- **CustomValidator** control

   The following code defines the **CustomValidator** control that calls the function **MyServerValidation**, which compares the input in **txtPhone1** with a database of telephone numbers:

```
<asp:CustomValidator
   id="CustomValidator1"
   OnServerValidate = "MyServerValidation"
   runat="server"
   ErrorMessage="This telephone number is not recognized"
   ControlToValidate="txtPhone1"
   Text="*">
</asp:CustomValidator>
```

Input Validation Controls

- **RequiredFieldValidator**
  - InitialValue
- **CompareValidator**
  - **ValueToCompare** or **ControlToCompare**
  - Type
  - Operator
- **RangeValidator**
  - MinimumValue
  - MaximumValue
  - Type

Code Examples

Introduction

The simplest validation controls are the **RequiredFieldValidator**, **CompareValidator**, and **RangeValidator** controls. All of these validation controls validate against fixed values or a second input control.

RequiredFieldValidator control

Use the **RequiredFieldValidator** control to force a user to provide input in an input control. Any character is a valid response with this validation control. Only no input (blank), or spaces, is invalid input with this control.

The **RequiredFieldValidator** control is typically used only on input controls that are required to complete a requested process. For example, a **RequiredFieldValidator** control would be used for the **username** and **password** fields on a sign-in page, but not for incidental information, such as an offer to become a preferred Web site visitor.

An option for the **RequiredFieldValidator** control is to have an initial value that is not an empty string (blank). It is useful to have an initial value when you have a default value for an input control and you want the user to enter a different value. To require a change to the initial value for the associated input control, set the **InitialValue** property to match the initial value of the input control.

In the following example, a **RequiredFieldValidator** control verifies that the **TextBox** control **txtName** value is not the initial value of **Enter your name**:

```
<asp:TextBox id="txtName" runat="server">
Enter your name</asp:TextBox>

<asp:RequiredFieldValidator id="txtNameValidator"
  runat="server"
  ControlToValidate="txtName"
  InitialValue="Enter your name"
  ErrorMessage="You must enter your name"
  Display="dynamic"
  Text="*">
</asp:RequiredFieldValidator>
```

Note Only the **RequiredFieldValidator** control requires that a value be entered into a control. The other validator controls will accept an empty control or a space as a valid response.

Using the CompareValidator control

Use the **CompareValidator** control to test the user's input against a specific value, or against a second input control. The **CompareValidator** control is often used where the risk of typographic errors is high, such as password fields that do not show the users actual input.

The **CompareValidator** control will evaluate an empty input control as valid.

The **CompareValidator** control uses the following properties:

- **ValueToCompare**

  Use the **ValueToCompare** property to reference against a constant value. Use the pipe character (|) to separate multiple values. This property is best used to validate against unchanging values, such as a minimum age limit. Use the **CustomValidator** control to compare against values that are likely to change.

- **ControlToCompare**

  Use the **ControlToCompare** property to identify another control to compare against. This property can be used to check for typographic errors by having the user enter the same data in two adjacent fields.

  If you set both the **ValueToCompare** and **ControlToCompare** properties, the **ControlToCompare** property takes precedence.

- **Type**

  The **Type** property is used to specify the data type. Use this property if you want to compare the value in an input control against a **DataType**.

- **Operator**

  The **Operator** property specifies the comparison operator to use. Operators are specified with the name of the comparison operators, such as **Equal**, **NotEqual**, **GreaterThan**, and **GreaterThanEqual**.

In the following example, a **CompareValidator** control verifies that the values of the **TextBox** controls, **txtPassword1** and **txtPassword2**, match:

```
<asp:TextBox id="txtPassword1" runat="server">
Enter your password </asp:TextBox>

<asp:TextBox id="txtPassword2" runat="server" >
Enter your password again </asp:TextBox>

<asp:CompareValidator id="CompareValidator1" runat="server"
  ErrorMessage="These fields do not match"
  ControlToCompare="txtPassword1"
  ControlToValidate="txtPassword2"
  Text="*">
</asp:CompareValidator>
```

Using the RangeValidator control

The **RangeValidator** control is used to test whether an input value is within a given range. The range measured is inclusive and the minimum and maximum values are considered valid. The **RangeValidator** control is typically used to verify that the value entered (for example: age, height, salary, or number of children) matches an expected range.

The **RangeValidator** control will evaluate an empty input control as valid.

The **RangeValidator** control has the following properties:

- **MinimumValue**

  The **MinimumValue** property specifies the minimum value of the valid range for numeric variables, or the minimum character length of the string for string variables.

- **MaximumValue**

  The **MaximumValue** property specifies the maximum value of the valid range for numeric variables, or the maximum character length of the string for string variables.

- **Type**

  The **Type** property is used to specify the data type of the values to compare. The values to compare are converted to this data type before any comparison is performed.

In the following example, a **RangeValidator** control verifies that the **TextBox** named **txtAge** has a value between 18 and 50:

```
<asp:textbox id="txtAge" runat="server">
Enter your age</asp:textbox>
<asp:RangeValidator id="txtAgeValidator" runat="server"
  ControlToValidate="txtAge"
  Type="Integer"
  MinimumValue="18"
  MaximumValue="50"
  ErrorMessage="Applicants must be between 18 and 50"
  Display="dynamic"
  Text="*">
</asp:RangeValidator>
```

Using the RegularExpressionValidator Control

- **Used when input must conform to a pre-defined pattern**

- **Visual Studio .NET includes patterns for:**

  - Telephone numbers

  - Postal codes

  - E-mail addresses

```
<asp:RegularExpressionValidator …
    ControlToValidate="US_PhoneNumber"…
    ValidationExpression="((\(\d{3}\) ?)|(\d{3}-))?\d{3}-\d{4} "
    …>*</asp:RegularExpressionValidator >
```

Code Example

Introduction

When you must verify that a user's input matches a pre-defined pattern, such as a telephone number, postal code, or e-mail address, you must use the **RegularExpressionValidator** control. This validation control compares the pattern of characters, digits, and symbols entered by the user with one or more patterns in the control.

When you click **ValidationExpression** in the Properties window, Visual Studio .NET provides a set of preset regular expression patterns. These patterns include e-mail and Web site addresses, telephone numbers, and postal codes. To create a new pattern, select the **Custom** template. The last pattern that was used will then be available for editing. This *last used* feature gives you a foundation from which to create your own pattern.

Regular expression characters

You build your own custom regular expressions by using the set of control characters that are shown on the following table.

Character	Definition
a	Must use the letter a in lower case. Any letter that is not preceded by a backslash (\), or part of a range, is a requirement for that literal value.
1	Must use the number 1. Any number that is not preceded by a backslash (\), or part of a range, is a requirement for that literal value.
?	0 or 1 item.
*	0 to N items.
+	1 to N items (at least 1).
[0-n]	Integer value range from 0 to n.
{n}	Length must be n characters.
|	Separates multiple valid patterns.
\	The following character is a command character.
\w	Must have a character.
\d	Must have a digit.
\.	Must have a period.

Note For more information about control characters, see "Introduction to Regular Expressions," in the online *JScript reference*.

Example of a simple expression

The following code example shows how you can use a **RegularExpressionValidator** control to check whether a user has entered a valid e-mail address:

```
<asp:TextBox id="txtEmail" runat="server" />

<asp:RegularExpressionValidator id="txtEmail_validation"
  runat="server"
  ControlToValidate="txtEmail"
  ErrorMessage="Use the format username@organization.xxx"
  ValidationExpression="\w+@\w+\.\w+"
  Text="*">
</asp:RegularExpressionValidator>
```

This **RegularExpression** validation control checks for a specific pattern, as shown in the following table.

Characters	Definition
\w+	A string of at least one character.
@	An at sign (@).
\w+	A string of at least one character.
\.	A period.
\w+	A string of at least one character.

A valid e-mail address for this control is: someone@example.com.

An invalid e-mail address for this control is: someone.com, or someone@.com.

Example of a complex expression

The default Visual Studio .NET e-mail regular expression is more complex than the preceding example. The default e-mail pattern also limits the separation of terms before and after the at sign (@) to xx.xx or xx-xx.

The default regular expression for e-mail addresses is as follows:

```
\w+([-+.]\w+)*@\w+([-.]\w+)*\.\w+([-.]\w+)*
```

This **RegularExpression** validation control checks for a specific pattern, as shown in the following table.

Characters	Definition
\w+	A string of at least one character.
([-+.]\w+)*	May have one or more hyphens or a period, and a string of at least one character.
@	An at sign (@).
\w+	A string of at least one character.
([-.]\w+)*	May have a hyphen or period, and a string of at least one character.
\.	A period.
\w+	A string of at least one character.
([-.]\w+)*	May have a hyphen or period, and a string of at least one character.

A valid e-mail address for this control is: some-one@example.company.com.

An invalid e-mail address for this control is:
some,one@example..company.com.

Demonstration: Using Validation Controls

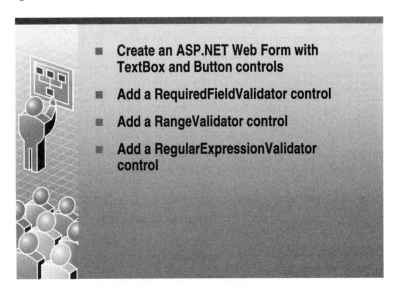

- **Create an ASP.NET Web Form with TextBox and Button controls**
- **Add a RequiredFieldValidator control**
- **Add a RangeValidator control**
- **Add a RegularExpressionValidator control**

In this demonstration, you will see how a **RequiredFieldValidator** control can be used to verify that a **TextBox** control is filled in before a Web Form is processed.

▶ **To run this demonstration**

Create an ASP.NET Web Form with TextBox and Button controls

1. Create a new Web application project named **ValidationTst1**.

2. Switch to **FlowLayout**.

3. Drag the following Web Controls from the Toolbox to the WebForm1: a **TextBox** and a **Button**.

Add a RequiredFieldValidator control

4. Add a **RequiredFieldValidator** control next to the **TextBox** input control.

5. Set the properties of the **RequiredFieldValidator** control in the Properties window, as shown in the following table.

Property	Value
ControlToValidate	TextBox1
ErrorMessage	Summary error message
Text	An input is required

6. Show that the property **Display** of the **RequiredFieldValidator** is set to **Static** by default.

7. Save, build and browse the page.

8. Leave the control blank and click the **Button1**.

   Notice that you get the **Text** error message, and not the **ErrorMessage** message.

Add a RangeValidator control

9. Add a **RangeValidator** control to the Web Form next to the **RequiredFieldValidator**.

10. Set the properties of the **RangeValidator** control in the Properties window, as shown in the following table.

Property	Value
ControlToValidate	TextBox1
ErrorMessage	Summary error message
Text	Out of range
MaximumValue	100
MinimumValue	16
Type	Integer

11. Save, build and browse the page.

12. Leave the value blank and click the **Button**.

    You should get the message **An input is required** from the **RequiredFieldValidator** control.

13. Type a value greater than 100 or less than 16, and then click the **Button**. You should get the text message **Out of range** from the **RangeValidator** control.

    Notice that the text message **Out of range** is not directly next to the input control. Because the page is in static display mode, the **RequiredFieldValidator** control holds a space for its text message.

14. Reopen the Web Form, select the **RequiredFieldValidator** control and change the property **Display** to **Dynamic**.

15. Save, build and browse the page.

16. Enter a value greater than 100 or less than 16, and then click the **Button**. You should get the text message **Out of range** from the **RangeValidator** control.

    Notice that this time the text message **Out of range** is directly next to the input control because the **RequiredFieldValidator** does not hold the space for its text message (dynamic display mode).

Add a second TextBox and a RegularExpression Validator control

17. Add a second **TextBox** control and a **RegularExpressionValidator** control next to it.

18. Right-click the **RegularExpressionValidator** control and click **Properties**, or click the **RegularExpressionValidator** control if the Properties window is still open, and enter the following properties:

    a. In the **ErrorMessage** property, type **Invalid E-mail address!**

    b. In the **ControlToValidate** property, select **TextBox2**.

    c. In the ValidationExpression property, select Internet E-mail Address.

19. Save, build and browse the page.

    Type an incorrect e-mail address in the second textbox and then click the **Button**. You should get the Text message **Invalid E-mail address!** from the **RegularExpressionValidator** control.

20. Select **View Source** and show the client-side validation HTML.

Using the CustomValidator Control

- **Can validate on client-side, server-side, or both**
  - **ClientValidationFunction**
  - **OnServerValidate**
- **Validate with:**
  - Formula
  - Data
  - COM objects
  - Web Service

Code Example

Introduction

Use the **CustomValidator** control when you want to use your own customized validation logic to check the user's input against a variable, formula, or input from a second source. The **CustomValidator** control is often used for situations, such as password verification, in which the user's input is compared with a password that is stored in a user database.

Client-side and server-side validation

The **CustomValidator** control validates on the server side, and it can validate on the client side if the browser supports validation. Unlike the other validation controls, where ASP.NET creates the client and server validation scripts, you must write the validation scripts for the **CustomValidator** control. You set the **CustomValidator** control as valid or invalid by using the **args.IsValid** property.

Properties of the **CustomValidator** control include:

- **ClientValidationFunction**

  The **ClientValidationFunction** property is the script that you want the **CustomValidator** control to run on the client side. Because you write your own client script, it is important to check for logical consistency with the server-side code.

- **OnServerValidate**

  The **OnServerValidate** property is the script that you want the **CustomValidator** to run on the server side. Because you write your own server code, it is important to check for logical consistency with the client-side script.

Example

The following code example shows the server-side and client-side procedures for a **CustomValidator** control and will verify that a number entered into an input control is even:

```
<asp: CustomValidator…
  ClientValidationFunction = "MyClientFunction"
  OnServerValidate = "MyServerFunction" />
```

- **Client-side procedure**

  The following JScript code is designed to run on Internet Explorer 6, and will verify that a number is even:

  ```
  <script language = "Jscript">
  function MyClientFunction(source, arguments) {
     alert("I am running on the client! ");
     var intValue = arguments.Value;
     if (intValue % 2 == 0) {
         arguments.IsValid = true;
         } else {
         arguments.IsValid = false;
     }
  }
  </script>
  ```

- **Server-side procedure**

  The following code is designed to run on a .NET server, and will verify that a number is even:

Visual Basic .NET

```
Sub MyServerFunction(objSource as Object, _
   args as ServerValidateEventArgs)
   Dim intValue As Integer = args.Value
   If intValue mod 2 = 0 Then
       args.IsValid = True
   Else
       args.IsValid = False
   End If
End Sub
```

C#

```
private void MyServerFunction(object objSource,
   ServerValidateEventArgs args)
{
   int intValue = Convert.ToInt16(args.Value);
   if (intValue%2 == 0)
   {
       args.IsValid = true;
   }
   else
   {
       args.IsValid = false;
   }
}
```

Demonstration: Using the CustomValidator Control

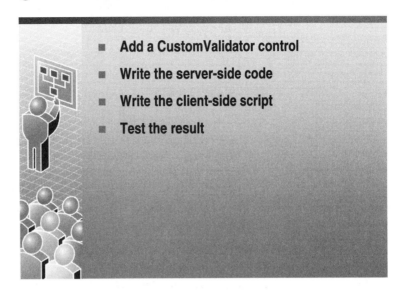

- Add a CustomValidator control
- Write the server-side code
- Write the client-side script
- Test the result

Introduction

In this demonstration, you will see how to use a **CustomValidator** control.

The starting code for this demonstration is in the Mod07VB or Mod07CS project within the 2310Demos solution.

▶ **To run this demonstration**

1. Open the Web Form named **CustomValidator.aspx** in Visual Studio .NET.

   The Web Form already has a **TextBox** and a **Button** control.

Add a CustomValidator control

2. Add a **CustomValidator** control to the Web Form.

3. In the **Text** property of the **CustomValidator** control, type **It's an odd number**.

4. Set the **ControlToValidate** property to **TextBox1**.

Write the server-side code

5. Double-click the CustomValidator to open the server-side event procedure and add the following code:

Visual Basic .NET

```
Dim intValue As Integer = args.Value
If intValue mod 2 = 0 Then
    args.IsValid = True
Else
    args.IsValid = False
End If
```

C#

```
int intValue = Convert.ToInt16(args.Value);
if (intValue % 2 == 0)
{
   args.IsValid = true;
}
else
{
   args.IsValid = false;
}
```

The server-side event procedure that was automatically created by Visual Studio .NET should have the name **CustomValidator1_ServerValidate**, and have two parameters: source (type **Object**) and args (type **ServerValidateEventArgs**).

Write the client-side script

6. In the ClientValidationFunction property of the CustomValidator control, type MyClientValidation.

7. Open the HTML source of the page CustomValidator.aspx (and not CustomValidator.aspx.vb).

8. Uncomment the following code that is located just after the <head> tag. This example is in JScript:

```
function MyClientValidation(source, arguments)
{
   alert("I am running on the client! ");
   var intValue = arguments.Value;
   if (intValue % 2 == 0)
   {
      arguments.IsValid = true;
      } else {
      arguments.IsValid = false;
   }
}
```

Test the result

9. Verify that the target browser is Internet Explorer 5.

   Right-click **CustomValidator.aspx** in Design view or HTML view, select **Properties**, and then verify that **Target Schema** is set to **Internet Explorer 5.0**.

10. Set the **EnableClientScript** property of the **CustomValidator** control to **True**.

   The client-side script will run before the server-side code to avoid the server round trip with the page if this property is set to **True** and the client browser is Internet Explorer 4 or later.

11. Build and browse **CustomValidator.aspx**.

12. Type a number into the text box.

13. You should get the message box **I am running on the client!** when you click the **Button**. In addition, you should get the message **It's an odd number** when the number is odd.

14. Set the **EnableClientScript** property of the **CustomValidator** control to **False**, so that only the server-side code will run.

15. Build and browse the page.

16. Now you should not get the message box because you are running the server-side code. However, you should still get the message **It's an odd number** when the number is odd.

Lesson: Page Validation

- Using the Page.IsValid Property

- Using the ValidationSummary Control

- Demonstration: Using the Page.IsValid Property and the ValidationSummary Control

---

Introduction

In this lesson, you will learn how to use the **Page.IsValid** property and the **ValidationSummary** control to verify that all validation controls on an ASP.NET Web Form are valid before processing is initiated.

Lesson objectives

After completing this lesson, you will be able to:

- Use the **Page.IsValid** property to determine if all input validation controls on a page are valid.

- Use the **ValidationSummary** control to display a summary of error messages on a page.

Using the Page.IsValid Property

```
Polls all validation controls

Sub cmdSubmit_Click(s As Object, e As EventArgs)
  If Page.IsValid Then
        Message.Text = "Page is valid!"
        ' Perform database updates or other logic here
  End If
End Sub
```

```
private void cmdSubmit_Click(object s, System.EventArgs e)
{ if (Page.IsValid)
    {     Message.Text = "Page is Valid!";
        // Perform database updates or other logic here
    }
}
```

Introduction

.NET enables you to verify that all of the controls on a page are valid before the controls perform some action. This verification of validity can be conducted on either the client or the server, depending on the browser being used. Client-side verification is done with the **ValidationSummary** control, while server-side verification is done with the **Page.IsValid** property.

Using the Page.IsValid property

To determine whether all of the validation controls on a page are currently valid, you check the **IsValid** property of the page at run time. The **IsValid** property rolls up the values of all the validation controls that are on the page (using a logical AND). If any one validation control is not valid, the **IsValid** property returns **False**. This property provides a simple way to determine whether the input controls on the Web Form are valid and whether the Web Form is ready to proceed with business logic.

Validation controls test user input, set an error state, and produce error messages. However, validation controls do not change the flow of page processing. For example, validation controls do not bypass your code if they detect a user input error. Instead, you test the state of the controls in your code before performing application-specific logic. If you detect an error, you prevent your own code from running; the page will continue to process and is returned to the user with error messages.

Note   Validation information is not available during a page's initialization or load stage. For details about page states, see "Web Forms Page Processing Stages," in the Visual Studio .NET documentation.

Example

The following example shows the event handler for a button. The code tests the **IsValid** property of the entire page. Note that there is no need for an **Else** clause, because the page will be returned automatically to the browser and the validation controls will display their own error messages:

Visual Basic .NET

```
Sub cmdSubmit_Click (s As Object, e As EventArgs)
    If Page.IsValid Then
        Message.Text = "Page is valid!"
        ' Perform database updates or other logic here
    End If
End Sub
```

C#

```
private void cmdSubmit_Click(object s, System.EventArgs e)
{
  if (Page.IsValid)
  {
      Message.Text = "Page is Valid!";
      // Perform database updates or other logic here
  }
}
```

Using the ValidationSummary Control

- Collects error messages from all validation controls on the page
- Can display text and error messages
- Use Text="*" to indicate the location of the error

```
<asp:ValidationSummary id="valSummary"
  runat="server"
  HeaderText="These errors were found:"
  ShowSummary="True"
  DisplayMode="List"/>
```

Introduction

The **ValidationSummary** control displays when the **Page.IsValid** property returns **False**. Each of the validation controls on the page is polled and the **ErrorMessage** messages are aggregated by the **ValidationSummary** control.

Displays text and error messages

The **ValidationSummary** control can display a message box or a text area, with a header and a list of errors, depending on the value of the **DisplayMode**, you can display the error list as a bulleted list or a single paragraph. **ValidationSummary** controls are typically placed near the **Submit** button so that all of the error messages will be highly visible to the user when the input validation controls are triggered.

The following HTML shows a typical **ValidationSummary** control:

```
<asp:ValidationSummary id="valSummary"
  runat="server"
  HeaderText="These errors were found:"
  ShowSummary="True"
  DisplayMode="List" />
```

Using * to locate errors

When the **ValidationSummary** control is used, the **Text** property (if used) is displayed at the location of the validation control, while the **ErrorMessage** property is displayed in the **ValidationSummary** control display.

A **Text** property with a red asterisk (*)is typically displayed to the right of the input control to warn the user that the input control is not correctly filled in. An **ErrorMessage** property, with a description of the input error, is displayed in the **ValidationSummary** control, which is typically placed near the event that is triggering the control.

Example

The following illustration shows a pair of password fields with several input validation controls and a **ValidationSummary** control.

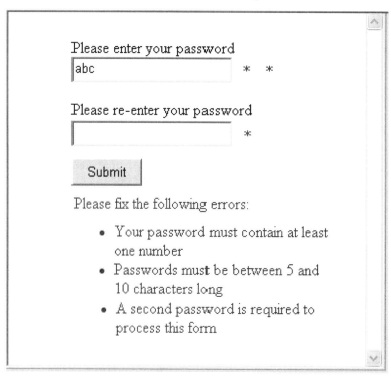

Demonstration: Using the Page.IsValid Property and the ValidationSummary Control

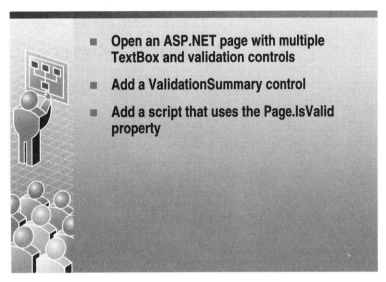

- Open an ASP.NET page with multiple TextBox and validation controls
- Add a ValidationSummary control
- Add a script that uses the Page.IsValid property

Introduction

In this demonstration, you will see how to use the **Page.IsValid** method and the **Validation Summary** control.

The files for this demonstration are in the Mod07VB or Mod07CS project in the 2310Demos solution.

▶ **To run this demonstration**

Open an ASP.NET page

1. Open the Web Form named **ValidationSummary.aspx** in Visual Studio .NET.

   The page already contains two **TextBox** controls. There is a **RequiredFieldValidator** and a **RangeValidator** control, which validate the first text box. The page also contains a **RequiredFieldValidator** control and a **RegularExpressionValidator** control, which validate the second text box. In addition, there is a **Submit** button and a **Label**.

Add a Validation Summary control

2. Drag a **ValidationSummary** control to the bottom of the page.

Add code to test the validity of the page

3. Double-click the **Button** control to open the **Click** event handler, and then uncomment the following code:

Visual Basic .NET

```
If Page.IsValid Then
    lblMessage.Text = "Page is valid!"
End If
```

C#

```
if (Page.IsValid)
{
    lblMessage.Text = "Page is valid!";
}
```

4. Save, build and browse the ValidationSummary.aspx page.

   You should see the message **Page is valid!** when the entire page is valid.

Review

- Overview of User Input Validation
- Using Validation Controls
- Page Validation

For the following questions, you will select the type of validation control(s) that should be used for each scenario.

The types of validation controls available for a Web Form include:

- **CompareValidator**
- **CustomValidator**
- **RangeValidator**
- **RegularExpressionValidator**
- **RequiredFieldValidator**
- **ValidationSummary**

▶ **Given the following user input fields, what kind of validation control(s) would you use?**

1. The user's age.

2. The user's telephone number.

3. The user's password, which is entered twice.

4. Whether an entered number is prime.

5. Whether all of the fields in a form are correctly filled in.

6. Whether the date format is correct.

7. Whether a new employee's requested e-mail address matches the company policy.

Lab 7: Validating User Input

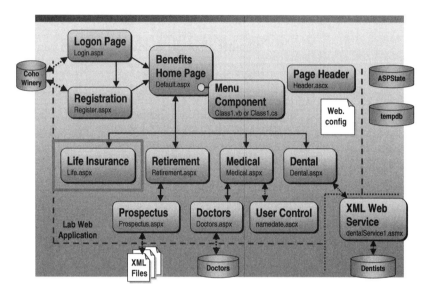

After completing this lab, you will be able to:

- Use validation controls to validate text box values in a Microsoft® ASP.NET Web Form.

- Use a **ValidationSummary** validation control to summarize validation errors on a Web Form.

Note   This lab focuses on the concepts in this module and as a result may not comply with Microsoft security recommendations.

Prerequisites

Before working on this lab, you must have:

- Knowledge of how to add Web controls to an ASP.NET Web Form.

- Knowledge of how to write a client-side Microsoft Visual Basic® Scripting Edition (VBScript) function.

- Knowledge of how to create an event procedure for a Web control.

ScenarioCoho Winery offers several benefits to its employees. In the labs for Course 2310B, *Developing Microsoft ASP.NET Web Applications Using Visual Studio .NET*, you will create a Web site that enables employees to select and set up their chosen benefits.

The Benefits Web application has a Web Form named life.aspx. This page is used for the life insurance benefit, and asks for a Name, a Birth date, and a Coverage amount from the user. In this lab, you will add validation controls to validate the entries in these text fields. You will also add a summary validation control to summarize the invalid entries on the page.

Estimated time to complete this lab: 15 minutes

Exercise 0
Lab Setup

To complete this lab, you must have created a Benefits Web Application project and a BenefitsList Class Library project. These projects may be created by using Visual Basic .NET or Microsoft Visual C#™ .NET.

If you have not created these projects, complete the following steps.

▶ **Create the 2310LabApplication solution**

Important Only perform this procedure if you have not created a 2310LabApplication solution file.

1. Using Microsoft Visual Studio® .NET, create a new blank solution named **2310LabApplication**:

   a. On the **File** menu, point to **New**, and then click **Blank Solution**.

   b. In the **New Project** dialog box, type **2310LabApplication** in the **Name** text box, and then click **OK**.

▶ **Create the Benefits project**

Important Only perform this procedure if you have not previously created a Benefits project, or if you have removed the Benefits project according to the steps in Appendix A, "Lab Recovery," in Course 2310B, *Developing Microsoft ASP.NET Web Applications Using Visual Studio .NET*.

1. Create a new ASP.NET Web Application project, named **BenefitsVB** or **BenefitsCS**, in the 2310LabApplication solution:

   a. On the **File** menu, point to **New**, and then click **Project**.

   b. In the **New Project** dialog box, in the **Project Types** list, click **Visual Basic Projects** or **Visual C# Projects**.

   c. In the **Templates** list, click **ASP.NET Web Application**. Set the **Location** to **http://localhost/BenefitsVB** for the Visual Basic .NET project or to **http://localhost/BenefitsCS** for the Visual C# .NET project.

   d. Click **Add to Solution**, and then click **OK**.

Caution When adding projects to the solution, the capitalization of the project name is important. Because you may be using some pre-built Web Forms in this and other labs in Course 2310B, *Developing Microsoft ASP.NET Web Applications Using Visual Studio .NET*, you must verify that you have capitalized the Benefits project as shown.

► **Update the Benefits project**

1. In Visual Studio .NET, open the 2310LabApplication solution file.

2. In Solution Explorer, right-click **BenefitsVB** or **BenefitsCS**, point to **Add**, and then click **Add Existing Item**.

For the Visual Basic .NET project

Browse to the *install folder*\Labfiles\Lab07\VB\Starter\BenefitsVB folder

For the Visual C# project

Browse to the *install folder*\Labfiles\Lab07\CS\Starter\BenefitsCS folder

3. In the **Files of type** box of the **Add Existing Item – Benefits** dialog box, click **All Files (*.*)**.

4. Select all of the files in this folder, and then click **Open**.

5. Click **Yes** if prompted to overwrite or reload files.

► **Create the BenefitsList class library**

Important   Only perform these steps if you have not previously created a BenefitsList project, or if you have removed the BenefitsList project according to the steps in Appendix A, "Lab Recovery," in Course 2310B, *Developing Microsoft ASP.NET Web Applications Using Visual Studio .NET*.

---

1. Create a Class Library project.

For the Visual Basic .NET project

Create a new Visual Basic .NET Class Library project, name it **BenefitsListVB**, and then add it to the 2310LabApplication solution:

a. On the **File** menu, point to **New**, and then click **Project**.

b. In the **New Project** dialog box, in the **Project Types** list, click **Visual Basic Projects**.

c. In the **Templates** list, click **Class Library**. Set the **Name** to **BenefitsListVB**.

d. Click **Add to Solution**, and then click **OK**.

For the Visual C# project

Create a new Visual C# .NET Class Library project, name it **BenefitsListCS**, and then add it to the 2310LabApplication solution:

a. On the **File** menu, point to **New**, and then click **Project**.

b. In the **New Project** dialog box, in the **Project Types** list, click **Visual C# Projects**.

c. In the **Templates** list, click **Class Library**. Set the **Name** to **BenefitsListCS**.

d. Click **Add to Solution**, and then click **OK**.

Important   Verify that you have capitalized the BenefitsList project as shown.

▶ **Update the BenefitsList project**

1. In Visual Studio .NET, open the 2310LabApplication solution file.

2. In Solution Explorer, right-click **BenefitsListVB** or **BenefitsListCS**, point to **Add**, and then click **Add Existing Item**.

3. Browse to the BenefitsList project.

For the Visual Basic .NET project

Browse to the *install folder*\Labfiles\Lab07\VB\Starter\BenefitsListVB folder.

For the Visual C# project

Browse to the *install folder*\Labfiles\Lab07\CS\Starter\BenefitsListCS folder.

4. In the Files of type box of the Add Existing Item – BenefitsList dialog box, click All Files (*.*).

5. Select all of the files in this folder, and then click **Open**.

6. Click **Yes** if prompted to overwrite or reload files.

▶ **Create a reference to the BenefitsList component in the Benefits project**

1. In the Benefits project in the 2310LabApplication solution, complete the following steps to add a reference to the BenefitsList component that you just created:

   a. Right-click the **BenefitsVB** or **BenefitsCS** project in Solution Explorer and then click **Add Reference**.

   b. In the **Add Reference** dialog box, on the **Projects** tab, double-click the **BenefitsListVB** or **BenefitsListCS** project.

   c. In the **Selected Components** list, select the **BenefitsListVB** or **BenefitsListCS** component, and then click **OK**.

   The component is added to the References folder in Solution Explorer.

Exercise 1
Using RequiredFieldValidator Controls

In this exercise, you will add **RequiredFieldValidator** controls for the **Name**, **Birth Date**, and **Coverage** text boxes on the life.aspx ASP.NET Web Form.

▶ **Add RequiredFieldValidator controls**

1. Open the life.aspx page in the Benefits project in the 2310LabApplication solution.

2. Using a drag-and-drop operation, place three **RequiredFieldValidator** controls onto the Web Form such that your form looks like the following illustration.

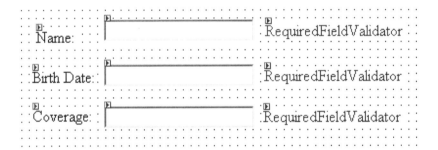

3. Set the properties of the three **RequiredFieldValidator** controls by using the values that are shown in the following table.

ID	Error Message	Text	ControlToValidate
vldName	Name cannot be blank	*	**txtName**
vldBirth	Birth date cannot be blank	*	**txtBirth**
vldCoverage	Coverage cannot be blank	*	**txtCoverage**

When you change the **Text** property of the controls, you will change the text that appears in Design view. Your page should now look like the following illustration.

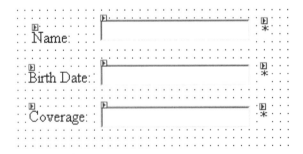

4. Build and browse the life.aspx page.

5. In the browser, leave the **Name**, **Birth Date**, and **Coverage** fields blank and then click **Save**.

    What happens and why?

    _____

    _____

6. In the browser, enter values for the **Name**, **Birth Date**, and **Coverage** fields and then click **Save**.

    What happens and why?

    _____

    _____

Exercise 2
Using the ValidationSummary Control

In this exercise, you will use a **ValidationSummary** control to summarize the validation errors for the life.aspx page.

▶ **Add a ValidationSummary control to the life.aspx page**

1. Using a drag-and-drop operation, place a **ValidationSummary** control onto the bottom of the life.aspx Web Form and set its **ID** property to **vldSummary**.

2. Set the **HeaderText** property of the **vldSummary** control to These errors were found:

   Your page should look like the following illustration.

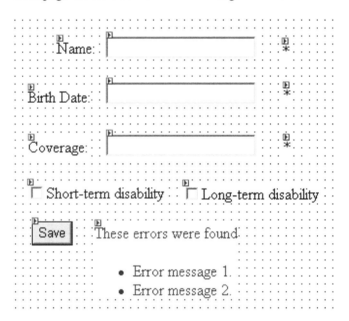

3. Build and browse the life.aspx page.

4. In the browser, leave the **Name**, **Birth Date**, and **Coverage** fields blank and then click **Save**.

   In addition to the red asterisk appearing next to the invalid entries, you now should see a summary of errors at the bottom of the page.

5. Where did the summary error messages come from?

   _____

   _____

▶ **Test if the page is valid**

1. Add a **Label** control to the bottom of the Web Form and set the control's **ID** property to **lblMessage** and then clear the default value of its **Text** property.

    Your page should look like the following illustration.

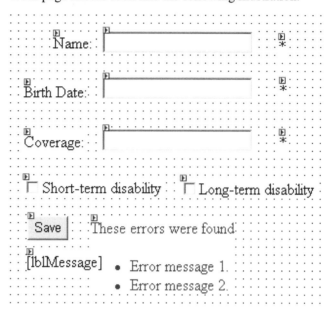

2. Open the **Click** event procedure for the **Save** button.

3. Modify the event procedure code to test if the controls on the page are valid, and, if they are, write a message in the **lblMessage** control indicating that the page is valid.

    Your code should look like the following:

Visual Basic .NET

```
If Page.IsValid Then
    lblMessage.Text = "The page is valid"
End If
```

C#

```
if (Page.IsValid)
{
    lblMessage.Text = "The page is valid";
}
```

4. Build and browse the life.aspx page.

5. In the browser, enter values for the **Name**, **Birth Date**, and **Coverage** fields and then click **Save**.

    Verify that the message **The page is valid** appears.

Exercise 3
Using the CompareValidator Control

In this exercise, you will use a **CompareValidator** control to validate the user entry into the **Birth Date** text field.

▶ **Add a CompareValidator control**

1. Using a drag-and-drop operation, place a **CompareValidator** control onto the life.aspx Web Form, next to the **vldBirth RequiredFieldValidator** control.

2. Set the properties for the **CompareValidator** control as shown in the following table.

Property	Value
ErrorMessage	Birth date format is invalid
Text	*
ControlToValidate	txtBirth
Operator	DataTypeCheck
Type	Date
ID	vldBirthType

Your page should look like the following illustration.

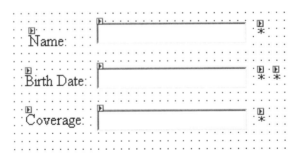

3. Build and browse the life.aspx page.

4. Enter an invalid date, such as **14/3/02** (month 14 is wrong here), in the **Birth Date** field, and then click **Save**.

   The red asterisk next to the **Birth Date** field should appear.

5. Enter a valid date, such as **12/3/02**, in the **Birth Date** field, and then click **Save**.

   The red asterisk next to the **Birth Date** field should now disappear.

Exercise 4
Using the RegularExpressionValidator Control

In this exercise, you will use a **RegularExpressionValidator** control to validate the user entry in the **Coverage** text field.

▶ **Add a RegularExpressionValidator control**

1. Using a drag-and-drop operation, place a **RegularExpressionValidator** control onto the life.aspx Web Form, next to the **vldCoverage RequiredFieldValidator** control.

2. Set the properties for the control as shown in the following table.

Property	Value
ErrorMessage	Coverage must be a currency value
Text	*
ControlToValidate	txtCoverage
ValidationExpression	\ d + (\ . \ d { 2 }) ?
ID	vldCoverageType

Your page should look like the following illustration.

3. What are the valid entries for the **Coverage** field?

_____

_____

4. Build and browse the life.aspx page.

5. Enter an incorrect value, such as **333.3,** into the **Coverage** field, and then click **Save**.

The red asterisk next to the **Coverage** field should appear.

6. Enter a correct value, such as **3.33**, into the **Coverage** field, and then click **Save**.

The red asterisk next to the **Coverage** field should now disappear.

msdn training

Module 8: Creating User Controls

Contents

Overview

- ■ **Adding User Controls to an ASP.NET Web Form**
- ■ **Creating User Controls**

In addition to Hypertext Markup Language (HTML) and Web server controls, you can easily create your own controls that can be reused across Web applications. These controls are called user controls. User controls provide an easy way to reuse common user interface (UI) components and code across a Web application.

Objectives

After completing this module, you will be able to:

- ■ Add a user control to a Microsoft® ASP.NET Web Form.
- ■ Create a user control.

Lesson: Adding User Controls to an ASP.NET Web Form

- **What is a User Control?**
- **Why Use User Controls?**
- **Practice: Listing User Controls**
- **Adding a User Control**
- **Demonstration: Creating a User Control**

Introduction

A user control is an ASP.NET page that can be imported as a server control by other ASP.NET Web Forms. Similar to Web server controls, which are components that run on the server, user controls provide UI and other related functionality. After you have created a user control, it can then be used by other pages in the same Web application.

In this lesson, you will learn what user controls are, why you should consider using them in your Web applications, how to reference a user control from an ASP.NET Web Form, and then learn how to access the properties in a user control.

Lesson objectives

After completing this lesson, you will be able to:

- Explain what a user control is and why you might use one.
- Add a user control in an ASP.NET page.
- Access user control properties in an ASP.NET page.

What is a User Control?

- **User controls simplify the reuse of code and UI components within a Web application**

- **A user control is a user-defined Web server control with an .ascx extension**

- **Contains HTML, but not the <HTML>, <BODY>, or <FORM> tags**

```
<%@ Control Language="vb" %>
```

or

```
<%@ Control Language="c#" %>
```

- **Contains code to handle its own events**

Introduction

Because user controls can simplify the reuse of code and common UI components, understanding what they are and how they work is an important part of learning about ASP.NET development.

Definition

User controls are ASP.NET pages with an .ascx file extension. User controls offer you an easy way to partition and reuse common UI functionality across your ASP.NET Web applications. Similar a Web Forms page, you can author these controls with any text editor, or develop them by using code-behind classes. Also, similar to a Web Forms page, user controls are compiled when first requested and then stored in server memory to reduce the response time for subsequent requests. Unlike Web Form pages, however, user controls cannot be requested independently; user controls must be included in a Web Forms page to work.

Note The Microsoft .NET Framework prevents files with the .ascx file extension from being viewed in a Web browser. This is a security measure that ensures that the user control cannot be viewed as a stand-alone ASP.NET page.

What is in a user control?

A user control consists of HTML and code, but because user controls are used by Web Forms, they do not contain the <HEAD>, <BODY>, or <FORM> HTML tags. Instead, these tags are included in each Web Form that uses the user control.

When a user control is used by a Web Form, the user control participates in the event life cycle for the Web Form. Also, because a user control is an ASP.NET page, it has its own page logic. For example, a user control can handle its own postback in its **Page_Load** event procedure.

Note User controls are different from custom server controls. To learn more about creating custom server controls, see "Developing ASP.NET Server Controls" in the Microsoft Visual Studio® .NET documentation.

User controls and their associated code-behind pages

Just as Web Forms have code-behind pages, user controls also have an associated code-behind page. The @ **Page** directive is used in Web Forms to associate a code-behind page, whereas the @ **Control** directive is used to reference a code-behind page from a user control page. The @ **Control** directive can only be used with user controls, and you can only include one @ **Control** directive per .ascx file. For example, to reference a code-behind page for a user control that is named WebUserControl1, in a Web application project named test, you use the following @ **Control** directive:

Visual Basic .NET

```
<%@ Control Language="vb" Codebehind="WebUserControl1.ascx.vb"
Inherits="test.WebUserControl1" %>
```

C#

```
<%@ Control Language="c#" Codebehind="WebUserControl1.ascx.cs"
Inherits="test.WebUserControl1" %>
```

Note The @ **Control** directive supports the same attributes as the @ **Page** directive, except for the **AspCompat** and **Trace** attributes. Because the @ **Control** directive does not use the **Trace** attribute, you must add the **Trace** attribute to the @ **Page** directive for the .aspx page that calls the user control, if you want to enable tracing for the user control.

User control vs. Web server control

A user control is not same as a Web server control. Web server controls include not only form-type controls, such as buttons and text boxes, but also include specific controls such as a calendar.

Note For more information about Web server controls, see Module 4, "Creating a Microsoft ASP.NET Web Form," in Course 2310B, *Developing Microsoft ASP.NET Web Applications Using Visual Studio .NET.*

Why Use User Controls?

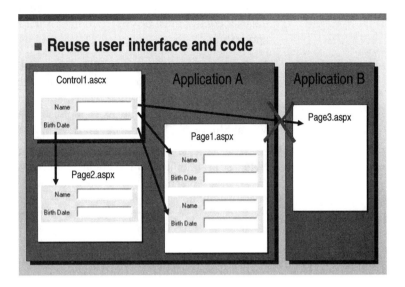

Introduction

There are several advantages to using user controls in your ASP.NET Web applications. User controls are self-contained, can be used multiple times, and can be written in a different language from the main hosting page.

Advantages to using user controls

User controls are used for numerous purposes, such as creating headers and navigation bars, and for repeating blocks of code in a Web application project.

Note In traditional Active Server Pages (ASP) Web pages, **include** files are used for code and UI reuse. In ASP.NET, user control pages replace the functionality of **include** files.

User controls offers many advantages when developing a Web application:

- User controls are self-contained. User controls provide separate variable namespaces, which means that none of the methods and properties of the user control conflict with any existing methods or properties of the hosting page.

- User controls can be used more than once within a hosting page, without causing property and method conflicts.

- User controls can be written in a different language from the main hosting page. For example, a user control that is written in Microsoft Visual C# can be used on a Web Form that is written in Microsoft Visual Basic® .NET.

Sharing user controls

A single user control can be shared amongst all pages within a Web application. However, .aspx pages in one Web application cannot host a user control from another Web application. To use a user control in multiple Web applications, the user control must be copied to the virtual root folder of each Web application.

To share controls amongst multiple Web applications, you can also create a Web custom control, which acts like a shareable user control. Web custom controls are more difficult to create than user controls, because, unlike user controls, Web custom controls cannot be created by using the visual tools of Visual Studio .NET; therefore, all development is done by code only.

Note For more information about user controls and Web custom controls, see "Web User Controls and Web Custom Controls" in the Visual Studio .NET documentation.

Practice: Listing User Controls

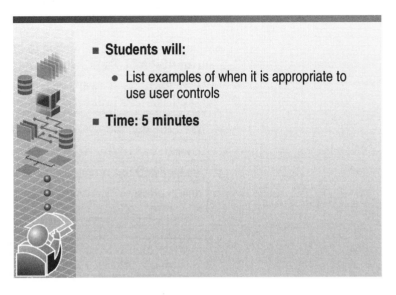

Introduction

In this practice, you will list ideas for when you would use user controls and then discuss these examples with the rest of the class.

List four examples where a user control simplifies Web page development

_____

_____

Adding a User Control

- **Use the @ Register directive to include a user control in an ASP.NET Page**

```
<%@ Register TagPrefix="demo"
TagName="validNum" Src="numberbox.ascx" %>
```

- **Insert the user control in a Web Form**

```
<demo:validNum id="num1" runat="server"/>
```

- **Use Get and Set properties of the user control**

```
num1.pNum = 5 'uses Set
x = num1.pNum 'uses Get
```

or

```
num1.pNum = 5; //uses Set
x = num1.pNum; //uses Get
```

Introduction

You can place a user control in any ASP.NET Web Form. The page that references the user control is called a host, and the control is included in that host.

Including user controls

User controls are included in an ASP.NET Web Form by using the @ **Register** directive, as shown in the following code:

```
<%@ Register TagPrefix="demo" TagName="validNum"
  Src="numberbox.ascx" %>
```

The **TagPrefix** attribute determines a unique namespace for the user control so that multiple user controls with the same name can be differentiated from each other. The **TagName** attribute is the unique name for the user control. The **Src** attribute is the virtual path to the user control file.

Using the user control

After registering the user control with the @ **Register** directive, you can place the user control tag in the Web Form just as you would place an ordinary Web server control, including using the **runat="server"** attribute. The following code example adds two user controls to a Web Form:

```
<demo:validNum id="num1" runat="server"/>
<demo:validNum id="num2" runat="server"/>
```

When the primary Web Form is requested, the runtime compiles the user control file and makes it available to the page.

Using the Get and Set properties

In event procedures on the host page, you can access the properties of the user control by adding declarations for the user control. The following code shows declarations for two **numberbox** user controls:

Visual Basic .NET

```
Protected num1 As numberbox
Protected num2 As numberbox
```

C#

```
protected numberbox num1;
protected numberbox num2;
```

In the preceding code examples, **numberBox** is the name of the class that implements the user control. The variable name (**num1** or **num2**) must be the same as the **id** attribute that is used when adding the user control to the Web Form.

The following example calls the **Get** property of the **num1** and **num2** user controls:

Visual Basic .NET

```
lblSum.Text = (num1.pNum + num2.pNum).ToString()
```

C#

```
lblSum.Text = (num1.pNum + num2.pNum).ToString();
```

The following example calls the **Set** property of the **num1** and **num2** user controls to display the constants 5 and 7 in the user control:

Visual Basic .NET

```
num1.pNum = 5
num2.pNum = 7
```

C#

```
num1.pNum = 5;
num2.pNum = 7;
```

Demonstration: Creating a User Control

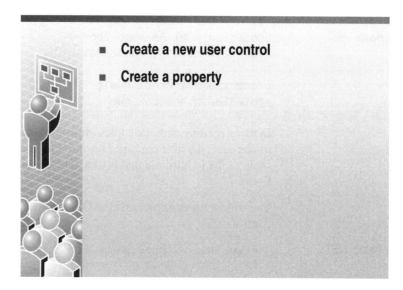

- Create a new user control
- Create a property

Introduction

In this demonstration, you will see how to create a user control by using Visual Studio .NET.

The completed code for this demonstration is in the numberbox.ascx file in the *install folder*\Democode\Mod08VB folder or *install folder*\Democode\ Mod08CS folder.

▶ **To run this demonstration**

1. Either create a new Web application project or use an existing project.

2. Add the beforeuser.aspx page to the Web application project.

For the Visual Basic .NET project

Add the *install folder*\Democode\Mod08VB\beforeuser.aspx page to the project.

For the Visual C# project

Add the *install folder*\Democode\Mod08CS\beforeuser.aspx page to the project.

3. Open the page and show the source HTML. The HTML uses the same combination of controls (a text box and two validation controls) in two places.

4. In design view, group select and copy the first set of text box and validation controls from the page.

5. Create a new user control by adding a new Web User Control to the project. Name it numberbox.ascx.

6. Show the HTML for the page and point out the @ **Control** directive that was created by Visual Studio .NET.

7. In design view, paste in the text box and validation controls.

8. Open the code-behind page for the new user control.

9. In the code-behind page named numberbox.ascx.vb or numberbox.ascx.cs, create a public property for the value of the text box, as shown in the following code example:

For the Visual Basic .NET Project

```
Public Property pNum() As Integer
    Get
        Return CInt(txtNum1.Text)
    End Get
    Set(ByVal Value As Integer)
        txtNum1.Text = Value.ToString()
    End Set
End Property
```

Point out that when you enter the header for the pNum property, Visual Studio .NET creates a template for the **Get** and **Set** properties.

For the Visual C# Project

```
public int pNum
{
    get
    {
        return Convert.ToInt32(txtNum1.Text);
    }
    set
    {
        txtNum1.Text = Convert.ToString(value);
    }
}
```

Point out that the **set** property does not take any arguments. The value being passed is automatically placed into a variable called **value**, which is accessible to the **set** property.

10. Save your changes to the numberbox.ascx page.

Lesson: Creating User Controls

- Creating a User Control
- Demonstration: Using a User Control

Introduction

After you create a user control, the user control can be used by other pages in the same Web application. In this lesson, you will learn how to create user controls.

Lesson objectives

After completing this lesson, you will be able to:

- Create a user control.
- Convert an existing Web Form to a user control.

Creating a User Control

- **Two methods for user control creation:**
  - Create a new user control using Visual Studio .NET
  - Convert an existing ASP.NET page to a user control
- **Host page interacts with the control using properties**
- **Host page should use flow layout**

```
Public Property pNum() As Integer
  Get
    Return Convert.ToInt32(txtNum.Text)
  End Get
  Set (ByVal value As Integer)
    txtNum.Text = CStr(value)
  End Set
End Property
```

```
public int pNum
{
  get
  {
    return
      Convert.ToInt32(txtNum.Text);
  }
  set
  {
    txtNum.Text =
      Convert.ToString(value);
  }
}
```

Introduction

You can create a new user control or convert an existing ASP.NET Web Form to a user control.

Creating a new user control

▶ **To create a new user control**

1. Right-click a Web application project in Solution Explorer in Visual Studio .NET, point to **Add**, and then click **Add Web User Control**.

2. Give the control a name and then click **Open**.

   A page with an .ascx extension is created.

   Note The page is created with the page layout set to the flow layout mode, and an @ **Control** directive. You can drag a Grid Layout Panel control from the HTML section of the toolbox if you need to build the user control with grid layout instead of flow layout.

3. Add the UI elements. You build the page just as you would build an ASP.NET Web Form, adding UI elements from the Toolbox in Visual Studio .NET or by writing the HTML.

   Note When you build the UI portion of a user control in Visual Studio .NET, you must use flow layout rather than grid layout.

4. Add event procedures for UI elements and Page events. Similar to building any other ASP.NET page, you add event procedures to the code-behind page.

5. Create properties for interacting with the host page. Properties allow the hosting Web Form to read and write values into the UI elements on the user control. Properties on the user control hide the implementation of the control.

Converting an existing Web Form to a user control

▶ **To convert an existing Web Form to a user control**

1. Remove all <HTML>, <BODY>, and <FORM> tags.

2. If there is an existing @ **Page** directive on the page, change it to an @ **Control** directive. Although most @ **Page** attributes are also supported by the @ **Control** directive, ensure that there are no unsupported attributes.

Note For more information on the attributes that are supported by the @ **Page** and @ **Control** directives, see "Directive Syntax" in the Visual Studio .NET documentation.

---

3. Add a className attribute to the @ **Control** directive. The className attribute allows the user control to be strongly typed when it is added to a page.

4. Rename the file to a name that reflects its purpose, and then change the file extension from .aspx to .ascx.

Host page

The host page is the Web Form that will include the user control. This page should be in flow layout to avoid overlap between the content of the user control and the content of the page.

The host page does not have direct access to the UI elements that are on a user control. Therefore, you use public properties in a user control to expose the UI elements that are in the control so that the host can use the UI elements.

For example, if a user control is composed of two text boxes, you would need a property for each text box so that the host page can read and write the value in each text box.

The following code is the HTML part of a Visual Basic .NET user control that includes a text box and two input validation controls:

```
<%@ Control Language="vb" Codebehind="WebUserControl1.ascx.vb"
    Inherits="test.WebUserControl1" %>
<asp:textbox id="txtNum" runat="server" />
<asp:RequiredFieldValidator id="txtNumValidator"
    runat="server"
    controlToValidate="txtNum"
    errorMessage="You must enter a value"
    display="dynamic">
</asp:RequiredFieldValidator>
<asp:RangeValidator id="txtNumRngValidator" runat="server"
    controlToValidate="txtNum"
    errorMessage="Please enter a number between 0 and 99"
    type="Integer"
    minimumValue="0"
    maximumValue="99"
    display="dynamic">
</asp:RangeValidator>
```

To expose the values of the text box to the host, you must create a public property. For example, the following code in the code-behind page creates a property named **pNum.** The **pNum** property exposes the **Text** property of the text box control in the user control:

Visual Basic .NET

```
Public Property pNum() As Integer
  Get
      Return CInt(txtNum.Text)
  End Get
  Set(ByVal Value As Integer)
      txtNum.Text = Value.ToString()
  End Set
End Property
```

C#

```
public int pNum
{
  get
  {
      return Convert.ToInt32(txtNum1.Text);
  }
  set
  {
      txtNum1.Text = Convert.ToString(value);
  }
}
```

All public variables, properties, and methods of a user control become the properties and methods of the control in the host page. From the preceding code examples, you can access the **pNum** property as a tag attribute on the host page. If the user control is named userText1, you can read and write the **userText1.pNum** property. Likewise, if you create a public function in the user control, it becomes a method that can be used from the host page.

Demonstration: Using a User Control

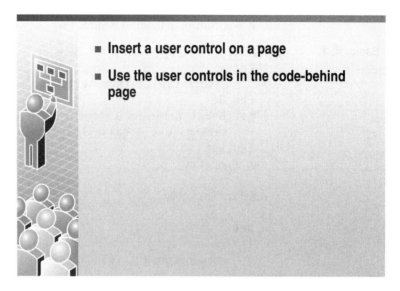

- Insert a user control on a page
- Use the user controls in the code-behind page

Introduction

In this demonstration, you will see how to use a user control on a host page.

The completed code for the Visual Basic .NET demonstration is in the *install folder*\Democode\Mod08VB\afteruser.aspx file.

The completed code for the Visual C# demonstration is in the *install folder*\Democode\Mod08CS\afteruser.aspx file.

Note This demonstration builds on the first demonstration in this module, "Creating a User Control."

▶ **To use a user control in a new ASP.NET page**

1. Edit the beforeuser.aspx page.

2. Delete the two sets of text boxes and validation controls (six controls in all).

3. Using a drag-and-drop operation, place the numberbox.ascx user control from Solution Explorer onto the Web Form at the location of the first set of controls that you just deleted.

4. View the HTML for the page; the @ **Register** directive was added by Visual Studio .NET, along with the tag for the user control, as shown in the following code example:

```
<%@ Register TagPrefix="uc1" TagName="numberbox"
Src="numberbox.ascx" %>
...
<uc1:numberbox id=Numberbox1 runat="server">
</uc1:numberbox>
...
```

5. Place a second numberbox.ascx control onto the beforeuser.aspx Web Form at the location of the second set of controls that you just deleted.

   Visual Studio .NET adds the following HTML to create the user control:

   ```
   <uc1:numberbox id=Numberbox2 runat="server">
   </uc1:numberbox>
   ```

6. In the code-behind page for the file beforeuser.aspx, add declarations for the two new controls:

Visual Basic .NET

```
Protected Numberbox1 As numberbox
Protected Numberbox2 As numberbox
```

Visual C#

```
protected numberbox Numberbox1;
protected numberbox Numberbox2;
```

Note   If your project name is not Mod08CS or Mod08VB, then you should change the name of the namespace in beforeuser.aspx.cs or .vb to match the project name.

---

7. Change the **Compute** button's event procedure to read the values from the user controls:

Visual Basic .NET

```
Sub Button1_Click(s As Object, e As EventArgs)
    If Page.IsValid Then
        lblSum.Text = _
            CStr(Numberbox1.pNum + Numberbox2.pNum)
    End If
End Sub
```

C#:

```
private void Button1_Click(object sender, System.EventArgs
e)
{
    if (Page.IsValid)
        lblSum.Text = Convert.ToString(Numberbox1.pNum +
            Numberbox2.pNum);
}
```

8. Build and browse the beforeuser.aspx page.

9. View the HTML source in the browser.

10. Notice how the user controls are rendered in HTML.

11. In the numberbox.ascx user control, add initialization code to the **Page_Load** event procedure:

Visual Basic .NET

```
If Not Page.IsPostBack Then
    txtNum1.Text = "0"
End If
```

C#

```
if (!Page.IsPostBack)
    txtNum1.Text = "0";
```

12. Build and browse the beforeuser.aspx page.

13. You will notice that the user control now has an initial value of 0.

Review

- ■ **Adding User Controls to an ASP.NET Web Form**
- ■ **Creating User Controls**

1. What are two differences between a user control and a component?

2. How do you access the properties of a user control's UI elements from the host page?

3. What are the four general steps in creating a user control?

4. How do you reference a user control from an ASP.NET Web Form?

5. Can you use two different user controls with the same name in the same ASP.NET page? Why or why not?

6. How can you use a user control in two different Web applications?

Lab 8: Creating User Controls

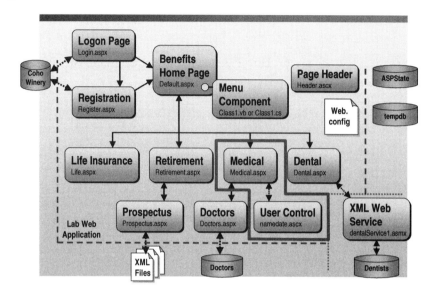

Objectives

After completing this lab, you will be able to:

- Create a user control.
- Use a user control on a Microsoft® ASP.NET Web Form.

Note This lab focuses on the concepts in this module and as a result may not comply with Microsoft security recommendations.

Prerequisites

Before working on this lab, you must have:

- Knowledge of how to use Web server controls on an ASP.NET Web Form.
- Knowledge of how to use validation controls on a Web Form.
- Knowledge of how to create event procedures for controls on a Web Form.
- Knowledge of how to create a property in Microsoft Visual Basic® .NET or C#.

Scenario

Coho Winery offers several benefits to its employees. In the labs for Course 2310B, *Developing Microsoft ASP.NET Web Applications Using Visual Studio .NET*, you will create a Web site that enables employees to select and set up their chosen benefits.

In many pages of your company's Web site, you are collecting the name and birth date from the user. In this lab, you will create a user control to collect that information and then use the user control on the medical.aspx page of the Web site.

Estimated time to complete this lab: 30 minutes

Exercise 0
Lab Setup

To complete this lab, you must have created a Benefits Web Application project. If you have not created this project, complete the following steps:

▶ Create the 2310LabApplication solution

Important Only perform this procedure if you have not created a 2310LabApplication solution file.

1. Using Microsoft Visual Studio® .NET, create a new blank solution named **2310LabApplication**:

   a. On the **File** menu, point to **New**, and then click **Blank Solution**.

   b. In the **New Project** dialog box, enter **2310LabApplication** in the **Name** text box, and then click **OK**.

▶ Create the Benefits project

Important Only perform this procedure if you have not previously created a Benefits project, or if you have removed the Benefits project according to the steps in Appendix A, "Lab Recovery," in Course 2310B, *Developing Microsoft ASP.NET Web Applications Using Visual Studio .NET*.

1. Create a new ASP.NET Web Application project, named **BenefitsVB** or **BenefitsCS**, in the 2310LabApplication solution:

   a. On the **File** menu, point to **New**, and then click **Project**.

   b. In the **New Project** dialog box, click **Visual Basic Projects** or **Visual C# Projects** in the **Project Types** list, click **ASP.NET Web Application** in the **Templates** list, set the **Location** to **http://localhost/BenefitsVB** for the Visual Basic .NET project or to **http://localhost/BenefitsCS** for the Visual C# project, click **Add to Solution**, and then click **OK**.

Caution When adding projects to the solution, the capitalization of the project name is important. Because you may be using some pre-built Web Forms in this and other labs in Course 2310B, *Developing Microsoft ASP.NET Web Applications Using Visual Studio .NET*, you must verify that you have capitalized the Benefits project as shown. Two versions of the project can be created; **BenefitsVB** would be a **Visual Basic .NET** solution and **BenefitsCS** would be a **Visual C#** solution.

▶ **Update the Benefits project**

1. In Visual Studio .NET, open the 2310LabApplication solution file.

2. In Solution Explorer, right-click **BenefitsVB** or **BenefitsCS**, point to **Add**, and then click **Add Existing Item**:

For the Visual Basic .NET Project

    a. Browse to *install folder*\Labfiles\Lab08\VB\Starter\BenefitsVB folder for the Visual Basic .NET files.

    b. In the **Files of type** box of the **Add Existing Item – BenefitsVB** dialog box, choose **All Files**.

For the Visual C# Project

    a. Browse to *install folder*\Labfiles\Lab08\CS\Starter\BenefitsCS folder for the Visual C# files.

    b. In the **Files of type** box of the Add **Existing Item – BenefitsCS** dialog box, choose **All Files**.

3. Select all of the files in this folder, and then click **Open**.

4. Click **Yes** if prompted to overwrite or reload files.

▶ **Create the BenefitsList class library**

Important   Only perform these steps if you have not previously created a BenefitsList project, or if you have removed the BenefitsList project according to the steps in Appendix A, "Lab Recovery," in Course 2310B, *Developing Microsoft ASP.NET Web Applications Using Visual Studio .NET*.

---

1. Create a new Visual Basic .NET Class Library project, name it **BenefitsListVB** or **BenefitsListCS**, and then add it to the 2310LabApplication solution:

    a. On the **File** menu, point to **New**, and then click **Project**.

    b. Create Class Library Project

For the Visual Basic .NET Project

    In the **New Project** dialog box, click **Visual Basic Projects** in the **Project Types** list, click **Class Library** in the **Templates** list, set the **Name** to **BenefitsListVB,** click **Add to Solution**, and then click **OK**.

For the Visual C# Project

    In the **New Project** dialog box, click **Visual C# Projects** in the **Project Types** list, click **Class Library** in the **Templates** list, set the **Name** to **BenefitsListCS**, click **Add to Solution**, and then click **OK**.

Caution   Verify that you have capitalized the BenefitsListVB or BenefitsListCS project as shown.

▶ **Update the BenefitsList project**

1. In Visual Studio .NET, open the 2310LabApplication solution file.

2. In Solution Explorer, right-click **BenefitsListVB** or **BenefitsListCS**, point to **Add**, and then click **Add Existing Item**.

3. Copy files from Labfiles folder.

For the Visual Basic .NET Project:

Browse to *install folder*\Labfiles\Lab08\VB\Starter\BenefitsListVB.

In the **Files of type** box of the **Add Existing Item – BenefitsListVB** dialog box, choose **All Files (*.*)**.

For the Visual C# Project:

Browse to *install folder*\Labfiles\Lab08\CS\Starter\BenefitsListCS folder.

In the **Files of type** box of the **Add Existing Item – BenefitsListCS** dialog box, choose **All Files (*.*)**.

4. Select all of the files in this folder, and then click **Open**.

5. Click **Yes** if prompted to overwrite or reload files.

▶ **Create a reference to the BenefitsList component in the Benefits project**

For the Visual Basic .NET project:

1. In the BenefitsVB project in the 2310LabApplication solution, complete the following steps to add a reference to the BenefitsListVB component that you just created:

   a. Right-click the **BenefitsVB** project in Solution Explorer and then click **Add Reference**.

   b. In the **Add Reference** dialog box, on the **Projects** tab, double-click the **BenefitsListVB** project.

   c. In the **Selected Components** list, select the BenefitsListVB component, and then click **OK**.

   The component is added to the References folder in Solution Explorer.

For the Visual C# project:

1. In the BenefitsCS project in the 2310LabApplication solution, complete the following steps to add a reference to the BenefitsListCS component that you just created:

   a. Right-click the **BenefitsCS** project in Solution Explorer and then click **Add Reference**.

   b. In the **Add Reference** dialog box, on the **Projects** tab, double-click the **BenefitsListCS** project.

   c. In the **Selected Components** list, select the BenefitsListCS component, and then click **OK**.

   The component is added to the **References** folder in Solution Explorer.

Exercise 1
Creating a User Control

In this exercise, you will create a user control from the **Name** and **Birth Date** controls on the life.aspx page.

▶ **Create the user interface**

1. Using Visual Studio .NET, open the 2310LabApplication solution.

2. Add a new user control to the BenefitsVB or BenefitsCS project named namedate.ascx:

   a. Right-click on the **Benefits** project, point to **Add**, and then click **Add Web User Control**.

   b. In the **Add New Item** dialog box, type **namedate.ascx** in the **Name** field, and then click **Open**.

3. Open the life.aspx page in the Benefits project.

4. Copy the **Label**, **TextBox**, and validation controls for the name and birth date input fields (seven controls in total).

5. Paste the controls that you just copied onto the namedate.ascx page.

6. Using the Enter key and spacebar, arrange the controls to look like the following illustration.

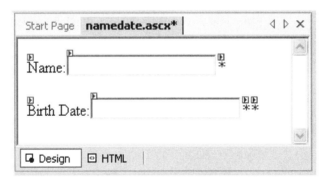

▶ **Create the properties for the user control**

1. Open the code-behind page for the namedate.ascx page, which is named namedate.ascx.vb or namedate.ascx.cs.

2. Add a property named **strName** of type **String** to read and write the **Text** property of the **txtName** control.

   Your code should look like the following:

Visual Basic .NET

```
Public Property strName() As String
    Get
        Return txtName.Text
    End Get
    Set(ByVal Value As String)
        txtName.Text = Value
    End Set
End Property
```

C#

```
public String strName
{
    get
    {
        return txtName.Text;
    }
    set
    {
        txtName.Text = value;
    }
}
```

Caution When using C#, the **set** and **get** keywords are specified in lowercase.

3. Add a property named **dtDate** to read and write the **Text** property of the **txtBirth** control.

Visual Basic .NET

Add a property named **dtDate** of type **Date** to read and write the **Text** property of the **txtBirth** control.

C#

Add a property named **dtDate** of type **DateTime** to read and write the **Text** property of the **txtBirth** control.

The data type of the **dtDate** property is **Date** for Visual Basic .NET and **DateTime** for C#, but the **txtBirth** control holds a **String** value. Therefore, in the **Get** property, you need to convert the control's value to a **Date** data type, and in the **Set** property, you need to convert the passed in value to a **String** data type.

Your code should look like the following:

Visual Basic .NET

```vbnet
Public Property dtDate() As Date
    Get
        Return CDate(txtBirth.Text)
    End Get
    Set(ByVal Value As Date)
        txtBirth.Text = Value.ToString()
    End Set
End Property
```

C#

```csharp
public DateTime dtDate
{
    get
    {
        return Convert.ToDateTime(txtBirth.Text);
    }
    set
    {
        txtBirth.Text = value.ToString();
    }
}
```

4. Save your changes.

Visual Basic .NET   Save your changes to the files namedate.ascx and namedate.ascx.vb.

C#   Save your changes to the files namedate.ascx and namedate.ascx.cs

You will test the user control in Exercise 2.

Exercise 2
Using the User Control

In this exercise, you will use the user control on the medical.aspx page to request the user's name and birth date.

▶ **Place user control on medical.aspx page**

1. Open the medical.aspx page in the BenefitsVB or BenefitsCS project.

2. Using a drag-and-drop operation, place the namedate.ascx control from Solution Explorer into the first row of the table on the medical.aspx page.

   Your page should look like the following illustration.

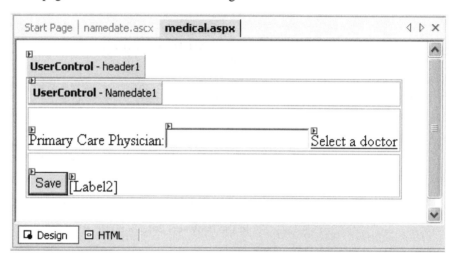

3. View the HTML created.

   Enter the @ **Register** directive that was created by Visual Studio .NET on the lines below.

   _____

   _____

   Enter the HTML that was created by Visual Studio .NET for the user control on the lines below.

   _____

   _____

4. Open the code-behind page for the medical.aspx Web Form, medical.aspx.vb or medical.aspx.cs.

5. Declare a **Protected** variable named **Namedate1** of data type **namedate**.

Visual Basic .NET

```
Protected Namedate1 As BenefitsVB.namedate
```

C#

```
protected BenefitsCS.namedate Namedate1;
```

6. Create a **Click** event procedure for the **Save** button.

   When the user clicks **Save**, the event procedure should output the name and birth date values from the user control into the **Label2** control on the medical.aspx page.

   Your code should look like the following:

Visual Basic .NET

```
Private Sub cmdSave_Click(ByVal sender As System.Object, _
    ByVal e As System.EventArgs) Handles cmdSave.Click

    Label2.Text = Namedate1.strName & " born on " & _
        Namedate1.dtDate.ToString()
End Sub
```

C#

```
private void cmdSave_Click(object sender, System.EventArgs
e)
{
    Label2.Text = Namedate1.strName + " born on " +
        Namedate1.dtDate.ToString();
}
```

7. Build and browse the medical.aspx page.

8. In the browser, enter a name and birth date, and then click **Save**.

msdn® training

Module 9: Accessing Relational Data Using Microsoft Visual Studio .NET

Contents

Overview

- ■ **Overview of ADO.NET**
- ■ **Creating a Connection to a Database**
- ■ **Displaying a DataSet in a List-Bound Control**

Introduction

Microsoft® ADO.NET is the technology that you use to connect Microsoft .NET-based Web applications and Microsoft Windows® applications to data sources, such as Microsoft SQL Server™ databases and Extensible Markup Language (XML) files. ADO.NET is specifically designed to work in disconnected environments, such as the Internet, and it provides a flexible and simple way for developers to integrate data access and data manipulation into their Web applications.

In this module, you will learn what ADO.NET is and how you can incorporate it into a Microsoft ASP.NET Web application by using data tools that are built into Microsoft Visual Studio® .NET.

Objectives

After completing this module, you will be able to:

- ■ Describe ADO.NET.
- ■ Create a connection to a database by using ADO.NET.
- ■ Display data in a Web Form by using a list-bound control.

Lesson: Overview of ADO.NET

- **What is ADO.NET?**
- **Using Namespaces**
- **The ADO.NET Object Model**
- **What is a DataSet?**
- **Accessing Data with ADO.NET**
- **Practice: Identifying ADO.NET Components**

Introduction

Because of the importance of data storage in Web applications, you should have a thorough understanding of the data access methods that ADO.NET provides for ASP.NET Web Forms. In this lesson, you will learn what ADO.NET is and how it works.

Lesson objectives

After completing this lesson, you will be able to:

- Import the appropriate ADO.NET namespaces into your Web application.
- Describe the purpose of individual objects in ADO.NET.
- Explain the purpose of a **DataSet**.
- Connect to a database by using ADO.NET.

What is ADO.NET?

ADO.NET provides a set of classes for working with data. ADO.NET provides:

- An evolutionary, more flexible successor to ADO

- A system designed for disconnected environments

- A programming model with advanced XML support

- A set of classes, interfaces, structures, and enumerations that manage data access from within the .NET Framework

Introduction

ADO.NET is a new technology that is based on the usefulness of Microsoft ActiveX® Data Objects (ADO). ADO.NET is not a revision of ADO; it is a completely new way to manipulate data, built on ADO. ADO.NET contains numerous improvements over the previous version of ADO, and it greatly simplifies the process of connecting your Web application to a database.

ADO.NET coexists with ADO. While most new .NET-based Web applications will be written by using ADO.NET, ADO remains available to the .NET programmer through the .NET COM interoperability services.

Definition

ADO.NET is a set of classes that you use to connect to and manipulate data sources. Unlike ADO, which relies on connections, uses OLE DB to access data, and is COM-based, ADO.NET is specifically designed for data-related connections in a disconnected environment, thereby making it the perfect choice for Internet-based Web applications. ADO.NET uses XML as the format for transmitting data to and from the database and your Web application, thereby ensuring greater compatibility and flexibility than ADO.

Using Namespaces

- Use the Imports or using statement to import namespaces

```
Imports System.Data
Imports System.Data.SqlClient
```

```
using System.Data;
using System.Data.SqlClient;
```

- Namespaces used with ADO.NET include:
  - System.Data
  - System.Data.SqlClient
  - System.Data.OleDb

Introduction

There are three namespaces that you import into your ASP.NET Web Form if you are using ADO.NET. You will always use the **System.Data** namespace; and you will also use either **System.Data.SqlClient** or **System.Data.OleDb**, depending on the data source.

ADO.NET namespaces

When using ADO.NET, you must import the **System.Data** namespace. To import this namespace, you use the **Imports** or **using** keyword:

Visual Basic .NET

```
Imports System.Data
```

C#

```
using System.Data;
```

If you are working with data in a SQL Server 2000 database, you also import the **System.Data.SqlClient** namespace. If you are working with data from other database sources, you need to import the **System.Data.OleDb** namespace. The following code example shows how to import both of these namespaces:

Visual Basic .NET

```
Imports System.Data.SqlClient
Imports System.Data.OleDb
```

C#

```
using System.Data.SqlClient;
using System.Data.OleDB;
```

The ADO.NET Object Model

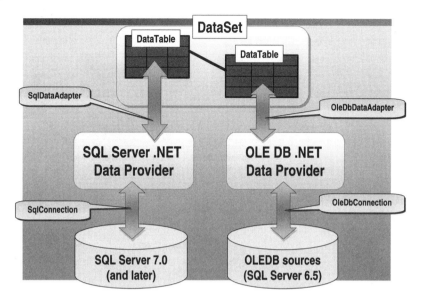

Introduction

The ADO.NET object model provides the structure for accessing data from different data sources. There are two main components of the ADO.NET object model: the **DataSet** and the .NET data provider.

ADO.NET components

A **DataSet** is made up of one or more **DataTables**, and it is designed for data access, regardless of the data source. For example, a **DataSet** may contain data from a SQL Server 2000 database, an OLE DB source, and an XML file. The **DataSet** may also use a **DataView**, which is a customizable view of a **DataTable**.

The .NET data provider provides the link between the data source and the **DataSet**. Examples of objects that are provided by the .NET data providers are listed in the following table.

.NET data provider objects	Purpose
Connection	Provides connectivity to the data source.
Command	Provides access to database commands.
DataReader	Provides data streaming from the source.
DataAdapter	Uses the **Connection** object to provide a link between the **DataSet** and the data provider. The **DataAdapter** object also reconciles changes that are made to the data in the **DataSet**.

Using the objects

The Microsoft .NET Framework includes the SQL Server .NET Data Provider (for SQL Server version 7.0 or later), and the OLE DB .NET Data Provider. You use the **SqlConnection**, **SqlCommand**, **SqlDataReader**, and **SqlDataAdapter** objects to read and manipulate data in a SQL Server 7.0 or later database. You use **OleDbConnection**, **OleDbCommand**, **OleDbDataReader**, and **OleDbDataAdapter** objects to read and manipulate data in all of the other types of databases.

What is a DataSet?

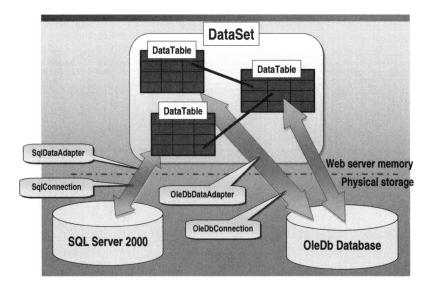

Introduction

A **DataSet** stores information in a disconnected environment. After you establish a connection to a database, you can then access its data. The **DataSet** object is the primary way to store that data when using ADO.NET.

DataSet object

The **DataSet** object allows you to store data, which has been collected from a data source, in your Web application. The data stored in a **DataSet** can be manipulated without the ASP.NET Web Form maintaining a connection to the data source. A connection is re-established only when the data source is updated with changes.

DataTables and DataRelations

The **DataSet** object stores the data in one or more **DataTables**. Each **DataTable** may be populated with data from a unique data source. You can also establish relationships between two **DataTables** by using a **DataRelation** object.

Note You will learn more about the **DataRelation** object in Module 10, "Accessing Data with Microsoft ADO.NET," in Course 2310B, *Developing Microsoft ASP.NET Web Applications Using Visual Studio .NET*.

Accessing Data with ADO.NET

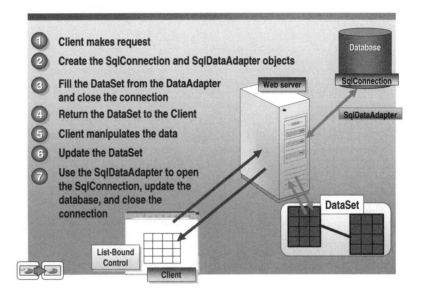

Introduction

There are typically three stages in data access: first, the accessing of the data from a data source and displaying it on an ASP.NET Web Form; second, manipulating the data; and third, sending the data updates back to the database.

Accessing data

In a typical scenario, a client makes a request to an ASP.NET page. The page creates the **SqlConection** and **SqlDataAdapter** objects, populates a **DataSet** from the database by using the **SqlDataAdapter** object, and then returns the **DataSet** to the client by means of a list-bound control.

The data is transferred as XML data. Although the **DataSet** is transmitted as XML, ASP.NET and ADO.NET automatically transform the XML data into a **DataSet**, thereby creating a complete, yet simplified, programming model.

Manipulating data

After the **DataSet** is populated, the client can view and manipulate the data. While the data is being viewed and manipulated there is no connection between the client and the Web server, nor is there a connection between the Web server and the database server. The design of the **DataSet** makes this disconnected environment easy to implement. Because the **DataSet** is stateless, it can be safely passed between the Web server and the client without tying up server resources, such as database connections.

Updating the database

When the user is finished viewing and modifying the data, the client passes the modified **DataSet** back to the ASP.NET page, which uses a **DataAdapter** to reconcile the changes in the returned **DataSet** with the original data that is in the database. The data is sent as XML data between the client and Web server, and then between the Web server and the database server.

Practice: Identifying ADO.NET Components

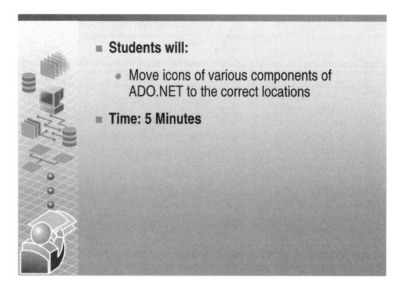

Introduction

In this practice, you will run a Macromedia Flash animation and construct a picture of the ADO.NET architecture.

To run the practice

1. Open the 2310B_09A001.htm page from the *install folder*\Practices\Mod09 folder.

2. Organize the pieces of the ADO.NET architecture onto the frame at the bottom of the page.

3. When you think you have the correct answer, click **Reveal**.

Lesson: Creating a Connection to a Database

- ■ **Using Server Explorer to Generate a Connection**
- ■ **The DataAdapter Object Model**
- ■ **Demonstration: Connecting to a Database**
- ■ **Generating a DataSet**
- ■ **Demonstration: Generating a DataSet**

Introduction

ADO.NET is used to connect a Web Form to a database. In this lesson, you will learn how to connect to different types of databases by using ADO.NET objects. You will also learn how to store data in a **DataSet**.

Lesson objectives

After completing this lesson, you will be able to:

- ■ Generate a connection to a database by using Server Explorer.
- ■ Explain how a **DataAdapter** works.
- ■ Generate a typed **DataSet** from a **DataAdapter**.

Using Server Explorer to Generate a Connection

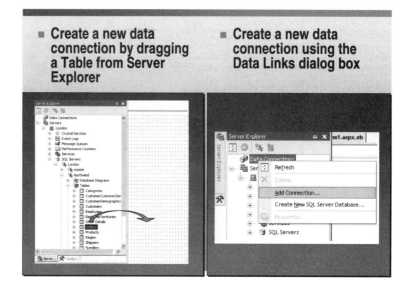

Introduction	You can establish a connection to a data source from within the Visual Studio .NET integrated development environment (IDE). By using the Visual Studio .NET IDE, you simplify the process of establishing a connection to a data source and have the opportunity to verify the connection during design time.
Create a connection	Server Explorer, which is part of the Visual Studio .NET IDE, allows you to browse for servers that are running SQL Server and other databases.

▶ **To connect to a database table**

1. In Server Explorer, expand the list of servers, expand the database that you want to use, and then expand the **Tables** list.

   Server Explorer displays the list of tables in the selected database, as shown in the following illustration. The server list in Server Explorer only displays servers that are running SQL Server 7.0 or later. If you need to connect to a different type of database, you use the **Data Links Properties** dialog box.

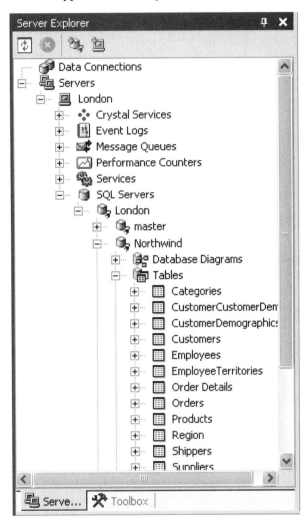

2. Within the list of tables, click the specific table that you want to connect to, and drag it to the open project.

Visual Studio .NET automatically configures a connection and a **DataAdapter** to connect to that table. A **SqlConnection** or **OleDbConnection** object is added to the project, and the object is then displayed at the bottom of the Web Form, as shown in the following illustration.

Data Link Properties dialog box

To add a connection to a database that is not running SQL Server, you use the **Data Connections** option, which is located at the top of the Server Explorer list. In Server Explorer, right-click **Data Connections** and then click **Add Connection**, as shown in the following illustration.

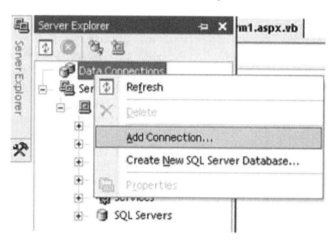

In the resulting **Data Link Properties** dialog box, select the data type that you will be connecting to, as shown in the following illustration.

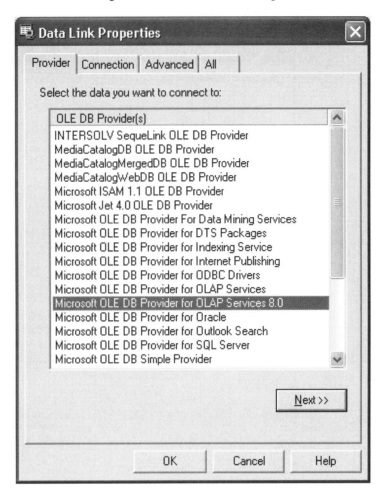

After selecting the data type, click **Next** or select the **Connection** tab and provide the necessary information to connect to the database, as shown in the following illustration.

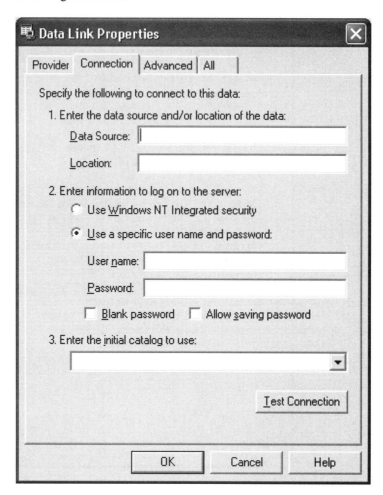

After you have created a connection from the **Data Link Properties** dialog box, you can click on the connection and drag it to the project, just as you would drag a connection from the SQL Servers list in Server Explorer.

The DataAdapter Object Model

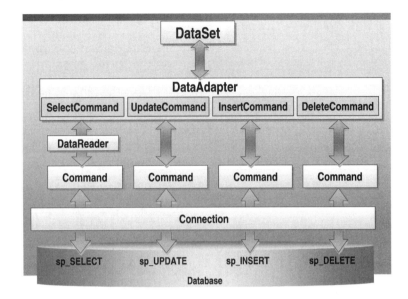

Introduction

When a **DataAdapter** connects to a database, it uses several other objects to communicate with the database.

DataAdapter definition

The **DataAdapter** object uses the **Connection** object to connect to a database, and it then uses **Command** objects to retrieve data and resolve changes to the database.

The **DataAdapter** object has properties. These properties are **SqlCommand** or **OleDbCommand** objects that contain SQL statements. The **DataAdapter** object has the following four **Command-type** properties:

- **SelectCommand**. This property issues a **SQL SELECT** statement.
- **UpdateCommand**. This property issues a **SQL UPDATE** statement.
- **InsertCommand**. This property issues a **SQL INSERT** statement.
- **DeleteCommand**. This property issues a **SQL DELETE** statement.

Each of these **DataAdapter** properties can have SQL statements or can be calls to stored procedures in the database. By using stored procedures, you reduce the amount of code that is required to perform SELECT, INSERT, UPDATE, and DELETE operations.

If your data connects to, or is generated from, a single database table, you can take advantage of the **CommandBuilder** object to automatically generate the **DeleteCommand**, **InsertCommand**, and **UpdateCommand** properties of the **DataAdapter**. Using the **CommandBuilder** object reduces development time.

Demonstration: Connecting to a Database

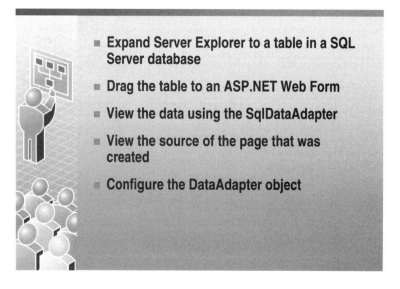

- ■ Expand Server Explorer to a table in a SQL Server database
- ■ Drag the table to an ASP.NET Web Form
- ■ View the data using the SqlDataAdapter
- ■ View the source of the page that was created
- ■ Configure the DataAdapter object

Introduction

In this demonstration, you will see how to add a **SqlConnection** object and a **SqlDataAdapter** object to a Web Form.

The completed code for this demonstration is in the DemoSolution.aspx page in the *install folder*\Democode\Mod09VB, *install folder*\Democode\Mod09CS folder, or in the 2310Demos solution.

▶ **To run the demonstration**

1. Open the Mod09VB or Mod09CS project in the 2310Demos solution.

2. Open the WebForm1.aspx page.

3. Open Server Explorer and expand the folders Servers, *machinename*, SQL Servers, *machinename*, pubs, and Tables.

4. Select the **authors** table and drag it onto the WebForm1.aspx page.

   This creates a **sqlConnection1** object and a **sqlDataAdapter1** object.

5. Right-click **sqlDataAdapter1**, and then click **Preview Data**.

6. In the **Data Adapter Preview** dialog box, click **Fill DataSet** to display the data from the database.

7. Close the **Data Adapter Preview** dialog box.

8. View the Hypertext Markup Language (HTML) for the page. There are no HTML tags for the **Connection** or **DataAdpater** objects.

9. View the code-behind page for the page. There is a lot of code that is generated by Visual Studio .NET that sets up the **DataAdapter** object to retrieve, modify, and delete data from the database that it is connected to.

Generating a DataSet

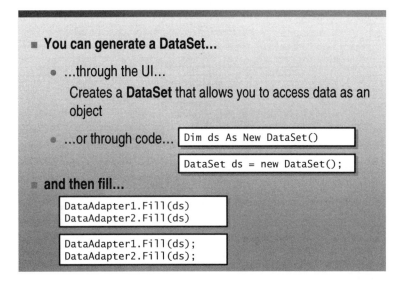

Introduction

When you drag a table from Server Explorer onto a Web Form, most of the code that is needed to create the **Connection** and **DataAdapter** objects is generated by Visual Studio .NET, in the code-behind page. However, you need to add code to populate the **DataSet**. You add this code to the **Page_Load** event procedure or to an event procedure of a control that uses the **DataAdapter** object.

Generating a DataSet

There are two ways to generate a **DataSet** in Visual Studio .NET. You can generate it graphically, through the user interface (UI), or with a single line of code.

▶ **To generate a DataSet from the UI**

1. On the ASP.NET page where you have created the **Connection** and **DataAdapter** objects, right-click the **DataAdapter** object and click **Generate Dataset**.

2. In the **Generate Dataset** dialog box, create a new typed **DataSet**, select **Add this dataset to the designer**, as shown in the following illustration, and then click **OK**.

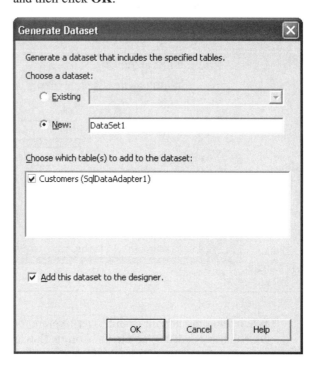

The **Generate Dataset** Dialog then creates a strongly typed **DataSet** in an .xsd file. This .xsd file allows you to reference tables and fields in the **Dataset** by name.

Note   You will learn more about using typed **DataSets** in Module 10, "Accessing Data with Microsoft ADO.NET," in Course 2310B, *Developing Microsoft ASP.NET Web Applications Using Visual Studio .NET*.

▶   **To generate a DataSet using code**

1. In the code-behind page, in the **Page_Load** event procedure, declare a new variable as a **DataSet**. The following code demonstrates how to create a new **DataSet** called **ds**:

Visual Basic .NET
```
Dim ds As New DataSet()
```

C#
```
DataSet ds = new DataSet();
```

Filling the DataSet
2. After you have a **DataSet** in your Web Form, you can fill it in with data by using the **Fill** method of the **DataAdapter**

Visual Basic .NET
```
DataAdapter1.Fill(ds)
```

C#
```
DataAdapter1.Fill(ds);
```

Demonstration: Generating a DataSet

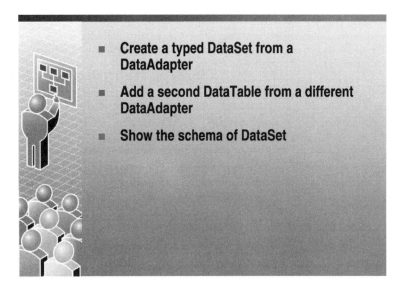

- Create a typed DataSet from a DataAdapter
- Add a second DataTable from a different DataAdapter
- Show the schema of DataSet

Introduction

In this demonstration, you will see how to generate a **Dataset** from a **DataAdapter** and then fill the **DataSet** with data.

The completed code for this demonstration is in the DemoSolution.aspx page in the *install folder*\Democode\Mod09VB, *install folder*\Democode\Mod09CS folder, or in the 2310Demos solution.

▶ **To run the demonstration**

1. In the Mod09VB or the Mod09CS project, open the WebForm1.aspx page that has the **sqlConnection** and **sqlDataAdapter** objects on it.

2. Right-click the **sqlDataAdapter1** object and then click **Generate Dataset**.

3. In the **Generate Dataset** dialog box, create a new **DataSet** named DataSet5.

   A file called DataSet5.xsd is created in the project.

4. Open the DataSet5.xsd file. This file contains the schema of the data that was retrieved by the **DataAdapter** object.

5. Close the DataSet5.xsd file.

Lesson: Displaying a DataSet in a List-Bound Control

- **What are List-Bound Controls?**
- **Displaying DataSet Data in List-Bound Controls**
- **Demonstration: Binding List-Bound Controls to a Database**
- **Practice: Using a DataGrid**
- **Demonstration: Customizing the DataGrid Control**

Introduction

In this lesson, you will learn how to display, on a Web Form, the data from an ADO.NET connection. You will specifically learn about list-bound controls, which are the controls that can be populated automatically with data from a data source.

Lesson objectives

After completing this lesson, you will be able to:

- Describe what list-bound controls are and how they are used.
- Use a **DataGrid** to display data.
- Customize the appearance of a **DataGrid**.

What are List-Bound Controls?

- **Controls that connect to a data source and display the data**
- **List-bound controls include the following:**
  - **DropDownList**
  - **ListBox**
  - **CheckBoxList**
  - **RadioButtonList**
  - **DataGrid**
  - **DataList**
  - **Repeater**

Introduction

You can directly link data-bound controls that are on a Web Form to a data source. There are two types of data-bound controls:

- Single-bound control
- List-bound control

Definition

List-bound controls are controls that connect to a data source and then display the data from that source. The list-bound controls are directly linked to a data source. ASP.NET automatically fills the list-bound control with data.

Examples of list-bound controls

The following table shows Web controls that are list-bound controls.

Control	Description
CheckBoxList	A multi-selection check box group that can be dynamically generated by using data binding.
DataGrid	A control that displays the fields of a data source as columns in a table.
DataList	A control that displays a template-defined data bound list.
DropDownList	A single selection, drop-down list control.
ListBox	A list control that allows single or multiple item selection.
RadioButtonList	A single-selection radio button group that can be dynamically generated through data binding.
Repeater	A data-bound list that uses a template. This control has no built-in layout or styles, so you must explicitly declare all HTML layout, formatting, and style tags within the control's templates.

Displaying DataSet Data in List-Bound Controls

■ **Set the properties**

Property	Description
DataSource	▪ The **DataSet** containing the data
DataMember	▪ The DataTable in the **DataSet**
DataTextField	▪ The field in the **DataTable** that is displayed
DataValueField	▪ The field in the **DataTable** that becomes the value of the selected item in the list

■ **Fill the DataSet, then call the DataBind method**

```
DataAdapter1.Fill(ds)
lstEmployees.DataBind()
```

```
DataAdapter1.Fill(ds);
lstEmployees.DataBind();
```

Introduction

You can connect a **DataSet** to a list-bound control, which automatically fills the list-bound control with the data from the **DataSet**.

Setting list-bond control properties

Each list-bound control in Visual Studio .NET has properties that are specific to list-bound controls. The following table describes the properties that you must set to bind a list-bound control to a **DataSet**.

Property	Description
DataSource	Specifies the **DataSet** containing the data.
DataMember	Specifies the **DataTable** in the **DataSet**.
DataTextField	Specifies the field in the **DataTable** that will be displayed in the list.
DataValueField	Specifies the field in the **DataTable** that becomes the value of the selected item in the list.

The **DataTextField** and **DataValueField** properties are used by the **ListBox**, **DropDownList**, **CheckBoxList**, and **RadioButtonList** controls because these controls can only display one field from a row of the **DataSet**.

Bind the data

After a **DataSet** has been filled with data, you call the **DataBind** method of the list-bound control to connect the control to the **DataSet**. The following code binds the data that is specified in the **DataSource** property to the **lstEmployees** list box:

Visual Basic .NET

```
lstEmployees.DataBind()
```

C#

```
lstEmployees.DataBind();
```

Demonstration: Binding List-Bound Controls to a Database

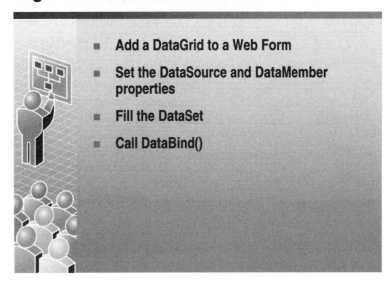

- Add a DataGrid to a Web Form
- Set the DataSource and DataMember properties
- Fill the DataSet
- Call DataBind()

Introduction

In this demonstration, you will see how to bind an existing **DataSet** to a **DataGrid** control that is on a Web Form.

The completed code for this demonstration is in the DemoSolution.aspx page in the *install folder*\Democode\Mod09VB, *install folder*\Democode\Mod09CS folder, or in the 2310Demos solution.

▶ **To run the demonstration**

1. In the Mod09 project, open the WebForm1.aspx page that has the **sqlConnection** objects, **sqlDataAdapter** objects, and the **DataSet** on it.

2. Using the Toolbox, put a **Button** control and a **DataGrid** control on WebForm1.aspx.

3. Select the **DataGrid** control and set the **DataSource** property to the **dataSet51 DataSet** and the **DataMember** property to the authors **DataTable** in the Properties window.

4. Create a **Click** event procedure for the **Button** control and add the following code to fill the **DataSet** and bind the authors table to the **DataGrid**:

Visual Basic .Net

```
SqlDataAdapter1.Fill(DataSet51)
DataGrid1.DataBind()
```

C#

```
sqlDataAdapter1.Fill(dataSet51);
DataGrid1.DataBind();
```

5. In Project Explorer, right-click the **WebForm1.aspx** page and click **Build and Browse**.

6. In the browser, click **Button1** on the **Web Form**.

   You see the data in the **DataGrid** control.

7. Double-click the Web Form in Design mode, this will ensure the **Page_Load** procedure is correctly bound to the page load event.

8. **Move** the two lines of code from the **Button1_Click** event procedure to the **Page_Load** event procedure and add an If Not Page.IsPostBack check:

Visual Basic .NET

```
Private Sub Page_Load(ByVal sender As System.Object, _
    ByVal e As System.EventArgs) Handles MyBase.Load

    If Not Page.IsPostBack Then
        SqlDataAdapter1.Fill(DataSet51)
        DataGrid1.DataBind()
    End If
End Sub
```

C#

```
private void Page_Load(object sender, System.EventArgs e)
{
    if (!Page.IsPostBack)
    {
        sqlDataAdapter1.Fill(dataSet51);
        DataGrid1.DataBind();
    }
}
```

9. In Project Explorer, right-click the **WebForm1.aspx** page and click **Build and Browse**.

10. In the browser, click **Button1** on the Web Form. The **DataGrid** control continues to show the data without re-reading the data from the database.

Using other list-bound controls

11. Open the ListboundControls.aspx page.

    The ListboundControls.aspx page has four list-bound controls that are bound to the same **DataSet**.

12. Build and browse the ListboundControls.aspx page.

13. Show the source of the page and point out the properties that you have to set to bind these list-bound controls to a **DataSet**. Compare the properties of the list-bound controls to the properties that you have to set for a **DataGrid** control.

Practice: Using a DataGrid

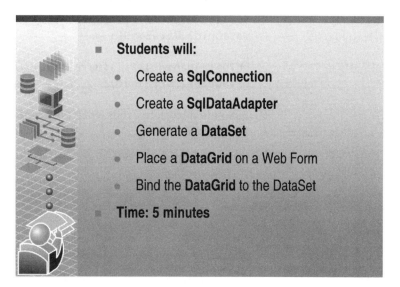

Students will:
- Create a **SqlConnection**
- Create a **SqlDataAdapter**
- Generate a **DataSet**
- Place a **DataGrid** on a Web Form
- Bind the **DataGrid** to the DataSet

Time: 5 minutes

Introduction

In this practice, you will create a **Connection** and a **DataAdapter** to connect to a table in a database, generate a **DataSet**, place a **DataGrid** control on a Web Form, and then bind the **DataGrid** control to the **DataSet**.

▶ **To display data in a DataGrid control**

1. Create a new Web application project and set the location to

   Visual Basic .NET   http://localhost/Mod09PracticeVB

   C#   http://localhost/Mod09PracticeCS

2. Open the WebForm1.aspx page.

3. Open Server Explorer and expand the folders *machinename*, SQL Servers, *machinename*, pubs, and Tables.

4. Click the **authors** table and drag it onto the WebForm1.aspx page.

   Visual Studio .NET creates a **sqlConnection** and a **sqlDataAdapter** object.

5. Right-click the **sqlDataAdapter** object and click **Generate DataSet**.

6. In the **Generate DataSet** dialog box, create a new **DataSet** named DataSet1 and click **OK**.

   A strongly typed **DataSet** and a file named DataSet1.xsd are created.

7. Using the Toolbox, put a **DataGrid** control on WebForm1.aspx.

8. Select the **DataGrid** control and set the **DataSource** property to the DataSet11 **DataSet** and the **DataMember** property to the authors table.

9. Create a **Page_Load** event procedure and add the following code to bind the authors table to the **DataGrid**:

Visual Basic .NET

```
SqlDataAdapter1.Fill(DataSet11)
DataGrid1.DataBind()
```

C#

```
sqlDataAdapter1.Fill(dataSet11);
DataGrid1.DataBind();
```

10. In Solution Explorer, right-click the **WebForm1.aspx** page and click **Build and Browse**.

Demonstration: Customizing the DataGrid Control

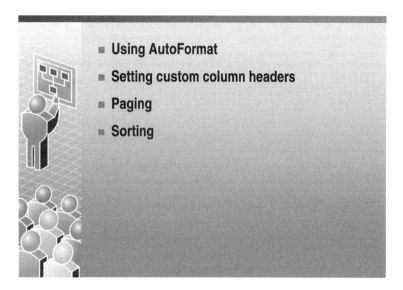

- **Using AutoFormat**
- **Setting custom column headers**
- **Paging**
- **Sorting**

Introduction

In this demonstration, you will see how to customize the look and feel of the **DataGrid** control.

The completed code for this demonstration is in the DemoSolution.aspx page in the *install folder*\Democode\Mod09VB, *install folder*\Democode\Mod09CS folder, or in the 2310Demos solution.

▶ **To run the demonstration**

1. In the Mod09 project, open the WebForm1.aspx page with the **SqlConnection**, **SqlDataAdapter**, **DataSet**, and **DataGrid** objects on it.

Auto Format

2. Select the **DataGrid** control and then select the **Auto Format** hyperlink in the Properties window.

3. In the **Auto Format** dialog box, select a format.

4. Save your changes and view the page in the browser. You do not have to rebuild the project because you did not change any code.

Custom Column Headers

   a. Select the **DataGrid** control and then click the **Property Builder** hyperlink in the Properties window.

5. In the **Properties** dialog box, on the **Columns** tab, do the following:

   a. Clear the **Create columns automatically at run time** check box.

   b. Select a couple of columns (such as au_lname, au_fname, or phone) and add them to the **Selected columns** list.

   c. Set the **Header text** for each column to be more "user friendly."

   d. Click **Apply** and then click **OK**.

6. Save your changes and view the page in the browser.

Paging

7. Select the **DataGrid** control and then click the **Property Builder** hyperlink in the Property window.

8. In the **Properties** dialog box, on the **Paging** tab:

    a. Select the **Allow paging** check box.

    b. Point out the **Allow custom paging** check box. This option lets you define the paging algorithm.

    c. Set the **Page size** field to **5**.

    d. Select the **Show navigation buttons** check box and set the position and mode for the navigation buttons. Set the **Mode** to **Page numbers**.

    e. Click **Apply** and then click **OK**.

9. In the code-behind page, for the WebForm1.aspx page, create a **PageIndexChanged** event procedure for the **DataGrid** control:

Visual Basic .NET

```
Private Sub DataGrid1_PageIndexChanged( _
  ByVal source As Object, _
  ByVal e As _
  System.Web.UI.WebControls.DataGridPageChangedEventArgs
  ) _
  Handles DataGrid1.PageIndexChanged

End Sub
```

C#

```
private void DataGrid1_PageIndexChanged(
  object source,
  System.Web.UI.WebControls.DataGridPageChangedEventArgs
  e)
{
}
```

Notice that the **EventArgs** argument is of type **DataGridPageChangedEventArgs**.

10. Add the following code to the **DataGrid1_PageIndexChanged** event procedure to implement paging:

Visual Basic .NET

```
DataGrid1.CurrentPageIndex = e.NewPageIndex
SqlDataAdapter1.Fill(DataSet51)
DataGrid1.DataBind()
```

C#

```
DataGrid1.CurrentPageIndex = e.NewPageIndex;
sqlDataAdapter1.Fill(dataSet51);
DataGrid1.DataBind();
```

11. Save your changes, build the project (because you added code), and then view the WebForm1.aspx page in the browser.

12. Click the page numbers to move through the **DataSet**.

Review

- Overview of ADO.NET
- Creating a Connection to a Database
- Displaying a DataSet in a List-Bound Control

1. How many **DataTables** can there be in a **DataSet**?

2. How do you create a connection to a database?

3. What namespaces do you use when accessing a SQL Server 2000 database?

4. When you create a **SqlDataAdapter** with the Visual Studio .NET tools, what are the **SelectCommand**, **UpdateCommand**, **InsertCommand**, and **DeleteCommand** properties set to?

5. How do you create a **DataSet**?

6. After you have created a **SqlConnection** object, a **SqlDataAdapter** object, and a **DataSet** object, how do you display the data in a **DataGrid** control?

Lab 9: Accessing Relational Data Using Microsoft Visual Studio .NET

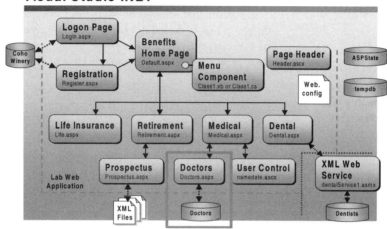

Lab 9: Accessing Relational Data Using Microsoft Visual Studio .NET

Objectives

After completing this lab, you will be able to:

- Create a connection to a Microsoft® SQL Server™ database.
- Read data from a SQL Server database into a **DataSet** object.
- Display **DataSet** data in a **DataGrid** control.
- Format a **DataGrid** control to display custom headers.
- Implement paging for a **DataGrid** control.

Note This lab focuses on the concepts in Module 9, "Accessing Relational Data Using Microsoft Visual Studio .NET," in Course 2310B, *Developing Microsoft ASP.NET Web Applications Using Visual Studio .NET*, and as a result may not comply with Microsoft security recommendations.

Prerequisites

Before working on this lab, you must have:

- Knowledge of how to use Web controls on a Microsoft ASP.NET Web Form.
- Knowledge of how to create event procedures for controls on a Web Form.

Scenario

Coho Winery offers several benefits to its employees. In the labs for Course 2310B, *Developing Microsoft ASP.NET Web Applications Using Visual Studio .NET*, you will create a Web site that enables employees to select and set up their chosen benefits.

One benefit that is offered by Coho Winery is medical insurance. When applying for medical insurance, a user must select a primary care physician. The doctors that are approved by your company are all listed in a SQL Server database that is called **doctors**. In this lab, you will create a page to display all of the doctors in the database and allow a user to select one of the doctors as their primary care physician.

Estimated time to complete this lab: 30 minutes

Exercise 0
Lab Setup

To complete this lab, you must have created a Benefits Web Application project and a BenefitsList Class Library project. These projects can be created by using Microsoft Visual Basic® .NET or Microsoft Visual C#™ .NET.

If you have not created these projects, complete the following steps:

▶ **Create the 2310LabApplication solution**

Important   Only perform this procedure if you have not created a 2310LabApplication solution file.

1. Using Microsoft Visual Studio® .NET, create a new blank solution named **2310LabApplication**:

   a. On the **File** menu, point to **New**, and then click **Blank Solution**.

   b. In the **New Project** dialog box, type **2310LabApplication** in the **Name** text box, and then click **OK**.

▶ **Create the Benefits project**

Important   Only perform this procedure if you have not previously created a Benefits project, or if you have removed the Benefits project according to the steps in Appendix A, "Lab Recovery," in Course 2310B, *Developing Microsoft ASP.NET Web Applications Using Visual Studio .NET.*

1. Create a new ASP.NET Web Application project, named **BenefitsVB** or **BenefitsCS**, in the 2310LabApplication solution:

   a. On the **File** menu, point to **New**, and then click **Project**.

   b. In the **New Project** dialog box, in the **Project Types** list, click **Visual Basic Projects** or **Visual C# Projects**.

   c. In the **Templates** list, click **ASP.NET Web Application.** Set the **Location** to **http://localhost/BenefitsVB** for the Visual Basic .NET project or to **http://localhost/BenefitsCS** for the Visual C# project.

   d. Click **Add to Solution**, and then click **OK**.

Caution   When adding projects to the solution, the capitalization of the project name is important. Because you may be using some pre-built Web Forms in this and other labs in Course 2310B, *Developing Microsoft ASP.NET Web Applications Using Visual Studio .NET*, you must verify that you have capitalized the Benefits project as shown.

▶ **Update the Benefits project**

1. In Visual Studio .NET, open the 2310LabApplication solution file.

2. In Solution Explorer, right-click **BenefitsVB** or **BenefitsCS**, point to **Add**, and then click **Add Existing Item**.

3. Browse for project files.

For the Visual Basic .NET project

Browse to the *install folder*\Labfiles\Lab09\VB\Starter\BenefitsVB folder.

For the Visual C# project

Browse to the *install folder*\Labfiles\Lab09\CS\Starter\BenefitsCS folder.

4. In the **Files of type** box of the **Add Existing Item – Benefits** dialog box, click **All Files (*.*)**.

5. Select all of the files in this folder, and then click **Open**.

6. Click **Yes** if prompted to overwrite or reload files.

▶ **Create the BenefitsList class library**

Important   Only perform these steps if you have not previously created a BenefitsList project, or if you have removed the BenefitsList project according to the steps in Appendix A, "Lab Recovery," in Course 2310B, *Developing Microsoft ASP.NET Web Applications Using Visual Studio .NET*.

---

1. Create a new Class Library Project.

For the Visual Basic .NET project

Create a new Visual Basic .NET Class Library project, name it **BenefitsListVB**, and then add it to the 2310LabApplication solution:

a. On the **File** menu, point to **New**, and then click **Project**.

b. In the **New Project** dialog box, in the **Project Types** list, click **Visual Basic Projects**.

c. In the **Templates** list, click **Class Library**, and then set the **Name** to **BenefitsListVB**.

d. Click **Add to Solution**, and then click **OK**.

For the Visual C# project

Create a new Visual C# .NET Class Library project, name it **BenefitsListCS**, and then add it to the 2310LabApplication solution:

a. On the **File** menu, point to **New**, and then click **Project**.

b. In the **New Project** dialog box, in the **Project Types** list, click **Visual C# Projects**.

c. in the **Templates** list, click **Class Library**, and then set the **Name** to **BenefitsListCS**.

d. Click **Add to Solution**, and then click **OK**.

Caution   Verify that you have capitalized the BenefitsList project as shown.

▶ **Update the BenefitsList project**

1. In Visual Studio .NET, open the 2310LabApplication solution file.

2. In Solution Explorer, right-click **BenefitsListVB** or **BenefitsListCS**, point to **Add**, and then click **Add Existing Item**.

3. Browse for project files:

**For the Visual Basic
.NET project**

Browse to the *install folder*\Labfiles\Lab09\VB\Starter\BenefitsListVB folder.

For the Visual C# project

Browse to the *install folder*\Labfiles\Lab09\CS\Starter\BenefitsListCS folder.

4. In the **Files of type** box of the **Add Existing Item – BenefitsList** dialog box, click **All Files (*.*)**.

5. Select all of the files in this folder, and then click **Open**.

6. Click **Yes** if prompted to overwrite or reload files.

▶ **Create a reference to the BenefitsList component in the Benefits project**

1. In the Benefits project in the 2310LabApplication solution, complete the following steps to add a reference to the BenefitsList component that you just created:

   a. Right-click the **BenefitsVB** or the **BenefitsCS** project in Solution Explorer and then click **Add Reference**.

   b. In the **Add Reference** dialog box, on the **Projects** tab, double-click the **BenefitsListVB** or **BenefitsListCS** project.

   c. In the **Selected Components** list, select the **BenefitsListVB** or **BenefitsListCS** component, and then click **OK**.

   The component is added to the References folder in Solution Explorer.

Exercise 1
Connecting to the Doctors Database

In this exercise, you will use Visual Studio .NET to connect to the Doctors database and display the data in a **DataGrid** control on the doctors.aspx page.

▶ **Create the connection and data adapter**

1. In Visual Studio .NET, open the 2310LabApplication solution.

2. Right click the **BenefitsVB** or **BenefitsCS** project, point to **Add**, and then click **Add Existing Item**.

3. Add the doctors.aspx file from:

Visual Basic .NET   The *install folder*\Labfiles\Lab09\VB\Starter\BenefitsVB folder.

C#   The *install folder*\Labfiles\Lab09\CS\Starter\BenefitsCS folder.

4. Expand Server Explorer to view the databases on the local SQL Server.

5. Using a drag-and-drop operation, place the doctors table, from the doctors database, onto the doctors.aspx page.

▶ **Create the DataSet**

1. Right-click the **sqlDataAdapter1** object on the doctors.aspx page and then click **Generate Dataset**.

2. In the **Generate Dataset** dialog box, create a new **DataSet** named **dsDoctors**, ensure that the **Add this dataset to the designer** option is selected, and then click **OK**.

▶ **Display the DataSet in a DataGrid control**

1. Drag a **DataGrid** control from the Toolbox onto the doctors.aspx page, so your page looks like the following illustration.

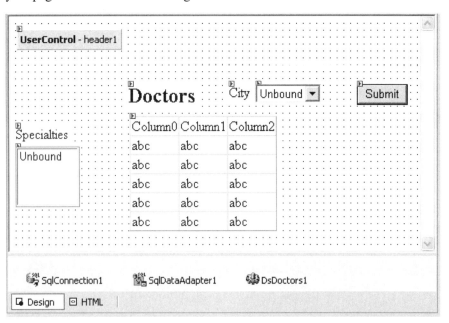

2. Set the properties of the **DataGrid** control in the Properties window, according to the information in the following table.

Property	Value
ID	dgDoctors
DataSource	dsDoctors1
DataMember	doctors

3. In the Properties window, click the **Auto Format** link below the list of properties.

4. In the **Auto Format** dialog box, click a formatting option, such as **Simple 1**, and then click **OK**.

5. Open the code-behind page for the doctors.aspx page and locate the following comment:

Visual Basic .NET

```
'TODO Lab 9: bind the datagrid to the doctors table
```

C#

```
//TODO Lab 9: bind the datagrid to the doctors table
```

6. Add the following code to display the **DataSet** data in the **DataGrid** control:

Visual Basic .NET

```
SqlDataAdapter1.Fill(DsDoctors1)
dgDoctors.DataBind()
```

C#

```
sqlDataAdapter1.Fill(dsDoctors1);
dgDoctors.DataBind();
```

7. Save your changes.

Exercise 2
Paging and Selection in a DataGrid Control

In this exercise, you will implement paging for the **DataGrid** control on the doctors.aspx page, and allow the user to select a doctor from the **DataGrid**.

▶ **Implement paging**

1. Open the doctors.aspx page in the Benefits project.

2. Select the **DataGrid** control and then click **Property Builder** in the Properties window.

3. In the **dgDoctors Properties** dialog box, on the **Paging** tab, set the properties, as shown in the following table, and then click **OK**.

Property	Value
Allow paging	Checked
Page size	5
Show navigation buttons	Checked
Position	Bottom
Mode	Page numbers
Numeric buttons	10

4. Click **Apply**, and then click **OK**.

5. Create a **PageIndexChanged** event procedure.

Visual Basic .NET

Open the code-behind page for the doctors.aspx page and create a **PageIndexChanged** event procedure for the **DataGrid** control:

a. In the code-behind page, click **dgDoctors** in the **Class Name** drop-down list.

b. Click **PageIndexChanged** in the **Method Name** drop-down list.

C#

In the properties for the **dgDoctors DataGrid** control, click the **events** button. Scroll down the list of events, double click the **PageIndexChanged** event.

6. Add the following code to the **dgDoctors_PageIndexChanged** event procedure to implement paging:

Visual Basic .NET

```
dgDoctors.CurrentPageIndex = e.NewPageIndex
SqlDataAdapter1.Fill(DsDoctors1)
dgDoctors.DataBind()
```

C#

```
dgDoctors.CurrentPageIndex = e.NewPageIndex;
sqlDataAdapter1.Fill(dsDoctors1);
dgDoctors.DataBind();
```

7. Build and browse the doctors.aspx page.

8. Click the page numbers on the **DataGrid** control to move through the pages of doctor names.

▶ **Add a select column**

1. Open the doctors.aspx page in the Benefits project.

2. Select the **DataGrid** control and then click **Property Builder** in the Properties window.

3. In the **dgDoctors Properties** dialog box, on the **Columns** tab, add a Select column:

    a. Expand the **Button Column** list in the **Available columns** list.

    b. Click **Select**, then click the > button to add it to the **Selected columns** list.

4. Set the **Header text** for the new column to **Select**, and then click **OK**.

▶ **Send the selected doctor to the medical.aspx page**

1. Open the doctors.aspx page in the Benefits project.

2. Create a **click** event procedure for the **cmdSubmit** button.

3. Add the following code to read the selected doctor's name and send it to the medical.aspx page:

Visual Basic .NET

```
Dim strDrName As String
strDrName = Trim(dgDoctors.Items _
    (dgDoctors.SelectedIndex).Cells(3).Text) & " " & _
    Trim(dgDoctors.Items _
    (dgDoctors.SelectedIndex).Cells(2).Text)
Response.Redirect("medical.aspx?pcp=" & strDrName)
```

C#

```
string strDrName;
strDrName = dgDoctors.Items
        [dgDoctors.SelectedIndex].Cells[3].Text
        .Trim() + " " +
        dgDoctors.Items[dgDoctors.SelectedIndex].Cells[2]
        .Text.Trim();
Response.Redirect("medical.aspx?pcp=" + strDrName);
```

4. Open the code-behind page for the medical.aspx page in the Benefits project.

5. Modify the **Page_Load** event procedure, so that if there is an argument on the Uniform Resource Locator (URL), display it in the **Primary Care Physician** text box:

Visual Basic .NET

```
If Not Page.IsPostBack Then
    If Request.QueryString("pcp") <> "" Then
        txtDoctor.Text = Request.QueryString("pcp")
    End If
End If
```

C#

```
if (!Page.IsPostBack)
{
    if (Request.QueryString["pcp"] != "")
    {
        txtDoctor.Text = Request.QueryString["pcp"];
    }
}
```

6. Save your changes to the doctors.aspx and medical.aspx pages.

7. Build and browse the medical.aspx page:

   a. In the browser, click the **Select a doctor** hyperlink.

      The hyperlink displays the doctors.aspx page.

   b. Move through the doctors on the doctors.aspx page and select a doctor by clicking **Select**.

   c. Click **Submit** to send your selection back to the medical.aspx page.

msdn training

Module 10: Accessing Data with Microsoft ADO.NET

Contents

Overview

- **Introduction to Using ADO.NET**
- **Connecting to a Database**
- **Accessing Data with DataSets**
- **Using Multiple Tables**
- **Accessing Data with DataReaders**

Introduction

Creating a dynamic Web site that responds to user requests with customized data may require you to link your Web application to various data sources. Microsoft® ADO.NET is the tool that allows you to programmatically access data sources from a Web Form.

In this module, you will learn how to use ADO.NET to add data access to your Microsoft ASP.NET Web application.

Lesson objectives

After completing this lesson, you will be able to:

- Describe the ADO.NET object model for accessing data.

- Create secure connections to a Microsoft SQL Server™ database by using the **SqlConnection** and **SqlDataAdapter** objects.

- Use **DataSet** objects to support the local data storage and manipulation requirements of Web Forms.

- Store multiple tables of data in a **DataSet** object, and then display that data in **DataGrid** controls.

- Programmatically read data from a SQL Server database by using a **SqlDataReader** object.

Lesson: Introduction to Using ADO.NET

- **Multimedia: The ADO.NET Object Model**
- **Using DataSets vs. DataReaders**
- **Practice: When to Use DataSets or DataReaders**

Introduction

ADO.NET is designed to load data from a data source and then work with that data in a disconnected state. This disconnected state allows the Web Form to operate semi-independently from data sources, thereby reducing network traffic. ADO.NET uses Extensible Markup Language (XML) as the universal transmission format, which guarantees interoperability with any platform where an XML parser is available.

In this lesson, you will learn about using the ADO.NET object model to access data. You will also learn about how to use **DataSet** and **DataReader** objects to access data.

Lesson objectives

After completing this lesson, you will be able to:

- Describe how **DataSet** and **DataReader** objects access data.
- Choose between **DataSet** and **DataReader** objects, depending on the data access needs of a Web application.

Multimedia: The ADO.NET Object Model

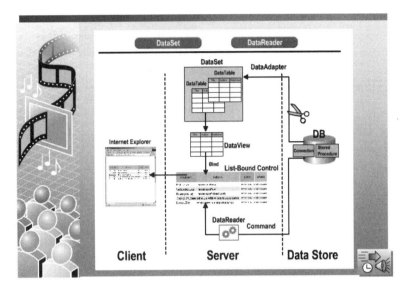

Introduction	In this animation, you will see how to use **DataSet** and **DataReader** objects to access data from a data source.
DataSet	■ When a user requests data, **DataSetCommand** pulls data out of a data store and pushes it into a **DataTable**.
	■ After the **DataTables** are on the server, the link can be severed.
	■ A **DataView** is then created and bound to a list-bound control to be displayed.
DataReader	■ When a user requests data, the **Command** retrieves data into the **DataReader**.
	■ The **DataReader** is a read-only, forward-only stream that is returned from the database.

Using DataSets vs. DataReaders

DataSet	DataReader
Read/write access to data	Read-only
Includes multiple tables from different databases	Based on one SQL statement from one database
Disconnected	Connected
Bind to multiple controls	Bind to one control only
Forward and backward scanning of data	Forward-only
Slower access	Faster access
Supported by Visual Studio .NET tools	Manually coded

Introduction

DataSet objects are complex objects that allow you to store multiple **DataTables** of data from a data source. **DataSet** objects are similar to a *virtual database* that is inside a Web Application. **DataSet** objects can also contain relationships between the data in the **DataTables**, and can use these relationships to retrieve data.

DataReader objects are light-weight objects that are used for reading data from a data source; **DataReader** objects provide forward-only, read-only access to the data in a database.

Using DataSets and DataReaders

The choice between using **DataSet** or **DataReader** objects should be based on your intended use for the data. Generally, **DataReader** objects are used for reading data in one-time, read-only situations, such as when accessing a stored password, or filling in a list-bound control. **DataSet** objects are used for more complicated data access, such as accessing a customer's entire order history.

Some of the data access issues to consider when selecting between **DataSet** and **DataReader** objects include:

- Access to data

  If you intend to both read from and write to your data source, you must use a **DataSet** object. **DataReader** objects are read-only connections and should only be used when the data will be used in a read-only situation.

- Access to multiple databases

  If you intend to combine tables from one or more databases, you must use a **DataSet** object. **DataReader** objects are based on a single SQL statement from a single database.

- Binding to controls

  If you intend to bind the data to more than one control, you must use a **DataSet** object. **DataReader** objects can only be bound to a single control.

■ Connection mode

If you intend to run in a disconnected mode, you must use a **DataSet** object. **DataReader** objects must run in a connected mode.

■ Data scanning

If you intend to scan both backwards and forwards through the data, you must use a **DataSet** object. **DataReader** objects must scan forwards as the data is streamed from the database.

■ Access speed

If you need high-speed access to your data source, use a **DataReader** object. **DataSet** objects are slower than **DataReader** objects when it comes to accessing data from a database because **DataSet** objects store the data in an object on the Web server. There is also more overhead in creating the **DataSet** object because of the ability to read and write data and scan forwards and backwards. **DataReader** objects are faster due to the light-weight nature of the object. There is very little overhead to the **DataReader** object since it is forward-only and read-only.

■ Tool support

If you intend to use Microsoft Visual Studio® .NET to create the data connection, use a **DataSet** object. With **DataSet** objects, you have the choice of writing your own code or using Visual Studio .NET machine code. With **DataReader** objects, you need to write all of the supporting code yourself.

Practice: When to Use DataSets or DataReaders

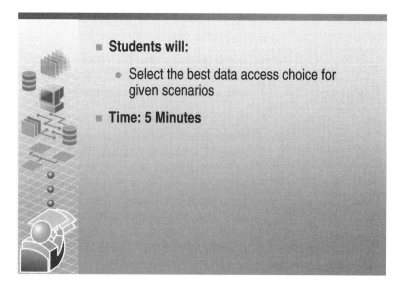

Read the following scenarios, and then decide whether to use a DataSet or DataReader object

You want to get information from two tables that are in two different databases, and then you want to display the tables to the user.

_____

_____

You want to get the information from one table in a database, allow the user to make changes to the data, and then save those changes back into the database.

_____

_____

You want to get information from two tables in the same database and then display that information to the user.

_____

_____

You want to get information from one table in a database and let the user view the data in many different configurations.

_____

_____

Lesson: Connecting to a Database

- SQL Server Security
- Creating the Connection
- Demonstration: Setting SQL Server Security

Introduction

The first step in using a database to support your Web application is to create a secure connection to the database. Non-secure connections may expose both the Web application and the database to malicious attacks.

In this lesson, you will learn how to create secure connections to a SQL Server database by using the **SqlConnection** and **SqlDataAdapter** objects.

Lesson objectives

After completing this lesson, you will be able to:

- Explain the difference between mixed-mode and Windows-only authentication.
- Create a connection, with Windows-only authentication, to a SQL Server database.

SQL Server Security

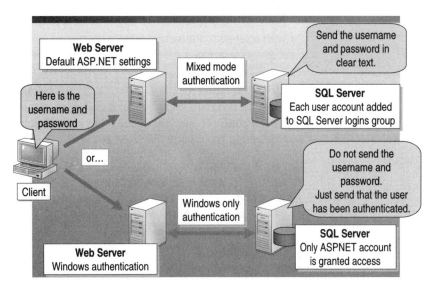

Introduction

From the user's perspective, accessing data from a SQL Server database is a two-step process. First, the user sends a request to the Web application, and then the Web application connects to the SQL Server database to comply with the request. There are two primary methods for connecting a Web application to a SQL Server database: mixed-mode authentication and Windows-only authentication. The preferred method is Windows-only authentication.

Mixed-mode authentication

Mixed-mode authentication uses the default ASP.NET and Web application settings. Each user of the Web application must have a user account added to the SQL Server Logins Group. The weakness of mixed-mode authentication is that the user names and passwords are sent to the computer running SQL Server in unencrypted Hypertext Markup Language (HTML). This exposed data could allow third parties to obtain logon credentials. In addition, you need to manage user accounts on both the Web Server and the computer running SQL Server.

To use mixed-mode authentication, set the SQL Server to mixed-mode authentication (SQL Server and Windows). The following code can be used to connect to a SQL Server with mixed-mode authentication:

Visual Basic .NET

```
Dim strConn As String = _
   "data source=localhost; " & _
   "initial catalog=northwind; " & _
   "user id=CohoUser;password=1Coho"
Dim conn As New SqlConnection(strConn)
```

C#

```
string strConn =
   "data source=localhost; " +
   "initial catalog=northwind; " +
   "user id=CohoUser; " +
   "password=1Coho";
SqlConnection conn = new SqlConnection(strConn);
```

> **Warning** Using mixed-mode authentication to access a SQL Server from a Web application is a security risk and it is not recommended. Mixed-mode authentication is discussed here only as a technique that may be used during Web application development.

Windows-only authentication

Windows-only authentication is the preferred method to use when connecting a Web application to a SQL Server database. When you use Windows-only authentication, the SQL Server does not need the user name and password. Only a confirmation that the user has been authenticated by a trusted source is required to process the database request.

The Windows-only authentication process uses a single account named ASPNET for all SQL Server access from the Web application. This single account eliminates the issues of transmitting unencrypted user names and passwords between the Web application and SQL Server, along with the need to keep user accounts on both servers.

With Windows-only authentication, users access the Web Form as anonymous users. ASP.NET then connects to the SQL Server and is authenticated by using the ASPNET user account. The requested data is returned from the SQL Server and it is used by the Web application. Finally, the Web Form that includes the requested data is returned to the user.

To use Windows-only authentication, you set the SQL Server with Windows-only authentication. The following code can be used to connect to a SQL Server with Windows-only authentication:

Visual Basic .NET

```
Dim strConn As String = _
  "data source=localhost; " & _
  "initial catalog=northwind; " & _
  "integrated security=true"
Dim conn As New SqlConnection(strConn)
```

C#

```
string strConn =
  "data source=localhost; " +
  "initial catalog=northwind; " +
  "integrated security=true";
SqlConnection conn = new SqlConnection(strConn);
```

Configuring the SQL Server to run mixed-mode or Windows-only authentication

When you use Windows-only authentication, you can leave SQL Server with the default authentication mode of Windows-only. If you use mixed-mode authentication, you need to change the authentication mode of the SQL Server.

To change the Authentication mode of the SQL Server

1. On the **Start** menu, right-click **My Computer** and then click **Manage**.

2. In the Computer Management console, expand the Services and Applications folder and then expand the Microsoft SQL Servers folder.

3. Right-click the **(local)** SQL Server and then click **Properties**.

4. In the **SQL Server Properties** dialog box, on the **Security** tab, click either the **SQL Server and Windows** option button or the **Windows only** option button in the **Authentication** section, and then click **OK**.

Note For more information on securing a Web application, see Module 16, "Securing a Microsoft ASP.NET Web Application," in Course 2310B, *Developing Microsoft ASP.NET Web Applications Using Visual Studio .NET.*

Creating the Connection

- **Using SqlConnection**

```
Dim strConn As String = "data source=localhost; " & _
    "initial catalog=northwind; integrated security=true"
Dim conn As New SqlConnection(strConn)
```

```
string strConn = "data source=localhost; " +
    "initial catalog=northwind; integrated security=true";
SqlConnection conn = new SqlConnection(strConn);
```

- **Setting connection string parameters**

  - Connection timeout   - Password

    Data source   - Persist security info

    Initial catalog   Provider

    Integrated security   User ID

Introduction

To move data between a database and your Web application, you must first have a connection to the database. To create a connection to a database, you need to identify the name of the database server, the name of the database, and the required login information.

Depending on the type of database that you are accessing, you can use either a **SqlConnection** or **OleDbConnection** object. You would use a **SqlConnection** object to connect to SQL Server 7.0 and later databases, and use **OleDbConnection** objects to connect to all other databases.

Creating a connection string

You create a **SqlConnection** object by passing in a connection string that provides the parameters needed to create a connection to a data source.

The following sample code creates a **SQLConnection** object to the Northwind SQL Server Database:

Visual Basic .NET

```
Dim strConn As String = _
  "data source=localhost; " & _
  "initial catalog=northwind; " & _
  "integrated security=true"
Dim conn As New SqlConnection(strConn)
```

C#

```
string strConn =
  "data source=localhost; " +
  "initial catalog=northwind; " +
  "integrated security=true";
SqlConnection conn = new SqlConnection(strConn);
```

Connection string parameters

The following table describes some of the commonly used parameters of a connection object:

Parameter	Description
Connection Timeout	The length of time, in seconds, to wait for a connection to the server before terminating the attempt and generating an exception. **15** seconds is the default length of time.
Data Source	The name of the SQL Server to be used when a connection is open, or the file name to be used when connecting to a Microsoft Access database.
Initial Catalog	The name of the database.
Integrated Security	The parameter that determines whether or not the connection is to be a secure connection. **True**, **False**, and **SSPI** are the possible values. **SSPI** is the equivalent of **True**.
Password	The login password for the SQL Server database.
Persist Security Info	When set to **False**, security-sensitive information, such as the password, is not returned as part of the connection, if the connection is open or has ever been in an open state. Setting this property to **True** can be a security risk. The default setting is **False**.
Provider	The property that is used to set or return the name of the provider for the connection; this parameter used only for **OleDbConnection** objects.
User ID	The SQL Server login account name.

Demonstration: Setting SQL Server Security

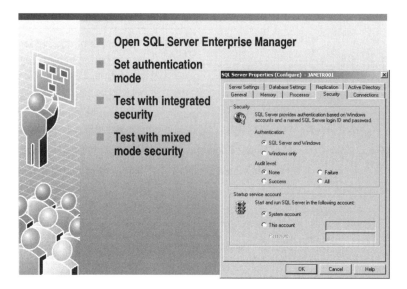

Introduction

In this demonstration, you will see how to set and test an integrated security connection between a Web application and a SQL Server.

To run this demonstration

Open SQL Server Enterprise Manager

1. On the **Start** menu, right-click **My Computer** and then click **Manage**.

2. In the **Computer Management** console, expand the **Services and Applications folder** and then expand the **Microsoft SQL Servers folder**.

3. Right-click the **(local)** SQL Server and then click **Properties**.

Set the authentication mode

4. In the **SQL Server Properties** dialog box, on the **Security** tab, click the **Windows only** option button in the **Authentication** section, and then click **OK**.

5. Open the SQLSecurityModes.aspx Web Form in the Mod10VB or Mod10CS project in the 2310Demos solution.

6. Build and browse the SQLSecurityModes.aspx page.

Test with integrated security

7. Click **Use integrated security**, and then click **Get Data**.

   The data is retrieved from the database and is displayed in the **DataGrid** control.

8. Click **Use standard security**, and then click **Get Data**.

   You get an error because the user does not exist in the SQL Server.

9. Create a new user for SQL Server:

   a. In the **Computer Management** console, expand the **(local)** SQL Server folder and then expand the **Security** folder.

   b. Right-click **Logins** and then click **New Login**.

   c. In the **SQL Server Login Properties** dialog box, type **CohoUser** in the **Name** field, click **SQL Server Authentication** in the **Authentication** section, type **1Coho** in the **Password** field, and then click **OK**.

   d. Type **1Coho** in the **Confirm Password** dialog box, and then click **OK**.

Test with mixed-mode security

10. Change the SQL Server authentication mode to mixed-mode.

   a. In the **Computer Management** console, right-click the **(local)** SQL Server and click **Properties**.

   b. In the **SQL Server Properties** dialog box, on the **Security** tab, click the **SQL Server and Windows** option button in the **Authentication** section, and then click **OK**.

   c. When prompted to restart the SQL Server service, click **Yes**.

11. View the SQLSecurityModes.aspx page in the browser again and test both methods of accessing the SQL Server. Both methods will now work.

Lesson: Accessing Data with DataSets

- Creating a DataAdapter
- Creating a DataSet
- Demonstration: Programmatically Using a DataSet
- Using a DataView
- Practice: Organizing Code to Create a DataSet
- Binding a DataSet to a List-Bound Control
- Instructor-Led Practice: Displaying a DataSet
- Handling Errors

Introduction

The **DataSet** object represents a local copy of data that comes from one or more data sources. Using a **DataSet** object allows a Web Form to run semi-independently from the data sources. The **DataSet** object can use a **DataAdapter** object to load data from a data source and can then disconnect from that data source. The user can then use and manipulate the data. When the data needs to be updated in the data source, a **DataAdapter** is used to reconnect and update the data source.

In this lesson, you will learn how to use **DataSet** objects to support the local data storage and the manipulation requirements of Web Forms.

Lesson objectives

After completing this lesson, you will be able to:

- Create a **DataAdapter** object to link a **DataSet** object to a data source.
- Create a **DataSet** object to hold data from a data source.
- Use **DataView** objects to hold a subset of data from a **DataSet** object.
- Bind a **DataSet** object and a **DataView** object to a list-bound control.
- Handle the typical errors that are encountered while accessing data.

Creating a DataAdapter

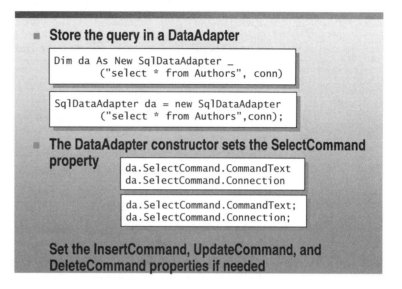

■ **Store the query in a DataAdapter**

```
Dim da As New SqlDataAdapter _
        ("select * from Authors", conn)
```

```
SqlDataAdapter da = new SqlDataAdapter
        ("select * from Authors",conn);
```

■ **The DataAdapter constructor sets the SelectCommand property**

```
da.SelectCommand.CommandText
da.SelectCommand.Connection
```

```
da.SelectCommand.CommandText;
da.SelectCommand.Connection;
```

Set the InsertCommand, UpdateCommand, and DeleteCommand properties if needed

Introduction

The **DataSet** object represents a local copy of data from a data source. When used without a data source, the **DataSet** object is useful for holding local data that Web Forms can access. However, to serve as an actual data-management tool, a **DataSet** object must be able to interact with one or more data sources. To accomplish this interaction, the Microsoft .NET Framework provides the **SqlDataAdapter** and **OleDbDataAdapter** classes.

DataAdapter

A **DataAdapter** object serves as a link between a **DataSet** object and a data source that can be used for retrieving and saving data. The **DataAdapter** class represents a set of database commands and a database connection that you use to fill a **DataSet** object and update the data source. Each **DataAdapter** object exchanges data between a single **DataTable** object in a **DataSet** object and a single result set from a SQL statement or stored procedure.

Visual Studio .NET makes two primary **DataAdapter** classes available for use with databases:

- **OleDbDataAdapter** class

  This class is suitable for use with any data source that is exposed by an OLE DB Data Provider.

- **SqlDataAdapter** class

  This class is specific to a SQL Server version 7.0 or later database. The **SqlDataAdapter** object is faster than the **OleDbDataAdapter** object because it works directly with SQL Server and does not go through an OLE DB Data Provider layer.

In addition, **DataAdapter** classes for other types of data sources can be integrated with Visual Studio .NET.

DataAdapter properties

When you use **DataAdapter** objects to exchange data between a **DataSet** object and a data source, you can specify the actions that you want to perform by using one of the four **DataAdapter** properties. The **DataAdapter** properties then execute a SQL statement or call a stored procedure.

The properties that are available with the **DataAdapter** class are shown in the following table.

Property	Function
SelectCommand	The **SelectCommand** property retrieves rows from the data source.
InsertCommand	The **InsertCommand** property writes inserted rows from the **DataSet** into the data source.
UpdateCommand	The **UpdateCommand** property writes modified rows from the **DataSet** into the data source.
DeleteCommand	The **DeleteCommand** property deletes rows in the data source.

SqlDataAdapter example

The following code example shows how to create a **SqlDataAdapter** object named **da** that contains a query statement:

Visual Basic .NET

```
'Create a connection
Dim conn As New SqlConnection _
  ("data source=localhost;initial catalog=pubs;" & _
  "integrated security=true;persist security info=True;")

'Create the DataAdapter
Dim da As New SqlDataAdapter _
    ("select * from Authors", conn)
```

C#

```
//Create a connection
SqlConnection conn = new SqlConnection
  ("data source=localhost; initial catalog=pubs; " +
  "integrated security=true; persist security info=True;");

//Create the DataAdapter
SqlDataAdapter da = new SqlDataAdapter
    ("select * from Authors", conn);
```

Creating a DataSet

> ■ **Create and populate a DataSet with DataTables**
>
>> ● **Fill** method executes the **SelectCommand**
>
> ```
> DataSet ds = new DataSet();
> da.Fill(ds, "Authors");
> ```
> ```
> Dim ds As New DataSet()
> da.Fill(ds, "Authors")
> ```
>
> ■ **Access a DataTable**
>
> ```
> ds.Tables["Authors"].Rows.Count;
> ```
> ```
> ds.Tables("Authors").Rows.Count
> ```
>
> ```
> string str="";
>
> foreach(DataRow r in
>     ds.Tables["Authors"].Rows)
> {
>   str += r[2];
>   str += r["au_lname"];
> }
> ```
> ```
> Dim r As DataRow
> Dim str As String
> For Each r in _
>     ds.Tables("Authors").Rows
>     str &= r(2)
>     str &= r("au_lname")
> Next
> ```

Introduction

To create a local copy of a database, you create and populate a **DataSet** object by using **DataTable** objects.

Create a DataSet

The first step in creating a **DataSet** object is to declare the **DataSet** object name. The following code creates a **DataSet** object named **ds**:

Visual Basic .NET

```
Dim ds As New DataSet()
```

C#

```
DataSet ds = new DataSet();
```

Fill the DataSet

After you create a **DataSet** object, you fill the **DataTable** objects by creating a **DataAdapter** object. You call the **Fill** method on the **DataAdapter** object and then specify the **DataTable** object that you want to fill. The following code fills the **Authors** table of the **ds DataSet** object by using a **DataAdapter** named **da**:

Visual Basic .NET

```
da.Fill(ds, "Authors")
```

C#

```
da.Fill(ds, "Authors");
```

The **Fill** method implicitly executes an SQL query in the **SelectCommand** property of the **DataAdapter** object. The results of the SQL query are used to define the structure of the **DataTable** object, and to populate the table with data.

The following code example shows how to create a **SqlDataAdapter** object **da**, and then call the **Fill** method to store the data in the **DataSet** object **ds**.

Visual Basic .NET

```
'Create a connection
Dim conn As New SqlConnection _
  ("data source=localhost;initial catalog=pubs;" & _
  "integrated security=SSPI;persist security info=True;")

'Create the DataSet
Dim ds As New DataSet()

'Create the DataAdapter
Dim da As New SqlDataAdapter _
      ("select * from Authors", conn)

'Fill the DataSet ds
da.Fill(ds, "Authors")
```

C#

```
//Create a connection
SqlConnection conn = new SqlConnection
  ("data source=localhost;initial catalog=pubs; " +
  "integrated security=SSPI;persist security info=True;");

//Create the DataSet
DataSet ds = new DataSet();

//Create the DataAdapter
SqlDataAdapter da = new SqlDataAdapter
      ("select * from Authors", conn);

//Fill the DataSet ds
da.Fill(ds, "Authors");
```

The second argument to the **Fill** method is a name for the **DataTable** object that is created. You use this name to access the returned data.

Accessing a DataTable

After you have placed data in a **DataSet** object, you can programmatically access the data. As shown in the following code, each **DataSet** object is comprised of one or more **DataTable** objects that you can refer to by name or by ordinal position:

Visual Basic .NET

```
ds.Tables("Authors")
-or-
ds.Tables(0)
```

C#

```
ds.Tables["Authors"];
-or-
ds.Tables[0];
```

The **DataRow** and **DataColumn** classes are primary components of a **DataTable** class. You would use a **DataRow** object and its properties and methods to retrieve and evaluate the values in a **DataTable** object. The **DataRowCollection** represents the actual **DataRow** objects that are in the **DataTable** object, and the **DataColumnCollection** contains the **DataColumn** objects that describe the schema of the **DataTable** object. The **Rows** property of the **DataTable** object provides programmatic access to the **DataRowCollection**. The **Columns** property of the **DataTable** object provides programmatic access to the **DataColumnCollection**.

The following sample code adds the column names from a **DataSet** object to the **ListBox** control named **lstItems**:

Visual Basic .NET

```
Dim col As DataColumn
For Each col In ds.Tables(0).Columns
  lstItems.Items.Add(col.ColumnName)
Next
```

C#

```
foreach(DataColumn col in ds.Tables[0].Columns)
{
  lstItems.Items.Add(col.ColumnName);
}
```

Both the **DataRowCollection** and **DataColumnCollection** objects have a **Count** property that Enables you to determine the number of rows or columns in a **DataTable** object, as shown in the following sample code:

Visual Basic .NET

```
ds.Tables("Authors").Rows.Count
ds.Tables("Authors").Columns.Count
```

C#

```
ds.Tables["Authors"].Rows.Count;
ds.Tables["Authors"].Columns.Count;
```

Counting the rows and columns of the **DataTable** object allows you to access individual fields in the **DataTable** object. You can either access fields by ordinal (0-based) position or by name. In the following code, X is the index of the row of data that you want to access:

Visual Basic .NET

```
DataSet.Tables(0).Rows(x)(1)
DataSet.Tables(0).Rows(x)("fieldname")
```

C#

```
ds.Tables["Authors"].Rows[x][1];
ds.Tables["Authors"].Rows[x]["fieldname"];
```

The following code loops through each row in the **DataTable** object named **Authors** and creates a string by using the second and **au_lname** fields in **Authors**:

Visual Basic .NET

```
Dim r As DataRow
Dim str As String
For Each r in ds.Tables("Authors").Rows
  str &= r(1)
  str &= r("au_lname")
Next
```

C#

```
string str = "";
foreach(DataRow r in ds.Tables["Authors"].Rows)
{
  str += r[1];
  str += r["au_lname"];
}
```

Demonstration: Programmatically Using a DataSet

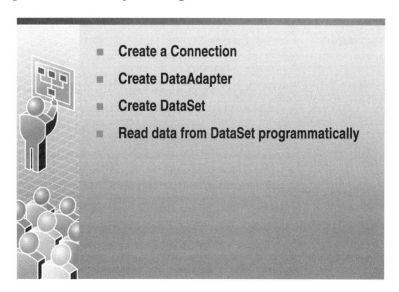

- **Create a Connection**
- **Create DataAdapter**
- **Create DataSet**
- **Read data from DataSet programmatically**

Introduction

In this demonstration, you will review code that creates and fills a **DataSet** object, and then see how that code dynamically fills a **ListBox** control from the **DataSet** object.

To run the demonstration

1. Open the UseDataSet.aspx page in the Mod10VB or Mod10CS project in the 2310Demos solution.

2. Build and browse the page.

   The first time the page is loaded, the **lstItems** list box is dynamically filled with the column names from the **DataSet**.

   The **Get Number of Rows** button and the **Get Values** button read information from the **DataSet**.

3. Click **Get Number of Rows**.

   The code in the click event procedure displays the **Count** property of the **Rows** collection.

4. Select a column in the list box and then click **Get Values**.

   The code in the click event procedure loops through the rows of the **DataSet** and displays the selected field.

5. In Visual Studio .NET, view the code-behind page for the UseDataSet.aspx page.

6. In the **Page_Load** event procedure, show the code that creates the following objects:

   - **SqlConnection**
   - **SqlDataAdapter**
   - **DataSet**

7. In the **Page_Load** event procedure, show how, the first time that the page is displayed, the **lstItems** list box is filled with column names only.

8. In the **cmdRows_Click** event procedure, show how the number of rows is retrieved from the **DataSet**.

9. In the **cmdGetValues_Click** event procedure, show how the selected field is retrieved from the **DataSet**.

Using a DataView

- A DataView can be customized to present a subset of data from a DataTable

- The DefaultView property returns the default DataView of the table

```
Dim dv As DataView = ds.Tables("Authors").DefaultView
```

```
DataView dv = ds.Tables["Authors"].DefaultView;
```

- Setting up a different view of a DataSet

```
Dim dv As New DataView (ds.Tables("Authors"))
dv.RowFilter = "state = 'CA'"
```

```
DataView dv = new DataView(ds.Tables["Authors"]);
dv.RowFilter = "state = 'CA'";
```

Introduction

To display the data that is held in a **DataSet** object, you can bind the **DataSet** object directly to a list-bound control or use a **DataView** object. A **DataView** object is a bindable, customized display of a single **DataTable** object. After you have created a **DataView** object, the user can use the **DataView** object for data sorting, filtering, searching, editing, and navigation.

DataViews as a subset of a DataTable

DataView objects can be customized to present a subset of data from a **DataTable** object. This customization allows you to have two controls that are bound to the same **DataTable** object, but with each control showing different versions of the data. For example, one control may be bound to a **DataView** object showing all of the rows in the table, while a second control is bound to another **DataView** object that is configured to display only the rows that have been deleted from the **DataTable** object.

DefaultView

Each **DataTable** object in a **DataSet** object has a **DefaultView** property, which returns the default view for the table. The following code shows how you can access the default **DataView** object dv, of a **DataTable** object named **Authors**:

Visual Basic .NET

```
Dim dv As DataView = ds.Tables("Authors").DefaultView
```

C#

```
DataView dv = ds.Tables["Authors"].DefaultView;
```

Customized DataView

You can also create a custom **DataView** object that is based on a subset of the data that is in a **DataTable** object. For example, you can set the **DataView RowFilter** property by using a filter expression. The filter expression must evaluate to **True** or **False**. You can also set the **DataView** object **Sort** property by using a sort expression. The sort expression can include the names of **DataColumn** objects or a calculation.

In the following code, the **RowFilter** property, of a **DataView** object **dv**, is set to retrieve only authors from the state of California, and it then sorts the results by last name:

Visual Basic .NET

```
Dim dv As New DataView(ds.Tables("Authors"))
dv.RowFilter = "state = 'CA'"
dv.Sort = "au_lname"
```

C#

```
DataView dv = new DataView(ds.Tables["Authors"]);
dv.RowFilter = "state = 'CA'";
dv.Sort = "au_lname";
```

Practice: Organizing Code to Create a DataSet

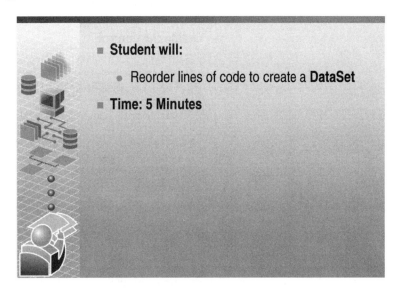

In this practice, you will rearrange lines of ADO.NET code into the correct order to create a **DataSet** object.

To run the practice

- View the http://localhost/Mod10VB/DataSetCode.aspx or http://localhost/Mod10CS/DataSetCode.aspx page and organize the lines of ADO.NET code into the correct order to create a **DataSet** object.

Note   There are several correct answers to this practice.

Binding a DataSet to a List-Bound Control

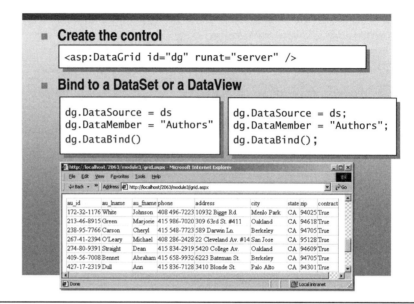

Introduction

ASP.NET includes a set of list-bound controls, such as the **DataGrid**, **DataList**, and **DataRepeater** controls, which make displaying data from a data source simple and flexible. Developers only need to bind these controls to a data source to display the selected data.

Create the control

The first step in binding the **DataSet** object to the list-bound control is to create the control. The following code shows how to create a **DataGrid** control **dg** that produces the HTML output that resembles a spreadsheet:

```
<asp:DataGrid id="dg" runat="server" />
```

Bind to a Dataset or DataView

To bind a **DataSet** object to a **DataGrid** control, you first need to set the **DataSource** property of the **DataGrid** control to a **DataSet**, **DataTable**, or **DataView** object, and then call the **DataBind** method.

If you set the **DataSource** property of the **DataGrid** control directly to a **DataSet** object, the **DataTable** object with the index of 0 is used by default. To specify a different **DataTable** object, set the **DataMember** property of the **DataGrid** control to the name of the desired **DataTable** object.

The following code example shows how to bind the **Authors** table, of the **ds** **DataSet** object, to a **DataGrid** control named **dg**:

Visual Basic .NET

```
dg.DataSource = ds
dg.DataMember = "Authors"
dg.DataBind()
```

C#

```
dg.DataSource = ds;
dg.DataMember = "Authors";
dg.DataBind();
```

The following code shows how you can also use the **Tables** collection of the **DataSet** object **ds** to assign the **DataTable** object **Authors** directly to the **DataSource** property of the **DataGrid** control named **dg**:

Visual Basic .NET

```
dg.DataSource = ds.Tables("Authors")
dg.DataBind()
```

C#

```
dg.DataSource = ds.Tables["Authors"];
dg.DataBind();
```

If you want to display a different view of the data in the **DataGrid** control, you will need to create a new **DataView** object from the **DataSet** object, and then bind that object to the control.

Example of Using a custom view

The following code example shows how to bind a **DataView** object **dv**, filtered for the state of California, to a **DataGrid** control **dg**:

Visual Basic .NET

```
Dim dv As New DataView(ds.Tables("Authors"))
dv.RowFilter = "state = 'CA'"
dg.DataSource = dv
dg.DataBind()
```

C#

```
DataView dv = new DataView(ds.Tables["Authors"]);
dv.RowFilter = "state = 'CA'";
dg.DataSource = dv;
dg.Databind();
```

The following illustration shows the default format of the **DataGrid** control, displaying data for authors who are living in the state of California.

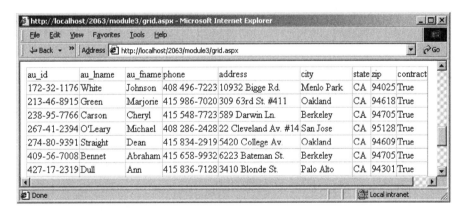

Instructor-Led Practice: Displaying a DataSet

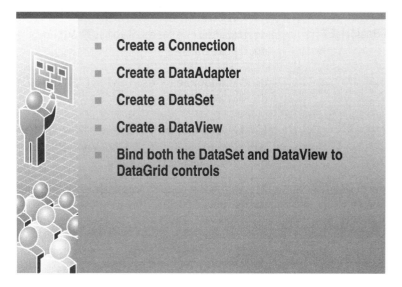

- Create a Connection
- Create a DataAdapter
- Create a DataSet
- Create a DataView
- Bind both the DataSet and DataView to DataGrid controls

Introduction

In this instructor-led practice, you will review code that creates and fills a **DataSet** object, creates a **DataView** object by using sorted and filtered data from the **DataSet** object, and then binds **DataGrid** controls to the **DataSet** and **DataView** objects.

To run the instructor-led practice

1. Open the UseGrid.aspx page in the Mod10VB or Mod10CS project in the 2310Demos solution.

2. Build and browse the UseGrid.aspx page.

   There are two **DataGrid** controls that are bound to the same **DataSet** object. The first **DataGrid** control shows all of the data in the **DataSet** object. The second **DataGrid** control is bound to a **DataView** object, which filters and sorts the data. The second **DataGrid** control also implements sorting by setting the **Sort** property of the **DataView** object.

3. In Visual Studio .NET, view the code-behind page for the UseGrid.aspx page.

4. In the Page_Load event procedure, show the code that does the following:

   - Creates the **SqlConnection** object.
   - Creates the **SqlDataAdapter** object.
   - Creates a **DataSet** object.
   - Binds the first **DataGrid** control to the **DataSet** object.
   - Creates a **DataView** object and sets the **RowFilter** and **Sort** properties.
   - Binds the second **DataGrid** control to the **DataView** object.

Handling Errors

- **Connection will not open**
  - Connection string is invalid
  - Server or database not found
  - Login failed
- **DataAdapter cannot create a DataSet**
  - Invalid SQL syntax
  - Invalid table or field name

Code Example

Introduction

There are two main sources of error when you try to access data from a Web Form by using ADO.NET: connection problems and misalignment with the database.

Connection will not open

More than one error can occur when the **Open** method call is made. As a result of the possibility of more than one error occurring, you must be able to handle multiple errors by using **Try...Catch...Finally** statements. If one or more **SqlException** exceptions occur, you can loop through all of the SQL exception objects that are returned to your Web application.

The following code shows how to use a **Try...Catch** statement to catch multiple types of exceptions. In this example, the code catches the **InvalidOperationException** type of exception, along with other exceptions, by using a generic exception handler:

Visual Basic .NET

```vbnet
Try
    Dim conn As New SqlConnection(...)
    Dim da As New SqlDataAdapter(..., conn)
    Dim ds As New DataSet()
        da.Fill(ds)

Catch ex1 As System.Data.SqlClient.SqlException
    Select Case ex1.Number
        Case 17
            lblErrors.Text = lblErrors.Text & _
                                        ("invalid Server name")
        Case 156, 170 'bad SQL syntax
            lblErrors.Text = lblErrors.Text & _
                                        ("incorrect syntax")
        Case 207 'bad field name in select
            lblErrors.Text = lblErrors.Text & _
                                        ("invalid column name")
        Case 208 'bad table name in select
            lblErrors.Text = lblErrors.Text & _
                                        ("invalid object name")
        Case 18452
            lblErrors.Text = lblErrors.Text & _
                                        ("invalid user name")
        Case 18456
            lblErrors.Text = lblErrors.Text & _
                                        ("invalid password")
        Case 4060
            lblErrors.Text = lblErrors.Text & _
                                        ("invalid database")
    End Select

Catch ex2 As System.Exception
    lblErrors.Text = lblErrors.Text & _
    ("Unexpected exception: " & ex2.Message & ". ")
End Try
```

C#

```
try
{
  SqlConnection conn = new SqlConnection("...");
  SqlDataAdapter da = new SqlDataAdapter("...",conn);
  DataSet ds = new DataSet();
  da.Fill(ds);
}
catch (System.Data.SqlClient.SqlException ex1)
{
  switch(ex1.Number)
  {
      case 17:
          lblErrors.Text = lblErrors.Text +
                          ("invalid Server name");
          break;
      case 156:
      case 170: //bad SQL syntax
          lblErrors.Text = lblErrors.Text +
                          ("incorrect syntax");
          break;
      case 207: //bad field name in select
          lblErrors.Text = lblErrors.Text +
                          ("invalid column name");
          break;
      case 208: //bad table name in select
          lblErrors.Text = lblErrors.Text +
                          ("invalid object name");
          break;
      case 18452:
          lblErrors.Text = lblErrors.Text +
                          ("invalid user name");
          break;
      case 18456:
          lblErrors.Text = lblErrors.Text +
                          ("invalid password");
          break;
      case 4060:
          lblErrors.Text = lblErrors.Text +
                          ("invalid database");
          break;
  }
}
catch (System.Exception ex2)
{
  lblErrors.Text = lblErrors.Text +
      ("Unexpected exception: " + ex2.Message + ". ");
}
```

DataAdapter cannot create a DataSet

The **SqlException** class contains the exception that is thrown when SQL Server returns a warning or error. This class is created whenever the SQL Server .NET Data Provider encounters a situation that it cannot handle. The **SqlException** class always contains at least one instance of a **SqlError** object. You can use the severity level of the class to help you determine the content of a message that is displayed by an exception.

To catch **SqlException** objects, you need to look for errors of type **System.Data.SqlClient.SqlException**. When a **SqlException** object occurs, the exception object contains an **Errors** collection.

The following example shows how you can loop through the **Errors** collection to find details about the errors that occurred:

Visual Basic .NET

```
Dim erData As SqlClient.SqlErrorCollection = ex1.Errors
Dim i As Integer
For i = 0 To erData.Count - 1
  lblErrors.Text &= ("Error " & i & ": " & _
      erData(i).Number & ", " & _
      erData(i).Class & ", " & _
      erData(i).Message & "<br>")
Next i
```

C#

```
SqlErrorCollection erData = ex1.Errors;
for(int i = 0; i < erData.Count; i++)
{
  lblErrors.Text += "Error" + i + ": " +
      erData[i].Number + ", " +
      erData[i].Class + ", " +
      erData[i].Message + "<br>";
}
```

SQL Server errors

SQL Server errors share common properties and are identified by number and severity level:

- The **SqlError** class and common properties

  Each **SqlError** object has the common properties that are shown in the following table.

Property	Description
Class	Gets the severity level of the error that was returned from the SQL Server.
LineNumber	Gets the line number within the Transact-SQL command batch or the stored procedure that contains the error.
Message	Gets the text describing the error.
Number	Gets a number that identifies the type of error.

  Note For a complete list of **SqlError** class properties, see the Visual Studio .NET documentation.

- SQL Server error numbers

  The **Number** property allows you to determine the specific error that occurred. For example, the following table lists some common SQL Server error numbers and their descriptions.

Number	Description
17	Invalid server name
4060	Invalid database name
18456	Invalid user name or password

- SQL Server severity levels

  The following table describes SQL Server error severity levels, which are accessed through the **Class** property, of the **SqlError** class.

Severity	Description	Action
11-16	Generated by user	Can be corrected by user.
17-19	Software or hardware errors	You can continue working, but you might not be able to execute a particular statement. **SqlConnection** remains open.
20-25	Software or hardware errors	The server closes **SqlConnection**. The user can reopen the connection.

Lesson: Using Multiple Tables

- Storing Multiple Tables

- Creating Relationships

- Programmatically Navigating Between Tables Using Relationships

- Visually Navigating Between Tables Using Relationships

- Instructor-Led Practice: Displaying Data from Multiple Tables

Introduction

One of the strengths of **DataSet** objects is that they can contain multiple **DataTable** objects, and each **DataTable** object can come from a different data source.

In this lesson, you will learn how to store multiple tables of data in a **DataSet** object and then learn how to display that data in **DataGrid** controls.

Lesson objectives

After completing this lesson, you will be able to:

- Store data in multiple tables from multiple sources.

- Create relationships between data from multiple data sources.

- Use relationships to navigate between tables of data from multiple sources.

Storing Multiple Tables

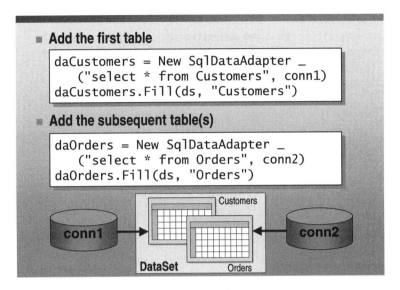

Introduction	To fill a **DataSet** object with multiple **DataTable** objects that come from one or more data sources, you need to use multiple **DataAdapter** objects. Each **DataAdapter** object fills a separate table in the **DataSet** object. Because the order of the **DataAdapter** objects controls the order of implementation, you can control the order in which updates are written to and from the database. This control over implementation order helps you to preserve referential integrity between related tables in the database.
Add first table	An example of controlling the order in which **DataTable** objects are created is a salesperson who needs to retrieve customer information, and information about purchase orders that were placed by each customer, from a central database. To meet this requirement, you could create a Web application that contains two **DataAdapter** objects, a first one to retrieve customer records, and a second one to retrieve purchase order records. By loading the customer data first, you can preserve the referential integrity between customers and their purchase orders.

The following code populates a **Customers DataTable** object by using a **DataAdapter** object named **daCustomers**:

Visual Basic .NET

```
Dim conn As SqlConnection
Dim daCustomers As SqlDataAdapter
Dim daOrders As SqlDataAdapter
Dim ds As New DataSet()

'create a connection to the Pubs database
conn = New SqlConnection("data source=localhost;" & _
  "integrated security=true;initial catalog=northwind")

'create the first DataTable
daCustomers = New SqlDataAdapter _
  ("select CustomerID, CompanyName from Customers", conn)
daCustomers.Fill(ds, "Customers")
```

C#

```
SqlConnection conn;
SqlDataAdapter daCustomers;
SqlDataAdapter daOrders;
DataSet ds = new DataSet();

// Create a connection to the Pubs database
conn = new SqlConnection("data source=localhost; " +
    "integrated security=true;initial catalog=northwind");

// Create the first DataTable
daCustomers = new SqlDataAdapter
  ("select CustomerID, CompanyName from Customers", conn);
daCustomers.Fill(ds, "Customers");
```

Add subsequent tables

After the first **DataTable** object is loaded, you can fill additional **DataTable** objects and define the relationships between the objects based on the initial **DataTable** object. Continuing with the preceding example, you would fill the **Orders DataTable** object.

The following code populates the **Orders DataTable** object by using a **DataAdapter** object named **daOrders**:

Visual Basic .NET

```
'Create the second DataTable
daOrders = New SqlDataAdapter _
  ("select CustomerID, OrderID, OrderDate, ShippedDate " & _
  "from Orders", conn)
daOrders.Fill(ds, "Orders")
```

C#

```
// Create the second DataTable
daOrders = new SqlDataAdapter
  ("select CustomerID, OrderID, OrderDate, ShippedDate " +
    "from Orders", conn);
daOrders.Fill(ds, "Orders");
```

Note   You should use a new **DataAdapter** object for each **DataTable** object in a **DataSet** object.

Creating Relationships

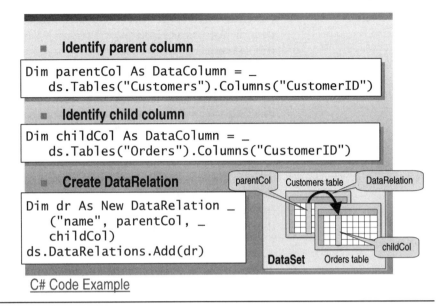

- **Identify parent column**

```
Dim parentCol As DataColumn = _
    ds.Tables("Customers").Columns("CustomerID")
```

- **Identify child column**

```
Dim childCol As DataColumn = _
    ds.Tables("Orders").Columns("CustomerID")
```

- **Create DataRelation**

```
Dim dr As New DataRelation _
    ("name", parentCol, _
    childCol)
ds.DataRelations.Add(dr)
```

C# Code Example

Introduction

A **DataRelation** object is used to reference two **DataTable** objects to each other through **DataColumn** objects. For example, in a Customer/Orders relationship, the Customers table is the parent of the relationship and the Orders table is the child of the relationship. This relationship is similar to a primary key/foreign key relationship. Relationships are created between matching columns in the parent and child tables. The **DataType** value for both columns must be identical.

DataRelation objects are contained in a **DataRelationCollection** object, which you can access not only through the **Relations** property of the **DataSet** object, but also through the **ChildRelations** and **ParentRelations** properties of the **DataTable** object.

To create a **DataRelation** object, you use the **DataRelation** constructor and the **Add** method of the **Relations** collection of a **DataSet** object.

DataRelation object example

The following example creates a **DataRelation** object **dr** and adds it to the **DataSet** object **ds**:

Visual Basic .NET

```
'Create DataRelation: each publisher publishes many titles
Dim dr As DataRelation
Dim parentCol As DataColumn
Dim childCol As DataColumn

parentCol = ds.Tables("Customers").Columns("CustomerID")
childCol = ds.Tables("Orders").Columns("CustomerID")
dr = New DataRelation("CustOrders", parentCol, childCol)
ds.Relations.Add(dr)
```

C#

```
// Create DataRelation: each publisher publishes many titles
DataRelation dr;
DataColumn parentCol;
DataColumn childCol;

parentCol = ds.Tables["Customers"].Columns["CustomerID"];
childCol = ds.Tables["Orders"].Columns["CustomerID"];
dr = new DataRelation("CustOrders", parentCol, childCol);
ds.Relations.Add(dr);
```

Note For more information on data relationships, see "Navigating a Relationship between Tables," in the Visual Studio .NET documentation.

Programmatically Navigating Between Tables Using Relationships

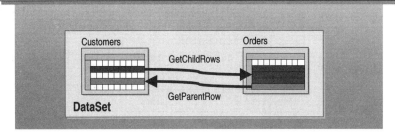

```
ds.Tables(index).Rows(index).GetChildRows("relation")
ds.Tables(index).Rows(index).GetParentRow("relation")
```

```
ds.Tables[index].Rows[index].GetChildRows("relation");
ds.Tables[index].Rows[index].GetParentRow("relation");
```

Customers   Orders
                GetChildRows
DataSet   GetParentRow

Introduction

In many Web application scenarios, you will want to work with data from more than one table, and often you will want to work with data from related tables. The relationship between a parent and child table is called a *master-detail* relationship. An example of this relationship would be retrieving a customer record and also viewing related customer order information.

The disconnected **DataSet** object model allows you to work with multiple **DataTables** objects in your Web application and to define a relationship between those **DataTable** objects. You can then use the relationship to navigate between related records in the tables.

Navigating programmatically

One of the primary functions of a **DataRelation** class is to allow navigation from one **DataTable** object to another **DataTable** object within a **DataSet** object. This ability to navigate allows you to retrieve all of the related **DataRow** objects in one **DataTable** object when you are given a single **DataRow** object from a related **DataTable** object. For example, after establishing a **DataRelation** object between a **DataTable** object of customers and a **DataTable** object of purchase orders, you can retrieve all of the order rows for a particular customer row by using the **DataRow.GetChildRows** method.

The **GetChildRows** method of a **DataRow** object retrieves related rows that are from a child **DataTable** object. The **GetParentRow** method of a **DataRow** object then retrieves the parent row from a parent **DataTable** object.

For example, you can have a **DataGrid** control named **dgCustomers** that is displaying data that is from the **DataTable** object **Customers**, which is in a **DataSet** object **ds**. The following code shows a loop through all the **childOrder** records to get a list of order numbers:

Visual Basic .NET

```
currentParentRow = ds.Tables("Customers"). _
  Rows(dgCustomers.SelectedIndex)
For Each r In currentParentRow.GetChildRows("CustOrders")
  Label1.Text &= r("OrderID") & ", "
Next
```

C#

```
currentParentRow = ds.Tables["Customers"].
  Rows[dgCustomers.SelectedIndex];
foreach(DataRow r
  in currentParentRow.GetChildRows("CustOrders"))
{
  Label1.Text += r["OrderID"] + ",";
}
```

Visually Navigating Between Tables Using Relationships

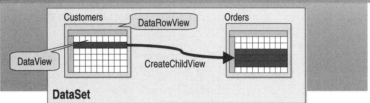

```vbnet
Dim tableView As DataView
Dim currentRowView As DataRowView

tableView = New DataView(ds.Tables("Customers"))
currentRowView = tableView(dgCustomers.SelectedIndex)
dgChild.DataSource = currentRowView.CreateChildView("CustOrders")
```

```csharp
DataView tableView;
DataRowView currentRowView;

tableView = new DataView(ds.Tables["Customers"]);
currentRowView = tableView[dgCustomers.SelectedIndex];
dgChild.DataSource = currentRowView.CreateChildView("CustOrders");
```

Customers   DataRowView   Orders

DataView   CreateChildView

DataSet

Navigating Visually

With Visual Studio .NET, you can also display relationships by dragging controls from the toolbox. If you want to display the child rows of a relationship in a separate list-bound control, you can use the **CreateChildView** method and then bind the list-bound control to the resulting **DataView** object.

To connect two list-bound controls through a **DataRelation** object, you need to get the **DataRowView** object of the selected row of the parent list-bound control, and then call the **CreateChildView** method of the **DataRowView** object.

The following code creates a **DataView** object from a **DataRelation** object to display child records in a **DataGrid** control:

Visual Basic .NET

```vbnet
Dim parentTableView As New _
                        DataView(ds.Tables("Customers"))
Dim currentRowView As DataRowView = _
                parentTableView(dgCustomers.SelectedIndex)
dgChild.DataSource = _
  currentRowView.CreateChildView("CustOrders")
dgChild.DataBind()
```

C#

```csharp
DataView parentTableView = new
                        DataView(ds.Tables["Customers"]);
DataRowView currentRowView =
                parentTableView[dgCustomers.SelectedIndex];

dgChild.DataSource =
  currentRowView.CreateChildView("CustOrders");
dgChild.DataBind();
```

Instructor-Led Practice: Displaying Data from Multiple Tables

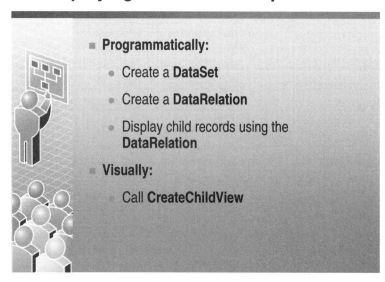

To run the instructor-led practice

1. Open the UseRelations.aspx page in the Mod10VB or the Mod10CS project in the 2310Demos solution.

2. Build and browse the UseRelations.aspx page.

   There are two **DataGrid** controls on the page. When you select a customer in the first **DataGrid** control, the event procedure reads the related rows from the Orders **DataTable** object, based on the relation and the displayed order numbers, and then builds a **DataView** for the child **DataGrid** control.

3. In Visual Studio .NET, view the code-behind page for the UseRelations.aspx page.

4. The **Page_Load** event procedure calls three sub procedures: **CreateDataSet, MakeDataRelation** ,and **BindToDataGrid**:

   • **CreateDataSet**. This sub procedure creates the **Connection** object, **DataAdapter** object, and **DataSet** object.

   • **MakeDataRelation**. This sub procedure creates the **DataRelation** object between the two tables. The relationship is Publishers to Titles.

   • **BindToDataGrid**. This sub procedure binds the **DataGrid** control to the parent table, Customers.

5. The **dgParent_SelectedIndexChanged** event procedure displays child rows in two ways: programmatically and visually:

   • Programmatically. The procedure calls the **GetChildRows** method of the current row and then loops through the returned records to output the **OrderID** field of each row.

   • Visually. The procedure calls the **CreateChildView** method of the view of the current row and then binds it to a second **DataGrid** control.

To demonstrate the Data Form Wizard

1. Right-click the **Mod10** project, click **Add**, and then click **Add New Item**.

2. In the **Add New Item** dialog box, click **Data Form Wizard** in the **Templates** list, type **CustOrders.aspx** in the **Name** field, and then click **Open**.

3. Complete the steps of the wizard as shown in the following table.

On this page	Do this
Welcome …	Click **Next**.
Choose the dataset you want to use	Click **Create a new dataset named**, then type **dsCustOrders** in the field, and then click **Next**.
Choose a data connection	Select an existing connection or create a new one to the Northwind database, and then click **Next**.
Choose tables or views	Add the Customers and Orders tables to the **Selected item(s)** list, and then click **Next**.
Create a relationship between tables	Enter **CustOrders** in the **Name** field, select **Customers** for the **Parent table**, select **Orders** for the **Child table**, select **CustomerID** for the **Key**, for both the parent and child tables, click the **>** button, and then click **Next**.
Choose tables and columns to display	Keep the defaults to display all of the columns in the Master and Detail tables, and then click **Finish**.

The Data Form Wizard creates a Web Form with a **DataGrid** control and a **Load** button.

4. Right-click the **CustOrders.aspx** page in Solution Explorer and then click **Build and Browse**.

5. In the browser, click **Load**.

   The **DataGrid** control is loaded with data from the Customers table and the data is displayed.

6. Click **Show Details** for one of the Customers, and then scroll to the bottom of the page.

   The detailed information for the selected customer is displayed in a separate table.

Lesson: Accessing Data with DataReaders

- **What is a DataReader?**

- **Creating a DataReader**

- **Reading Data from a DataReader**

- **Binding a DataReader to a List-Bound Control**

- **Practice: Organizing Code to Create a DataReader**

- **Demonstration: Displaying Data Using DataReaders**

Introduction

The benefit of using a **DataSet** object is that it gives you a disconnected copy of the database. For long-running Web applications, using a **DataSet** object is often the best approach. However, developers often perform short and simple operations, such as displaying a single set of data directly to the user or accessing a single password, with each data request. For such operations, developers do not need to maintain a **DataSet** object; instead, they can use a **DataReader** object.

In this section, you will learn how to read data from a data source by using the **DataReader** class.

Lesson objectives

After completing this lesson, you will be able to:

- Explain how the **DataReader** class works.

- Create a **DataReader** object.

- Read data from a **DataReader** object.

- Bind a list-bound server control to a **DataReader** object.

What is a DataReader?

- Forward-only, read-only
- Fast access to data
- Connected to a data source
- Manage the connection yourself
- Manage the data yourself, or bind it to a list-bound control
- Uses fewer server resources

Introduction

When a large amount of data is being retrieved from a data source, holding memory open becomes an issue. For example, reading 10,000 rows out of a database causes a **DataTable** object to allocate and maintain memory for those 10,000 rows for the lifetime of the table. If 1,000 users do this against the same computer at the same time, memory usage becomes critical. To address such memory usage situations, the **DataReader** class is designed to produce a read-only, forward-only data stream that is returned from the database. Therefore, only one record at a time is ever in server memory.

Forward-only, read-only

The **DataReader** class provides a read-only, forward-only transfer of data that can be bound to a single list-bound control. For example, if you only want to show the results of a database query in a single list-bound control, and if you will not be manipulating that data, a **DataReader** class is an ideal way to accomplish this.

Fast access to data

DataReader objects are faster than **DataSet** objects due to the light-weight nature of the **DataReader** class. There is more overhead in creating the **DataSet** object because **DataSet** objects have the ability to read and write data and scan forwards and backwards. There is very little overhead to a **DataReader** object because it is forward-only and read-only. This relative lack of overhead means that accessing data with a **DataReader** object is faster than accessing data with a **DataSet** object.

Connected to data source

ADO.NET includes two types of **DataReader** objects: the **SqlDataReader** object for SQL Server version 7.0 or later data, and the **OleDbDataReader** object for OLE DB Data Provider data. You use the **OleDbCommand** and **SqlCommand** objects, and the **ExecuteReader** method, to transfer data into a **DataReader** object.

Manage the connection yourself

Unlike a **DataAdapter** object that opens and closes automatically, you need to manage the **DataReader** object connection yourself. The **DataReader** class is similar to the **DataAdapter** class in that you create a **Command** object from a SQL statement and a connection. However, with the **DataReader Command** object, you must explicitly open and close the **Connection** object.

Manage the data yourself

You have the option of looping through the **DataReader** object data and displaying it programmatically, or you can bind a **DataReader** object to a list-bound control. In both cases, you must write the code yourself.

Uses fewer server resources

Because the **DataReader** is not an in-memory representation of the data, using a **DataReader** has little effect on the availability of server resources.

Creating a DataReader

> ■ **To use a DataReader:**
>
> ① Create and open the database connection
>
> ② Create a **Command** object
>
> ③ Create a **DataReader** from the **Command** object
>
> ④ Call the **ExecuteReader** method
>
> ⑤ Use the **DataReader** object
>
> ⑥ Close the **DataReader** object
>
> ⑦ Close the **Connection** object
>
> **Use Try...Catch...Finally error handling**

Code Example

Introduction

To use a **SqlDataReader** object, you need to create a **SqlCommand** object instead of a **SqlDataAdapter** object, which was what was needed with **DataSet** objects. The **SqlCommand** object exposes an **ExecuteReader** method that returns a **SqlDataReader** object.

Similar to a **DataAdapter** object, you create a **Command** object from a SQL statement and a connection. However, with the **DataReader Command** object, you must explicitly open and close the **Connection** object.

To use a DataReader

To use a **DataReader** object, you need to manually code the entire connection process. The following steps are required to use a **DataReader** object:

1. Create and open the database connection.

2. Create a **Command** object.

3. Create the **DataReader** object from the **Command** object.

4. Call the **ExecuteReader** method.

5. Use the **DataReader** object.

6. Close the **DataReader** object.

7. Close the **Connection** object.

The following sample code opens a connection to a database, creates a
DataReader object from a **Command** object, and then loops through the
DataReader object and adds fields from the records to a **ListBox** control:

Visual Basic .NET

```
'Create connection and command objects
Dim conn As New SqlConnection _
  ("data source=localhost;integrated security=true;" & _
  "initial catalog=pubs")
Dim cmdAuthors As New SqlCommand _
                             ("select * from Authors", conn)
conn.Open()

'create DataReader and display data
Dim dr As SqlDataReader
dr = cmdAuthors.ExecuteReader()
Do While dr.Read()
    lstBuiltNames.Items.Add(dr("au_lname") + ", " + _
                             dr("au_fname"))
Loop

'close DataReader and Connection
dr.Close()
conn.Close()
```

C#

```
// Open Connection and create command
SqlConnection conn = new SqlConnection
  ("data source=localhost; integrated security=true; " +
    "initial catalog=pubs;");
SqlCommand cmdAuthors = new SqlCommand
                             ("select * from Authors", conn);
conn.Open();

// Create DataReader and read data
SqlDataReader dr;
dr = cmdAuthors.ExecuteReader();
while (dr.Read())
{
  lstBuiltNames.Items.Add(dr["au_lname"] + ", " +
                             dr["au_fname"]);
}

// Close DataReader and Connection
dr.Close();
conn.Close();
```

Use Try...Catch...Finally error handling

When using connections with the **DataReader** object, you need to always use a **Try...Catch...Finally** statement to ensure that if anything fails, the connection will be closed. Otherwise, the connection may be left open indefinitely.

The following code for a **DataReader** object catches errors and closes the connection:

Visual Basic .NET

```
Try
  conn.Open()
  dr = cmdAuthors.ExecuteReader()
  'use the returned data in the DataReaders
Catch e As Exception
  'handle the error
Finally
  dr.Close()
  conn.Close()
End Try
```

C#

```
try
{
  conn.Open();
  dr = cmdAuthors.ExecuteReader();
  // use the returned data in the DataReaders
}
catch(Exception e)
{
  // Handle error
}
finally
{
  dr.Close();
  conn.Close();
}
```

Reading Data from a DataReader

- **Call Read for each record**
  - Returns false when there are no more records
- **Access fields**
  - Parameter is the ordinal position or name of the field
  - **Get** functions give best performance

```
Do While myReader.Read()
   str &= myReader(1)
   str &= myReader("field")
   str &= myReader.GetDateTime(2)
Loop
```

```
while (myReader.Read())
{
   str += myReader[1];
   str += myReader["field"];
   str += myReader.GetDateTime(2);
}
```

Close the DataReader

Close the connection

Call Read for each record

After you have called the **ExecuteReader** method of the **Command** object, you can access a record in the **DataReader** object by calling the **Read** method. The default positioning in the **DataReader** object is before the first record; therefore, you must call the **Read** method before accessing any data. When there are no more records available, the **Read** method returns a null value.

The following code loops through all of the records in a **DataReader** object **dr,** and displays the **au_fname** field in the **Label** control **lblName**:

Visual Basic .NET

```
Do While dr.Read()
   lblName.Text &= dr("au_fname")
Loop
```

C#

```
while (dr.Read())
{
   lblName.Text += dr["au_name"];
}
```

Access fields

To get the data from the fields in the current record, you can access a field by ordinal position, by name, or by calling an appropriate **Get** method, such as **GetDateTime**, **GetDouble**, **GetInt32**, or **GetString**.

Tip Using a specific **Get** method is faster than accessing by ordinal position or by name because the **DataReader** does not need to check the data format.

For example, the following sample code reads the first name and last name fields, both string values, from the first record of the **DataReader** object **dr**, by using the **GetString()** method:

Visual Basic .NET

```
dr.Read()
lblName.Text = dr.GetString(1) + ", " + _
    dr.GetString(2)
```

C#

```
dr.Read();
lblName.Text = dr.GetString(1) + ", " +
    dr.GetString(2);
```

You can also reference, by name, the fields of data in the current record of the **DataReader** object. You can then call an appropriate conversion function, as shown in the following example code:

Visual Basic .NET

```
myReader("au_fname")
```

C#

```
myReader["au_fname"];
```

Close the DataReader

While the **DataReader** object is in use, the associated connection is busy serving the **DataReader** object. Therefore, you must call the **Close** method to close the **DataReader** object when you are finished using it, as shown in the following code example:

Visual Basic .NET

```
myReader.Close()
```

C#

```
myReader.Close();
```

Close the Connection

The **DataReader** does not automatically close the connection. You must explicitly call the **Close** method to close the connection when you are finished using it, as shown in the following code example:

Visual Basic .NET

```
conn.Close()
```

C#

```
conn.Close();
```

Binding a DataReader to a List-Bound Control

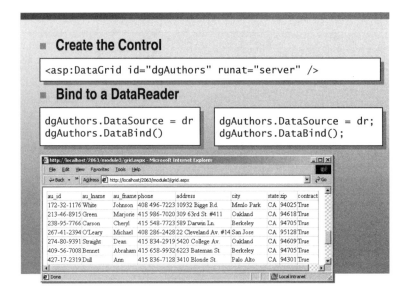

Introduction	In addition to looping through **DataReader** object data and displaying it programmatically, you can bind a **DataReader** object to a list-bound control.

To bind a **DataReader** object to a list-bound control, you set the **DataSource** property of the list-bound control to the **DataReader** object. The following sample code creates a **DataReader** object **dr**, binds it to a **ListBox** control **au_lname**, and then closes the **DataReader** and **Connection** objects:

Visual Basic .NET

```vbnet
Dim conn As New SqlConnection _
   ("data source=localhost;integrated security=true;" & _
   "initial catalog=pubs")
conn.Open()
Dim cmdAuthors As New SQLCommand _
   ("select * from Authors", conn)

'bind the datareader to a listbox
Dim dr As SqlDataReader
dr = cmdAuthors.ExecuteReader()
lstBoundNames.DataSource = dr
lstBoundNames.DataTextField = "au_lname"
lstBoundNames.DataBind()

'close the datareader and the connection
dr.Close()
conn.Close()
```

C#

```
SqlConnection conn = new SqlConnection
  ("data source=localhost; integrated security=true; " +
    "initial catalog=pubs");
conn.Open();

SqlCommand cmdAuthors = new SqlCommand
  ("select * from Authors", conn);

//bind the datareader to a listbox
SqlDataReader dr;
dr = cmdAuthors.ExecuteReader();
lstBoundNames.DataSource = dr;
lstBoundNames.DataTextField = "au_lname";
lstBoundNames.DataBind();

//close the datareader and the connection
dr.Close();
conn.Close();
```

Practice: Organizing Code to Create a DataReader

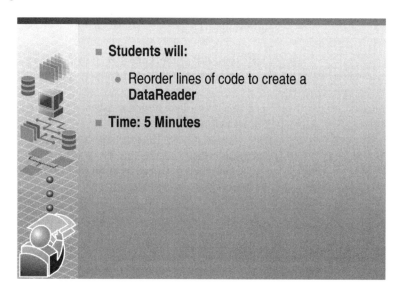

In this practice, you will rearrange the lines of ADO.NET code into the correct order to create a **DataReader** object.

To run the practice

- View the http://localhost/Mod10VB/DataReaderCode.aspx or http://localhost/Mod10CS/DataReaderCode.aspx page and organize the lines of ADO.NET code into the correct order to create a **DataReader** object.

Note There are several correct answers to this practice.

Demonstration: Displaying Data Using DataReaders

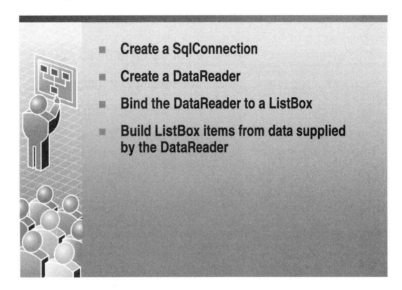

- Create a SqlConnection
- Create a DataReader
- Bind the DataReader to a ListBox
- Build ListBox items from data supplied by the DataReader

Introduction

In this demonstration, you will review code that creates and fills a **DataReader** object by using a **SQLCommand** object that binds the **DataReader** object to one **ListBox** control, and that then recreates the **DataReader** to bind it to a second **ListBox** control.

To run the demonstration

1. Open the datareader.aspx page in the Mod10VB or Mod10CS project in the 2310Demos solution.

2. Build and browse the datareader.aspx page.

   There are two list boxes that are displaying the same data. The first list box is bound to a **DataReader** object, while the second list box is built by looping through the records in the **DataReader** object and programmatically building each **ListBox** control entry.

3. In Visual Studio .NET, view the code-behind page for the datareader.aspx page.

4. In the **Page_Load** event procedure, show the code that does the following:

   - Creates a **SqlConnection** object.

   - Creates a **SqlCommand** object.

   - Creates a **DataReader** object.

   - Binds the **DataReader** object to the first **ListBox** control.

   - Closes the **DataReader** object and then creates it again.

     This step is necessary because a **DataReader** object is a forward-only view of the data and you had already reached the end of the data when the **DataReader** object was bound to the **ListBox** control.

   - Steps through the **DataReader** object and adds two fields for each item in the second **ListBox** control.

Review

- Introduction to Using ADO.NET
- Connecting to a Database
- Accessing Data with DataSets
- Using Multiple Tables
- Accessing Data with DataReaders

1. What is the code that is used to create a connection to a database named Coho, on the local SQL Server, using integrated security?

2. What is the difference between a **DataSet** and a **DataView** object?

3. What is the difference between a **DataSet** and a **DataReader** object?

4. What is the purpose of the **DataAdapter** object?

5. Which method is used to populate a **DataSet** object with the results from a query?

6. How do you add multiple tables into a **DataSet** object?

7. How do you create a relationship between two **DataTable** objects in a **DataSet** object?

Lab 10: Accessing Data with Microsoft ADO.NET

Lab 10: Accessing Data with Microsoft ADO.NET

Objectives

After completing this lab, you will be able to:

- Retrieve data from a Microsoft® SQL Server™ database by using the **SqlConnection** and **SqlDataAdapter** objects.

- Store data in a **DataSet** object and then display that data to users in a **DataGrid** control.

- Retrieve data from a SQL Server database by using **SqlConnection** and **SqlDataReader** objects.

- Bind a **SqlDataReader** object to a **DataGrid** control to display data.

Note   This lab focuses on the concepts in this module and as a result may not comply with Microsoft security recommendations. For instance, this lab does not comply with the recommendation that all data access be done through stored procedures.

Prerequisites

Before working on this lab, you must have:

- Knowledge of how to use Microsoft ADO.NET **SqlConnection**, **SqlDataAdapter**, **SqlDataReader**, and **DataSet** objects to read data from a SQL Server database.

- Knowledge of how to display **DataSet** data in a **DataGrid** control.

Scenario

Coho Winery offers several benefits to its employees. In the labs for Course 2310B, *Developing Microsoft ASP.NET Web Applications Using Visual Studio .NET*, you will create a Web site that enables employees to select and set up their chosen benefits.

One benefit that is offered by Coho Winery is medical insurance. When applying for medical insurance, a user must select a primary care physician. The doctors that are approved by your company are all listed in a SQL Server database named doctors. The doctors' addresses are also in the database. In this lab, you will enhance the doctors.aspx page in the Coho Winery Web site to allow users to list doctors that are in specific cities.

Estimated time to complete this lab: 30 minutes

Exercise 0
Lab Setup

To complete this lab, you must have created a Benefits Web Application project and a BenefitsList Class Library project. These projects can be created by using Microsoft Visual Basic® .NET or Microsoft Visual C#™ .NET.

If you have not created these projects, complete the following steps:

Create the 2310LabApplication solution

Important Only perform this procedure if you have not created 2310LabApplication solution file.

1. Using Microsoft Visual Studio® .NET, create a new blank solution named **2310LabApplication**:

   a. On the **File** menu, point to **New**, and then click **Blank Solution**.

   b. In the **New Project** dialog box, type **2310LabApplication** in the **Name** text box, and then click **OK**.

Create the Benefits project

Important Only perform this procedure if you have not previously created a Benefits project, or if you have removed the Benefits project according to the steps in Appendix A, "Lab Recovery," in Course 2310B, *Developing Microsoft ASP.NET Web Applications Using Visual Studio .NET*.

1. Create a new Microsoft ASP.NET Web Application project, named **BenefitsVB** or **BenefitsCS**, in the 2310LabApplication solution:

   a. On the **File** menu, point to **New**, and then click **Project**.

   b. In the **New Project** dialog box, in the **Project Types** list, click **Visual Basic Projects** or **Visual C# Projects**.

   c. In the **Templates** list click **ASP.NET Web Application**, set the **Location** to **http://localhost/BenefitsVB** for the Visual Basic .NET project or to **http:/localhost/BenefitsCS** for the Visual C# project.

   d. Click **Add to Solution**, and then click **OK**.

Caution When adding projects to the solution, the capitalization of the project name is important. Because you may be using some pre-built Web Forms in this and other labs in Course 2310B, *Developing Microsoft ASP.NET Web Applications Using Visual Studio .NET*, you must verify that you have capitalized the Benefits project as shown.

Update the Benefits project

1. In Visual Studio .NET, open the 2310LabApplication solution file.

2. In Solution Explorer, right-click **BenefitsVB** or **BenefitsCS**, point to **Add**, and then click **Add Existing Item**.

3. Browse for project files.

For the Visual Basic .NET project

Browse to the *install folder*\Labfiles\Lab10\VB\Starter\BenefitsVB folder for the Visual Basic .NET files.

For the Visual C# project

Browse to the *install folder*\Labfiles\Lab10\CS\Starter\BenefitsCS folder for the Visual C# files.

4. In the **Files of type** box of the **Add Existing Item – Benefits** dialog box, click **All Files (*.*)**.

5. Select all of the files in this folder, and then click **Open**.

6. Click **Yes** if prompted to overwrite or reload files.

Create the BenefitsList class library

Important   Only perform these steps if you have not previously created a BenefitsList project, or if you have removed the BenefitsList project according to the steps in Appendix A, "Lab Recovery," in Course 2310B, *Developing Microsoft ASP.NET Web Applications Using Visual Studio .NET*.

---

1. Create a new Class Library Project.

For the Visual Basic .NET project

Create a new Microsoft Visual Basic® .NET Class Library project, named **BenefitsListVB**, and then add it to the 2310LabApplication solution:

a. On the **File** menu, point to **New**, and then click **Project**.

b. In the **New Project** dialog box, in the **Project Types** list, click **Visual Basic Projects**.

c. In the **Templates** list, click **Class Library**, and then set the **Name** to **BenefitsListVB**.

d. Click **Add to Solution**, and then click **OK**.

For the Visual C# project

Create a new Microsoft Visual C#™ .NET Class Library project, name it **BenefitsListCS**, and then add it to the 2310LabApplication solution:

a. On the **File** menu, point to **New**, and then click **Project**.

b. In the **New Project** dialog box, in the **Project Types** list, click **Visual C# Projects**.

c. In the Templates list, click **Class Library**, and then set the **Name** to **BenefitsListCS**.

d. Click **Add to Solution**, and then click **OK**.

Caution   Verify that you have capitalized the BenefitsList project as shown.

▶ **Update the BenefitsList project**

1. In Visual Studio .NET, open the 2310LabApplication solution file.

2. In Solution Explorer, right-click **BenefitsListVB** or **BenefitsListCS**, point to **Add**, and then click **Add Existing Item**.

3. Browse for the project files:

For the Visual Basic .NET project

Browse to the *install folder*\Labfiles\Lab10\VB\Starter\BenefitsListVB folder.

For the Visual C# project

Browse to the *install folder*\Labfiles\Lab10\CS\Starter\BenefitsListCS folder.

4. In the **Files of type** box of the **Add Existing Item – BenefitsList** dialog box, click **All Files (*.*)**.

5. Select all of the files in this folder, and then click **Open**.

6. Click **Yes** if prompted to overwrite or reload files.

▶ **Create a reference to the BenefitsList component in the Benefits project**

1. In the Benefits project in the 2310LabApplication solution, complete the following steps to add a reference to the BenefitsList component that you just created:

    a. Right-click the **BenefitsVB** or **BenefitsCS** project in Solution Explorer and then click **Add Reference**.

    b. In the **Add Reference** dialog box, on the **Projects** tab, double-click the **BenefitsListVB** or **BenefitsListCS** project.

    c. In the **Selected Components** list, select the **BenefitsListVB** or the **BenefitsListCS** component, and then click **OK**.

    The component is added to the References folder in Solution Explorer.

Exercise 1
Using a SqlDataReader

In this exercise, you will fill in a list box on the doctors.aspx page with the cities where the doctors are located. When the user selects a city, you will create a new view of the **DataSet** data and display the data in the **DataGrid**.

▶ **Add the list box**

1. Open the doctors.aspx page in the BenefitsVB or the BenefitsCS project.

2. Using a drag-and-drop operation, place a **DropDownList** control on the doctors.aspx page, as shown in the following illustration. This list box will display the cities where the doctors are located.

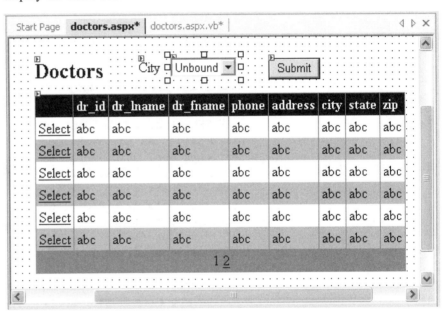

3. Set the **ID** property of the **DropDownList** control to **lstCities**.

▶ **Read the list of cities from the doctors database**

1. Open the code-behind page for the doctors.aspx page, doctors.aspx.vb or doctors.aspx.cs, and go to the **Page_Load** event procedure.

Visual C#
2. If you are using C# to complete this lab enter the following **using** statement after the **using** statements at the top of the doctors.aspx.cs file.

```
using System.Data.SqlClient;
```

3. Locate the following comment:

Visual Basic .NET
```
'TODO Lab10: bind the listbox to city field in the doctors
table
```

C#
```
//TODO Lab10: bind the listbox to city field in the doctors
table
```

4. Write code to create a **SqlCommand** object to read the city field from the doctors table in the **doctors** SQL Server database. Use the **SqlConnection** object that is already created in the page.

   The **SqlCommand** should be **"SELECT city FROM doctors."**

5. Write code to open the database connection.

6. Write code to create a **SqlDataReader** object from the **SqlCommand** object by calling the **ExecuteReader** method of the **SqlCommand** object.

7. Write code to set the properties of the **lstCities** drop-down list box as shown in the following table.

Property	Value
DataSource	**SqlDataReader** object
DataTextField	"city"

8. Write code to call the **DataBind** method of the **lstCities** drop-down list box.

9. Write code to close the **DataReader** and **Connection** objects.

   Your code should look like the following:

Visual Basic .NET

```
Dim cmdCities As New SqlCommand _
    ("SELECT city FROM doctors", SqlConnection1)
Dim drCities As SqlDataReader
SqlConnection1.Open()
drCities = cmdCities.ExecuteReader()
lstCities.DataSource = drCities
lstCities.DataTextField = "city"
lstCities.DataBind()
drCities.Close()
SqlConnection1.Close()
```

C#

```
SqlCommand cmdCities = new SqlCommand
    ("Select city FROM doctors", sqlConnection1);
sqlDataReader drCities;
sqlConnection1.Open();
drCities = cmdCities.ExecuteReader();
lstCities.DataSource = drCities;
lstCities.DataTextField = "city";
lstCities.DataBind();
drCities.Close();
sqlConnection1.Close();
```

10. Build and browse the doctors.aspx page.

The **City** drop-down list box should display the list of cities where the doctors are located.

Notice that the **City** list box shows a city for every row in the database. Although this method works, it is not the most user-friendly way to display the city information. What can you do to improve the display?

_____

_____

Note One solution for this problem is presented in Lab 11, "Calling Stored Procedures with Microsoft ADO.NET," in Course 2310B, *Developing Microsoft ASP.NET Web Applications Using Visual Studio .NET.*

▶ **Create a DataView for the DataGrid**

1. Set the **AutoPostBack** property of the **lstCities** drop-down list box to **true**.

2. Create a **SelectedIndexChanged** event procedure for the **lstCities** drop-down list box.

   In the **SelectedIndexChanged** event procedure, you will add the code to display only the doctors from the selected city in the **DataGrid** control. For example, if **Seattle** is selected in the drop-down list box, the **DataGrid** control will only display doctors from the city of Seattle.

3. Read the city that is selected in the **lstCities** drop-down list box and store the city name in a **String** variable named **strCity**.

4. Fill the DsDoctors1 **DataSet** by using the sqlDataAdapter1 **DataAdapter**.

5. Create a new **DataView** from Table(0) of the **DataSet**.

6. Set the **RowFilter** property of the **DataView** to display only the records where the **city** field is equal to the city that is selected in the **lstCities** drop-down list box.

7. Set the **DataSource** property of the **DataGrid** control to the new **DataView**.

8. Call the **DataBind** method of the **DataGrid** control.

   Your code should look like the following:

Visual Basic .NET

```
Dim strCity As String = Trim(lstCities.SelectedItem.Value)
SqlDataAdapter1.Fill(DsDoctors1)
Dim dvDocs As New DataView(DsDoctors1.Tables(0))
dvDocs.RowFilter = "city = '" & strCity & "'"
dgDoctors.DataSource = dvDocs
dgDoctors.DataBind()
```

C#

```
string strCity = lstCities.SelectedItem.Value.Trim();
sqlDataAdapter1.Fill(dsDoctors1);
DataView dvDocs = new DataView(dsDoctors1.Tables[0]);
dvDocs.RowFilter = "City = '" + strCity + "' ";
dgDoctors.DataSource = dvDocs;
dgDoctors.DataBind();
```

9. In Design view, remove the **DataSource** and **DataMember** property settings for the **DataGrid** control:

   a. On the doctors.aspx page, select the dgDoctors **DataGrid** control.

   b. In the Properties window, select **DataMember**, highlight the value **doctors**, and then press DELETE.

   c. In the Properties window, select **DataSource**, highlight the value **dsDoctors1**, and then press DELETE.

   Note You are removing these property settings because they conflict with the code that you added in the preceding steps. When properties are set in both the code and user interface (UI), you will get unpredictable results.

   ---

10. In the **Page_Load** event procedure, immediately after the code to fill the dsDoctors1 **DataSet** object, set the **DataSource** of the dgDoctors **DataGrid** to the DsDoctors1 **DataSet** object. Your code should look like the following, with the newly-added line in bold font:

Visual Basic .NET

```
SqlDataAdapter1.Fill(DsDoctors1)
dgDoctors.DataSource = DsDoctors1
dgDoctors.DataBind()
```

C#

```
sqlDataAdapter1.Fill(dsDoctors1);
dgDoctors.DataSource = dsDoctors1;
dgDoctors.DataBind();
```

11. Build and browse the doctors.aspx page.

    When you select a city in the **City** list box, the **dgDoctors** DataGrid will display only the doctors that are located in the selected city.

Exercise 2
Viewing Doctors from All Cities

In this exercise, you will add the **All** option to the **City** drop-down list box and reset functionality to the doctors.aspx Web page, which will then reset the **DataGrid** and **Specialties** list box controls to a default configuration.

▶ **Add an [All] item to the list box**

1. Open the code-behind page for the doctors.aspx page, doctors.aspx.vb or doctors.aspx.cs, and go to the **Page_Load** event procedure.

2. Locate the following comment:

Visual Basic .NET

```
'TODO Lab10: add the "All" item to the list and select it
```

C#

```
//TODO Lab10: add the "All" item to the list and select it
```

3. Call the **Add** method of the **lstCities.Items** collection to add a new item to the list named **[All]**.

4. Set the **SelectedIndex** property of the **lstCities** drop-down list box to the last item in the list (which is the **[All]** item that you just added).

Your code should look like the following:

Visual Basic .NET

```
lstCities.Items.Add("[All]")
lstCities.SelectedIndex = lstCities.Items.Count - 1
```

C#

```
lstCities.Items.Add("[All]");
lstCities.SelectedIndex = lstCities.Items.Count - 1;
```

▶ **Check for the [All] selection in the SelectedIndexChanged event procedure**

1. In the doctors.aspx.vb or the doctors.aspx.cs file, go to the **lstCities_SelectedIndexChanged** event procedure.

2. Add a test to the **lstCities_SelectedIndexChanged** event procedure, after filling the **DataSet**, but before calling the **DataBind** method, to see if the **[All]** item was selected.

3. If the **[All]** item is selected, set the **DataSource** of the **dgDoctors DataGrid** control to the entire DsDoctors1 **DataSet**.

4. If a city is selected in the **lstCities** drop-down list box, create a **DataView** to display only doctors that are located in that city, and then set the **DataSource** of the **dgDoctors DataGrid** to the **DataView**.

5. Call the **reset** function to remove any page or selection from the **DataGrid**.

   The **reset** function is already in the doctors.aspx.vb or the doctors.aspx.cs code-behind page.

The **lstCities_SelectedIndexChanged** event procedure should look like the following:

Visual Basic .NET

```
Private Sub lstCities_SelectedIndexChanged(...
    Dim strCity As String = _
        Trim(lstCities.SelectedItem.Value)
    SqlDataAdapter1.Fill(DsDoctors1)

    If strCity = "[All]" Then
        dgDoctors.DataSource = DsDoctors1
    Else
        Dim dvDocs As New DataView(DsDoctors1.Tables(0))
        dvDocs.RowFilter = "city = '" & strCity & "'"
        dgDoctors.DataSource = dvDocs
    End If

    reset()
    dgDoctors.DataBind()
End Sub
```

C#

```
private void lstCities_SelectedIndexChanged(...
{
    string strCity =
        lstCities.SelectedItem.Value.Trim();
    sqlDataAdapter1.Fill(dsDoctors1);

    if (strCity == "[All]")
    {
        dgDoctors.DataSource = dsDoctors1;
    }
    else
    {
        DataView dvDocs =
                new DataView(dsDoctors1.Tables[0]);
        dvDocs.RowFilter = "city = '" + strCity + "'";
        dgDoctors.DataSource = dvDocs;
    }

    reset();
    dgDoctors.DataBind();
}
```

6. Build and browse the doctors.aspx page.

7. Click a city in the **City** drop-down list box.

   You should see only doctors that are from that city.

8. Click **[All]** in the **City** drop-down list box.

   You should see all of the doctors in the **doctors** database.

▶ **Paging with city selection**

1. In the doctors.aspx.vb or the doctors.aspx.cs file, go to the existing **dgDoctors_PageIndexChanged** event procedure.

2. Retrieve the currently selected item from the **lstCities** drop-down list box and save it in a variable named **strCity**.

3. Add a test, after filling the **DataSet**, but before calling the **DataBind** method, to see if the **[All]** item was selected.

4. If the **[All]** item is selected, set the **DataSource** property of the **dgDoctors DataGrid** to the entire DsDoctors1 **DataSet**.

5. If a city is selected in the **lstCities** drop-down list box, create a **DataView** to display only doctors that are located in that city, and then set the **DataSource** property of the **dgDoctors DataGrid** to the **DataView**.

When complete, the entire **dgDoctors_PageIndexChanged** event procedure should look like the following:

Visual Basic .NET

```
Private Sub dgDoctors_PageIndexChanged(...
    Dim strCity As String = _
        Trim(lstCities.SelectedItem.Value)
    dgDoctors.CurrentPageIndex = e.NewPageIndex
    SqlDataAdapter1.Fill(DsDoctors1)

    If strCity = "[All]" Then
        dgDoctors.DataSource = DsDoctors1
    Else
        Dim dvDocs As New DataView(DsDoctors1.Tables(0))
        dvDocs.RowFilter = "city = '" & strCity & "'"
        dgDoctors.DataSource = dvDocs
    End If
    dgDoctors.DataBind()
End Sub
```

C#

```
private void dgDoctors_PageIndexChanged(...
{
    string strCity =
        lstCities.SelectedItem.Value.Trim();
    dgDoctors.CurrentPageIndex = e.NewPageIndex;
    sqlDataAdapter1.Fill(dsDoctors1);

    if (strCity == "[All]")
    {
        dgDoctors.DataSource = dsDoctors1;
    }
    else
    {
        DataView dvDocs =
                new DataView(dsDoctors1.Tables[0]);
        dvDocs.RowFilter = "city = '" + strCity + "'";
        dgDoctors.DataSource = dvDocs;
    }
    dgDoctors.DataBind();
}
```

6. Build and browse the doctors.aspx page.

Test by selecting a city and then a page number.

msdn training

Module 11: Calling Stored Procedures with Microsoft ADO.NET

Contents

Microsoft

Overview

- Overview of Stored Procedures
- Calling Stored Procedures

Introduction

Directly accessing and manipulating data in a database from a Web Form can be a very inefficient use of resources, and may create security risks. One way of improving the efficiency and security of database access is to create stored procedures on the database server, and then call these stored procedures from your Web Form. Accessing a database through a stored procedure limits the Web Form code and the network bandwidth that you have to use when performing complicated tasks. Accessing a database through a stored procedure also protects the database by limiting direct access to the database to trusted, local stored procedures.

In this module, you will learn how to accomplish data access tasks from Web applications by using Microsoft® ADO.NET to access stored procedures.

Objectives

After completing this module, you will be able to:

- Explain what a stored procedure is and the reasons for using stored procedures when accessing a database.

- Call stored procedures.

Lesson: Overview of Stored Procedures

- ■ **What Is a Stored Procedure?**
- ■ **Why Use Stored Procedures?**
- ■ **Practice: Select the Correct Stored Procedure**

Introduction

One alternative to directly accessing databases from your Web application is to call a stored procedure that will access the database for you. Using stored procedures has several advantages over direct database access, including efficiency, security, and the protection of the database.

In this lesson, you will learn what a stored procedure is and the reasons for calling stored procedures when accessing a database.

Lesson objectives

After completing this lesson, you will be able to:

- ■ Describe what a stored procedure is.
- ■ Explain the reasons for using stored procedures to access and manipulate databases.

What Is a Stored Procedure?

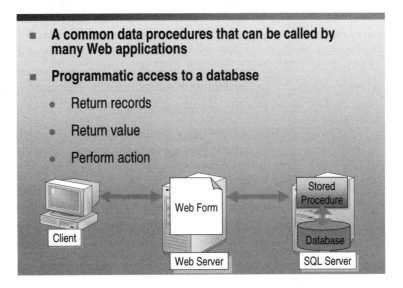

- **A common data procedures that can be called by many Web applications**
- **Programmatic access to a database**
  - Return records
  - Return value
  - Perform action

Introduction

A stored procedure is a database procedure that a database developer writes for use with a specific database. Other Web applications can then call these stored procedures to access and manipulate data in the database.

Programmatic access to a database

Stored procedures allow you to access a database by calling an existing procedure rather than having to write your own SQL statements. Stored procedures are built from sequences of Transact-SQL statements, and they function similarly to procedures in a Web application in that the statements are called by name, and can have both input and output parameters.

The three types of stored procedures are:

- Return records stored procedures

  Return records stored procedures are used to find specific records, sort and filter those records, and then return the result of the find, sort and filter operations to a **DataSet** object or to a list-bound control. These stored procedures are based on SQL Select statements.

  An example of a return records stored procedure is a request for the amount, date, and recipient of the last three checks that have been processed in a bank account. This data could be loaded into a **DataSet** object for further processing, or displayed directly to the user in a **ListBox** control.

■ Return value stored procedures, also known as scalar stored procedures

Return value stored procedures are used to execute a database command or function that returns a single value. Because only a value is returned, return value stored procedures are often used in code and then the result is displayed to users.

An example of a return value stored procedure is to return the total value of the last three checks that have been processed in a bank account.

■ Action stored procedures

Action stored procedures are used to perform some function in the database, but not return a record or a value. These database functions may include updating, editing, or modifying the data.

An example of an action stored procedure is a request to update a single mailing address in a company's customer database.

Why Use Stored Procedures?

- Modular programming
- Distribution of work
- Database security
- Faster execution
- Reduces network traffic
- Provides flexibility

Introduction

It is easier, more efficient, and more secure to use a stored procedure than it is to write the code that is required to connect directly to a database and run your own Transact-SQL statements. Calling a stored procedure does not require that you understand how the database is designed, and the database is only accessed by a tested procedure.

Modular programming

Stored procedures are classic examples of modular programming. You create the procedure once, test it once, store it on the database server, and then call it any number of times from multiple applications. Any updates or changes to the database are hidden from all of the accessing applications by the stored procedure.

Distribution of work

Stored procedures can be created independently by a developer who specializes in database programming, while the Web applications that will use the stored procedure can be created in parallel by other developers. This distribution of work allows each developer to focus on their own specialty, and meet their own deadlines.

Increase database security

Using stored procedures provides increased security for a database by limiting direct access. Only the tested and proven stored procedures that are developed by the owner of the database directly access the database. Because other Web applications and developers do not directly access the database, there is a minimum risk of accidental damage to the structure or to the content of the database.

Using SQL or Transact-SQL statements directly in the Microsoft ASP.NET code is also a security risk because the statements can give a hacker information about the database and its structure. In addition, with direct access to a database, you also have the security issue of trying to determine what kind of permissions you should give to the Webuser account on the individual tables.

Faster execution

If a procedure requires a large amount of Transact-SQL code or if it is performed repetitively, using stored procedures can be faster than direct database access with Transact-SQL code. Stored procedures are parsed and optimized when they are created, and an in-memory version of the procedure can be used after the procedure is executed for the first time.

Direct access through Transact-SQL statements requires that the statements be sent from the client each time they run. The statements are then compiled and optimized every time they are executed by the database server.

Reduce network traffic

An operation requiring hundreds of lines of Transact-SQL code can sometimes be performed through a single statement that calls a stored procedure. Sending one call over the network, rather than hundreds of lines of code, reduces network traffic.

Provides flexibility

Because database access is through the stored procedure, the database developer can change the structure of the database without breaking the Web applications that use it. This protection allows for continual improvement of the database without putting the rest of the system at risk.

Practice: Select the Correct Stored Procedure

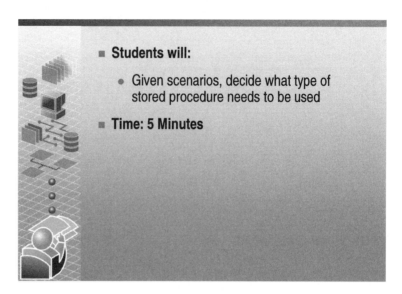

▶ **Read the following scenarios and decide what type of the following stored procedure would be used:**

■ Return records

■ Return value

■ Perform action

You need to determine the top 10 best sellers of the company.

_____

_____

You need to determine the net profit for a given quarter.

_____

_____

You need to change all the 425 United States telephone area codes to 415.

_____

_____

You need to determine which records have 425 United States telephone area codes.

_____

_____

You need to delete all of the items that have been discontinued in a given category.

_____

_____

Lesson: Calling Stored Procedures

- **Calling Stored Procedures**
- **Demonstration: Calling a Stored Procedure**
- **Practice: Displaying Data from a Stored Procedure**
- **Using Parameters**
- **Passing Input Parameters**
- **Using Output Parameters**
- **Demonstration: Passing Parameters**

Introduction

Before you can call a stored procedure, you need to have identified the procedure name and the available parameters. After you have identified the stored procedure, you can call the procedure, pass any input parameters that are required to process your request, and handle the output parameters that are included in the response.

In this lesson, you will learn how to call stored procedures, pass input parameters, and handle output parameters.

Lesson objectives

After completing this lesson, you will be able to:

- Call a stored procedure from a Web Form.
- Identify the type of parameters that are available when calling stored procedures.
- Pass input parameters when calling stored procedures from a Web Form.
- Use output parameters from a stored procedure.

Calling Stored Procedures

- Identify the stored procedure

- Set up the SelectCommand property of the DataAdapter

```
Dim daCategory As New SqlDataAdapter()
daCategory.SelectCommand = New SqlCommand()
daCategory.SelectCommand.Connection = conn
daCategory.SelectCommand.CommandText = "ProductCategoryList"
daCategory.SelectCommand.CommandType = CommandType.StoredProcedure
```

```
SqlDataAdapter daCategory = new SqlDataAdapter();
daCategory.SelectCommand = new SqlCommand();
daCategory.SelectCommand.Connection = conn;
daCategory.SelectCommand.CommandText = "ProductCategoryList";
daCategory.SelectCommand.CommandType = CommandType.StoredProcedure;
```

- Run the stored procedure and store returned records

```
daCategory.Fill(ds, "Categories")
```

```
daCategory.Fill(ds, "Categories");
```

Introduction

To call a stored procedure, you first need to identify the stored procedure, create a **DataAdapter** object, and point the **DataAdapter** object to the database connection. You then set the **CommandText** property to the name of the identified stored procedure, and finally, you set the **CommandType** property to **CommandType.StoredProcedure**.

Identify the stored procedure

The first step in using a stored procedure is to identify the type and name of the stored procedure. You can use a **DataAdapter** object or a **DataReader** object to call all three types of stored procedures. The method that you call to execute the stored procedure will vary depending on the type of stored procedure that you are calling:

- Return records stored procedures

  When you call a stored procedure that returns a set of records, you need to store that set of records either in a **DataSet**, or directly into a list-bound control by using a **DataReader**. If you want to use a **DataSet**, you need to use a **DataAdapter** and the **Fill** method. If you want to use a **DataReader**, you need to use a **Command** object and the **ExecuteReader** method, and then bind the returned record into a list-bound control.

- Return value stored procedures

  When you call a stored procedure that returns a value, call the **ExecuteScalar** method of the **Command** object, and save the result in a variable of the appropriate data type.

- Perform action stored procedures

  When you call a stored procedure that performs some action on the database but does not return a set of records or a value, use the **ExecuteNonQuery** method of the **Command** object.

Set the SelectCommand property

To set up the call to the stored procedure, you need to create a **SqlCommand** object and save it as the **SelectCommand** property of a **DataAdapter**. Then, you need to set the **Connection**, **CommandText**, and **CommandType** properties.

You can set up the call to a stored procedure visually by using the stored procedure tools in the Microsoft Visual Studio® .NET Toolbox, or you can manually write the code to call the stored procedure. The following examples use manual code to show both the complete code and the logical process of calling a stored procedure.

The following examples calls the **ProductCategoryList** stored procedure. The **ProductCategoryList** stored procedure returns a list of category IDs and category names from the **Categories** table:

```
Procedure ProductCategoryList
As
  SELECT CategoryID,CategoryName
  FROM Categories
```

The following code uses a **Connection** object and a **DataAdapter** object to call the **ProductCategoryList** return records stored procedure:

Visual Basic .NET

```
Dim daCategory as New SqlDataAdapter()
daCategory.SelectCommand = New SqlCommand()
daCategory.SelectCommand.Connection = conn
daCategory.SelectCommand.CommandText = _
  "ProductCategoryList"
daCategory.SelectCommand.CommandType = _
  CommandType.StoredProcedure
```

C#

```
SqlDataAdapter daCategory = new SqlDataAdapter();
daCategory.SelectCommand = new SqlCommand();
daCategory.SelectCommand.Connection = conn;
daCategory.SelectCommand.CommandText =
  "ProductCategoryList";
daCategory.SelectCommand.CommandType =
  CommandType.StoredProcedure;
```

Note You can also directly set the connection and command text when you create the **SqlDataAdapter** object. The following code performs the same task as the preceding code:

Visual Basic .NET

```
Dim daCategory As New SqlDataAdapter _
  ("ProductCategoryList", conn)
daCategory.SelectCommand.CommandType = _
  CommandType.StoredProcedure
```

C#

```
SqlDataAdapter daCategory = new SqlDataAdapter
  ("ProductCategoryList", conn);
daCategory.SelectCommand.CommandType =
  CommandType.StoredProcedure;
```

Run the stored procedure

To execute the stored procedure and save the returned records in a **DataSet**, call the **Fill** method of the **SqlDataAdapter** object. This method fills a **DataTable** object with the returned records of the stored procedure.

For example, the following code fills the **DataSet** object **ds** with the records that were returned from the **ProductCategoryList** stored procedure by using the **daCategory SqlDataAdapter**:

Visual Basic .NET

```
daCategory.Fill(ds, "Categories")
```

C#

```
daCategory.Fill(ds, "Categories");
```

After you have filled a **DataTable** with the results of a **Select** stored procedure, you can bind the **DataTable** to a list-bound control to display the data.

Demonstration: Calling a Stored Procedure

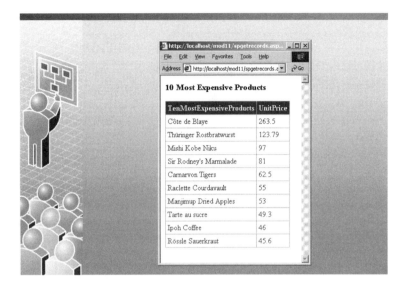

Introduction

In this demonstration, you will see how to call a stored procedure in a Microsoft SQL Server™ database, and then bind the results to a **DataGrid**.

▶ **To run the demonstration**

1. Open the SPGetRecords.aspx page in the Mod11VB or Mod11CS project in the 2310Demos solution.

2. Build and browse the page.

   The **DataGrid** is bound to the **Ten Most Expensive Products** stored procedure in the Northwind Traders database.

3. In Visual Studio .NET, view the code-behind page for the SPGetRecords.aspx page.

4. In the **Page_Load** event procedure, show the code that does the following:

   • Creates the **SqlConnection**.

   • Creates the **SqlDataAdapter** and **SqlCommand**.

   • Sets the properties of the **SqlCommand** object to call the stored procedure.

   • Creates a new **DataSet** and fills that **DataSet** from the **DataAdapter**.

Practice: Displaying Data from a Stored Procedure

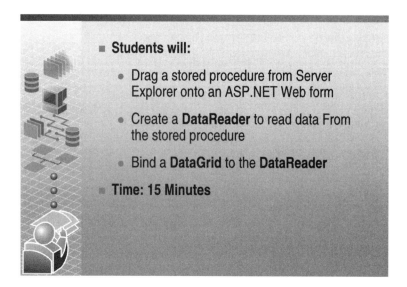

Students will:
- Drag a stored procedure from Server Explorer onto an ASP.NET Web form
- Create a **DataReader** to read data From the stored procedure
- Bind a **DataGrid** to the **DataReader**

Time: 15 Minutes

Introduction

In this practice, you will create a **DataReader** to call a stored procedure in a SQL Server database, and then bind the results to a **DataGrid**.

▶ **To run the practice**

1. Create a new Web application project and set location to

Visual Basic .NET   http://localhost/Mod11PracticeVB

C#   http://localhost/Mod11PracticeCS

2. Open the WebForm1.aspx page.

3. Open Server Explorer and expand the following folders: *machinename*, SQL Servers, *machinename*, Northwind, and Stored Procedures.

4. Click the **Ten Most Expensive Products** stored procedure and drag it onto the WebForm1.aspx page.

   Visual Studio .NET automatically creates a **SqlConnection** object named **sqlConnection1** and a **SqlCommand** object named **sqlCommand1**.

5. Using the Toolbox, put a **DataGrid** control on WebForm1.aspx page.

6. Create a **Page_Load** event procedure and add the following code to create a **DataReader** from the **SqlCommand** object and bind it to the **DataGrid**:

Visual Basic .NET

```
Dim dr As SqlClient.SqlDataReader
SqlConnection1.Open()
dr = SqlCommand1.ExecuteReader()
DataGrid1.DataSource = dr
DataGrid1.DataBind()
dr.Close()
SqlConnection1.Close()
```

C#

```
SqlDataReader dr;
sqlConnection1.Open();
dr = sqlCommand1.ExecuteReader();
DataGrid1.DataSource = dr;
DataGrid1.DataBind();
dr.Close();
sqlConnection1.Close();
```

C#

7. If you are using C# to build this project, you must enter the following code at the start of the code-behind page.

```
using System.Data.SqlClient;
```

8. Build and browse the WebForm1.aspx page.

Using Parameters

> ■ **Identify the available parameters**
>
>   ● **Input**
>
>   ● **Output**
>
>   ● **InputOutput**
>
>   ● **ReturnValue**
>
> ■ **Include parameters in the parameters collection**
>
> **or**
>
> ■ **Include parameter values in the command string**

Introduction

When you are using stored procedures on a SQL Server database or on another procedure-based database, parameters can be used to pass and retrieve information from the stored procedure.

When you use parameters with a SQL Server database, the names of the parameters that are added to the **Parameters** collection of the **Command** object must match the names of the parameters that are in the stored procedure; however, the order of the parameters is flexible.

Note When using parameters in an OLE DB database, the order of the parameters in the **Parameters** collection must match the order of the parameters that are defined in the stored procedure.

The following table describes the types of parameters that are available with stored procedures.

Parameter	Use
Input	Used by your Web application to send specific data values to a stored procedure.
Output	Used by a stored procedure to send specific values back to the calling Web application.
InputOutput	Used by a stored procedure to both retrieve information that was sent by your Web application and to send specific values back to the Web application.
ReturnValue	Used by a stored procedure to send a return value back to the calling application.

Passing Input Parameters

- **Create parameter, set direction and value, add to the Parameters collection**

```
param = New SqlParameter _
    ("@Beginning_Date", SQLDbType.DateTime)
param.Direction = ParameterDirection.Input
param.Value = CDate(txtStartDate.Text)
da.SelectCommand.Parameters.Add(param)
```

- **Run stored procedure and store returned records**

```
ds = New DataSet()
da.Fill(ds, "Products")
```

Code Examples

Introduction

After you have identified the parameters that a stored procedure supports, you need to add the parameters you will be using to the **Parameters** collection of the **Command** object.

Creating a parameter

To create a parameter, create a new **SqlParameter** object with the name and data type of the parameter, as specified by the stored procedure. Next, set the **Direction** property of the new parameter to indicate how the parameter is used by the stored procedure. If the stored procedure returns a return value, create a parameter named **returnValue**. If the parameter is an input parameter, set the **Value** property to specify the data that should be sent to the SQL Server.

For example, the **ProductsByCategory** stored procedure takes one input parameter, named **@CategoryID** of type **int**, as shown in the following code:

```
Procedure ProductsByCategory (
    @CategoryID int )
As
  SELECT ProductID, ModelName, UnitCost, ProductImage,
      Chairman
  FROM Products
  WHERE CategoryID=@CategoryID
```

To call the **ProductsByCategory** stored procedure, create an input parameter named **@CategoryID** and set its value to the value of a text box:

Visual Basic .NET

```
Dim workParam1 As New SqlParameter _
  ("@CategoryID", SqlDbType.Int)
workParam1.Direction = ParameterDirection.Input
workParam1.Value = Cint(txtStartDate.Text)
```

C#

```
SqlParameter workParam1 = new SqlParameter
  ("@CategoryID", SqlDbType.Int);
workParam1.Direction = ParameterDirection.Input;
workParam1.Value = Convert.ToInt16(txtStartDate.Text);
```

Note You should always validate the contents of a text box before sending the user input to the stored procedure. For simplicity, the preceding code does not do this.

After you have created the **Parameter** object, use the **Add** method of the **Parameters** collection of the **SelectCommand** object. If a stored procedure has more than one parameter, it does not matter in what order you add them because you create them by name:

Visual Basic .NET

```
Dim daSales as New SqlDataAdapter()
daSales.SelectCommand = New SqlCommand()
daSales.SelectCommand.Connection = conn
daSales.SelectCommand.CommandText = "ProductsByCategory"
daSales.SelectCommand.CommandType = _
  CommandType.StoredProcedure
daSales.SelectCommand.Parameters.Add(workParam1)
```

C#

```
SqlDataAdapter daSales = new SqlDataAdapter();
daSales.SelectCommand = new SqlCommand();
daSales.SelectCommand.Connection = conn;
daSales.SelectCommand.CommandText = "ProductsByCategory";
daSales.SelectCommand.CommandType =
  CommandType.StoredProcedure;
daSales.SelectCommand.Parameters.Add(workParam1);
```

Running a stored procedure

After you have created the **Command** object, you use the **Fill** method to run the stored procedure and retrieve the records:

Visual Basic .NET

```
ds = New DataSet()
daSales.Fill(ds, "Products")
```

C#

```
ds = new DataSet();
daSales.Fill(ds, "Products");
```

Using Output Parameters

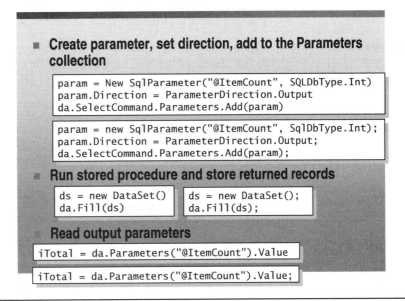

- **Create parameter, set direction, add to the Parameters collection**

```
param = New SqlParameter("@ItemCount", SQLDbType.Int)
param.Direction = ParameterDirection.Output
da.SelectCommand.Parameters.Add(param)
```

```
param = new SqlParameter("@ItemCount", SqlDbType.Int);
param.Direction = ParameterDirection.Output;
da.SelectCommand.Parameters.Add(param);
```

- **Run stored procedure and store returned records**

```
ds = new DataSet()
da.Fill(ds)
```
```
ds = new DataSet();
da.Fill(ds);
```

- **Read output parameters**

```
iTotal = da.Parameters("@ItemCount").Value
```

```
iTotal = da.Parameters("@ItemCount").Value;
```

Introduction

To read the value of an output parameter, or to read a returned value from a return records stored procedure, you need to access the value of the output parameter in the **Parameters** collection after the stored procedure has executed.

Example of using output parameters

The **OrdersCount** stored procedure takes a customer's **ID** and returns the number of outstanding orders that the customer has, but not the actual orders. The stored procedure uses the input parameters **@CustomerID**, and the output parameter **@ItemCount**, both of type **int**, as shown in the following stored procedure:

```
Procedure OrdersCount (
     @CustomerID int,
     @ItemCount int OUTPUT )
As
  SELECT @ItemCount=COUNT(OrderID)
  FROM Orders
  WHERE CustomerID=@CustomerID
```

Because the preceding stored procedure returns the *number* of rows, and it does not return the data in those rows, you do not need to use a **DataAdapter** object. Instead, you can use a **Command** object directly, and call the **ExecuteNonQuery** method to run the stored procedure.

Calling a return value stored procedure

To call the **OrdersCount** stored procedure, you need to create an input parameter named **@CustomerID**, and an output parameter named **@ItemCount**, add them to the **Parameters** collection of a **Command** object, and then call **ExecuteNonQuery** to run the stored procedure:

Visual Basic .NET

```
Dim myCmd As SqlCommand = New SqlCommand("OrdersCount", conn)
myCmd.CommandType = CommandType.StoredProcedure

'add an input parameter
Dim workParam as SqlParameter
workParam = New SqlParameter("@CustomerID", SqlDbType.Int)
workParam.Direction = ParameterDirection.Input
workParam.Value = CInt(txtCustID.Text)
myCmd.Parameters.Add (workParam)

'add an output parameter
workParam = New SqlParameter("@ItemCount", SqlDbType.Int)
workParam.Direction = ParameterDirection.Output
myCmd.Parameters.Add (workParam)
```

C#

```
SqlCommand myCmd = new SqlCommand("OrdersCount", conn);
myCmd.CommandType = CommandType.StoredProcedure;

// add an input parameter
SqlParameter workParam;
workParam = new SqlParameter("@CustomerID", SqlDbType.Int);
workParam.Direction = ParameterDirection.Input;
workParam.Value = Convert.ToInt16(txtCustID.Text);
myCmd.Parameters.Add(workParam);

// add an output parameter
workParam = new SqlParameter("@ItemCount", SqlDbType.Int);
workParam.Direction = ParameterDirection.Output;
myCmd.Parameters.Add(workParam);
```

Running the stored procedure

The following code runs the **MyCmd** stored procedure:

Visual Basic .NET

```
conn.Open()
myCmd.ExecuteNonQuery()
conn.Close()
```

C#

```
conn.Open();
myCmd.ExecuteNonQuery();
conn.Close();
```

Reading output parameters

If you are retrieving a value from a stored procedure that returns a value or sets an output parameter, you need to use the **Value** method of the returned parameter in the **Parameters** collection. You can reference the value of the output parameter by name or index. The following example code retrieves the value of the **@ItemCount** output parameter by name:

Visual Basic .NET

```
curSales = myCmd.Parameters("@ItemCount").Value
```

C#

```
curSales = myCmd.Parameters["@ItemCount"].Value;
```

Demonstration: Passing Parameters

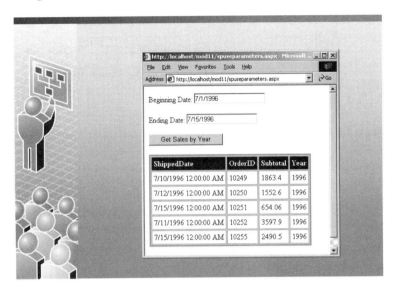

Introduction

In this demonstration, you will see how to call a stored procedure with two input parameters, and then bind the results to a **DataGrid**.

▶ **To run the demonstration**

1. Open the SPUseParameters.aspx page in the Mod11VB or Mod11CS project in the 2310Demos solution.

2. **Build and Browse**.

    Enter dates for the **Beginning Date** and **Ending Date**, and then click **Get Sales by Year**.

    A **DataGrid** is bound to the **Sales by Year** stored procedure in the Northwind Traders database.

3. In Visual Studio .NET, view the code-behind page for the SPUseParameters.aspx page.

4. In the **cmdSale_Click** event procedure, show the code that does the following:

    • Creates the **SqlConnection**.

    • Creates the **SqlDataAdapter** and sets properties of the **SelectCommand** to call the **Sales by Year** stored procedure.

    • Creates two input parameters.

    • Creates a new **DataSet** and fills the **DataSet** from the **DataAdapter**.

Review

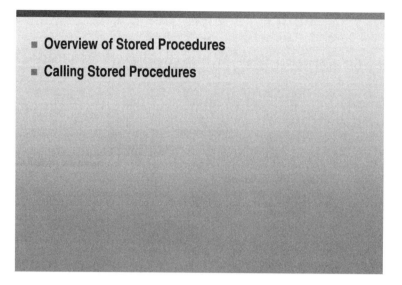

1. What type of stored procedure would you use to select and retrieve a customer's billing record?

2. What are the three steps in calling a stored procedure?

3. Do the parameter names and the order of the names in the **Parameters** collection have to match the stored procedure when working with a data source?

4. What method of the **Command** object do you use when calling a return value stored procedure?

5. What are the four types of stored procedure parameters?

Lab 11: Calling Stored Procedures with Microsoft ADO.NET

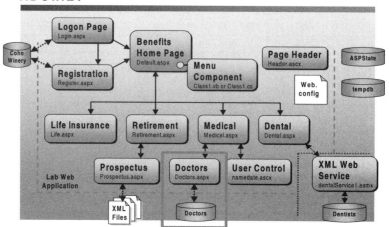

Objectives

After completing this lab, you will be able to:

- Retrieve data from a Microsoft® SQL Server™ database by using stored procedures.

- Access stored procedures by using **SqlCommand** and **SqlDataReader** objects.

- Bind a **SqlDataReader** object to a list box.

Note This lab focuses on the concepts in this module and as a result may not comply with Microsoft security recommendations.

Prerequisites

Before working on this lab, you must have:

- Knowledge of how to use Microsoft ADO.NET **SqlConnection**, **SqlDataAdapter**, **SqlDataReader**, and **SqlCommand** objects to read data from a SQL Server database by using stored procedures.

- Knowledge of how to create event procedures for server controls.

- Knowledge of how to display **DataSet** and **DataReader** data in a list-bound control.

Scenario

Coho Winery offers several benefits to its employees. In the labs for Course 2310B, *Developing Microsoft ASP.NET Web Applications Using Visual Studio .NET*, you will create a Web site that enables employees to select and set up their chosen benefits.

One benefit that is offered by Coho Winery is medical insurance. When applying for medical insurance, a user must select a primary care physician. The doctors that are approved by your company are all listed in a SQL Server database that is named doctors. The doctors' specialties are also in the database. In this lab, you will enhance the doctors.aspx page on the Coho Winery Web site to allow users to view the list of specialties of a selected doctor.

Estimated time to complete this lab: 30 minutes

Exercise 0
Lab Setup

To complete this lab, you must have created a Benefits Web Application project and a BenefitsList Class Library project. These projects can be created by using Microsoft Visual Basic® .NET or Microsoft Visual C#™ .NET.

If you have not created these projects, complete the following steps:

▶ **Create the 2310LabApplication solution**

Important   Only perform this procedure if you have not created a 2310LabApplication solution file.

1. Using Microsoft Visual Studio® .NET, create a new blank solution named **2310LabApplication**:

  a. On the **File** menu, point to **New**, and then click **Blank Solution**.

  b. In the **New Project** dialog box, type **2310LabApplication** in the **Name** text box, and then click **OK**.

▶ **Create the Benefits project**

Important   Only perform this procedure if you have not previously created a Benefits project, or if you have removed the Benefits project according to the steps in Appendix A, "Lab Recovery," in Course 2310B, *Developing Microsoft ASP.NET Web Applications Using Visual Studio .NET.*

1. Create a new Microsoft ASP.NET Web Application project, named **BenefitsVB** or **BenefitsCS**, in the 2310LabApplication solution:

  a. On the **File** menu, point to **New**, and then click **Project**.

  b. In the **New Project** dialog box, in the **Project Types** list, click **Visual Basic Projects** or **Visual C# Projects**.

  c. In the **Templates** list, click **ASP.NET Web Application**. Set the **Location** to **http://localhost/BenefitsVB** for the Visual Basic .NET project or to **http:/localhost/BenefitsCS** for the Visual C# project.

  d. Click **Add to Solution**, and then click **OK**.

Caution   When adding projects to the solution, the capitalization of the project name is important. Because you may be using some pre-built Web Forms in this and other labs in Course 2310B, *Developing Microsoft ASP.NET Web Applications Using Visual Studio .NET*, you must verify that you have capitalized the Benefits project as shown.

▶ **Update the Benefits project**

1. In Visual Studio .NET, open the 2310LabApplication solution file.

2. In Solution Explorer, right-click **BenefitsVB** or **BenefitsCS**, point to **Add**, and then click **Add Existing Item**.

3. Browse for project files.

For the Visual Basic .NET project

Browse to *install folder*\Labfiles\Lab11\VB\Starter\BenefitsVB folder for the Visual Basic .NET files.

For the Visual C# project

Browse to *install folder*\Labfiles\Lab11\CS\Starter\BenefitsCS folder for the Visual C# files.

4. In the **Files of type** box of the **Add Existing Item – Benefits** dialog box, click **All Files (*.*)**.

5. Select all of the files in this folder, and then click **Open**.

6. Click **Yes** if prompted to overwrite or reload files.

▶ **Create the BenefitsList class library**

Important   Only perform these steps if you have not previously created a BenefitsList project, or if you have removed the BenefitsList project according to the steps in Appendix A, "Lab Recovery," in Course 2310B, *Developing Microsoft ASP.NET Web Applications Using Visual Studio .NET*.

1. Create a new Class Library Project

For the Visual Basic .NET project

Create a new Visual Basic .NET Class Library project, name it **BenefitsListVB**, and then add it to the 2310LabApplication solution:

a. On the **File** menu, point to **New**, and then click **Project**.

b. In the **New Project** dialog box, in the **Project Types** list, click **Visual Basic Projects**.

c. In the **Templates** list, click **Class Library**, and then set the **Name** to **BenefitsListVB**.

d. Click **Add to Solution**, and then click **OK**.

For the Visual C# project

Create a new Visual C# .NET Class Library project, name it **BenefitsListCS**, and then add it to the 2310LabApplication solution:

a. On the **File** menu, point to **New**, and then click **Project**.

b. In the **New Project** dialog box, in the **Project Types** list, click **Visual C# Projects**.

c. In the **Templates** list, click **Class Library** and then set the **Name** to **BenefitsListCS**.

d. Click **Add to Solution**, and then click **OK**.

Caution   Verify that you have capitalized the BenefitsList project as shown.

▶ **Update the BenefitsList project**

1. In Visual Studio .NET, open the 2310LabApplication solution file.

2. In Solution Explorer, right-click **BenefitsListVB** or **BenefitsListCS**, point to **Add**, and then click **Add Existing Item**.

3. Browse for project files:

For the Visual Basic .NET project

Browse to the *install folder*\Labfiles\Lab11\VB\Starter\BenefitsListVB folder.

For the Visual C# project

Browse to the *install folder*\Labfiles\Lab11\CS\Starter\BenefitsListCS folder.

4. In the **Files of type** box of the **Add Existing Item – BenefitsList** dialog box, click **All Files (*.*)**.

5. Select all of the files in this folder, and then click **Open**.

6. Click **Yes** if prompted to overwrite or reload files.

▶ **Create a reference to the BenefitsList component in the Benefits project**

1. In the Benefits project in the 2310LabApplication solution, complete the following steps to add a reference to the BenefitsList component that you just created:

   a. Right-click the **BenefitsVB** or **BenefitsCS** project in Solution Explorer and then click **Add Reference**.

   b. In the **Add Reference** dialog box, on the **Projects** tab, double-click the **BenefitsListVB** or **BenefitsListCS** project.

   c. In the **Selected Components** list, select the **BenefitsListVB** or **BenefitsListCS** component, and then click **OK**.

   The component is added to the References folder in Solution Explorer.

Exercise 1
Get Unique City Names

In this exercise, you will bind the **lstCities** drop-down list box on the doctors.aspx page so that the drop-down list box displays only unique city names from the doctors database. When the user selects a city, the code will create a new view of the **DataSet** data and display the data in the **DataGrid**.

The **lstCities** drop-down list box is currently bound to the city field in the **doctors** table by using a **SqlCommand** object. This binding results in all cities being displayed in the drop-down list box. In this exercise, you will use a stored procedure to select only unique city names from the **doctors** table.

Because the **lstCities** drop-down list box is currently bound, you must first remove that binding before using the stored procedure.

▶ **Remove existing binding code**

1. Open the doctors.aspx.vb page in the BenefitsVB project or the doctors.aspc.cs page in the BenefitsCS project.

2. In the **Page_Load** event procedure, find the following code:

Visual Basic .NET

```
'TODO: Lab10: bind the listbox to city field
'in the doctors
table
Dim cmdCities As New SqlCommand _
    ("Select city from doctors", SqlConnection1)
Dim drCities As SqlDataReader
SqlConnection1.Open()
drCities = cmdCities.ExecuteReader()
lstCities.DataSource = drCities
lstCities.DataTextField = "city"
lstCities.DataBind()
drCities.Close()
SqlConnection1.Close()
```

C#

```
//TODO Lab10: bind the listbox to city field
//in the doctors table
SqlCommand cmdCities = new SqlCommand
    ("Select city from doctors", sqlConnection1);
sqlDataReader drCities;
sqlConnection1.Open();
drCities = cmdCities.ExecuteReader();
lstCities.DataSource = drCities;
lstCities.DataTextField = "City";
lstCities.DataBind();
drCities.Close();
sqlConnection1.Close();
```

3. Comment this code by selecting all of the lines of code, and then clicking the Comment icon ▦ on the toolbar.

▶ **Bind the drop-down list box using a stored procedure**

1. Locate the following comment:

   ```
   TODO: Lab11: bind the listbox to the getUniqueCities stored
   procedure
   ```

2. Create a new **SqlCommand** object named **cmdCities** that uses the **sqlConnection1** object to call the **getUniqueCities** stored procedure.

3. Set the **CommandType** for the **cmdCities** object to **Stored Procedure**.

4. Open the sqlConnection1 SqlConnection object.

5. Create a **SqlDataReader** object from the **SqlCommand** object by calling the **ExecuteReader** method of the **SqlCommand** object. Name the **SqlDataReader** object **drCities**.

6. In the code, set the properties of the **lstCities** drop-down list box as shown in the following table.

Property	Value
DataSource	drCities
DataTextField	"City"

7. Call the **DataBind** method of the **lstCities** drop-down list box.

8. Close the **DataReader** and the **Connection** objects.

   Your code should look like the following:

Visual Basic .NET

```
Dim cmdCities As SqlCommand = New _
    SqlCommand("getUniqueCities", SqlConnection1)
cmdCities.CommandType = CommandType.StoredProcedure
SqlConnection1.Open()
Dim drCities As SqlDataReader
drCities = cmdCities.ExecuteReader()
lstCities.DataSource = drCities
lstCities.DataTextField = "City"
lstCities.DataBind()
drCities.Close()
SqlConnection1.Close()
```

C#

```
SqlCommand cmdCities = new SqlCommand
    ("getUniqueCities", sqlConnection1);
cmdCities.CommandType = CommandType.StoredProcedure;
sqlConnection1.Open();
sqlDataReader drCities;
drCities = cmdCities.ExecuteReader();
lstCities.DataSource = drCities;
lstCities.DataTextField = "City";
lstCities.DataBind();
drCities.Close();
sqlConnection1.Close();
```

9. Build and browse the doctors.aspx page.

   The **City** drop-down list box displays the list of cities where the doctors are located. There are no duplicate cities listed.

Exercise 2
Get Doctor Specialties

In this exercise, you will display a doctor's specialties in a list box. When a doctor is selected in the **dgDoctors DataGrid** object, call the **getDoctorSpecialty** stored procedure and display the results in the **lstSpecialties** list box.

▶ **Call the getDrSpecialty stored procedure**

1. Create **SelectedIndexChanged** event procedure.

Visual Basic .NET

Open the code-behind page for the doctors.aspx page and create a **SelectedIndexChanged** event procedure for the **DataGrid** control:

a. In the code-behind page, in the **Class Name** drop-down list, click **dgDoctors**.

b. In the **Method Name** drop-down list, click **SelectedIndexChanged**.

C#

In the properties for the **dgDoctors DataGrid** control, click **Events**. Scroll down the list of events, and then double click the **SelectedIndexChanged** event.

2. Create a string variable named *strDrID* to hold the value of the **dr_id** column for the row that was selected by the user.

3. Using the **Cells** collection of the **SelectedItem** of the **dgDoctors DataGrid**, read the value of the *dr_id* field and store it in the *strDrID* variable.

Your code should look like the following:

Visual Basic .NET

```
Dim strDrID As String
strDrID = dgDoctors.SelectedItem.Cells.Item(1).Text
```

C#

```
string strDrID;
strDrID = dgDoctors.SelectedItem.Cells[1].Text;
```

4. Create a new **SqlCommand** object named **cmdSpecialty** that uses the **sqlConnection1** object to call the **getDrSpecialty** stored procedure.

5. Set the **SqlCommand** command type to a stored procedure.

Your code should look like the following:

Visual Basic .NET

```
Dim cmdSpecialty As New _
    SqlCommand("getDrSpecialty", SqlConnection1)
cmdSpecialty.CommandType = CommandType.StoredProcedure
```

C#

```
SqlCommand cmdSpecialty = new
    SqlCommand("getDrSpecialty", sqlConnection1);
cmdSpecialty.CommandType = CommandType.StoredProcedure;
```

6. Create a **SqlParameter** object named **paramSpecialty** by using the parameter that is shown in the following table.

Parameter name	Data type	Size
@dr_id	SqlDbType.Char	4

7. Set the Direction property of the **SqlParameter** to **Input**.

8. Set the value of the **SqlParameter** to the variable **strDrID**.

9. Add the parameter to the **SqlCommand** object by using the **Add** method.

   Your code should look like the following:

Visual Basic .NET

```
Dim paramSpecialty As New SqlParameter _
    ("@dr_id", SqlDbType.Char, 4)
paramSpecialty.Direction = ParameterDirection.Input
paramSpecialty.Value = strDrID
cmdSpecialty.Parameters.Add(paramSpecialty)
```

C#

```
SqlParameter paramSpecialty = new SqlParameter
    ("@dr_id", SqlDbType.Char, 4);
paramSpecialty.Direction = ParameterDirection.Input;
paramSpecialty.Value = strDrID;
cmdSpecialty.Parameters.Add(paramSpecialty);
```

10. Open the sqlConnection1 SqlConnection object.

11. Create a new **SqlDataReader** object named **drSpecialty**.

12. Fill the **SqlDataReader** object from the **SqlCommand** object by calling the **ExecuteReader** method of the **SqlCommand** object.

   Your code should look like the following:

Visual Basic .NET

```
SqlConnection1.Open()
Dim drSpecialty As SqlDataReader
drSpecialty = cmdSpecialty.ExecuteReader()
```

C#

```
sqlConnection1.Open();
sqlDataReader drSpecialty;
drSpecialty = cmdSpecialty.ExecuteReader();
```

▶ **Bind the lstSpecialties list box to the drSpecialties DataReader and make the list box visible**

1. In your code, set the properties for the **lstSpecialties** list box as shown in the following table.

Property	Value
DataSource	drSpecialty
DataTextField	"Specialty"

2. Call the **DataBind** method of the list box.

3. Close the **SqlDataReader** and **SqlConnection** objects.

Your code should look like the following:

Visual Basic .NET

```
lstSpecialties.DataSource = drSpecialty
lstSpecialties.DataTextField = "Specialty"
lstSpecialties.DataBind()
drSpecialty.Close()
SqlConnection1.Close()
```

C#

```
lstSpecialties.DataSource = drSpecialty;
lstSpecialties.DataTextField = "Specialty";
lstSpecialties.DataBind();
drSpecialty.Close();
sqlConnection1.Close();
```

4. Add code to make the **lstSpecialties** list box and **lblSpecialties** label visible, but only if there are specialties in the **DataReader**.

Your code should look like the following:

Visual Basic .NET

```
If Not IsDBNull(drSpecialty) Then
    lstSpecialties.Visible = True
    lblSpecialties.Visible = True
End If
```

C#

```
if (drSpecialty != null)
{
    lstSpecialties.Visible = true;
    lblSpecialties.Visible = true;
}
```

5. Build and browse the doctors.aspx page:

   a. In the browser, select a doctor from the list.

   The **Specialties** list box displays the specialties for the selected doctor.

   b. Choose a city from the **City** drop-down list box, and then select a new doctor.

   The **Specialties** list box may display a different list of specialties. If it does not, select a different doctor to ensure that your code is working properly.

   c. Click **Submit**.

   You are redirected to the medical.aspx page, and the selected doctor's name displays in the **Primary Care Physician** text box.

msdn® training

Module 12: Reading and Writing XML Data

Contents

Overview

- Overview of XML Architecture in ASP.NET
- XML and the DataSet Object
- Working with XML Data
- Using the XML Web Server Control

Introduction

Although a lot of data is stored in Microsoft® SQL Server™ databases and managed through Microsoft ADO.NET, Extensible Markup Language (XML) has recently become a strong standard for storage, management, and transmission of data. XML has two big advantages when it comes to storing and transferring data:

- XML is an accepted industry standard.
- XML is only plain text.

In this module, you will learn how to read, write, and display XML data.

Objectives

After completing this module, you will be able to:

- Describe XML architecture in Microsoft ASP.NET.
- Read and write XML data into a **DataSet** object.
- Identify how to store, retrieve, and transform XML data by using **XmlDataDocument** and **XslTransform** objects.
- Use the XML Web server control to display, load, and save XML data.

Lesson: Overview of XML Architecture in ASP.NET

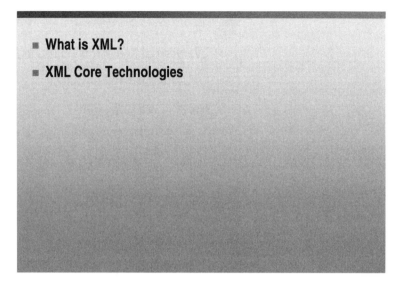

Introduction

ASP.NET provides various types of classes and objects that can be used to access and synchronize XML data. These classes and objects represent low-level XML processing components that integrate XML into ASP.NET Web applications.

In this lesson, you will learn about what comprises an XML document. You will also learn about XML core technologies. You will then learn about the classes and objects that are used to read and write XML data.

Lesson objectives

After completing this lesson, you will be able to:

- Distinguish between valid and well-formed XML.
- Describe the XML core technologies.

What is XML?

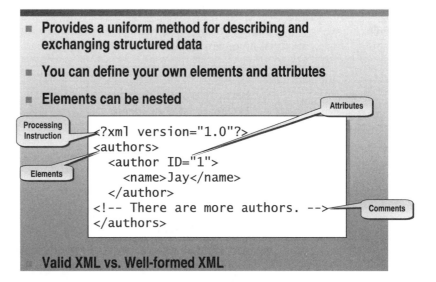

■ **Provides a uniform method for describing and exchanging structured data**

■ **You can define your own elements and attributes**

■ **Elements can be nested**

```
<?xml version="1.0"?>
<authors>
   <author ID="1">
      <name>Jay</name>
   </author>
<!-- There are more authors. -->
</authors>
```

Processing Instruction   Attributes   Elements   Comments

■ **Valid XML vs. Well-formed XML**

Introduction

Currently, companies confront many problems when it comes to organizing data because they need to fulfill the following requirements:

■ Data must be readable by both computers and users.

■ Both the content and the structure of the data must be defined.

■ The structure of the data must be separate from the presentation of the data.

■ The structure of the data must be open and extensible.

XML fulfills all of these requirements, thereby assisting companies in the organization of data.

Definition

XML is the universal format that is used for describing and exchanging structured documents and data on the Internet. XML is a subset of the Standard Generalized Markup Language (SGML), and it is defined by the World Wide Web Consortium (W3C), thereby ensuring that the structured data will be uniform and independent of Web applications or vendors.

XML defines the structure of data in an open and self-describing manner. The open and self-describing manner allows data to be easily transferred over a network and to be consistently processed by the receiver. XML describes how the data is structured, not how it should be displayed or used, similar to Hypertext Markup Language (HTML). XML documents contain tags that assign meaning to the content of the document. These tags allow programmers to find the data that they need in the XML document.

Parts of an XML document

The parts of an XML document include:

■ Processing Instruction

■ Elements

■ Attributes

■ Comments

Processing instruction

Most XML documents begin with a processing instruction to the XML processor that the document is formed according to the W3C XML Recommendation.

Elements

A set of nested elements can be defined following the processing instruction. With regard to elements:

- An element usually consists of a start tag and a closing tag pair.

- Between the start tag and closing tag pair, an element can contain data content or other elements.

- An element can consist of just the closing tag.

- The first element that the XML processor encounters must consist of a start tag and a closing tag. This first element contains all of the other elements and it is called the root element.

- All other elements, after the first element, but within the root element, are called child elements.

- Any child element may nest subsequent child elements. Most of the content data in XML is stored between the start tag and closing tag of the child elements.

Attributes

Any element can contain attributes. Using attributes is an alternative to using elements to store content. Attributes define data that belongs to a single element. With regard to attributes:

- Create an attribute in the start tag of an element.

- Declare the name of the attribute, followed by a value assignment.

- Use either single or double quotation marks to set the value of an attribute.

Comments

Comments are optional.

Well-formed XML

A well-formed XML document conforms to specifications that are listed in the W3C Recommendation for XML 1.0. An XML document is considered well-formed if:

- It contains exactly one root element (the document element).

- All of the child elements are nested properly within each other.

- The beginning and end tags of a given element exist within the body of the same parent element.

Example of well-formed XML:

```
<Temp>22</Temp>
```

Example of non-well-formed XML:

```
<Temp>22</temp>
```

The error in the preceding example is that the closing tag <temp> does not match the start tag <Temp>.

Valid XML

XML is valid if its vocabulary conforms to a set of requirements that are listed in a schema:

- In XML, a schema is a description of an XML document.

- A schema is used to validate XML documents. An XML document that you validate with a schema is called an instance document. If an instance document matches the schema definition, the instance document is said to be valid.

There are three types of schemas that can be used for validating an XML instance document, as shown in the following table.

Type of schema	Description
Document Type Definition (DTD)	DTD is the original validation method that is described in W3C XML Recommendation version 1.0. XML Schema Definition (XSD) superceded the DTD. DTDs are not based on XML.
XML-Data Reduced (XDR schema)	XDR is an interim schema technology that was developed by Microsoft. While XDR is similar to XSD, XDR schemas are written in XML.
XML Schema Definition language (XSD)	XSD is the W3C Recommendation for validating XML Schemas. XSD replaces both DTDs and XDR schemas. XSD schemas are written in XML.

XSD is the most commonly used schema in the Microsoft .NET Framework.

XML Core Technologies

- **XML Schema definition**
    - Defines the required structure of a valid XML document
- **Extensible Stylesheet Language Transformation**
    - Transforms the content of a source XML document into another document that is different in format or structure
- **XML Path Language**
    - Addresses parts of an XML document
- **Document Object Model**
    - Object model for programmatically working with XML documents in memory
- **XML Query**
    - Easily implementable language in which queries are concise and easily understood

Introduction

Since its inception, XML has initiated other technology innovations and developments that work with XML to manipulate data. The core technologies related to XML, which are all W3C recommendations, include:

- XML Schema definition (XSD)
- Extensible Stylesheet Language Transformation (XSLT)
- XML Path Language (XPath)
- Document Object Model (DOM)
- XML Query (XQuery)

XSD

XSD is the current schema definition standard that defines the required structure of a valid XML document. You can create an XSD schema as a stand-alone document that is referenced by instance documents. An instance document is an XML document validated by an XML schema. You can also include an XSD schema in an XML document. The extension of a stand-alone schema file is .xsd.

Schema definition

You can define an XML document as a schema by using the <xsd:schema> element. The W3C schema namespace qualifies the xsd: prefix. Each element you identify with the xsd: prefix belongs to the XSD namespace.

In XSD, you can reference multiple namespaces (xmlns). For example, the following schema definition references two namespaces, the first for the W3C XML Schema, and the second for a Microsoft Office 10 data schema:

```
<xsd:schema xmlns:xsd="http://www.w3c.org/2000/10/XMLSchema"
xmlns:od="urn:schemas-microsoft-com:officedata">
```

Element and attribute declarations

You use element and attribute declarations to define the use of elements and attributes in an XML document. The following properties can be defined for an element or attribute: name, contents, number, sequence of occurrences, data type.

In the following example, the name of the element is declared as <LastName>. Within the document, <LastName> can occur 0 or more times. The element type is string:

```
<xsd:element name="LastName" minOccurs="0" maxOccurs="*"
type="string"></xsd:element>
```

XSLT

For many purposes, XML data must be transformed into other forms and variants. W3C has produced XSLT as one of the programming languages that can be used to transform data. XSLT is a part of Extensible Stylesheet Language (XSL).

XSLT is an XML-based language that performs transformations of XML documents into arbitrary text-based formats, which may or may not be XML.

The following three documents are used with XSLT:

- The source document

  The source document is simply a well-formed XML document that provides the input for the transformation. For example, the following code is a sample of an XML source document:

```
<?xml version="1.0" ?>
<?xml-stylesheet type="text/xsl" href="Employees1.xsl"?>
<employees>
    <employee>
        <name>Stuart Munson</name>
        <jobtitle>Programmer</jobtitle>
    </employee>
    <employee>
        <name>Robert Brown</name>
        <jobtitle>Tester</jobtitle>
    </employee>
</employees>
```

- The XSLT style sheet document

  The XSLT style sheet document is an XML document that uses the XSLT vocabulary for expressing transformation rules. For example, the following code is the XSLT style sheet document (Employees1.xsl) that will be applied to the source document in the preceding code:

```xml
<xsl:stylesheet
xmlns:xsl="http://www.w3.org/1999/XSL/Transform"
version="1.0">
   <xsl:template match="/">
      <xsl:apply-templates select="//employee" />
   </xsl:template>
   <xsl:template match="employee">
      <P>
         <xsl:apply-templates />
         <HR />
      </P>
   </xsl:template>
   <xsl:template match="name">
      <FONT COLOR="red" />
      <B>
         <xsl:value-of select="." />
      </B>
   </xsl:template>
   <xsl:template match="jobtitle">
      <BR/>
      <FONT COLOR="blue" />
      <xsl:value-of select="." />
   </xsl:template>
</xsl:stylesheet>
```

- The result document

  The result document is a text document that is produced by running the source document through the transformations that are found in the XSLT style sheet. For example, by running the source document in the preceding code through the preceding XSLT style sheet Employees1.xsl, the following result document is produced:

Stuart Munson
Programmer

Robert Brown
Tester

Note For more information about XSLT, see Course 1913, *Exchanging and Transforming Data Using XML and XSLT.*

XPath

XPath is a comprehensive language that is used referencing elements in an XML documents. XPath version 2.0 is a W3C recommendation.

The XPath language specifies an object model for XML documents. In the XPath object model, an XML document is represented as a tree of nodes. You query an XML source by using its XPath node properties.

DOM

The DOM is an in-memory cache tree representation of an XML document. The DOM enables the navigation and editing of the XML document. W3C defines the properties, methods, and events of the DOM.

With ASP.NET, you can write script that runs on the Web server and then uses the DOM to create an XML document that will be sent to the browser. Alternatively, you can write client-side script that builds an XML document at the client and then submits the XML data to the Web server, when appropriate.

XQuery

As increasing amounts of information are stored, exchanged, and presented by using XML, the ability to intelligently query XML data sources becomes increasingly important. XQuery provides features for retrieving and interpreting information from these data sources:

- XQuery is designed to be an easily implementable language in which queries are concise and easily understood.

- XQuery is flexible enough to query a broad spectrum of XML information sources, including both databases and documents.

- XQuery is based on several other W3C technologies. For example, XQuery uses path statements from the XPath 2.0 Recommendation.

- XQuery greatly depends upon XPath to target its queries within a particular XML source. XQuery also borrows its object model from XPath.

Note For more information about XML core technologies, see Module 4, "Technologies for Handling XML Data," in Course 2500, *Introduction to XML and the Microsoft .NET Platform,* and see the W3C Web site at http://www.w3c.org.

Lesson: XML and the DataSet Object

- **Why use XML with DataSets?**

- **Overview of XML and DataSets**

- **The XML-Based Methods of the DataSet Object**

- **Demonstration: Reading and Writing XML to and from a DataSet**

- **Practice: Using the ReadXml Method**

- **Creating Nested XML Data**

- **Demonstration: Creating Nested XML**

Introduction

XML and **DataSets** share a close connection with each other. **DataSets** are the basis for disconnected storage and the manipulation of relational data. **DataSets** are also a container for one or more data tables. XML is the standard format for data that is present in **DataSets**.

Lesson objectives

After completing this lesson, you will be able to:

- Describe the use of XML with DataSets.

- Identify the relationship of XML with DataSets.

- Identify the use of the **ReadXml**, **WriteXml** and **GetXml** methods.

- Create nested XML data.

Why Use XML with DataSets?

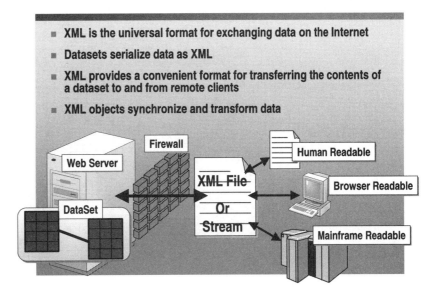

- XML is the universal format for exchanging data on the Internet
- Datasets serialize data as XML
- XML provides a convenient format for transferring the contents of a dataset to and from remote clients
- XML objects synchronize and transform data

Introduction

XML is a universal format that is used for exchanging data on the Internet and a **DataSet** is a relational view of data that can be represented in XML. XML is used with the DataSets in the following ways:

- Serialize data

  DataSets can serialize data as XML. The schema of a DataSet that includes tables, columns, data types, and constraints is defined by using an XML Schema (.xsd file).

- XML and XML Schema

  XML and XML Schemas provide a convenient format for transferring the contents of a DataSet to and from remote clients. You can infer XML Schemas from existing DataSets and create DataSets from existing XML Schemas.

- Synchronize and transform data

  You can use different XML objects to synchronize and transform data that is represented by DataSets.

Overview of XML and DataSets

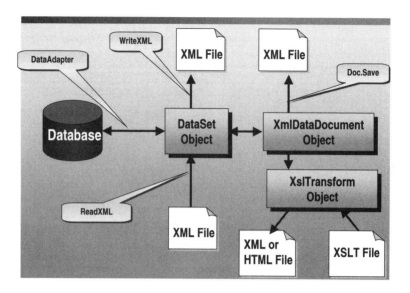

Introduction

XML plays an important role in the way that data is handled in the .NET Framework. XML is the format that is used in the .NET Framework for storing and transmitting all kinds of data. **DataSets** are able to store and transmit data in XML format. Regarding **DataSets** and XML features:

- Structure of a DataSet can be defined in an XML Schema

  The structure of a DataSet that includes tables, columns, relationships, and constraints can be defined by using an XML Schema. XML Schemas are a standards-based format of the W3C that can be used for defining the structure of XML data.

- Generate a DataSet class

  You can generate a DataSet class that incorporates schema information to define its data structures (such as tables and columns) as class members.

- DataSet methods

  You can read an XML document or stream it into a DataSet by using the **ReadXML** method of the DataSet and then write a DataSet in XML by using the **WriteXML** method of the DataSet. Because XML is a standard interchange format for data between different Web applications, you can load a DataSet with XML-formatted information that was sent by other applications. Similarly, a DataSet can write out its data as an XML stream or document that will be shared with other applications or simply stored as an XML document.

■ Create an XML view of the contents of a DataSet

You can create an XML view (an **XmlDataDocument** object) of the contents of a DataSet, and then view and manipulate the data by using either relational methods (by means of the DataSet) or XML methods. The two views are automatically synchronized as they are changed.

■ Transformation of data

You can use the **XSLTransform** object to load an .xsl style sheet file and apply the transformation. The resulting document can be an XML or HTML file.

Note DataSets can read and write schemas that store structured information by using the **ReadXmlSchema** and **WriteXmlSchema** methods. If no schema is available, the DataSet can infer one, by means of its **InferXmlSchema** method, from the data that is in an XML document that is structured in a relational way.

The XML-Based Methods of the DataSet Object

- ■ **Use ReadXml to load data from a file or stream**

```
DataSet ds = new DataSet();
ds.ReadXml(Server.MapPath("filename.xml"));
```

- ■ **Use WriteXml to write XML data to a file or stream**

```
DataSet ds = new DataSet();
SqlDataAdapter da = new SqlDataAdapter("select * from
        Authors", conn);
da.Fill(ds);
ds.WriteXml(Server.MapPath("filename.xml"));
```

- ■ **Use GetXml to write data to a string variable**

```
string strXmlDS = ds.GetXml();
```

Visual Basic .NET Code Example

Introduction

The contents of a **DataSet** can be created from an XML stream or document. In addition, with the .NET Framework, you have great flexibility over what information is loaded from XML, and how the schema or relational structure of the **DataSet** is created.

ReadXML

To fill a **DataSet** with data from XML, you use the **ReadXml** method of the **DataSet** object. The **ReadXml** method reads from a file, a stream, or an **XmlReader**.

The **ReadXml** method reads the contents of the XML stream or document and then loads the **DataSet** with that data. **ReadXml** also creates the relational schema of the **DataSet**, depending on the **XmlReadMode** that is specified and whether or not a relational schema already exists.

The following code shows how to fill a DataSet with data:

Microsoft Visual Basic® .NET

```
Dim ds As New DataSet()
ds.ReadXml(Server.MapPath("filename.xml"))
```

C#

```
DataSet ds = new DataSet();
ds.ReadXml(Server.MapPath("filename.xml"));
```

Note The **Server.MapPath** method returns the physical file path, which corresponds to the specified virtual path on the Web server.

WriteXML

To write a **DataSet** to a file, stream, or **XmlWriter**, use the **WriteXml** method. The first parameter you pass to **WriteXml** is the destination of the XML output. For example, you could pass a string containing a file name, a **System.IO.TextWriter** object, and so on. You can pass an optional second parameter of an **XmlWriteMode** to specify how the XML output is to be written.

The following code examples show how to write a DataSet:

Visual Basic .NET

```
Dim ds As New DataSet()
Dim da As New SqlDataAdapter( _
  "select * from Authors", conn)
da.Fill(ds)
ds.WriteXml(Server.MapPath("filename.xml"))
```

C#

```
DataSet ds = new DataSet();
SqlDataAdapter da = new SqlDataAdapter
  ("select * from Authors", conn);
da.Fill(ds);
ds.WriteXml(Server.MapPath("filename.xml"));
```

GetXML

The XML representation of the **DataSet** can be written to a file, a stream, an **XmlWriter**, or to a string. These choices provide great flexibility for how you transport the XML representation of the **DataSet**. To obtain the XML representation of the **DataSet** as a string, you would use the **GetXml** method, as shown in the following code examples:

Visual Basic .NET

```
Dim strXmlDS As String = ds.GetXml()
```

C#

```
string strXmlDS = ds.GetXml();
```

GetXml returns the XML representation of the **DataSet** without schema information. To write the schema information from the **DataSet** (as XML Schema) to a string, you use **GetXmlSchema**.

Demonstration: Reading and Writing XML to and from a DataSet

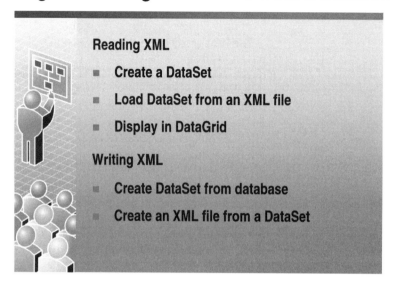

Reading XML

- Create a DataSet
- Load DataSet from an XML file
- Display in DataGrid

Writing XML

- Create DataSet from database
- Create an XML file from a DataSet

Introduction

In this demonstration, you will see how to read and write XML to and from a **DataSet**.

The files for this demonstration are in the Mod12CS and Mod12VB projects in the 2310Demos solution.

▶ **To run the demonstration**

Reading XML data

1. Open the file Books.xml in Microsoft Visual Studio® .NET.

   This file contains the data that will be displayed.

2. Build and browse the DisplayXML.aspx page.

3. In the text box, click **Books.xml** and then click **Load**.

4. In the text box, click **Employees.xml** and then click **Load**.

5. Open the code-behind file DisplayXML.aspx.vb or DisplayXML.aspx.cs in Visual Studio .NET.

6. In the **cmdLoad_Click** event procedure, show the code that reads an XML file into a **DataSet** and then binds the **DataGrid** to the **DataSet**.

Note The **DataGrid** can only handle one level of elements in an XML file.

If there is too much nesting of elements, the data will not be displayed. You can demonstrate excessive nesting by adding an author element to the book elements in the Books.xml file:

```
<book>
    ...
    <author>
        <firstname>Jay</firstname>
        <lastname>Bird</lastname>
    </author>
</book>
```

7. Build and browse the DisplayXML.aspx page.

   The data is not displayed due to excessive nesting.

Writing XML data

8. Build and browse the SaveAsXML.aspx page.

   The **DataGrid** displays the **DataSet** data that will be saved into an XML file.

9. Click **Save as XML**, and then click the **View XML** hyperlink.

   This is the XML data that was created from the **DataSet**.

10. Open one of the code-behind files SaveAsXml.aspx.vb or SaveAsXml.aspc.cs in Visual Studio .NET.

    There is a function called **CreateDataSet** that builds the **DataSet** from a SQL Server database.

11. To create an XML file, show the code in the **cmdSave_Click** event procedure that calls the **WriteXml** method of the **DataSet**.

12. To create an XSD schema file, show the code in the **cmdSchema_Click** event procedure that calls the **WriteXmlSchema** method of the **DataSet**.

Practice: Using the ReadXml Method

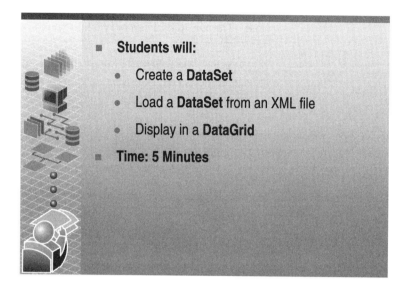

Introduction

In this practice, you will learn how to use the **ReadXml** method.

The files for this practice are in the Mod12VB and Mod12CS projects in the 2310Demos solution.

▶ **To run the practice**

1. Open the Employees.xml file in Visual Studio .NET. In the following steps you will create a webform to display the data found in Employees.xml.

2. Create a new Web Form in the Mod12VB or Mod12CS project named ReadXmlForm.aspx.

3. Drag a **DataGrid** control into the Web Form. Set its **ID** property to **dgEmployees**.

4. In the **Page_Load** event procedure, create a **DataSet**, call **ReadXml** to read the XML data from the Employees.xml file into the **DataSet**, and then bind the **DataGrid** to the **DataSet**.

   Your code should look like the following:

Visual Basic .NET

```
Dim ds As New DataSet()
ds.ReadXml(Server.MapPath("Employees.xml"))
dgEmployees.DataSource = ds
dgEmployees.DataBind()
```

C#

```
DataSet ds = new DataSet();
ds.ReadXml(Server.MapPath("Employees.xml"));
dgEmployees.DataSource = ds;
dgEmployees.DataBind();
```

5. Build and browse your page.

Creating Nested XML Data

- **By default, the output of DataTables is sequential**

- **To make XML nested, make the DataRelation nested**

```
Dim dr As New DataRelation _
    ("name", parentCol, childCol)
dr.Nested = True
ds.Relations.Add(dr)
```

```
DataRelation dr = new
    DataRelation("name",
    parentCol,
    childCol);
dr.Nested = true;
ds.Relations.Add(dr);
```

Sequential

Nested

```
<Title name="title1" />
<Title name="title2" />
<Title name="title3" />
<Publisher name="pub1" />
<Publisher name="pub2" />
```

```
<Publisher name="pub1" >
    <Title name="title1" />
    <Title name="title3" />
</Publisher>
<Publisher name="pub2" >
    <Title name="title2" />
</Publisher>
```

Introduction

In a relational representation of data, individual tables contain rows that are related to one another by using a column or a set of columns. In the ADO.NET **DataSet**, the relationship between tables is implemented by using a **DataRelation**.

DataRelation

When you create a **DataRelation**, the parent-child relationships are managed only through the relation between the rows and columns. The tables and columns are separate entities. In the hierarchical representation of data that XML provides, the parent-child relationships are represented by parent elements that contain nested child elements.

Note When using nested relationships, a child element can have only one parent element.

To facilitate the nesting of child objects when a **DataSet** is synchronized with an **XmlDataDocument**, or when it is written as XML data by using **WriteXml**, the **DataRelation** exposes a **Nested** property.

Setting the **Nested** property of a **DataRelation** to **true** causes the child rows of the relation to be nested within the parent column when the **DataSet** is written as XML data or is synchronized with an **XmlDataDocument**. The **Nested** property of the **DataRelation** is set to **false** by default.

In the following illustration of a **DataSet**, you will see how to write the code when the **Nested** property of the **DataRelation** is set to **false**, in addition to when the **Nested** property of the **DataRelation** is set to **true**. You will also see the output of the result from calling **WriteXml** on the **DataSet**.

DataSet

The following code demonstrates how to set the **Nested** property of the **DataRelation** to **false**:

Visual Basic .NET

```
Dim ds As New DataSet()
'fill the DataSet
...
Dim parentCol As DataColumn = _
  ds.Tables("Publishers").Columns("pub_id")
Dim childCol As DataColumn = _
  ds.Tables("Titles").Columns("pub_id")
Dim dr As New DataRelation _
  ("TitlePublishers", parentCol, childCol)
ds.Relations.Add(dr)
ds.WriteXml(Server.MapPath("PubTitlesNotNested.xml"), _
  XmlWriteMode.IgnoreSchema)
```

C#

```
DataSet ds = new DataSet();
//fill the DataSet
...
DataColumn parentCol =
  ds.Tables["Publishers"].Columns["pub_id"];
DataColumn childCol= ds.Tables["Titles"].Columns["pub_id"];
DataRelation dr =  new DataRelation ("TitlePublishers",
  parentCol, childCol);
ds.Relations.Add(dr);
ds.WriteXml(Server.MapPath("PubTitlesNotNested.xml"),
  XmlWriteMode.IgnoreSchema);
```

Because the **Nested** property of the **DataRelation** object is not set to **true** for the preceding **DataSet**, the child objects will not be nested within the parent elements when this **DataSet** is represented as XML data.

The following XML example shows the output that will result from calling **WriteXml** on the **DataSet**:

```xml
<?xml version = "1.0" standalone = "yes"?>
<NewDataSet>
  <Titles>
      <title>title1</title>
      <pub_id>1</pub_id>
      <price>40.00</price>
  </Titles>
  <Titles>
      <title>title2</title>
      <pub_id>2</pub_id>
      <price>60.00</price>
  </Titles>
  <Titles>
      <title>title3</title>
      <pub_id>1</pub_id>
      <price>30.00</price>
  </Titles>
  <Publishers>
      <pub_id>1</pub_id>
      <pub_name>pub1</pub_name>
  </Publishers>
  <Publishers>
      <pub_id>2</pub_id>
      <pub_name>pub2</pub_name>
  </Publishers>
</NewDataSet>
```

Note that the **Titles** element and the **Publishers** elements are shown as sequential elements. To have the **Titles** elements show up as children of their respective parent elements, the **Nested** property of the **DataRelation** would need to be set to **true** and you would add the following code:

Visual Basic .NET

```vb
...
Dim dr As New DataRelation _
  ("TitlePublishers", parentCol, childCol)
dr.Nested = True
ds.Relations.Add(dr)
ds.WriteXML(Server.MapPath("PubTitlesNested.xml"), _
  XmlWriteMode.IgnoreSchema)
```

C#

```csharp
...
DataRelation dr = new DataRelation("TitlePublishers",
  parentCol, childCol);
dr.Nested = true;
ds.Relations.Add(dr);
ds.WriteXML(Server.MapPath("PubTitlesNested.xml"),
  XmlWriteMode.IgnoreSchema);
```

The following XML shows what the resulting output would look like with the **Titles** elements nested within their respective parent elements:

```xml
<?xml version = "1.0"standalone = "yes"?>
<NewDataSet>
  <Publishers>
      <pub_id>1</pub_id>
      <pub_name>pub1</pub_name>
      <Titles>
          <title>title1</title>
          <pub_id>1</pub_id>
          <price>40.00</price>
      </Titles>
      <Titles>
          <title>title3</title>
          <pub_id>1</pub_id>
          <price>30.00</price>
      </Titles>
  </Publishers>
  <Publishers>
      <pub_id>2</pub_id>
      <pub_name>pub2</pub_name>
      <Titles>
          <title>title2</title>
          <pub_id>2</pub_id>
          <price>60.00</price>
      </Titles>
  </Publishers>
</NewDataSet>
```

Demonstration: Creating Nested XML

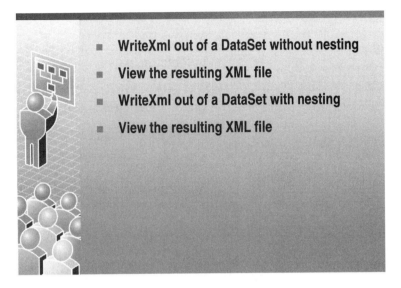

- WriteXml out of a DataSet without nesting
- View the resulting XML file
- WriteXml out of a DataSet with nesting
- View the resulting XML file

Introduction

In this demonstration, you will learn how to create a nested XML document.

The files for this demonstration are in the Mod12VB or Mod12CS project in the 2310Demos solution.

▶ **To run the demonstration**

1. Open the SaveNestedXML.aspx page in Visual Studio .NET.

2. View the code-behind page, explain the code, and make note of the following:

   a. In the **CreateDataSet** function, a **DataSet** with two **DataTables** is created.

   b. In the **MakeDataRelation** function, a **DataRelation** is created between the two tables, setting the **Nested** property to **True** or **False**, depending on the argument to the function.

   c. In the **cmdSave_Click** event procedure, the **DataRelation** is created with **Nested** set to **false**, and then the **DataSet** is written to an XML file.

   d. In the **cmdSaveNested_Click** event procedure, the **DataRelation** is created with the **Nested** property set to **true**, and then the **DataSet** is written to an XML file.

3. Build and browse the SaveNestedXML.aspx page.

4. Click **Save as XML**, and then click the **View XML** hyperlink.

   This is the XML data that was created from the **DataSet** with the **Nested** property set to **false**. Notice that the **Titles** elements are all listed, followed by the **Publishers** elements.

5. Click **Save as Nested XML**, and then click the **View Nested XML** hyperlink.

   This is the XML data that was created from the DataSet with the Nested property set to **True**. Notice that the Titles elements are nested inside the related Publishers elements.

Lesson: Working with XML Data

- Overview of Synchronizing a DataSet with an XmlDataDocument

- How to Synchronize a DataSet with an XmlDataDocument

- Working with an XmlDataDocument

- Transforming XML Data with XSLT

- Demonstration: Transforming Data with XSLT

Introduction

The **XmlDataDocument** class allows XML documents to be stored, retrieved, and manipulated through a relational **DataSet**. **XmlDataDocument** has a close affiliation with the **DataSet** class, which provides a relational view of the loaded XML document. Any changes that are made to the **XmlDataDocument** are reflected in the **DataSet** and vice versa.

Similarly, to transform the contents of a source XML document into another format, such as XML or HTML, you can use XSLT Transformation.

In this lesson, you will learn how to synchronize a **DataSet** with an **XmlDataDocument**. You will also learn how to use **XmlDataDocument**. Finally, you will learn how to transform XML data by using the **XslTransform** object.

Lesson objectives

After completing this lesson, you will be able to:

- Identify the different ways that are available for synchronizing a **DataSet** with an **XmlDataDocument**.

- Identify how to synchronize a **DataSet** with an **XmlDataDocument**.

- Use an **XmlDataDocument**.

- Transform XML data by using the **XslTransform** object.

Overview of Synchronizing a DataSet with an XmlDataDocument

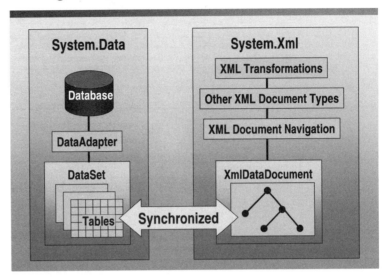

Introduction

DataSets provide you with a relational representation of data. For hierarchical data access, you can use the XML classes that are available in the .NET Framework. Previously, hierarchical and relational representations of data have been used separately. However, the .NET Framework enables real-time, synchronous access to both the relational and hierarchical representations of data through the **DataSet** object and the **XmlDataDocument** object, respectively.

Single set of data

When a **DataSet** is synchronized with an **XmlDataDocument**, both objects are working with a single set of data. This means that if a change is made to the **DataSet**, the change will be reflected in the **XmlDataDocument**, and vice versa.

The relationship between the **DataSet** and the **XmlDataDocument** creates great flexibility by allowing a single application, using a single set of data, to access the entire suite of services that are built around the **DataSet**.

Synchronizing an **XmlDataDocument** with a **DataSet** preserves the fidelity of an XML document. If the **DataSet** is populated from an XML document by using **ReadXml**, the data may differ dramatically from the original XML document when the data is written back as an XML document by using **WriteXml**. The data can be different because the **DataSet** does not maintain formatting, such as white space, or hierarchical information, such as element order, from the original XML document. The **DataSet** also does not contain elements from the XML document that were ignored because they did not match the schema of the **DataSet**. Synchronizing an **XmlDataDocument** with a **DataSet** allows the formatting and hierarchical element structure of the original XML document to be maintained in the **XmlDataDocument**, while the **DataSet** contains only the data and schema information that is appropriate to the **DataSet**.

How to Synchronize a DataSet with an XmlDataDocument

■ **Store XML Data into an XmlDataDocument**

```
Dim objXmlDataDoc As New XmlDataDocument()
objXmlDataDoc.Load(Server.MapPath ("file.xml"))
                         -or-
objXmlDataDoc.DataSet.ReadXml(Server.MapPath ("file.xml"))
```

```
XmlDataDocument objXmlDataDoc = new XmlDataDocument();
objXmlDataDoc.Load(Server.MapPath ("file.xml"));
                         -or-
objXmlDataDoc.DataSet.ReadXml(Server.MapPath ("file.xml"));
```

■ **Store a DataSet in an XmlDataDocument**

```
Dim ds As New DataSet()
'fill in ds
Dim objXmlDataDoc As New XmlDataDocument(ds)
```

```
DataSet ds = new DataSet();
//fill in ds
objXmlDataDoc = new XmlDataDocument(ds);
```

Introduction

There are two ways to synchronize a **DataSet** with an **XmlDataDocument**. You can:

- Store XML data into an **XmlDataDocument**.
- Store a **DataSet** in an **XmlDataDocument**.

Store XML Data into an XmlDataDocument

The following code samples demonstrate how to store XML data in an **XmlDataDocument**:

Visual Basic .NET

```
Dim objXmlDataDoc As New XmlDataDocument()
objXmlDataDoc.Load(Server.MapPath("file.xml"))
```

C#

```
XmlDataDocument objXmlDataDoc = new XmlDataDocument();
objXmlDataDoc.Load(Server.MapPath("file.xml"));
```

While the first line of the preceding code creates an **XmlDataDocument** object, the second line of the preceding code loads the XML file into the **XmlDataDocument** object.

You can also store XML data into an **XmlDataDocument** by using one line of code as shown in the following examples:

Visual Basic .NET

```
objXmlDataDoc.DataSet.ReadXml(Server.MapPath("file.xml"))
```

C#

```
objXmlDataDoc.DataSet.ReadXml(Server.MapPath("file.xml"));
```

Store a DataSet in an XmlDataDocument

The following code samples demonstrate how to store a **DataSet** in an **XmlDataDocument**:

Visual Basic .NET

```
Dim ds As New DataSet()
'fill in ds
...
Dim objXmlDataDoc As New XmlDataDocument(ds)
```

C#

```
DataSet ds = new DataSet();
//fill in ds
...
XmlDataDocument objXmlDataDoc = new XmlDataDocument(ds);
```

The first line of the preceding code creates a new **DataSet** called **ds**. The last line of the preceding code creates an object called **XmlDataDocument** and passes **ds**, a **DataSet**, as a parameter. The process of filling **ds** has been omitted from the example.

Working with an XmlDataDocument

- **Display data in a list-bound control**

  ```
  dg.DataSource = objXmlDataDoc.DataSet
  ```

  ```
  dg.DataSource = objXmlDataDoc.DataSet;
  ```

- **Extract Dataset rows as XML**

  ```
  Dim elem As XmlElement
  elem = objXmlDataDoc.GetElementFromRow _
      (ds.Tables(0).Rows(1))
  ```

  ```
  XmlElement elem;
  elem = objXmlDataDoc.GetElementFromRow(ds.Tables[0].Rows[1]);
  ```

  - **XmlDataDocument** inherits from **XmlDocument**
- **Apply an XSLT transformation**
  - **XslTransform** object

Introduction

The **DataSet** represents a relational data source in ADO.NET. The **XmlDocument** implements the DOM in XML, and the **XmlDataDocument** unifies ADO.NET and XML by representing relational data from a **DataSet** and synchronizing that data with the XML document model.

Display data in list-bound control

The **DataGrid** control displays all of the rows in the table within the **DataSet**. The following code demonstrates how to assign the **DataSet** object (**objXmlDataDoc.DataSet**) to the **DataGrid** control (**dg**):

Visual Basic .NET

```
dg.DataSource = objXmlDataDoc.DataSet
```

C#

```
dg.DataSource = objXmlDataDoc.DataSet;
```

Extract DataSet Rows

To extract individual rows as XML, you need to query the **DataSet**. To query the **DataSet**, you use the **GetElementFromRow** method. The following code demonstrates how the **GetElementFromRow** method of **XmlDataDocument** returns an **XmlElement** object:

Visual Basic .NET

```
Dim elem As XmlElement
elem = objXmlDataDoc.GetElementFromRow _
    (ds.Tables(0).Rows(1))
```

C#

```
XmlElement elem;
elem = objXmlDataDoc.GetElementFromRow(ds.Tables[0].Rows[1]);
```

Use XML DOM methods

The.NET Framework implements the XML DOM to provide access to data in XML documents and to provide access to the additional classes to read, write, and navigate within XML documents. The **XmlDataDocument** provides relational access to data with its ability to synchronize with the relational data in the **DataSet**.

The **XmlDataDocument** class extends the **XmlDocument** class. Because the **XmlDocument** class implements the DOM, it enables you to load either relational data or XML data. The **XmlDataDocument** also allows you to manipulate that data by using the DOM.

Apply an XSLT Transformation

If data is stored in a relational structure and you want it to be input into an XSLT transformation, you can load the relational data into a **DataSet** and then associate it with the **XmlDataDocument**.

By taking relational data, loading it into a **DataSet**, and using the synchronizing within the **XmlDataDocument**, the relational data can have XSLT transformations performed on it. The **XslTransform** object transforms XML data by using an XSLT style sheet.

Transforming XML Data with XSLT

- **Create XmlDataDocument**

```
Dim ds As New DataSet()
'fill in DataSet
...
Dim xmlDoc As New XmlDataDocument(ds)
```

- **Create XSLTransform object and call Transform method**

```
Dim xslTran As New XslTransform()
xslTran.Load(Server.MapPath("PubTitles.xsl"))
Dim writer As New XmlTextWriter _
   (Server.MapPath("PubTitles_output.html"), _
   System.Text.Encoding.UTF8)
xslTran.Transform(xmlDoc, Nothing, writer)
writer.Close()
```
C# Code Example

Introduction

The objective of the XSLT Transformation is to transform the content of a source XML document into another document that is different in format or structure. For example, to transform XML into HTML for use on a Web site or to transform XML into a document that contains only the fields that are required by an application.

In the .NET Framework, the **XslTransform** class is the XSLT processor that transforms one XML document into another.

Create XmlDataDocument

Before transforming XML data, you need to create a DataSet and an **XmlDataDocument** object:

Visual Basic .NET

```
Dim ds As New DataSet()
'fill in DataSet
...
Dim xmlDoc As New XmlDataDocument(ds)
```

C#

```
DataSet ds = new DataSet();
//fill in DataSet
...
XmlDataDocument xmlDoc = new XmlDataDocument(ds);
```

The first line of the preceding code creates the DataSet. The next line of code (code not displayed; instead, the comment is present) fills the DataSet. The last line of the preceding code creates an **XmlDataDocument** object that is called **xmlDoc** and it passes a parameter to **xmlDoc**, the DataSet **ds**.

Create the XslTransform object and call the Transform method

The following steps demonstrate the process of transforming XML data by creating a **XslTransform** object and calling the **Transform** method:

1. Create an **XslTransform** object:

Visual Basic .NET
```
Dim xslTran As New XslTransform()
```

C#
```
XslTransform xslTran = new XslTransform();
```

2. Use the **Load** method to load the .xsl style sheet file for the transformation:

Visual Basic .NET
```
xslTran.Load(Server.MapPath("PubTitles.xsl"))
```

C#
```
xslTran.Load(Server.MapPath("PubTitles.xsl"));
```

3. Create an **XmlTextWriter** object to output the document:

Visual Basic .NET
```
Dim writer As New XmlTextWriter _
    (Server.MapPath("PubTitles_output.html"), _
    System.Text.Encoding.UTF8)
```

C#
```
XmlTextWriter writer = new XmlTextWriter
    (Server.MapPath("PubTitles_output.html"),
    System.Text.Encoding.UTF8);
```

4. Use the **Transform** method of the **XslTransform** object to transform the data. The **Transform** method has several overloads and can handle different types of input and output.

   Notice that the **XmlDoc** variable of the **XmlDataDocument** type is one of the parameters that was passed to the **Transform** method:

Visual Basic .NET
```
xslTran.Transform(xmlDoc, Nothing, writer)
```

C#
```
xslTran.Transform(xmlDoc, null, writer);
```

5. Close the **XmlTextWriter**:

Visual Basic .NET
```
writer.Close()
```

C#
```
writer.Close();
```

Note The transformation process is specified by the W3C XSLT Version 1.0 recommendation. For more information, see www.w3c.org/TR/xslt.

Demonstration: Transforming Data with XSLT

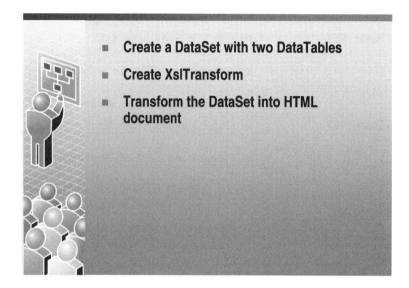

- Create a DataSet with two DataTables
- Create XslTransform
- Transform the DataSet into HTML document

Introduction

In this demonstration, you will see how to transform data by using the **XslTranform** object.

The files for this demonstration are in the Mod12VB or Mod12CS project in the 2310Demos solution.

▶ **To run the demonstration**

1. Open the TransformPubTitles.aspx page.

   The two **DataGrid** controls display the two **DataTables** in the **DataSet**.

2. View the code-behind page.

3. Show the code in the **cmdTransform_Click** event procedure and explain the code:

   a. The **DataSet** is created by calling **CreateDataSet** to create the **DataSet**, and then it calls the **MakeDataRelation** to create the **DataRelation**. However, for the **XmlDataDocument** mapping to work, the parent table, **Publishers**, must be added to the **DataSet** first, before the **Titles** table.

   b. An **XmlDataDocument** is created from the **DataSet**.

   c. An **XslTransform** object is created and loaded with the PubTitles.xsl style sheet.

   d. The **Transform** method of the **XslTransform** object is called to apply the style sheet to the **XmlDocument**.

Note The **Transform** method can only output to an **XmlReader**, a **TextReader**, or to **XmlWriter** objects.

---

4. View the page in a browser.

5. Click **Transform Data**, and then click the **View Transform Output** hyperlink.

    This is the HTML page that was created from **DataSet** data.

6. Open the **Transform.aspx** page in Visual Studio .NET.

7. View the code-behind page.

8. Show the code in the **cmdTransform_Click** event procedure and explain the code:

    a. The **DataSet** is created by calling **CreateCustOrdersDataSet** to create the **DataSet** and the **DataRelation**.

    b. An **XmlDataDocument** is created from the **DataSet**.

    c. An **XslTransform** object is created and loaded with the CustomerOrders.xslt style sheet.

    d. The **Transform** method of the **XslTransform** object is called to apply the style sheet to the **XmlDocument**.

9. Open the PubTitles.xsl style sheet to show how it works.

Lesson: Using the XML Web Server Control

- **What is the XML Web Server Control?**
- **Loading and Saving XML Data**
- **Demonstration: Using the XML Web Server Control**

Introduction

Information in an XML file is raw, containing only the data and no indication about how to format or display it. To display XML data in a Web Forms page, you must provide formatting and display information.

In this lesson, you will learn how to display, load, and save XML data.

Lesson objectives

After completing this lesson, you will be able to:

- Describe the XML Web server control.
- Load and save XML data.

What is the XML Web Server Control?

- **Write to an XML document**

- **Writes the results of an XSLT Transformations into a Web page**

```
<asp:Xml id="Xml1"
    Document="XmlDocument object to display"
    DocumentContent="String of XML"
    DocumentSource="Path to XML Document"
    Transform="XslTransform object"
    TransformSource="Path to XSL Document"
    runat="server"/>
```

Introduction

To present XML data in a Web Forms page, you need to specify the tags, such as the <TABLE> tags, <P> tags, or any other tags that you would like to use to display the data. You must also provide instructions for how the data from the XML file fits into these tags, for example whether each element in the XML file should be displayed as a table row or a column and so on.

XSLT Transformation language

One way to provide all of these instructions is to use the XSLT Transformation language and create XSLT files. After you have XSLT Transformations, you must apply them to the XML file. The output is a new file with the XML information formatted according to the transformation file.

Use the XML Web server control to write an XML document

You can use the XML Web server control to write an XML document, or to write the results of an XSLT Transformations, into a Web page. The XML output appears in the Web page at the location of the control.

The XML and the XSLT information can be in external documents, or you can include the XML inline. There are two ways to reference external documents by using the property settings in the XML Web server control. You can provide a path to the XML document in the control tag, or you can load the XML and XSLT documents as objects and then pass them to the control. If you prefer to include the XML inline, you must write it between the opening and closing tags of the control.

The following code sample shows how to use the XML Web server control to display the contents of an XML document or the results of an XSLT Transformation:

```
<asp:Xml id="Xml1"
    Document="XmlDocument object to display"
    DocumentContent="String of XML"
    DocumentSource="Path to XML Document"
    Transform="XslTransform object"
    TransformSource="Path to XSL Transform Document"
    runat="server">
```

Loading and Saving XML Data

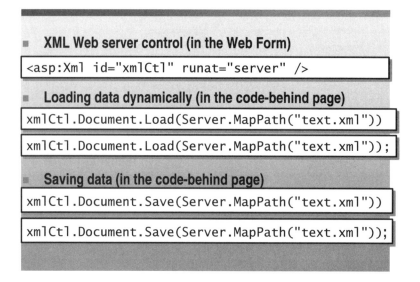

XML Web server control (in the Web Form)

```
<asp:Xml id="xmlCtl" runat="server" />
```

Loading data dynamically (in the code-behind page)

```
xmlCtl.Document.Load(Server.MapPath("text.xml"))
```

```
xmlCtl.Document.Load(Server.MapPath("text.xml"));
```

Saving data (in the code-behind page)

```
xmlCtl.Document.Save(Server.MapPath("text.xml"))
```

```
xmlCtl.Document.Save(Server.MapPath("text.xml"));
```

Introduction

Before loading and saving XML data into a Web application, you need to add the XML Web server control to the Web Forms page, in the location where you want the output to appear.

To add an XML Web server control to a Web Forms page

There are two ways to add an XML Web server control to a Web Forms page:

1. Drag an **XML** control from the **Web Forms** tab of the Toolbox onto the Design view, as shown in the following illustration.

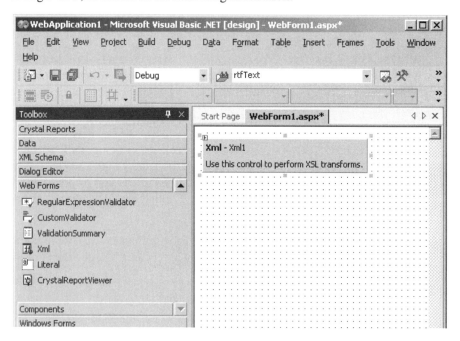

2. To add an XML Web server control programmatically, in HTML view, add the following line of code:

```
<asp:Xml id="xmlCtl" runat="server" />
```

To load XML data into the XML Web server control

There are three ways to load XML data into a Web application. You can:

■ Provide a path to an external XML document by using the **DocumentSource** property.

■ Load an XML document as an object and pass it to the control, using the **Load** method in the **Page_Load** event, and then assigning the document to the **Document** property of the **XML** control.

■ Include the XML content inline, between the opening and closing tags of the XML Web server control.

To provide a path to an external XML document

To provide a path to an external XML document, perform the following steps:

1. Set the **DocumentSource** property of the XML Web server control to the path of the XML source document.

2. The XML document will be written directly to the output stream unless you also specify the **TransformSource** property. **TransformSource** must be a valid XSLT Transformations document, which will be used to transform the XML document before its contents are written to the output stream. The following example shows how to refer to source documents by using a relative path:

```
<body>
    <h3>XML Example</h3>
    <form runat="server">
        <asp:Xml id="xml1" DocumentSource="MySource.xml"
            TransformSource="MyStyle.xsl" runat="server" />
    </form>
</body>
```

To load an XML document as an object and pass it to the control

To load an XML document as an object and pass it to the control, perform the following steps:

1. On the **View** menu, click **Code**. In the Code Editor, find the **Page_Load** event procedure.

2. Add code to load the XML source document, and then assign the source to the **Document** property of the control. For example:

Visual Basic .NET

```
Private Sub Page_Load(ByVal sender As System.Object, _
    ByVal e As System.EventArgs) Handles MyBase.Load
    Dim xmlDoc As System.Xml.XmlDocument = _
        New System.Xml.XmlDocument()
    xmlDoc.Load(Server.MapPath("MySource.xml"))
    Dim xslTran As System.Xml.Xsl.XslTransform = _
        New System.Xml.Xsl.XslTransform()
    xslTran.Load(Server.MapPath("MyStyle.xsl"))
    Xml1.Document = xmlDoc
    Xml1.Transform = xslTran
End Sub
```

C#

```csharp
private void Page_Load(object sender, System.EventArgs e)
{
    System.Xml.XmlDocument xmlDoc = new
        System.Xml.XmlDocument();
    xmlDoc.Load(Server.MapPath("MySource.xml"));
    System.Xml.Xsl.XslTransform xslTran = new
        System.Xml.Xsl.XslTransform();
    xslTran.Load(Server.MapPath("MyStyle.xsl"));
    Xml1.Document = xmlDoc;
    Xml1.Transform = xslTran;
}
```

To include the XML content inline

To include the XML content inline, perform the following steps:

1. In HTML view, find the <asp:Xml> and </asp:Xml> tags.

2. Add your XML code between these two tags. For example:

```
<asp:xml TransformSource="MyStyle.xsl" runat="server">
    <clients>
        <name>Frank Miller</name>
        <name>Judy Lew</name>
    </clients>
</asp:xml>
```

To save XML data

You can save the XML data by using the **Save** method, as shown in the following code examples:

Visual Basic .NET

```
XmlCtl.Document.Save(Server.MapPath("xmlResult.xml"))
```

C#

```csharp
XmlCtl.Document.Save(Server.MapPath("xmlResult.xml"));
```

Demonstration: Using the XML Web Server Control

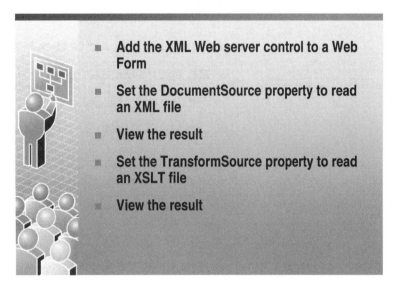

Introduction	In this demonstration, you will learn how to use the XML Web Server control.
	The files for this demonstration are in the Mod12VB and Mod12CS projects in the 2310Demos solution.
	The completed code for this demonstration is in the UseXmlControl.aspx file.

▶ **To run the demonstration**

1. Open the PubTitlesData.xml file.

   This file contains the data that will be displayed from the ASPX page.

2. Create a new Web Form in the Mod12VB or Mod12CS project named MyUseXmlControl.aspx.

3. Drag the **XML** control from the Toolbox onto the Web Form.

4. Set the **DocumentSource** property of the **XML** control to the PubTitlesData.xml file.

5. Build and browse.

   This is the default view of the data as set by the control. The default view of the data is unformatted.

6. Set the **TransformSource** property of the **XML** control to the PubTitles.xsl file.

7. Build and browse the page again.

   This is the view of the data as set by the **PubTitles.xsl** style sheet.

Review

- Overview of XML Architecture in ASP.NET
- XML and the DataSet Object
- Working with XML Data
- Using the XML Web Server Control

1. What is the advantage of using XML to manage data?

2. What is the difference between a well-formed and XML document and a valid XML document?

3. Which of the following code samples is a well-formed XML sample?

   a. `<employee>12</employee>`

   b. `<employee>12</Employee>`

   c. `<Employee>12</employee>`

4. What is the importance of XSD?

5. What is the role of the **XmlDataDocument** class in the XML architecture?

6. Write the Visual Basic .NET or C# code that reads the XML file named titles.xml into the existing **DataSet** object named **dsTitles**.

   The file title.xml is located in the same folder as the Web Form and the code-behind page that is executing the code.

Lab 12: Reading XML Data

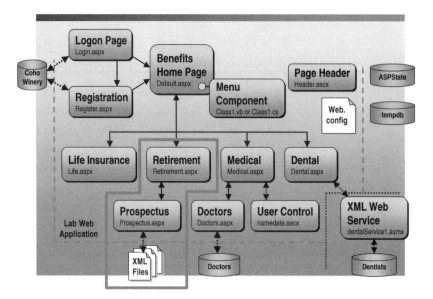

Objectives

After completing this lab, you will be able to:

- Read an Extensible Markup Language (XML) file and store it in a DataSet.
- Apply transformation to an XML file.

Prerequisites

Before working on this lab, you must have:

- Knowledge of how to use a **DataGrid** control.
- Knowledge of how to create event procedures for Web server controls.

Scenario

Coho Winery offers several benefits to its employees. In the labs for Course 2310B, *Developing Microsoft ASP.NET Web Applications Using Visual Studio .NET*, you will create a Web site that enables employees to select and set up their chosen benefits.

One benefit that is offered by Coho Winery is the retirement benefit. When applying for the retirement benefit, employees can view the prospectuses of several mutual funds that are offered by Coho Winery.

Estimated time to complete this lab: 30 minutes

Exercise 0
Lab Setup

To complete this lab, you must have created a Benefits Web Application project and a BenefitsList Class Library project. These projects may be created by using Microsoft® Visual Basic® .NET or Microsoft Visual C#™.

If you have not created these projects, complete the following steps:

▶ **Create the 2310LabApplication solution**

Important Only perform this procedure if you have not created a 2310LabApplication solution file.

1. Using Microsoft Visual Studio® .NET, create a new blank solution named **2310LabApplication**:

   a. On the **File** menu, point to **New**, and then click **Blank Solution**.

   b. In the **New Project** dialog box, type **2310LabApplication** in the **Name** text box, and then click **OK**.

▶ **Create the Benefits project**

Important Only perform this procedure if you have not previously created a Benefits project, or if you have removed the Benefits project according to the steps in Appendix A, "Lab Recovery," in Course 2310B, *Developing Microsoft ASP.NET Web Applications Using Visual Studio .NET*.

1. Create a new Microsoft ASP.NET Web Application project, named **BenefitsVB** or **BenefitsCS**, in the 2310LabApplication solution:

   a. On the **File** menu, point to **New**, and then click **Project**.

   b. In the **New Project** dialog box, in the **Project Types** list, click **Visual Basic Projects** or **Visual C# Projects**.

   c. In the **Templates** list, click **ASP.NET Web Application**. Set the **Location** to **http://localhost/BenefitsVB** for the Visual Basic .NET project or to **http://localhost/BenefitsCS** for the Visual C# project.

   d. Click **Add to Solution**, and then click **OK**.

Caution When adding projects to the solution, the capitalization of the project name is important. Because you may be using some pre-built Web Forms in this and other labs in Course 2310B, *Developing Microsoft ASP.NET Web Applications Using Visual Studio .NET*, you must verify that you have capitalized the Benefits project as shown.

▶ **Update the Benefits project**

1. In Visual Studio .NET, open the 2310LabApplication solution file.

2. In Solution Explorer, right-click **BenefitsVB** or **BenefitsCS**, point to **Add**, and then click **Add Existing Item**.

3. Browse for project files.

For the Visual Basic .NET Project

Browse to the *install folder*\Labfiles\Lab12\VB\Starter\BenefitsVB folder for the Visual Basic .NET files.

For the Visual C# Project

Browse to the *install folder*\Labfiles\Lab12\CS\Starter\BenefitsCS folder for the Visual C# files.

4. In the **Files of type** box of the **Add Existing Item – Benefits** dialog box, click **All Files (*.*)**.

5. Select all of the files in this folder, and then click **Open**.

6. Click **Yes** if prompted to overwrite or reload files.

▶ **Create the BenefitsList class library**

Important   Only perform these steps if you have not previously created a BenefitsList project, or if you have removed the BenefitsList project according to the steps in Appendix A, "Lab Recovery," in Course 2310B, *Developing Microsoft ASP.NET Web Applications Using Visual Studio .NET.*

1. Create a new Class Library Project:

For the Visual Basic .NET Project

Create a new Visual Basic .NET Class Library project, name it **BenefitsListVB**, and then add it to the 2310LabApplication solution:

a. On the **File** menu, point to **New**, and then click **Project**.

b. In the **New Project** dialog box, in the **Project Types** list, click **Visual Basic Projects**.

c. In the **Templates** list, click **Class Library** and then set the **Name** to **BenefitsListVB**.

d. Click **Add to Solution**, and then click **OK**.

For the Visual C# Project

Create a new Visual C# .NET Class Library project, name it **BenefitsListCS**, and then add it to the 2310LabApplication solution:

a. On the **File** menu, point to **New**, and then click **Project**.

b. In the **New Project** dialog box, in the **Project Types** list, click **Visual C# Projects**.

c. In the **Templates** list, click **Class Library**, and then set the **Name** to **BenefitsListCS**.

d. Click **Add to Solution**, and then click **OK**.

Caution   Verify that you have capitalized the BenefitsList project as shown.

▶ **Update the BenefitsList project**

1. In Visual Studio .NET, open the 2310LabApplication solution file.

2. In Solution Explorer, right-click **BenefitsListVB** or **BenefitsListCS**, point to **Add**, and then click **Add Existing Item**.

3. Browse for project files:

For the Visual Basic .NET project

Browse to the *install folder*\Labfiles\Lab12\VB\Starter\BenefitsListVB folder.

For the Visual C# project

Browse to the *install folder*\Labfiles\Lab12\CS\Starter\BenefitsListCS folder.

4. In the **Files of type** box of the **Add Existing Item – BenefitsList** dialog box, click **All Files (*.*)**.

5. Select all of the files in this folder, and then click **Open**.

6. Click **Yes** if prompted to overwrite or reload files.

▶ **Create a reference to the BenefitsList component in the Benefits project**

1. In the Benefits project in the 2310LabApplication solution, complete the following steps to add a reference to the BenefitsList component that you just created:

   a. Right-click the **BenefitsVB** or **BenefitsCS** project in Solution Explorer and then click **Add Reference**.

   b. In the **Add Reference** dialog box, on the **Projects** tab, double-click the **BenefitsListVB** or **BenefitsListCS** project.

   c. In the **Selected Components** list, select the **BenefitsListVB** or **BenefitsListCS** component, and then click **OK**.

   The component is added to the References folder in Solution Explorer.

Exercise 1
Reading a List of Mutual Funds from an XML File

In this exercise, you will read a list of mutual funds from the mutual_funds.xml file and store them in a **DataSet**. You will then display the **DataSet** in a **DataGrid** control.

▶ **Read a list of mutual funds**

1. Open the Benefits project in the 2310LabApplication Visual Studio .NET solution.

2. Add files to the Benefits project:

   a. In Solution Explorer, right-click **BenefitsVB** or **BenefitsCS**, point to **Add**, and then choose **Add Existing Item**.

   b. Browse to the benefits folder:

   install folder\Labfiles\Lab12\VB\Starter\BenefitsVB folder.

   install folder\Labfiles\Lab12\CS\Starter\BenefitsCS folder.

   c. In the **Files of type** drop-down list box, click **All Files (*.*)**.

   d. Select the following files, and then click **Open**:

   - retirement.aspx
   - prospectus.aspx
   - mutual_funds.xml
   - lgcap.xml
   - growth.xml
   - midcap.xml
   - smcap.xml
   - prospectus_style.xsl

3. Open the mutual_funds.xml file and examine its contents. What are the two fields (elements) of each fund?

   _____

   _____

4. Open the retirement.aspx Web Form.

   A **DataGrid** control has already been added to the page. This **DataGrid** has two custom columns, a **Name** column for displaying the name of a mutual fund, and a **Link to prospectus** column, which contains a hyperlink to the prospectus.aspx Web Form. In the following steps, you will fill this **DataGrid** with data from an XML file.

Visual Basic .NET

C#

5. Open the retirement.aspx.vb or retirement.aspx.cs code-behind page and locate the following comment in the **Page_Load** event procedure:

Visual Basic .NET

```
'TODO Lab 12: Create a DataSet, fill it with the
'XML file, and display it
```

C#

```
//TODO Lab 12: Create a DataSet, fill it with the
//XML file, and display it
```

6. Fill the **DataSet** with the data in the XML file and display the **DataSet** in the dgRetirement **DataGrid** control:

   a. Create a **DataSet** named **dsRetirement**.

   b. Call the **ReadXml** method of the **DataSet** to read the mutual_funds.xml file.

   c. Set the data source of the dgRetirement **DataGrid** to **dsRetirement**.

   d. Call the **DataBind** method of the **DataGrid**.

   Your code should look like the following:

Visual Basic .NET

```
Dim dsRetirement As New DataSet()
dsRetirement.ReadXml( _
   Server.MapPath("mutual_funds.xml"))
dgRetirement.DataSource = dsRetirement
dgRetirement.DataBind()
```

C#

```
DataSet dsRetirement = new DataSet();
dsRetirement.ReadXml(Server.MapPath("mutual_funds.xml"));
dgRetirement.DataSource = dsRetirement;
dgRetirement.DataBind();
```

What is the purpose of the **Server.MapPath** method?

_____

_____

7. Save your changes.

8. Build and browse the retirement.aspx page.

   You should see all of the mutual fund names, in addition to links to the mutual fund prospectuses in the **DataGrid**.

   Although the links to the prospectuses currently do not work, the links will open a page called prospectus.aspx and pass to it a prospectus id in the **ProspID** parameter. You will build the prospectus.aspx page to display the requested prospectus in Exercise 2.

Exercise 2
Reading, Transforming, and Displaying XML

In this exercise, you will use the **Xml** control to read, transform, and display a prospectus for a given mutual fund.

▶ **Read and display a prospectus**

1. Open the lgcap.xml file and examine its contents.

   What are the three fields (elements) of a prospectus?

   _____

   _____

2. Open the prospectus_style.xsl file and examine its content.

   Prospectus_style.xsl is an XML style sheet file that uses XSLT to display XML data. What will the title of the prospectus page be? What color will be used to display the text **General Description**?

   _____

   _____

3. Open the prospectus.aspx Web Form.

   This page currently contains the header.ascx user control and a single hyperlink.

4. Drag an **Xml** control from the Toolbox onto the prospectus.aspx page, so that your page looks like the following illustration.

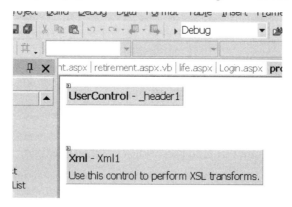

5. Set the properties of the **Xml** control in the Properties window, as shown in the following table.

Property	Value
ID	xmlProspectus
DocumentSource	lgcap.xml

6. Build and browse the prospectus.aspx page.

   You should see the content of the lgcap.xml prospectus as a continuous, unformatted string of text.

▶ **Apply a transformation to the prospectus**

1. Open the prospectus.aspx Web Form.

2. Set the **TransformSource** property of the **xmlProspectus** control to **prospectus_style.xsl**.

3. Build and browse the prospectus.aspx page.

   You should see now the content of the lgcap.xml prospectus as formatted Hypertext Markup Language (HTML).

▶ **Modify the DocumentSource property of the Xml control dynamically**

You will now use a string parameter named **ProspID** to select which prospectus will be displayed:

1. Open the prospectus.aspx Web Form.

2. In the Properties window, clear the **DocumentSource** property of the **xmlProspectus** control.

3. Open the prospectus code-behind page.

Visual Basic .NET

Open the prospectus.aspx.vb page and locate the following comment in the **Page_Load** event procedure:

```
'TODO Lab 12: Dynamically select the prospectus
```

C#

Open the prospectus.aspx.cs page and locate the following comment in the **Page_Load** event procedure:

```
//TODO Lab 12: Dynamically select the prospectus
```

4. Read the **ProspID** parameter from the requested query string and store the parameter in a variable named **strProspID**.

   Your code should look like the following:

Visual Basic .NET

```
Dim strProspID As String = Request.Params("ProspID")
```

C#

```
string strProspID = Request.Params["ProspID"];
```

5. In the code, set the **DocumentSource** property of the **xmlProspectus** control to the value of the variable **strProspID**, concatenated with an **.xml** extension.

Your code should look like the following:

Visual Basic .NET

```
xmlProspectus.DocumentSource = strProspID & ".xml"
```

C#

```
xmlProspectus.DocumentSource = strProspID + ".xml";
```

6. Save your changes to the prospectus.aspx page.

7. Build and browse the retirement.aspx page.

8. Click the **Prospectus** link that is next to **Large cap stocks**.

You should see the prospectus for the **Large cap stocks** mutual fund.

9. Click the **Back to retirement page** link.

10. Test the **Prospectus** links for the **Growth stocks**, **Mid-cap stocks**, and **Small-cap stocks**.

Exercise 3 (If Time Permits)
Nested Data

In this exercise, you will experiment with the generation of nested XML data from a Microsoft SQL Server™ database.

▶ **Generate sequential data**

1. Add the nestedData.aspx Web Form from the benefits folder. This file can be found at:

Visual Basic .NET

install folder\Labfiles\Lab12\VB\Starter\BenefitsVB folder to the Benefits project.

C#

install folder\Labfiles\Lab12\CS\Starter\BenefitsCS folder to the Benefits project.

2. Open the nestedData.aspx Web Form.

3. Open the nestedData.aspx.vb or the nestedData.aspx.cs code-behind page and examine the code.

   The code generates a **DataSet** named **dsDoctorsSpecialities**, which contains three **DataTable** objects: **doctors**, **drspecialties**, and **specialties**. The code then creates relationships between the three tables.

   What column links the doctors and drspecialties **DataTable** objects together in the relation1 **DataRelation**? What is the parent **DataTable** of this relationship?

   _____

   _____

4. Build and browse the nestedData.aspx page and analyze the XML that was created.

   Is the data nested?

   _____

   _____

5. Locate the following comment in the **Page_Load** event procedure:

Visual Basic .NET

```
'TODO Lab 12: Create a nested relationship between the
doctors and drspecialties DataTable objects
```

C#

```
//TODO Lab 12: Create a nested relationship between the
doctors and drspecialties DataTable objects
```

6. Uncomment the following line of code to create a nested relationship between the **doctors** and **drspecialties DataTable** objects:

Visual Basic .NET

```
'dr1.Nested = True
```

C#

```
//dr1.Nested = true;
```

7. Build and browse nestedData.aspx and analyze the XML that was created.

Tip You may need to refresh the browser after the page loads to see the changes to the XML data.

What has changed from the preceding XML response?

_____

_____

8. Comment out the line of code that you uncommented in Step 6.

9. Locate the following comment in the **Page_Load** event procedure:

Visual Basic .NET

```
'TODO Lab 12: Create a nested relationship between the
specialties and drspecialties DataTable objects
```

C#

```
//TODO Lab 12: Create a nested relationship between the
specialties and drspecialties DataTable objects
```

10. Uncomment the following line of code to create a nested relationship between the **specialties** and **drspecialties DataTable** objects:

Visual Basic .NET

```
'dr2.Nested = True
```

C#

```
//dr2.Nested = true;
```

11. Build and browse the nestedData.aspx page and analyze the XML that was created.

> **Tip** You may need to refresh the browser after the page loads to see the changes to the XML data.

What has changed from the preceding XML response?

_____

_____

> **Note** You cannot use the two nested relationships at the same time because the same **DataTable** (drspecialties) cannot be a child in two nested relations.

msdn® training

Module 13: Consuming and Creating XML Web Services

Contents

Overview

- Overview of Using XML Web Services
- Calling an XML Web Service Using HTTP
- Using a Proxy to Call an XML Web Service
- Creating an XML Web Service

Introduction

The Internet has helped to facilitate better communication within and between companies by providing fast access to information. However, for many companies, browsing data-driven pages do not adequately satisfy their business needs. Programmable Web sites that directly link organizations, applications, and services would better meet their business needs. This direct linking of applications is the role of the Extensible Markup Language (XML) Web service. By linking your Web sites and applications to XML Web services, you have the opportunity to expand the functionality your Web site offers to users.

In this module, you will learn how to call an XML Web service directly with a browser and by proxy from a Web Form. You will also learn how to create and publish XML Web services by using Microsoft® Visual Studio® .NET.

Objectives

After completing this module, you will be able to:

- Describe the purpose and process behind calling an XML Web service from a Web Form.

- Call an XML Web service directly from a browser by using Hypertext Transfer Protocol (HTTP).

- Create a Web reference proxy for an XML Web service method, and call that Web method from a Web Form.

- Use the templates in Visual Studio .NET to create an XML Web service.

Lesson: Overview of Using XML Web Services

- **What is an XML Web Service?**
- **Why use XML Web Services?**
- **Finding an XML Web Service**
- **Multimedia: XML Web Service Execution Model**

Introduction

One of the challenges that you may encounter in creating feature-rich Web sites is application integration. You often need to combine a number of applications into a single, easy-to-use solution. The problem with trying to achieve a single, easy-to-use solution is that the applications you want to combine may be on a variety of platforms, each running different operating system. The applications also might have been created in several different programming languages.

XML Web services provide a simple, flexible, standards-based model for connecting applications together over the Internet. XML Web services allow you to take advantage of the existing Internet infrastructure, and link applications, regardless of which platforms, programming languages, or object models have been used to implement them.

In this lesson, you will learn the purpose and process behind calling an XML Web service from a Web Form.

Lesson objectives

After completing this lesson, you will be able to:

- Explain what an XML Web service is.
- Explain why XML Web services are important to Web application developers.
- Describe how to find existing XML Web services.
- Identify the process by which XML Web services are integrated into Web sites.

What is an XML Web Service?

- **Programmable logic accessible by standard Web protocols**
  - Allows applications to send and receive information across the Internet
  - Language, protocol, and platform independent
  - Stateless architecture
  - Can be asynchronous
- **Based on an evolving W3C standard**

Introduction

XML Web services are similar to components in that they represent black-box functionality that developers can use to add features to a Web Form, Microsoft Windows® applications, or even another XML Web service, without worrying about how the supporting service is implemented.

Application–to-application communication across the Internet

XML Web services are designed to interact directly with other applications over the Internet. As a result, XML Web services do not have user interfaces (UIs); instead, XML Web services provide standard defined interfaces called *contracts* that describe the services that they provide.

An XML Web service can be used internally by a single application, or it can be used externally by many applications that access it through the Internet.

Language independent

A connection to an XML Web service can be written in any Microsoft .NET-based language. As a result of this flexibility, you do not need to learn a new language every time you want to use an XML Web service.

Protocol independent

Unlike current component technologies, XML Web services do not use protocols that are specific to certain object models, such as the Distributed Component Object Model (DCOM). XML Web services communicate by using standard Web protocols and data formats, such as HTTP, XML, and Simple Object Access Protocol (SOAP). Any server that supports these Web standards can access or host XML Web services.

Platform independent

Because XML Web services are accessible through a standard interface, they allow disparate systems to work together. Servers that can support Web Forms can also support XML Web services.

Stateless architecture

The XML Web Services model assumes a stateless service architecture. Stateless architectures are generally more scalable than statefull architectures. Each response from the XML Web service is a new object, with a new state. Unless the XML Web services uses Microsoft ASP.NET State Management services to maintain state between requests, the state of the response is lost on the XML Web service server.

Note For more information about saving state, see Module 14, "Managing State," in Course 2310B, *Developing Microsoft ASP.NET Web Applications Using Visual Studio .NET.*

Asynchronous

XML Web services are asynchronous, because the request object from the client application and response object from the XML Web service are unique SOAP envelopes that do not require a shared connection. Interactions between the client application and the XML Web service can be further split into an initial request and response to start the XML Web service method, and a second request and response to collect the results. This asynchronous communication allows both the requesting application and the XML Web service the opportunity to continue processing while the interaction is ongoing.

Based on W3C

XML Web services are based on a World Wide Web Consortium (W3C) standard that is still evolving. As a result, the generic features of XML Web services are fixed; however, new features may be added in the future.

Note For more information on the W3C XML Web service standard, see the official W3C Web site, at http://www.w3c.org.

Why Use XML Web Services?

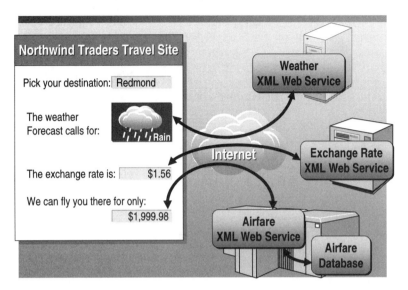

Introduction

XML Web services enable you to share programming logic and capabilities with numerous Web and Windows applications, with applications that are running on other platforms. Consider an XML Web service as a component that can expose its methods through the Web.

XML Web services are also based on W3C standards. XML Web services also offer the use of a standard Web protocols and the support tools that are available in Visual Studio .NET. With Visual Studio .NET, XML Web services are extremely easy to develop and to consume.

Adding XML Web services to Web applications

You can imagine an infinite number of XML Web services that you can use to add features to you Web applications. The following table lists some of the XML Web services that can be used.

XML Web Service	Features
Authentication services	Provides user authentication.
	For example, Microsoft Passport.
Weather reports	Provides updated weather reports for selected locations.
	For example, a Web site could provide local weather forecasts for a given city or area by consuming a weather report XML Web service.
Exchange rates	Provides updated exchange rates for all currencies.
	For example, a travel Web site could provide exchange rates for likely vacation destinations based on user profiles, by consuming an exchange rates XML Web service.
Airfare quotes	Provides updated airfares from one or more airlines.
	For example, a travel Web site could offer automatically discounted prices from preferred airlines by consuming an airfare quotes XML Web service.

(continued)

XML Web Service	Features
Stock quotes	Provides updated stock market quotes.
	For example, a company could offer to post their own stock price on their Web site by consuming a stock quotes XML Web service.
Partnering services	Provides business partners the opportunity to access your services on their Web site.
	For example, Convention Web sites could offer hotel registration services.
News headlines	Provides updated news headlines.
	For example, a company could post headlines from their business market on their Web site by consuming a news headline XML Web service.
Order tracking	Provides status of orders by linking existing enterprise resource management (ERP) systems to internal and external Web sites.
	For example, coupling results from internal ERP applications with suppliers and shipping companies order tracking XML Web services would give customers a complete view of their order's status.

XML Web service example

The preceding illustration shows a hypothetical travel Web site that offers several features that are based on XML Web services. In this scenario, the user enters a destination city name, and the Web Form uses the city name as a parameter in calls to several XML Web services. From the user's perspective, this is a highly featured travel Web site. From a code perspective, the Web site is more of a graphical interface combining a number of XML Web services from unrelated companies.

This travel agency Web site, by using XML Web services, provides advantages to both the consuming Web site, and the various XML Web services:

- Advantages for the Web site:

  - The applications that the travel agency has access to are not limited by the agency developer's programming skills, availability, or subject expertise.

  - The travel agency does not bear the high maintenance costs of keeping data, such as weather reports or exchange rates, up-to-date.

  - XML Web services use the Internet, so the travel agency does not have to create or maintain dedicated connections to offer the service.

  - XML Web services are language, protocol, and platform-independent, so the travel agency developers do not need to learn how the XML Web service was built and deployed to be able to use it.

  - The Web site may be able to charge the XML Web service providers for the right to offer services to the travel agency Web site customer base.

- Advantages for the XML Web service providers:

  Creating new applications as XML Web services, and updating existing applications with XML Web services, offers a number of advantages to service providers:

  - The XML Web service provider may be able to charge the Web site for the use of the service.

  - By offering an application, such as an exchange rate calculator, as an XML Web service, a bank can access the customer base of a number of travel agencies.

  - The XML Web service provider does not bear the high cost of developing and marketing a Web site to the traveling public.

  - Because XML Web services use the Internet to communicate, the service providers do not need expensive dedicated connections to offer your service.

  - Because XML Web services are language-independent, protocol-independent, and platform-independent, the XML Web service can be consumed by a wide variety of applications.

Finding an XML Web Service

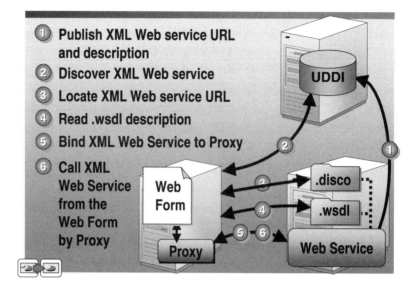

Introduction

You can find existing XML Web services to add to your Web site by using one or more of a series of discovery services. These discovery services are evolving and changing rapidly as the development and use of XML Web services gains acceptance in the Internet community.

Finding an XML Web service

The process for finding and binding to an XML Web service is as follows:

1. XML Web service developers publish descriptions and locations for their XML Web services to a Universal Description, Discovery, and Integration (UDDI) Web site.

2. You query the UDDI Web site to find the available XML Web services that meet your requirements. The UDDI Web site provides a listing of XML Web services that includes the Discovery file (DISCO) document Uniform Resource Locators (URLs) for the XML Web services.

3. You select an XML Web service and access the DISCO document to locate the XML Web service URL and the related Web Services Description Language (WSDL) document URLs.

4. You build a proxy object from the WSDL document.

    A proxy class is code that looks exactly like the class it is meant to represent; however, the proxy class does not contain any of the application logic. Instead, the proxy class contains marshaling and transport logic. A proxy object allows a client to access an XML Web service as if it were a local COM object.

5. You use the proxy object to bind the XML Web service.

6. You call the XML Web service from the Web Form by using the proxy.

UDDI

The UDDI specification defines a way to publish and discover information about XML Web services and the companies that supply them.

Companies individually register information about the XML Web services that they expose for other businesses to then use. After the data has been registered, it becomes freely available to anyone who needs to discover which XML Web services are exposed by a particular business.

Note For more information on UDDI, see the UDDI Web site at http://www.uddi.org or the Microsoft UDDI Project Web site at http://uddi.microsoft.com.

DISCO files

Discovery (DISCO) files are used to group common services together on a Web server. Discovery files, .disco and .vsdisco, are XML-based files that contain links in the form of URLs to resources that provide discovery information for an XML Web service. These files enable programmatic discovery of XML Web services. The following examples show the difference between static and dynamic discovery files:

■ .disco files

A static discovery (.disco) file is an XML document that contains links to other resources that describe XML Web services. .disco files are automatically generated for an XML Web service when the service is accessed by using a URL with **?DISCO** provided in the query string.

The following code shows an example of a .disco file:

```
<?xml version="1.0" ?>
<disco:discovery
xmlns:disco="http://schemas.xmlsoap.org/disco"
xmlns:wsdl="http://schemas.xmlsoap.org/disco/wsdl">
    <wsdl:contractRef
    ref="http://MyWebServer/UserName.asmx?WSDL"/>
</disco:discovery>
```

■ .vsdisco files

Dynamic discovery (.vsdisco) files are dynamic discovery documents that are automatically generated by Visual Studio .NET during the development phase of an XML Web service.

A .vsdisco file is an XML-based file with a root node called <dynamicDiscovery>. This node can contain <exclude> nodes. Each <exclude> node contains a path that the dynamic discovery process should not search.

Caution To maintain control over which XML Web services clients can discover, you should only use dynamic discovery on development Web servers.

The following code shows an example of a .vsdisco file:

```
<?xml version="1.0" encoding="utf-8" ?>
<dynamicDiscovery xmlns="urn:schemas-
dynamicdiscovery:disco.2000-03-17">
    <exclude path="_vti_cnf" />
    <exclude path="_vti_pvt" />
    <exclude path="_vti_log" />
    <exclude path="_vti_script" />
    <exclude path="_vti_txt" />
    <exclude path="Web References" />
</dynamicDiscovery>
```

WSDL files

A WSDL file defines the XML grammar that is used for communicating with an XML Web service. Visual Studio .NET uses the WSDL file to build proxy objects to communicate with an XML Web service.

WSDL files contain the following information about an XML Web service:

- Where to find the URL.

- XML Web service methods and properties.

- Data types used.

- Communication protocols.

Note For more information on DISCO and WSDL files, see "XML Web service discovery" in the Visual Studio .NET documentation.

Multimedia: XML Web Service Execution Model

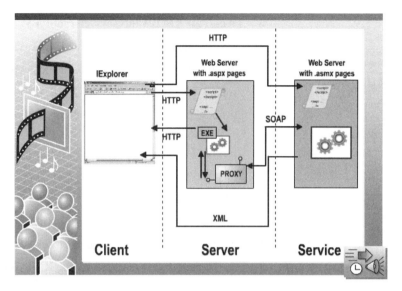

Introduction

In this animation, you will see how XML Web services interact with browsers and other Web Forms.

XML Web service model

▶ **To create an XML Web service**

1. Create the .asmx file that includes the namespace, classes, properties, and Web methods of the XML Web service.

2. Declare methods as XML Web service methods, which can then be accessed over the Internet.

Access from a browser

Direct access to an XML Web service involves a user sending the URL request in HTTP by using a browser. The XML Web service responds with a list of the designed methods and properties in XML. The user then has the opportunity to send a request directly to the XML Web service and receive results in XML.

This direct access process is not recommended for normal use, but it does allow you to test the XML Web service's functionality.

▶ **To directly access an XML Web service**

1. Call the XML Web service from the browser to determine which methods are available.

    When you call an XML Web service from a browser, you access the Hypertext Markup Language (HTML) description page, which lists the methods that are included in the XML Web service. The protocol that is used in this case is HTTP, and the data is returned as XML.

2. Call a method of the XML Web service from the browser.

    When you call a method of an XML Web service from a browser, the protocol that is used is HTTP, and the data is returned as XML.

Access from a Web Form

You can also call methods of the XML Web service by using code on a Web Form.

▶ **To call an XML Web service from a Web Form**

1. Find out which XML Web services are available.

   This involves finding the URL for the XML Web service.

2. Create a WebReference to the XML Web service.

   This creates a .vb or .cs file that contains the source code for the proxy as created by Visual Studio .NET.

3. Compile the project, which in turn compiles the proxy.

   The proxy is compiled into the Web application assembly in the /bin folder.

4. Open a Web Form.

5. Create an instance of the WebReference.

6. Call the methods of the XML Web service.

7. Use the data that is returned by the XML Web service.

Lesson: Calling an XML Web Service Using HTTP

- **How to Call an XML Web Service Using HTTP**
- **Practice: Calling an XML Web Service Using HTTP**

Introduction

In this lesson, you will learn how to access an XML Web service directly from a browser by using HTTP-Get. This process, called *direct access*, is typically used by developers at design time to identify and test XML Web services. Direct access lets you view the methods, properties, and output of an XML Web service in a developer-friendly environment.

Lesson objectives

After completing this lesson, you will be able to:

- Call an XML Web service with a browser by using HTTP-GET protocol direct access.
- Identify the Web methods that are available from an XML Web service.
- Invoke Web methods from an XML Web service by using HTTP_GET protocol direct access, and then view the response.

How to Call an XML Web Service Using HTTP

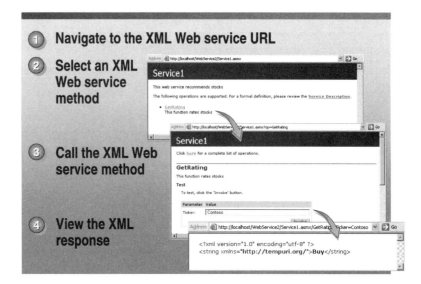

Introduction

When you access an XML Web service directly with a browser, you first access the HTML description page, DefaultWsdlHelpGenerator.aspx. From this page, you can select from the available XML Web service methods and call the method with parameters. You will then receive a response in XML.

You can also use the HTTP-POST protocol to access an XML Web service. You will not access the default page, DefaultWsdlHelpGenerator.aspx; however, the final response from the XML Web service will be identical to an HTTP-GET request.

Navigate to the XML Web service URL

After you have found an XML Web service on UDDI, you use the .asmx URL to navigate to the HTML description page. This description page provides information about what an XML Web service does, the available Web methods it contains, the Web method parameters, and responses. In addition, you can use the HTML description page to test the functionality of the XML Web service.

The following illustration shows the browser view of the XML Web service **Stocks** that is used in the demonstrations in this module.

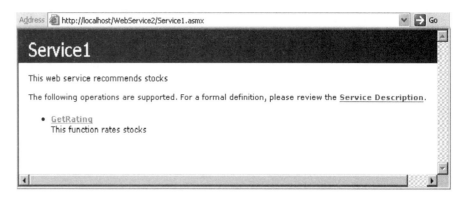

Select an XML Web service method

When you access the HTML description page for an XML Web service, the browser displays the available XML Web service methods. Click a Web method to view the available parameters for that Web method.

The following illustration shows the browser view resulting from the selection of the **GetRating** Web method in the XML Web service **Stocks**.

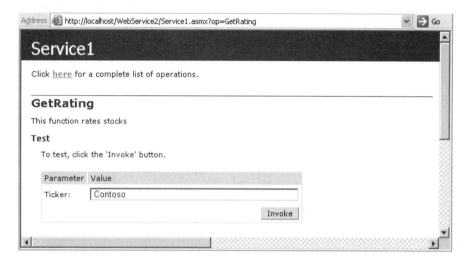

You can also click the **Service Description** link at the top of the HTML description page to view the WSDL contract, which contains an XML description of the XML Web service and its contents.

Call the Web method

To call a Web method, you fill in the form and then click **Invoke**. The Web Form passes the name of the method, the required parameters, and the values of the parameters to the URL of the XML Web service.

View the XML response

XML Web services always return data in XML format. The following illustration shows the browser view resulting from invoking the XML Web service **Stocks** with the parameter **Contoso**.

Practice: Calling an XML Web Service Using HTTP

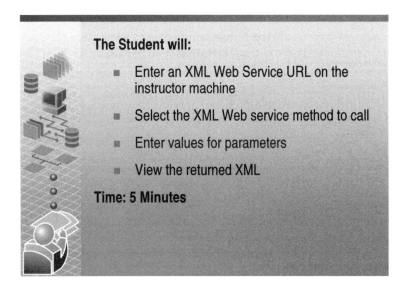

The Student will:

- Enter an XML Web Service URL on the instructor machine
- Select the XML Web service method to call
- Enter values for parameters
- View the returned XML

Time: 5 Minutes

Introduction

In this practice, you will access an XML Web service on the Instructor's computer and test the three available Web methods.

▶ **To access this XML Web service**

1. Open **http://*Instructorsmachine*/Mod13VB/WeatherService.asmx** or **http://*Instructorsmachine*/Mod13CS/WeatherService.asmx** in a browser.

Call the WeatherByCity Web method

2. Click **WeatherByCity**.

3. In the **City** field, type the name of a city, such as **Seattle**, for which you would like to have tomorrow's weather prediction.

4. Click **Invoke**.

   Enter the XML response on the following lines.

   _____

   _____

5. Call the **WeatherByCity** Web method again, this time passing another city name, such as **London**, as a parameter in the **City** field.

   Note the XML response.

   Note also that with city names other than Seattle, you will receive a random weather forecast of **sun**, **cloudy**, or **rain**. When Seattle is entered in the **City** field, you will always receive the weather forecast of **sun**.

Call the TemperatureByCity Web method

6. Return to the http://*Instructorsmachine*/Mod13VB/WeatherService.asmx or the http://*Instructorsmachine*/Mod13CS/WeatherService.asmx introductory page.

7. Click **TemperatureByCity**.

8. In the **City** field, enter the name of a city for which you would like to have the present temperature.

9. Click **Invoke**.

   The result value should be a random value between 31 and 60 degrees Fahrenheit.

Call the TravelAdviceByCity Web method

10. Return to the http:**//*Instructorsmachine*/Mod13VB/WeatherService.asmx** or the **http://*Instructorsmachine*/Mod13CS/WeatherService.asmx** introductory page.

11. Click **TravelAdviceByCity**.

12. In the **City** field, type the name of a city, such as **Seattle**, for which you would like to have travel advice.

13. Click **Invoke**.

   Note the XML response.

14. Call the **TravelAdviceByCity** Web method again, this time passing another city name, such as **London**, as a parameter in the **City** field.

15. Note the XML response.

Lesson: Using a Proxy to Call an XML Web Service

- ■ **Using Proxies to Call XML Web Services**

- ■ **How to Use a Proxy to Call an XML Web Service**

- ■ **Instructor-Led Practice: Using a Proxy to Call an XML Web Service**

- ■ **XML Web Service Error Handling**

- ■ **Demonstration: Testing the Availability of an XML Web Service**

Introduction

To programmatically call an XML Web service from a Web Form, you need to create a proxy to handle the call. In this lesson, you will learn how to create a Web reference proxy for an XML Web service method, and call the Web method from a Web Form.

Lesson objectives

After completing this lesson, you will be able to:

- ■ Explain how a proxy calls an XML Web service.

- ■ Create a proxy to call an XML Web service.

- ■ Incorporate content from an XML Web service into a Web site.

- ■ Handle errors from an XML Web service.

- ■ Test the availability of an XML Web service.

Using Proxies to Call XML Web Services

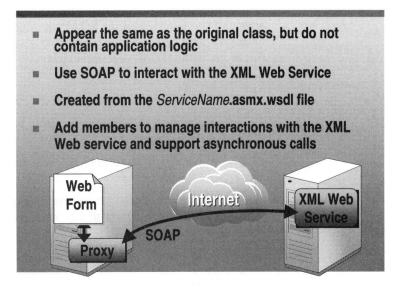

Introduction

To call an XML Web service from a Web Form, you need to create a Web reference to the XML Web service in your Web Application project. The Web reference creates the proxy object that is used to communicate with the XML Web service by using SOAP.

What is a proxy?

A proxy class is code that looks exactly like the class it is meant to represent, but it does not contain any of the application logic. Instead, the proxy class contains marshaling and transport logic. A proxy object allows a client to access an XML Web service as if it were a local COM object. The proxy must be on the computer that has the Web application.

Visual Studio .NET automatically creates a proxy named reference.vb or reference.cs when you add a Web reference to an XML Web service. When you create the Web reference, Visual Studio .NET creates the reference file, which is the proxy code.

Interact with SOAP

Proxies and XML Web services interact by using SOAP, which is an XML protocol that is used for exchanging structured and typed information.

Note To see a preview of the SOAP messages from an XML Web service, access the XML Web service URL directly and review the code that is displayed by the HTML description page.

The process of accessing an XML Web service by using a proxy is:

1. The user sends a URL request to a Web Form that requires a call to an XML Web service.

2. The Web Form instantiates the proxy, which then calls the XML Web service by using SOAP.

   The following is the SOAP request for the **GetRating** Web method in a **Stocks** XML Web service that is passing the argument *Contoso:*

   ```
   <?xml version="1.0" encoding="utf-8"?>
   <soap:Envelope xmlns:xsi="http://www.w3.org/2001/XMLSchema-
   instance" xmlns:xsd="http://www.w3.org/2001/XMLSchema"
   xmlns:soap="http://schemas.xmlsoap.org/soap/envelope/">
     <soap:Body>
       <GetRating xmlns="http://tempuri.org/">
         <Ticker>Contoso</Ticker>
       </GetRating>
     </soap:Body>
   </soap:Envelope>
   ```

3. The XML Web service sends a response to the proxy by using SOAP.

   The following is the SOAP response from the **GetRating** XML Web service:

   ```
   <?xml version="1.0" encoding="utf-8"?>
   <soap:Envelope xmlns:xsi="http://www.w3.org/2001/XMLSchema-
   instance" xmlns:xsd="http://www.w3.org/2001/XMLSchema"
   xmlns:soap="http://schemas.xmlsoap.org/soap/envelope/">
     <soap:Body>
       <GetRatingResponse xmlns="http://tempuri.org/">
         <GetRatingResult>Buy</GetRatingResult>
       </GetRatingResponse>
     </soap:Body>
   </soap:Envelope>
   ```

4. The ASP.NET Web Form consumes the response from the XML Web service.

Created from the .asmx.wsdl file

Visual Studio .NET automatically creates a proxy when you select **Add Web Reference** from the **Project** menu and enter the XML Web service URL. The .asmx.wsdl file on the XML Web service server is used to identify the Web methods and parameters that are available in the XML Web service.

When you create a proxy by using Visual Studio .NET, a number of methods and properties that support programmatic access to the XML Web service are available. The members that are available to a proxy include:

- Members built into the proxy

  The infrastructure for making asynchronous calls from a Web Form to an XML Web service is built into the proxy class that is created automatically by Visual Studio .NET, when you add a Web reference. A **Begin***WebMethodName* method and an **End***WebMethodName* method are automatically created in the proxy for every Web method of the XML Web service:

  - **Begin***WebMethodName*

    The **Begin** method is used to start asynchronous communication with an XML Web service method *WebMethodName*.

  - **End***WebMethodName*

    The **End** method is used to finish an asynchronous communication with an XML Web service method *WebMethodName*, and retrieve the completed reply from the XML Web service method.

  For example, creating a Web reference to the **Stocks** XML Web service creates a proxy with two additional methods: **BeginGetRating** and **EndGetRating**.

  Note For more information on asynchronously calling an XML Web service, see "Communicating With XML Web Services Asynchronously," in the Visual Studio .NET documentation.

- Members Inherited from **SoapHttpClientProtocol**

  A proxy inherits a number of methods and properties from the **System.Web.Services.Protocols.SoapHttpClientProtocol** class that can be used to manage interactions with the XML Web service. Some of the proxy properties include:

  - **Timeout**

    The **Timeout** property indicates the amount of time, in milliseconds, an XML Web service client waits for a synchronous XML Web service request to complete.

  - **Url**

    The **Url** property gets or sets the base URL of the XML Web service that the client is requesting.

  Note For more information on **SoapHttpClientProtocol** members, see "SoapHttpClientProtocol Members," in the Visual Studio .NET documentation.

How to Use a Proxy to Call an XML Web Service

> 1. **Create a Web reference for the XML Web Service**
>
> 2. **Create an instance of the XML Web Service**
>
> 3. **Call the Web methods of the XML Web Service**
>
> 4. **Build the ASP.NET Web Application**
>
> ```
> Sub Button1_Click(s As Object, e As EventArgs)...
>   Dim ProxyGetStocks As New _
>       GetStocks.localhost.Service1()
>   lblResults.Text = _
>       ProxyGetStocks.GetRating("Contoso")
> End Sub
> ```
>
> C# Code Example

Introduction

To use an XML Web service from a Web Form that was created in Visual Studio .NET, you must first identify the XML Web service URL, and then create a Web reference.

▶ **To create a proxy to call an XML Web service from a Web Form**

1. Open the Web application and the Web Form from which you will be calling the XML Web service, and then create a Web reference for the XML Web service:

   a. On the **Project** menu, click **Add Web Reference**.

   b. In the **Address** field of the **Add Web Reference** dialog box, type the URL of the XML Web service that you are accessing, press ENTER, and then click **Add Reference**.

   Visual Studio .NET creates a Web reference to the XML Web service, with the name of the server that is hosting the XML Web service.

   For example, if you created a Web reference to the http://localhost/Stocks/Service1.asmx, Visual Studio .NET will name the Web reference **localhost** by default.

Note   Visual Studio .NET is optimized for XML Web services that are created by Visual Studio .NET. ASP.NET may not read .wsdl files that are created with other programs, if the files include null terminated strings.

---

2. In an event procedure in the Web Form, create an instance of the proxy of the XML Web service.

For example, if you have a button to call the **GetRating** method of the **Stocks** XML Web service, use the following code in the **Click** event procedure **GetStocks.localhost.Service1**:

Visual Basic .NET

```
Dim ProxyGetStocks As New GetStocks.localhost.Service1()
```

C#

```
GetStocks.localhost.Service1 ProxyGetStocks =
                        new GetStocks.localhost.Service1();
```

GetStocks is the name of the Web application, **localhost** is the name of the Web reference, and **Service1** is the name of the Web service.

3. Call the Web methods of the XML Web service:

Visual Basic .NET

```
Label1.Text = ProxyGetStocks.GetRating("Contoso")
```

C#

```
Label1.Text = ProxyGetStocks.GetRating("Contoso");
```

The complete code in a **button_Click** event procedure would look like:

Visual Basic .NET

```
Sub Button1_Click(s As Object, e As EventArgs) _
    Handles Button1.Click
  Dim ProxyGetStocks As New _
     GetStocks.localhost.Service1()
  lblResults.Text = ProxyGetStocks.GetRating("Contoso")
End Sub
```

C#

```
private void Button1_Click(object sender,
   System.EventArgs e)
{
   GetStocks.localhost.Service1 ProxyGetStocks = new
      GetStocks.localhost.Service1();
   lblResults.Text = ProxyGetStocks.GetRating("Contoso");
}
```

4. Build the ASP.NET Web Application project.

Compile the Web application by clicking **Build** on the **Build** menu.

Instructor-Led Practice: Using a Proxy to Call an XML Web Service

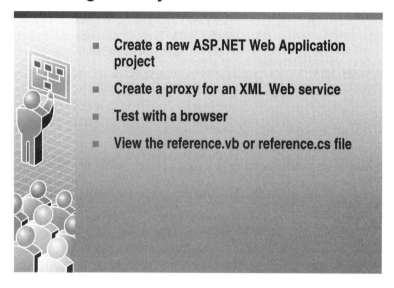

- Create a new ASP.NET Web Application project
- Create a proxy for an XML Web service
- Test with a browser
- View the reference.vb or reference.cs file

Introduction

In this practice, you will use a proxy to call an XML Web service.

▶ **To run the instructor-led practice**

Create a new project

1. Create a new ASP.NET Web Application project called **GetWeatherVB** or **GetWeatherCS** in Visual Studio .NET.

Create a proxy

2. Add a Web Reference to the XML Web service located at **http://localhost/Mod13VB/WeatherService.asmx** or **http://localhost/Mod13CS/WeatherService.asmx**.

   The Web reference you are adding will create a proxy and a new Web Reference called **localhost** in Solution Explorer.

   Note that the proxy is created in the language of your project. For instance, if you are using Microsoft Visual Basic®, the proxy will be created in Visual Basic.

3. In Solution Explorer, view the files that were automatically created for you by Visual Studio .NET.

4. Rename the Web Reference in Solution Explorer to **WeatherWebRef**.

5. Open the default Webform1.aspx page in Design view and add a **Text Box** control, a **Button** control, and a **Label** control to the Web Form. Keep the default properties for each control.

6. Create a **Click** event procedure for the **Button1** button, and add the following code:

Visual Basic .NET

```
Private Sub Button1_Click( _
   ByVal sender As System.Object, _
   ByVal e As System.EventArgs) Handles Button1.Click
   Dim ProxyGetWeather As New _
      GetWeatherVB.WeatherWebRef.WeatherService()
   Label1.Text = _
      ProxyGetWeather.WeatherByCity(TextBox1.Text)
End Sub
```

C#

```
private void Button1_Click(object sender,
   System.EventArgs e)
{
   GetWeatherCS.WeatherWebRef.WeatherService
      ProxyGetWeather = new
         GetWeatherCS.WeatherWebRef.WeatherService();
   Label1.Text =
      ProxyGetWeather.WeatherByCity(TextBox1.Text);
}
```

Test with a browser

7. Build and Browse Webform1.aspx.

8. To test the XML Web service, type **Seattle** in the text box and then click the button. Next, type another city name, such as **London**, in the text box and click the button again.

   Entering **Seattle** should result in a weather forecast of **sun**.

   Entering any other city name should result in a random weather forecast of: **sun, cloudy**, or **rain**.

View the reference file

9. View the reference.vb or the reference.cs file. The Reference.vb or Reference.cs file can be found by clicking **Show All Files** in **Solution Explorer** and expanding **Web References**, **WeatherWebRef**, and **Reference map**.

   Note that the reference file is the source code of the proxy that was automatically generated by Visual Studio .NET. The proxy has **Begin** and **End** methods for the asynchronous calling of every Web method in the XML Web service.

XML Web Service Error Handling

- **Service unavailable**

```
GetStocks.StockWebRef.Service1 ProxyGetStocks = new
    GetStocks.StockWebRef.Service1();
ProxyGetStocks.Timeout = 10000;
try
{
  lblMessage.Text =
    ProxyGetStocks.GetRating(TextBox1.Text);
}
catch (Exception err)
{
  lblMessage.Text = err.Message;
}
```

- **SOAP exceptions from XML Web Services**

Visual Basic .NET Code Example

Introduction

There are three major sources of error when you use an XML Web service: unavailable service, long response delays, and errors that are internal to the XML Web service, thereby resulting in error messages from the service in the form of SOAP exceptions. Your Web Form needs to be able to identify and handle all three of these errors types.

XML Web service unavailable

To test the availability of an XML Web service from an ASP.NET Web Form, you need to set a timeout for the XML Web service proxy. You need to use a **Try...Catch...Finally** statement to handle the timeout exception:

- Set the timeout parameter in the proxy

  Set the **Timeout** property of the XML Web service proxy to a value in milliseconds, as shown in the following code:

  ```
  ProxyName.Timeout = value in millisec
  ```

- Handle any timeout exceptions

  The following code calls the XML Web service, catches any exception, and displays an error message in Label1:

Visual Basic .NET

```
Try
    'call the XML Web service
Catch err As Exception
    Label1.Text = err.Message
End Try
```

C#

```
try
{
    //call the XML Web service
}
catch (Exception err)
{
    Label1.Text = err.Message;
}
```

SOAP Exceptions from XML Web services

If an XML Web service is unable to process a request, it may return an error message by using an instance of the **System.Web.Services** class **SoapException** object. To handle these exceptions, you need to use a **Try...Catch...Finally** statement.

The following code catches the exception and displays an error message in Label1:

Visual Basic .NET

```
Try
  'call your XML Web service
Catch err As SoapException
  Label1.Text = "Unable to process your request"
End Try
```

C#

```
try
{
    //call your XML Web service
}
catch (SoapException err)
{
    Label1.Text = "Unable to process your request";
}
```

Demonstration: Testing the Availability of an XML Web Service

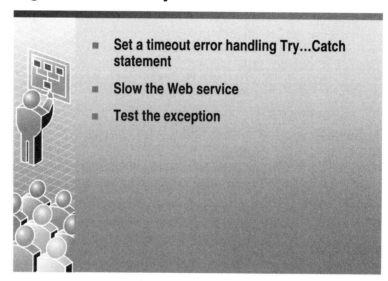

- Set a timeout error handling Try...Catch statement
- Slow the Web service
- Test the exception

Introduction

In this demonstration, you will learn how to test if the XML Web service is available.

▶ **To run the demonstration**

1. Reopen the **GetWeather** project from the previous Instructor-led Practice.

Set the timeout try...catch

2. Modify the code of the button event handler to set a timeout of 10 seconds (10,000) and add code to the button event handler to add a **try...catch** statement around the call to the XML Web service.

   Your code should look like the following:

Visual Basic .NET

```
Private Sub Button1_Click( _
    ByVal sender As System.Object, _
    ByVal e As System.EventArgs) Handles Button1.Click
  Dim ProxyGetWeather As New _
    GetWeatherVB.WeatherWebRef.WeatherService()
  ProxyGetWeather.Timeout = 10000
  Try
    Label1.Text = _
      ProxyGetWeather.WeatherByCity(TextBox1.Text)
  Catch err As Exception
    Label1.Text = err.Message
  End Try
End Sub
```

C#

```
private void Button1_Click(object sender,
   System.EventArgs e)
{
  GetWeatherCS.WeatherWebRef.WeatherService
    ProxyGetWeather = new
    GetWeatherCS.WeatherWebRef.WeatherService();
  ProxyGetWeather.Timeout = 10000;
  try
  {
    Label1.Text =
      ProxyGetWeather.WeatherByCity(TextBox1.Text);
  }
  catch (Exception err)
  {
    Label1.Text = err.Message;
  }
}
```

3. **Build and Browse** WebForm1.aspx.

4. Test the XML Web service by entering **Seattle** in the text box and clicking the button to verify that the application is still working as before.

Slow the XML Web service

5. Open the **Mod13** project in the **2310Demos** solution that contains the XML Web service.

6. At the top of the WeatherService.asmx.vb or the WeatherService.asmx.cs page, add the following import statement:

Visual Basic .NET

```
Imports System.Threading
```

C#

```
using System.Threading;
```

7. At the beginning of the **WeatherByCity** Web method, add the following code to slow the response to 40 seconds:

Visual Basic .NET

```
Thread.Sleep(40000)
```

C#

```
Thread.Sleep(40000);
```

This code will force the XML Web service to operate very slowly to simulate an XML Web service that is not online or is operating very slow.

Test the exception

8. Build the Web application by right-clicking **Mod13VB** or **Mod13CS** in Solution Explorer, and then clicking **Build**.

9. In the GetWeather project, view the WebForm1.aspx page in the browser.

10. To test the XML Web service by, type **Seattle** in the text box and click the button.

After 10 seconds, you should get the message "**The operation has timed-out**" in the label.

Lesson: Creating an XML Web Service

- How to Create an XML Web Service
- XML Web Service Code
- Instructor-Led Practice: Creating an XML Web Service

Introduction

Visual Studio .NET provides the templates that make developing XML Web services easy. In this lesson, you will learn how to use these templates to create an XML Web service.

Lesson objectives

After completing this lesson, you will be able to:

- Create an XML Web service by using Visual Studio .NET.
- Describe the classes and structures that are used in an XML Web service project that is built by using ASP.NET.
- Explain the code that is generated when you create a new XML Web service project by using ASP.NET.

How to Create an XML Web Service

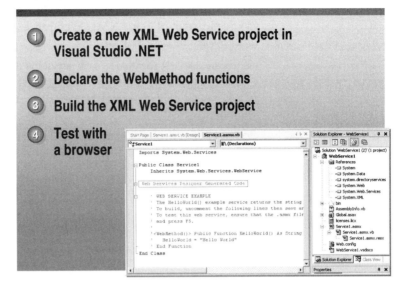

1. Create a new XML Web Service project in Visual Studio .NET

2. Declare the WebMethod functions

3. Build the XML Web Service project

4. Test with a browser

Introduction

Visual Studio .NET provides templates and a default XML Web service method to help you get started in creating XML Web services.

▶ **To create an XML Web service in Visual Studio .NET**

1. Open Visual Studio .NET, and create a new ASP.NET Web service project.

   Visual Studio .NET will automatically create the required folders, files, and the XML Web service page. Renaming the project and the XML Web service is recommended to help identify and maintain the project and files.

2. Declare the Web-callable functions.

   Visual Studio .NET creates a default "Hello World" function on the XML Web service page. The function can be activated by removing the comment tags.

   Almost any kind of function can be written as an XML Web service method function, from a simple local calculation to a complex database query.

3. Build the ASP.NET Web service project.

   After your functions are written, you need to build the Web Service before you can test the logic. As with Web Forms, ASP.NET compiles the XML Web service into Microsoft Intermediate Language (MSIL) for later execution.

4. Test with a browser.

    To verify that your functions work correctly, you can test them by accessing the XML Web service directly with a browser. In Visual Studio .NET, you do this by right-clicking **XML Web service** in Solution Explorer and then clicking **Build and Browse**.

    You can also test the XML Web service with a remote browser, from Visual Studio .NET, by right-clicking **XML Web service** in Solution Explorer and then clicking **Browse with…**, or by opening the browser and entering the Web service URL:

    ```
    http://serverName/WebService1/Service1.asmx
    ```

XML Web Service Code

> ■ **.asmx page**
>
> ```
> <%@ WebService Language="vb"
>     Codebehind="Service1.asmx.vb"
>     Class="XMLWebServiceName.Service1" %>
> ```
>
> ■ **.asmx.vb page**
>
> ```
> Imports System
> Imports System.Web.Services
>
> Class Service1
> <WebMethod()> Public Function function1() As type
>     'function_here
> End Function
> End Class
> ```
>
> C# Code Example

Introduction

When you create an XML Web service with Visual Studio .NET, two primary files are created that comprise the XML Web service: the .asmx file and the .asmx.vb or .asmx.cs file. The .asmx file identifies the Web page as an XML Web service, while the .asmx.vb or .asmx.cs file, also known as the code-behind page, contains the XML Web service logic.

.asmx page

Because there is no UI on an XML Web service, the .asmx page only contains the file type information and a directive to the code-behind page.

The code in an .asmx page is as follows:

Visual Basic .NET

```
<%@ WebService Language="vb" Codebehind="Service1.asmx.vb"
Class="XMLWebServiceName.Service1" %>
```

C#

```
<%@ WebService Language="c#" Codebehind="Service1.asmx.cs"
Class="XMLWebServiceName.Service1" %>
```

.asmx pages have the following attributes:

■ **@ Web Service**

The @ **Web Service** attribute identifies the file as an XML Web service.

■ **Language**

The **Language** attribute defines the language in which the script on the Web page is written. Some of the values for this attribute are: **vb**, **c#**, and **JScript**™.

- **Codebehind page**

  The **Codebehind** attribute identifies name and location of the .asmx.vb or .asmx.cs code-behind page that contains the logic of the XML Web Service.

- **Class**

  The **Class** attribute identifies the base class that supports this instance of an XML Web service.

  In the .asmx file, you must define a class that encapsulates the functionality of the XML Web Service. This defined class should be public, and should inherit from the XML Web service base class.

  The default XML Web service class is:

Visual Basic .NET

```
Class Service1
```

C#

```
class Service1
```

Code-behind page

The code-behind file is the page that caries the XML Web service logic.

The default code for a code-behind page is:

Visual Basic .NET

```
Imports System.Web.Services

<WebService(Namespace := "http://tempuri.org/")> _
Public Class Service1
    Inherits System.Web.Services.WebService

'<WebMethod()> Public Function HelloWorld() As String
'    HelloWorld = "Hello World"
' End Function

End Class
```

C#

```
using System;
using System.Collections;
using System.ComponentModel;
using System.Data;
using System.Diagnostics;
using System.Web;
using System.Web.Services;

namespace Service1
{
  public class Service1 : System.Web.Services.WebService
  {
      public Service1()
      {
         //CODEGEN: This call is required by the ASP.NET Web
Services Designer
         InitializeComponent();
      }

//        [WebMethod]
//        public string HelloWorld()
//        {
//             return "Hello World";
//        }
  }
}
```

Code-behind pages have the following attributes:

- Namespaces

Visual Basic .NET

XML Web services import the **System** and the **System.Web.Services** namespaces:

- **Imports System**

  The ASP.NET **System** namespace contains the classes that support general ASP.NET classes.

- **Imports System.Web.Services**

  The ASP.NET **Web.Services** namespace contains the methods and properties classes that support XML Web services.

C#

XML Web services import the **System** and the **System.Web.Services** namespaces:

- **using System**

  The ASP.NET **System** namespace contains the classes that support general ASP.NET classes.

- **using System.Web.Services**

  The ASP.NET **Web.Services** namespace contains the methods and properties classes that support XML Web services.

- **using System.Collections**

- **using System.ComponentModel**

- **using System.Data**

- **using System.Diagnostics**

- **using System.Web**

■ Class

The **Class** attribute identifies the base class that supports this instance of an XML Web service.

The default XML Web service class is Service1.

■ XML Web service methods

Each method that will be exposed from the XML Web service must be flagged with a custom **<WebMethod()>**attribute. This attribute is required to create a Web-callable method. If the method does not have the **<WebMethod()>** custom attribute, the method will not be exposed from the XML Web service.

Visual Studio .NET creates a default **"Hello World"** Web method, which can be activated by removing the comment tags on the XML Web service page. You can edit the default function, or add your own functions.

The following code is the default Visual Studio .NET XML Web service method:

Visual Basic .NET

```
<WebMethod()> Public Function HelloWorld() As String
    HelloWorld = "Hello World"
End Function
```

C#

```
[WebMethod]
public string HelloWorld()
{
    return "Hello World";
}
```

Instructor-Led Practice: Creating an XML Web Service

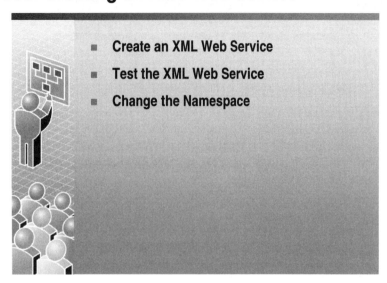

- ■ Create an XML Web Service
- ■ Test the XML Web Service
- ■ Change the Namespace

Introduction

In this practice, you will create a simple stock market rating service. This rating service returns a **Buy** value if the company name **Contoso** is entered as an input parameter. All of the other company names should return a **Sell** value.

▶ **To run this practice**

Create an XML Web service

1. Create a new ASP.NET Web Service project in Visual Studio .NET and then specify the location of the Web service as

Visual Basic .NET   **http://localhost/StocksVB**

C#   **http://localhost/StockCS**.

A StocksVB or StocksCS folder is automatically created in the \Inetpub\wwwroot folder.

2. Open the default .asmx file, Service1.asmx, in Code view by right-clicking the file in Solution Explorer and clicking **View Code**.

Note that the default name of the class is Service1, and Visual Studio .NET has automatically opened the code-behind file Sevice1.asmx.vb or Sevice1.asmx.cs.

3. Create a **GetRating** function as follows:

Visual Basic .NET

```
<WebMethod()> Public Function GetRating( _
   ByVal Ticker As String) As String
   If Ticker ="Contoso" Then
       Return "Buy"
   Else
       Return "Sell"
   End If
End Function
```

C#

```
[WebMethod]
public string GetRating(String Ticker)
{
   if (Ticker == "Contoso")
       return "Buy";
   else
       return "Sell";
}
```

4. Save the file.

Test the XML Web service

5. Build and browse the XML Web service in Microsoft Internet Explorer by viewing

Visual Basic .NET

http://localhost/StocksVB/Service1.asmx.

C#

http://localhost/StocksCS/Service1.asmx.

To open the XML Web service, you can also right-click **Service1.asmx** in Solution Explorer and then click **View in Browser**.

Note that there is a comment about the namespace.

6. Click **GetRating**.

7. Type the name of a company for which you would like a stock recommendation, such as **Contoso** or **Northwind Traders**, in the **Ticker** field, and then click **Invoke**.

Change or add the namespace

To prevent the namespace comment from appearing when you browse the XML Web service, you must change the namespace URL. If you are using Visual Basic .NET, you change the default URL that Visual Studio .NET provides. If you are using C#, Visual Studio .NET does not generate a default namespace. You must add a WebService attribute and then add the namespace directive to it.

8. Add or modify the WebService attribute.

Visual Basic .NET

Modify the namespace directive in Sevice1.asmx.vb to use http://microsoft.com/webservices/:

```
<WebService(Namespace:= _
    "http://microsoft.com/webservices/")> _
```

C#

Add the WebService attribute and namespace directive below the summary information in Service1.asmx.cs.

Your C# code should look like the following (with the new code that you must add in bold font):

```
/// Summary description for WeatherService
/// </summary>
///
[WebService(Namespace="http://microsoft.com/webservices/")]
public class Service1 : System.Web.Services.WebService
```

9. Save and rebuild the file.

10. Browse the Web service in Internet Explorer by viewing

Visual Basic .NET

http://localhost/StocksVB/Service1.asmx.

C#

http://localhost/StocksCS/Service1.asmx.

Note that the comment about the namespace disappears.

Add a description to the class and Web method

11. Add a description for the **Class**. Your code should look like the following:

Visual Basic .NET

```
<WebService(Namespace:= _
    "http://microsoft.com/webservices/", _
    Description:="My class description...")> _
```

C#

```
[WebService(Namespace=
    "http://microsoft.com/webservices/",
    Description="My class description...")]
```

12. Add a description to the **WebMethod** directive. Your code should look like the following:

Visual Basic .NET

```
<WebMethod(Description:="My WebMethod description...")>
```

C#

```
[WebMethod(Description="My WebMethod description...")]
```

13. Save and rebuild the file.

14. Browse the Web service in Internet Explorer at

Visual Basic .NET

http://localhost/StocksVB/Service1.asmx.

C#

http://localhost/StocksCS/Service1.asmx.

and verify that the descriptions appear.

Review

- **Overview of Using XML Web Services**
- **Calling an XML Web Service Using HTTP**
- **Using a Proxy to Call an XML Web Service**
- **Creating an XML Web Service**

1. Does an XML Web Service have a user interface?

2. Where would you look for information about available XML Web services?

3. How could you quickly test an XML Web service to see what Web methods and parameters are available?

4. How do you access an XML Web service from a Web Form?

5. How do you check to see if an XML Web service is available for use at runtime?

6. What is the protocol that is used to communicate between a proxy and an XML Web service?

7. What attribute do you add to methods that you want to be exposed to the Web from your XML Web service?

8. What is the difference between the .asmx and .asmx.vb (or .asmx.cs) files?

Lab 13: Consuming and Creating XML Web Services

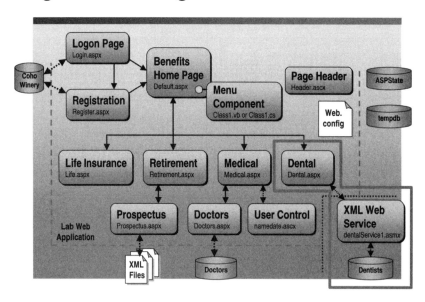

Objectives

After completing this lab, you will be able to:

- Create an XML Web service that returns complex data types.
- Test an XML Web service by using a browser.

Prerequisites

Before working on this lab, you must have:

- Knowledge of how to add a Microsoft® SQL Server™ table to a project.
- An understanding of Microsoft ADO.NET.
- Knowledge of how to add a Web reference to a Web Form.
- Knowledge of how to use a **DataGrid** control.
- Knowledge of how to create event procedures for server controls.

Scenario

Coho Winery offers several benefits to its employees. In the labs for Course 2310B, *Developing Microsoft ASP.NET Web Applications Using Visual Studio .NET*, you will create a Web site that enables employees to select and set up their chosen benefits.

In this lab, you will:

- Create an XML Web Service that enables you to retrieve the list of all of the dentists that are used by Coho Winery.
- Retrieve the list of dentists for a given postal code.
- Consume the Web service from the dental.aspx page.

Estimated time to complete this lab: 60 minutes

Exercise 0
Lab Setup

To complete this lab, you must have created a Benefits Web Application project and a BenefitsList Class Library project. These projects can be created by using Microsoft Visual Basic® .NET or Microsoft Visual C#™ .NET.

If you have not created these projects, complete the following steps:

▶ **Create the 2310LabApplication solution**

Important Only perform this procedure if you have not created a 2310LabApplication solution file.

1. Using Microsoft Visual Studio® .NET, create a new blank solution named **2310LabApplication**:

   a. On the **File** menu, point to **New**, and then click **Blank Solution**.

   b. In the **New Project** dialog box, type **2310LabApplication** in the **Name** text box, and then click **OK**.

▶ **Create the Benefits project**

Important Only perform this procedure if you have not previously created a Benefits project, or if you have removed the Benefits project according to the steps in Appendix A, "Lab Recovery," in Course 2310B, *Developing Microsoft ASP.NET Web Applications Using Visual Studio .NET*.

1. Create a new Microsoft ASP.NET Web Application project, named **BenefitsVB** or **BenefitsCS**, in the 2310LabApplication solution:

   a. On the **File** menu, point to **New**, and then click **Project**.

   b. In the **New Project** dialog box, in the **Project Types** list, click **Visual Basic Projects** or **Visual C# Projects**.

   c. In the **Templates** list, click **ASP.NET Web Application**. Set the **Location** to **http://localhost/BenefitsVB** for the Visual Basic .NET project or to **http:/localhost/BenefitsCS** for the Visual C# project.

   d. Click **Add to Solution**, and then click **OK**.

Caution When adding projects to the solution, the capitalization of the project name is important. Because you may be using some pre-built Web Forms in this and other labs in Course 2310B, *Developing Microsoft ASP.NET Web Applications Using Visual Studio .NET*, you must verify that you have capitalized the Benefits project as shown.

▶ **Update the Benefits project**

1. In Visual Studio .NET, open the 2310LabApplication solution file.

2. In Solution Explorer, right-click **BenefitsVB** or **BenefitsCS**, point to **Add**, and then click **Add Existing Item**.

3. Browse for project files:

For the Visual Basic .NET project

Browse to the *install folder*\Labfiles\Lab13\VB\Starter\BenefitsVB folder.

For the Visual C# project

Browse to the *install folder*\Labfiles\Lab13\Starter\BenefitsCS folder.

4. In the **Files of type** box of the **Add Existing Item – Benefits** dialog box, click **All Files (*.*)**.

5. Select all of the files in this folder, and then click **Open**.

6. Click **Yes** if prompted to overwrite or reload files.

▶ **Create the BenefitsList class library**

Important   Only perform these steps if you have not previously created a BenefitsList project, or if you have removed the BenefitsList project according to the steps in Appendix A, "Lab Recovery," in Course 2310B, *Developing Microsoft ASP.NET Web Applications Using Visual Studio .NET.*

---

1. Create a new Class Library Project

For the Visual Basic .NET project

Create a new Visual Basic .NET Class Library project, name it **BenefitsListVB**, and then add it to the 2310LabApplication solution:

   a. On the **File** menu, point to **New**, and then click **Project**.

   b. In the **New Project** dialog box, in the **Project Types** list, click **Visual Basic Projects**.

   c. In the **Templates** list, click **Class Library**, and then set the **Name** to **BenefitsListVB**.

   d. Click **Add to Solution**, and then click **OK**.

For the Visual C# project

Create a new Visual C# .NET Class Library project, name it **BenefitsListCS**, and then add it to the 2310LabApplication solution:

   a. On the **File** menu, point to **New**, and then click **Project**.

   b. In the **New Project** dialog box, in the **Project Types** list, click **Visual C#** Projects.

   c. In the **Templates** list, click **Class Library**, and then set the **Name** to **BenefitsListCS**.

   d. Click **Add to Solution**, and then click **OK**.

Caution   Verify that you have capitalized the BenefitsList project as shown.

► **Update the BenefitsList project**

1. In Visual Studio .NET, open the 2310LabApplication solution file.

2. In Solution Explorer, right-click **BenefitsListVB** or **BenefitsListCS**, point to **Add**, and then click **Add Existing Item**.

3. Browse for project files:

For the Visual Basic .NET project

Browse to the *install folder*\Labfiles\Lab13\VB\Starter\BenefitsListVB folder.

For the Visual C# project

Browse to the install folder\Labfiles\Lab13\CS\Starter\BenefitsListCS folder.

4. In the **Files of type** box of the **Add Existing Item – BenefitsList** dialog box, click **All Files (*.*)**.

5. Select all of the files in this folder, and then click **Open**.

6. Click **Yes** if prompted to overwrite or reload files.

► **Create a reference to the BenefitsList component in the Benefits project**

1. In the Benefits project in the 2310LabApplication solution, complete the following steps to add a reference to the BenefitsList component that you just created:

   a. Right-click the **BenefitsVB** or **BenefitsCS** project in Solution Explorer and then click **Add Reference**.

   b. In the **Add Reference** dialog box, on the **Projects** tab, double-click the **BenefitsListVB** or **BenefitsListCS** project.

   c. In the **Selected Components** list, select the **BenefitsListVB** or **BenefitsListCS** component, and then click **OK**.

   The component is added to the References folder in Solution Explorer.

Exercise 1
Create the Dentist XML Web Service GetAllDentists XML Web Service Method

In this exercise, you will use Visual Studio .NET to create an XML Web service.

▶ **Create an XML Web service**

1. Using Visual Studio .NET, open the 2310LabApplication solution.

2. Create a new ASP.NET Web Service project, named **DentalServiceVB** or **DentalServiceCS**, in the 2310LabApplication solution:

   a. On the **File** menu, click **New**, and then click **Project**.

   b. In the **New Project** dialog box, in the **Project Types** list, click **Visual Basic Projects** or **Visual C# Projects**.

   c. In the **Templates** list, click **ASP.NET Web Service**. Set the **Location** to **http://localhost/DentalServiceVB** for a Visual Basic project or to **http://localhost/DentalServiceCS** for a Visual C# project.

   d. Click **Add to Solution**, and then click **OK**.

3. In Solution Explorer, right-click **Service1.asmx** and rename it **DentalService1.asmx**

4. In Solution Explorer, make sure that the DentalService1.asmx file is open, and then double-click the design surface to open the code-behind page.

5. Change the name of the class:

Visual Basic .NET

In the DentalService1.asmx.vb file, change the name of the class from Service1 to DentalService1.

C#

In the DentalService1.asmx.cs file, change the name of the class and the constructor from Service1 to DentalService1.

▶ **Create the Connection and DataAdapter**

1. In Server Explorer, expand **Servers**, expand *machinename*, expand **SQL Servers**, expand *machinename*, expand **dentists**, and then expand **tables** to view the tables of the **dentists** database.

2. In Design mode, use a drag-and-drop operation to place the **Dentists** table from the **dentists** database onto the DentalService1.asmx page.

Visual Basic .NET

A **SqlConnection1** object and a **SqlDataAdapter1** object are created and are placed on the design surface of the DentalService1.asmx XML Web service.

C#

A **sqlConnection1** object and a **sqlDataAdapter1** object are created and are placed on the design surface of the DentalService1.asmx XML Web service.

▶ **Create the DataSet**

1. Click anywhere on the design surface to unselect the **SqlConnection1** and **SqlDataAdapter1** objects.

2. Right-click the **SqlDataAdapter1** object on the DentalService1.asmx page and click **Generate Dataset**.

3. In the **Generate Dataset** dialog box, create a new **DataSet** named **dsDentists**, ensure that the **Add this dataset to the designer** option is selected, and then click **OK**.

   A **dsDentists** object is created and is placed on the Design view of the DentalService1.asmx page, and a new schema file named dsDentists.xsd is added to the DentalService project in Solution Explorer.

   Note When creating the **dsDentists DataSet**, Visual Basic .NET will create a dsDentists instance named "DsDentists1" whereas Visual C# will create a dsDentists instance named "dsDentists1".

▶ **Create the GetAllDentists XML Web service method**

1. In the code-behind page of the DentalService1.asmx page, DentalService1.asmx.vb or DentalService1.asmx.cs, create an XML Web service method named **GetAllDentists**, which returns a **DataSet** object.

2. In the XML Web service method, call the **Fill** method of the **SqlDataAdapter1** object to fill the **DataSet, dsDentists1**, and then return the **DataSet**.

   Your code should look like the following:

Visual Basic .NET

```
<WebMethod()> _
    Public Function GetAllDentists() As DataSet
    SqlDataAdapter1.Fill(DsDentists1)
    Return DsDentists1
End Function
```

C#

```
[WebMethod()]
    public DataSet GetAllDentists()
{
    sqlDataAdapter1.Fill(dsDentists1);
    return dsDentists1;
}
```

3. Save your changes.

4. Build and browse the DentalService1.asmx page.

The description page of the XML Web service is displayed.

Where does this description page come from?

_____

_____

Note There is a warning message at the bottom of the page about the use of tempuri.org. The warning is here because this temporary URL is the temporary namespace of the XML Web service and it is used for testing purposes only.

5. In the browser, click the **GetAllDentists** link and then click **Invoke**.

The browser displays the XML response from the XML Web service.

What is the purpose of the content between the <xs:schema> and </xs:schema> tags?

_____

_____

▶ **Modify the output of the XML Web service**

1. In the DentalService1.asmx code-behind page, set the attributes of the Web service according to the following table. If you are working in C#, you will need to create the WebService attribute.

Attribute	Value
Namespace	http://microsoft.com/webservices/
Description	This XML Web service contains information about the dentists

Your code should look like the following:

Visual Basic .NET

```
<WebService( _
Namespace:="http://microsoft.com/webservices/", _
Description:="This XML Web service contains " & _
"information about the dentists.")> _
Public Class DentalService1
    Inherits System.Web.Services.WebService
```

C#

```
[WebService(Namespace="http://microsoft.com/webservices/",
    Description="This XML Web service contains " +
    "information about the dentists.")]
public class DentalService1 :
        System.Web.Services.WebService
```

2. Add a **description** attribute to the **GetAllDentists** XML Web service method and set it to **This XML Web service method returns all the dentists**.

   Your code should look like the following:

Visual Basic .NET

```
<WebMethod(Description:= _
"This XML Web service method returns all the dentists")> _
    Public Function GetAllDentists() As DataSet
```

C#

```
[WebMethod(Description= "This XML Web service method
returns all the dentists")]
public DataSet GetAllDentists()
```

3. Build and browse the DentalService1.asmx page.

4. In the browser, notice that the description of the XML Web service and that the description of the XML Web service method have changed. In addition, notice that the warning message at the bottom of the page, regarding the use of tempuri.org, no longer appears because you changed the namespace of the service.

▶ **Test your neighbor's XML Web service**

1. In Microsoft Internet Explorer, navigate to your neighbor's DentalService XML Web service by navigating to the following URL, where *MachineName* is the name of another student's computer: http://*MachineName*/**DentalServiceVB/DentalService1.asmx** or http://*MachineName*/**DentalServiceCS/DentalService1.asmx**

Note   You can also use the Instructor computer named London.

---

2. Invoke the **GetAllDentists** XML Web service method.

Exercise 2
Create the GetDentistsByPostalCode XML Web Service Method

In this exercise, you will add another XML Web service method to your DentistService XML Web service. The new XML Web service method is named **GetDentistsByPostalCode** and returns a **DataSet** containing all of the dentists that are in a given postal code. In this exercise, you will write code that uses ADO.NET to call a SQL Server stored procedure.

▶ **Create the GetDentistsByPostalCode XML Web service method**

1. In the DentalService1.asmx.vb or DentalService1.asmx.cs file, import the **System.Data.SqlClient** namespace.

   Your code should look like the following:

Visual Basic .NET
```
Imports System.Data.SqlClient
```

C#
```
using System.Data.SqlClient;
```

2. Create an XML Web service method named **GetDentistsByPostalCode** that has one **String** parameter that is passed by the value named **strPostalCode** and returns a **DataSet**.

3. Set the description of the XML Web service method to **This XML Web service method returns the dentists from a supplied postal code**.

   Your code should look like the following:

Visual Basic .NET
```
<WebMethod(Description:= _
   "This XML Web service method returns the " & _
   "dentists from a supplied postal code.")> _
Public Function GetDentistsByPostalCode( _
   ByVal strPostalCode As String) As DataSet

End Function
```

C#
```
[WebMethod(Description=
   "This XML Web service method returns the " +
   "dentists from a supplied postal code.")]
public DataSet GetDentistsByPostalCode(
   String strPostalCode)
{
}
```

4. Inside the **GetDentistsByPostalCode** XML Web service method, add code to fill a new **DataSet**, with the dentists that are in a given a postal code, by calling the **DentistByPostalCode** stored procedure.

Your code should look like the following:

Note You can copy and paste this code from: the file *install folder*\Labfiles \Lab13\VB\Starter\DentalServiceVB\DentistsPoCode.txt, or *install folder*\ Labfiles\Lab13\CS\Starter\DentalServiceCS\DentistsPoCode.txt.

Visual Basic .NET

```
Dim conn As New SqlConnection _
   ("data source=localhost; " & _
   "initial catalog=Dentists; " & _
   "integrated security=true")
Dim daDentistsPoCode As SqlDataAdapter
Dim dsDentistsPoCode As New DataSet()
Dim workParam As SqlParameter = Nothing

'call the DentistsByState stored procedure
daDentistsPoCode = _
   New SqlDataAdapter("DentistsByPostalCode", conn)
daDentistsPoCode.SelectCommand.CommandType = _
   CommandType.StoredProcedure

'add the postal code input parameter
workParam = New SqlParameter("@PostalCode", _
   System.Data.SqlDbType.NVarChar)
workParam.Direction = ParameterDirection.Input
workParam.Value = strPostalCode
daDentistsPoCode.SelectCommand.Parameters.Add(workParam)

'run the stored procedure and fill a dataset
daDentistsPoCode.Fill(dsDentistsPoCode, _
   "DentistsPoCode")

'close the connection
conn.Close()

Return dsDentistsPoCode
```

C#

```csharp
SqlConnection conn = new SqlConnection
    ("data source=localhost;" +
    "initial catalog=Dentists;" +
    "integrated security=true");
SqlDataAdapter daDentistsPoCode;
DataSet dsDentistsPoCode = new DataSet();
SqlParameter workParam  = null;

//call the DentistsByState stored procedure
daDentistsPoCode = new
    SqlDataAdapter("DentistsByPostalCode", conn);
daDentistsPoCode.SelectCommand.CommandType =
    CommandType.StoredProcedure;

//add the postal code input parameter
workParam = new SqlParameter("@PostalCode",
    System.Data.SqlDbType.NVarChar);
workParam.Direction = ParameterDirection.Input;
workParam.Value = strPostalCode;
daDentistsPoCode.SelectCommand.Parameters.Add(workParam);

//run the stored procedure and fill a dataset
daDentistsPoCode.Fill(dsDentistsPoCode, "DentistsPoCode");

//close the connection
conn.Close();

return dsDentistsPoCode;
```

5. Save your changes.

6. Build and browse the DentalService1.asmx page.

7. In the browser, click the **GetDentistsByPostalCode** link, type **98052** in the **strPostalCode** field, and then click **Invoke**.

    You should see all of the dentists for the postal code 98052. There should be six dentists for this postal code.

8. Test the **GetDentistsByPostalCode** XML Web service method again with the postal code 94111.

    Now, you should see all of the dentists for the postal code 94111. There should be three dentists for this postal code.

9. Test the **GetDentistsByPostalCode** XML Web service method again with the postal code 02703.

    You should see no dentists.

Exercise 3
Consume the GetAllDentists XML Web Service Method

In this exercise, you will call the **GetAllDentists** XML Web service method of the DentalService XML Web service. You will then display the resulted **DataSet** in a **DataGrid** control.

▶ **Consume the DentalService XML Web service**

1. Open the BenefitsVB or BenefitsCS project in the 2310LabApplication Visual Studio .NET solution.

2. Add the dental.aspx Web Form from the *install folder*\Labfiles\Lab13\VB\Starter\BenefitsVB or *install folder*\Labfiles\Lab13\CS\Starter\BenefitsCS folder to the BenefitsVB or BenefitsCS project.

3. Add a Web reference to the DentalService XML Web service. The XML Web service should be located at http://localhost/DentalServiceVB/DentalService1.asmx or http://localhost/DentalServiceCS/DentalService1.asmx

   a. In Solution Explorer, right-click **BenefitsVB** or **BenefitsCS**, then click **Add Web Reference**.

   b. In the **Address** field of the **Add Web Reference** dialog box, type **http://localhost/DentalServiceVB/DentalService1.asmx** or **http://localhost/DentalServiceCS/DentalService1.asmx**, and then press ENTER.

   c. Click **Add Reference**.

   A new folder named Web References is automatically created in the **BenefitsVB** or **BenefitsCS** project, inside Solution Explorer. The Web References folder contains a proxy and a new Web Reference named **localhost**.

> **Note** The proxy is created in the default language of your project settings. For instance, if you are using Visual Basic .NET, the proxy will be created in Visual Basic .NET, and its name will be Reference.vb.

4. Click the **Show All Files** icon 📄 in Solution Explorer.

5. In Solution Explorer, rename the Web Reference from **localhost** to **DentalWebRef**.

6. Expand **Web References**, expand **DentalWebRef**, and then click the **Reference.map** icon in Solution Explorer.

7. Open the Reference.vb or Reference.cs file.

   What is the purpose of the **BeginGetAllDentists** and **EndGetAllDentists** methods?

   _____

   _____

8. Close Reference.vb or Reference.cs.

▶ **Call the GetAllDentists XML Web service method**

1. Open the dental.aspx Web Form.

   There are already **TextBox**, **Button**, and **DataGrid** controls on the page.

2. Open the dental.aspx code-behind page and locate the following comment in the **cmdGetAllDentists_Click** event procedure:

Visual Basic .NET

```
'TODO Lab 13: call the XML Web service method
'GetAllDentists
```

C#

```
//TODO Lab 13: call the XML Web service method
//GetAllDentists
```

3. Write the code to consume the **GetAllDentists** XML Web service method:

   a. Create a DentalService proxy named **ProxyGetAllDentists**.

   b. Create a **DataSet** named **dsAllDentists**.

   c. Call the **GetAllDentists** XML Web service method and save the results in **dsAllDentists**.

   d. Set the data source of the **dgDentists** DataGrid to **dsAllDentists**.

   e. Bind the **DataSet** to the **DataGrid**.

Your code should look like the following:

Visual Basic .NET

```
Dim ProxyGetAllDentists As New _
    BenefitsVB.DentalWebRef.DentalService1()
Dim dsAllDentists As New DataSet()
dsAllDentists = _
        ProxyGetAllDentists.GetAllDentists()
dgDentists.DataSource = dsAllDentists.Tables(0)
dgDentists.DataBind()
```

C#

```
BenefitsCS.DentalWebRef.DentalService1 ProxyGetAllDentists
    = new BenefitsCS.DentalWebRef.DentalService1();
DataSet dsAllDentists = new DataSet();
dsAllDentists = ProxyGetAllDentists.GetAllDentists();
dgDentists.DataSource = dsAllDentists.Tables[0];
dgDentists.DataBind();
```

Note If the **DentalWebRef** displays as **localhost** in Microsoft IntelliSense®, you need to close Visual Studio .NET and reopen it before writing the code to consume the XML Web service methods from the Web Reference.

---

4. Save your changes.

5. Build and browse the dental.aspx page.

6. In the browser, click **Get All Dentists**.

   You should see all the dentists in the **DataGrid**.

Exercise 4
Consume the GetDentistsByPostalCode XML Web Service Method

In this exercise, you will call the **GetDentistsByPostalCode** XML Web service method of the Dentists.asmx XML Web Service. You will use a **DataGrid** to display the resulting **DataSet** of the dentists for a given postal code.

▶ **Call the GetDentistsByPostalCode XML Web service method**

1. Open the dental.aspx code-behind page and locate the following comment in the **cmdSubmit_Click** event procedure:

Visual Basic .NET

```
'TODO Lab 13: call the XML Web service methods
'GetDentistsByPostalCode
```

C#

```
//TODO Lab 13: call the XML Web service methods
//GetDentistsByPostalCode
```

2. Write the code to call the **GetDentistsByPostalCode** XML Web service method:

   a. Create a proxy named **ProxyGetDentistsByPostalCode**.

   b. Create a **DataSet** named **dsDentistsByPostalCode**.

   c. Call the **GetDentistsByPostalCode** XML Web service method, passing to it the content of the **txtPostalCode** text box, and then save the resulting **DataSet** in the DataSet **dsDentistsByPostalCode**.

   d. Set the **DataSource** of the dgDentists **DataGrid** to **dsDentistsByPostalCode**.

   e. Bind the **DataSet** to the **DataGrid**.

   Your code should look like the following:

Visual Basic .NET

```
Dim ProxyGetDentistsByPostalCode As New _
  BenefitsVB.DentalWebRef.DentalService1()
Dim dsDentistsByPostalCode As New DataSet()
dsDentistsByPostalCode = _
  ProxyGetDentistsByPostalCode. _
  GetDentistsByPostalCode(txtPostalCode.Text)
dgDentists.DataSource = dsDentistsByPostalCode.Tables(0)
dgDentists.DataBind()
```

C#

```
BenefitsCS.DentalWebRef.DentalService1
  ProxyGetDentistsByPostalCode = new
  BenefitsCS.DentalWebRef.DentalService1();
DataSet dsDentistsByPostalCode = new DataSet();
dsDentistsByPostalCode =
  ProxyGetDentistsByPostalCode.GetDentistsByPostalCode
    (txtPostalCode.Text);
dgDentists.DataSource = dsDentistsByPostalCode.Tables[0];
dgDentists.DataBind();
```

3. Save your changes.

4. Build and browse dental.aspx.

5. Type **98052** in the **Postal Code** text box, and then click **Submit**.

   You should see all of the dentists for the postal code 98052 in the **DataGrid**.

6. Type **94111** in the **Postal Code** text box, and then click **Submit**.

   You will see all the dentists for the postal code 94111 in the **DataGrid**.

msdn® training

Module 14:
Managing State

Contents

Overview

- State Management
- Application and Session Variables
- Cookies and Cookieless Sessions

Introduction   Microsoft® ASP.NET enables you to manage state in a Web application. State is the ability of a Web application to retain user information.

In this module, you will learn how to manage state in an ASP.NET Web application.

Objectives   After completing this module, you will be able to:

- Describe state management and its different types of options that are available to manage state in an ASP.NET Web application.

- Use application and session variables to manage state in ASP.NET Web applications.

- Use cookies and cookieless sessions to manage state in ASP.NET Web applications.

Lesson: State Management

- **What is State Management?**
- **Types of State Management**
- **Server-Side State Management**
- **Client-Side State Management**
- **The Global.asax File**

Introduction

The connection that is established between a user (the client computer) and a Web server is called a session. Sessions can span multiple Web pages and are tracked through state management.

State management is the process by which you maintain the same information throughout multiple requests for the same or different Web pages.

In this lesson, you will begin to understand in detail what state management is and why it is important to manage state. You will learn about server-side state management and client-side state management. You will also learn about the global.asax file.

Lesson objectives

After completing this lesson, you will be able to:

- Describe state management.
- Identify the different types of state management options.
- Describe server-side state management.
- Describe client-side state management.
- Describe the different events that are handled by the global.asax file.

What is State Management?

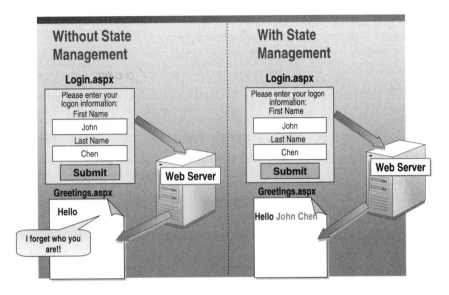

Introduction	As is true for any Hypertext Transfer Protocol (HTTP)-based technology, Web Forms are stateless, which means that they do not automatically indicate whether the requests in a sequence are all from the same client or even whether a single browser instance is still actively viewing a Web page or a Web site. Furthermore, Web pages are destroyed and then recreated with each new request to the Web server; therefore, page information does not exist beyond the life cycle of a single page.
State Management	ASP.NET provides state management that saves information on the server between pages, which helps to maintain the continuity of user information (state) throughout a visit to a Web Site.
	If state is maintained between pages, the information that is originally supplied by users can be reused; consequently, users do not need to reenter the same information multiple times each time a page is sent back to the server.
Example	For example, in the preceding illustration, the user, John Chen, enters his name in the login.aspx form. After he enters his personal details, that information is sent to the server and the next page, the greetings.aspx form, is displayed. Without state management, the details that were entered by the user on the first page are lost.
	However, with state management being used in your Web application, you can maintain state across multiple Web pages. Therefore, when the user's personal information is sent to the server, the second page, which is the greetings.aspx form, welcomes the user by his name, John Chen, which he entered in the login.aspx form, which is the first page of the Web application.

Types of State Management

Server-Side State Management	Client-Side State Management
Application state *Cache* ■ Information is available to all users of a Web application	**Cookies** ■ Text file stores information to maintain state
Session state ■ Information is available only to a user of a specific session	**The ViewState property** ■ Retains values between multiple requests for the same page
Database ■ In some cases, use database support to maintain state on your Web site	**Query strings** ■ Information appended to the end of a URL

Introduction

ASP.NET provides two types of state management that can be used to maintain state between server roundtrips. Choosing between the two types of state management that are available in ASP.NET depends mostly on the nature of your Web application.

Server-side and client-side state management

The two types of state management are:

■ Server-side

Server-side state management options use server resources to store state information. These options have higher security than client-side.

■ Client-side

Client-side state management does not use server resources to store state information. Client-side options tend to have minimal security, but they do offer fast server performance because the demand on the server to maintain state is none.

Server-side

Server-side state management further contains different options to choose from, including:

■ Application state

In application state, information is available to all of the users of a Web application; for example, storing the number of visitors to a Web application.

■ Session state

In session state, information is available only to a user of a specific session of a Web application; for example, storing the preferred color scheme of a user.

- Microsoft SQL Server™ database or a state server

  Another option of server-side state management is using the database technology. You can use a SQL Server database or a state server to store user-specific information when the information store is large. The SQL Server database or a state server can be used in conjunction with session state and cookies.

- The **Cache** object

  You can also use the **Cache** object to manage state at the application level.

Note For more information about the **Cache** object, see Module 15, "Configuring, Optimizing, and Deploying a Microsoft ASP.NET Web Application," in Course 2310B, *Developing Microsoft ASP.NET Web Applications Using Visual Studio .NET.*

Client-side

Client-side state management also offers different options to maintain state. These options include:

- Cookies

  A cookie is a text file that can be used to store small amounts of information that is needed to maintain state.

- The **ViewState** property

  Web Forms provide the **ViewState** property as a built-in structure for automatically retaining values between multiple requests for the same page. The **ViewState** property is maintained as a hidden field in the page.

- Query strings

  A query string is information that is appended to the end of a Uniform Resource Locator (URL). A typical example might look like the following:

  http://www.contoso.com/listwidgets.aspx?category=basic&price=100

  In the preceding URL path, the query string starts with the question mark (**?**) and includes two attribute-value pairs, category and price.

Note This module covers information pertaining to cookies only. For more information about **ViewState** and query strings, see the Microsoft Visual Studio® .NET documentation.

Server-Side State Management

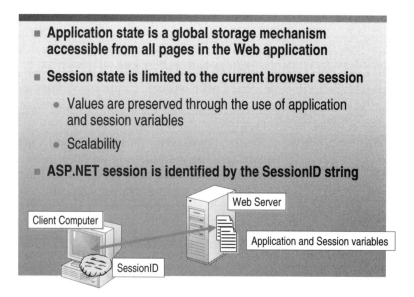

- Application state is a global storage mechanism accessible from all pages in the Web application

- Session state is limited to the current browser session
  - Values are preserved through the use of application and session variables
  - Scalability

- ASP.NET session is identified by the SessionID string

Introduction

ASP.NET offers several options to implement server-side state management. The application and session states are two of those options. This topic covers the application and session states in greater detail.

Application state

ASP.NET provides application state by using an instance of the **HttpApplicationState** class for each active Web application. Application state is a global storage mechanism that is accessible from all of the pages in the Web application, and it is therefore useful for storing user information that must be maintained between server round trips and between pages.

Application state is a key-value dictionary structure that is created during each request to a specific URL. You can add the application-specific information to this structure to store it between page requests. After you add the application-specific information to application state, the server manages it.

Application variables

ASP.NET provides the application variables that maintain application state. The ideal data to insert into application variables is the data that is shared by multiple sessions and does not change often.

Session state

ASP.NET provides session state by using an instance of the **HttpSessionState** class for each active Web application session.

Session state is similar to application state, except that it is limited to the current browser session. If different users are using a Web application, each user will have a different session state. In addition, if the same user leaves the Web application and then returns later, that user will also have a different session state than the one he or she had previously.

Session state is structured as a key-value dictionary structure that is used for storing session-specific information that needs to be maintained between server round trips and between requests for pages. After you add the application-specific information to session state, the server manages it. You can configure ASP.NET to automatically serialize and store session information in a SQL Server database or in a state server.

Session variables

ASP.NET provides the session variables that are needed to maintain session state. The ideal data to store in session state variables is short-lived, sensitive data that is specific to an individual session.

Note The application and session states are implemented as a hashtable, and store data based on key/value pair combinations. Hashtable is similar to the concept of a **dictionary** object.

Scalability

With ASP.NET, session state can be used in both multicomputer and multiprocess configurations; thereby optimizing the scalability scenarios of a Web application.

Identifying and tracking a session

Each active Web application session is identified and tracked by using a 120-bit **SessionID** string containing only the ASCII characters that are allowed in the URLs. The **SessionID** strings are communicated across client-server requests, either by means of an HTTP cookie or a modified URL, with the **SessionID** string embedded, commonly called cookieless **SessionID**, depending on how you configure the Web application settings.

Server-side state management requires a cookie to store the **SessionID** on the client computer. Because the life duration of a **SessionID** is very short, just the duration of a session, the mechanism that is used by ASP.NET to store session information, either in a SQL Server database or in a state server, is also used to allow the application to be scalable, but not for long-term storage. If you want to implement long-term storage of user session information, you must require the users to enter their personal information, and then you need to implement your own storage solution by using a database that permanently stores the personal information of registered users.

Client-Side State Management

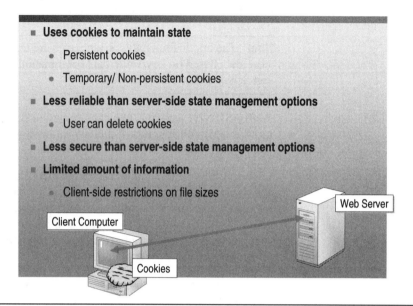

Introduction	Most Web applications use cookies for client-side state management.
Cookies	A cookie is a small amount of data that is stored either in a text file on the file system of the client computer or in-memory in the client-browser session. A cookie contains page-specific information that the server sends to the client, along with page output.
	You can use cookies to store information about a particular client, session, or application. The cookies are stored on the client computer, and when the browser requests a page, it sends the information in the cookie, along with the request information. The server is authorized to read the cookie and extract its value. Every cookie contains the information of the domain that issued the cookie. You can have several cookies issued for one domain.
Types of cookies	The two types of cookies are:

- Temporary

   Temporary cookies, also called the session or non-persistent cookies, exist only in the memory of the browser. When the browser is shut down, any temporary cookies that were added to the browser are lost.

- Persistent

   Persistent cookies are similar to temporary cookies, except that persistent cookies have a definite expiration period. When a browser requests a page that creates a persistent cookie, the browser saves that cookie to the user's hard disk. You can create a persistent cookie that last months, or even years, on the client computer. With Microsoft Internet Explorer, persistent cookies are stored in a file named username@domainname.txt, which is created on the client's hard disk.

Expiration

Cookies can expire when the browser session ends (temporary cookies), or they can exist indefinitely on the client computer, subject to the expiration rules on the client (persistent cookies).

Users can also choose to delete cookies from their computer before the cookie expires. Therefore, there is no guarantee that a persistent cookie will remain on a user's computer for the period of time that is specified.

Security

Cookies are less secure as compared to server-side state management options. Cookies are also subject to tampering. Users can manipulate cookies on their computer, which can potentially represent a security compromise or can cause the application that is dependent on the cookie to fail.

Limited information

There is also a limit on how much information you can store in a cookie because client computers have restrictions on file sizes. In addition, each individual cookie can contain a limited amount of information, no more than 4 kilobytes (KB).

The Global.asax File

- Only one Global.asax file per Web application
- Stored in the virtual root of the Web application
- Used to handle application and session events
- The Global.asax file is optional

Introduction

The global.asax file is a declarative file that is used to handle events while your Web application is running.

Some of the features of the global.asax file are:

- Every ASP.NET Web application supports one global.asax file per Web application.

- The global.asax file is stored in the virtual root of the Web application.

- The global.asax file can handle application and session (start and end) events that can be used to initialize application and sessions variables.

- The global.asax file is optional. If you do not define the file, the ASP.NET page framework assumes that you have not defined any application or session event handlers.

The Global.asax File (*continued*)

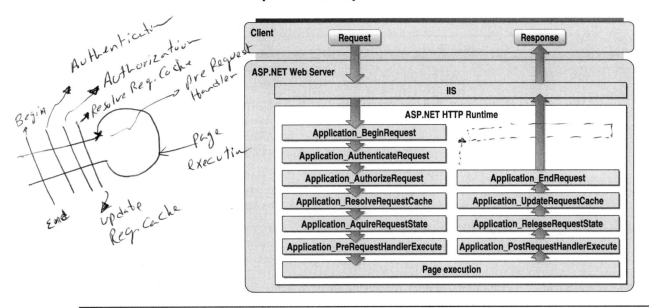

Introduction	The global.asax file is a declarative file that is used to handle events while your Web application is running.
Categories of events	The global.asax file supports three categories of events:
	■ Events that are fired when a page is requested.
	■ Events that are fired when the requested page is sent.
	■ Conditional application events.
Events that are fired when a page is requested	The following table lists the events that are fired when a page is requested.

Event Name	Description
Application_BeginRequest	This event is fired whenever a new request is received.
Application_AuthenticateRequest	This event indicates that the request is ready to be authenticated.
Application_AuthorizeRequest	This event signals that the request is ready to be authorized.
Application_ResolveRequestCache	This event is used by the output cache module to stop the processing of requests that have been cached.
Application_AcquireRequestState	This event signals that per-request state should be obtained.
Application_PreRequestHandlerExecute	This event signals that the request handler is about to execute.

Events that are fired when the requested page is sent

Global.asax also includes events that are fired when the requested page is sent back to the client. The following table lists these events.

Event Name	Description
Application_PostRequestHandlerExecute	This event is first available after the handler, such as an ASP.NET page or a Web service, has completed its work.
Application_ReleaseRequestState	This event is called when the request state should be stored, because the ASP.NET Web application is finished with it.
Application_UpdateRequestCache	This event signals that code processing is complete and that the file is ready to be added to the ASP.NET cache.
Application_EndRequest	This event is the last event that is called when the ASP.NET Web application ends.

Conditional application events

Conditional application events are events that may or may not be raised during the processing of a request. Some of the common conditional applications events are listed in the following table.

Event Name	Description
Application_Start	This event is raised when an ASP.NET Web application starts.
Application_End	This event is another single occurrence event. This event is the reciprocal event to **Application_Start**; this event is raised when the ASP.NET Web application is shutting down.
Session_Start	This event is raised when a user's **Session** begins within an ASP.NET Web application.
Session_End	This event is a reciprocal event to **Session_Start**; this event is raised when a user's session ends.
Application_Error	This event is fired when an unhandled error occurs within an ASP.NET Web application.

Lesson: Application and Session Variables

- Initializing Application and Session Variables
- Using Application and Session Variables
- Demonstration: Using Session Variables
- Application and Session Variable Duration
- Scalable Storage of Application and Session Variables
- Saving Application and Session Variables in a Database

Introduction

You can use the application and session variables to share information between the pages of an ASP.NET Web application. In this lesson, you will learn how to initialize and use the application and session variables. You will also learn how to specify the duration for the application and session variables and learn how the application and session variables impact scalable storage. Finally, you will learn how to save the application and session variables in a database.

Lesson objectives

After completing this lesson, you will be able to:

- Initialize application and session variables.
- Set and read application and session variables.
- Modify the application and session variable duration.
- Describe the in process and out of process methods that are used to store session state.
- Save application and session variables in a database.

Initializing Application and Session Variables

- **Variables are initialized in Global.asax**

    - The **Application** object shares information among all
      users of a Web application

```
Sub Application_Start(s As Object,e As EventArgs)
    Application("NumberofVisitors") = 0
End Sub
```

```
protected void Application_Start(Object sender,EventArgs e)
{
    Application["NumberofVisitors"] = 0;
}
```

    - The **Session** object stores information for a particular
      user session

Introduction

You initialize session and application variables in the **Start** event procedures of the **Application** and **Session** objects in the global.asax file.

Session variables

You use the **Session** object to store the information that is needed for a particular user session. Variables that are stored in the **Session** object will not be discarded when the user goes between the different pages in the Web application. Instead, these variables will persist for the entire user session.

The following code example illustrates how session variables are used to store the preferred color scheme of a particular user session:

Visual Basic® .NET

```
Sub Session_Start(ByVal Sender As Object, _
    ByVal e As EventArgs)
    Session("BackColor") = "beige"
    Session("ForeColor") = "black"
End Sub
```

C#

```
protected void Session_Start(Object sender, EventArgs e)
{
    Session["BackColor"] = "beige";
    Session["ForeColor"] = "black";
}
```

Application variables

You can use the **Application** object to share state information among all of the users of a Web application. An **Application** object is created when the first user of the Web application requests an .aspx file. The **Application** object is destroyed when all users have exited the Web application and the Web application is then unloaded.

For example, you might store the total number of visitors to a Web site in an application-level variable:

Visual Basic .NET

```
Sub Application_Start(ByVal Sender As Object, _
    ByVal e As EventArgs)
  Application("NumberofVisitors") = 0
End Sub
```

C#

```
protected void Application_Start(Object sender, EventArgs e)
{
  Application["NumberofVisitors"] = 0;
}
```

Using Application and Session Variables

- **Set session and application variables**

```
Session("BackColor") = "blue"
Application.Lock()
Application("NumberOfVisitors") += 1
Application.UnLock()
```

```
Session["BackColor"] = "blue";
Application.Lock();
Application["NumberOfVisitors"] =
                (int)Application["NumberOfVisitors"]  + 1;
Application.UnLock();
```

- **Read session and application variables**

```
strBgColor = Session("BackColor")
lblNbVisitor.Text = Application("NumberOfVisitors")
```

```
strBgColor = (string)Session["BackColor"];
lblNbVisitor.Text = Application["NumberOfVisitors"].ToString();
```

Introduction

To use application and session variables in ASP.NET, you simply use a string key and set a value.

Set session and application variables

To set the session variable, you must provide a key, which identifies the item that you are storing, by using a statement such as the following:

```
Session("BackColor") = "blue"
```

The preceding statement adds a key, named **BackColor**, to the session state with a value of **blue**.

Since application variables are accessible in a multi-user environment, whenever **Application** data is updated, you must prevent other users or applications from updating the data simultaneously. ASP.NET provides a simple set of locking methods, **Application.Lock()** and **Application.UnLock()**, which can be used to prevent multiple, concurrent access of the application variable. The following code demonstrates the use of the **Application.Lock()** and **Application.UnLock()** methods:

Visual Basic .NET

```
Application.Lock()
Application("NumberOfVisitors") += 1
Application.UnLock()
```

C#

```
Application.Lock();
Application["NumberofVisitors"] =
                (int)Application["NumberOfVisitors"] + 1;
Application.UnLock();
```

Read session and application variables

To use a session or application variable in an ASP.NET page, you simply need to read the value from the **Session** or **Application** object:

Visual Basic.NET

```
strBgColor = Session("BackColor")
lblNbVisitor.Text = Application("NumberOfVisitors")
```

C#

```
strBgColor = (string)Session["BackColor"];
lblNbVistitor.Text =
                Application["NumberofVisitors"].ToString();
```

Demonstration: Using Session Variables

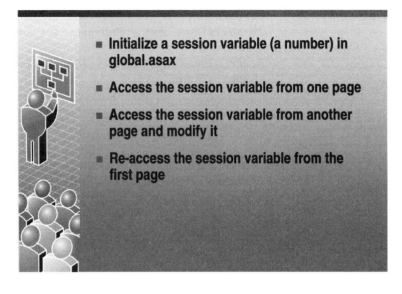

- Initialize a session variable (a number) in global.asax
- Access the session variable from one page
- Access the session variable from another page and modify it
- Re-access the session variable from the first page

Introduction

In this demonstration, you will learn to use session variables.

The code for this demonstration is in the Mod14VB and Mod14CS projects in the 2310Demos Solution.

▶ **To run the demonstration**

1. Open the Mod14VB or Mod14CS project in the 2310Demos solution.

2. Open the code-behind page for global.asax.

3. Initialize a session variable, named **intNumber**, to **3** by adding the following code to the **Session_Start** event procedure:

Visual Basic .NET

```
Session("intNumber") = 3
```

C#

```
Session["intNumber"] = 3;
```

4. Open the UsingSessionVar1.aspx and the UsingSessionVar2.aspx files.

   The session variable is retrieved and displayed in the **Page_Load** event procedure.

5. Build and browse the UsingSessionVar1 page.

   The value of the session variable, 3, is displayed.

6. Click Next Page.

   The UsingSessionVar2.aspx page opens, increments the session variable by 4, and then displays the new value, 7.

7. Click **Previous Page** to return to the UsingSessionVar1.aspx, which displays the new value of the session variable.

Application and Session Variable Duration

- **Session variables have a set duration after last access**
  - Default is 20 minutes
- **Session duration can be changed in Web.config:**

```
<configuration>
  <system.web>
      <sessionState timeout="10" />
  </system.web>
</configuration>
```

- **Application variables persist until the Application_End event is fired**

Introduction

HTTP is a stateless protocol. A Web server has no means of detecting when a user leaves a Web site. Instead, the Web server detects that a certain period of time has passed without the user requesting a page. At that point, the Web server assumes that the user has left the Web site, and it removes all of the items in session state that are associated with that user.

Default session duration

By default, a session times out when a user has not requested a page for more than 20 minutes. If the same user requests a page after a 20 minutes, that user is treated as a new user.

Note Setting smaller session duration makes your Web site save resources on your Web server. Conversely, if you expect the user to spend more than 20 minutes at your Web site, you should set a longer session duration.

Modify session duration

You can modify the session duration in the Web.config file. Web.config files are standard, human-readable Extensible Markup Language (XML) files that you can open and modify with any text editor. For example, in the following Web.config file, the session duration is set to10 minutes:

```
<configuration>
  <system.web>
      <sessionState timeout="10" />
  </system.web>
</configuration>
```

Application variable

Application variables persist until the **Application_End** event is fired. **Application_End** is raised immediately before the end of all application instances.

Scalable Storage of Application and Session Variables

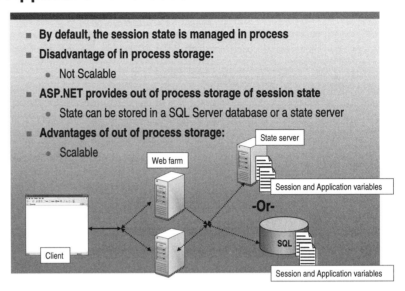

- **By default, the session state is managed in process**
- **Disadvantage of in process storage:**
  - Not Scalable
- **ASP.NET provides out of process storage of session state**
  - State can be stored in a SQL Server database or a state server
- **Advantages of out of process storage:**
  - Scalable

State server

Web farm

Session and Application variables

-Or-

Client

SQL

Session and Application variables

Introduction	By default, the session state is managed *in process*. In process means that all of the information that is added to a session state is stored in the same Web server that is running the ASP.NET Web application. However, storing session state in process has some significant disadvantages.
Disadvantage of in process	One of the major disadvantages in storing session state in process is that it limits the scalability of your Web site. You cannot configure multiple servers to handle requests.
Out of process	ASP.NET provides two methods that can be used to store session state out of process. You can:

- Manage session state with a SQL Server database.

- Manage session state with a separate state server.

    A state server can be any Microsoft Windows®-based server.

To store session state out of process, you must modify the Web.config file to set the **sessionstate** mode to the value **sqlserver** or **stateserver**, and then specify the location of the server. The **sqlserver** option is similar to the **stateserver** option, except that in the former the information persists to SQL Server rather than being stored in the computer's memory.

Advantage of out of process
The main advantage of separating the storage of session state from the Web application is that you can use an external state server or a computer running SQL Server to store session state, thereby making the Web application scalable. To have scalable ASP.NET Web applications, session state is shared across multiple servers that are supporting the Web farm scenario. In a Web farm scenario, multiple servers are configured to handle user requests and as a result, users can be routed dynamically from one server to another without losing the application and session variables. Moreover, session variables can be retrieved from any server of the Web farm because they are stored in a separate computer running SQL Server or state server.

Saving Application and Session Variables in a Database

① Configure the session state in Web.config

- Mode is set to **sqlserver** or **stateserver**

```
<sessionState mode="SQLServer"
    sqlConnectionString="data source=SQLServerName;
    Integrated security=true" />
```

② Then, configure the SQL server

```
c:\> OSQL -S SQLServerName -E <InstallSqlState.sql
```

- OSQL creates several stored procedures and
  temporary databases for storing the variables

Introduction

To save application and session variables in a SQL Server database or in a state server, you have to perform two steps:

1. Configure the session state in the Web.config file of your Web server.
2. Configure the SQL Server or the state server.

Configure the session state in the Web.config file of your ASP.NET Web server

In the Web.config file, you need to modify the configuration settings to set the **mode** attribute of the **sessionstate** to **sqlserver** or **stateserver**. Then, you need to modify the **sqlconnectionstring** attribute to identify the name of the computer running SQL Server or the state server.

For example, if you are using the **sqlserver** mode with integrated security, you must set the session state in Web.config as shown in the following code:

```
<sessionState mode="SQLServer"
    sqlConnectionString="data source=SQLServerName;
        Integrated security=true" />
```

Configure the SQL Server

To configure the SQL Server, you must use the command line tool that SQL Server provides, OSQL.exe.

OSQL.exe installs the database that is called ASPState, which is used to save the application and session variables.

To install the ASPState database by using integrated security, use the following syntax:

```
c:\> OSQL -S SQLServerName -E <InstallSqlState.sql
```

Important   The switches for the OSQL command are case-sensitive.

If you use a state server instead of SQL Server, you must start the ASP.NET Windows service instead of installing a database.

Lesson: Cookies and Cookieless Sessions

- ■ **Using Cookies to Store Session Data**
- ■ **Instructor-Led Practice: Using Variables and Cookies**
- ■ **Retrieving Information from a Cookie**
- ■ **Using Cookieless Sessions**
- ■ **Setting Up Cookieless Sessions**

Introduction

Cookies are a means by which the Web application running on the Web server can cause a client to return information to the Web server with each HTTP request. The returning of the information can be used to maintain state with the client across multiple requests. Cookies are sent to the client as part of the HTTP header in a client request, or are sent in a server response.

In this lesson, you will learn how to use cookies to store session data, and then learn how to retrieve that data from a cookie. You will also learn about cookieless sessions and setting up cookieless sessions.

Lesson objectives

After completing this lesson, you will be able to:

- ■ Use cookies to store session data.
- ■ Retrieve information from a cookie.
- ■ Describe cookieless sessions.
- ■ Set up a cookieless session.

Using Cookies to Store Session Data

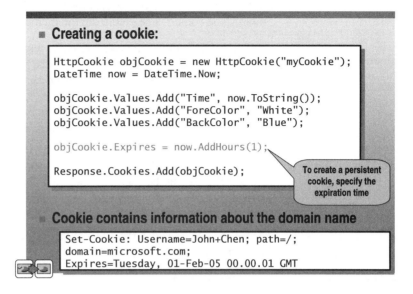

- **Creating a cookie:**

```
HttpCookie objCookie = new HttpCookie("myCookie");
DateTime now = DateTime.Now;

objCookie.Values.Add("Time", now.ToString());
objCookie.Values.Add("ForeColor", "White");
objCookie.Values.Add("BackColor", "Blue");

objCookie.Expires = now.AddHours(1);

Response.Cookies.Add(objCookie);
```

To create a persistent cookie, specify the expiration time

- **Cookie contains information about the domain name**

```
Set-Cookie: Username=John+Chen; path=/;
domain=microsoft.com;
Expires=Tuesday, 01-Feb-05 00.00.01 GMT
```

Introduction	You can create cookies by using the **Cookies** property of the **Response** object and **Request** class. The **Cookies** property represents a collection of cookies and is an instance of the **HttpCookieCollection** class.
Creating a cookie	The following code creates a new cookie named **myCookie**:
Visual Basic .NET	`Dim objCookie As New HttpCookie("myCookie")` `Dim now As DateTime = DateTime.Now`

C#	`HttpCookie objCookie = new HttpCookie("MyCookie");`
	`DateTime now = DateTime.Now;`
	
	The following code adds a pair of keys and values:

Visual Basic .NET	`objCookie.Values.Add("Time", now.ToString())`
	`objCookie.Values.Add("ForeColor", "White")`
	`objCookie.Values.Add("BackColor", "Blue")`

C#	`objCookie.Values.Add("Time", now.ToString());`
	`objCookie.Values.Add("ForeColor", "White");`
	`objCookie.Values.Add("BackColor", "Blue");`

Making a cookie persistent	The following code sets the expiration time of the cookie to one hour:
Visual Basic .NET	`objCookie.Expires = now.AddHours(1)`
C#	`objCookie.Expires = now.AddHours(1);`

If you do not add the preceding code while creating a cookie, the cookie that is created is a temporary cookie. The temporary cookie is added to the memory of the browser, but it will not be recorded to a file. When the user shuts down the browser, the cookie is deleted from the memory.

Adding the expiration time code turns the temporary cookie into a persistent cookie. The persistent cookie is saved to the hard disk. With a persistent cookie, if the user closes the browser and opens it again, the user can access the same Web page again until the persistent cookie expires. The expiration of the persistent cookie depends on the expiration time that was set in the code. In the preceding code, the persistent cookie will be deleted after one hour.

Note Persistent cookies are often used to store information about user names and user IDs so that the server can identify the same users when they return to the Web site.

The following code adds the new cookie to the cookie collection of the **Response** object:

Visual Basic .NET

```
Response.Cookies.Add(objCookie)
```

C#

```
Response.Cookies.Add(objCookie);
```

How cookies work

Suppose you want to create a cookie, named Username, which contains the name of a visitor to your Web site. To create this cookie, the Web server will send an HTTP header as shown in the following code:

```
Set-Cookie: Username=John+Chen; path=/; domain=microsoft.com;
Expires=Tuesday, 01-Feb-05 00.00.01 GMT
```

The header in the preceding code example instructs the browser to add an entry to its cookie file. The browser adds the cookie, named Username, with the value John Chen.

The **domain** attribute in the preceding code example restricts where the cookie can be sent by the browser. In the preceding code example, the cookie can be sent only to the Microsoft.com Web site. The cookie will never be sent to any other Web site on the Internet.

After the Web server creates a cookie, the browser returns the cookie in every request that it makes to that Web site. The browser returns the cookie in a header that looks like the following:

```
Cookie: Username: John+Chen
```

The cookies that are stored in a text file format are the persistent cookies. By default, this file is stored in the folder \Documents and Settings\ *Username*\Cookies.

When persistent cookies are stored by using Internet Explorer, the format of the text file is:

```
Username@DomainName.txt
```

Instructor-Led Practice: Using Variables and Cookies

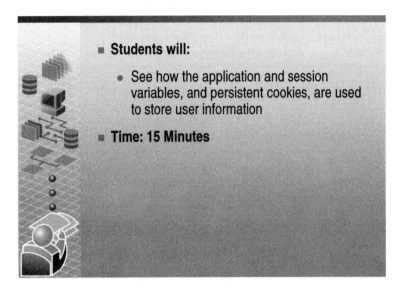

Introduction

In this practice, you will see how application and session variables, and persistent cookies, are used to store user information.

Testing functionality

▶ **Log on to the Web application**

1. Open Internet Explorer and browse to:

   http://*instructorsmachine*/Mod14VB/default.aspx or

   http://*instructorsmachine*/Mod14CS/default.aspx.

2. Type your name in the text box, select a color from the drop-down list box, and then click **Submit**.

   You are redirected to results.aspx, which displays your name, selected color, and the date and time when you last accessed default.aspx. The results.aspx also displays the number of visitors.

3. Refresh the browser a few times.

   Each refresh results in the number of visitors increasing, but your name and color selection remain.

4. Close Internet Explorer.

5. Reopen Internet Explorer and browse to:

   http://*instructorsmachine*/Mod14VB/results.aspx or

   http://*instructorsmachine*/Mod14CS/results.aspx.

   Your name appears, but the color you previously chose is not displayed. The date and time you last accessed default.aspx is also displayed.

6. Close Internet Explorer.

   Why do you think that your name is remembered when you revisit the site, but not your color choice?

   _____

   _____

   How is the page keeping track of the number of visitors?

   _____

   _____

   ▶ **Viewing the code**

   1. In the address box of Windows Explorer, type:

      instructorsmachine\c$\inetpub\wwwroot\mod14VB or

      instructorsmachine\c$\inetpub\wwwroot\mod14CS

      and then press ENTER.

   2. Open the code-behind page for the **Default.aspx** page.

      In the **btnSubmit_Click** event procedure, what two actions occur?

      _____

      _____

   3. In Windows Explorer, double-click **results.aspx.vb** or **results.aspx.cs** to open the results.aspc code-behind page file in Visual Studio .NET.

      In the **Page_Load** event procedure, how are the numbers of visits to the page stored?

      _____

      _____

      Why is the code placed in an **If** statement in the **Page_Load** event procedure?

      _____

      _____

   4. Close Visual Studio .NET.

▶ **View the cookie**

1. In Windows Explorer, browse to the following directory on your computer:

   c:\Documents and Settings\Student\Cookies

   Note If you are logged on as someone other than Student, browse to the Cookies folder for that user account.

   ---

2. Double-click to open the cookie named **student**@*instructorsmachine*[*n*]**.txt**, where *n* is an instance number.

   What information can you find in this cookie?

   _____

   _____

3. Close Microsoft Notepad and Windows Explorer.

Retrieving Information from a Cookie

■ **Read the cookie**

```
Dim objCookie As HttpCookie = Request.Cookies("myCookie")
```

```
HttpCookie objCookie = Request.Cookies["myCookie"];
```

■ **Retrieve values from the cookie**

```
lblTime.Text = objCookie.Values("Time")
lblTime.ForeColor = System.Drawing.Color.FromName _
                              (objCookie.Values("ForeColor"))
lblTime.BackColor = System.Drawing.Color.FromName _
                              (objCookie.Values("BackColor"))
```

```
lblTime.Text = objCookie.Values["Time"];
lblTime.ForeColor = System.Drawing.Color.FromName
                              (objCookie.Values["ForeColor"]);
lblTime.BackColor = System.Drawing.Color.FromName
                              (objCookie.Values["BackColor"]);
```

Introduction	Retrieving information from a cookie involves reading a cookie and retrieving the key/value pairs from the cookie.
Read a cookie	A cookie is returned to the server by the client in an HTTP **"Cookie:"** header. Multiple cookies, separated by semicolons, can appear in this header. To read an existing cookie, you access the cookies collection of the **Request** object, as shown in the following code:

Visual Basic

```
Dim objCookie As HttpCookie = Request.Cookies("myCookie")
```

C#

```
HttpCookie objCookie = Request.Cookies["myCookie"];
```

Retrieve values from the cookie

The following code displays the values that need to be retrieved from a cookie:

Visual Basic .NET

```
lblTime.Text = objCookie.Values("Time")
lblTime.ForeColor = System.Drawing.Color.FromName _
                              (objCookie.Values("ForeColor"))
lblTime.BackColor = System.Drawing.Color.FromName _
                              (objCookie.Values("BackColor"))
```

C#

```
lblTime.Text = objCookie.Values["Time"];
lblTime.ForeColor = System.Drawing.Color.FromName
                              (objCookie.Values["ForeColor"]);
lblTime.BackColor = System.Drawing.Color.FromName
                              (objCookie.Values["BackColor"]);
```

Using Cookieless Sessions

- **Each active session is identified and tracked using session IDs**

- **Session IDs are communicated across client-server requests using an HTTP cookie or included in the URL**

- **Cookieless sessions**

  - Session ID information is encoded into URLs

  `http://server/(h44a1e55c0breu552yrecob1)/page.aspx`

  - Cannot use absolute URLs

  - Most browsers limit the URL size to 255 characters, which limits use of cookieless Session IDs

Introduction

Each active session is identified and tracked using a **SessionID**. The **SessionID** is communicated across client-server requests by using an HTTP cookie or by including it in the URL. By default, **SessionID** is stored in cookies.

Users can, however, disable cookies through a setting in their browsers. If the cookie cannot be added to a user's browser, every request that is made by the user starts a new user session. Any session data that was associated with that user is lost when a new page is requested.

Cookieless sessions

The ASP.NET page framework includes an option to enable cookieless sessions. Cookieless sessions enable you to take advantage of session state even with browsers that have cookie support disabled.

When a user makes the first request to a Web site with cookieless sessions enabled, the URL that is used for the request is automatically modified to include the user's SessionID. For example, when a user makes a request for http://server/page.aspx, the request is automatically modified to:

`http://server/(h44a1e55c0breu552yrecob1)/page.aspx`

The part of the URL that appears in parentheses is the SessionID for the current user.

After the SessionID is embedded in the URL of the first page request, the SessionID tracks the user throughout his or her visit to the Web site.

Limitation of cookieless sessions

There are certain limitations to using cookieless sessions:

- If you choose to use cookieless sessions, you cannot use absolute URLs when linking between pages. You must design your Web site in a way that every link uses a URL that is relative to the current page.

- Most browsers limit the URL size to 255 characters.

Setting Up Cookieless Sessions

- Session state is configured in the <SessionState> section of Web.config

- Set cookieless = true

```
<sessionState cookieless="true" />
```

Introduction

You enable cookieless sessions by modifying a single attribute in the Web.config file.

Setting up a cookieless session

In the Web.config file, in the **<sessionstate>** section, the **cookieless** attribute is set to the value **true**. Setting this value is the only thing that you need to do enable cookieless sessions, as shown in the following code:

```
<sessionState cookieless="true" />
```

Review

- State Management
- Application and Session Variables
- Cookies and Cookieless Sessions

1. How do you set up a Web application to use cookieless sessions?

2. What are the three categories of events that are handled in the global.asax file?

3. Where is global.asax file of an application located?

4. Can there be more than one global.asax file for a single Web application?

5. What are the two steps that need to be performed with ASP.NET to use session variables in a Web farm?

6. What is the difference between a temporary cookie and a persistent cookie?

7. What is used to retain the **SessionID** of a session variable?

Lab 14: Storing Application and Session Data

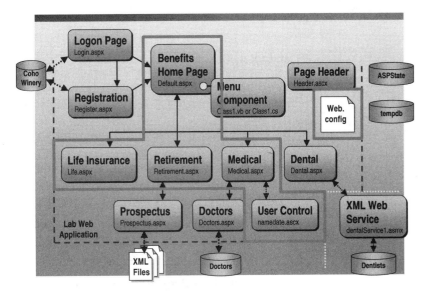

Objectives

After completing this lab, you will be able to:

- Create session and application variables and then use them to store and retrieve information.

- Create, read to, and write from persistent cookies.

- Store session variables in a Microsoft® SQL Server™ database.

Note This lab focuses on the concepts in this module and as a result may not comply with Microsoft security recommendations.

Prerequisites

Before working on this lab, you must have:

- Knowledge of how to create session and application variables.

- Knowledge of how to create cookies.

Scenario

Coho Winery offers several benefits to its employees. In the labs for Course 2310B, *Developing Microsoft ASP.NET Web Applications Using Visual Studio .NET*, you will create a Web site that enables employees to select and set up their chosen benefits.

In this lab, you will use session and application variables to enhance the users experience for when they are browsing the benefits Web site.

Estimated time to complete this lab: 90 minutes

Exercise 0
Lab Setup

To complete this lab, you must have created a Benefits Web Application project and a BenefitsList Class Library project. These projects can be created by using Microsoft Visual Basic® .NET or Microsoft Visual C#™ .NET.

If you have not created these projects, complete the following steps:

▶ **Create the 2310LabApplication solution**

Important   Only perform this procedure if you have not created a 2310LabApplication solution file.

---

1. Using Microsoft Visual Studio® .NET, create a new blank solution named **2310LabApplication**:

   a. On the **File** menu, point to **New**, and then click **Blank Solution**.

   b. In the **New Project** dialog box, type **2310LabApplication** in the **Name** text box, and then click **OK**.

▶ **Create the Benefits project**

Important   Only perform this procedure if you have not previously created a Benefits project, or if you have removed the Benefits project according to the steps in Appendix A, "Lab Recovery," in Course 2310B, *Developing Microsoft ASP.NET Web Applications Using Visual Studio .NET.*

---

1. Create a new Microsoft ASP.NET Web Application project, named **BenefitsVB** or **BenefitsCS**, in the 2310LabApplication solution:

   a. On the **File** menu, point to **New**, and then click **Project**.

   b. In the **New Project** dialog box, in the **Project Types** list, click **Visual Basic Projects** or **Visual C# Projects**.

   c. In the **Templates** list, click **ASP.NET Web Application**. Set the **Location** to **http://localhost/BenefitsVB** for the Visual Basic .NET project or to **http:/localhost/BenefitsCS** for the Microsoft Visual C#™ project.

   d. Click **Add to Solution**, and then click **OK**.

Caution   When adding projects to the solution, the capitalization of the project name is important. Because you may be using some pre-built Web Forms in this and other labs in Course 2310B, *Developing Microsoft ASP.NET Web Applications Using Visual Studio .NET*, you must verify that you have capitalized the Benefits project as shown.

▶ **Update the Benefits project**

1. In Visual Studio .NET, open the 2310LabApplication solution file.

2. In Solution Explorer, right-click **BenefitsVB** or **BenefitsCS**, point to **Add**, and then click **Add Existing Item**.

3. Browse for project files:

For the Visual Basic .NET project

Browse to the *install folder*\Labfiles\Lab14\VB\Starter\BenefitsVB folder.

For the Visual C# project

Browse to the *install folder*\Labfiles\Lab14\CS\Starter\BenefitsCS folder.

4. In the **Files of type** box of the **Add Existing Item – Benefits** dialog box, click **All Files (*.*)**.

5. Select all of the files in this folder, and then click **Open**.

6. Click **Yes** if prompted to overwrite or reload files.

▶ **Create the BenefitsList class library**

Important Only perform these steps if you have not previously created a BenefitsList project, or if you have removed the BenefitsList project according to the steps in Appendix A, "Lab Recovery," in Course 2310B, *Developing Microsoft ASP.NET Web Applications Using Visual Studio .NET*.

---

1. Create a new Class Library Project.

For the Visual Basic .NET project

Create a new Visual Basic .NET Class Library project, name it **BenefitsListVB**, and then add it to the 2310LabApplication solution:

a. On the **File** menu, point to **New**, and then click **Project**.

b. In the **New Project** dialog box, in the **Project Types list**, click **Visual Basic Projects**.

c. In the **Templates** list, click **Class Library** set the **Name** to **BenefitsListVB**.

d. Click **Add to Solution**, and then click **OK**.

For the Visual C# project

Create a new Visual C# .NET Class Library project, name it **BenefitsListCS**, and then add it to the 2310LabApplication solution:

a. On the **File** menu, point to **New**, and then click **Project**.

b. In the **New Project** dialog box, in the **Project Types** list, click **Visual C# Projects**.

c. In the **Templates** list, click **Class Library**, and then set the **Name** to **BenefitsListCS**.

d. Click **Add to Solution**, and then click **OK**.

Caution Verify that you have capitalized the BenefitsList project as shown.

▶ **Update the BenefitsList project**

1. In Visual Studio .NET, open the 2310LabApplication solution file.

2. In Solution Explorer, right-click **BenefitsListVB** or **BenefitsListCS**, point to **Add**, and then click **Add Existing Item**.

3. Browse for project files:

For the Visual Basic .NET project

Browse to the *install folder*\Labfiles\Lab14\VB\Starter\BenefitsListVB folder.

For the Visual C# Project

Browse to the *install folder*\Labfiles\Lab14\CS\Starter\BenefitsListCS folder.

4. In the **Files of type** box of the **Add Existing Item – BenefitsList** dialog box, click **All Files (*.*)**.

5. Select all of the files in this folder, and then click **Open**.

6. Click **Yes** if prompted to overwrite or reload files.

▶ **Create a reference to the BenefitsList component in the Benefits project**

1. In the Benefits project in the 2310LabApplication solution, complete the following steps to add a reference to the BenefitsList component that you just created:

   a. Right-click the **BenefitsVB** or **BenefitsCS** project in Solution Explorer and then click **Add Reference**.

   b. In the **Add Reference** dialog box, on the **Projects** tab, double-click the **BenefitsListVB** or **BenefitsListCS** project.

   c. In the **Selected Components** list, select the **BenefitsListVB** or **BenefitsListCS** component, and then click **OK**.

      The component is added to the References folder in Solution Explorer.

▶ **Create the Dental XML Web Service**

Important   Only perform this procedure if you have not previously created the DentalService project, or if you have removed the DentalService project according to the steps in Appendix A, "Lab Recovery," in Course 2310B, *Developing Microsoft ASP.NET Web Applications Using Visual Studio .NET*.

---

1. Create a new XML Web Service project.

For Visual Basic .NET Project

Create a new Visual Basic .NET XML Web Service project, named **DentalServiceVB**, and then add it to the 2310LabApplication solution:

   a. On the **File** menu, point to **New**, and then click **Project**.

   b. In the **New Project** dialog box, in the **Project Types** list, click **Visual Basic Projects**.

   c. In the **Templates** list, click **ASP.NET Web Service**, and then set the **Location** to **http://localhost/DentalServiceVB**.

   d. Click **Add to Solution**, and then click **OK**.

Caution   Verify that you have capitalized the DentalServiceVB project as shown.

For Visual C# .NET Project

Create a new Visual C# .NET XML Web Service project named **DentalServiceCS**, and then add it to the 2310LabApplication solution:

a. On the **File** menu, point to **New**, and then click **Project**.

b. In the **New Project** dialog box, in the **Project Types** list, click **Visual Basic Projects**.

c. In the **Templates** list, click **ASP.NET Web Service**, and then set the **Location** to **http://localhost/DentalServiceCS**.

d. Click **Add to Solution**, and then click **OK**.

Caution   Verify that you have capitalized the DentalServiceCS project as shown.

▶ **Update the DentalService project**

1. In Visual Studio .NET, open the 2310LabApplication solution file.

2. In Solution Explorer, right-click **DentalServiceVB** or **DentalServiceCS**, point to **Add**, and then click **Add Existing Item**.

3. Browse for project files:

For Visual Basic .NET Project

Browse to the *install folder*\Labfiles\Lab14\VB\Starter\DentalServiceVB folder.

For Visual C# .NET Project

Browse to the *install folder*\Labfiles\Lab14\CS\Starter\DentalServiceCS folder.

4. In the **Files of type** box of the **Add Existing Item – DentalService** dialog, click **All Files (*.*)**.

5. Select all of the files in this folder, and then click **Open**.

6. Click **Yes** if prompted to overwrite or reload files.

7. Build the DentalService XML Web service by right-clicking the **DentalServiceVB** or **DentalServiceCS** project in Solution Explorer and clicking **Build**.

► **Add a Web reference in the Benefits project to the DentalService Web service**

1. In the Benefits project in the 2310LabApplication solution, complete the following steps to add a Web reference to the DentalService XML Web service:

   a. In Solution Explorer, right-click **BenefitsVB** or **BenefitsCS** and then click **Add Web Reference**.

   b. In the Address text box, type **http://localhost/DentalServiceVB/DentalService1.asmx** or **http://localhost/DentalServiceCS/DentalService1.asmx** and then press ENTER.

   The DentalService1 Web reference will then be displayed.

   c. Click **Add Reference**.

   The Web reference is added to the project in the Web References folder.

2. In Solution Explorer, expand **Web References**, right-click **localhost**, and then click **Rename**.

3. Type **DentalWebRef**, and then press ENTER.

4. Build the solution by clicking **Build Solution** on the **Build** menu.

Exercise 1
Using Session Variables

Scenario

In this exercise, you will store the user's name and birth date in session variables. Both the namedate.ascx user control and the life.aspx page will look for the session variables and then fill the appropriate text boxes with the information, if it is available. If the session variables do not yet exist, either page will create the session variables.

In the current Web application, a user must enter redundant information on multiple pages. For example, the user is required to supply their name and birth date on both the medical page and the life insurance page. To simplify using the Web application, you will use a cookie to store this information in session variables so that the user only needs to enter this information once.

▶ **Get and set session variables in life.aspx**

1. In Visual Studio .NET, open the life.aspx code behind page in the Benefits project.

2. Add code to the **Page_Load** event procedure that gets the **Name** and **Birth** session variables, but only when the page is not being posted back.

3. Set the **Text** property for the **txtName** text box to the content of the **Name** session variable, and set the **Text** property of the **txtBirth** text box to the content of the **Birth** session variable.

4. Your code should look like the following:

Visual Basic .NET

```
If Not (Page.IsPostBack) Then
    Dim strName As String = CStr(Session("Name"))
    Dim strBirth As String = CStr(Session("Birth"))
    txtName.Text = strName
    txtBirth.Text = strBirth
End If
```

Visual C#

```
if (!Page.IsPostBack)
{
    string strName = (string)Session["Name"];
    string strBirth = (string)Session["Birth"];
    txtName.Text = strName;
    txtBirth.Text = strBirth;
}
```

5. In the **cmdSave_Click** event procedure, find the following comment:

Visual Basic .NET

```
'TODO Lab 14: Set Session Variables
```

Visual C#

```
//TODO Lab 14: Set Session Variables
```

Note If this code section is not in your life.aspx file, you can copy the code from the life.aspx file in the
install folder\Labfiles\Lab14\VB\Starter\BenefitsVB or
install folder\Labfiles\Lab14\CS\Starter\BenefitsCS folder.

6. Add code below this comment that assigns the text in the **txtName** text box to the **Name** session variable, and assigns the text in the **txtBirth** text box to the **Birth** session variable.

7. Your code should look like the following:

Visual Basic .NET

```
Session("Name") = txtName.Text
Session("Birth") = txtBirth.Text
```

Visual C#

```
Session["Name"] = txtName.Text;
Session["Birth"] = txtBirth.Text;
```

▶ **Get and set session variables in namedate.ascx code-behind page**

1. Open namedate.ascx.vb or namedate.ascx.cs.

   This is the user control that displays the name and birth date on the medical.aspx Web Form.

2. Add code to the **Page_Load** event procedure that retrieves the **Name** and **Birth** session variables, but only when the page is not being posted back.

3. Set the **Text** property for the **txtName** text box to the content of the **Name** session variable, and set the **Text** property of the **txtBirth** text box to the content of the **Birth** session variable.

4. Your code should look like the following:

Visual Basic .NET

```
If Not (Page.IsPostBack) Then
    Dim strName As String = CStr(Session("Name"))
    Dim strBirth As String = CStr(Session("Birth"))
    txtName.Text = strName
    txtBirth.Text = strBirth
End If
```

Visual C#

```
if (!Page.IsPostBack)
{
    string strName = (string)Session["Name"];
    string strBirth = (string)Session["Birth"];
    txtName.Text = strName;
    txtBirth.Text = strBirth;
}
```

5. In the **Get** statement for the Public Property **strName**, add a line of code preceding the **Return** statement that sets the **Name** session variable to the text that is in the **txtName** text box.

   The **Get** statement should look like the following:

Visual Basic .NET

```
Get
    Session("Name") = txtName.Text
    Return txtName.Text
End Get
```

Visual C#

```
get
{
    Session["Name"] = txtName.Text;
    return txtName.Text;
}
```

6. In the **Get** statement for the Public Property **dtDate**, add a line of code preceding the **Return** statement that sets the **Birth** session variable to the text that is in the **txtBirth** text box.

   The **Get** statement should look like the following:

Visual Basic .NET

```
Get
    Session("Birth") = txtBirth.Text
    Return CDate(txtBirth.Text)
End Get
```

Visual C#

```
get
{
    Session["Birth"] = txtBirth.Text;
    return Convert.ToDateTime(txtBirth.Text);
}
```

⬐ Test the code

1. Build and browse life.aspx.

2. In the browser, type your name in the **Name** text box, type your birth date in the **Birthdate** text box, and then type **400** in the **Coverage** text box.

3. Click **Save**.

4. At the top of the life.aspx Web Form, click the link for Medical.

   In the **medical.aspx** Web Form, your name and birth date appear. These values were obtained from the session variables.

5. Change your name in the text box, and then click **Save**.

6. Click the link to Life Insurance and verify that your name has changed in the life.aspx Web Form.

Exercise 2
Using Cookies

In this exercise, you will use cookies to store all of the user's benefits selections. When the user returns to the default.aspx page, his or her selections are listed on the page.

Scenario

Before the user completes the benefits registration process, he or she should be able to see his or her selections on a single page. You have chosen to list the selected benefits on the default.aspx page. You will show all of the selected benefits on the default.aspx page by using a persistent cookie.

For both the medical.aspx and life.aspx pages, you will add code that reads the existing values from the cookie, and then updates the values and re-writes the cookie.

▶ **Configure the home page**

1. Open the default.aspx page.

2. Add two labels and two text box controls to the bottom of the Web Form, so that the Web Form looks like the following illustration.

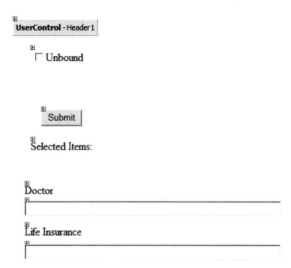

3. Name the first text box **txtDoctor** and the second text box **txtLife**.

4. Open default.aspx.vb or default.aspx.cs.

5. In the **Page_Load** event procedure, add code to read from a cookie named **Benefits**. This code should be added after the existing **Page.IsPostBack** condition.

6. Declare two variables, **strDoc** and **strLife**, which will hold the **doctors** and **life** values from the **Benefits** cookie.

7. If the cookie exists and is not empty, set the **Text** property of the **txtDoctors** text box to **strDoc**, and set the text property of **txtLife** to **strLife**.

Your code should look like the following:

Visual Basic .NET

```
Dim objGetCookie As HttpCookie = _
        Request.Cookies("Benefits")
Dim strDoc As String
Dim strLife As String

If Not objGetCookie Is Nothing Then
    strDoc = objGetCookie.Values("doctor")
    strLife = objGetCookie.Values("life")
    txtDoctor.Text = strDoc
    txtLife.Text = strLife
End If
```

Visual C#

```
HttpCookie objGetCookie =
        Request.Cookies["Benefits"];
string strDoc;
string strLife;

if (objGetCookie != null)
{
    strDoc = objGetCookie.Values["doctor"];
    strLife = objGetCookie.Values["life"];
    txtDoctor.Text = strDoc;
    txtLife.Text = strLife;
}
```

8. Save default.aspx.

▶ **Store the doctor selection**

1. Open medical.aspx.vb or medical.aspx.cs.

2. In the **cmdSave_Click** event procedure, add code that retrieves all of the information from the Benefits cookie, but only if the cookie exists and contains information.

   This added code should include two string variables that hold the doctor and life insurance values from the cookie. Your code should look like the following:

Visual Basic .NET

```
Dim objCookie As HttpCookie = Request.Cookies("Benefits")
Dim strDoc As String
Dim strLife As String

If Not objCookie Is Nothing Then
   strDoc = objCookie.Values("doctor")
   strLife = objCookie.Values("life")
End If
```

Visual C#

```
HttpCookie objGetCookie = Request.Cookies["Benefits"];
string strDoc ="";
string strLife ="";

if (objGetCookie != null)
{
   strDoc = objGetCookie.Values["doctor"];
   strLife = objGetCookie.Values["life"];
}
```

3. Add code to do the following tasks:

   a. Update the value of the **strDoc** variable to the text that is contained in the **txtDoctor** text box.

   b. Create a new cookie object, **objNewCookie,** with a cookie name of **Benefits**.

      This will replace the existing Benefits cookie with a new cookie that contains the updated information.

   c. Set the expiration date for the Benefits cookie to 30 days from the present date.

   d. Add two values, named **doctor** and **life**, to the cookie. These values will hold **strDoc** and **strLife**, respectively.

   e. Write the **objNewCookie** cookie.

Your code should look like the following:

Visual Basic .NET

```
strDoc = txtDoctor.Text
Dim objNewCookie As New HttpCookie("Benefits")
objNewCookie.Expires = DateTime.Now.AddDays(30)
objNewCookie.Values.Add("doctor", strDoc)
objNewCookie.Values.Add("life", strLife)
Response.Cookies.Add(objNewCookie)
```

Visual C#

```
strDoc = txtDoctor.Text;
HttpCookie objNewCookie = new HttpCookie("Benefits");
objNewCookie.Expires = DateTime.Now.AddDays(30);
objNewCookie.Values.Add("doctor", strDoc);
objNewCookie.Values.Add("life", strLife);
Response.Cookies.Add(objNewCookie);
```

4. Finally, you must add code to the **cmdSave_Click** event procedure that redirects the user back to the default.aspx page. Your added code should look like the following:

Visual Basic .NET

```
Response.Redirect("default.aspx")
```

Visual C#

```
Response.Redirect("default.aspx");
```

5. Save the medical.aspx.vb or medical.aspx.cs file.

▶ **Store the life insurance selections**

1. Open life.aspx.vb or life.aspx.cs.

2. In the **cmdSave_Click** event procedure, add code that retrieves all of the information from the Benefits cookie, but only if the cookie exists and it is not empty.

   This code is identical to the code that you added to medical.aspx.

3. Find the following line of code:

Visual Basic .NET

```
'TODO Lab 14: Build the string
```

Visual C#

```
//TODO Lab 14: Build the string
```

Note If this code section is not in your life.aspx file, you can copy the code from the life.aspx file in the
install folder\Labfiles\Lab14\VB\Starter\BenefitsVB or
install folder\Labfiles\Lab14\CS\Starter\BenefitsCS folder.

---

4. Uncomment the code below this comment.

   This code builds a string that includes the selected life insurance options and the value that was entered for the coverage amount.

5. Add code to create and write the Benefits cookie.

   This code is identical to the code that you added in medical.aspx.

6. Add code to redirect the page back to the default.aspx page.

7. When finished, the entire **cmdSave_Click** event procedure for life.aspx should look like the following:

Visual Basic .NET

```
If Page.IsValid Then
    lblMessage.Text = "Valid!"

    'TODO Lab 14: Set Session Variables
    Session("Name") = txtName.Text
    Session("Birth") = txtBirth.Text

    Dim objCookie As HttpCookie = _
        Request.Cookies("Benefits")
    Dim strDoc As String
    Dim strLife As String

    If Not objCookie Is Nothing Then
        strDoc = objCookie.Values("doctor")
        strLife = objCookie.Values("life")
    End If

    If (chkShortTerm.Checked) Then
        If (chkLongTerm.Checked) Then
            strLife = "Short Term and Long Term"
        Else
            strLife = "Short Term"
        End If
    ElseIf (chkLongTerm.Checked) Then
        strLife = "Long Term"
    End If
    strLife &= ": Coverage = $" & txtCoverage.Text

    Dim objNewCookie As New HttpCookie("Benefits")
    objNewCookie.Expires = DateTime.Now.AddDays(30)
    objNewCookie.Values.Add("doctor", strDoc)
    objNewCookie.Values.Add("life", strLife)
    Response.Cookies.Add(objNewCookie)
    Response.Redirect("default.aspx")

End If
```

Note You can copy and paste this code from the file *install folder*\LabFiles\Lab14\VB\Starter\life.txt.

Visual C#

```csharp
if (Page.IsValid)
{
    lblMessage.Text = "Valid!";

    //TODO Lab 14: Set Session Variables
    Session["Name"] = txtName.Text;
    Session["Birth"] = txtBirth.Text;

    HttpCookie objCookie =
        Request.Cookies["Benefits"];
    string strDoc = "";
    string strLife = "";

    if (objCookie != null)
    {
        strDoc = objCookie.Values["doctor"];
        strLife = objCookie.Values["life"];
    }

    if (chkShortTerm.Checked)
    {
        if (chkLongTerm.Checked)
        {
            strLife = "Short Term and Long Term";
        }
        else
        {
            strLife = "Short Term";
        }
    }
    else if (chkLongTerm.Checked)
    {
        strLife = "Long Term";
    }

    strLife += ": Coverage = $" + txtCoverage.Text;

    HttpCookie objNewCookie = new HttpCookie("Benefits");
    objNewCookie.Expires = DateTime.Now.AddDays(30);
    objNewCookie.Values.Add("doctor", strDoc);
    objNewCookie.Values.Add("life", strLife);
    Response.Cookies.Add(objNewCookie);
    Response.Redirect("default.aspx");
}
```

Note You can copy and paste this code from the file
install folder\LabFiles\Lab14\CS\Starter\life.txt.

8. Save the life.aspx.vb or life.aspx.cs file.

▶ **Test the cookie**

1. Build and browse default.aspx.

2. Click the link for **Medical**.

3. Fill in the required information, and then click **Save**.

4. You are then returned to default.aspx, and the doctor information has been filled in.

5. Click the **Life Insurance** link.

6. Fill in the required information, select one or both of the term coverage options, and then click **Save**.

7. You are returned to default.aspx and the life insurance information has been filled in.

Exercise 3
Using Application Variables

In this exercise, you will add a page counter to the retirement.aspx page.

Scenario

You want to provide a quick and easy way for management to see how many employees are accessing the new Benefits Web site. As such, you have decided to implement a page counter on the default.aspx page by using an application variable. You want to ensure that the counter is not increased when a page postback occurs, but rather only counts unique visits to the page.

▶ **Add user interface (UI) components**

1. Open the retirement.aspx page.

2. Add two labels and a text box to the bottom of the form, so that the Web Form resembles the following illustration.

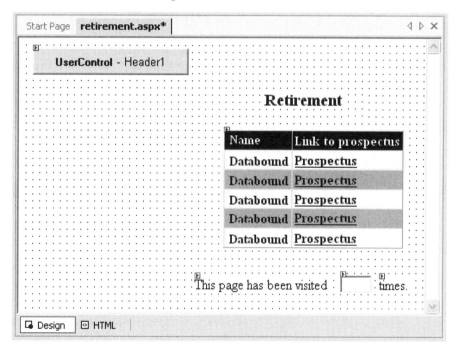

3. Name the new text box **txtVisits**.

▶ **Add the code**

1. In the **Page_Load** event procedure, add code that increments the value of the application variable **Visits** by one.

2. The code should lock the application variable before incrementing it, and the code should then unlock it after incrementing it. Place the code so that it runs only when the page is not posted back.

3. Add code to set the **Text** property of **txtVisits** to the value that is stored in the **Visits** application variable. This code should run with every page load.

4. When complete, the **Page_Load** event procedure should look like the following:

Visual Basic .NET

```
If Not Page.IsPostBack Then
   Dim dsRetirement As New DataSet()
   dsRetirement.ReadXml( _
      Server.MapPath("mutual_funds.xml"))
   dgRetirement.DataSource = dsRetirement
   dgRetirement.DataBind()

   Application.Lock()
   Application("Visits") = CInt(Application("Visits")) + 1
   Application.UnLock()
End If

txtVisits.Text = CStr(Application("Visits"))
```

Visual C#

```
if (!Page.IsPostBack)
{
   DataSet dsRetirement = new DataSet();
   dsRetirement.ReadXml(
      Server.MapPath["mutual_funds.xml"]);
   dgRetirement.DataSource = dsRetirement;
   dgRetirement.DataBind();

   Application.Lock();
   Application["Visits"]
=Convert.ToInt16(Application["Visits"]) + 1;
   Application.UnLock();
}

txtVisits.Text = Application["Visits"].ToString();
```

▶ **Test the application variable**

1. Build and browse the retirement.aspx page.

2. Refresh the browser.

3. The page counter increases with each refresh of the page.

Exercise 4
Storing Session Variables In a Database

In this exercise, you will store the user name and birth date session variables in a SQL Server database.

Scenario

To prepare your Web site for deployment on a Web form, you want the session variables to be stored in a central location. You have chosen to use a SQL Server database for this short-term storage solution.

▶ **Configure Web.config**

1. Open the Web.config file for the Benefits Web application.

2. Find the **sessionState** element.

3. Change the mode for the **sessionState** to **SQLServer**, and then set the connection string to use integrated security to connect to **localhost**.

   When complete, the **sessionState** element should look like the following:

   ```
   <sessionState
        mode="SQLServer"
        stateConnectionString="tcpip=127.0.0.1:42424"
        sqlConnectionString="data source=127.0.0.1;
            Integrated Security=SSPI"
        cookieless="false"
        timeout="20"
   />
   ```

   Important   Because the Web.config file is an Extensible Markup Language (XML) file, proper capitalization of the element and attribute names is critical.

   ---

4. Save the Web.config file.

▶ **Install and configure the databases**

Session variables are stored in two pre-configured databases, which are named **ASPState** and **tempdb**. To install and configure the databases, you must perform the following steps:

1. From the **Start** menu, point to **All Programs**, point to **Accessories**, and then click **Command Prompt**.

   A command window opens.

2. At the command prompt, type the following command, where *version* is the latest version of the Microsoft .NET Framework that is installed on your computer, and then press ENTER:

   ```
   cd\WINDOWS\Microsoft.NET\Framework\version\
   ```

   The command prompt changes to the new directory.

3. At the command prompt, type the following command, and then press ENTER:

```
OSQL -S localhost -E <InstallSqlState.sql
```

The command window displays a series of numbers and messages, and then returns to the command prompt. The **ASPState** and **tempdb** databases have been restored.

4. Close the command prompt, and then open Windows Explorer.

5. Browse to the following directory:

Visual Basic .NET

installfolder\LabFiles\lab14\VB\Starter

Visual C#

installfolder\LabFiles\lab14\CS\Starter

6. Double-click **Lab14.bat**.

This batch file runs an SQL query that configures security for the **ASPState** and **tempdb** databases.

7. Close Windows Explorer.

▶ **Test the Web application**

1. Build and browse the default.aspx page to test the Benefits Web application.

2. Click the link to **Medical**, enter the necessary information, and then click **Save**.

3. Click the link for **Life Insurance**.

Verify that the session variables that hold your name and birth date work properly.

msdn® training

Module 15: Configuring, Optimizing, and Deploying a Microsoft ASP.NET Web Application

Contents

Overview

- Using the Cache Object
- Using ASP.NET Output Caching
- Configuring an ASP.NET Web Application
- Deploying an ASP.NET Web Application

Introduction

After you have finished development of your Microsoft® ASP.NET Web application, you can deploy it on a production server. However, before deployment, you may want to optimize the Web application to improve performance.

You can optimize and then deploy the Web application by:

- Setting up the **Cache** object and the output cache to optimize response times for the Web application.

- Organizing the application settings in the Machine.config and Web.config files to both support and protect the Web site.

- Selecting the files that are necessary to run the Web site and then copying those files to the production server.

Objectives

After completing this module, you will be able to:

- Use the **Cache** object to store information.

- Use ASP.NET output caching to store Web pages and Web page fragments.

- Configure an ASP.NET Web application by using the Machine.config and Web.config files.

- Deploy an ASP.NET Web application.

Lesson: Using the Cache Object

- **What Is the Cache Object?**
- **Advantages of Using the Cache Object**
- **How to Use the Cache Object**
- **Removing Items from the Cache Object**
- **Demonstration: Using the Cache Object**

Introduction

One of most effective ways to increase the performance of an ASP.NET Web application is to use the ASP.NET **Cache** object. The **Cache** object allows you to place items in server memory so that they can be quickly retrieved. However, loading too many items into the **Cache** object can slow down server response times by reducing the available memory on the server.

In this lesson, you will learn how to set up the **Cache** object to optimize the response times for a Web application.

Lesson objectives

After completing this lesson, you will be able to:

- Explain what a **Cache** object is.
- Explain the advantages and disadvantages of using a **Cache** object.
- Use a **Cache** object to store and retrieve items that are used by your Web application.
- Remove items from a **Cache** object after a period of time, or when the item changes, to limit memory use.

What Is the Cache Object?

- **An object used to store information**
  - One **Cache** object per Web Application
  - An alternative to application variables
  - Not used to store information in session variables
- **Uses key-value pairs to store and retrieve items**

```
Cache("myKey") = myValue
```

```
Cache["myKey"] = myValue;
```

Introduction

An issue that you will encounter when building high-performance Web applications is the need to avoid duplication. A **Cache** object allows you to cache (store) items in memory the first time they are requested, and then use the cached copy for later requests. Using the cached copy allows you to avoid recreating information that satisfied a previous request, particularly information that demands significant processor time on the server every time it is created.

In addition to caching individual items, such as computational results in the **Cache** object, ASP.NET offers an output cache that can be used for storing Web pages and user controls. The **Cache** object and the output cache are distinct objects with unique roles and properties.

An object used to store information

ASP.NET provides a full-featured cache engine that can be used to store and retrieve pieces of information. The **Cache** object has no information about the content of the items it contains. The **Cache** object merely holds a reference to those objects and provides a process for tracking their dependencies and setting expiration policies.

The **Cache** object also provides a method to pass values between pages in the same Web application. The cache methods implement automatic locking; therefore, it is safe for values to be accessed concurrently from more than one page.

How the Cache object works

The process for using the **Cache** object is:

1. A page requests an item that has been identified as being stored in the **Cache** object.

2. ASP.NET checks the **Cache** object and uses the cached version if it is available.

3. If a cached version is not available, ASP.NET recreates the item, uses that item, and then stores that item in the **Cache** object for future use.

One Cache object per Web application

ASP.NET creates a single **Cache** object for each Web application. The items stored in the **Cache** object are unique to the Web application and cannot be accessed by other Web applications that are running on the same server or on other servers. As a result, the use of the **Cache** object to increase Web application performance is not scalable above the single Web application level.

The lifetime of the cache is the same as the lifetime of the Web application. When the Web application is restarted, the cache is then recreated.

Storing variables

The **Cache** object can be used to store information that could also be stored in application variables. Rather than recreating the value each time you use it, a single cached value can be accessed by any page in the Web application.

The **Cache** object cannot be used to store information that is found in session variables. Session variables can be stored in cookies, the page Uniform Resource Locator (URL), or the hidden **ViewState** control.

Note For more information about application and session variables, see Module 14, "Managing State," in Course 2310B, *Developing Microsoft ASP.NET Web Applications Using Visual Studio .NET.*

Uses key-value pairs

The **Cache** object uses key-value pairs to store and retrieve objects. The *key* is the cache key string that is used to reference the object. The *value* is the object to be cached. In the simplest case, placing an item in the cache and retrieving it is exactly like adding an item to a dictionary.

To add an item into a **Cache** object:

Microsoft Visual Basic® .NET

```
Cache("mykey") = myValue
```

C#

```
Cache["mykey"] = myValue;
```

To retrieve an item from a **Cache** object:

Visual Basic .NET

```
myValue = Cache("myKey")
```

C#

```
myValue = Cache["myKey"];
```

Advantages of Using the Cache Object

- **Faster than creating a new object for each request**
- **Supports internal locking**
- **Automatic cache resource management**
- **Supports callback functions**
- **Supports removal based on dependencies**

Introduction	The **Cache** object provides a simple dictionary interface that allows you to easily insert values and then retrieve them later. Using the **Cache** object to store values has several advantages.
Faster than creating a new object for each request	An item that is stored in memory can be retrieved much more quickly than it can be rebuilt. For example, a DataSet filled with data from a computer running Microsoft SQL Server™ must reconnect to the SQL Server for each page request. Placing the DataSet in the **Cache** object provides much more rapid access to that data.
Supports internal locking	The **Cache** object provides automatic lock management on items that are in the cache; therefore, concurrent requests for an item cannot modify the object. Automatic lock management protects in-process transactions when items are being updated.
Automatically manages cache resources	ASP.NET automatically removes items from the cache on a regular schedule. This automatic removal is an improvement over earlier cache versions where the developer had to manually manage cache resources.
Supports callback functions	Callback functions are code that runs when an item is removed from the cache. For example, you can use a callback function to place the newest version of an object in cache as soon as the old version is removed.
Supports removal based on dependencies	If an item in a cache has a dependency on another cached item or a file, you can set the **Cache** object to remove that item when the dependency meets certain requirements. For example, if you store data from an Extensible Markup Language (XML) file in the cache, you can remove the cached data when the XML document changes.

How to Use the Cache Object

- **Writing to the Cache object:**

```
'Implicit method
Cache("myKey") = myValue

'Explicit method
Cache.Insert("myKey", myValue, Dependency, AbsoluteExpiration, _
    SlidingExpiration, CacheItemPriority, CacheItemRemovedCallBack)
```

```
//Implicit method
Cache["myKey"] = myValue;

//Explicit method
Cache.Insert("myKey", myValue, Dependency, AbsoluteExpiration,
    SlidingExpiration, CacheItemPriority, CacheItemRemovedCallBack);
```

- **Retrieving values from the Cache object:**

```
myValue = Cache("myKey")
```
```
myValue = Cache["myKey"];
```

Introduction

To use the **Cache** object, you use key-value pairs to store and retrieve items. The *key* is the Cache key string that is used to reference the item. The *value* is the item to be cached.

Writing to the Cache object

You can write an item into a **Cache** object implicitly, as shown in the following code:

Visual Basic .NET

```
Cache("mykey") = myValue
```

C#

```
Cache["mykey"] = myValue;
```

You can also supply parameters, such as a time limit for storage in the **Cache** object, when inserting an item into the **Cache** object. The following code shows the explicit **Insert** method with parameters:

Visual Basic .NET

```
Cache.Insert("myKey", myValue, _
    Dependency, AbsoluteExpiration, SlidingExpiration, _
    CacheItemPriority, CacheItemRemovedCallBack)
```

C#

```
Cache.Insert("myKey", myValue,
    Dependency, AbsoluteExpiration, SlidingExpiration,
    CacheItemPriority, CacheItemRemovedCallBack);
```

Retrieving values from the Cache object

Retrieving values from the **Cache** object is equally simple in that you only need to provide the correct key to receive the value.

The following code uses the key **myKey** to retrieve the value **myValue** and then displays **myValue** if it is not empty:

Visual Basic .NET

```
myValue = Cache("mykey")
If myValue <> Nothing Then
    DisplayData(myValue)
End If
```

C#

```
myValue = Cache["mykey"];
if (myValue != null)
    DisplayData(myValue);
```

Removing Items from the Cache Object

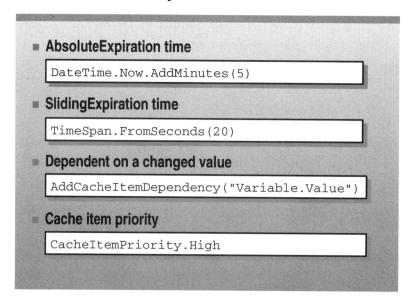

- **AbsoluteExpiration time**

  ```
  DateTime.Now.AddMinutes(5)
  ```

- **SlidingExpiration time**

  ```
  TimeSpan.FromSeconds(20)
  ```

- **Dependent on a changed value**

  ```
  AddCacheItemDependency("Variable.Value")
  ```

- **Cache item priority**

  ```
  CacheItemPriority.High
  ```

Introduction

The ASP.NET **Cache** object is designed to ensure that it does not use too much of the server's memory. As a result, the **Cache** object automatically removes the least used items when available memory becomes scarce. You can influence how the **Cache** object saves and removes items by defining time limits, dependencies, and priorities for items that are in the **Cache** object.

Items in the **Cache** object are removed as soon as a dependency or time limit is triggered. Attempts to retrieve the removed items will return **null** value unless the item is added to the **Cache** object again.

AbsoluteExpiration

You can define the maximum absolute lifetime for an item by using the **AbsoluteExpiration** parameter. This parameter is a **DateTime** type parameter that allows you to specify the time at which the item will expire.

The following code specifies that **myValue** be removed from the **Cache** object exactly five minutes after it is created:

Visual Basic .NET

```
Cache.Insert("myKey", myValue, Nothing, _
    DateTime.Now.AddMinutes(5), Nothing)
```

C#

```
Cache.Insert("myKey", myValue, null, _
    DateTime.Now.AddMinutes(5), Cache.NoSlidingExpiration);
```

SlidingExpiration

You can define the maximum relative lifetime for an item by using the **SlidingExpiration** parameter. This is a **TimeSpan** type parameter that allows you to specify the time interval between the time the cached object was last accessed and when the object expires.

The following code specifies that **myValue** be removed from the **Cache** object exactly 20 seconds after it is last accessed:

Visual Basic .NET

```
Cache.Insert("myKey", myValue, Nothing, _
    Nothing, TimeSpan.FromSeconds(20))
```

C#

```
Cache.Insert("myKey", myValue, null, _
    null, TimeSpan.FromSeconds(20));
```

Dependencies

There are times when you want an object to be removed from the **Cache** object because a supporting item, such as a file, has changed. ASP.NET allows you to define the validity of a cached item, based on file dependencies or another cached item. Dependencies based on external files and directories are referred to as file dependencies, dependencies based on another cached item are referred to as a key dependencies. If a dependency changes, the cached item is invalidated and removed from the **Cache** object.

The following code specifies that **myValue** be removed from the **Cache** object when the myDoc.xml file changes:

Visual Basic .NET

```
Cache.Insert("myKey", myValue, _
    new CacheDependency(Server.MapPath("myDoc.xml")))
```

C#

```
Cache.Insert("myKey", myValue, new
CacheDependency(Server.MapPath("myDoc.xml")));
```

Cache item priority

When the Web server runs low on memory, the **Cache** object selectively removes items to free up system memory. Items that you assign higher priority values to are less likely to be removed from the cache, whereas the items to which you assign lower priority values are more likely to be removed.

The following code specifies that **myValue** has a high priority and should be one of the last items removed from the **Cache** object when the server memory becomes limited:

Visual Basic .NET

```
Cache.Insert("myKey", myValue, Nothing, Nothing, _
    Nothing, CacheItemPriority.High, onRemove)
```

C#

```
Cache.Insert("myKey", myValue, null, null,
Cache.NoSlidingExpiration, CacheItemPriority.High, onRemove);
```

Example of setting the parameters in Cache.Insert

The following code inserts a value for **MyBook** into the **Cache** object with a number of parameter arguments. The following dependency or timeout event that occurs first will be the dependency or timeout event that removes the item from the **Cache** object:

- Remove the item 5 minutes after being stored.

- Remove the item 30 seconds after the latest access.

- Remove the item if the Books.xml file changes.

- Make the priority of the item high so that it is removed last if server resources become a problem.

- When the item is removed from the **Cache** object, the callback function **onRemove** runs.

Visual Basic .NET

```
Cache.Insert("MyBook.CurrentBook", CurrentBook, _
   new CacheDependency(Server.MapPath("Books.xml")), _
   DateTime.Now.AddMinutes(5), _
   TimeSpan.FromSeconds(30), _
   CacheItemPriority.High, onRemove)
```

C#

```
Cache.Insert("MyBook.CurrentBook", CurrentBook,
   new CacheDependency(Server.MapPath("Books.xml")),
   DateTime.Now.AddMinutes(5),
   TimeSpan.FromSeconds(30),
   CacheItemPriority.High, onRemove);
```

Demonstration: Using the Cache Object

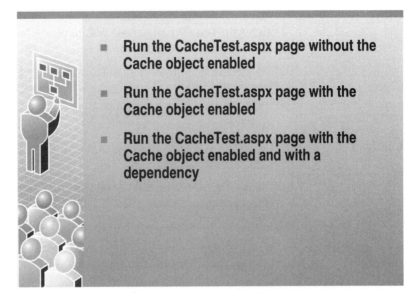

- Run the CacheTest.aspx page without the Cache object enabled
- Run the CacheTest.aspx page with the Cache object enabled
- Run the CacheTest.aspx page with the Cache object enabled and with a dependency

Introduction

In this demonstration, you will see how to use the **Cache** object with a **DataGrid**.

All files for this demonstration are in the Mod15CS or Mod15VB project in the 2310Demos solution.

▶ **To run the demonstration**

Run without caching

1. Open the CacheTest.aspx page.

2. Show the code-behind page.

   Point out that the **DataSet** reads an XML file and that the **DataGrid** is filled with the XML file.

3. Set the Mod15 project as the StartUp project, set the CacheTest.aspx page as the Start Page for the project, and then browse to the page in Microsoft Internet Explorer.

Note Because of feature differences between the built-in browser in Microsoft Visual Studio® .NET and Internet Explorer, it is important to use Internet Explorer for this demonstration.

Enable caching

4. In CacheTest.aspx.vb or CacheTest.aspx.cs, comment out the lines that are marked with the following comment in both the **Page_Load** and the **dgXML_PageIndexChanged** event procedures:

Visual Basic .NET

```
'comment this line for caching
```

C#

```
//comment this line for caching
```

5. Uncomment all remaining code in both the **Page_Load** and **dgXML_PageIndexChanged** event procedures.

   Explain how this additional code creates a new cache key **dsCache**, which places the **DataSet** object **dsXML** in the cache and sets the absolute expiration time at two minutes.

6. Click **Start** to build the CacheTest.aspx page and view it in Internet Explorer.

   Verify that the **DataGrid** is populated with the XML data and that the paging feature works.

Test the caching

7. Leave Internet Explorer open, and in Visual Studio .NET, open the pubs.xml file.

8. Change the title of the first book listed to a title that the students can easily detect and then save the file.

9. In Internet Explorer, switch to Page 1 of the **DataGrid**.

   If you are already viewing Page 1, switch to another page and then go back to Page 1.

10. Show the students that the title of the first book listed did not change because the information is coming from cache.

11. Switch to another page, wait at least two minutes, and then switch back to the first page.

    The **DataGrid** will now display the new title for the first book.

12. Close Internet Explorer.

Add a dependency

13. Open the CacheTest.aspx.vb or the CacheTest.aspx.cs page.

14. For both of the Cache.Insert lines of code in the CacheTest.aspx.vb or CacheTest.aspx.cs pages, add a dependency on the pubs.xml file. Your code should look like the following:

Visual Basic .NET

```
Cache.Insert("dsCache", dsXML, New _
    System.Web.Caching.CacheDependency _
    (Server.MapPath("pubs.xml")), _
    DateTime.Now.AddMinutes(1), Nothing)
```

C#

```
Cache.Insert("dsCache", dsXML, new
    System.Web.Caching.CacheDependency
    (Server.MapPath("pubs.xml")),
    DateTime.Now.AddMinutes(1), Cache.NoSlidingExpiration);
```

15. Right-click the **Mod15VB** or **Mod15CS** project in Solution Explorer and click **Build**.

16. Right-click **CacheTest.aspx**, and then click **Browse With...** In the **Browse With** dialog box, click **Microsoft Internet Explorer**, and then click **Browse**.

17. Click **Start** to build the CacheTest.aspx page and view it in Internet Explorer.

18. Leave Internet Explorer open, and in Visual Studio .NET, open the pubs.xml file.

19. Change the title of the first book listed to a title that the students can easily detect. Save the pubs.xml file.

20. In Internet Explorer, switch to Page 1 of the **DataGrid**.

    If you are already viewing Page 1, switch to another page and then go back to Page 1.

21. Show the students that the information in the **DataGrid** changes to reflect the change that was made in the pubs.xml file, because the cache is dependent on that file.

Lesson: Using ASP.NET Output Caching

- Multimedia: Output Caching
- Output Cache Types
- How to Use Page Output Caches
- Demonstration: Page Output Caching
- How to Use Fragment Caching

Introduction

One factor developers must consider in creating high-performance Web applications is the need for minimizing the response time to page requests. By storing a page, or parts of a page, in memory the first time they are requested, and then using that stored page, or parts of that page, for later requests, you can avoid the processing time required to recreate the page.

In this lesson, you will learn how to set up the output cache to minimize page response times for a Web application.

Lesson objectives

After completing this lesson, you will be able to:

- Explain why you would use output caching.
- Explain the different output cache types.
- Use page output caching.
- Use page fragment output caching.

Multimedia: Output Caching

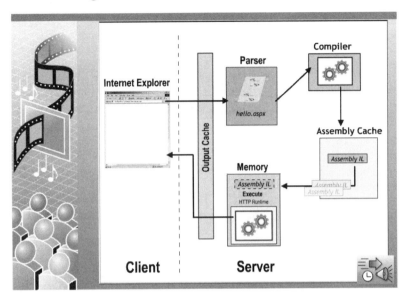

Introduction   In this animation, you will see how the page output cache affects server response times when an ASP.NET Web Form is requested more than once.

Output Cache Types

- Page caching

- Page fragment caching as a user control

- XML Web service caching

Introduction

ASP.NET provides page output caching, which allows you to store entire Web Forms and user controls in server memory. After the first request, the Web Form, user control, or XML Web service code is not executed; instead, the cached output is used to satisfy the request.

ASP.NET creates a single output cache for each Web server. The pages and page fragments that are stored in the output cache are unique to the Web server and cannot be accessed by other servers in a Web server farm. As a result, the use of the output cache to increase server performance is not scalable above the single Web server level.

Page caching

Page caching allows you to cache dynamic content. When a Web Form is requested for the first time, the page is compiled and cached in the output cache, and it is then available to serve the next request. This cached page is removed when the source file is changed or the cache time-out is reached.

Page fragment caching as a user control

Sometimes it is impractical to cache an entire page, because portions of the page may need to be dynamically created for each request. In these situations, it may be worthwhile for you to identify the objects or data that are associated with the page request that do not change often, and therefore do not require significant server resources to construct. After you identify these objects or data, you can isolate them from the rest of the page by creating them as user controls, and then caching the user controls with the page output cache.

An example of a page fragment that would be worthwhile to cache is a page header that contains static graphics, or a sidebar menu system.

XML Web service caching

XML Web services also support caching to increase response performance. In the **WebMethod** attribute, you add the **CacheDuration** property and set the value to the number of seconds that the results for the XML Web service method will remain in the output cache.

For example, the following code places the results from the WebMethod **CachedInfo** into the output cache for five minutes:

Visual Basic .NET

```
<WebMethod(CacheDuration:=300)> _
Public Function CachedInfo() As String
    ...
End Function
```

C#

```
[WebMethod(CacheDuration=300)]
public string CachedInfo()
{
    ...
}
```

Important Creating an output cache for an application should be your final task in Web application development. Otherwise, when you debug your pages, you may get out-of-date pages that are stored in the output cache instead of getting new and modified pages.

How to Use Page Output Caches

- **Cache content is generated from dynamic pages**

- **Entire Web page is available in cache**

- **Set cache duration in seconds**

- **Set the VaryByParam property to control the number of page variations in the cache**

```
<%@ OutputCache Duration="900"
  VaryByParam="none" %>
```

Introduction

ASP.NET provides page output caching, which allows you to store requested Web Forms in server memory. After the first request, the Web Form code is not executed; instead the cached output is used to satisfy the request.

Cache content from dynamic pages

To load a page into the output cache, you must add the **OutputCache** directive to the Web Form. The **OutputCache** directive includes two properties: a **Duration** property that sets the maximum storage time for the cached page in seconds, and a **VaryByParam** property that determines when a new copy of the page is created in the cache, based on parameters that are passed to the page.

Entire Web page is available in cache

Output caching allows requests for a particular page to be satisfied from the cache so that the code that initially creates the page does not have to be run on subsequent page requests. Using output caching to store your Web site's most frequently accessed pages can substantially reduce your Web server's page response time.

Set the cache duration

You can specify the cache time-out value for a page by setting the **OutputCache** page directive. For example, to cache an ASP.NET page for 15 minutes, add the following **OutputCache** page directive to the .aspx page:

```
<%@ OutputCache Duration="900" VaryByParam="None"%>
```

The unit of time for the **Duration** property is seconds. The default is 0 seconds, which means the response is not cached.

Set VaryByParam

The **VaryByParam** property is used to determine whether ASP.NET should create different versions of the cached page in situations in which page requests pass specific parameters. Setting the **VaryByParam** property to **"none"** means that only one version of the page will be cached. Setting the property to **"*"** means that any variation in page parameters will result in a new version of the page being cached. Identifying one or more parameters means that only changes to these parameters will result in new pages being cached.

For example, the following directive in an .aspx file sets an expiration of 60 seconds for the cached output of each dynamically generated page, and therefore requires the creation of a new page in the output cache for each new **productID**:

```
<%@ OutputCache Duration="60" VaryByParam="productID"%>
```

Caution   When you use the **OutputCache** directive, the **Duration** and **VaryByParam** attributes are required. If you do not include those attributes, a parser error occurs when the page is first requested. If you do not want to use the functionality that the **VaryByParam** attribute provides, you must set its value to **"none"**.

Demonstration: Page Output Caching

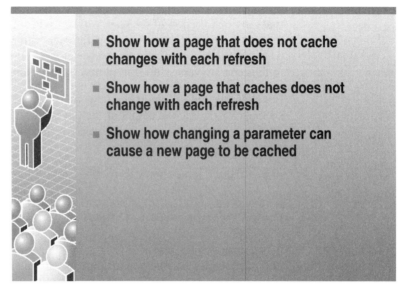

Introduction

In this demonstration, you will see how page output caching affects the user's experience. First, you will see a page running a clock function that does not cache. Next you will see the same page with a 10-second output cache duration. Finally, you will see how changing the **VaryByParam** property controls the caching of different versions of the page.

All files for this demonstration are in the Mod15CS or Mod15VB project in the 2310Demos solution.

▶ **To run the demonstration**

Show how a page that does not cache changes with each refresh

1. Open the OutputCache.aspx page in the Mod15project in Visual Studio .NET.

2. Show the code that gets the current time and date, and then displays the code in a label.

3. Build and browse the page.

4. Reload the page several times consecutively to show that the seconds are changing.

Show how a page that caches does not change with each refresh

5. Add the following directive to the page, after the line of code that contains the page directive.

    ```
    <%@ OutputCache Duration="10" VaryByParam="none"%>
    ```

6. Build and browse the page.

7. Reload the page several times consecutively to show that the seconds are changing only after a 10-second interval.

8. You can add a dummy parameter **?Name=Someone** to show that there is no impact on the caching. The page is cached regardless of the value of the parameter.

Show how changing a parameter can cause a new page to be cached

9. Open the OutputCacheVaryByParam.aspx page.

10. Show the **OutputCache** directive with the **VaryByParam** property.

11. Build and browse the page.

12. At the end of the URL, add the parameter **?Name=Someone**.

13. Show the effect on the output cache when changing the value of the **?Name=Someone** parameter to a **?Name=Someone2** parameter.

How to Use Fragment Caching

- **Convert the page fragment into a user control**

- **Set the Duration and varyByParam properties**

```
<%@ OutputCache Duration="120"
   VaryByParam="none" %>
```

Introduction

To cache only parts of a page, you must isolate those parts from the rest of the page by placing them in a user control. You then cache the user control for a period of time that you specify, which is known as fragment caching.

Fragment caching allows you to separate the portions of a page—such as database queries, which take up valuable processor time—from the rest of the page. With fragment caching, you can choose to allow only the parts of the page that require fewer server resources, or the parts of a page that must be created with every request, to be generated dynamically for each request.

Items that are good candidates for fragment caching include headers, footers, and drop-down lists that are used by multiple pages.

Convert fragment to a user control

After you identify the parts of the page that you want to cache, you must create user controls that encapsulate each one of those fragments.

Note   For more information on creating user controls, see Module 8, "Creating User Controls," in Course 2310B, *Developing Microsoft ASP.NET Web Applications Using Visual Studio .NET.*

Set Duration the and VaryByParam properties

You set the caching policies for the user controls, such as the duration and the number of variations stored, the same way that you set page output caching policies. You set these caching policies declaratively, by using the **OutputCache** directive.

For example, if you include the following directive at the top of a user control file, a version of the user control is stored in the output cache for two minutes, and only one version of the user control will be cached:

```
<%@ OutputCache Duration="120" VaryByParam="none"%>
```

Lesson: Configuring an ASP.NET Web Application

- **Overview of Configuration Methods**
- **Configuring a Web Server Using Machine.config**
- **Configuring an Application Using Web.config**
- **Understanding Configuration Inheritance**
- **Demonstration: Configuration Inheritance**
- **Practice: Determining Configuration Inheritance**
- **Storing and Retrieving Data in Web.config**
- **Using Dynamic Properties**
- **Demonstration: Using Dynamic Properties**

Introduction

Before you can deploy your ASP.NET Web application, you must organize the Web application settings in the Machine.config and Web.config files. In this lesson, you will learn how to configure an ASP.NET Web application.

Lesson objectives

After completing this lesson, you will be able to:

- Explain how to configure a Web application.
- Configure a Web server by using the Machine.config file.
- Configure an application by using Web.config files.
- Explain how Web.config files inherit from the Machine.config file and other Web.config files.
- Store and retrieve data by using Web.config files.
- Use dynamic properties to store property values.

Overview of Configuration Methods

- **Machine.config file**
  - Machine-level settings
- **Web.config files**
  - Application and directory-level settings
- **Both Machine.config and Web.config files are:**
  - Well-formed XML
  - camelCase
  - Extendable

Introduction	Configuration information for ASP.NET resources is contained in a collection of configuration files. Each configuration file contains a nested hierarchy of XML tags and subtags with attributes that specify the configuration settings.

The ASP.NET configuration infrastructure makes no assumptions about the types of configuration data that the infrastructure supports. |
Machine.config	Machine-level configuration settings are stored in the Machine.config file. There is only one Machine.config file on each Web server. As a result, the Machine.config file can be used to store settings that apply to all of the ASP.NET Web applications that are residing on that Web server.
Web.config	Application and directory-level settings are stored in Web.config files. Each Web application has at least one Web.config file. Virtual directories can have their own Web.config files containing settings that are specific to that directory.
.config file attributes	Because the tags in Machine.config and Web.config files must be well-formed XML, the tags, subtags, and attributes are case-sensitive. Tag names and attribute names are camelCased, which means that the first character of a tag name is lowercase and the first letter of any subsequent concatenated words is uppercase. All configuration information in a .config file resides between the **<configuration>** and **</configuration>** root XML tags.

Configuring a Web Server Using Machine.config

- **Settings in the Machine.config file affect all Web applications on the server**
  - Only one Machine.config file per Web server
  - Most settings can be overridden at the application level using Web.config files

Introduction

The machine configuration file, Machine.config, contains settings that apply to an entire computer. There is only one Machine.config file for each Web server.

The Machine.config file is located in the following directory, where *version* is the Microsoft .NET Framework version that is installed on the Web server:

C:\WINDOWS\Microsoft .NET \Framework*version*\CONFIG\Machine.config

Settings affect all Web applications

Settings in the Machine.config file affect all of the Web applications that are located on the server. The configuration system first looks in the Machine.config file for the **<appSettings>** element, and then looks for local overriding settings in the application's Web.config files.

Placing Web application settings in the Machine.config file has advantages and disadvantages:

- Advantages of the Machine.config file

  Placing settings in the Machine.config file can make your system more maintainable because you only have one configuration file to search, edit, and maintain.

- Disadvantages of the Machine.config file

  When you deploy a Web application to a new server, the Web application settings that are in the Machine.config file will not be copied to the new Web server.

Configuring an Application Using Web.config

- **One or more Web.config files per Web application**

- **All configuration information for the application is contained in the Web.config files**

- **Contains a section for each major category of ASP.NET functionality**
  - Security
  - Mode
  - General application settings
  - Tracing

Introduction

In ASP.NET, you can share the information and settings between Web pages by storing Web application settings in a central location called the Web.config file. You can also store local information and settings in virtual directories by creating additional local Web.config files.

A single Web.config file is always located in the root folder of the Web application. Additional Web.config files can be located in the folder of the virtual directory to which they belong.

One or more Web.config files per Web application

The presence of a Web.config file within a given directory is optional. If a Web.config file is not present, all configuration settings for the directory are automatically inherited from the parent directory, Webconfig file.

Contains a section for each major category of ASP.NET functionality

In a Web.config file, there are sections for each major category of ASP.NET functionality, as shown in the following table.

Section name	Description
<browserCaps>	Responsible for controlling the settings of the browser capabilities component.
<compilation>	Responsible for all compilation settings that are used by ASP.NET.
<globalization>	Responsible for configuring the globalization settings of an application.
<httpModules>	Responsible for configuring Hypertext Transfer Protocol (HTTP) modules within an application. HTTP modules participate in the processing of every request to an application. Common uses include security and logging.
<httpHandlers>	Responsible for mapping incoming URLs to **IHttpHandler** classes. Subdirectories do not inherit these settings.

(continued)

Section name	Description
\<processModel\>	Responsible for configuring the ASP.NET process model settings on Internet Information Services (IIS) Web server systems.
\<authentication\> **\<identity\>** **\<authorization\>**	Responsible for all security settings that are used by the ASP.NET security **httpModule**.
\<sessionState\>	Responsible for configuring the session state **httpModule**.
\<trace\>	Responsible for configuring the ASP.NET Trace service.

Note For more information on setting up security in the Web.config file, see Module 16, "Securing a Microsoft ASP.NET Web Application," in Course 2310B, *Developing Microsoft ASP.NET Web Applications Using Visual Studio .NET.*

Understanding Configuration Inheritance

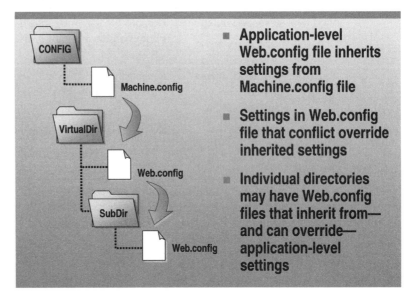

- **Application-level Web.config file inherits settings from Machine.config file**

- **Settings in Web.config file that conflict override inherited settings**

- **Individual directories may have Web.config files that inherit from— and can override— application-level settings**

Introduction

When a Web server receives a request for a particular Web resource, ASP.NET determines the configuration settings for that resource hierarchically. ASP.NET uses all of the configuration files that are located in the virtual directory path for the requested resource. The lowest level configuration setting may override the settings that were provided in the parent directory configuration files.

The following are the rules of inheritance for configuration files:

- Application-level Web.config files inherit settings from the Machine.config file.

- Conflicting settings in a child Web.config file that override inherited settings.

- Individual directories can have Web.config files that inherit from, and can override, application-level Web.config file settings.

Machine.config

The highest-level file is named Machine.config. The settings in this file apply to all ASP.NET directories and subdirectories. Machine.config is installed with the .NET Framework, and contains many default ASP.NET settings.

For example, the default setting for the security configuration section of the Machine.config file allows all users to access all URL resources. As a result, every Web application allows access to all URL resources unless the setting is overridden in Web.config.

Web.config

Additional configuration information for an ASP.NET Web application is contained in configuration files that are named Web.config, which are located in the same directories as the application files. Child directories inherit the settings of the parent directories, unless the settings of the parent directory are overridden by a Web.config file in the child directory.

For example, if the Web.config file in the root directory (**VirtualDir**) of a Web application contains a security configuration section that allows access only to certain users, the subdirectory **SubDir** inherits that security setting. As a result, all users have access to the ASP.NET resources in the application root directory, **VirtualDir**, but only certain users have access to the ASP.NET resources in **SubDir**.

Web.config files for the application in **VirtualDir** and the subdirectory **SubDir** are located in:

C:\Inetpub\wwwroot*VirtualDir*\Web.config

C:\Inetpub\wwwroot*VirtualDir**SubDir*\Web.config

Demonstration: Configuration Inheritance

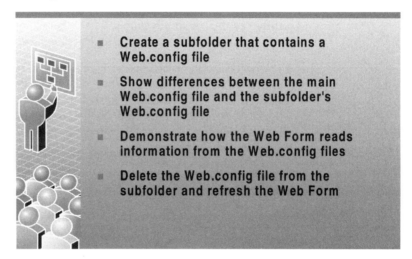

- Create a subfolder that contains a Web.config file
- Show differences between the main Web.config file and the subfolder's Web.config file
- Demonstrate how the Web Form reads information from the Web.config files
- Delete the Web.config file from the subfolder and refresh the Web Form

Introduction

In this demonstration, you will see how configuration settings are inherited from one Web.config file to a second Web.config file that is located in a subdirectory.

All files for this demonstration are in the Mod15CS or Mod15VB project in the 2310Demos solution.

▶ **To run the demonstration**

Create a subfolder that contains Web.config

1. Open the 2310Demos solution.

Show differences between the main Web.config and the subfolder's Web.config

2. In Visual Studio .NET, show the code of the Web.config file and GetConfigMainFolder.aspx in the main folder.

   Point out the value that is stored in the Web.config file.

3. Show the code of the Web.config file and GetConfigSubFolder.aspx in the SubFolder folder.

   Point out that the value that is stored in the Web.config file is different.

4. Build and browse the GetConfigMainFolder.aspx page, and highlight the value that was retrieved from the Web.config file.

5. Click **Next** to open the GetConfigSubFolder.aspx page that is located in the SubFolder folder and emphasize the fact that the value is different here.

Delete Web.config from the subfolder and refresh the Web Form

6. In the SubFolder folder, rename the Web.config file to oldWeb.config.

7. Build and browse the GetConfigMainFolder.aspx page, and highlight the value that was retrieved from the Web.config file.

8. Click **Next** to open the GetConfigSubFolder.aspx page in the SubFolder folder, and point out that the value is the same as the value in the Web.config file in the main directory.

Practice: Determining Configuration Inheritance

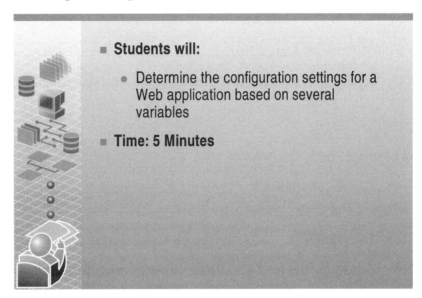

- **Students will:**
  - Determine the configuration settings for a Web application based on several variables
- **Time: 5 Minutes**

Introduction

In this practice, you will review a Machine.config file and two Web.config files to determine the configuration settings for the Web server, the Web application, and the Web application subdirectory.

Review the following code from the Machine.config file. After reviewing the code, answer the questions.

```
<configuration>
  <appSettings>
      <add key="Default XML File Name"
        value="Default.xml" />
      <add key="Default Text File Name"
        value="Default.txt" />
  </appSettings>
  <authentication mode="Windows">
    <forms name=".ASPXAUTH"
        loginUrl="login.aspx"
        protection="All"
        timeout="30"
        path="/">
    </forms>
  </authentication>
  <system.web>
     <trace
        enabled="false"
        localOnly="true"
        pageOutput="false"
        requestLimit="10"
        traceMode="SortByTime"
     />
  </system.web>
</configuration>
```

At this level, what is the configuration setting for the authentication mechanism?

_____

_____

Is there a configuration setting for a connection string? If so, what is it?

_____

_____

Are there other application configuration settings? If so, what are their values?

_____

_____

Is there a configuration setting to enable tracing for the Web application? If so, is it possible to trace from an external computer?

_____

_____

Review the following code from a Web.config file that is located in the virtual root directory of the Web application. After reviewing the code, answer the questions. Consider the preceding code example when answering the questions.

```
<configuration>
  <appSettings>
      <add key="northwind"
          value="data source=localhost;
          initial catalog=northwind;
          integrated security=true;" />
  </appSettings>
<system.web>
    <trace
      enabled="true"
      localOnly="true"
      pageOutput="false"
      requestLimit="30"
      traceMode="SortByCategory"
    />
  </system.web>
</configuration>
```

At this level, what is the authentication mechanism?

_____

_____

Is there a connection string? If so, what is it?

_____

_____

Are there other application settings? If so, what are their values?

_____

_____

Is tracing enabled for the Web application? If so, is it possible to trace from an external computer?

_____

_____

34   Module 15: Configuring, Optimizing, and Deploying a Microsoft ASP.NET Web Application

Review the following code from a Web.config file that is located in a subfolder of the Web application. After reviewing the code, answer the questions. Consider the preceding code example when answering the questions.

```xml
<configuration>
  <appSettings>
      <add key="Northwind"
          value="data source=SQLServ01;
          initial catalog=northwind;
          integrated security=true;" />
  </appSettings>
  <authentication mode="Forms">
    <forms name=".ASPXAUTH"
        loginUrl="loginPage.aspx"
        timeout="30"
        path="/">
        …
    </forms>
  </authentication>
<system.web>
    <trace
      enabled="true"
      localOnly="false"
      pageOutput="false"
      requestLimit="40"
      traceMode="SortByTime"
    />
  </system.web>
</configuration>
```

At this level, what is the authentication mechanism?

_____

_____

Is there a connection string? If so, what is it?

_____

_____

Are there other application settings? If so, what are their values?

_____

_____

Is tracing enabled for the Web application? If so, is it possible to trace from an external computer?

_____

_____

Storing and Retrieving Data in Web.config

■ **Storing application settings in a Web.config file**

```
<configuration>
  <appSettings>
    <add key="pubs" value="server=localhost;
      integrated security=true; database=pubs"/>
  </appSettings>
</configuration>
```

■ **Retrieving application settings from a Web.config file**

```
Dim strPubs As String = _
  ConfigurationSettings.AppSettings("pubs")
```

```
AppSettingsReader App = new AppSettingsReader();

string strPubs =  (string)App.GetValue("pubs",
  typeof(string));
```

Introduction

You can use the **<appSettings>** section of the Web.config file as a repository for application settings. In the **<appSettings>** section, you can create key-value pairs for data that is commonly used throughout your Web application. Creating key-value pairs for data is very useful because you can define all application configuration data in a central location. For example, you can store a database connection string for an application in a central location, instead of having it in each ASP.NET page.

Storing application settings in Web.config

You store application settings by entering a key-value pair for the information that you want to store. The following Web.config file creates two key-value pairs for the connection strings for databases that are used in a Web application:

```
configuration>
 <appSettings>
  <add key="pubs"
     value="data source=localhost;
     initial catalog=pubs;
     integrated security=SSPI" />
  <add key="northwind"
     value="data source=localhost;
     initial catalog=northwind;
     integrated security=SSPI" />
 </appSettings>
</configuration>
```

Retrieving application settings from Web.config

To retrieve application settings from Web.config files, you use the **ConfigurationSettings.AppSettings** static string collection.

For example, the following sample code reads the value of the **pubs** key from the **<appSettings>** section:

Visual Basic .NET

```
Dim strPubs As String = _
    ConfigurationSettings.AppSettings("pubs")
```

C#

```
string strPubs = System.Configuration.
    ConfigurationSettings.AppSettings["pubs"];
```

Using Dynamic Properties

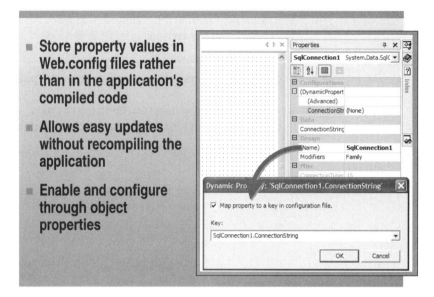

■ Store property values in Web.config files rather than in the application's compiled code

■ Allows easy updates without recompiling the application

■ Enable and configure through object properties

Introduction

Dynamic properties allow you to configure your application so that its property values are stored in an external configuration file, for example Web.config, rather than being stored in the application's compiled code. Storing in an external configuration file can reduce the total cost of maintaining an application, after the application has been deployed, by providing administrators with the means to update property values that may change over time.

Store property values in Web.config

While the properties of most components and controls in a Web application can be handled dynamically, some properties are better suited to be handled dynamically than others. For example, you will likely use dynamic properties to store and retrieve the properties that are connected to external resources that might change, such as databases.

Allows easy updates

For example, suppose you are building a Web application that uses a test database during the development process and you must switch the Web application to a production database when you deploy it. If you store the property values inside the Web application, you have to manually change all of the database settings before you can deploy the database, and then you will need to recompile the source code. If you store these property values externally, you can make a single change in the external file and the Web application will use the new values the next time it runs.

Enable and configure through object properties

You configure an object to use dynamic properties in the Properties window of the object in Visual Studio .NET. Select the **DynamicProperties** check box in the configuration section of the Properties window, and then set the property to a key in Web.config.

Demonstration: Using Dynamic Properties

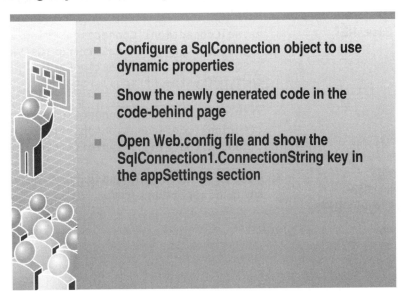

- Configure a SqlConnection object to use dynamic properties

- Show the newly generated code in the code-behind page

- Open Web.config file and show the SqlConnection1.ConnectionString key in the appSettings section

---

Introduction

In this demonstration, you will see how to enable and configure a **SqlConnection** object to use dynamic properties.

All files for this demonstration are in the Mod15CS or Mod15VB project in the 2310Demos solution.

▶ **To run the demonstration**

Configure a SqlConnection object to use dynamic properties

1. Open the DataAccess.aspx page in the Mod15VB or Mod15CS project in Visual Studio .NET.

2. Select the **SqlConnection** object and view the **Properties** window.

3. Expand the **DynamicProperties** property.

   Notice that the **ConnectionString** property can be a dynamic property.

4. Select the **ConnectionString** property and then click the "**...**" button.

5. In the **Dynamic Property** dialog box, make the property a dynamic property with the default key name by selecting **Map property to a key in configuration file**, and then click **OK**.

6. In the Properties window, notice the blue glyph next to the **<original> ConnectionString** property of the **SqlConnection** object. The glyph indicates that this is a dynamic property.

**Show the newly
generated code**

7. View the newly generated code in the code-behind page and look for the
   line of code that sets the **ConnectionString** property of the **SqlConnection**
   object:

Visual Basic .NET

```
Me.SqlConnection1.ConnectionString = _
CType(configurationAppSettings.GetValue _
("SqlConnection1.ConnectionString", _
GetType(System.String)), String)
```

C#

```
this.SqlConnection1.ConnectionString =
((string)(configurationAppSettings.GetValue("SqlConnection1
.ConnectionString", typeof(string))));
```

**Show the
SqlConnection1.
ConnectionString key**

8. Open the Web.config file and find the **SqlConnection1.ConnectionString**
   key in the **appSettings** section.

Lesson: Deploying an ASP.NET Web Application

- Web Application Deployment

- Preparing a Web Application for Deployment

- Practice: Selecting Necessary Files

- Sharing Assemblies in the Global Assembly Cache

- Updating Your Web Application

Introduction

After you have set up **Cache** objects and the output cache, and organized the Web application settings between the Machine.config and Web.config files, you are ready to deploy your ASP.NET Web application.

In this lesson, you will learn how to select the files that are necessary to run the Web application and then use XCOPY or file transfer protocol (FTP) to copy these files to the production directory.

Lesson objectives

After completing this lesson, you will be able to:

- Explain how to deploy a Web application.

- Prepare your Web application for deployment by selecting only the files that are necessary for running the Web application.

- Share assemblies in the Global Assembly Cache (GAC).

- Update an ASP.NET Web application.

Web Application Deployment

- **Copy files locally or FTP files remotely**
- **Configure the target folder as a virtual directory in IIS**
- **Copy all necessary files, including the \bin directory and content**
  - No need to register components

Introduction

To deploy an ASP.NET Web application to a production directory or server, you must copy all of the necessary files to their proper location. This copying is typically done by using either Windows Explorer for local copies, or the FTP for remote deployments. This type of copying is often referred to as XCOPY deployment, after the Microsoft MS-DOS® utility XCOPY, which copies all of the files and folders within a directory.

Configure the target folder as a virtual directory in IIS

Before you can deploy a Web application to a production directory, the folder to which you will deploy your Web application must be configured as a virtual directory in IIS.

▶ **To Configure a folder as a virtual directory in IIS**

1. On the **Start** menu, right-click **My Computer** and then click **Manage**.
2. Expand **Services and Applications**, and then expand **Internet Information Services**.
3. In the left pane of the IIS console, browse to the folder that you want to convert to a Web application directory.
4. Right-click the folder and then click **Properties**.
5. On the **Directory** tab, in the **Application Settings** section, click **Create**.
6. Click **OK**.

Copy all necessary files

Only subsets of the files that are required to build a Web application are required to run the Web application in the production directory. The final step before copying the Web application should be to build the Web application and then remove all of the unnecessary files.

Because common language runtime applications are self-describing and require no registry entries, you do not need to register components before or after copying files. The Web application is ready to accept requests after it has been copied to a folder that has been configured in IIS as a Web application directory.

Preparing a Web Application for Deployment

1. **Build the Web application**

2. **Do not select unnecessary files**

   - Visual Studio .NET solution files (.vbproj, .vbproj.webinfo, .csproj, .csproj.webinfo, etc.)

   - Resource (.resx) files

   - Code-behind pages (.vb, .cs)

3. **Copy or FTP necessary files to the production directory**

Introduction

There are three major steps required to move your Web application from the development environment to a production directory or server:

1. Build the Web application.
2. Remove all of the unnecessary files from the Web application.
3. Copy the files to the production environment.

Build the application

The first step is to build, or *compile*, your Web application. This compilation creates a dynamic-link library (DLL) file in the \bin directory that contains all of the code for the Web application. One *ApplicationName*.dll file is created for each Web application; this file contains the code from all of the resource and code-behind files.

Do not select unnecessary files

The second step in deploying a Web application is to select only the necessary files from the directory that contains the Web application. By not copying unnecessary files, you increase the security of your production environment by limiting the exposure of uncompiled code.

The files that are not needed in the production directory include:

- Visual Studio .NET solution files (.vbproj, .vbproj.webinfo, .csproj, and so on)

  These files are only required by Visual Studio .NET to develop the Web application and are not required to run the Web application in production.

- Resource (.resx) files

  These files are compiled into the DLL file.

- Code-behind pages (.vb, .cs)

  These files are compiled into the DLL file.

Note   You must copy the code-behind pages if you are using dynamic compilation in your Web application. Dynamic compilation is enabled by using the **src** attribute in the @ **Page** directive.

Required files

The files that are required on the production server include:

- The \bin directory and the DLL files that are within it.

  These files are the compiled resource files and code-behind pages.

- All Web Form, user control, and XML Web service files (.aspx, .ascx, .asmx).

  These are the user and application interface files.

- Configuration files, including Web.config and global.asax.

  If you have changed configuration settings in the Machine.config file on the development computer, you must make the same changes in the Machine.config file on the production server.

- Any additional support files that are in the directory (such as XML files).

Copy or FTP the files

After you have compiled the Web application and removed all of the unnecessary files, you need only copy or FTP all of the remaining Web application files in the development directory to the production directory.

Practice: Selecting Necessary Files

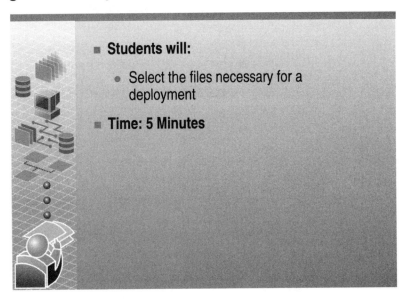

In this practice, you will select the necessary files that you need to copy to the production directory

Visual Basic .NET File	Microsoft Visual C#™ File	Keep	Remove
.vbproj	.csproj		
.vbproj.webinfo	.csproj.webinfo		
.resx	.resx		
.dll	.dll		
.aspx	.aspx		
\bin directory and content	\bin directory and content		
.aspx.vb	.aspx.cs		
.csproj	.vbproj		
Global.asax	Global.asax		
.exe	.exe		
.ascx	.ascx		
.xml	.xml		
Web.config	Web.config		

Sharing Assemblies in the Global Assembly Cache

- **The global assembly cache provides storage for assemblies you need to share**

  - Machine-wide cache for code

  - Because DLL files are not registered, they are not easily shared between Web applications

Introduction

Each computer with the common language runtime installed also has a computer-wide code cache called the global assembly cache. After you have deployed your Web application to a production Web server, you can use the GAC to share code among Web applications on the Web server.

Storage for assemblies you need to share

Although the ASP.NET **Cache** object is used for short-term storage of information within a Web application, the GAC can be used to share code across the entire Web server. The GAC stores assemblies that are specifically designated to be shared by several Web applications on a server. An assembly is a collection of resources in a single file (for example, a dll file).

There are several reasons why you might want to install an assembly into the GAC, including:

- Shared location

  Assemblies used by multiple applications can be put in the GAC.

- File security

  The GAC is installed in the WINNT directory, which typically has access restrictions to its contents.

- Side-by-side versioning

  Multiple copies of assemblies with the same name, but with different version information, can be maintained in the GAC.

Updating Your Web Application

- **Copy or FTP files to update the Web application**
  - Do not need to stop and restart IIS
  - .dll files can be updated while the site is still running
- **Output cache protects existing users**

Introduction

After your Web application is running on a production directory, you can update the Web application at any time without restarting the server, IIS, or the Web application.

Copy or FTP files

With ASP.NET, when you have a new version of the Web application, you need only copy the new files to the directory, thereby overwriting the existing files. When the next user connects to your Web application, they receive the most up-to-date files. Unlike earlier versions of Active Server Pages (ASP), updating an ASP.NET Web site does not require you to stop and restart IIS.

Output cache protects existing users

If you enable page output caching for the Web Forms, users will continue to receive the older versions of the pages until the cache expires. After the cached pages expire, users will receive an updated version of that page.

Review

> ■ Using the Cache Object
>
> ■ Using ASP.NET Output Caching
>
> ■ Configuring an ASP.NET Web Application
>
> ■ Deploying an ASP.NET Web Application

1. What is the difference between the **Cache** object and page output caching?

2. What sort of caching would you use to place a **DataSet** into cache?

3. Which files can you use to configure an ASP.NET Web application?

4. What are the three main steps to deploying an ASP.NET Web application?

5. What is the purpose of the global assembly cache?

6. Why can you remove the code-behind pages (.aspx.vb and .aspx.cs) when deploying your Web application?

7. Why would you consider using dynamic properties to store the URL to an XML Web service in Web.config?

Lab 15: Configuring, Optimizing, and Deploying a Microsoft ASP.NET Web Application

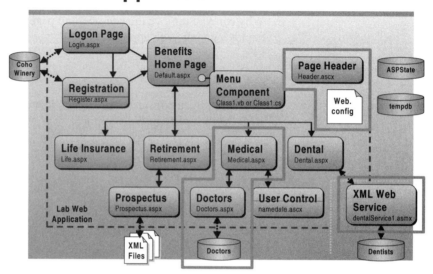

Objectives

After completing this lab, you will be able to:

- Use the **Cache** object to cache a **DataSet**.

- Use dynamic properties.
- Use page output caching to cache a Web Form and a user control.
- Use the **VaryByParam** property to manipulate page caching.
- Deploy a Microsoft® ASP.NET Web application on a remote server.

Note This lab focuses on the concepts in this module and as a result may not comply with Microsoft security recommendations.

Prerequisites

Before working on this lab, you must have:

- Knowledge about how to use the **Cache** object.
- Knowledge about how page output caching works.
- Knowledge about using Internet Information Services (IIS).

Scenario

Coho Winery offers several benefits to its employees. In the labs for Course 2310B, *Developing Microsoft ASP.NET Web Applications Using Visual Studio .NET*, you will create a Web site that enables employees to select and set up their chosen benefits.

In this lab, you will:

- Use the **Cache** object to cache a **DataSet**.
- Use the output cache to cache a Web Form and a user control.
- Use dynamic properties to store the Uniform Resource Locator (URL) for an XML Web service.
- Deploy the 2310LabApplication Web site on a remote server.

Estimated time to complete this lab: 90 minutes

Exercise 0
Lab Setup

To complete this lab, you must have created a Benefits Web Application project and a BenefitsList Class Library project. These projects can be created by using Microsoft Visual Basic® .NET or Microsoft Visual C#™ .NET.

If you have not created these projects, complete the following steps:

▶ **Create the 2310LabApplication solution**

Important Only perform this procedure if you have not created a 2310LabApplication solution file.

1. Using Microsoft Visual Studio® .NET, create a new blank solution named **2310LabApplication**:

   a. On the **File** menu, point to **New**, and then click **Blank Solution**.

   b. In the **New Project** dialog box, type **2310LabApplication** in the **Name** text box, and then click **OK**.

▶ **Create the Benefits project**

Important Only perform this procedure if you have not previously created a Benefits project, or if you have removed the Benefits project according to the steps in Appendix A, "Lab Recovery," in Course 2310B, *Developing Microsoft ASP.NET Web Applications Using Visual Studio .NET*.

1. Create a new ASP.NET Web Application project, named **BenefitsVB** or **BenefitsCS**, in the 2310LabApplication solution:

   a. On the **File** menu, point to **New**, and then click **Project**.

   b. In the **New Project** dialog box, in the **Project Types** list, click **Visual Basic Projects** or **Visual C# Projects**.

   c. In the **Templates** list, click **ASP.NET Web Application**. Set the **Location** to **http://localhost/BenefitsVB** for the Visual Basic .NET project or to **http:/localhost/BenefitsCS** for the Visual C# project.

   d. Click **Add to Solution**, and then click **OK**.

Caution When adding projects to the solution, the capitalization of the project name is important. Because you may be using some pre-built Web Forms in this and other labs in Course 2310B, *Developing Microsoft ASP.NET Web Applications Using Visual Studio .NET*, you must verify that you have capitalized the Benefits project as shown.

▶ **Update the Benefits project**

1. In Visual Studio .NET, open the 2310LabApplication solution file.

2. In Solution Explorer, right-click **BenefitsVB** or **BenefitsCS**, point to **Add**, and then click **Add Existing Item**.

3. Browse for project files:

For the Visual Basic .NET project

Browse to the *install folder*\Labfiles\Lab15\VB\Starter\BenefitsVB folders.

For the Visual C# project

Browse to the *install folder*\Labfiles\Lab15\CS\Starter\BenefitsCS folder.

4. In the **Files of type** box of the **Add Existing Item – Benefits** dialog box, click **All Files (*.*)**.

5. Select all of the files in this folder, and then click **Open**.

6. Click **Yes** if prompted to overwrite or reload files.

▶ **Create the BenefitsList class library**

Important Only perform these steps if you have not previously created a BenefitsList project, or if you have removed the BenefitsList project according to the steps in Appendix A, "Lab Recovery," in Course 2310B, *Developing Microsoft ASP.NET Web Applications Using Visual Studio .NET.*

1. Create a new Class Library Project.

For the Visual Basic .NET project

Create a new Visual Basic .NET Class Library project, name it **BenefitsListVB**, and then add it to the 2310LabApplication solution:

a. On the **File** menu, point to **New**, and then click **Project**.

b. In the **New Project** dialog box, in the **Project Types** list, click **Visual Basic Projects**.

c. In the **Templates** list, click **Class Library** and then set the **Name** to **BenefitsListVB**.

d. Click **Add to Solution**, and then click **OK**.

For the Visual C# project

Create a new Visual C# .NET Class Library project, name it **BenefitsListCS**, and then add it to the 2310LabApplication solution:

a. On the **File** menu, point to **New**, and then click **Project**.

b. In the **New Project** dialog box, in the **Project Types** list, click **Visual C# Projects**.

c. In the **Templates** list, click **Class Library**, and then set the **Name** to **BenefitsListCS**.

d. Click **Add to Solution**, and then click **OK**.

Caution Verify that you have capitalized the BenefitsList project as shown.

▶ **Update the BenefitsList project**

1. In Visual Studio .NET, open the 2310LabApplication solution file.

2. In Solution Explorer, right-click **BenefitsListVB** or **BenefitsListCS**, point to **Add**, and then click **Add Existing Item**.

3. Browse for project files:

For the Visual Basic .NET project

Browse to the *install folder*\Labfiles\Lab15\VB\Starter\BenefitsListVB folder.

For the Visual C# project

Browse to the *install folder*\Labfiles\Lab15\CS\Starter\BenefitsListCS folder.

4. In the **Files of type** box of the **Add Existing Item – BenefitsList** dialog box, click **All Files (*.*)**.

5. Select all of the files in this folder, and then click **Open**.

6. Click **Yes** if prompted to overwrite or reload files.

▶ **Create a reference to the BenefitsList component in the Benefits project**

1. In the Benefits project in the 2310LabApplication solution, complete the following steps to add a reference to the BenefitsList component that you just created:

   a. Right-click the **BenefitsVB** or **BenefitsCS** project in Solution Explorer and then click **Add Reference**.

   b. In the **Add Reference** dialog box, on the **Projects** tab, double-click the **BenefitsListVB** or **BenefitsListCS** project.

   c. In the **Selected Components** list, select the **BenefitsListVB** or **BenefitsListCS** component, and then click **OK**.

      The component is added to the References folder in Solution Explorer.

▶ **Create the Dental XML Web Service**

Important   Perform this procedure only if you have not previously created the DentalService project, or if you have removed the DentalService project according to the steps in Appendix A, "Lab Recovery," in Course 2310B, *Developing Microsoft ASP.NET Web Applications Using Visual Studio .NET*.

---

1. Create a new XML Web Service project, named **DentalServiceVB** or **DentalServiceCS**, and then add it to the 2310LabApplication solution:

   a. On the **File** menu, point to **New**, and then click **Project**.

   b. In the **New Project** dialog box, in the **Project Types** list, click **Visual Basic Projects**.

   c. In the **Templates** list, click **ASP.NET Web Service** and then set the **Location** to **http://localhost/DentalServiceVB** or to **http://localhost/DentalServiceCS**.

   d. Click **Add to Solution**, and then click **OK**.

Caution   Verify that you have capitalized the DentalService project name as shown.

▶ **Update the DentalService project**

1. In Visual Studio .NET, open the 2310LabApplication solution file.

2. In Solution Explorer, right-click **DentalServiceVB** or **DentalServiceCS**, point to **Add**, and then click **Add Existing Item**.

3. Browse to the DentalService folder:

Visual Basic .NET   Browse to the *install folder*\Labfiles\Lab15\VB\Starter\DentalServiceVB.

Visual C#   Browse to the *install folder*\Labfiles\Lab15\CS\Starter\DentalServiceCS.

4. Add files to the project:

Visual Basic .NET   In the **Files of type** box of the **Add Existing Item – DentalServiceVB** dialog box, click **All Files (*.*)**.

Visual C#   In the **Files of type** box of the **Add Existing Item – DentalServiceCS** dialog box, click **All Files (*.*)**.

5. Select all of the files in this folder, and then click **Open**.

6. Click **Yes** if prompted to overwrite or reload files.

7. Build the DentalService XML Web service by right-clicking the **DentalService** project in Solution Explorer and clicking **Build**.

▶ **Add a Web reference in the Benefits project to the DentalService Web service**

1. In the Benefits project in the 2310LabApplication solution, complete the following steps to add a Web reference to the DentalService XML Web service:

   a. In Solution Explorer, right-click **BenefitsVB** or **BenefitsCS** and then click **Add Web Reference**.

   b. In the **Address** text box, type:

Visual Basic .NET   http://localhost/DentalServiceVB/DentalService.asmx

Visual C#   http://localhost/DentalServiceCS/DentalService.asmx

   and then press ENTER.

   The DentalService Web reference is displayed.

   c. Click **Add Reference**.

   The Web reference is added to the project in the Web References folder.

2. In Solution Explorer, expand **Web References**, right-click **localhost**, and then choose **Rename**.

3. Type **DentalWebRef** and then press ENTER.

4. Build the solution by clicking **Build Solution** on the **Build** menu.

▶ **Install and configure the session state databases**

1. From the **Start** menu, point to **All Programs**, point to **Accessories**, and then click **Command Prompt**.

   A command window opens.

2. At the command prompt, type the following command, where *version* is the latest version of the Microsoft .NET Framework that is installed on your computer, and then press ENTER:

   ```
   cd\WINDOWS\Microsoft.NET\Framework\version\
   ```

   The command prompt changes to the new directory.

3. At the command prompt, type the following command, and then press ENTER:

   ```
   OSQL -S localhost -E <InstallSqlState.sql
   ```

   The command window displays a series of numbers and messages, and then returns to the command prompt. The **ASPState** and **tempdb** databases have been restored.

4. Close the command prompt, and then open Windows Explorer.

5. Browse to the following directory:

   Visual Basic .NET   *install folder*\LabFiles\Lab15\VB\Starter

   Visual C#   *install folder*\LabFiles\Lab15\CS\Starter

6. Double-click **Lab15.bat**.

   This batch file runs an SQL query that configures security for the **ASPState** and **tempdb** databases.

7. Close Windows Explorer.

Exercise 1
Using the Cache Object

In this exercise, you will use the **Cache** object to cache the **DataSet** object **doctors**. Placing a **DataSet** in cache reduces the number of times a Web Form needs to connect to the data source, in this case Microsoft SQL Server™, to fill the **DataGrid**.

Because the **DataGrid** uses **DataViews** that are based on the city name selected from the list box, you will implement caching in the **Page_Load** event procedure, and in the list box's **SelectedIndexCached** event procedure.

The **DataGrid** also implements paging. To reduce the amount of code that you add in this lab, you will disable this feature of the **DataGrid**.

▶ **Turn off paging**

1. Open the doctors.aspx file.

2. Right-click the **DataGrid** object **dgDoctors,** and then choose **Property Builder**.

3. Select the **Paging** tab, and then clear the **Allow paging** check box.

   This will disable paging for the **DataGrid**. All data that is returned from the data source will be displayed.

4. Click **OK**.

▶ **Cache the DataSet in the Page_Load event procedure**

1. Open the doctors.aspx.vb or doctors.aspx.cs file.

2. In the **Page_Load** event for doctors.aspx, find the following line of code:

Visual Basic .NET
```
If Not Page.IsPostBack Then
```

C#
```
if (!Page.IsPostBack)
```

3. Add code, immediately preceding this line, that checks the cache for a key named **doctors**. The code should check to see if this key is empty or does not exist.

4. If the **doctors** cache key is empty or does not exist, fill the **DataSet** object **dsDoctors1** by using the existing **DataAdapter** object **sqlDataAdapter1**, and then insert a new **doctors** key into the cache that contains the new **DataSet**. Use the information in the following table to write your code.

Property	Visual Basic .NET Value	C#
Key name	doctors	doctors
Value	DsDoctors1	dsDoctors1
Dependencies	Nothing	null
Absolute Expiration	Four minutes	Four minutes
Sliding Expiration	Nothing	Caching.Cache.NoSlidingExpiration

Your code should look like the following:

Visual Basic .NET

```
If (Cache("doctors") Is Nothing) Then
    SqlDataAdapter1.Fill(DsDoctors1)
    Cache.Insert("doctors", DsDoctors1, Nothing, _
        DateTime.Now.AddMinutes(4), Nothing)
End If
```

C#

```
if (Cache["doctors"] == null)
{
    sqlDataAdapter1.Fill(dsDoctors1);
    Cache.Insert("doctors", dsDoctors1, null,
        DateTime.Now.AddMinutes(4),
        System.Web.Caching.Cache.NoSlidingExpiration);
}
```

5. In the **Page_Load** event procedure, locate the following comment:

   ```
   TODO Lab 9: bind the datagrid to the doctors table
   ```

   Beneath the comment, delete or comment out the following line of code:

Visual Basic .NET

```
SqlDataAdapter1.Fill(DsDoctors1)
```

C#

```
sqlDataAdapter1.Fill(dsDoctors1);
```

6. In the **Page_Load** event procedure, find the following line of code:

Visual Basic .NET

```
dgDoctors.DataSource = DsDoctors1
```

C#

```
dgDoctors.DataSource = dsDoctors1;
```

7. Set the **DataSource** property of **dgDoctors** to the cached **DataSet**.

   Your code should look like the following:

Visual Basic .NET

```
dgDoctors.DataSource = Cache("doctors")
```

C#

```
dgDoctors.DataSource = Cache["doctors"];
```

▶ **Cache the DataSet in the lstCities_SelectedIndexChanged event procedure**

1. In the **lstCities_SelectedIndexChanged** event procedure for doctors.aspx, find the following line of code:

Visual Basic .NET

```
SqlDataAdapter1.Fill(DsDoctors1)
```

C#

```
sqlDataAdapter1.Fill(DsDoctors1);
```

2. Remove this line of code and replace it with the same code that you added to the **Page_Load** event procedure. That code checks for the presence of the **doctors** cache key, and creates a new key if the **doctors** key does not exist or if it is empty.

3. In the remaining code in the **lstCities_SelectedIndexChanged** event procedure, change any occurrences of **dsDoctors1** to the **doctors** cache key and convert it to a **DataSet** type.

When complete, the entire **lstCities_SelectedIndexChanged** event procedure should look like the following:

Visual Basic .NET

```
Dim strCity As String = _
    Trim(lstCities.SelectedItem.Value)

If (Cache("doctors") Is Nothing) Then
    SqlDataAdapter1.Fill(DsDoctors1)
    Cache.Insert("doctors", DsDoctors1, Nothing, _
        DateTime.Now.AddMinutes(4), Nothing)
End If

If strCity = "[All]" Then
    dgDoctors.DataSource = Cache("doctors")
Else
    Dim dvDocs As New DataView(CType(Cache("doctors"), _
        DataSet).Tables(0))
    dvDocs.RowFilter = "city = '" & strCity & "'"
    dgDoctors.DataSource = dvDocs
End If
reset()
dgDoctors.DataBind()
```

C#

```
string strCity = (lstCities.SelectedItem.Text).Trim();
if (Cache["doctors"] == null)
{
    sqlDataAdapter1.Fill(dsDoctors1);
    Cache.Insert("doctors",dsDoctors1, null,
        DateTime.Now.AddMinutes(4),
        System.Web.Caching.Cache.NoSlidingExpiration);
}

if (strCity == "[All]")
    dgDoctors.DataSource = Cache["doctors"];
else
{
    DataView dvDocs = new
        DataView(((DataSet)Cache["doctors"]).Tables[0]);
    dvDocs.RowFilter = "city = '" + strCity + "'";
    dgDoctors.DataSource = dvDocs;
}
reset();
dgDoctors.DataBind();
```

Note When using a cache key with a **DataView** object, you must perform an explicit data type conversion because the Benefits project has Option Strict enabled.

▶ **Test the Page**

1. Save doctors.aspx.vb or doctors.aspx.cs, and then build and browse the page.

   If you receive a SQL Permission error when trying to browse the Benefits Web site, close Internet Explorer, open Windows Explorer, browse to *install folder*\LabFiles\Lab15\VB\Starter or *install folder*\LabFiles\Lab15\CS\Starter and then double-click **Lab15.bat**.

2. Test the drop-down list box of city names by selecting different city names.

▶ **If time permits**

1. Add a new row to the **DataTable** object **doctors** of the **DataBase** object **doctors** by using SQL Server Enterprise Manager. You must include a value for the dr_id, dr_fname, and dr_lname columns.

2. Refresh doctors.aspx in the browser.

   Note that the new item does not appear in the **DataGrid**.

3. Select any city in the drop-down list box, and then select **All**.

   Note that the new item still does not appear in the **DataGrid**.

4. Wait at least four minutes, and then repeat Step 3.

   Note that the new row now displays in the **DataGrid**.

5. In SQL Server Enterprise Manager, delete the row that you added.

   Note that the deleted item still appears in the **DataGrid**. If you wait four minutes and then refresh the page, the deleted item no longer displays.

Exercise 2
Using the Page Output Cache

In this exercise, you will cache a Web Form by using the **OutputCache** directive. You will also alter the **VaryByParam** attribute.

Scenario

The medical.aspx page displays the user's name, birth date, and the doctor the user has selected from the doctors.aspx page. To reduce response times for this page, you should cache the entire page by using page output caching.

▶ **Cache the medical.aspx page**

1. Open the medical.aspx page and switch to Hypertext Markup Language (HTML) view.

2. Add an **OutputCache** directive that enables output caching for the entire page. The page should remain in the cache for two minutes and should not be updated based on the parameters that are passed to the page. You code should look like the following:

   ```
   <%@ OutputCache Duration="120" VaryByParam="none"%>
   ```

3. Save and browse the medical.aspx page.

4. Click the **Select a doctor** link.

5. In the doctors.aspx page, select a doctor from the **DataGrid**, and then click **Submit**.

   You are returned to the medical.aspx page, but the selected doctor's name does not appear next to **Primary Care Physician**. Why?

   _____

   _____

▶ **Use the VaryByParam attribute**

1. Return to the HTML view for the medical.aspx page.

2. Edit the **OutputCache** directive you added, and change the code to create a new cached version of the page when a different doctor is selected from the doctors.aspx page.

   What is the name of the parameter that is passed from the doctors.aspx page to the medical.aspx page?

   _____

   _____

Your code should look like the following:

```
<%@ OutputCache Duration="120" VaryByParam="pcp"%>
```

3. Save the medical.aspx page and view it in a browser.

4. Click the **Select a doctor** link.

5. In Doctors.aspx, select a doctor from the **DataGrid**, and then click **Submit**.

   You are returned to medical.aspx, and the selected doctor's name appears next to **Primary Care Physician**.

6. Again, click **Select a doctor**.

7. Select a different doctor in the **DataGrid**, and then click **Submit**.

   When you are returned to medical.aspx, the **Primary Care Physician** box now shows the newly selected doctor's name.

Exercise 3
Partial Page Caching

In this exercise, you will use the page output cache to cache the user control header.ascx. You will first add a time stamp to the header to verify that the cache is working properly.

Scenario

The user control header.ascx displays a banner at the top of each page in your Web application. Because this information typically does not change and is required for every page request, you should cache the information for quick retrieval.

▶ **Add a time stamp to the header**

1. Open the header.ascx file.

2. Using a click-and-drag operation, drag a **label** control to the right of the text "Benefits Selection Site." Rename the new label control **lblTime**.

3. In the code-behind page for header.ascx, at the end of the **Page_Load** event procedure, add code to make the **lblTime** label show the current time. Your code should look like the following:

Visual Basic .NET

```
lblTime.Text = DateTime.Now.TimeOfDay.ToString()
```

C#

```
lblTime.Text = DateTime.Now.TimeOfDay.ToString();
```

4. Save and then build header.ascx.

5. Browse the doctors.aspx Web Form.

   Because header.ascx cannot be viewed in a browser, you must view a page that uses the user control.

   Why can you not browse header.ascx directly?

   _____

   _____

6. Refresh the browser several times.

   Note that the time displayed in header.ascx changes with every refresh of the doctors.aspx page.

▶ **Add caching to the header file**

1. Open header.ascx and switch to HTML view.

2. Add an **Output Cache** directive to the page that enables page caching with a duration of two minutes. The cache should not change based on any parameters that are passed. Your code should look like the following:

   ```
   <%@ OutputCache Duration="120" VaryByParam="none"%>
   ```

3. Save and then build header.ascx.

4. Browse the doctors.aspx page.

   Note that you do not need to rebuild doctors.aspx, because no changes were made to this file.

5. Refresh the browser several times.

   Notice that the time in header.ascx does not change with each refresh. If time allows, wait more than two minutes and then refresh the page once more. The header will display the current time.

Exercise 4
Using Dynamic Properties

In this exercise, you will use dynamic properties to place the URL for the DentalService XML Web service in the Web.config file.

Scenario

An XML Web service may have a URL that changes with time. If your Web application connects to an XML Web service, you can place the URL of that Web service in the Web.config file of your Web application. If the URL for the XML Web service changes, you only need to update the Web.config file, rather than changing the proxy information and rebuilding the project. Changing the Web.config file does not require rebuilding of the Web application.

▶ **View the current settings of the proxy**

1. Open the proxy file for the DentalService XML Web service.

    The proxy file is named Reference.vb or Reference.cs, and is found in Solution Explorer under Web References\DentalWebRef\Reference.map.

    Tip If you do not see a file listed under the Reference.map file, you must click the **Show All Files** icon at the top of Solution Explorer or click **Show All Files** on the **Project** menu.

    ---

2. In Reference.vb, find the constructor named **New**. In Reference.cs, find the constructor named **DentalService**.

    What does this method do?

    _____

    _____

3. In Solution Explorer, right-click the **Web reference** and choose **Properties**.

    The Web reference is named **DentalWebRef** and is located in the Web References folder.

4. In the Properties window, change the **URL Behavior** property setting from **Static** to **Dynamic**.

5. When the dialog box opens, notifying you that the Reference.vb or Reference.cs file has changed, click **Yes** to reload the file.

6. In Reference.vb or Reference.cs, find the constructor again.

    What has changed in the constructor? What does the added code do?

    _____

    _____

7. In Solution Explorer, open the Web.config file for the Benefits project.

Note   Be sure to open the Web.config file for the Benefits project, not the Web.config file that is associated with the DentalService XML Web service.

---

8. Scroll to the end of Web.config and find the **appSettings** element.

What information is included in the **appSettings** element?

_____

_____

Exercise 5
Deploying Your Site

In this exercise, you will deploy your Web site on another server. You will use your class partner's computer as a deployment server.

▶ **Prepare the folder for deployment**

These steps must be completed on your class partner's computer.

1. Open Windows Explorer and browse to the directory C:\Inetpub\wwwroot.

2. Right-click **Lab15VB** or **Lab15CS**, and then click **Sharing**.

3. In the **Lab15VB** or **Lab15CS Properties** window, click **Share this folder**, and then click **OK**.

Important   The default sharing permissions in Microsoft Windows® XP grant the **Everyone** group full control of the shared folder. In a controlled laboratory environment, used for testing purposes only, this is an acceptable setting. On a production server, you should never grant the **Everyone** group access to shared folders.

▶ **Prepare the project for deployment**

1. In Visual Studio .NET, on the **Debug** toolbar shortcut menu,
   `Debug ▾`, click **Release**.

2. On the **Build** menu, click **Rebuild Solution**.

3. Close Visual Studio .NET.

▶ **Select and copy files for deployment**

1. Open Windows Explorer and browse to the directory C:\Inetpub\wwwroot\BenefitsVB or C:\Inetpub\wwwroot\BenefitsCS.

2. Select all of the files and folders in the Benefits folder.

3. On the **Edit** menu, click **Copy**.

4. In the address box in Windows Explorer, type ***partner*\Lab15VB** or ***partner*\Lab15CS,** where *partner* is the name of your class partner's computer, and then press ENTER.

5. On the **Edit** menu, click **Paste**.

   If you receive an "Access Denied" error while copying the files, you and your partner need to complete the following steps:

   a. Open Windows Explorer and browse to the C:\Inetpub\wwwroot folder.

   b. Right-click **Lab15VB** or **Lab15CS**, and then choose **Properties**.

   c. Clear the **Read-only** attribute, and then click **OK**.

   d. In the **Confirm Attribute Changes** dialog box, click **Apply changes to this folder, subfolders, and files**, and then click **OK**.

   After your partner has completed these four steps, repeat the file copy procedure in Step 5.

6. Open the Lab15VB or Lab15CS folder.

   The folder contains all of the files from your Web site.

7. Delete the files that are not needed for deployment. Files that you can delete include all files with the following extensions:

   - .resx

   - .vbproj

   - .vb

   - .webinfo

   - .vsdisco

   - .csproj

   - .cs

   Note Normally, you would delete these files before copying them to the production server. In this lab, you delete them after copying so that you are not deleting any files that you may use in other labs in Course 2310B, *Developing Microsoft ASP.NET Web Applications Using Visual Studio .Net*.

8. Close Windows Explorer.

▶ **Test the deployment**

1. Open Internet Explorer.

2. In the address bar, type **http://*partner*/Lab15VB** or **http://*partner*/Lab15CS**, where *partner* is the name of your partner's computer.

   The Default.aspx page displays.

3. Browse through the site to ensure that all of the pages appear and function as expected.

   Note The Lab15CS and Lab15VB folders were configured as application directories during classroom setup. Ordinarily, you would need access to the Web server to configure this folder as a Web application.

Course Evaluation

Your evaluation of this course will help Microsoft understand the quality of your learning experience.

At a convenient time between now and the end of the course, please complete a course evaluation, which is available at http://www.CourseSurvey.com

Microsoft will keep your evaluation strictly confidential and will use your responses to improve your future learning experience.

msdn® training

Module 16: Securing a Microsoft ASP.NET Web Application

Contents

Overview

- Web Application Security Overview
- Working with Windows-Based Authentication
- Working with Forms-Based Authentication
- Overview of Microsoft Passport Authentication

Introduction

Securing Web applications is a critical and a complex matter for Web developers. A secure system requires careful planning, and Web site administrators and developers must have an unambiguous understanding of the options that are available to them when securing their Web applications.

Microsoft® ASP.NET synchronizes with the Microsoft .NET Framework and Internet Information Services (IIS) to provide Web application security.

This module covers, in detail, the various Web application security methods.

Objectives

After completing this module, you will be able to:

- Describe the ASP.NET and IIS authentication methods.
- Use Windows-based authentication to secure ASP.NET Web applications.
- Use Forms-based authentication to secure ASP.NET Web applications.
- Use Microsoft Passport to secure ASP.NET Web applications.

Lesson: Web Application Security Overview

- **Authentication vs. Authorization**
- **What Are ASP.NET Authentication Methods?**
- **Multimedia: ASP.NET Authentication Methods**
- **Comparing the ASP.NET Authentication Methods**
- **What Are the IIS Authentication Mechanisms?**
- **Demonstration: Using IIS Authentication Mechanisms**
- **What Is Secure Sockets Layer?**

Introduction

By definition, Web applications give users access to a central resource, the Web server, and access through it, to database servers. By understanding and implementing suitable security measures for your Web application, you can protect your own resources, in addition to providing a secure environment in which your users are comfortable working.

This lesson provides an overview of different security concepts: authentication, authorization, and IIS authentication mechanisms. You will also learn about Secure Sockets Layer (SSL).

Lesson objectives

After completing this lesson, you will be able to:

- Describe the two fundamental security concepts for securing a Web application.
- Describe the three ASP.NET authentication methods.
- Distinguish between the three ASP.NET authentication methods.
- Describe the four IIS authentication mechanisms.
- Describe SSL.

Authentication vs. Authorization

- **Authentication**
  - Accepts credentials from a user
  - Validates the credentials
- **Authorization**
  - Given the authentication credentials supplied, determines the right to access a resource
  - Can be assigned by user name or by role

Introduction

To work with security, you should be familiar with the two fundamental security concepts for securing a Web application:

- Authentication
- Authorization

Authentication

Authentication is the process of obtaining identification credentials, such as a name and a password, from a user and validating those credentials against some authority, such as a database. If the credentials are valid, the entity that submitted the credentials is considered an authenticated identity.

For example, all users must provide a user name and password every time they log on to a network. These credentials are then validated against an authority, such as a database or a Microsoft Windows®–based domain server.

Authorization

After an identity has been authenticated, the authorization process determines whether that identity has access to a specified resource. The authorization process limits access rights by granting or denying specific permissions to an authenticated identity.

For example, you can authorize user Robert Brown to access the color printer, but deny access to user Bob Hohman. Similarly, you can authorize only the users of the Media group to be able to access the color printer and deny access to the rest of the users.

What Are ASP.NET Authentication Methods?

- **Windows-based authentication**
  - Relies on the Windows operating system and IIS
  - User requests a secure Web page and the request goes through IIS
  - After credentials are verified by IIS, the secure Web page is returned
- **Forms-based authentication**
  - Unauthenticated requests are redirected to an HTML form
  - User provides credentials and submits the HTML form
  - After credentials are verified, an authentication cookie is issued
- **Microsoft Passport authentication**
  - Centralized authentication service that offers a single logon option
  - Microsoft Passport is an XML Web service

Introduction

ASP.NET implements authentication through authentication methods. ASP.NET authentication methods contain the code that is necessary to authenticate the user's credentials.

Authentication methods

ASP.NET supports three types of authentication methods:

- Windows-based authentication
- Forms-based authentication
- Microsoft Passport authentication

Windows-based authentication

With Windows-based authentication, the ASP.NET Web application relies on the Windows operating system to authenticate the user. ASP.NET uses Windows-based authentication in conjunction with IIS authentication.

With Windows-based authentication, the user requests a secure Web page from the Web application, and the request then goes through IIS. If the user's credentials do not match those of an authorized user, IIS rejects the request. The user then has to enter his or her name and password in the logon form. The credentials are again verified by IIS. If correct, IIS directs the original request to the Web application. The secure Web page is then returned to the user.

Forms-based authentication

Forms-based authentication refers to a system where non-authenticated requests are redirected to a Hypertext Markup Language (HTML) form by using Hypertext Transfer Protocol (HTTP) client-side redirection. The user provides credentials and submits the form. If the application validates the credentials on the form, the system issues an authentication cookie to the user. Subsequent requests from the user are issued with the authentication cookie in the request headers, and then the user is authenticated based on those request headers.

Microsoft Passport authentication

Passport authentication is a centralized authentication service, provided by Microsoft, which offers a single logon option and core profile services for member sites. Users that sign up to use Passport are authenticated to access Web sites by using a single Passport account. Microsoft Passport is an XML Web service, and it is an integral part of the .NET Framework.

Multimedia: ASP.NET Authentication Methods

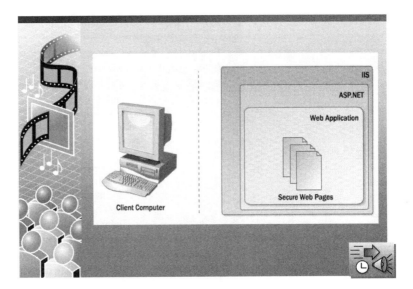

Introduction

In this animation, you will see the three types of authentication methods that you can use to secure ASP.NET Web applications:

- Windows-based authentication
- Forms-based authentication
- Microsoft Passport authentication

Comparing the ASP.NET Authentication Methods

Method	Advantages	Disadvantages
Windows-based Authentication	• Uses existing Windows infrastructure • Controls access to sensitive information	• Not appropriate for most Internet applications
Forms-based Authentication	• Good for Internet applications • Supports all client types	• Based on cookies
Microsoft Passport Authentication	• Single sign in for many Internet sites • No need to maintain a database to store user information • Allows developers to customize the appearance of the registration page	• Based on cookies • Fees involved

Introduction

Each of the three authentication methods supported by ASP.NET, Windows-based, Forms-based, and Microsoft Passport, are best suited for specific situations. Each method has significant advantages and disadvantages.

Windows-based authentication

Windows-based authentication uses the existing Windows infrastructure, and, therefore, it is best suited to situations in which you have a fixed number of users with existing Windows user accounts. Two such situations are:

■ If you are developing an intranet for your organization. Your organization might already have Windows user accounts configured for each employee.

■ If you need to control access to sensitive information. For example, you might want users in the Human Resources group to have access to directories containing employee resumes and salary details. You can use Windows-based authentication to prevent employees in other Windows groups, such as the Developers group, from accessing these sensitive documents.

The disadvantage of Windows-based authentication is that it is not suitable for most Internet applications. For example, if you are building a public user registration and password system, Windows-based authentication is not a good authentication option. With Windows-based authentication, a valid Windows user account must be configured for each user who accesses a restricted page. The process of adding new user accounts cannot be easily automated.

Forms-based authentication

Forms-based authentication is a good solution if you want to set up a custom user registration system for your Web site. The advantage of this type of authentication is that it enables you to store user names and passwords in whatever storage mechanism you want, such as the Web.config file, an Extensible Markup Language (XML) file, or a database table.

Forms-based authentication relies on cookies to determine the identity of the user. After Forms-based authentication is enabled, the requested page cannot be accessed by the user unless a specific cookie is found on the client. If this cookie is not found, or if the cookie is invalid, ASP.NET rejects the request and returns a logon page.

Microsoft Passport authentication

Microsoft Passport authentication has several advantages, including:

- It allows users to use the same user name and password to sign into many Web sites; therefore, users are less likely to forget their passwords. For example, both Microsoft Hotmail® and Microsoft MSN® use Microsoft Passport to authenticate users.

- You do not need to set up and maintain a database to store user registration information. Microsoft does all of that maintenance for you.

- It provides you with options to customize the appearance of the registration and sign-in pages by supplying templates.

There are two disadvantages with using Microsoft Passport authentication. First, there is a subscription fee to use the Microsoft Passport service. Second, Microsoft Passport authentication is based on cookies.

What Are the IIS Authentication Mechanisms?

Mechanisms	Security Level	Description
Anonymous	None	▪ No authentication occurs
Basic	Low (Medium with SSL)	▪ Client sends username and password as clear text ▪ Can be encrypted by using SSL ▪ Part of the HTTP specification and supported by most browsers
Digest	Medium	▪ Sends information as encoded hash ▪ Requires Internet Explorer 5 or later ▪ Requires Active Directory
Integrated Windows	High	▪ Uses either NTLM or Kerberos ▪ Generally good for intranets, not Internet ▪ Does not work through most firewalls

Introduction

Before you can use Windows-based authentication, you must first configure IIS. When a user requests a page that requires authorization, the user must be authenticated through IIS.

IIS provides several mechanisms that can be used for establishing authentication, including:

- Anonymous access
- Basic authentication
- Digest authentication
- Integrated Windows security

Anonymous access

For Web applications where unknown users will be making requests, typically public Web applications, IIS supports an anonymous user, one who has no authentication credentials. When IIS gets a request from an anonymous user, IIS in turn makes the request to Windows by using the default IUSR_*machinename* account.

Note The default account IUSR_*machinename* can be changed through the IIS snap-in.

Basic authentication

IIS also supports a Basic authentication model. In Basic authentication, users without credentials are prompted to supply a user name and password. These details are returned to IIS where they become available to the Web application. The advantage of Basic authentication is that it is part of the HTTP specification and it is supported by most browsers. Basic authentication provides a useful way to provide restricted access to a public Web application.

However, because the user passes a user name and password to IIS as clear text, Basic authentication is not highly secure. To increase the security level, use SSL to encrypt user names and passwords as they are transmitted across the network.

Digest authentication

Digest authentication is similar to Basic authentication, but it uses encryption to send user information to the server. If Anonymous access is disabled, users are prompted for their credentials (logon information). The browser combines this logon information with the other information that is stored on the client, and then sends an encoded hash called an MD5 hash (also known as Message Digest) to the server. The server already has a copy of this information and it recreates the original details from its own hash and authenticates the user. This mechanism works only with Microsoft Internet Explorer 5 and later, but it does pass through firewalls, proxy servers, and over the Internet.

However, Digest authentication only works with Active Directory® directory service domain accounts.

Note For more information about configuring Active Directory domain accounts to allow Digest authentication, see the IIS documentation.

Integrated Windows security

If the user making the request has already been authenticated in a Windows-based network, IIS can pass the user's credentials through when requesting access to a resource. The credentials do not include the user name and password, only an encrypted token indicating the user's security status.

Integrated Windows security works with Microsoft Windows NT® Local Area Network (LAN) Manager or Kerberos. Integrated Windows security also uses a hash algorithm to code and decode the user's credentials.

However, Integrated Windows security is not practical in Web applications that must go through firewalls. Therefore, it is best suited for a corporate intranet scenario.

Note When you configure IIS, you can use multiple IIS authentication mechanisms. You can check Anonymous and other authentication methods, such as Basic, Digest, or Integrated Windows. If you use multiple IIS authentication mechanisms, and if Anonymous authentication fails, the Web server attempts to use Basic, Digest, or Integrated Windows authentication, depending on which ones are selected.

Demonstration: Using IIS Authentication Mechanisms

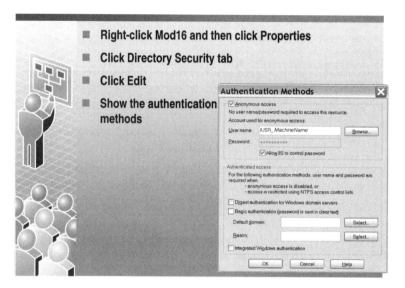

- Right-click Mod16 and then click Properties
- Click Directory Security tab
- Click Edit
- Show the authentication methods

Introduction

In this demonstration, you will see the dialog box that is used to set up the IIS authentication mechanisms.

▶ **To run the demonstration**

1. On the **Start** menu, right-click **My Computer** and then click **Manage**.

2. In the **Computer Management** console, **expand Services and Applications**, expand **Internet Information Services**, expand **Web Sites**, and then expand **Default Web Site**.

3. Right-click the **Mod16VB** or **Mod16CS** Web application and then click **Properties**.

4. In the **Mod16VB** or **Mod16CS Properties** dialog box, on the **Directory Security** tab, in the **Anonymous access and authentication control section**, click **Edit**.

5. Show the authentication methods available.

What Is Secure Sockets Layer?

- **SSL is a protocol used for transmitting data securely across a network. SSL secures data through:**

  - Data encryption
    - Ensures that the data sent is read only by a secure target server

  - Server authentication
    - Ensures that data is sent to the correct server
    - Uses the server and client certificates

  - Data integrity
    - Protects the integrity of the data
    - Includes a message authentication code that detects whether a message is altered

- **Uses Hypertext Transfer Protocol Secure to retrieve an ASP.NET Web page**

Introduction

IIS provides users with a secure communication channel by supporting the SSL protocol and RSA Data Security encryption on both the server and client.

Note RSA stands for Rivest, Shamir, and Adleman, which are the names of the scientists who created this algorithm.

What is SSL?

SSL is a protocol that is used for transmitting data securely across a network. SSL secures data communication through:

- Data encryption
- Server authentication
- Data integrity

Data encryption

When you enter information into an HTML form and submit it to a Web site, the information is then transmitted from your browser to the Web site server. As the information is transmitted, the data entered into the form can be intercepted and read.

SSL encrypts the information as it is transmitted back and forth between a Web server and a Web browser. The information is encrypted by using a publicly known algorithm and a session key. The Web server generates a public key that any client can use. The client generates a session key and uses the public key to encrypt it before sending it to the Web server. Data is transferred by using this session key.

The number of bits in the session key determines the strength of encryption. By default, IIS supports a 40-bit session key. However you have the option of upgrading IIS to use a stronger 128-bit session key.

The following table shows the advantages and disadvantages of using 40-bit and 128-bit session keys.

Session key	Advantage	Disadvantage
40-bit session key	Communication is much faster.	Not very secure, messages have been cracked.
128-bit session key	Very secure, messages encrypted with 128-bit session key are considered unbreakable.	Communication is significantly slowed; the longer the key, the more work the server and browser must perform to encrypt and decrypt the message.

Server authentication

Server authentication ensures that the data is sent to the correct server and that the server is secure.

For example, you may visit a Web site that appears to be an e-commerce Web site that you often access. The Web site appears to be the same familiar Web site in every way and you provide your credit card information to buy an item. However, a person who wants to deceive you could create a Web site that is identical to the genuine e-commerce Web site and steal your credit card information.

Server certificate

To prevent one Web site from impersonating another, you would use SSL to authenticate a Web site. When you install SSL on your Web server, you must install a server certificate. The server certificate contains information about your organization, your Web site, and the issuer of the certificate.

To work as a digital ID, a server certificate must be signed by a certificate authority. A certificate authority acts as a trusted third-party that verifies the identity of a Web site for its users.

Client certificate

SSL also supports client certificates. The client certificates are used to authenticate Web browsers instead of Web servers.

Data integrity

SSL protects the integrity of the data as it is passed between the Web server and Web browsers. SSL ensures that the data that was received by the target server is not altered in any way.

When messages are transmitted with SSL, they include a message authentication code. This code detects whether a message has been altered.

Using SSL in ASP.NET pages

After you configure your server to use SSL, you can request any page from your Web site by using a secure connection. To retrieve a Web page, SSL uses Hypertext Transfer Protocol Secure (HTTPS). For example, an address with the form https://www.yourdomain.com/login.aspx rather than http://www.yourdomain.com/page.aspx.

This form works for any page on your Web site.

Note ASP.NET provides the **Request.IsSecureConnection** property that allows you to determine if you are on a secure https connection or not.

Lesson: Working with Windows-Based Authentication

- How to Enable Windows-Based Authentication
- Reading User Information
- Demonstration: Using Windows-Based Authentication

Introduction

Windows-based authentication should be used to secure Web applications when you know which users will be accessing your Web site.

In this lesson, you will learn the procedure to use Windows-based authentication to secure your Web applications.

Lesson objectives

After completing this lesson, you will be able to:

- Use Windows-based authentication to secure Web applications.
- Read the identity of the user who is authenticated by using Windows-based authentication.

How to Enable Windows-Based Authentication

> **①** **Configure IIS to use one or more of the following authentication mechanisms:**
>
> - Basic
>
> - Digest
>
> - Integrated Windows security
>
> **②** **Set Windows-based authentication in Web.config**
>
> ```
> <system.web>
>   <authentication mode="Windows" />
> </system.web>
> ```

Introduction

Securing Web applications by using Windows-based authentication is a four-step process:

1. Configure IIS.
2. Set up authentication in Web.config.
3. Set up authorization in Web.config.
4. IIS requests logon information from the users.

Configure IIS

The first step in securing Web applications by using Windows-based authentication involves configuring IIS by using one or more of its three authentication mechanisms:

- Basic authentication
- Digest authentication
- Integrated Windows security

Note Typically, you enable either Basic authentication or Integrated Windows. If you want your Web application to be compatible with Netscape browsers, you should use Basic authentication. If you are not using a firewall or proxy server, you can use Integrated Windows.

Set up authentication

The second step in securing Web applications by using Windows-based authentication is to set ASP.NET security to Windows-based authentication in Web.config. The security settings in Web.config are included in the <authentication>, <authorization>, and <identity> sections.

Set the authentication method to "Windows" for the application in an <authentication> subsection of the <system.web> section in Web.config, as shown in the following example:

```
<system.web>
  <authentication mode="Windows" />
</system.web>
```

How to Enable Windows-Based Authentication *(continued)*

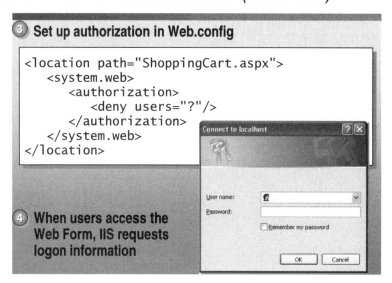

③ **Set up authorization in Web.config**

```
<location path="ShoppingCart.aspx">
    <system.web>
        <authorization>
            <deny users="?"/>
        </authorization>
    </system.web>
</location>
```

④ **When users access the Web Form, IIS requests logon information**

Introduction	Securing Web applications by using Windows-based authentication is a four-step process:

1. Configure IIS.
2. Set up authentication in Web.config.
3. Set up authorization in Web.config.
4. IIS requests logon information from the users.

You learned about the first two steps in the previous topic. This topic covers the last two steps.

Set up authorization

To indicate that only specific pages are secure, you must create a <location> section with <system.web> and <authorization> subsections for each secure page in your Web application:

```
<location path="ShoppingCart.aspx">
  <system.web>
      <authorization>
          <deny users="?" />
      </authorization>
  </system.web>
</location>
```

Any configuration settings that are contained in the <location> section will be directed to the file or directory that is indicated in the **path** attribute. There can be multiple <location> sections within the <configuration> section.

Note The <location>section can be an ASP.NET Web Form or a folder. If you specify a folder name, all of the subfolders under it are secure. If you want to secure multiple Web Forms or folders, use multiple <location> sections.

In the <system.web> section, you create an <authorization> subsection to specify what type of authorization will be enforced. Create <allow> or <deny> tags to allow or deny users access to a page. Within these tags, "**?**" indicates anonymous users, whereas "*****" means all users.

For example, the following code denies access to all anonymous users:

```
<authorization>
  <deny users="?" />
</authorization>
```

The following code allows the user "Mary" access to a page:

```
<authorization>
  <allow users="Mary" />
</authorization>
```

Note It is not advisable to authorize users individually, because this process may disclose sensitive information if the Web.config file is stolen. In addition, hard coding users in the Web.config file is not a flexible approach because you cannot modify this information programmatically at runtime. Hard coding users in the Web.config file is suitable for testing purposes only.

The following code denies all anonymous users access to the ShoppingCart.aspx page:

```
<location path="ShoppingCart.aspx">
  <system.web>
     <authorization>
        <deny users="?" />
     </authorization>
  </system.web>
</location>
```

After specifying the authentication mode, you need to either mark the entire Web application as needing authorization, or specify which pages are secure and therefore require authorization.

To mark the entire application as secure, create an <authorization> section within the <system.web> section, as shown in the following code example:

```
<system.web>
  <authorization>
     <deny users="?" />
  </authorization>
</system.web>
```

You use the <identity> element to enable impersonation. Impersonation allows the server to execute code under the security context of a request entity or as an anonymous user. In ASP.NET, impersonation is optional, and, by default, it is disabled.

The <identity> element must be under the <system.web> section in the Web.config or Machine.config file. The following code shows the syntax that is used with the <identity> element:

```
<identity impersonate="true|false"
     username="username"
     password="password" />
```

In the preceding code, the **username** and **password** attributes specify the credentials to use if **impersonate** is set to **true**.

A special Windows account named **ASPNET** is used if **impersonate** is set to **false**, which is the default value.

IIS requests logon information from users

The last step in the process of enabling Windows-based authentication is when users try to access a Web Form from your Web application and IIS requests logon information from the user. The user must provide his or her user name and password. If the user's credentials are approved by IIS, the user gets access to the requested, secure Web page.

Reading User Information

- **After authentication, the Web server can read the user identity**

```
lblAuthUser.Text = User.Identity.Name
lblAuthType.Text = User.Identity.AuthenticationType
lblIsAuth.Text = User.Identity.IsAuthenticated
```

```
lblAuthUser.Text = User.Identity.Name;
lblAuthType.Text = User.Identity.AuthenticationType;
lblIsAuth.Text = User.Identity.IsAuthenticated;
```

Introduction

After the process of Windows-based authentication is complete, the Web server can read the user identity from any Web page of the Web application.

The Web server can read the user identity by using **User.Identity.Name**. The Web server can also identify the IIS authentication mechanism that is used to authenticate the user by using **User.Identity.AuthenticationType**. In addition, the Web server can also test if the user is authenticated by using **User.Identity.IsAuthenticated**.

The following code example shows how to write the code to allow the Web server to read user identity:

Visual Basic .NET

```
lblAuthUser.Text = User.Identity.Name
lblAuthType.Text = User.Identity.AuthenticationType
lblIsAuth.Text = User.Identity.IsAuthenticated
```

C#

```
lblAuthUser.Text = User.Identity.Name;
lblAuthType.Text = User.Identity.AuthenticationType;
lblIsAuth.Text = User.Identity.IsAuthenticated;
```

Note **User.Identity** is an object of the **WindowsIdentity** class.

Demonstration: Using Windows-Based Authentication

- Open IIS and configure with Anonymous authentication only

- Create a new user on the local machine

- Open Web.config and configure it for authentication and authorization

- Run the secure ASP.NET Web application

  - Students can access the secure ASP.NET Web application on the Instructor machine

Introduction

In this demonstration, you will see how to set up IIS to use Windows-based authentication with Basic IIS authentication. You will then see how to create a new user on the local server, and how to set up authentication and authorization in Web.config. Then, you will see some demonstrations of accessing secure and non-secure pages. Finally, you will be able to connect to a secure page on the Instructor computer.

The files for this demonstration are in the Mod16VB or Mod16CS project in the 2310Demos solution.

▶ **To run the demonstration**

Set IIS with Basic authentication

1. Right click **My Computer** and then click **Manage**.

2. Expand **Services and Applications**, expand **Internet Information Services**, and then click **Web Sites**.

3. Right click **Default Web Site** and then click **Properties**.

4. Click the **Directory Security** tab, and then click **Edit** to open the **Authentication Methods** dialog box in IIS.

5. Select the Basic authentication (password is sent in clear text) check box and click Yes in the Internet Service Manager dialog box.

Note   Make sure that the **Anonymous access** check box is selected. Verify that the **Digest authentication for Windows domain servers** check box and the **Integrated Windows authentication** check box are cleared.

---

6. Type *machinename* in the **Default domain** field, because this demonstration will be done with a local account that was created on this computer.

7. Click **OK** to close the **Authentication Methods** dialog box of IIS.

8. Click **OK** to close the **Default Web Site Properties** dialog box. In the **Inheritance Overrides** dialog box, click **OK**.

Create a new user on the local computer

9. In the Computer Management console, expand System Tools, and then expand Local Users and Groups.

10. Right-click the **Users** folder and then click **New User**:

   Enter the following information in the **New User** dialog box.

Field Name	Value
User name	someone
Full name	someone
Description	someone demo account
Password	Secret1
Confirm password	Secret1

   a. Clear the **User must change password** at next logon check box.

   b. Select the **User cannot change password** check box.

   c. Click **Create** and then click **Close**.

   In the right-hand window of the **Computer Management** dialog box, you should see the user **someone**.

Show the security settings in the Web.config file

11. Open the Mod16VB or Mod16CS project and view the Web.config file in Microsoft Visual Studio® .NET.

   There is an <authentication> section set up with Windows-based authentication.

   There are two <location> sections that are needed to secure two pages: SecurePageDemo1.aspx and SecurePageDemo2.aspx. With the current IIS setting, if a user tries to access one of these pages, Basic authentication will be used. If a user tries to access the other pages, Anonymous authentication will be used.

Display the name and authentication type on a Web Form.

12. Open the SecurePageDemo1.aspx code-behind page and explain the code **User.Identity.Name** and **User.Identity.AuthenticationType**.

Note   No **Imports** statement is required to use **User.Identity.xxx**.

---

13. Build the Mod16VB or Mod16CS project in the 2310Demos solution.

14. Open a new browser and browse to:

Visual Basic .NET   http://localhost/Mod16VB/NonSecurePageDemo.aspx

C#   http://localhost/Mod16CS/NonSecurePageDemo.aspx

15. Browse to:

Visual Basic .NET   http://localhost/Mod16VB/SecurePageDemo1.aspx

C#   http://localhost/Mod16CS/SecurePageDemo1.aspx

   Show that the **Connect to localhost** dialog box appears.

16. Click **Cancel** and show that you get a Server Error because access is denied.

17. Browse to:

Visual Basic .NET   http://localhost/Mod16VB/SecurePageDemo2.aspx

C#   http://localhost/Mod16CS/SecurePageDemo2.aspx

   Show that the **Connect to localhost** dialog box also appears.

18. Type the credentials **User name** as **someone** and **Password** as **Secret1** and then click **OK**.

19. You should see the user name **someone** and authentication type **Basic** displayed on the SecurePageDemo2.aspx page.

    You can now access any secured pages, as long as you do not close the browser. If you close the browser, you have to go through the authentication process again.

20. Browse to :

Visual Basic .NET   http://localhost/Mod16VB/SecurePageDemo1.aspx

C#   http://localhost/Mod16CS/SecurePageDemo1.aspx

    Show that this time you are not asked to enter your credentials.

Students access the instructor computer   21. Tell the students to browse to:

Visual Basic .NET   http://*Instructormachinename*/Mod16VB/SecurePageDemo1.aspx

C#   http://*Instructormachinename*/Mod16CS/SecurePageDemo1.aspx

    Type the credentials **someone** and **Secret1** when prompted.

    After entering the credentials, students should be able to see SecurePageDemo1.aspx and SecurePageDemo2.aspx.

Lesson: Working with Forms-Based Authentication

- Overview of Forms-Based Authentication
- Multimedia: Forms-Based Authentication
- How to Enable Forms-Based Authentication
- Creating a Logon Page
- Demonstration: Using Forms-Based Authentication

Introduction

The most commonly used authentication method to secure ASP.NET Web applications is Forms-based authentication.

In this lesson, you will learn about the Forms-based architecture, and learn the steps to enable Forms-based authentication. You will also learn how to set up security in Web.config, and to create a logon page.

Lesson objectives

After completing this lesson, you will be able to:

- Identify the set of events that takes place during Forms-based authentication.
- Identify the steps to enable Forms-based authentication.
- Set up authentication and authorization in a Web.config file.
- Describe how to create a logon page.

Overview of Forms-Based Authentication

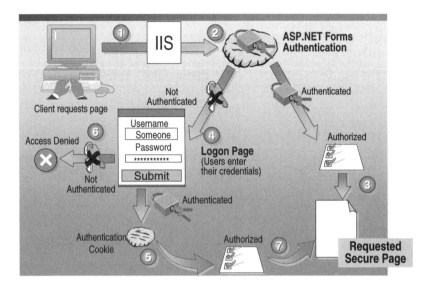

Introduction

When a user requests a Web page that is protected by Forms-based authentication, the request must first go through IIS. Therefore, you must set IIS authentication to Anonymous access. Setting IIS to anonymous requires that all requests go through ASP.NET before being authenticated.

Set of events that takes place during Forms-based authentication

The following is the set of events that takes place during Forms-based authentication:

1. A client generates a request for a protected .aspx page.

2. IIS receives the request and passes it to ASP.NET. Because the authentication mode is set to Anonymous access, the request goes directly through IIS.

3. ASP.NET checks to see if a valid authentication cookie is attached to the request. If it is, this means that the user's credentials have already been confirmed, and that the request is tested for authorization. The authorization test is performed by ASP.NET, and it is accomplished by comparing the credentials that are contained in the request's authorization cookie to the authorization settings that are in the Web.config file. If the user is authorized, access to the requested secure page is granted.

4. If there is no cookie attached to the request, ASP.NET redirects the request to a logon page (the path of which resides in the application's configuration file), where the user enters the required credentials, usually a name and password.

5. The application code on the logon page checks the credentials to confirm their authenticity and, if authenticated, attaches a cookie containing the credentials to the request.

6. If authentication fails, the request is returned with an "Access Denied" message.

7. If the user is authenticated, ASP.NET checks authorization, as in Step 3, and can then either allow access to the originally requested secure page or redirect the request to another page, depending on the design of the application.

   Alternatively, ASP.NET can direct the request to some custom form of authorization where the credentials are tested for authorization to the protected page. Usually if authorization fails, the request is returned with an "Access Denied" message.

Multimedia: Forms-Based Authentication

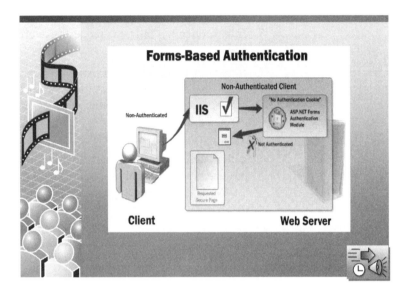

Introduction

In this animation, you will see how Forms-based authentication works with a non-authenticated client, and with an authenticated client. The steps are as follows:

1. When a non-authenticated client requests a secure page on the Web server, the request first goes through IIS.

2. Because IIS must be configured as Anonymous to use Forms-based authentication, the request goes straight to the ASP.NET Forms authentication module.

3. ASP.NET checks if the client has an authentication cookie. Because this is the users' first visit to the page, he or she will not yet have a cookie. If the client does not have an authentication cookie, the client is redirected to a logon page.

4. The users can then enter their credentials in the logon page.

5. At this point, the user credentials are checked. In a large number of applications, the user's credentials are tested against a database of users.

6. If the credentials are not recognized by the application, then access is denied.

7. If the credentials are recognized by the application, an authentication cookie is created and the client is authorized to access the page. The client is then redirected to the page that the user originally wanted to access.

8. When an authenticated client requests a page on the Web server, the authentication cookie travels with the request.

9. The request goes first through IIS and then goes straight to the ASP.NET Forms authentication module because IIS is still set to Anonymous access.

10. The ASP.NET Forms authentication module checks the authentication cookie, and if the cookie is valid the client is authorized to see the requested secure page.

How to Enable Forms-Based Authentication

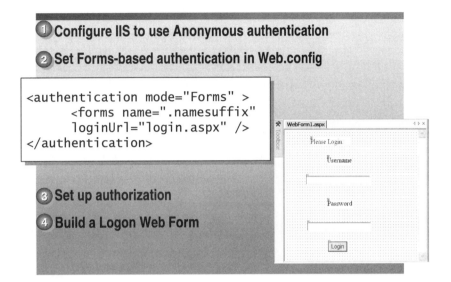

Introduction	To enable Forms-based authentication for your Web application, you must complete the following four steps:
Enabling Forms-based authentication	1. Configure IIS to use Anonymous authentication so that the user is authenticated by ASP.NET and not by IIS.
Setting up authentication	2. Set the authentication method to Forms-based for the application in an <authentication> subsection of the <system.web> section in Web.config, as shown in the following example:

```
<system.web>
    <authentication mode="Forms">
        <forms name=".namesuffix" loginUrl="login.aspx" />
    </authentication>
</system.web>
```

If you set the authentication mode to "Forms", you must add a <forms> element to the <authentication> section, as shown in the preceding example.

In the <forms> section, you configure the settings of the cookie. Set the **name** attribute to the suffix to be used for the cookies and the **loginUrl** attribute to the Uniform Resource Locator (URL) of the page to which unauthenticated requests are redirected.

Setting up authorization	3. Set up the <authorization> section in Web.config. The process of setting up authorization for Forms-based authentication is identical to the one you learned with Windows-based authentication.

By setting the <authorization> section in Web.config, you can deny or allow users access to your Web application. You can also mark the entire Web application as needing authorization or specify which pages are secure and therefore require authorization.

Build a logon Web Form	4. Build a logon Web Form, login.aspx. Login.aspx can be a simple page with two fields for a user name and a password. Login.aspx requires the users to enter their user name and password to establish authentication and to access your Web application.

Creating a Logon Page

- Reference System.Web.Security
- Logon page verifies and checks the credentials of a user

```
private void cmdLogin_Click(object sender, EventArgs e)
{
  if (login(txtEmail.Text, txtPassword.Text))
    FormsAuthentication.RedirectFromLoginPage(txtEmail.Text, false);
}
```

```
Sub cmdLogin_Click(s As Object, e As eventArgs)
  If (login(txtEmail.Text, txtPassword.Text))
    FormsAuthentication.RedirectFromLoginPage(txtEmail.Text, False)
  End If
End Sub
```

- Reading user credentials from a cookie
  - User.Identity.Name returns the value saved by FormsAuthentication.RedirectFromLoginPage

Introduction

During authentication, all requests are redirected to the logon page that is specified in the **loginUrl** attribute of the <forms> tag. The logon page verifies and checks the credentials of a user.

How does a logon page work?

If the authentication mode is set to "Forms", ASP.NET looks for an authentication cookie attached to a request for a secure page. If ASP.NET does not find the authentication cookie, it redirects the request to the specified logon page.

On the logon page, the user enters the required credentials. The page checks the entered credentials, either through application-specific code or by calling **FormsAuthentication.Authenticate**. If the credentials are valid, a cookie is generated and the user is redirected to the originally requested page by calling **FormsAuthentication.RedirectFromLoginPage**. However, if the credentials are not valid, the user stays on the logon page and is given a message that indicates that the logon credentials are invalid.

The **RedirectFromLoginPage** method takes two parameters: **userName**, which specifies the name of the user for Forms-based authentication purposes, and **createPersistentCookie**. If the value of **createPersistentCookie** is **true**, a *persistent authentication cookie*, a cookie that is written to the client file system, is created on the user's computer. Otherwise, a temporary (non-persistent) authentication cookie is created.

The following table lists all of the methods of the **FormsAuthentication** object, which can be used in the authentication process.

Method	Function
Authenticate	Given the supplied credentials, this method attempts to validate the credentials against those that are contained in the configured credential store.
GetAuthCookie	Creates an authentication cookie for a given user name. This does not set the cookie as part of the outgoing response; therefore, an application can have more control over how the cookie is issued.
GetRedirectUrl	Returns the redirected URL for the original request that caused the redirect to the logon page.
RedirectFromLoginPage	Redirects authenticated users back to the original URL that they requested.
SetAuthCookie	Creates an authentication ticket for the given **userName** and attaches it to the cookies collection of the outgoing response. It does not perform a redirect.
SignOut	Given an authenticated user, calling **SignOut** removes the authentication ticket by doing a **SetCookie** with an empty value. This removes either durable or session cookies.

Creating a logon page

To be able to use the **FormsAuthentication** class, you should reference the **System.Web.Security** library using **Imports** or **using**.

A logon page is simply an ASP.NET page with an HTML form, a **Submit** button, and a **Click** event procedure for the **Submit** button.

The following is an example of a form on a logon page:

```
<form id="Login" method="post" runat="server">
  <P>Email:  <asp:TextBox id="txtEmail" runat="server">
          </asp:TextBox></P>
  <P>Password<asp:TextBox id="txtPassword" TextMode="password"
              runat="server">
          </asp:TextBox></P>
  <P><asp:Button id="cmdLogin" Text="Sign In Now"
OnClick="cmdLogin_Click"
        runat="server">
      </asp:Button></P>
  <P><asp:Label id="lblInfo" runat="server">
      </asp:Label></P>
</form>
```

In the **Click** event procedure of the **Submit** button, you validate the information that is entered in the form, and then if it is valid, call **FormsAuthentication.RedirectFromLoginPage**. The **RedirectFromLoginPage** method issues the cookie and then redirects the user to their originally requested page.

The following sample code uses a custom function named **Login** to validate the user name and password, and then calls **RedirectFromLoginPage** if the user name and password are valid:

Visual Basic .NET

```
Private Sub cmdLogin_Click( _
  ByVal sender As System.Object, _
  ByVal e As System.EventArgs) _
  Handles cmdLogin.Click

  Dim strCustomerId As String
  'Validate User Credentials
  strCustomerId = Login(txtEmail.Text, txtPassword.Text)

  If (strCustomerId <> "") Then
      FormsAuthentication.RedirectFromLoginPage _
          (strCustomerId, False)
  Else
      lblInfo.Text = "Invalid Credentials: Please try again"
  End If

End Sub
```

C#

```
private void cmdLogin_Click(object sender, EventArgs e)
{
    string strCustomerId;
    //Validate User Credentials
    strCustomerId = Login(txtEmail.Text, txtPassword.Text);

    if (strCustomerId != "")
    {
        FormsAuthentication.RedirectFromLoginPage
            (strCustomerId, false);
    }
    else
    {
        lblInfo.Text = "Invalid Credentials: Please try again";
    }
}
```

Reading credentials from cookies

After a user has been authenticated, you can obtain the user name of the authenticated user programmatically by using the **User.Identity.Name** property. This property is useful to build an application that uses the user's name as a key to save information in a database table or directory resource.

You can also identify the authentication mechanism (**Forms** in this case) dynamically by using **User.Identity.AuthenticationType** and then test if the user is authenticated by using **User.Identity.IsAuthenticated**.

With Forms-based authentication, **User.Identity** is an object of the **FormsIdentity** class.

Note   While using Forms-based authentication, the password that a user enters in the logon page is sent over the network in clear text. It is important to use SSL to encrypt these passwords.

Demonstration: Using Forms-Based Authentication

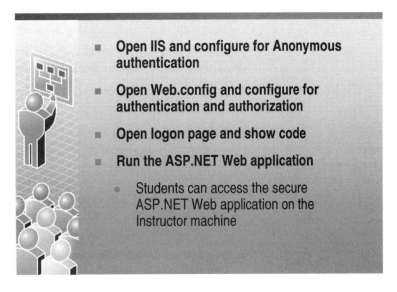

- Open IIS and configure for Anonymous authentication
- Open Web.config and configure for authentication and authorization
- Open logon page and show code
- Run the ASP.NET Web application
  - Students can access the secure ASP.NET Web application on the Instructor machine

Introduction

In this demonstration, you will see how to set up IIS to use Forms-based authentication with Anonymous authentication, then you will see how to set up authentication and authorization in the Web.config file. You will then see how the logon page works, along with some demonstrations of accessing secure and non-secure pages. Finally, you will be able to connect to a secure page on the Instructor computer.

The files for this demonstration are in the Mod16VB or Mob16CS project in the 2310Demos solution.

▶ **To run the demonstration**

Set up IIS for Anonymous access

1. Right click **My Computer** and then click **Manage**.

2. Navigate to **Services and Applications**, expand **Internet Information Services**, and then click **Web Sites**.

3. Right click Default Web Site and click Properties.

4. Click the **Directory Security** tab and then click **Edit** to open the **Authentication Methods** dialog box in IIS.

5. Clear the **Basic authentication** (password is sent in clear text) check box.

Note Verify that the check boxes **Digest authentication for Windows domain servers** and **Integrated Windows authentication** are cleared and that the **Anonymous access** check box is selected.

---

6. Click **OK**.

7. Click **OK**.

8. Click **OK** on the **Inheritance Overides** dialog box.

Set up the security in the Web.config file

9. Open the Web.config file.

    Using the **<!--** and **-->** comments, comment the <system.web> section containing the "Windows" authentication mode and uncomment the <system.web> section containing the authentication mode "Forms".

    Explain the new <authentication> section that redirects all non-authenticated requests to the LoginDemo.aspx page.

    The same two pages (SecurePageDemo1.aspx and SecurePageDemo2.aspx) have been set up as secure pages.

10. Save the changes.

Show the LoginDemo.aspx page

11. Open the LoginDemo.aspx.vb or LoginDemo.asox.cs code-behind page.

    Show the following:

    - The **cmdLogin_Click** event procedure that validates the user name and password by calling the **Login** function, and then calling **RedirectFromLoginPage**, if the credentials are valid.

    - The first parameter of **RedirectFromLoginPage** is the user identity that you want to save is in the cookie. After that, during the session, this identity can then be read from any page by using **User.Identity.Name**.

    - The **RedirectFromLoginPage** creates a temporary (non-persistent) authentication cookie (second parameter set to **false**).

    - To use **RedirectFromLoginPage**, you have to import **System.Web.Security**.

    - The code of the **Login** function. Show how the **Login** function calls the **EmployeeLogin** stored procedure to verify the entered credentials against the database.

    - Open the Microsoft SQL Server™ Enterprise Manager, then open the **Coho** database and show the record in the **Logins** table. Finally, show the **EmployeeLogin** stored procedure.

    Important   When you see the **Coho** database, notice that with Forms-based authentication, unlike with Windows-based authentication, it is up to you as the developer to design and manage a database of users.

    ---

12. Build the project.

13. Open a new browser and browse to:

Visual Basic .NET

> http://localhost/Mod16VB/NonSecurePageDemo.aspx

C#

> http://localhost/Mod16CS/NonSecurePageDemo.aspx

14. Browse to:

Visual Basic .NET

> http://localhost/Mod16VB/SecurePageDemo1.aspx

C#

> http://localhost/Mod16CS/SecurePageDemo1.aspx

    Show that you are automatically redirected to the LoginDemo.aspx page.

    Show that the URL, which contains the SecurePageDemo1.aspx page, is the page that is needed to redirect the user to the requested page, if the credentials are correct.

15. Type the credentials **User Name (Email)** name as **someone@cohowinery.com**, enter an invalid password, and then click **Sign In Now**.

   The sign-in will fail because the password is invalid.

16. Enter the credentials **User Name (Email)** name as **someone@cohowinery.com** and enter the **Password** as **someone**, and then click **Sign In Now** again. You will be redirected to the SecurePageDemo1.aspx page.

17. You should see the user name **1** (which is the identity that is stored in the cookie in LoginDemo.aspx) and the authentication type **Forms** displayed on the SecurePageDemo1.aspx page.

   You can now access any secured pages, as long as you do not close the browser. If you close the browser, you have to go through the authentication process again because the cookie is temporary (non-persistent).

18. Browse to:

Visual Basic .NET   http://localhost/Mod16VB/SecurePageDemo2.aspx

C#   http://localhost/Mod16CS/SecurePageDemo2.aspx

   Show that this time you are not asked to enter your credentials.

Students access the Instructor computer   19. Tell the students to browse to:

Visual Basic .NET   http://*Instructormachinename*/Mod16VB/SecurePageDemo1.aspx

C#   http://*Instructormachinename*/Mod16CS/SecurePageDemo1.aspx

   Type the following credentials, name: **someone@cohowinery.com**, and password: **someone**, when prompted.

   After entering the credentials, students should be able to see SecurePageDemo1.aspx and SecurePageDemo2.aspx.

Lesson: Overview of Microsoft Passport Authentication

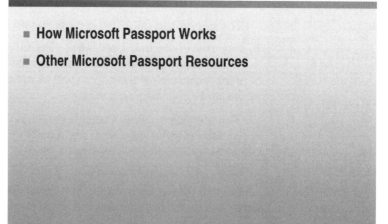

- How Microsoft Passport Works
- Other Microsoft Passport Resources

Introduction

The power of Microsoft Passport is that users can present the same credentials to any participating Web site, and they only have to log on once during a session. When users close their browser or indicate that they want to log off, the cookie is destroyed and the user must log on again to access any resources on any of the participating sites.

In this lesson, you will learn about the set of events that takes place during Microsoft Passport authentication. You will also learn how to implement Microsoft Passport authentication.

Lesson objectives

After completing this lesson, you will be able to:

- Describe the set of events that takes place during Microsoft Passport authentication.
- Identify other Microsoft Passport resources.

How Microsoft Passport Works

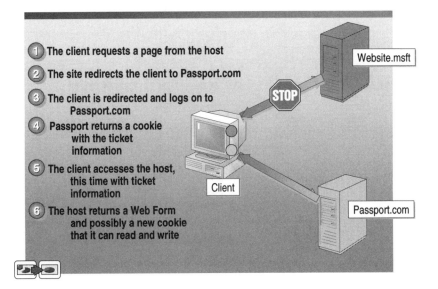

1. The client requests a page from the host
2. The site redirects the client to Passport.com
3. The client is redirected and logs on to Passport.com
4. Passport returns a cookie with the ticket information
5. The client accesses the host, this time with ticket information
6. The host returns a Web Form and possibly a new cookie that it can read and write

Introduction

There is a set of events that takes place during the authentication of users by using Microsoft Passport.

Set of events that take place in Microsoft Passport authentication

1. When the client requests a secure page from the Web site (host), the request is first sent to IIS. IIS authenticates the user as anonymous and passes the request to ASP.NET.

2. ASP.NET checks for a special cookie on the client. If the cookie is not present, the request is rejected, and the client is redirected to the Passport.com Web site for authentication.

3. Passport generates a logon form that it sends back to the client. The user provides the appropriate logon information and submits this information back to the Passport site.

4. If the supplied credentials match those in the Passport database, Passport authenticates the user and returns a cookie, with an authentication ticket, to the client.

5. The client then sends the initial request, this time with the authentication ticket information, back to the ASP.NET Web application.

6. Again, IIS authenticates the user as anonymous. ASP.NET authenticates the user based on the authentication ticket, and then returns the secure Web Form to the client.

After the user is authenticated with Passport, access may be granted to other Web sites that also use Microsoft Passport authentication.

Other Microsoft Passport Resources

Introduction

While learning about Microsoft Passport, you may need to access resources to find answers to specific questions. The following two Web sites are intended to give you a starting point to find more information about Microsoft Passport.

Web sites

You can find information about Microsoft Passport at the following sites:

- The Developer Information link at http://www.passport.com
- The resources at http://msdn.microsoft.com

Review

- Web Application Security Overview
- Working with Windows-Based Authentication
- Working with Forms-Based Authentication
- Overview of Microsoft Passport Authentication

1. What are the three authentication methods provided with ASP.NET?

2. What is the difference between authentication and authorization?

3. What is the main advantage of using Basic authentication instead of Digest authentication or Integrated Windows security?

4. What is the most important thing to remember when using Basic authentication?

5. Which authentication methods, Basic, Digest, or Integrated Windows, required Active Directory?

6. Is Forms-based authentication or Microsoft Passport authentication based on cookies? Or both?

7. How does ASP.NET know to which page you have to be redirected when using the **RedirectFromLoginPage** method?

Lab 16: Securing a Microsoft ASP.NET Web Application

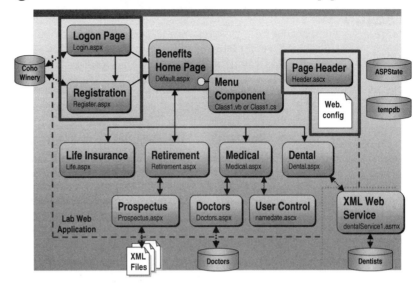

Objectives

After completing this lab, you will be able to:

- Secure a Microsoft® ASP.NET Web application by using Microsoft Windows®–based authentication.

- Secure a Web application by using Forms-based authentication.

- Create logon and registration pages.

Prerequisites

Before working on this lab, you must have:

- Knowledge of how a Web.config file is structured.

- Knowledge of how to use stored procedures for server controls.

- Knowledge of how validation controls work.

Scenario

Coho Winery offers several benefits to its employees. In the labs for Course 2310B, *Developing Microsoft ASP.NET Web Applications Using Visual Studio .NET*, you will create a Web site that enables employees to select and set up their chosen benefits.

Now that you have implemented all of the benefits, you want to allow only registered users to access the Web application. You will first secure the site by using Windows-based authentication, and you will then change it to Forms-based authentication. Then you will implement the registration page to give new employees the opportunity to register to the Coho Winery Benefits Web site. Finally, you will implement the sign-out page.

Estimated time to complete this lab: 45 minutes

Exercise 0
Lab Setup

To complete this lab, you must have created a Benefits Web Application project and a BenefitsList Class Library project. These projects can be created by using Microsoft Visual Basic® .NET or Microsoft Visual C#™ .NET.

If you have not created these projects, complete the following steps:

▶ **Create the 2310LabApplication solution**

Important   Only perform this procedure if you have not created
a 2310LabApplication solution file.

---

1. Using Microsoft Visual Studio® .NET, create a new blank solution
    named **2310LabApplication**:

    a. On the **File** menu, click **New**, and then click **Blank Solution**.

    b. In the **New Project** dialog box, type **2310LabApplication** in the **Name**
        text box, and then click **OK**.

▶ **Create the Benefits project**

Important   Only perform this procedure if you have not previously created a
Benefits project, or if you have removed the Benefits project according to the
steps in Appendix A, "Lab Recovery," in Course 2310B, *Developing Microsoft
ASP.NET Web Applications Using Visual Studio .NET.*

---

1. Create a new ASP.NET Web Application project, named **BenefitsVB** or
    BenefitsCS, in the 2310LabApplication solution:

    a. On the **File** menu, click **New**, and then click **Project**.

    b. In the **New Project** dialog box, in the **Project Types** list, click
        Visual Basic Projects or **Visual C# Projects**.

    c. In the **Templates** list, click **ASP.NET Web Application**. Set the
        Location to **http://localhost/BenefitsVB** for the Visual Basic .NET
        project or to **http:/localhost/BenefitsCS** for the Visual C# project.

    d. Click **Add to Solution**, and then click **OK**.

Caution   When adding projects to the solution, the capitalization of the
project name is important. Because you may be using some pre-built Web
Forms in this and other labs in Course 2310B, *Developing Microsoft
ASP.NET Web Applications Using Visual Studio .NET*, you must verify that
you have capitalized the Benefits project as shown.

▶ **Update the Benefits project**

1. In Visual Studio .NET, open the 2310LabApplication solution file.

2. In Solution Explorer, right-click **BenefitsVB** or **BenefitsCS**, point to **Add**, and then click **Add Existing Item**.

3. Browse for project files:

For the Visual Basic .NET project

Browse to the *install folder*\Labfiles\Lab16\VB\Starter\BenefitsVB folder.

For the Visual C# project

Browse to the *install folder*\Labfiles\Lab16\CS\Starter\BenefitsCS folder.

4. In the **Files of type** box in the **Add Existing Item – Benefits** dialog box, click **All Files (*.*)**.

5. Select all of the files in this folder, and then click **Open**.

6. Click **Yes** if prompted to overwrite or reload files.

▶ **Create the BenefitsList class library**

Important   Only perform these steps if you have not previously created a BenefitsList project, or if you have removed the BenefitsList project according to the steps in Appendix A, "Lab Recovery," in Course 2310B, *Developing Microsoft ASP.NET Web Applications Using Visual Studio .NET*.

1. Create a new Class Library Project.

For the Visual Basic .NET project

Create a new Visual Basic .NET Class Library project, name it **BenefitsListVB**, and then add it to the 2310LabApplication solution:

a. On the **File** menu, click **New**, and then click **Project**.

b. In the **New Project** dialog box, in the **Project Types** list, click **Visual Basic Projects**.

c. In the **Templates** list, click **Class Library**, and then set the **Name** to **BenefitsListVB**.

d. Click **Add to Solution**, and then click **OK**.

For the Visual C# project

Create a new Visual C# .NET Class Library project, name it **BenefitsListCS**, and then add it to the 2310LabApplication solution:

a. On the **File** menu, click **New**, and then click **Project**.

b. In the **New Project** dialog box, in the **Project Types** list, click **Visual C# Projects**.

c. In the **Templates** list, click **Class Library**, and then set the **Name** to **BenefitsListCS**.

d. Click **Add to Solution**, and then click **OK**.

Caution   Verify that you have capitalized the BenefitsList project as shown.

42 **Module 16: Securing a Microsoft ASP.NET Web Application**

▶ **Update the BenefitsList project**

1. In Visual Studio .NET, open the 2310LabApplication solution file.

2. In Solution Explorer, right-click **BenefitsListVB** or **BenefitsListCS**, point to **Add**, and then click **Add Existing Item**.

3. Browse for project files:

For the Visual Basic .NET project

Browse to the *install folder*\Labfiles\Lab16\VB\Starter\BenefitsListVB folder.

For the Visual C# project

Browse to the *install folder*\Labfiles\Lab16\CS\Starter\BenefitsListCS folder.

4. In the **Files of type** box of the **Add Existing Item – BenefitsList** dialog box, click **All Files (*.*)**.

5. Select all of the files in this folder, and then click **Open**.

6. Click **Yes** if prompted to overwrite or reload files.

▶ **Create a reference to the BenefitsList component in the Benefits project**

1. In the Benefits project in the 2310LabApplication solution, complete the following steps to add a reference to the BenefitsList component that you just created:

   a. Right-click the **BenefitsVB** or **BenefitsCS** project in Solution Explorer and then click **Add Reference**.

   b. In the **Add Reference** dialog box, on the **Projects** tab, double-click the **BenefitsListVB** or **BenefitsListCS** project.

   c. In the **Selected Components** list, select the **BenefitsListVB** or **BenefitsListCS** component, and then click **OK**.

   The component is added to the References folder in Solution Explorer.

▶ **Create the Dental XML Web Service**

Important Only perform this procedure if you have not previously created the DentalService project, or if you have removed the DentalService project according to the steps in Appendix A, "Lab Recovery," in Course 2310B, *Developing Microsoft ASP.NET Web Applications Using Visual Studio .NET.*

1. Create a new XML Web Service project.

For Visual Basic .NET project

Create a new Visual Basic .NET XML Web Service project, named **DentalServiceVB**, and then add it to the 2310LabApplication solution:

   a. On the **File** menu, click **New**, and then click **Project**.

   b. In the **New Project** dialog box, in the **Project Types** list, click **Visual Basic Projects**.

   c. In the **Templates** list, click **ASP.NET Web Service** and then set the **Location** to **http://localhost/DentalServiceVB**.

   d. Click **Add to Solution**, and then click **OK**.

Caution Verify that you have capitalized the DentalServiceVB project as shown.

For Visual C# .NET project

Create a new Visual C# .NET XML Web Service project, named **DentalServiceCS**, and then add it to the 2310LabApplication solution:

a. On the **File** menu, click **New**, and then click **Project**.

b. In the **New Project** dialog box, in the **Project Types** list, click **Visual Basic Projects**.

c. In the **Templates** list, click **ASP.NET Web Service**, and then set the **Location** to **http://localhost/DentalServiceCS**.

d. Click **Add to Solution**, and then click **OK**.

Caution   Verify that you have capitalized the DentalServiceVB project as shown.

▶ **Update the DentalService project**

1. In Visual Studio .NET, open the 2310LabApplication solution file.

2. In Solution Explorer, right-click **DentalServiceVB** or **DentalServiceCS**, point to **Add**, and then click **Add Existing Item**.

3. Browse for project files:

For Visual Basic .NET project

Browse to the *install folder*\Labfiles\Lab16\VB\Starter\DentalServiceVB folder.

For Visual C# .NET project

Browse to the *install folder*\Labfiles\Lab16\CS\Starter\DentalServiceCS folder.

4. In the **Files of type** box of the **Add Existing Item – DentalService** dialog box, click **All Files (*.*)**.

5. Select all of the files in this folder, and then click **Open**.

6. Click **Yes** if prompted to overwrite or reload files.

7. Build the DentalService XML Web service by right-clicking the **DentalServiceVB** or **DentalServiceCS** project in Solution Explorer and clicking **Build**.

▶ **Add a Web reference in the Benefits project to the DentalService Web service**

1. In the Benefits project in the 2310LabApplication solution, complete the following steps to add a Web reference to the DentalService XML Web service:

a. In Solution Explorer, right-click **BenefitsVB** or **BenefitsCS** and then click **Add Web Reference**.

b. In the Address text box, type

Visual Basic .NET project

http://localhost/DentalServiceVB/DentalService1.asmx

Visual C# project

http://localhost/DentalServiceCS/DentalService1.asmx

and then press ENTER.

The DentalService1 Web reference is displayed.

c. Click **Add Reference**.

The Web reference is added to the project in the Web References folder.

2. In Solution Explorer, expand **Web References**, right-click **localhost**, and then click **Rename**.

3. Type **DentalWebRef**, and then press ENTER.

4. Build the solution by clicking **Build Solution** on the **Build** menu.

▶ **Install and configure the session state databases**

1. On the **Start** menu, point to **All Programs**, point to **Accessories**, and then click **Command Prompt**.

   A command window opens.

2. At the command prompt, type the following command, where *version* is the latest version of the Microsoft .NET Framework that is installed on your computer, and then press ENTER:

   ```
   cd\WINDOWS\Microsoft.NET\Framework\version\
   ```

   The command prompt changes to the new directory.

3. At the command prompt, type the following command, and then press ENTER:

   ```
   OSQL -S localhost -E <InstallSqlState.sql
   ```

   The command window displays a series of numbers and messages, and then returns to the command prompt. The **ASPState** and **tempdb** databases have been restored.

4. Close the command prompt, and then open Windows Explorer.

5. Browse to the following directory:

Visual Basic .NET project

   C:\Program Files\MSDNTrain\2310\LabFiles\Lab16\VB\Starter

Visual C# project

   C:\Program Files\MSDNTrain\2310\LabFiles\Lab16\CS\Starter

6. Double-click **Lab16.bat**.

   This batch file runs an SQL query that configures security for the **ASPState** and **tempdb** databases.

7. Close Windows Explorer.

Exercise 1
Securing Your Web Site Using Windows-Based Authentication

In this exercise, you will set up Internet Information Services (IIS) to use Basic authentication to gain access to secured pages, and use Anonymous authentication to gain access to non-secured pages. You will then edit the Web.config file to deny non-authenticated users access to the medical.aspx and doctors.aspx pages. Finally, you will deny non-authenticated users access to any page of the Coho Winery Web site.

▶ **Configure IIS Authentication**

1. On the **Start** menu, right-click **My Computer** and then click **Manage**.

2. In the **Computer Management** console, expand **Services and Applications**, expand **Internet Information Services**, expand **Web Sites**, and then expand **Default Web Site**.

3. Right-click the **BenefitsVB** or **BenefitsCS** Web application and then click **Properties**.

4. In the **BenefitsVB** or **BenefitsCS Properties** dialog box, on the **Directory Security** tab, in the **Anonymous access and authentication control section**, click **Edit**.

5. In the **Authentication Methods** dialog box, verify that **Anonymous access** is selected, and that **Integrated Windows authentication** is not selected, and then select the **Basic authentication** (password is sent in clear text) check box.

6. When you receive the security warning about enabling Basic authentication, click **Yes**. Your configuration looks like the following illustration.

Security Note   Anonymous access is enabled so that you can have both secure and non-secure pages in the same Web application.

For this exercise, Basic authentication without using Secure Sockets Layer (SSL) has been enabled, which means passwords are sent by using clear text. In a real-world scenario, to be secure, you must get a server certificate and use SSL when you are using Basic authentication.

---

7. Click **OK**, click **OK** again, and then close the **Computer Management** console.

▶ **Add a page to output the security information**

1. Open the BenefitsVB or BenefitsCS project in the 2310LabApplication Visual Studio .NET solution.

2. Add the securitytest.aspx Web Form to the Benefits project from the

    Visual Basic .NET   *install folder*\Labfiles\Lab16\VB\Starter\BenefitsVB folder.

    Visual C#   *install folder*\Labfiles\Lab16\CS\Starter\BenefitsCS folder.

3. Open the securitytest.aspx.vb or securitytest.aspx.cs file and examine its contents. What is the purpose of the two lines of code in the **Page_Load** event procedure?

    _____

    _____

▶ **Configure security in the Web.config file for some of the pages in the Benefits project**

1. Open the Web.config file in the BenefitsVB or BenefitsCS project.

2. Find the <authentication> section and verify that the mode is set to Windows authentication.

    Your configuration should have the following:

    ```
    <authentication mode="Windows" />
    ```

3. For the Visual Basic .NET Project, remove the existing <authorization> section of Web.config.

4. Deny access to anonymous users for the medical.aspx and the doctors.aspx pages. Enter your configuration at the end of the Web.config file, after the </system.web> tag, but before the </configuration> tag.

    Your configuration should look like the following:

    ```
    <location path="medical.aspx">
       <system.web>
          <authorization>
             <deny users="?" />
          </authorization>
       </system.web>
    </location>

    <location path="doctors.aspx">
       <system.web>
          <authorization>
             <deny users="?" />
          </authorization>
       </system.web>
    </location>
    ```

▶ **Save and test**

1. Save your changes.

2. Build the **BenefitsVB** or **BenefitsCS** project.

3. Open a new browser and browse to http://localhost/BenefitsVB/default.aspx or http://localhost/BenefitsCS/default.aspx.

Note If you receive a SQL permission error when trying to browse the Benefits Web site, open Windows Explorer, browse to C:\Program Files\MSDNTrain\2310\LabFiles\Lab16VB\Starter and then double-click **Lab16.bat**. Close Windows Explorer, and then refresh Microsoft Internet Explorer.

---

4. Click **Life Insurance** and verify that the life.aspx page opens without asking for any user credentials.

5. Browse to http://localhost/BenefitsVB/SecurityTest.aspx or http://localhost/BenefitsCS/SecurityTest.aspx.

   No authentication information is displayed on this page because you are not yet authenticated.

6. Browse to http://localhost/BenefitsVB/Medical.aspx or http://localhost/BenefitsCS/Medical.aspx. You should see the **Connect to localhost** dialog box.

7. Enter your *machinename\username* and your classroom password.

   You are now able to browse the medical.aspx page.

8. Browse again to http://localhost/BenefitsVB/SecurityTest.aspx or http://localhost/BenefitsCS/SecurityTest.aspx.

   The page now displays your authentication information. If your authentication information is not displayed, refresh the page.

9. Close the browser.

▶ **Configure the security for the BenefitsVB or BenefitsCS Web site folder in the Web.config file**

1. Open the Web.config file.

2. Deny access to anonymous users to the entire Benefits folder. To do this, you need to remove the two <location> sections that were previously added and create a new section to deny access to anonymous users to the whole folder, just after the <authentication> element in the Web.config file.

   Your configuration should look like the following:

```
<authorization>
   <deny users="?" />
</authorization>
```

▶ **Save and test**

1. Save your changes.

   You do not need to rebuild the BenefitsVB or BenefitsCS project since no code has been changed. As soon as you save the Web.config file, changes will take effect.

2. Open a new browser and browse to http://localhost/BenefitsVB/default.aspx or http://localhost/BenefitsCS/default.aspx.

   > **Note** Make sure that you open a new browser. If you are still on the previous authenticated session, you will not be able to test whether the security works.

   This time you should immediately see the **Connect to localhost** dialog box, because all of the pages are secured, including default.aspx.

3. Enter your *machinename\username* and your classroom password, and then click **OK**.

   You can now browse all of the pages that are within the Benefits Web application.

▶ **Access your neighbor's Coho Winery Web site**

1. Open a new browser and browse to: http://*Neighbormachinename*/BenefitsVB/default.aspx or http://*Neighbormachinename*/BenefitsCS/default.aspx

2. You should see the **Connect to localhost** dialog box.

3. Enter your *machine_name\username* and your classroom password, and then click **OK**.

   You can now browse all of the pages of your neighbor's Coho Winery Web site.

Exercise 2
Securing Your Web Site Using Forms-Based Authentication

In this exercise, you will reconfigure IIS to use Anonymous authentication only, and then use Forms-based authentication to manage access to secure pages in the Benefits Web application. You will configure the Web.config file to use Forms-based authentication by denying non-authenticated users access to any page of the Benefits project folder. Finally, you will create the login.aspx page and validate user credentials against those that are in the **Logins** table of the **Coho** database.

▶ **Configure IIS to use only Anonymous authentication**

1. On the **Start** menu, right-click **My Computer** and then click **Manage**.

2. In the **Computer Management** console, expand **Services and Applications**, expand **Internet Information Services**, expand **Web Sites**, and then expand **Default Web Site**.

3. Right-click the **BenefitsVB** or **BenefitsCS** Web application and then click **Properties**.

4. In the **BenefitsVB** or **BenefitsCS Properties** dialog box, on the **Directory Security** tab, in the **Anonymous access and authentication** control section, click **Edit**.

5. In the **Authentication Methods** dialog box, verify that the Anonymous **access** check box is selected, and then clear the **Basic authentication** (password is sent in clear text) check box.

6. Click **OK**, click **OK** again, and then close the **Computer Management** console.

▶ **Configure Forms-based authentication in the Web.config file**

1. Open the Web.config file in the BenefitsVB or BenefitsCS project.

2. Find the <authentication> section and change it to use Forms-based authentication. You want to create a cookie named .ASPXAUTH, and redirect the user to a page named login.aspx if the user is not authenticated.

Your configuration should look like the following:

```
<authentication mode="Forms">
  <forms name=".ASPXAUTH" loginUrl="login.aspx" />
</authentication>
```

▶ **Add a connection string to the Coho database in the Web.config file**

1. In the Web.config file, add an <appSettings> section. Your configuration must be placed at the end of the Web.config file, after the </system.web> tag, but before the </configuration> tag.

Note If the Web.config file already has an <appSettings> section, do not create a second one. Continue with the following steps and add your new code to the existing <appSettings> section.

---

2. Add a new key named **conStrCoho** with a connection string that uses Integrated Windows security to access the local **Coho** database. Your addition to the Web.config file should look like the following:

```
<appSettings>
    <add key="conStrCoho" value="data source=localhost;
        initial catalog=Coho; integrated security=true" />
</appSettings>
```

▶ **Add a login.aspx Web Form to enter the credentials**

1. Add the **login.aspx** Web Form from the *install folder*\Labfiles\Lab16\VB\Starter\BenefitsVB or *install folder*\Labfiles\Lab16\CS\Starter\BenefitsCS folder to the BenefitsVB or BenefitsCS project.

   This page contains a text box to enter the e-mail address, a password box, a **Submit** button, two labels, and a hyperlink.

   Open the code-behind page for the login.aspx Web Form and locate the following comment in the **Imports** section at the beginning of the page:

   ```
   TODO Lab 16: add the Imports for forms-based auth
   ```

2. For this exercise, you will use the **FormsAuthentication** class. Using the Help documents, determine which namespace you have to import to use this class, and then write the import statement.

   Your code should look like the following:

Visual Basic .NET

```
Imports System.Web.Security
```

Visual C#

```
using System.Web.Security;
```

3. Locate the **Login** function and investigate its contents.

What is the name of the method that is used to retrieve the connection string to the **Coho** database from the **<appSettings>** section of the Web.config file?

_____

_____

What is the name of the stored procedure that is used for the login?

_____

_____

4. Locate the following comment in the **cmdLogin_Click** event procedure:

TODO Lab 16: Call the Login function

5. Call the **Login** function, passing the value in the **txtEmail TextBox** and the value in the **txtPassword TextBox.** Store the returned value in the **strEmployeeID** variable.

Your code should look like the following:

Visual Basic .NET

```
strEmployeeId = Login(txtEmail.Text, txtPassword.Text)
```

Visual C#

```
strEmployeeId = Login(txtEmail.Text, txtPassword.Text);
```

6. Locate the following comment in the **cmdLogin_Click** event procedure:

TODO Lab 16: Login users and generate an auth. cookie

7. Write the code to authenticate users, create a temporary (non-persistent) authentication cookie, and then redirect the user to the page that was originally requested:

a. Test if the variable **strEmployeeId** is not an empty string. This means whether the employee's e-mail address and password have been found in the database.

b. If the variable **strEmployeeId** is not an empty string, redirect the user to the requested page and create a temporary (non-persistent) cookie with the identity string **strEmployeeId**.

c. If the variable **strEmployeeId** is an empty string, redirect, and display the message "Login Failed!" in the **lblInfo** label on the login.aspx page.

Your code should look like the following:

Visual Basic .NET

```
If (strEmployeeId <> "") Then
    FormsAuthentication.RedirectFromLoginPage _
        (strEmployeeId, False)
Else 'Login failed
    lblInfo.Text = "Login Failed!"
End If
```

Visual C#

```
if (strEmployeeId != "")
{
    FormsAuthentication.RedirectFromLoginPage
        (strEmployeeId, false);
}
else //Login failed
{
    lblInfo.Text = "Login Failed!";
}
```

What is the difference between creating a temporary (non-persistent) cookie and a persistent cookie?

_____

_____

What method do you use to read the identity of the authenticated user, which is stored in the authentication cookie, from any Web Form of the ASP.NET Web application?

_____

_____

▶ **Save and test**

1. Save your changes.

2. Build the BenefitsVB or BenefitsCS project.

3. Open a new browser and browse to http://localhost/BenefitsVB/default.aspx or to http://localhost/BenefitsCS/default.aspx.

   You should be redirected to the login.aspx page because all of the pages are secured, including default.aspx.

4. Investigate the Uniform Resource Locator (URL) in the browser. What do you see? Why?

   _____

   _____

5. Enter the e-mail address and password of an employee who is already in the **Logins** table of the **Coho** database (e-mail address **someone@cohowinery.com**, and the password **someone**), and then click **Sign In Now**.

   You are now able to browse all of the pages.

6. Click the **Life Insurance** link and verify that the life.aspx page opens without asking for your credentials.

7. Browse to http://localhost/BenefitsVB/SecurityTest.aspx or to http://localhost/BenefitsCS/SecurityTest.aspx. You should see the employee ID 1, which corresponds to the someone@cohowinery.com e-mail address. You will also see that you are authenticated with Forms-based authentication.

8. Close the browser.

Security Note When using Forms-based authentication, the password that that is entered in the login page is sent in plain text over the network. In a real-world scenario, to prevent the possibility of someone obtaining the password, you must use an SSL connection.

Exercise 3 (If Time Permits)
Registering New Users

In this exercise, you will add code to the register.aspx page, which allows users to add a new employee to the **Logins** table of the **Coho** database.

▶ **Add a register.aspx Web Form to enter new employees**

1. Open the Benefits project in the 2310LabApplication Visual Studio .NET solution.

2. Add the **register.aspx** Web Form from the *install folder*\Labfiles\Lab16\VB\Starter\BenefitsVB or *install folder*\Labfiles\Lab16\CS\Starter\BenefitsCS folder to the BenefitsVB or BenefitsCS project.

3. Open the register.aspx Web Form and investigate its content. Which types of validation controls are used in this Web Form?

   _____

   _____

4. Open the register.aspx.vb or register.aspx.cs code-behind page. The code-behind page contains a function named **AddEmployee** that looks very similar to the **Login** function of the login page, but it calls a different stored procedure, named **EmployeeAdd**, which adds a new employee to the **Logins** table of the **Coho** database.

5. Locate the following comment in the **cmdValidation_Click** event procedure:

   ```
   TODO Lab 16: Call the AddEmployee function
   ```

6. Call the **AddEmployee** function, passing to it the value in the **txtEmail TextBox** and to the value in the **txtPassword TextBox**. Store the returned value in the **strEmployeeID** variable.

   Your code should look like the following:

Visual Basic .NET
```
strEmployeeId = _
    AddEmployee(txtEmail.Text, txtPassword.Text)
```

Visual C#
```
strEmployeeId =
    AddEmployee(txtEmail.Text, txtPassword.Text);
```

7. Locate the following comment in the **cmdValidation_Click** event procedure:

   ```
   TODO Lab 16: Login users and generate an auth. cookie
   ```

8. Within the **If** statement, write the code to authenticate users, create a temporary (non-persistent) authentication cookie, and then redirect the user to the default.aspx Web Form.

    Your code should look like the following:

Visual Basic .NET

```
FormsAuthentication.SetAuthCookie( _
    strEmployeeId, False)
Response.Redirect("default.aspx")
```

Visual C#

```
FormsAuthentication.SetAuthCookie(
    strEmployeeId, false);
Response.Redirect("default.aspx");
```

9. Why are you using the method **SetAuthCookie** here and not **RedirectFromLoginPage**?

    _____

    _____

▶ **Save and test**

1. Save your changes.

2. Build the BenefitsVB or BenefitsCS project.

3. Open a new browser and browse to http://localhost/BenefitsVB/default.aspx or to http://localhost/BenefitsCS/default.aspx.

    You should promptly be redirected to the **login.aspx** page because all of the pages are secured, and, therefore, **default.aspx** is a secure page.

4. Click **Click here!** to open the registration.aspx Web Form to register a new employee.

    What do you observe? Why? How should you fix it?

    _____

    _____

▶ **Configure the security for the register.aspx page in the Web.config file**

1. Open the Web.config file in the BenefitsVB or BenefitsCS project.

2. Enter the configuration information to authorize everyone to access the register.aspx Web Form. Place this information at the end of the Web.config file, just after the </appSettings> tag, but before the </configuration> tag.

   Your configuration should looks like the following:

   ```
   <location path="register.aspx">
      <system.web>
         <authorization>
            <allow users="*" />
         </authorization>
      </system.web>
   </location>
   ```

▶ **Save and test**

1. Save your changes.

   Note   You do not need to rebuild the project because you only changed the Web.config file.
   ---

2. Open a new browser and browse to http://localhost/BenefitsVB/default.aspx or to http://localhost/BenefitsCS/default.aspx.

   You should be redirected to the login.aspx page.

3. Click **Click here!** to open the registration.aspx Web Form and register a new employee. Now you should see the register.aspx Web Form.

4. Enter your e-mail address and a password of your choice to add yourself to the database as a new employee. Click **Submit**.

   You are redirected to the default.aspx page, and are able to browse all of the pages.

5. Click the **Life Insurance** link and verify that the life.aspx page opens without asking for your credentials.

6. Browse to http://localhost/BenefitsVB/SecurityTest.aspx or to http://localhost/BenefitsCS/SecurityTest.aspx. You should see your employee ID and that you are authenticated with Forms-based authentication.

7. Close the browser, open a new browser, and browse to http://localhost/BenefitsVB/default.aspx or to http://localhost/BenefitsCS/default.aspx.

8. On the login.aspx page, log on with your new credentials.

▶ **Register yourself as a new employee on your neighbor's Coho Winery Web site**

1. Open a new browser and browse to
   http://*Neighbormachinename*/BenefitsVB/default.aspx or to
   http://*Neighbormachinename*/BenefitsCS/default.aspx.

   You should be redirected to the login.aspx page of your neighbor's Coho
   Winery Web site.

2. Click **Click here!** to open the registration.aspx Web Form and register a
   new employee. Now you should see the register.aspx Web Form.

3. Enter your e-mail address and a password of your choice to add yourself to
   the database as a new employee. Click **Submit**.

   Now you should be able to see the all the pages of your neighbor's Benefits
   Web site.

Exercise 4 (If Time Permits)
Permitting Users to Sign Out

In this exercise, you will add code to the signout.aspx page that allows users to sign out of the Coho Winery Web site. Signing out can be useful if a user shares a computer with another user and if that user wants to make sure that the other user cannot access private information.

▶ **Update the header.ascx user control and add the signout.aspx Web Form**

1. Open the BenefitsVB or BenefitsCS project in the 2310LabApplication Visual Studio .NET solution.

2. In Solution Explorer, delete the header.ascx user control.

3. Add the header.ascx user control and the signout.aspx Web Form from the *install folder*\Labfiles\Lab16\VB\Starter\BenefitsVB or *install folder*\Labfiles\Lab16\CS\Starter\BenefitsCS folder to the BenefitsVB or BenefitsCS project.

4. The updated header.ascx user control contains a new link named **Sign out** that opens the signout.aspx Web Form.

5. Open the signout.aspx Web Form. The Web Form contains text notifying the user that they will be signed out and a **Sign Out** button.

6. Open the signout.aspx.vb or signout.aspx.cs code-behind page and locate the following comment in the **cmdSignout_Click** event procedure:

   ```
   TODO Lab 16: Implement the signout
   ```

7. Write the code to sign the users out and redirect them to the login.aspx Web Form.

   Your code should look like the following:

Visual Basic .NET

```
FormsAuthentication.SignOut()
Response.Redirect("login.aspx")
```

Visual C#

```
FormsAuthentication.SignOut();
Response.Redirect("login.aspx");
```

▶ **Save and test**

1. Save your changes.

2. Build the BenefitsVB or BenefitsCS project.

3. Open a new browser and browse to http://localhost/BenefitsVB/default.aspx or http://localhost/BenefitsCS/default.aspx.

   You should be redirected to the login.aspx page.

4. Enter your e-mail address and a password, and then click **Sign In Now**.

5. Click the **Life Insurance** link and verify that the life.aspx page opens without asking for your credentials.

6. Click the **signout** hyperlink, and then click **Sign Out**.

   You are redirected to the login.aspx page.

7. Without closing the browser, browse again to http://localhost/BenefitsVB/default.aspx or to http://localhost/BenefitsCS/default.aspx. Refresh your browser. You should be returned to the login.aspx page.

msdn training

Module 17: Review

Contents

Microsoft

Overview

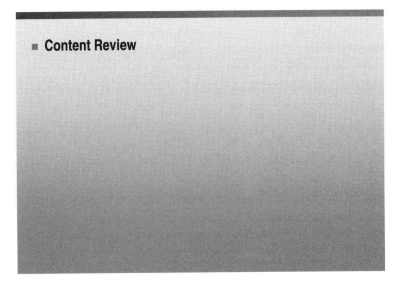

Introduction

Throughout Course 2310B, *Developing Microsoft ASP.NET Web Applications Using Visual Studio .NET*, you learned many of the skills that are needed to develop, secure, test, and deploy a complete Microsoft® ASP.NET Web application. You also learned how Microsoft Visual Studio® .NET can significantly reduce Web application development time by simplifying the development process.

In this module, you will review the main concepts and procedures you have learned throughout this course. You will also have the opportunity to apply your new knowledge in Lab 17, which is an interactive review game.

Content Review

■ **Topics covered:**

● Module 1: Overview of the Microsoft .NET Framework

● Module 2: Using Microsoft Visual Studio .NET

● Module 3: Using Microsoft .NET-Based Languages

● Module 4: Creating a Microsoft ASP.NET Web Form

● Module 5: Adding Code to a Microsoft ASP.NET Web Form

● Module 6: Tracing in Microsoft ASP.NET Web Applications

● Module 7: Validating User Input

● Module 8: Creating User Controls

Introduction

Throughout Course 2310B, *Developing Microsoft ASP.NET Web Applications Using Visual Studio .NET*, you have learned how to develop an ASP.NET Web application. The knowledge you have gained throughout this course includes the following:

■ In Module 1, "Overview of the Microsoft .NET Framework," you learned how the Microsoft .NET Framework works, and how it helps developers build ASP.NET Web applications.

■ In Module 2, "Using Microsoft Visual Studio .NET," you learned how to use the primary features of Visual Studio .NET to create ASP.NET Web applications.

■ In Module 3, "Using Microsoft .NET-Based Languages," you learned how the .NET Framework supports different development languages. You also learned about some of the differences between C# and Microsoft Visual Basic® .NET, and some of the fundamental Visual Basic .NET code procedures.

■ In Module 4, "Creating a Microsoft ASP.NET Web Form," you learned how to create and populate a Web Form.

■ In Module 5, "Adding Code to a Microsoft ASP.NET Web Form," you learned how to add code to a Web Form by using code-behind pages.

■ In Module 6, "Tracing in Microsoft ASP.NET Web Applications," you learned how to debug and trace through a Web application.

■ In Module 7, "Validating User Input," you learned how to use validation controls to ensure the correct input from the user.

■ In Module 8, "Creating User Controls," you learned how to build user controls to provide reusable code and user interface (UI) components that can be used across a Web application.

Content Review *(continued)*

> ■ **Topics covered:**
>
>   ● Modules 9, 10, and 11: Data Access Methods
>
>   ● Module 12: Reading and Writing XML Data
>
>   ● Module 13: Consuming and Creating XML Web Services
>
>   ● Module 14: Managing State
>
>   ● Module 15: Configuring, Optimizing, and Deploying a Microsoft ASP.NET Web Application
>
>   ● Module 16: Securing a Microsoft ASP.NET Web Application

Introduction

Throughout Course 2310B, *Developing Microsoft ASP.NET Web Applications Using Visual Studio .NET*, you have learned how to develop an ASP.NET Web application. The knowledge you have gained throughout this course includes the following:

■ In Modules 9, "Accessing Relational Data Using Microsoft Visual Studio .NET," Module 10, "Accessing Data with Microsoft ADO.NET," and Module 11, "Calling Stored Procedures with Microsoft ADO.NET," you learned how to use Microsoft ADO.NET to implement data-handling in a Web application.

■ In Module 12, "Reading and Writing XML Data," you learned how to read, write, and display Extensible Markup Language (XML) data in a Web Form.

■ In Module 13, "Consuming and Creating XML Web Services," you learned how to create and connect to XML Web services.

■ In Module 14, "Managing State," you learned how to maintain state in an ASP.NET Web application by using session and application variables, cookies, and cookieless sessions.

■ In Module 15, "Configuring, Optimizing, and Deploying a Microsoft ASP.NET Web Application," you learned how to configure your Web application by using Machine.config and Web.config files. In Module 15, you also learned how to:

  ● Optimize Web application performance by using caching.

  ● Deploy your Web application to a production server.

■ In Module 16, "Securing a Microsoft ASP.NET Web Application," you learned how to secure your Web application.

Lab 17: Review Game

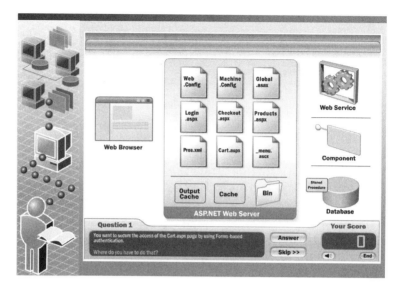

Overview

In this lab, you will run an interactive review game to test your understanding of the concepts and procedures that were presented throughout this course. The game is self-paced and can be run multiple times.

As you progress through the game, you will find that the questions become more technical and more difficult, building on previous questions. Therefore, it is important to fully understand the answer to the current question before proceeding on to the next.

Running the game

When you run the game for the first time, you will see a welcome screen in which you choose whether to play the game in Microsoft Visual Basic® .NET or C#. After selecting a development language, you will see a graphical representation of a Microsoft ASP.NET Web application. The illustration includes icons that represent many of the major components of an ASP.NET Web application.

The questions are displayed automatically in the bottom left corner of the game. Each question has three parts to it.

Part 1

The first part of the question requires you to select the appropriate icon on the screen, based on the question displayed. After you select the correct icon, a code window appears.

Part 2

The code window is the second part of the question. In this code window, you will add the necessary code to complete the task stated in the question. To enter code in the code window, click any placeholder (represented by three dashes, ---), and then type your code. Your code will appear as you type.

When you think you have entered the correct code, click **Verify**. If you have any errors, the game engine points to the areas of code that are incorrect.

Tip You can drag the error pointers away from the code so you can read the code more clearly.

You will then need to click the incorrect areas and correct the code.

Tip   If you do not know the answer, click **Answer**. The correct code will be supplied in the code window.

Part 3

After you have the correct code, click **Continue**. The third part of the question is a brief animation that shows which components are affected by the changes that you made. A pop-up window provides an explanation of the animation. You can control the animation by using the navigation buttons (Play/Pause, Forward, Back, and Skip), which are located in the pop-up window.

The game engine then returns to the initial screen and displays a new question for you to answer.

Scoring

There are 20 questions in the game.

Every question in Part 1 is worth 5 points; every incorrect guess subtracts 1 point from that initial 5 points. If you continue to guess after 5 incorrect answers, you will not earn any points, but you will not lose any points from your total score.

Every question in Part 2 has 10 points; every incorrect guess subtracts 2 points from that initial 10 points. If you continue to guess after 5 incorrect answers, you will not earn any points, but you will not lose any points from your total score.

In Parts 1 and 2, if you skip a question or ask for the answer, you will not earn any points for that question.

Part 3 is an explanation and animation on the picture of what you just changed; therefore, no points are awarded for this part of the game.

At the end of the game, you receive a **Game Over** message that displays your final score.

Course Evaluation

Course Evaluation

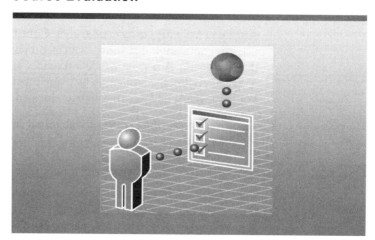

Your evaluation of this course will help Microsoft understand the quality of your learning experience.

To complete a course evaluation, go to http://www.CourseSurvey.com.

Microsoft will keep your evaluation strictly confidential and will use your responses to improve your future learning experience.

msdn®training

Appendix A:
Lab Recovery

Microsoft®

Removing Lab Files

Because of the way that Microsoft® Visual Studio® .NET keeps track of files, it can be difficult to recover from a broken lab in this course. By using the following steps, you can remove the parts of your 2310LabApplication solution that are likely to cause problems during a rebuild. You can then rebuild the 2310LabApplication solution by beginning with Exercise 0 in any lab in Course 2310B, *Developing Microsoft ASP.NET Web Applications Using Visual Studio .NET*. In Exercise 0 you will be replacing the deleted files with solution files that will support the remaining labs.

Note These steps will permanently delete the files that you have built while completing the labs in Course 2310B, *Developing Microsoft ASP.NET Web Applications Using Visual Studio .NET*. Any modifications to the labs that you made on your own will be lost.

▶ **To remove the BenefitsVB project**

1. In Visual Studio .NET, open the 2310LabApplication solution.
2. In Solution Explorer, right-click **BenefitsVB** and then click **Remove**.
3. Click **OK**.
4. Open Windows Explorer.
5. Browse to C:\Inetpub\wwwroot.
6. Right-click the **BenefitsVB** folder and then choose **Properties**.
7. Clear the **Read-only** attribute if it is selected, and then click **OK**.
8. In the **Confirm Attribute Changes** dialog box, select **Apply changes to this folder, subfolders, and files**, and then click **OK**.
9. In Windows Explorer, right-click **BenefitsVB** and then click **Delete**.
10. Click **Yes** to confirm deletion.

▶ **To remove the BenefitsListVB project**

1. In Visual Studio .NET, open the 2310LabApplication solution.
2. In Solution Explorer, right-click **BenefitsListVB** and then click **Remove**.
3. Click **OK**.
4. Open Windows Explorer.
5. Browse to My Documents\Visual Studio Projects\2310LabApplication.
6. Right-click **BenefitsListVB** and then choose **Delete**.
7. Click **Yes** to confirm deletion.

▶ **To remove the DentalServiceVB project**

1. In Visual Studio .NET, open the 2310LabApplication solution.
2. In Solution Explorer, right-click **DentalServiceVB** and then click **Remove**.
3. Click **OK**.
4. Open Windows Explorer.
5. Browse to C:\Inetpub\wwwroot.

6. Right-click the **DentalServiceVB** folder and then choose **Properties**.

7. Clear the **Read-only** attribute if it is selected, and then click **OK**.

8. In the **Confirm Attribute Changes** dialog, select **Apply changes to this folder, subfolders, and files**, and then click **OK**.

9. In Windows Explorer, right-click **DentalServiceVB** and then click **Delete**.

10. Click **Yes** to confirm deletion.

▶ **To remove the BenefitsCS project**

1. In Visual Studio .NET, open the 2310LabApplication solution.

2. In Solution Explorer, right-click **BenefitsCS** and then click **Remove**.

3. Click **OK**.

4. Open Windows Explorer.

5. Browse to C:\Inetpub\wwwroot

6. Right-click the **BenefitsCS** folder and then choose **Properties**.

7. Clear the **Read-only** attribute if it is selected, and then click **OK**.

8. In the **Confirm Attribute Changes** dialog box, select **Apply changes to this folder, subfolders, and files**, and then click **OK**.

9. In Windows Explorer, right-click **BenefitsCS** and then click **Delete**.

10. Click **Yes** to confirm deletion.

▶ **To remove the BenefitsListCS project**

1. In Visual Studio .NET, open the 2310LabApplication solution.

2. In Solution Explorer, right-click **BenefitsListCS** and then click **Remove**.

3. Click **OK**.

4. Open Windows Explorer.

5. Browse to My Documents\Visual Studio Projects\2310LabApplication.

6. Right-click **BenefitsListCS** and then choose **Delete**.

7. Click **Yes** to confirm deletion.

▶ **To remove the DentalServiceCS project**

1. In Visual Studio .NET, open the 2310LabApplication solution.

2. In Solution Explorer, right-click **DentalServiceCS** and then click **Remove**.

3. Click **OK**.

4. Open Windows Explorer.

5. Browse to C:\Inetpub\wwwroot.

6. Right-click the **DentalServiceCS** folder and then choose **Properties**.

7. Clear the **Read-only** attribute if it is selected, and then click **OK**.

8. In the **Confirm Attribute Changes** dialog box, select **Apply changes to this folder, subfolders, and files**, and then click **OK**.

9. In Windows Explorer, right-click **DentalServiceCS** and then click **Delete**.

10. Click **Yes** to confirm deletion.

msdn training

Appendix B: Debugging with Microsoft Visual Studio .NET

Microsoft

Lesson: Debugging with Microsoft Visual Studio .NET

- **What Is Debugging?**
- **Debugging with Visual Studio .NET**
- **Configuring for Debugging**
- **Demonstration: Debugging with Visual Studio .NET**
- **Demonstration: Using the Debug Object**

Introduction

Before deploying your Web application, thereby making it available to client requests, you first must debug it. Debugging your Web application is an important step in ensuring that the Web application works properly. In this appendix, you will learn how to debug a Web application by using Microsoft® Visual Studio® .NET. You will also learn how to perform remote debugging, in which you can debug, from a client computer, Microsoft ASP.NET Web applications that are located on a development server.

Lesson objectives

After completing this lesson, you will be able to:

- Explain how debugging works and why it is important.
- Use the debugging features of Visual Studio .NET.
- Configure debug options in Visual Studio .NET.
- Remotely debug a Web application.

What Is Debugging?

- Finding design-time errors (not runtime errors)
- Finding logic errors
- Finding coding errors that are not caught by Try...Catch...Finally blocks
- Viewing variables as their values change
- Testing the limits of the Web application

Introduction

As you develop Web applications, you may enter code that is not valid or you may not thoroughly consider the programming logic in a method. Debugging a Web application allows you to find design-time and logic errors before publishing the Web application. Debugging also allows you to watch variables that you have used and see how their values change.

What is debugging?

Debugging is the process of searching for and removing errors from your code. Because you use the same tools to create Web applications as Microsoft Windows® applications, you can use the powerful built-in debugging tools of Visual Studio .NET to debug your Web applications.

Why debug?

Debugging a Web application allows you to check for errors before users of the Web application find them. When you debug a Web application, you catch the following types of errors:

- *Design-time errors*. As you code an .aspx page, you may make typographical mistakes or forget to explicitly declare variables. For example, if you are using C#, you may have capitalization errors. These types of design-time errors are caught by the compiler when you build the project.

- *Logic errors*. Do you have a For loop that cannot be exited? Do you have code that can never be reached because of a loop? Perhaps you have an algorithm that is used for computing when a value is incorrect. You can find these types of logic errors by running the Web application in debug mode.

- *Code errors*. You should use **Try...Catch...Finally** blocks in your code to catch errors that may be generated when the Web application is run. However, you may not think of all of the possible places where exceptions may be thrown, or you may forget to place the code in a **Try** block. Debugging helps you to find and solve these errors.

Debugging also allows you to do the following:

- *View variables*. For each variable that you assign in your Web application, you can track the value of that variable as the Web application runs. This tracking is a useful way to ensure that variables are changing as you expect, which would be according to your programming logic.

- *Test application limits*. While debugging, you can test whether parts of your Web application work when users enter information that extends beyond what you would normally expect, or when users try to use the interface in a non-standard way.

Debugging with Visual Studio .NET

- **Visual Studio .NET offers integrated debugging in the runtime**
- **Debugging an ASP.NET Page**
  - Set breakpoints
  - Step through code
  - View values of variables
  - Change variable values

Introduction

For debugging Web applications, Visual Studio .NET offers integrated debugging in the common language runtime (hereafter referred to as "runtime"), thereby simplifying the debugging process.

Debugging

Because debugging is integrated in the runtime, you can debug all of the files in a solution, regardless of the language in which they were written. You can also debug components and even XML Web services, as long as they are included as part of the solution and are running on the same computer as the Web application.

When you debug an ASP.NET page, you can perform the following procedures:

- Set breakpoints.

  You set breakpoints by clicking in the left margin next to the line of code. When code execution reaches that line of code, execution pauses.

- Step through code.

  After execution has paused, control is returned to Visual Studio .NET. From the Visual Studio .NET IDE you can step through the code one line at a time.

- View the value of a variable.

  The Visual Studio .NET IDE includes a watch window. From the watch window, you can enter the name of a variable and then watch how the value of the variable changes as you step through the code. You can also pause the mouse over a variable name in the code and a tool tip will appear, displaying the variable's value.

- Change variable values.

  In the watch window, you can change the value that is assigned to a variable, and you can then watch how the value changes or how the other variables change as you step through the code.

Configuring for Debugging

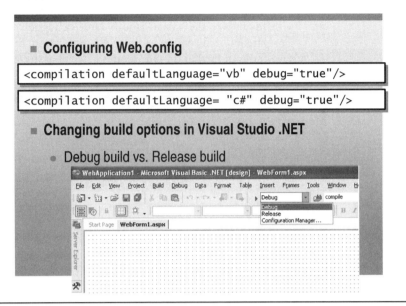

Introduction

When debugging a Web application, you need to configure the Web.config file for the Web application and change the build options in Visual Studio .NET.

Configuring Web.config

Each ASP.NET Web application has a configuration file named Web.config. Web.config is an Extensible Markup Language (XML) file that contains configuration settings for the Web application.

Note For more information about the Web.config file, see Module 15, "Configuring, Optimizing, and Deploying a Microsoft ASP.NET Application," in Course 2310B, *Developing Microsoft ASP.NET Web Applications Using Visual Studio .NET.*

Within the Web.config file, there is a **compilation** element. This element includes all of the compilation settings that ASP.NET uses. One attribute of the compilation element is **debug**. To enable debugging for a Web application, set the **debug** attribute to **true**, as shown in the following code:

Visual Basic .NET

```
<compilation defaultLanguage="vb" debug="true"/>
```

C#

```
<compilation defaultLanguage="c#" debug="true"/>
```

Note For more information on the **compilation** element, see "<compilation> Element" in the Visual Studio .NET documentation.

Visual Studio .NET build options

Within Visual Studio .NET, you can build Web applications in either debug mode or release mode. Debug mode adds more processing requirements to the Web application, thereby reducing performance, but it does allow you to use the features of the Visual Studio .NET debugger. Release mode builds a more streamlined version of the Web application, but it does not allow for debugging. You set the build mode from the tool bar, as shown in the following illustration.

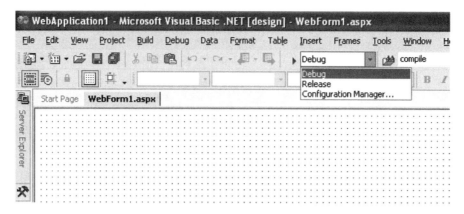

You can also choose to run the Web application in debug or release mode from the **Debug** menu. To run a Web application in debug mode, you must first select a Startup Project and Startup Page from Solution Explorer. In Solution Explorer, right-click on a project, choose **Set as Startup Project**, and then right-click a page and choose **Set as Start Page**.

In the **Debug** menu, you have two choices for running the Web application: **Start** or **Start Without Debugging**. These options are shown in the following illustration.

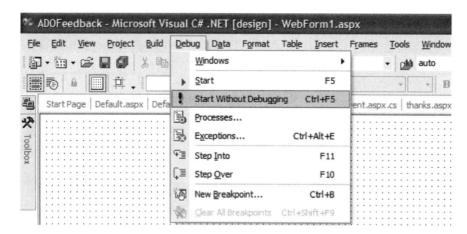

To debug a Web application, you need to build in debug mode and then choose **Start** from the **Debug** menu or from the toolbar. When you choose to **Build and Browse** or **View in Browser** from Solution Explorer, you will not be running the Web application in debug mode.

Demonstration: Debugging with Visual Studio .NET

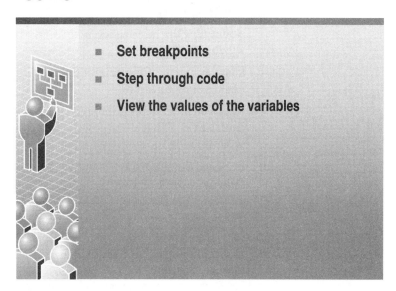

- Set breakpoints
- Step through code
- View the values of the variables

In this demonstration, you will see how to use the Visual Studio .NET debugger.

▶ **To run the demonstration**

1. Open the 2310Demos solution.

2. Set the CallClassVB or the CallClassCS project as the startup project and the CallClassLibraries.aspx page as the Start Page.

3. Set a breakpoint in the **cmdUseVB_Click** event procedure in the CallClassLibraries.aspx.vb or CallClassLibraries.aspx.cs page by clicking in the left-hand margin next to the following line of code:

Visual Basic .NET

```
Dim x As New VBClassLibrary.Class1()
```

C#

```
VBClassLibrary.Class1 x = new VBClassLibrary.Class1();
```

4. Run the Web application in debug mode by clicking **Start** on the **Debug** menu, or by clicking **Start** on the toolbar.

5. Enter a price in the **Price** field and then click **VB .NET Shipping Cost**.

   Visual Studio .NET enters the debugger at the breakpoint in the **cmdUseVB_Click** event procedure.

   Notice the information that is displayed in the following windows:

   - The Call Stack window displays the names of functions on the call stack.

   - The Autos window displays the names and values of variables in the current and previous statements.

   - The Locals window displays the names and values of all local variables in the current scope.

6. Pause the mouse on the variable x to show its current value.

7. Click **Step Into**. There is no constructor for the VBClassLibrary component, so the context does not change.

8. Click **Step Into** again. The next line of code calls the **ComputeShipping** method of the component and changes the view in the debugger to the VBClassLibrary.

    Notice how the information in the Call Stack window and the Locals window has changed.

9. Step through the **ComputeShipping** method to follow the logic and return to the calling function.

10. After you have stepped through all of the statements in the **cmdUseVB_Click** event procedure, the browser window becomes active again, waiting for more user input.

11. In Visual Studio .NET, set another breakpoint on the **cmdUseWS_Click** event procedure.

Note   You are adding this breakpoint while the debugger is running.

---

12. In the ShippingCS or ShippingVB project, set another breakpoint in the ComputeShipping XML Web service method in the Service1.asmx.vb or the Service1.asmx.cs page by clicking in the left margin, next to the following line of code:

Visual Basic .NET

```
If sngPrice > 15 Then
```

C#

```
if (sngPrice > 15)
```

13. In the browser, click **Web Service Shipping Cost**.

    Visual Studio .NET enters the debugger at the breakpoint in the **cmdUseWS_Click** event procedure.

14. Step through the **cmdUseWS_Click** event procedure.

    This time the Visual Studio .NET debugger will step into the Service1.asmx Web service.

    Notice that the information in the Call Stack and Locals windows has changed.

15. Click **Continue** to run the rest of the Web service and to return to the calling page.

16. End the debugging session by clicking **Stop Debugging**.

17. Disable the breakpoints by right-clicking on them and clicking **Disable Breakpoint**. This action keeps the breakpoint, but the debugger will not stop on them.

18. Show how you can disable, clear, and enable all breakpoints from the **Debug** menu.

Demonstration: Using the Debug Object

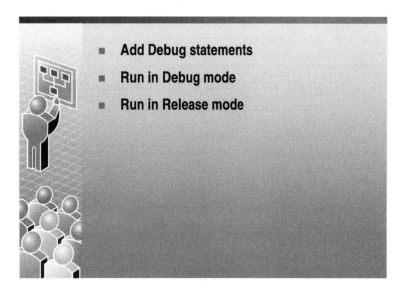

- Add Debug statements
- Run in Debug mode
- Run in Release mode

In this demonstration, you will see how to use the **Debug** object in a Web application.

▶ **To run the demonstration**

1. Open the 2310Demos solution.

2. Ensure that CallClassVB or CallClassCS is set to the startup project and CallClassLibraries.aspx is set to the start page.

3. In the CallClassLibraries.aspx.vb or the CallClassLibraries.aspx.cs page, add a debug message to the **cmdUseVB_Click** event as shown in the following code:

Visual Basic .NET

```
Debug.Write("UseVB", "price = " & CStr(TextBox1.Text))
```

C#

```
Debug.Write("UseVB", "price = " +
(TextBox1.Text).ToString());
```

4. In the CallClassLibraries.aspx.vb or the CallClassLibraries.aspx.cs page, add an **Imports** statement to import the **System.Diagnostics** namespace, as shown in the following code:

Visual Basic .NET

```
Imports System.Diagnostics
```

C#

```
using System.Diagnostics;
```

5. Run the Web application in debug mode by clicking **Start** on the toolbar.

6. In the browser, enter a price and then click **VB .NET Shipping Cost**.

   The debug message is displayed in the Output window of the debugger.

7. Stop debugging the Web application.

8. Run the Web application again, this time without debugging, by either right-clicking the CallClassLibraries.aspx page and clicking **View in Browser**, or by clicking **Start Without Debugging** on the **Debug** menu.

9. In the browser, enter a price and then click **VB .NET Shipping Cost**.

   The debug message is not displayed.

msdn training

Appendix C: Using Templates with List-Bound Controls

Microsoft

Lesson: Using Templates with List-Bound Controls

- Displaying Data in the Repeater and DataList Controls
- Using Templates
- Demonstration: Using a DataList Control

Introduction

Unlike the **DataGrid** control, the **DataList** and **Repeater** list-bound controls do not have a built-in user interface (UI). However, you can easily customize the appearance of these list-bound controls in Microsoft® ASP.NET by using templates. In this lesson, you will learn how to apply templates to the **DataList** and **Repeater** list-bound controls.

Lesson objectives

After completing this lesson, you will be able to:

- Display data in a **Repeater** or **DataList** control.
- Use a template to customize the appearance of a **Repeater** or **DataList** control.

Displaying Data in the Repeater and DataList Controls

- ■ **Create the control and bind it to a DataSet**

- ■ **Set custom properties**
  - ● Autoformat
  - ● Columns (horizontal vs. vertical columns)

- ■ **Display data in templates**

```
<asp:Repeater id="repList" runat="server">
<ItemTemplate>
  <%#DataBinder.Eval(Container.DataItem, "au_lname")%>
</ItemTemplate>
</asp:Repeater>
```

Introduction

The **DataList** and **Repeater** controls are list-bound controls that do not have a specific, predefined appearance. When you use these list-bound controls, you get greater flexibility in presenting data on your ASP.NET Web Form.

Using the DataList and Repeater controls

There are three basic steps to using a **Repeater** or **DataList** control. First, you bind the control to a **DataSet**. You then set custom properties, and finally, you associate the control with a template. The templates then determine how the data is displayed on the Web Form.

To use a **DataList** or **Repeater** control, the first step is to bind the control to a **DataSet** by setting the **DataSource** and **DataMember** properties in the Properties window. Then, in an event on the page, you need to call the **DataBind** method of the control, as shown in the following code:

Visual Basic .NET

```
repeater.DataBind()
```

C#

```
repeater.DataBind();
```

Custom properties

The second step in using a **Repeater** or **DataList** control is to define custom properties. The **DataList** control has the following custom properties, which determine the way that the list will be displayed:

- ■ **RepeatColumns**. This property sets the number of columns that will be displayed in the **DataList**.

- ■ **RepeatDirection**. This property determines whether the data in the **DataList** control is displayed horizontally (as rows) or vertically (as columns).

- ■ **RepeatLayout**. This property sets whether the data in the **DataList** control is displayed as a table or in **FlowLayout.**

In addition, like the **DataGrid** control, the **DataList** control has an AutoFormat option, which adds formatting to the otherwise unformatted control.

Displaying the data

The third step in using a **Repeater** or **DataList** control is the binding of the data that is held in the **Repeater** or **DataList** control to templates that describe how to display the data. For example, to display a list of authors' last names, use the following binding syntax in an **ItemTemplate** template:

```
<asp:Repeater id="repeater" runat="server">
  <ItemTemplate>
    <%# DataBinder.Eval(Container.DataItem, "au_lname") %><BR>
  </ItemTemplate>
</asp:Repeater>
```

In the preceding code, the <% %> is the syntax that is used for inline server-side code and # is the binding expression. The **Container** object refers to the current record of the **Repeater** control, and the **DataItem** method refers to a field in that record.

Using Templates

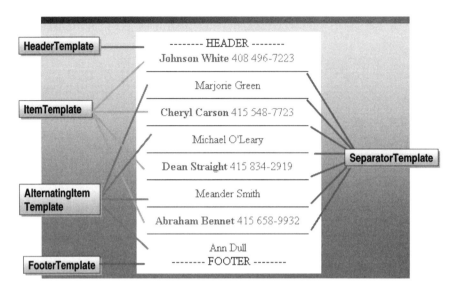

Introduction

Most ASP.NET controls have a standard appearance, but there are times when you may require a different appearance for your controls. ASP.NET allows you to customize the appearance of some controls by using templates. When a control supports a template, you add the ASP.NET template elements. Then, within the template, you insert the elements and controls that you want to display.

Template types

List-bound controls support five types of templates. The **Repeater** and **DataList** controls can use these templates directly. The **DataGrid** control can use these templates only if they are bound to a column. The following table describes the five template types.

Template	Use
HeaderTemplate	Contains elements that are displayed once before any data-bound rows are displayed. A typical use is to create the header row of a table.
ItemTemplate	Contains elements that are rendered once for each row in the data source.
AlternatingItemTemplate	Contains elements that are displayed as every other row in the **Repeater** control.
SeparatorTemplate	Contains elements that display between each row. These are typically line breaks (tags) and lines (<HR/> tags).
FooterTemplate	Contains elements that are displayed once when all data-bound rows have been rendered. A typical use is to close an element that was opened in the HeaderTemplate item (with a tag such as </TABLE>).

Using a template with a DataList control

The following sample code uses templates, combined with data in a **DataList** control named **DataList1**, to display the first name, last name, and telephone number fields in the data. The **DataList** uses the ItemTemplate and the SeparatorTemplate template types:

```
<asp:DataList id="DataList1" runat="server">
<ItemTemplate>
  <font color="#009966">
    <p align="center">
      <b>
        <%# DataBinder.Eval(Container.DataItem, "au_fname") %>
        <%# DataBinder.Eval(Container.DataItem, "au_lname") %>
      </b>
      <%# DataBinder.Eval(Container.DataItem, "phone") %>
    </p>
  </font>
</ItemTemplate>
<SeparatorTemplate>
  <hr color="#3300ff" size="1">
</SeparatorTemplate>
</asp:DataList>
```

The following illustration shows the list that was created by the preceding code.

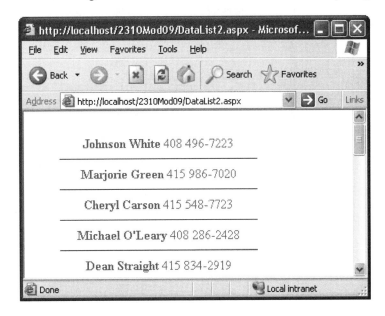

Using the AlternatingItemTemplate with a DataList control

The **DataList** and **Repeater** controls can use templates directly. The following code is an example of using the **AlternatingItemTemplate** with a **DataList** control. The **AlternatingItemTemplate** changes the color and the data in alternate lines:

```
<AlternatingItemTemplate>
  <font color=#cc3300>
    <p align="center">
      <%# DataBinder.Eval(Container.DataItem, "au_fname") %>
      <%# DataBinder.Eval(Container.DataItem, "au_lname") %>
    </p>
  </font>
</AlternatingItemTemplate>
```

The following illustration shows the table with the **AlternatingItemTemplate**.

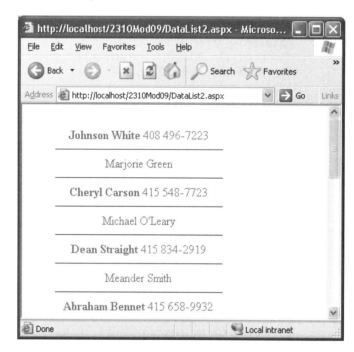

Demonstration: Using a DataList Control

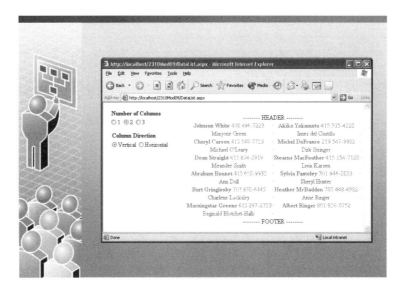

Introduction

In this demonstration, you will see how to use the **DataList** control to display data.

▶ **To run the demonstration**

1. Build and browse the DataList.aspx page in the Mod09VB or Mod09CS project in the 2310Demos solution.

   Notice that different data is shown for the alternating rows of the **DataList** control.

   Click the option buttons to change the layout of the **DataList** control.

2. View the page in Microsoft Visual Studio® .NET.

   There is a **SqlConnection**, a **SqlDataAdapter**, and a **DataSet** for the authors table in the Pubs database.

3. View the Hypertext Markup Language (HTML) for the page.

   There are **ItemTemplate** and **AlternatingItemTemplate** tags that are set up for the **DataList** control.

4. View the code for the page.

   In the **Page_Load** event, the **DataList** control is bound to the **DataSet**.

   In the **SelectedIndexChanged** events for the two sets of radio buttons, the **RepeatColumns** and **RepeatDirection** properties of the **DataList** control are set.

msdn® training

Appendix D: XML Web Service Responses

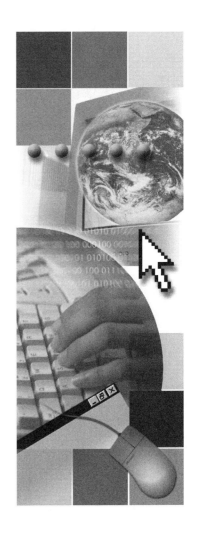

Microsoft®

Lesson: XML Web Service Responses

- **XML Web Service Responses**
- **Default Formatted XML Web Service Responses**
- **Reshaping XML Web Service Responses**
- **Demonstration: Reshaping XML Web Service Responses**

Introduction

XML Web services respond to calls with formatted Extensible Markup Language (XML). In this appendix, you will learn how XML Web service responses are formatted and how you can reshape these responses.

Lesson objectives

After completing this lesson, you will be able to:

- Describe the response format options that are available for XML Web services.
- Describe the default XML formatting of complex data that is created by an XML Web service.
- Reshape the XML response of an XML Web service.

XML Web Service Responses

- **Web services respond to direct HTTP-GET calls with simple XML documents**

- **Web services respond to application-to-application calls with SOAP envelopes**
  - Envelope definition
  - Encoding rules
  - RPC representation
  - Protocol bindings

Introduction

XML Web services support three request protocols: HTTP-GET, HTTP-POST, and Simple Object Access Protocol (SOAP). Replies to HTTP-GET and HTTP-POST requests are sent as simple XML documents. Replies to SOAP requests are sent as SOAP envelopes that contain the XML documents.

HTTP-GET and HTTP-POST calls

When you access an XML Web service directly from a browser by using the HTTP-GET protocol, the Web server that hosts the XML Web service will generate a description page for the requested XML Web service. This description page lists all of the available XML Web service methods and their parameters. When you then call an XML Web service method from this page, you receive the response in simple XML.

You could also use the HTTP-POST protocol to access the XML Web service without the default access page. The response from the XML Web service would be identical to an HTTP-GET request.

The following XML shows the response to an HTTP-GET or an HTTP-POST call to the default XML Web service method that was created by using Microsoft® Visual Studio® .NET:

```
<?xml version="1.0" encoding="utf-8"?>
  <string xmlns="http://tempuri.org/">Hello World</string>
```

Application-to-application calls

When you access a Microsoft ASP.NET Web service by using a proxy from another Web application, both the request and the response are in SOAP.

SOAP is a simple, lightweight, XML-based protocol that is used for exchanging structured and type information over the Internet. SOAP defines a messaging framework that contains no application or transport semantics. As a result, the protocol is modular and extensible.

A SOAP response from an XML Web service may include the following sections:

- Envelope definition

  The SOAP envelope defines a SOAP message and it is the basic unit of exchange between SOAP message processors.

- Encoding rules

  The encoding rules define the data encoding that is used to represent the application-defined data types and the directed graphs.

- RPC representation

  The RPC representation defines the (request/response) message exchange pattern.

- Protocol bindings

  Protocol bindings define the binding between SOAP and Hypertext Transfer Protocol (HTTP). You can use SOAP in combination with any transport protocol or mechanism, including Simple Mail Transfer Protocol (SMTP), File Transfer Protocol (FTP), or even a floppy disk that is able to transport the SOAP envelope.

Default Formatted XML Web Service Responses

■ **XML Web service code for an array**

```
Public Structure Contact
  Public name As String
  Public address As String
End Structure

<WebMethod()>Public Function _
  GetContacts() As Contact()
  Dim x(1) As Contact
  x(0).name = "Janet"
  x(0).address = "Seattle, WA"
  x(1).name = "Joe"
  x(1).address = "Attleboro, MA"
  Return x
End Function
```

```
public struct Contact
{
  public string name;
  public string address;
}

[WebMethod()]public Contact[]
  GetContacts()
{
  Contact[] x;
  x = new Contact[2];
  x[0].name = "Janet";
  x[0].address = "Seattle, WA";
  x[1].name = "Joe";
  x[1].address = "Attleboro, MA";
  return x;
}
```

Introduction

XML Web services use SOAP to communicate with other Web applications. The default SOAP XML data formatting can handle multiple data structures, but you need to be aware of how the default format treats complex data structures, such as arrays.

XML Web service code

The following code example shows a data array that is used inside an XML Web service:

Microsoft Visual Basic® .NET

```
Public Structure Contact
      Public name As String
      Public address As String
End Structure

<WebMethod()>Public Function GetContacts() _
  As Contact()
      Dim x(1) As Contact
      x(0).name = "Janet"
      x(0).address = "Seattle, WA"
      x(1).name = "Joe"
      x(1).address = "Attleboro, MA"
      Return x
End Function
```

C#

```csharp
public struct Contact
{
  public string name;
  public string address;
}

[WebMethod()]public Contact[] GetContacts()
{
  Contact[] x;
  X = new Contact[2];
  x[0].name = "Janet";
  x[0].address = "Seattle, WA";
  x[1].name = "Joe";
  x[1].address = "Attleboro, MA";
  return x;
}
```

Default SOAP response

When the XML Web service receives a request from another Web application, it responds with data that is formatted according to the SOAP protocol.

The following XML shows the default formatted XML data that was created from the preceding array:

```xml
<?xml version="1.0" encoding="utf-8"?>
<ArrayOfContact>
  <Contact>
    <name>Janet</name>
    <address>Seattle, WA</address>
  </Contact>
  <Contact>
    <name>Joe</name>
    <address>Attleboro, MA</address>
  </Contact>
</ArrayOfContact>
```

Reshaping XML Web Service Responses

```
■   XML Web service revised code
<XmlType("MyContact")>Public Structure Contact
  <XmlAttributeAttribute("ContactName")> _
        Public name As String
  <XmlAttributeAttribute("ContactAddress")> _
        Public address As String
End Structure
```
```
[XmlType("MyContact")]public struct Contact{
   [XmlAttributeAttribute("ContactName")]
      public string name;
   [XmlAttributeAttribute("ContactAddress")]
      public String address;
}
```
```
■  Resulting  XML response
<?xml version="1.0" encoding="utf-8"?>
<ArrayOfMyContact>
  <MyContact ContactName="Janet"
       ContactAddress="Seattle, WA" />
  <MyContact ContactName ="Joe"
       ContactAddress="Attleboro, MA" />
</ArrayOfMyContact>
```

Introduction

An indented list of XML tags and items is not the appropriate input format for all applications. If you have an application that requires a unique input structure, you then need to *shape* your XML Web service response. You adjust the *shape* of the XML Web service output by specifying XML attributes.

XML Web service code

In the following example, the item **MyContact** has the sub-attributes **ContactName** and **ContactAddress**:

Visual Basic .NET

```
<XmlType("MyContact")>Public Structure Contact
  <XmlAttributeAttribute("ContactName")> _
      Public name As String
  <XmlAttributeAttribute("ContactAddress")> _
      Public address As String
End Structure
```

C#

```
[XmlType("MyContact")]public struct Contact
{
   [XmlAttributeAttribute("ContactName")]
      public string name;
   [XmlAttributeAttribute("ContactAddress")]
      public String address;
}
```

XML response

The following XML shows the formatting that results from the preceding XML Web service:

```xml
<?xml version="1.0" encoding="utf-8"?>
<ArrayOfMyContact>
  <MyContact ContactName="Janet"
      ContactAddress="Seattle, WA" />
  <MyContact ContactName ="Joe"
      ContactAddress="Attleboro, MA" />
</ArrayOfMyContact>
```

Note For more information on how to implement an XML Web service that supports complex data types, see Module 5, "Implementing a Simple XML Web Service," in Course 2524, *Developing XML Web Services Using Microsoft ASP.NET*

Demonstration: Reshaping XML Web Service Responses

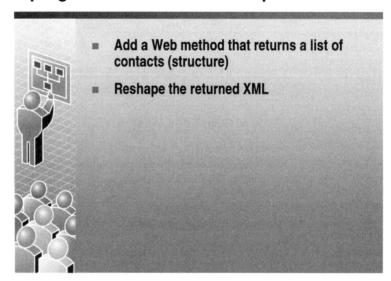

In this demonstration, you will learn how to create and return complex data.

The files GetContacts.txt and XMLReshaping.txt are in the *install folder*/Democode/Mod13VB or *install folder*/Democode/Mod13CS folder, and the Service1.asmx.vb or Service1.asmx.cs file is in the project called **StocksVB** or **StocksCS**. This XML Web service was created in the Instructor-Led Practice, "Creating an XML Web Service," in Module 13, "Consuming and Creating XML Web Services," in Course 2310B, *Developing Microsoft ASP.NET Web Applications Using Visual Studio .NET*.

▶ **To run this demonstration**

Add a Web method

1. Copy the contents of the GetContacts.txt file into the Service1.asmx.vb or Service1.asmx.cs file. Place the contents after the WebMethod attribute **GetRating** of the XML Web service.

2. Save the file.

3. Build and browse Service1.asmx.

4. Invoke the **GetContacts** method and view the result in XML.

Reshape the returned XML

5. Add the following import code at the beginning of the Service1.asmx.vb or Service1.asmx.cs file:

Visual Basic .NET

```
Imports System.Xml.Serialization
```

C#

```
using System.Xml.Serialization;
```

6. Copy the content of the XMLReshaping.txt file and paste it over the existing **Contact** structure in the Service1.asmx.vb or Service1.asmx.cs file.

7. Build and browse Service1.asmx.

8. Invoke the **GetContacts** method and show the new shape of the XML response.

Course 2310: Index

A

AbsoluteExpiration parameter 15.8
Active Directory 16.9
Active Server Pages. *See* ASP (Active Server Pages)
Add method 10.39, 11.18
Add Reference dialog box 3.25
Add Web Form option 4.8
Add Web Reference dialog box 13.22
ADO.NET
    connection object 10.12
    data access 9.7, 10.46–10.54
    DataAdapter object 9.15, 10.17
    database connections 9.9–9.14, 10.8–10.13
    database updates 9.7
    DataSet object 9.6, 9.17, 10.4, 10.19-10.22,12.10-12.24,
    DataReader object 10.4, 10.47-10.55
    DataRelation object 10.39-10.43,12.19
    DataView object 10.25
    described 1.6, 9.3, 9.4, 10.2, 10.3
    errors 10.31, 10.34
    list-bound controls 9.20-9.22
    manipulate data 9.7
    namespaces 9.4
    object model 9.5, 10.3
    properties 10.18
    relationships 10.39–10.43
    security 10.8
    stored procedures 11.10
    tables 10.36-10.38
    XML 12.29
Application object 14.15, 14.17
application services 1.6
application state
    described 14.4
    hashtable 14.7
application variables
    described 14.6, 14.13–14.19
    duration 14.19
    initialize 14.14, 14.15
    save 14.21
    scalable storage 14.20
Application_End event 14.19
Application.Lock method 14.16
Application.UnLock method 14.16
ASCII (American Standard Code for Information Interchange) 14.7
ASP (Active Server Pages)
    application updates 15.47
    inline code 5.4
    mixed code 5.3
    include files 8.5
AspCompat attribute 8.4

ASP.NET
    authentication 16.4–16.7, 16.15, 16.18, 16.23–16.24, 16.26, 16.28, 16.35
    browsers 3.16
    described 1.6, 1.12-1.14
    execution model 1.16
    Global.asax 14.10
    impersonation 16.18
    parser 1.16
    resources 1.23, 1.24
    server controls 4.12–4.18
    state management 13.4, 14.3, 14.4, 14.6
    validation 7.2, 7.5, 7.7
ASP.NET pages (see also Web Forms)
    described 4.3
    creating 4.2, 4.8, 4.9
    debugging 6.5-6.11
    add controls to 4.21-4.24
    event procedures 5.2–5.24, 5.31
    user controls 8.2, 8.3
assemblies. *See also* DLLs (dynamic-link libraries)
    create 2.23, 2.28
    described 2.23, 2.28
    GAC 15.41, 15.46
    shared 15.41, 15.46
Assembly.Info.cs 2.27
Assembly.Info.vb 2.27
Authenticate method 16.29
authentication
    SQL Server 10.9, 10.10, 10.11
    anonymous access 16.17, 16.24, 16.26
    Basic 16.8, 16.9, 16.14
    data transfer 9.7
    described 16.3
    digest 16.8, 16.9, 16.14
    enable 16.14–16.18, 16.27
    forms-based 16.4, 16.7, 16.23–16.28
    integrated Windows 16.8, 16.9, 16.14
    mechanisms 16.8, 16.9
    methods 16.4-16.7
    Microsoft Passport 16.4, 16.7, 16.34, 16.35–16.36
    mixed-mode 10.9-10.11
    SSL 16.11, 16.12
    Windows-based 16.4, 16.6, 16.13, 16.14–16.18
    XML Web services 13.5
authorization
    configuration 16.16, 16.27
    described 16.3
Auto Hide button 2.12
AutoEventWireup attribute 5.14
AutoPostBack property 5.23, 5.24, 5.32

Notes

Notes

Notes

Notes

Notes

Notes

Notes

Notes

Notes

Notes

Notes

Notes

MSM2310BCP/C90-02019